Jones Very

Jones Very
The Complete Poems

EDITED BY HELEN R. DEESE

The University of Georgia Press   Athens & London

© 1993 by the

University of Georgia Press

Athens, Georgia 30602

All rights reserved

Set in Galliard by Tseng Information Systems, Inc.

Printed and bound by Thomson-Shore, Inc.

The paper in this book meets the guidelines for permanence

and durability of the Committee on Production Guidelines

for Book Longevity of the Council on Library Resources.

Printed in the United States of America

97 96 95 94 93 C 5 4 3 2 1

Library of Congress Cataloging in Publication Data

Very, Jones, 1813–1880.

[Poems]

Jones Very : the complete poems /

edited by Helen R. Deese.

p.   cm.

Includes bibliographical references and index.

ISBN 0-8203-1481-1 (alk. paper)

I. Deese, Helen.   II. Title.

PS3126.D44   1993

811'.3—dc20   92-9301

CIP

British Library Cataloging in Publication Data available

This book has been supported by a grant from the National

Endowment for the Humanities, an independent federal

agency.

FOR MY PARENTS

CONTENTS

ACKNOWLEDGMENTS

I AM GRATEFUL to the National Endowment for the Humanities, an independent federal agency, and to the American Philosophical Society for grants and to Tennessee Technological University for released time that helped make possible this edition.

The staffs of many libraries have graciously assisted me in this project; I wish to thank especially the staffs of the Houghton Library and the Harvard University Archives at Harvard University; the James Duncan Phillips Library of the Essex Institute; the Wellesley College Library; the Massachusetts Historical Society; and the John Hay Library at Brown University, where Mark N. Brown and Barbara Filipac were extraordinarily helpful. I am grateful to the following for permission to publish materials in their collections: American Antiquarian Society; Brown University Library; Trustees of the Boston Public Library; Very Family Papers, Essex Institute, Salem, Massachusetts; Parkman Dexter Howe Library, Rare Books and Manuscripts, University of Florida; Harvard University Archives and the Houghton Library; Charles Roberts Autograph Collection, Haverford College Library; Lincoln Public Library; Massachusetts Historical Society; Collection of Joel Myerson; Bryant-Godwin Papers and Duyckinck Family Papers (Astor, Lenox and Tilden Foundations), Rare Books and Manuscripts Division, The New York Public Library; Pennsylvania Historical Society; The Pierpont Morgan Library, New York (MA 925); The University of Tennessee Library; Jones Very Collection, Clifton Waller Barrett Library, Manuscripts Division, Special Collections Department, University of Virginia Library; Wellesley College Library, English Poetry Collection; and Yale Collection of American Literature, Beinecke Rare Book and Manuscript Library, Yale University. An earlier version of a portion of the introduction appeared as "Jones Very Among His Contemporaries" in *Postscript: Publication of the Philological Association of the Carolinas* 8 (1991): 71–79.

I acknowledge great indebtedness to many friends, colleagues, and scholars who have had a hand in a wide variety of ways in making this edition possible: David Balise, Sarah Clayton, Ludwig Deringer, Philip Eppard, Shirley Laird, Joseph Lerner, Marcia Moss, Glenn Nicholls, Edmund P. Schofield, Alan Seaburg, Chris Steele, Stephen Tabachnick, G. Thomas Tanselle, David Viera, Michael Winship, and Elizabeth Witherell have all made significant contributions. Student workers who have toiled uncomplainingly on this project include Zhou Hongguang, Macy Hitt, Teresa Moore, Cindy Green, and Kevin J. Carrico. Guy R. Woodall, my colleague and mentor, is responsible for having excited my interest in Very and has been a regular and indispensable source of information, guidance, and encouragement. I am grateful to Walter Harding, director of the NEH seminar in which I participated, for vital support and counsel. Joel Myerson has over a long period provided often crucial encouragement for the project. I am immensely indebted and grateful to David Robinson and Gary Collison for their critical readings of the Introduction. My husband Pat has contributed to this work in every conceivable area, from facilitating my research trips to checking scriptural allusions to questioning my intellectual assumptions. To all of these I express my sincerest thanks.

INTRODUCTION

JONES VERY WAS IN MANY WAYS AN ENIGMA. To Ralph Waldo Emerson he was, for a time, one of Emerson's personal pantheon of discovered geniuses, a golden boy, stimulating company, an instance of the genius cropping out unexpectedly everywhere. To the Harvard College administration and the conservative Unitarians he was a dangerous enthusiast, a madman. Even among the Transcendentalists he excited mixed responses: for many of them he was a kind of personification of their doctrine of total reliance upon the inner spirit, but others were eager to dissociate his bizarre behavior from their own tenets. He was the author of both an extraordinary body of innovative and spirit-filled poetry and a larger body of verse that is, especially by contrast, remarkably mundane. He was both a mystic and a less than dynamic preacher. For a brief period he thrust himself into the limelight in Cambridge, Salem, and Concord; but most of his life is best characterized by its uneventfulness. Twentieth-century scholars have variously depicted him as Calvinist, Unitarian, or Transcendentalist.

VERY AMONG HIS CONTEMPORARIES

In the introduction to his selection of Jones Very's poetry in *The Oxford Book of American Verse*, F. O. Matthiessen remarks that "Jones Very was as little familiar to his contemporaries as he is to us." Yet while few contemporaries of any mystic could claim to understand him fully, Jones Very the man was a familiar fact of life for some time in the Harvard College, Salem, and Concord communities. Since he was a figure whose unconventional behavior as well as his genius made him impossible to ignore, a good many of Very's associates did comment on and attempt to analyze him. Since the appearance of the two biographies of Very, William I. Bartlett's in 1942 and Edwin Gittleman's in 1967, considerable, though fragmentary, new biographical material has surfaced, some of it having appeared in articles, some of it still unpublished.[1]

Very's life (1813–80) falls into four distinct stages: his youth and early manhood in Salem and as an undergraduate at Harvard; a period of religious crisis—a mystical experience—beginning in his senior year at Harvard and culminating in his stay in McLean Asylum, September–October 1838; from that date, a period of no longer than eighteen months during which he produced some three hundred ecstatic poems; and the remaining forty years of his life, during which he served as Unitarian supply preacher, wrote religious and nature poetry and a good deal of occasional verse, and lived in relative retirement in Salem.

Son of Salem sea captain Jones Very and his first cousin Lydia Very, the younger Jones Very entered with the sophomore class of Harvard College in September 1833. By then he had already shown a literary bent, having published three sentimental poems in the *Salem Observer* under the signature "I." All three poems are in heroic couplets and are strongly influenced by English romanticism. As a student at Harvard, Very was fully involved in the college life. His interests as an undergraduate took a decidedly religious and literary turn; he attended weekly meetings of a "Society for Religious Improvement" organized by Henry Ware, Jr., and he sometimes spent Sunday evenings singing hymns with his roommates, James Chisholm and Thomas Bernard West, with whom he occupied "the whole upper story of the third entry, in Holworthy."[2] Obviously a serious student, Very wrote the prize-winning Bowdoin essay in both his junior and senior years, the first Harvard student ever to do so, and finished second in his class. And his poetry, which continued to appear occasionally in the *Salem Observer*, now could be found as well not only in the student literary publication, *Harvardiana*, but also in the *Knickerbocker*.[3] He composed both the sophomore and senior class songs. There seems to be nothing of the later mystic or the religious fanatic in either of them; the earlier is a hearty drinking song, which includes the following lines:

> Then fill your cups my hearty friends,
> We'll have a cheerfull time;
> We'll use the gifts that Bacchus sends,
> And drink t' auld lang syne.
> > ("Song . . . to be Sung at the Class-Supper
> > of the Sophomore Class of 1834")

All of this seems normal and unremarkable behavior for an undergraduate. At about the same time Very seems to have been participating in civic affairs in his home town of Salem. He served as clerk of the volunteer Fire Club, recording and reporting minutes of its meetings to the local newspaper (*Salem Observer*, 16 July 1836).

In his senior year of college Very experienced a religious phenomenon which was the first of several stages of a mystical experience that was to affect profoundly his life and poetry. He underwent, by his own description, "what is commonly called a *change of heart,* which tells us that all we have belongs to God and that we ought to have no *will* of our own." Although this change brought him "great happiness," he "could not rest in it," but struggled to overcome his own will: "as long as I had a thought of what I ought to banish I felt that some of my will remained. To this I was continually prone and against it I continually strove."[4] This experience may well have been bound up with a sexual crisis, if there is any truth to the "strange stories" that one of his classmates recalled having heard of Very; these were rumors "of unbridled passions overcome by monkish austerity & self-denial. <But—he was so given to women,> that he had made himself a law <never to speak> not to speak (or look at <them> women, I forget which)—to them."[5]

After his graduation in 1836 Very accepted a position at Harvard as tutor in Greek. He was also a semiofficial student at the Divinity School, taking an active part for a time in a student organization called the Philanthropic Society.[6] He continued to write poetry; by the time he left Harvard he had approximately sixty poems to his credit. The relationships that Very established with many of the students with whom he studied at Harvard and especially those whom he tutored seem to have been among the strongest of his life. Among his papers at Brown University are copies of poems by several of these students, as well as by Henry David Thoreau, who was also a Harvard undergraduate, though not a student of Very. Some fifteen of Very's manuscript poems turned up several years ago in the papers of his classmate Charles Stearns Wheeler.[7] Among the several undergraduates who were significantly touched by Very while he was a tutor were Frederick G. Tuckerman, the poet, who wrote Very more than twenty years later asking for a volume of his verse;[8] the future Transcendentalist Samuel Johnson, like Very a Salem native, who was to include several of Very's poems in the hymnbook that he and Samuel Longfellow compiled;[9] James Elliot Cabot (later Emerson's secretary), who over fifty years later remembered the special interest Very took in students;[10] Abraham Jackson, who told Emerson in 1863 that he "owed more to Jones Very, who was Greek Tutor, than to almost any or all others in the [Harvard] faculty";[11] Claudius B. Farnsworth, a lawyer who five years after Very left Harvard published in a New Bedford newspaper three poems that Very had given him which until now have remained uncollected;[12] and William Orne White, for whom Very had been "the ideal instructor," "singling out among the freshmen those with whom he might take long walks, whom he could visit at their rooms, and who would call upon him."[13] Even after he was forced to leave Harvard, Very maintained his ties for at least a time with a number of students, writing them letters and sending them manuscript poems. Among his fellow Divinity School students Very was particularly close to Sylvester Judd and Robert C. Waterston, to whom he gave some of his manuscript poems,[14] and George Frederick Simmons. Simmons, an 1838 graduate of the Divinity School, was himself the subject of an enigmatic poem by Very.[15]

During his second year as tutor the arena of Very's personal acquaintances was significantly expanded, thanks to Elizabeth Palmer Peabody, to include most of the Transcendentalists. A resident of Salem herself at the time, she heard Very deliver his lecture on epic poetry at the Salem Lyceum on 27 December 1837, took him home with her, and immediately became his friend. She queried him "on all the current subjects of the day, which were mainly the transcendental topics" and was interested to learn that he was working on a piece on Shakespeare and was "an enthusiastic listener to Mr. Emerson."[16] Peabody at once made it her business to establish a personal connection between the two, writing Emerson that he should ask Very to lecture at the Concord Lyceum. Emerson did so, marking the beginning of a relationship that proved brief but profitable to both parties.

Emerson seems first to have thought of Jones Very as a bright and promising young mind. After Very's lecture in Concord in April 1838, Emerson wrote to Peabody "to thank again your sagacity that detects such wise men as Mr. Very, from whose conversation and lecture I have had a true and high satisfaction. I heartily congratulate myself on being, as it were, anew in such company."[17] The Emersons had entertained the lecturer in their home, and Lidian Emerson was also favorably impressed; she wrote her sister: "This morning Mr. *Very*—a young Cambridge Tutor—took his departure from our castle where we had entertained him a day and a night—But as Carlyle said of mine own *angel*-man—he left us not as he found us; but rejoicing in the existence of so high souled—pure—loving—and lovely a being. He is a sweeter spirit if possible than G.[eorge] P.[artridge] B.[radford] whom he most reminds me of. Mr. E. loves him as well as I do."[18] Very must himself have been pleased with the visit, for he returned some two weeks later along with Professor Cornelius C. Felton and two other Harvard students. They told Emerson "fine hopeful things of their mates in the senior class" and, partly on the basis of this interview, Emerson found his spirits soaring; he began "to conceive hopes of the Republic" (*JMN*, 5:475). A few days after the visit he wrote in his journal: "Have I said it before in these pages, then I will say it again, that it is a curious commentary on society that the expression of a devout sentiment by any young man who lives in society strikes me with surprise & has all the air & effect of genius; as when J. Very spoke of 'sin' & of 'love' & so on" (*JMN*, 5:480). By this time it is likely that Very was discussing with Emerson, as he had with Elizabeth Peabody on first meeting, ideas for his as yet embryonic essay on Shakespeare. So intriguing did Emerson find his new friend that he was invited to the next meeting (on May 20) of the

Transcendental Club at the home of Caleb Stetson in Medford. The topic for discussion—Is Mysticism an Element of Christianity?—was to prove, in the case of Very, curiously prophetic. In June Very attended another gathering of the club, this one at Cyrus Bartol's house in Boston, at which "the character and genius of Goethe" and miscellaneous topics were discussed.[19]

Meantime, throughout the two years of Very's tutoring and studying divinity, his religious crisis continued. He was still striving, with some success, he believed, to rid himself of his own will:

> During the two years succeeding my senior . . . I maintained this conflict—it began with the day and was continued into the night—the enemy gradually yielded and I went on rejoicing to the close[.] Towards the end of the second year I felt that I was going about all my engagements without any interest in them of my own and yet I felt very happy for I had so long persevered in this course that it had wrought out for me much peace and content. I began to be happy in simply trying to do and think good. I had nothing more to give up to I had given all I had yet I did not know this then as I do now.
>
> (Letter to Bellows)

He felt "a gradual increase of joy" and his life "was more and more regularly a sacrifice in all things." Very assumed that this would be a permanent state and "had no expectation of another change never having heard of any other" (Letter to Bellows).

Very was still on Emerson's mind as the tumultuous summer of his Divinity School Address (1838) came to an end. In the letter accompanying the copy of the address that he sent to his aunt Mary Moody Emerson, he wrote, testifying to Very's independence of thought: "There is a young man at Cambridge named Jones Very who I think would interest you & will presently finish & probably publish an Essay on S. and from a point of view quite novel & religious. He has been here twice yet be not uneasy on that account for he does not agree to my dogmatism" (1 September 1838, *Letters of R.W.E.*, 2:154).

By the fall of 1838, the beginning of Very's third year as tutor, his growing religious enthusiasm was attracting notice at Harvard. One of his students, James W. Boyden, recorded in his diary an account of one of Very's classes that consisted of less Greek than moral instruction:

> . . . at ten, we went to Very, where we were sure to get a *moral* lecture, averaging from fifteen to twenty minutes extent.
>
> But one sentence had been read before he commenced. He told us the motives, which influenced Darius, the Persian King to extend his power and to make an expedition into Greece that they were wrong, and that we should never entertain such feelings etc. etc.

According to Boyden's account a few days later, Very was also conducting his own Sunday school, "where were assembled twenty Freshmen, who read two verses each of John, 1st Chapter, which Mr. V. then explained to us."[20] Freshman Samuel Johnson on September 6 wrote to his father in Salem defending his tutor's behavior, which was by now clearly suspect, a topic of gossip "among a set of thoughtless and ignorant young fellows, who make him a butt for their ridicule."[21] Jones Very was being carefully observed.

From Very's own perspective, what was occurring was the culmination of the religious experience that had begun in his senior year. He recounted that this occurred "about the third week" in the term when

> I felt within me a new will something which came some time in the week but I could not tell what day exactly. It seemed like my old will only it was to the good—it was not a feeling of my own but a sensible will that was not my own. Accompanying this was another feeling as it were a consciousness which seemed to say—"That which creates you creates also that which you see or him to whom you speak," as it might be.
>
> (Letter to Bellows)

His newfound "two consciousnesses" continued for two or three weeks, he wrote; during that time "I was moved entirely by the Spirit within me to declare to all that the coming of Christ was at hand" (Letter to Bellows). On the evening of September 13 he made this declaration to Professor Henry Ware, Jr. When Ware objected to his interpretation of Matthew 24, Very said that "he was willing to yield, but the spirit would not let him . . . he had fully given up his own will, and now only did the will of the Father." He had been making similar assertions to "a great many" at the college. On the following day Very used his classroom as a forum to proclaim to his students that they should "flee to the mountains, for the end of all things is at hand." That evening he made a speech to a debating society at the college claiming that the Holy Spirit was speaking through him. George Moore, a divinity student who was an eyewitness to Very's strange behavior on both this occasion and at the interview with Henry Ware, was impressed with Very's sincerity but puzzled as to how to explain the phenomenon: "It is almost fearful to look upon him, and see his deep earnestness, exhibited in his face, and to hear the tremulous tones of voice as he utters himself—and at the same time to think that he is fully possessed with this great idea that the Spirit is revealing itself in him. I hardly know what to think of the man."[22]

President Josiah Quincy of Harvard College took immediate and decisive action: on this same evening (September 14) he asked Charles Stearns Wheeler to take over Very's position as tutor. On the next day Very was taken home to Salem by his brother. On September 17, after making similar declarations in Salem, Jones Very was sent ("contrary to my will," he wrote [Letter to Bellows]) to the McLean Asylum in Charlestown, where he would remain for one month. Though he was reputed "a highly approved Tutor,"[23] Very's career at Harvard was irrevocably finished.

This sensational news spread quickly. Reports of Very's spiritual-emotional crisis shortly reached Emerson, and he was much concerned. Very had managed to send him his now completed "Shakespeare" essay just as he was being evicted from Cambridge. To his friend William H. Furness in Philadelphia Emerson expressed his anxiety: "There is a young man at Cambridge a Tutor, Jones Very, who has written a noble paper / (MS) / <a>on Shakspeare, which I have just been reading. Yet I am distressed to hear that he is feared to be [in]sane. His critique certainly is not" (20 September 1838, *Letters of R.W.E.*, 7:319). And to Margaret Fuller he elaborated:

> Ha[ve] you heard of the calamity of poor Very, the tutor at Cambridge? He is at the Charlestown Asylum & his case tho't a very unpromising one. A fortnight ago tomorrow—I received from him his Dissertation on Shakspeare. The letter accompanying it betrayed the state of his mind; but the Essay is a noble production: not consecutive, filled with one thought; but that so deep & true & illustrated so happily & even grandly, that I account it an addition to our really scanty stock of adequate criticism on Shakspear. Such a mind cannot be lost.
>
> (28 September 1838, *Letters of R.W.E.*, 2:164–65)

In Salem Elizabeth Peabody took a proprietary interest in the Emerson-Very connection, writing Emerson extended accounts of Very's behavior in Salem both before he entered and after his release from the asylum and liberally dispensing advice as to how Emerson should deal with the transformed Very. Peabody herself was one of the first persons to be the target of Very's "mission" during the brief period Very was in Salem between when he was dismissed at Harvard and when he was sent to the asylum:

> One morning I answered <the> a ring at a door, and <found> Mr. Very walked in—He looked much flushed and his eyes very brilliant, and unwinking—It struck me at once that there was something unnatural—and dangerous in his air—As soon as we were within the parlor door he laid his hand on my head,—and said "I come to baptize you with the Holy Ghost & with fire"—and then he prayed—I cannot remember his words but they were thrilling—and as I stood under his hand, I trembled to the centre—But it was my instinct—not to antagonize but to be perfectly quiet—I felt he was beside himself and I was alone in the lower story of the house.—When he had done I sat down and he at a little distance, did the same—and there was a dead silence.— Soon he said,—with a slightly uneasy misgiving said, How do you feel? I

replied gently, "I feel no change"—"But you will"—said he hurriedly—
"I am the Second Coming—Give me a Bible"—There was one in the
room to which I pointed. He went to the table where it was and turned
to Christ's prophecy of the Second Coming—and read it ending with
the words, "This day is this fulfilled in your hearing"—I was silent but
respectful even tenderly so—I thought this was perhaps a passing frenzy
caused by overtaxing his brain in the attempt to look from the standpoint
of Absolute Spirit.

(Letters of E.P.P., p. 406)

Peabody advised Emerson after Very's release that Very was planning a visit
to him (*Letters of E.P.P.*, pp. 215–16). As she had warned, one week after his
release from the asylum on October 17, Very set out, his freshly completed
essay "Hamlet" in hand, for a five-day visit with Emerson. His state of mind
did not make him an ordinary or compliant house guest, but Emerson claimed
to have been "very happy in his visit as soon as I came to understand his
vocabulary" (*Letters of R.W.E.*, 7:325). Very declared the last day of his visit a
"day of hate" in which, Emerson wrote, he "discerns the bad element in every
person whom he meets which repels him: he even shrinks a little to give the
hand,—the sign of <love> receiving. . . . A very accurate discernment of
spirits belongs to his state, & he detects at once the <diff> presence of an
alien element though he cannot tell whence, how, or whereto it is" (*JMN*,
7:122). Overawed not even by Emerson, Very cited the chief spiritual defect
of his host: "He thinks me covetous in my hold of truth, of seeing truth sepa-
rate, & of receiving or taking it instead of merely obeying. The Will is to him
all, as to me (<in> ↑ after ↓ my own showing,) Truth. He is sensible in me
of a little colder air than that he breathes. He says you do not disobey be-
cause you do the wrong act, but you <disobe> do the wrong act, because
you disobey" (*JMN*, 7:122–23). But the *pièce de résistance* of the visit, from
Emerson's point of view, was Very's confronting a preacher who was present
at a meeting of Sunday school teachers at Emerson's house:

> I ought not to omit recording the astonishment which seized all the
> company when our brave saint the other day fronted the presiding
> preacher. The preacher began to tower & dogmatize with many words.
> Instantly I foresaw that his doom was fixed; and as quick as he ceased
> speaking, the Saint set him right & blew away all his words in an in-
> stant—unhorsed him I may say & tumbled him along the ground in utter
> dismay like my Angel of Heliodorus. Never was discomfiture more com-
> plete. <He> In tones of genuine pathos he "bid him wonder at the Love
> which suffered him to speak there in his chair, of things he knew nothing
> of; one might expect to see ↑ the book taken from his hands & ↓ him
> thrust out of the room,—& yet he was allowed to sit & talk whilst every

word he spoke was a step of departure from the truth, and of this he commanded himself to bear witness!"

(JMN, 7:127–28)

Emerson was obviously delighted; to Elizabeth Peabody he summarized his assessment of Very during this visit: "he is profoundly sane" (*Letters of R.W.E.*, 7:325). Very was in fact acting out Emerson's privately recorded remonstrances against contemporary preachers, Barzillai Frost in particular (who most likely was Very's victim in this story),[24] and fulfilling Emerson's plea in his Divinity School Address to reject a tradition-bound religion. Shortly after Very had left, Emerson reflected in his journal: "And he is gone into the multitude as solitary as Jesus. In dismissing him I seem to have discharged an arrow into the heart of society. Wherever that young enthusiast goes he will astonish & disconcert men by dividing for them the cloud that covers the profound gulf that is in man" (*JMN*, 7:123). In Jones Very, Emerson was meeting his own ideas in the flesh.

Because from our perspective we tend to think of Emerson as the editor of Very's poetry, it is an easily overlooked but significant fact, as Gittleman observes, that Emerson's fascination with Very up to this point had nothing whatever to do with his talents as a poet.[25] There is no indication that Emerson was aware that Very even wrote poetry, though it was on October 27, while Very was still in Concord, that "The New Birth," the first of the new ecstatic poems, appeared in the *Salem Observer*. But soon after returning to Salem from Concord Very sent Emerson a clipping from the *Observer* of two poems which appeared there on November 10—"'In Him we live, & move, & have our being'" and "Enoch." Emerson appears to have been caught by surprise at this unsuspected dimension of his newfound prophet. He immediately responded with his typical generosity and gracious encouragement upon discovering a new prodigy:

> I have also to thank you for the two sonnets sent me in the Salem Observer. I love them & read them to all who have ears to hear. Do not, I beg you, let a whisper or sigh of the muse go unattended to or unrecorded The sentiment which inspires your poetry is so deep & true, & the expression so simple, that I am sure you will find your audience very large as soon as the verses first take air & get abroad. And a man should be very happy & grateful who is the bringer to his fellow men of a good so excellent as poetry.
>
> (18 November 1838, *Letters of R.W.E.*, 7:326)

He further proposed that "after a little more writing" Very consider publishing a volume of his prose and poetry "& make the bookseller give you bread for the same. And let me help you with some of my recent experience in the matter" (pp. 326–27). It is somewhat surprising that although Very had published more than fifty poems by this time, he had apparently not considered them significant enough to mention to Emerson. But the sort of poetry that he had been writing for about a month now was markedly different from his earlier work, and Very obviously valued it much more highly.

Elizabeth Peabody too was soon made aware of Very the poet. He appeared at the Peabody home one evening[26] and "unfolded a monstrous folio sheet of paper, on which were four double columns of sonnets—which he said 'the Spirit had enabled' him to write . . . as the utterances of the Holy Ghost." Peabody "read them with wonder" and later urged Emerson (who had already independently had the same idea) to help Very publish them (*Letters of E.P.P.*, pp. 407, 220).

Though sympathizing with Very and treating him with great kindness and consideration throughout this crisis, both before and after his stay at the asylum, Peabody considered Very unequivocally, though perhaps temporarily, insane. (Among the Transcendentalists, she was in the minority; most were either ambivalent about Very's sanity or strongly defended it.) In addition to her anxiety for Very himself, her major concern was that Very's insanity was being associated with Emerson's Transcendentalism. She was herself eager to establish a distinction between the two: "I wonder whether something might not be written by a believer in the doctrine of Spirituality—which would show the difference between trusting the Soul & giving up one's mind to these *individual illuminations*" (*Letters of E.P.P.*, pp. 208–9). Others in Salem "have taken it [Very's strange behavior] all—as nothing but *transcendentalism*—which shows how very entirely they do *not* apprehend *the ground* of a *real belief* in *Inspiration*.—What a frightful shallowness of thought in the community—that sees no difference between the evidence of the most manifest insanity & the Ideas of Reason!" (*Letters of E.P.P.*, pp. 209–10).

After Very's return to his Salem home (which he shared with his widowed mother and his younger brother and two sisters) from McLean Asylum and from his visit to Emerson, he continued to insist upon calling on various ministers in Salem, pointing out to them the error of their ways and the righteousness of his own. The result was his making a formidable enemy in John Brazer, minister at Salem's Unitarian North Church, who taunted Very by challenging him to perform miracles or yield the point that he was insane (*Letters of E.P.P.*, p. 216). Brazer further frightened Very with threats of sending him away again, to sea or back to the asylum. The Harvard authorities and the Salem ministers continued to associate Very's dangerous doctrines with those recently proclaimed in Emerson's radical Divinity School Address and even with those of the convicted blasphemer Abner Kneeland.[27]

At this point the entire Peabody family, including Elizabeth's sisters Mary and Sophia, her brother George, and her mother and father, rallied to Very's defense. Their sensitive and sympathetic response to his perilous situation is evident in two letters written by Mary Peabody in Salem to her sister Elizabeth in Boston.[28] The Peabodys urged Very's mother not to bow to demands that her son be sent away. Mary concluded the first letter by writing that "there is no time to be lost in defending him against the wolves & bears." Very was not without other supporters in Salem; among the citizens whom Mary mentions as apparent admirers and defenders of Very are Judge Daniel A. White, one of Salem's leading citizens; Nancy Gay, Salem socialite and bluestocking; and Nathaniel Hawthorne. Very himself is shown in the letters to be capable of fairly normal social intercourse in polite society but deeply disturbed by his persecution by his "enemies." His behavior is depicted as gentle—he specifically rejected violence as an alternative in his present crisis. He was spending his time in the weeks following his institutionalization in writing sonnets, tutoring his brother Washington (a freshman at Harvard), and calling on both friend and foe. His appearance was "melancholy persecuted grieved," in Mary Peabody's words; and she closed her second letter to Elizabeth defiantly: "I don't feel quite easy yet & shall not till Mr. B. is in the Insane Hospital." As the Peabodys had urged, Very's mother stood firm, and no deportation occurred.[29]

The eventual result of Emerson's proposal in November 1838 to help Very publish his poems was, of course, *Essays and Poems*, but the road to its publication in early September 1839 was not smooth. Though initially interested in Emerson's offer, Very—after several months of extroversion during which he had regularly called upon the Peabodys, Nathaniel Hawthorne, and others in Salem, attended Emerson's lectures in Boston, and met with the Transcendental Club once again in December—suddenly went into seclusion in the spring of 1839. He sent word to Emerson, by way of a letter dictated to his brother on June 3, that he could not make him a visit but would send him what he had written and that Emerson could make his own selections "from the unpublished pieces." Then Very abruptly changed his mind about abdicating all authority to Emerson and left for Concord on June 14 for a three-day editorial conference from which he was to emerge the loser. Though Very objected to any correction of the poems, Emerson eventually prevailed, arguing, "we cannot permit the Holy Ghost to be careless (& in one instance) to talk bad grammar" (*Letters of E.P.P.*, p. 409). And, according to Emerson's own account to Elizabeth Peabody, "he [Emerson] selects and combines with sovereign will, 'and shall,' he says, 'make out quite a little gem of a volume'" (*Letters of E.P.P.*, p. 226). An examination of the Historical Collation in this edition actually reveals few instances of major alterations by Emerson of Very's own versions. There are a few, however, and to Very of course *any* alteration was major.[30]

As Very's editor Emerson is to be faulted less for his correction of the

Spirit's parsing and spelling (*Letters of R.W.E.*, 2:331) than for his "select[ing] . . . with sovereign will." For among the two hundred poems from which he selected sixty-five "that really possess rare merit" (*Letters of R.W.E.*, 2:209) were surely the radical "deific" poems, those in which the poet takes on the persona of the Godhead.[31] These poems, which recent critics have found so intriguing, were rejected at this point by Emerson, suppressed by later editors, and remained unpublished until Bartlett's biography of 1942. Chosen instead by Emerson for *Essays and Poems* were a number of early innocuous sentimental poems such as "The Humming-Bird" ("I cannot heal that green gold breast, / Where deep those cruel teeth have prest") and "The Canary Bird" ("Alas! that with thy music's gentle swell / Past days of joy should through thy memory throng, / And each to thee their words of sorrow tell"). Nearly one-fourth of the poems in Emerson's collection were composed before the culmination of Very's mystical experience. In producing *Essays and Poems* Emerson, evincing a surprising conservatism, toned down and cleaned up his brave saint.

The volume appeared in early September, with no acknowledgment of Emerson as its editor, and once it was published Emerson seemed curiously detached from it. On September 28 he wrote the cryptic entry in his journal: "Also I hate Early Poems" (*JMN*, 7:249). Almost two years later he finally wrote a brief review of the book for the *Dial*;[32] it is favorable, but the tone seems mildly patronizing:

> The genius of this little book is religious, and reaches an extraordinary depth of sentiment. The author, plainly a man of a pure and kindly temper, casts himself into the state of the high and transcendental obedience to the inward Spirit. He has apparently made up his mind to follow all its leadings, though he should be taxed with absurdity or even with insanity. In this enthusiasm he writes most of these verses, which rather flow through him than from him.

And thus the review goes on to glorify Very the saint at the expense of Very the poet:

> There is no *composition*, no elaboration, no artifice in the structure of the rhyme, no variety in the imagery; in short, no pretension to literary merit, for this would be departure from his singleness, and followed by loss of insight. He is not at liberty even to correct these unpremeditated poems for the press; but if another will publish them, he offers no objection. . . . They are the breathings of a certain entranced devotion.

Emerson points out, correctly, the narrowness of scope and tone in the poems:

These sonnets have little range of topics, no extent of observation, no playfulness; there is even a certain torpidity in the concluding lines of some of them, which reminds one of church hymns; but, whilst they flow with great sweetness, they have the sublime unity of the Decalogue or the Code of Menu, and if as monotonous, yet are they almost as pure as the sounds of Surrounding Nature.[33]

In the course of the review Emerson seems to acknowledge the inferiority of the earlier poems in the collection when he writes, "*With the exception of the few first poems,* which appear to be of an earlier date, all these verses bear the unquestionable stamp of grandeur" (emphasis mine). This is a curious comment from one who had selected these poems "with sovereign will" when he had his choice of scores of the mystical poems.

As Jones Very's religious enthusiasm faded away, so did the interest of Emerson and the other Transcendentalists in him. "When all was over," Emerson wrote in 1845, Very "remained in the thin porridge <of Unitari> or cold tea of Unitarianism" (*JMN*, 9:339). Yet Very continued to echo through Emerson's journals for decades and was the model for this striking passage in his essay "Friendship":

> I knew a man who, under a certain religious frenzy, cast off this drapery [hypocrisy], and omitting all compliment and commonplace, spoke to the conscience of every person he encountered, and that with great insight and beauty. At first he was resisted, and all men agreed he was mad. But persisting, as indeed he could not help doing, for some time in this course, he attained to the advantage of bringing every man of his acquaintance into true relations with him. No man would think of speaking falsely with him, or of putting him off with any chat of markets or reading-rooms. But every man was constrained by so much sincerity to the like plaindealing, and what love of nature, what poetry, what symbol of truth he had, he did certainly show him. But to most of us society shows not its face and eye, but its side and its back. To stand in true relations with men in a false age, is worth a fit of insanity, is it not?[34]

In the long term Emerson's lasting fascination was with the man Jones Very (the *saint,* as Emerson called him), not the poet; the man who had spent five days at his house straight out of an insane asylum and was utterly without pretense or cant, who functioned as a touchstone to reveal the pretense in others. Emerson's journals for years afterward are haunted by his memory of the man who "had an illumination that enabled him to excel every body in wit & to see farthest in every company & quite easily to bring the proudest to confession [misreading of "confusion"?]" (*JMN*, 9:339); who, "in his constant sense of the divine presence, thought it an honor to wash his own face"

(*JMN*, 16:89); who talked, like Jesus, "*ab intra*" (*JMN*, 7:157); who was evidence that "the revolutionary force in intellect is never absent" (*JMN*, 15:450); who was among the "silent minorities of one" (*JMN*, 15:357); who was "concealed, as Swedenborg was . . . buried in light, as the stars are by day" (*JMN*, 15:96); who represented "the outcropping of the granite which is the core of the world" (*JMN*, 11:53); and who alone could "get any advantage" of Alcott in conversation (*JMN*, 8:212). And although it is clear that Emerson had been genuinely attracted to Very's poetry when he first saw it, once his editorial duties were over he seems to have felt well rid of it. He appears to have pushed the poetry largely out of his consciousness in favor of the ideal man that Very represented. No doubt the disputes with Very over editorial authority were not pleasant. But it seems likely that at least a part of the explanation for this repression lies elsewhere: on some level Emerson surely realized that he himself had been responsible for suppressing the fullest expression of that ideal man. Emerson, as he must himself have recognized, had presented in *Essays and Poems* a somewhat subdued version of the man whose radicalism he had celebrated.

The relationship between Very and Elizabeth Peabody was allowed to lapse as well. The problem in this case seems to have been pecuniary. Several months after the publication of *Essays and Poems* Very asked Emerson for an accounting of the disposition of the copies. Emerson responded promptly and, Very wrote, satisfactorily. But by November 1842 he was again concerned and asked that the account with Little and Brown be transferred from Emerson's name to his own. What was probably bothering Very were some missing or unpaid for copies that, it turned out, could be traced to Elizabeth Peabody's bookshop. (Very had thanked Emerson in November 1841 for placing some of his books on her shelves.) [35] At first Peabody denied having had a certain number of the books and then, when presented with evidence that she had handled them, had no money to pay for them. Very's sisters were forever bitter toward Peabody on this account and rebuffed her friendly overtures after Very's death, writing her that "an acquaintance so long interrupted had better not be renewed." Very himself, they said, had more charitably attributed the incident simply to Peabody's incompetence in business affairs. [36] In any case the dispute seems to have effectively destroyed the relationship: there is no evidence of any communication between Very and Peabody for nearly the last forty years of his life. [37]

The record of Very's association with Transcendentalists other than Emerson and Elizabeth Peabody is in most cases fragmentary. Margaret Fuller was reading Very's "sonnets and pieces" as early as March 1839, Emerson having sent her a "roll" of the sonnets in mid-January and the "dissertations" ("Shakespeare" and "Hamlet"), which had been "wandering in Boston" among other friends, in mid-February. In a letter to Emerson she critiqued the essay "Hamlet," saying that she found "excellent things there and its tone is very noble," but observing that "the subject seems rather probed at an inquiring distance than grasped." Yet she professed to be "greatly interested in Mr. Very," and enclosed "a little sketch of him by Cary on the 3d page of this which I think one of her good letters. Does not the little sketch give the idea of him?—or no!"[38] ("Cary" is Caroline Sturgis; her sketch of Jones Very has unfortunately not been recovered.) But the letter suggests the extent to which Very had become a figure of central interest among the other Transcendentalists. He had attended by this time three meetings of the Transcendental Club.[39] After the publication of Very's *Essays and Poems* in September of 1839, Fuller published a review of it the following January in Orestes Brownson's *Boston Quarterly Review*, the first notice of the work to appear in print.

James Freeman Clarke, a Transcendentalist-Unitarian minister who settled in Louisville, Kentucky, met Very during a visit to Boston in 1838.[40] After his return to the West Very sent him a number of manuscript poems, which Clarke published in the *Western Messenger*, along with a defense of Very's sanity and a sharp indictment of his critics:

> The charge of Insanity is almost always brought against any man who endeavors to introduce to the common mind any very original ideas. . . . He who insists on taking us out of the sphere of thought which is habitual to us, into a higher and purer one, is regarded by us with alarm and dissatisfaction. We must either yield ourselves to him, and suffer our minds to be taken out of their customary routine, which is always painful, or we must find some way to set aside his appeals to our reason and conscience and disarm them of their force. The easiest way is to call him insane. . . . Nobody is obliged to attend to the "insane ravings" of a maniac. The moment therefore this word is applied to a man, were he sage, prophet, or apostle—were he Socrates or Solon, were he Jesus or Paul—all men are authorized to look down upon him with pity.

Clarke himself asserted that he had seen in Very "no evidence even of . . . partial derangement." He described a meeting that he witnessed between Very and the Rev. William Ellery Channing, who was greatly interested in the Very phenomenon and who was sent Very's manuscript sonnets by Elizabeth Peabody.[41] After Very's death Clarke collaborated with Very's sisters to publish what was meant to be a complete edition of Very's poems and essays.

Little is known about Very's personal relationship with Henry Thoreau, less in fact than we had previously thought that we knew, since a letter by Thoreau to an unnamed correspondent (formerly believed to be Very) that indicates a friendship as late as the 1850s is now believed to have been addressed to John Lewis Russell of Salem. But it is clear nevertheless that Thoreau was also an admirer of Very's poems. He chose Very's *Essays and Poems* as a gift for

Ellen Sewell's father;[42] and in his journal (25 August 1843) Thoreau ranked Very's works with those of Emerson, William Ellery Channing II, and "the best pieces of Bryant," observing that "he who is not touched" by such poetry "may be sure he has not drunk deep of the Pierian spring."[43] Among the other Transcendentalists, Convers Francis on occasion quoted in his sermons from Very's poems.[44] Cyrus Bartol, at whose home Very had met with the Transcendental Club, was another who expressed interest in Very's poems, requesting copies of them from Very (Alcott Journal, December 1838, p. 445). More than forty years later Bartol wrote the preface to Clarke's edition of Very's poems. Orestes Brownson, on the other hand, was a Transcendentalist who felt little affinity for Very. Alcott, who had hosted them both at dinner, commented on the "wide polarity" between the two that was comical to behold. "They tried to speak, but Very was unintelligible to the proud Philistine" (Alcott Journal, 10 June 1839, p. 880).

Bronson Alcott was among the most sympathetic of Very's friends during the period of Very's regular association with the Transcendentalists. Yet Alcott felt ambivalent about both Very's poetry and his mental condition, writing during the height of Very's ecstatic state: "His poetry, like himself, is quite unequal. I see him, at times, and am much impressed by the soul of the man. I reverence it. I feel myself, in the presence of a superiour creature. He upbraids me; he rebukes me. I feel whatsoever of pretence, of show, there may be in me. At other times, he seems wild, mystical, and I rather pity than worship the presence before me. I am the insane now, and now the sane soul. What does this mean?" (Alcott Journal, December 1838, pp. 465–66). Alcott felt Very's essay on Shakespeare to be "one of the remarkable things of the day. It is better than anything I have seen, aside from 'Nature' and the 'Growth of the Mind,' of modern origin" (Alcott Journal, December 1838, p. 498). After having seen Very at a lecture by Emerson in January 1839, Alcott compared the two in his journal: "Very is a gifted saint. Emerson a gifted scholar. Both are men of Genius. The one represents life in the form of Truth, or Thought: the other in that of good, or obedience, and both in images of graceful Beauty. I get more from these men than from others now extant" (16 January 1839, p. 103). In late January 1839 Alcott was conducting a conversation at Lynn, in which Very participated. He and Alcott spent the night following the conversation in the same room, and Alcott's observations on his mental condition led him to predict that Very would soon die. But he marveled, "He is a psychological phenomenon of rare occurrence" (Alcott Journal, 29 January 1839, p. 208). About a month later Very spent the day with Alcott; "He is more spectral than ever," Alcott wrote; "Obviously he has not long to stay in the body." Later that afternoon the two of them called on John Sullivan Dwight (Alcott Journal, 27 February 1839, p. 382). In March Alcott wrote that Very was sending him sonnets every week (28 March 1839, p. 550). By June of the same year

Alcott observed that Very, who had dined with him, was much better in body and soul, his interest in man and nature reviving. Alcott wrote to Emerson, "J. Very is to live, and aid in that new organization of the Soul presignified by all the Functions and Aspects of the Times."[45]

For Emerson and a number of the other Transcendentalists Jones Very in his ecstatic state was a *cause célèbre*, the personification of the Transcendentalist poet who listened only to the inner voice of the spirit. Yet at the same time, close association with one who insisted on pointing out frankly the spiritual insufficiencies of everyone within range was bound to be problematic. And both Emerson and Alcott complained about Very's antiquated Hebraic diction, borrowed from the Bible.[46]

Among the Very-watchers outside the Transcendentalist circle was another Salemite, Nathaniel Hawthorne, who noted that Very's calls upon him were often overly long; but when Very "delivered his mission" to Hawthorne, Elizabeth Peabody records that Hawthorne "received it in the loveliest manner," repressing his natural inclination to petulance, "and talked with him beautifully." She continues, "[Hawthorne] says that Very was always *vain* in his eyes—though it was always an innocent vanity—arising greatly from want of sense of the ludicrous & sanctified by his real piety & goodness. He says he had better remain as he is—however—one organ in the world of the impersonal Spirit—at least as long as he can write such good sonnets" (*Letters of E.P.P.*, p. 221). Commenting on various of his contemporaries in "The Hall of Fantasy," Hawthorne imagined that "in the same part of the hall [with Emerson], Jones Very stood alone, within a circle which no other of mortal race could enter, nor himself escape from."[47]

Very also attracted the attention of others in the literary community, among whom was Richard H. Dana, Sr. Dana wrote in 1840 to William Cullen Bryant, to whom he sent a copy of Very's *Essays and Poems*, that he believed Very to be insane, and understood that he had been so for the past two years. Like many others, he connected Very's insanity with his association with the Transcendentalists: "His is quite intimate with Emerson & the other Spiritualists, or Supernaturalists, or whatever they are called, or may be pleased to call themselves; & his insanity has taken <that> shape accordingly. I am told that some of them are absurd enough to say that he is not insane—but that the world does not understand him. Would their insanity were no worse than his; but 'madness is in their *hearts*.'"[48] Bryant later included a number of Very's poems in his *Poets and Poetry in America* and referred in the *New York Evening Post* to Very's poems as "some of the very finest sonnets in the English language." Dana also, some twenty-five years following publication of *Essays and Poems*, gave it favorable notice; in 1865 Very thanked him for his "kind remembrance of me and my volume after so many years." Very added that he had not been in Boston "for a few years past."[49]

Those words remind us of Very's relative seclusion after what Gittleman has called "the effective years" ending in 1840. This retirement has contributed to the aura of mystery surrounding him. But the evidence shows that Very's isolation was far from complete; in the early 1840s Very was still communicating with Emerson, receiving copies of the *Dial* from Emerson when Emerson was its editor.[50] He attended Harvard commencement ceremonies and visited the experimental Brook Farm community in August 1841.[51] Much of the remainder of Very's life was devoted to his work as a supply preacher at Unitarian congregations in Maine, Massachusetts, and Rhode Island.[52] That Very did not forget or repudiate the associations of his earlier years is evidenced in numerous examples. In 1849 he, along with Thomas Treadwell Stone and Nathaniel and Sophia Hawthorne, helped arrange a series of conversations for Alcott in Salem.[53] In 1852 he participated with Alcott, Emerson, Thoreau, and others in a series of Sunday lectures or sermons at Plymouth that were organized in part by Marston Watson, who had been his friend and student at Harvard twenty-five years earlier.[54] According to Franklin Benjamin Sanborn, he, Alcott, Emerson, and Very were together at Emerson's house in 1854 discussing Shakespeare's religion.[55] Sanborn also recalled having visited with Very in Salem about 1861 and having discussed with him the resurrection of the body, in which Very "fully and literally believed."[56] Very apparently made a visit to Concord in his later years; he wrote a sonnet in 1875 on visiting the graves of Hawthorne and Thoreau.[57]

Upon Very's death in 1880 at the age of sixty-seven, the Essex Institute, in which he had been active, organized a memorial service in his honor. Emerson, who was asked to attend or contribute something to the service, was slipping into senility and unable to do so; there were, however, written testimonies from James Freeman Clarke, Thomas Wentworth Higginson, and a number of Unitarian ministers including Robert C. Waterston, Charles T. Brooks, and Edwin M. Stone. The proceedings of this service were published by the Essex Institute.[58] And Very's memory was not neglected by his townspeople even many years after his death. It is a long forgotten fact that a tribute to Very—an exhibition complete with such artifacts as Emerson's early letter to Very urging that he not "let a whisper or sigh of the Muse go unattended to or unrecorded,"[59] and Very's own manuscript poems and sermons borrowed from Brown University—was held at the North Church in Salem in 1913, as a centenary celebration of Very's birth.[60]

Jones Very was not, as we perhaps have sometimes imagined, a phantom persona, unknown and unknowable; he was a flesh-and-blood figure, familiar to many associates throughout his life. Yet I am not suggesting that it is possible to erase entirely the mystique that has surrounded this poet who believed himself the voice of the Holy Spirit. For eighteen months or so between the fall of 1838 and the spring of 1840 Very was a dynamo of poetic energy, producing in this brief period nearly one-third of the nearly nine hundred poems that he would write over a span of almost fifty years. Although there has been much speculation, beginning with Emerson and Elizabeth Peabody and Bronson Alcott, which has attempted to explain this phenomenon, and although we today are tempted to postulate such explanations as manic-depressive syndrome or temporal lobe epilepsy, Very's period of inspiration remains a mystery that we cannot finally penetrate. Despite the accumulating biographical fragments that yield us snatches of his personality, we have not yet plucked out the heart of Jones Very's mystery.

VERY'S MYSTICISM

A considerable portion of twentieth-century commentary on Very focuses on the question of his religious-philosophical orientation: Was he Calvinist, Unitarian, or Transcendentalist? Yvor Winters sees him as Calvinist as opposed to Transcendentalist, James A. Levernier allows him a Transcendentalism subsumed by an all-encompassing Calvinism, David Robinson considers him more Unitarian than Transcendentalist, Nathan Lyons calls him a Quietist rather than a Transcendentalist, and virtually all literary histories place him among the Transcendentalists.[61] Historically speaking, it is clear, as the foregoing discussion of his relationship with Emerson and his circle demonstrates, that Very was a Transcendentalist, at least in the sense that for a period of some two years he was closely associated with the Transcendental circle. It was in fact largely within the context of this circle that Very made his mark in his own day, though it is also true that his views and his actions were at times perhaps an embarrassment to some members of the group.[62]

It must be remembered, however, that Transcendentalism as it appeared in Concord-Boston-Cambridge-Salem in the 1830s and 1840s was not a rigid monolithic philosophical system, but a loose association of thinkers who espoused many differing and conflicting shades of religious and philosophical opinions but held in common a trust in man's intuitive powers as a source of truth. For a time Very was part of that association, and he undeniably placed great faith in the voice within. For Very, however, the voice within was in a certain sense not the voice of his own self, for that self had been effaced to make place for the divine.

Robinson's arguments linking Very to the pietistic tradition of Unitarianism are compelling. Although Calvinism and Unitarianism held certain basic doctrines in common, it is clear that on the chief point of contention between the two, the question of whether man is arbitrarily chosen either for election or damnation by God or whether he has himself a choice, Very solidly, in both his poems and his sermons, comes down on the side of choice. And one can hardly overlook the fact that for nearly forty years Very was a licensed supply preacher in Unitarian churches. The Unitarians treated Very (for a few years before and for decades after his mystical period) as a Unitarian, and the Transcendentalists treated him for a few years during the height of the movement as a Transcendentalist.

But during the most significant period of his poetic production, such categories are to a large extent irrelevant. During that time Jones Very, believing himself to have experienced a spiritual rebirth and union with the Divine, was essentially a mystic, a classification that cuts across lines of dogma. He was of course a Christian mystic, and the form that his mysticism took was no doubt influenced by the Calvinistic milieu of New England, as well as his more immediate Unitarian and Transcendental environment. Very's only extant direct statement on this experience is contained in a letter to Henry W. Bellows, formerly one of Very's fellow students at Harvard, and at the time of the writing (29 December 1838) a Unitarian minister in New York City.[63] This document, central to an understanding of Very's mystical state, appears in its entirety in the Appendix to the Introduction. In this letter Very describes himself as having gone through several stages in reaching the state of complete union with God's will. Sometime during the 1835–36 school year he had experienced a "change of heart" that manifested itself in his desire to "banish" his own will; he continued for the next two years to strive against his own will until he eventually "had nothing more to give up." He assumed that he would continue in this state, "never having heard of any other." But in the third week of his third year as tutor in Cambridge (September 1838) he experienced in himself the presence of another will, not his own, as well as a sense of union with all creation.

This account is a classic description of mystical experience. Harry L. Jones sees in it three typical stages described in Evelyn Underhill's study of mysticism: illumination, purgation, and union.[64] The illumination he equates with Very's "change of heart" in his senior year; the purgation with his striving through the next two years to rid himself of his own will; and the final stage, or union, with his consciousness in September 1838 of having been subsumed into the divine will. Jones also finds these various stages recapitulated in the sonnets of this period. "The Son," is, Jones feels, one of the poems descriptive of the initial state, a statement of Very's conviction of the reality of the supernatural order and his longing for the fulfillment of that conviction in union with the divine will. Jones believes that the stage between this initial one and the final one of union, often characterized in traditional mystical literature as the "dark night of the soul," is depicted in Very's sonnet "Relief":

> Oh give me of thy waters pure and clear
> For my soul pants beneath this sultry hour

> There is no spring nor running river near
> That can assuage the burning fever's power.

The final stage of divine union Very described, Jones believes, in (among other poems) "The New World," in which the awaking sleeper

> beholds around the earth and sky
> That ever real stands; the rolling spheres,
> And heaving billows of the boundless main,
> That show though time is past no trace of years,
> And earth restored he sees as his again;
> The earth that fades not, and the heavens that stand;
> Their strong foundations laid by God's right hand!

A more obscure depiction by Very of his own state, from a spiritual rather than a psychological point of view, is to be found in three prose epistles addressed "To the Unborn." Unpublished until recently, these works were among Emerson's papers.[65] Why Very gave them to Emerson is unknown. They may have been an attempt on Very's part to convert Emerson, one of the unborn, to his own newly discovered spiritual insights. Emerson mentions a letter from Very accompanying the essay on Shakespeare (sent to him on the day that Very was forced to leave Harvard) that "betrayed the state of his mind"[66]—that is, betrayed it as being disturbed; if these epistles are actually the "letter" referred to, then they were written in September 1838. An alternative explanation is that they were intended, as Gittleman assumes, as an introduction to the edition of Very's essays and poems that Emerson was preparing and were considered by Emerson unsuitable for publication. In this case they could have been written at any time between September 1838 and the summer of 1839.

In these epistles, which are packed with scriptural allusions and in which the logic is associative at best, two points that bespeak his mystical experience are quite clear: Very distinguishes between himself and the unregenerated world that has not passed through the stages of mystical rebirth as he has done; and he identifies himself with Christ. He describes the spiritual condition of those to whom he addresses himself, the "unborn":

> To me, you were *dead* or *still born* into *what you call* the world; that is *your* bodies were begotten in enjoyment; and what you call your spirits naturally, as you would say, seek enjoyment. . . . By your still birth you are by inheritance opposed to the universal relations into which you are thrown, and this opposition continues until it ends in giving you a new body and spirit by which you recognize *God* as a parent. *This* is *the Birth;* the other was the *dead*-birth.[67]

The unborn therefore are not competent to interpret the scriptures:

> Remember therefore that with the real meaning of Scripture, as with the commonest thing about you, *you* can as yet have nothing to do. . . . Those of whom you there read, or *think you read,* as well as the commonest things of your daily life, move and are, as I have thus shown you, in other worlds than your own, and only exhibited to your sight that you may be led to aspire to communion with them. . . . *You* must then *be born into the world,* before you can have to do with those who are there [i.e., in Scripture], or learn to use the gifts of it.[68]

Very, on the other hand, has not only been *born,* but *born again* and is potentially the father of the born. He thus assumes a Christ-like role, coming "in person with authority to claim you as mine. *I* am the Resurrection." When those now unborn have been spiritually born, they will "know it was *I* who called you forth from the grave; it was *I* who raised you from the bed of sickness."[69]

Very's description of his spiritual status in the "Epistles to the Unborn" and his account of his experience in the letter to Bellows bear all the hallmarks of mysticism described in William James's study of the phenomenon.[70] The first of these is *ineffability,* the impossibility of expressing the experience. The tortured syntax of both Very's epistles and his letter to Bellows demonstrates the difficulty of communicating his experience. James's second mark is *noetic quality:* the mystical state seems to the one who experiences it to be illuminative, to provide access to truths previously hidden. Thus Very claims to know things that others do not and cannot know, such as how to understand Scripture. He now understands, what he himself did not understand before, that the first stage of his experience, his "change of heart," was only what "is commonly called the new birth," only the preparative state corresponding to John the Baptist's ministry. James's third hallmark is *transiency:* the mystical state at its height is usually not sustained for more than a few hours. According to his own account, Very's seems to have lasted for "two or three weeks." This would cover the period when he was proclaiming the coming of Christ in Cambridge to Henry Ware, Jr., and to his students at Harvard; and, after his dismissal there, in Salem to Elizabeth Peabody and various Salem ministers; and part of his stay at McLean Asylum. James's elaboration on *passivity,* his final mark of mysticism, perfectly coincides with Very's state of mind as he conveyed it in the letter to Bellows, in conversations with all his acquaintances, and in his poems: "the mystic feels as if his own will were in abeyance, and indeed sometimes as if he were grasped and held by a superior power."[71] Very's sonnet "The Son" is one of many expressions of this idea:

Father! I wait thy word—the sun doth stand,
Beneath the mingling line of night and day,
A listening servant waiting thy command
To roll rejoycing on its silent way;
The tongue of time abides the appointed hour,
Till on our ear its solemn warnings fall;
The heavy cloud withholds the pelting shower,
Then every drop speeds onward at thy call;
The bird reposes on the yielding bough
With breast unswollen by the tide of song;
So does my spirit wait thy presence now
To pour thy praise in quickening life along
Chiding with voice divine man's lengthened sleep,
While round the Unuttered Word and Love their vigils keep.

Contemporaneous accounts and estimates of Very's behavior tend to con-
firm the classification of him as mystic, at least among sympathetic associates
who did not immediately brand him as insane. Bronson Alcott wrote such an
evaluation in describing Very's contributions to an informal gathering of the
Transcendental Club. The meeting, which took place at Cyrus Bartol's home
following a lecture by Emerson in Boston on 5 December 1838, had as its pur-
pose "further talk on the Doctrine of Life" (Alcott Journal, December 1838,
pp. 429–39).

> He said much that was true, and expressed himself with great beauty.
> His language is that of an Oriental, and one might almost fancy himself
> in the presence of St John, whose words he affects. He is a phenomenon
> quite remarkable in this age of sensualism and idolatry. He is a mystic of
> the most ideal class; a pietist of the transcendental order. How few there
> are of sufficient insight into the soul to apprehend the facts of which he
> speaks, divested of the oriental dialect in which he puts them. He will be
> deemed insane by nearly every man.
>   (Alcott Journal, December 1838, p. 446)

If one concedes the possibility of the mystical state, Jones Very must surely
be admitted to it. No evidence exists that any one of his contemporaries,
friend or foe, doubted his sincerity when he was at the height of his ecstasy.
Those who considered him insane were manifestly convinced of his earnest-
ness. One might, of course, pose various explanations for Very's arriving in
September 1838 at the state that caused him to astound the Harvard and
Salem communities and begin producing remarkable poetry. Edwin Gittle-
man postulates a psychological condition deriving largely from Very's feelings

toward his mother, whose unconventional common law marriage and reputed atheism must have generated shame and guilt in her son. Modern psychiatry might well suspect bipolar (manic-depressive) syndrome as a contributing factor, pointing to the alternating periods of extroversion and seclusion during the critical period, both apparently accompanied by frenzied writing of poems. Temporal-lobe-epilepsy, a condition suffered, according to some estimates, by as many as one in every one hundred adults, is characterized by a syndrome including the following symptoms: hyperreligiosity; hypergraphia, the uncontrollable compulsion to write; "stickiness," the reluctance to end conversations (cf. Hawthorne's remark that Very "is somewhat unconscionable as to the length of his calls");[72] transient aggressiveness, rarely leading to violence; and altered or decreased interest in sex. Very manifested most if not all of these symptoms during this period. Some members of the medical community speculate that a number of major writers and artists have suffered from this condition, including Dostoevsky, Flaubert, Lewis Carroll, Eugene O'Neill, Arthur Inman, and Vincent Van Gogh.[73] In Very's case, however, no accounts of any seizures, which typically mark this condition, have survived.

All such theories are of course speculative. What is less speculative is that Very's condition of mind leading up to his heightened state was surely influenced by some of the more significant experiences he had had over the previous months. During this period he had shown signs of increasing interest not only in religion but also in the Transcendentalist approach to it. He owned a copy of Emerson's *Nature*, published in September 1836, with its memorable account of "the currents of the Universal Being circulat[ing] through" the author, making him "part or particle with God," and had read and carefully marked it. He no doubt regularly heard Emerson lecture or preach, for Elizabeth Peabody had found him in December 1837 already "an enthusiastic listener to Mr. Emerson" (*Letters of E.P.P.*, pp. 404–5). In April 1838 he had met Emerson, visited in his home, and Emerson had inscribed his copy of *Nature*. In May he must have felt honored by the invitation to attend his first meeting of the Transcendental Club, and he no doubt found provocative the topic for discussion ("Is Mysticism an Element of Christianity?"). Two months later, on July 15, Emerson delivered his address to the graduating class of the Divinity School, attacking the worn-out dogmas and forms of the church. The strong likelihood is that Very, a student himself at the Divinity School (though not a member of the graduating class) and one who must have been by now considering Emerson a mentor, was present for the address; in any case he would certainly have obtained a copy soon after its publication on August 21. In urging each of the students to become a "new-born bard of the Holy Ghost," Emerson gave a precise description of what in a matter of two months Jones Very would believe himself to have become.

The cumulative effect of such experiences as his study of Emerson's *Nature*, his participation in the Transcendental Club's discussion of mysticism, and the hearing or reading of Emerson's Divinity School Address may have been to set Very up for his psychological-religious crisis in mid-September. Indeed, it is possible that there is a certain sense in which the Unitarian establishment of Cambridge and Salem were correct in tying Very's ecstatic state to his association with Emerson and the Transcendentalists. It seems likely that his recent close affiliation with them, combined no doubt with other psychological and religious influences and pressures, to at least some extent functioned to "program" Very for the experience of mystical union. But whatever may have triggered it, the evidence is persuasive that Jones Very was in 1838 undergoing such an experience. And while almost all critics agree that Very was a mystic, few—Jones, Lyons, and Warner B. Berthoff[74] being the most notable exceptions—have read the poems in light of the mystical tradition. I believe that this perspective is the most fruitful one from which to view the poetry of the ecstatic period, as well as for understanding how and why the poetry written earlier and later differs from it.

VERY AS POET

Two facts that have not been generally recognized are basic to the understanding of Very's poetry: the poems written during an approximately eighteen-month period in 1838–40 were composed under the direct influence of a recent overwhelming mystical experience undergone by the author, whatever its origin; those composed earlier or later were not. Failure to appreciate this distinction has marred a good deal of the criticism of Very's poetry. Critics have frequently puzzled over inconsistencies between ecstatic poems and those written earlier or later. But these differences should not be surprising, for in a very real sense it was not the same mind that produced the poems of the different periods.

Very wrote poetry from the early 1830s to shortly before his death in 1880. Most of this verse is not dated either in the editions or in the two biographies of Very, and the student of Very's poetry is likely to be baffled by an overwhelming quantity of work of widely varying quality, with little way of knowing what was written when.[75] Side by side with poetic ecstatic utterances are quite mundane verses on the potato blight and the dangers of the camphene lamp. The present edition arranges Very's poems chronologically as far as possible. This chronological arrangement has been immensely illuminating in making sense of the variations in style and quality of the verse. Students of Very will now be able to trace his development from an ambitious, aspiring young poet writing poems on secular themes with a view to publication; to the voice of the "Spirit," as he conceived himself for a time, writing intensely religious verse and attracting the attention of Emerson and his circle; to his final stage as a rather conventional writer of occasional and religious verse.

The verse that Very wrote between mid-1833 when he was twenty years old and the late summer of 1838 is largely imitative of English late neoclassical and romantic poets, notably Wordsworth, and is often sentimental. The very earliest poems, often in the form of long blank verse meditations, and sometimes in heroic couplets or rhymed quatrains, give way toward the later part of this period to the form that was to become his favorite, the sonnet. The poems of this early period, which reveal a self-conscious and ambitious young poet struggling to find his voice, were published in Very's hometown newspaper, the *Salem Observer*, in a college publication, *Harvardiana*, in the *Knickerbocker*, and in Emerson's edition of Very's poetry. An examination of the extant manuscripts from this period reveals something of Very's composition habits: he revised heavily and sometimes produced multiple drafts of particular poems. With the exception of a few poems ("Beauty," "The Columbine") written late in this period that have intrinsic aesthetic merit, the interest that the poetry of this early period holds for the reader will be largely in terms of what it reveals of Very's biography and of his poetic development. Its contrast with the poetry of the succeeding period is particularly striking.

At the point of Very's religious awakening his poetry takes on an entirely new character. The conventional, sentimental, often forced nature poetry of early 1838 is suddenly supplanted by a poetry of exaltation. In the following sonnet, "The New Birth," Very both announces and demonstrates his new style, subject matter, and new manner of composition:

> 'Tis a new life—thoughts move not as they did
> With slow uncertain steps across my mind,
> In thronging haste fast pressing on they bid
> The portals open to the viewless wind;
> That comes not, save when in the dust is laid 5
> The crown of pride that gilds each mortal brow,
> And from before man's vision melting fade
> The heavens and earth—Their walls are falling now—
> Fast crowding on each thought claims utterance strong,
> Storm-lifted waves swift rushing to the shore 10
> On from the sea they send their shouts along,
> Back through the cave-worn rocks their thunders roar,
> And I a child of God by Christ made free
> Start from death's slumbers to eternity.

Very's mystical experience, which this poem attempts to communicate, has radically altered the nature of his poetry. The extraordinary intensity of the poem's tone and its apocalyptic theme are a significant departure from the earlier poems. It has been perhaps the most dramatic accomplishment of this project to make possible the pinpointing of this transformation almost to the day,[76] or at least to the poem.

"The New Birth" marks a watershed in terms of the poet's habits of composition as well as of subject and style. The manuscripts that survive from this period reflect the "thronging haste" and "fast crowding on" of thoughts and words described in this poem. They show very little if any revision, and in many cases punctuation is entirely absent. Sometimes a large number of sonnets written in small script and in pencil are crowded on a single sheet of paper. This sort of composition was clearly not slow and laborious but spontaneous, close perhaps to automatic writing, at times an almost frenzied recording of the voice of the Muse, or, as Very would have it, the Spirit. Very's output during these months was remarkable. Elizabeth Peabody reported to Emerson on 3 December 1838 that the poems "flow from him— impromptu—one or two per day" (*Letters of E.P.P.*, p. 220). Very began publishing them in the *Salem Observer* at the rate of two per week. At the height of this creative period four or six were appearing each week, and the editor of the *Observer* eventually created a new column for Very's poetry. Other poems of this period were published in James Freeman Clarke's *Western Messenger*, and approximately three-fourths of the sixty-five poems of Emerson's edition of Very belong to this period.

It is on the poetry of the ecstatic period that Jones Very's distinctive contribution to American literature must rest. The poems written at this time were almost exclusively religious. Very's chief concern in them was more evangelistic than aesthetic: they are his attempts to deliver the message that came, in whatever way, to him. Yet it is in fact Very's belief in the divine origin of his words that accounts for both some of the strengths and some of the weaknesses of the poems. A number of them are little more than paraphrases of Scripture—the sayings of Jesus, often, put into verse. A number of critics from Emerson forward have noted Very's lack of polish and craftsmanship in the writing of individual lines, especially his proclivity for "frequent inversions that twist the natural order of speech for the sake of rhyme" and the frequent failure of these poems to live up to their arresting openings.[77] The note of egotism inherent in the poetry of one who feels himself a special mouthpiece of God is sometimes, to some readers, offensive. A concomitant note of paranoia also is sometimes irritating, though the reader should bear in mind that Very was indeed persecuted (by the Harvard authorities and by the Salem ministers) for delivering his revelations. But the special nature of this poetry is also responsible for the breathless intensity of the verse. At its best, as in "The New Birth," "The Dead," and "Hope," Very's poetry is a highly charged utterance, or, in another vein (as in "The Son" and "The Prayer" [No. 829]) is striking in its depiction of a serene passiveness of the soul before

God. It is Very's poetry of this period that has attracted most of the critical interest.

The history of Very criticism in this century begins with Yvor Winters. In a 1936 article that was reprinted and became more widely known in collections of 1938 and 1943,[78] Winters proposed Jones Very as the third major rediscovery in this century of neglected nineteenth-century American writers, following Emily Dickinson and Herman Melville. He suggested that Very's nascent reputation had been ruined by the appearance of Clarke's "complete" edition of 1886, which contained "an enormous amount of dead materials."[79] It was mainly the poetry of the mystical, ecstatic period that interested Winters; he praised the "quality of intense personal conviction" in such poems ("The Created" he thought his best work) and judged Very "one of the finest devotional poets in English."[80] Winters argued that Very was "not a Transcendentalist at all, but a Christian, and a dogmatic one," "whose theological and spiritual affiliations were with the earlier Puritans and Quakers rather than with the Unitarians or with the friends of Emerson."[81] The force of Winters's promotion of Very was vitiated by the fact that his enthusiasm for Very was used as a springboard for an assault on Emerson. Winters asserted that Very had had the experience which Emerson merely preached; that Emerson was really "a fraud and a sentimentalist," not a mystic; that his guiding spirit was "instinct and personal whim."[82]

Winters's call for elevating Very to his rightful place in American literary history was responded to in 1942 by William I. Bartlett's biography *Jones Very: Emerson's "Brave Saint,"* which established the essential biographical facts of Very's life. Perhaps just as important, Bartlett presented seventy-one previously unpublished poems, most of them from the ecstatic period, and thirty-eight poems previously published in periodicals but not included in any edition of Very's poetry.

Warner B. Berthoff followed with a sound consideration of Very's thought, taking into its compass his essays, poems, and sermons. Berthoff noted as Very's major themes "the importance of submission to God's will; the lifelessness of the world without God's spirit; the light that floods the world when man wills his obedience; the brotherhood of the regenerate, and their sense of militant mission; and divine illumination." He concluded that Very "is the one figure of his generation who succeeded in translating the power of religious vision into formal poetry."[83]

Three important considerations of Very appeared in 1966–67. The first of these was Nathan Lyons's introduction to his selected edition of Very's poems. This study emphasizes Very's "Quietist" side, demonstrated in his insistence on will-lessness. Lyons sees "The Hand and the Foot" as the central statement of Very's thought. Especially valuable is Lyons's stylistic analysis of a number of the ecstatic poems, particularly his treatment of Very's use of paradox.

Harry L. Jones's 1967 dissertation analyzes the symbolism in 182 of Very's poems written during his ecstatic period. Because by its very nature such an experience defies expression, Jones notes, mystics frequently have resorted to symbolic language in an effort to convey their experience as fully as possible. Jones's approach is quite useful in interpreting the poems of this ecstatic period, particularly his convincing orientation of these works within the mystical tradition; his readings of the poems in light of traditional mystical symbols have the great merit of making sense of a number of enigmatic poems. Jones's analysis shows that Very uses symbols traditionally associated with Christian mysticism as well as some personal symbols.[84]

Jones further argues that the ecstatic poems constitute a "mystical sonnet sequence"; that they go through a logical progression from describing Very's own mystical journey, through his comments on the unregenerate, to his mission to convert them and finally, Jones believes, to the eventual abandonment of that mission (he cites "The Complaint"). Jones admits, however, that the sequence as he conceives it "is logical, not temporal, for there is no way of knowing whether or not the sonnets were composed in that order."[85] It is true that while most of these sonnets may be approximately dated by their publication dates (as they are in this edition), a number of them were not published in Very's lifetime, though it is clear from subject, style, and tone that they belong to this period. And no doubt for a time at least, because of the rate at which Very was writing, there must have been a backlog of unpublished poems. In other words, many of these poems were written so nearly contemporaneously that it is impossible to determine the exact order of their composition. Yet I find Jones's suggestion of a nicely ordered "mystical sonnet sequence" to be the imposition of too simple and neat a structure on what is a great mass of outpourings of various moods, voices, and forms.

One problem is that Jones's study is based upon only 182 of approximately 300 poems written during this period, and he does not explain his basis for choosing these particular "mystical sonnets." A number of the remaining contemporaneous or nearly contemporaneous poems he no doubt excluded because they are not sonnets, and a small additional number had not been discovered at the time of his study. But it is difficult to understand why such sonnets as "The Coming," "The Flight," "Thy Better Self," "I am the Way," "My Church," "The Message," "The Foe," "Comfort," and many others clearly written during this period and under the same sort of imperative as those that Jones designates as "mystical sonnets" should have been excluded. Jones has usefully described the mystical environment of a number of the poems of this period, but not nearly all of them; he particularly neglects those poems in which the speaker is apparently a member of the Godhead (the ones that Lawrence Buell finds most interesting),[86] and those not written in the sonnet form, probably composed for the most part near the end of the ecstatic period.

In 1967 appeared Edwin Gittleman's critical biography of Very. This work, concentrating on Very's "effective years" (1833–40), is an exhaustive examination of the existing documentary evidence for those years. It analyzes Very's behavior, essays, and poetry from, to a large extent, a psychological point of view, giving great significance to the fact that Very's parents were never formally married and that his mother was further known for her atheism. Since the validity of Gittleman's interpretation of certain poems in light of specific biographical events rests on the accuracy of his dating of the poems, his biographical reading of the poems is occasionally flawed by incomplete information or unfounded assumptions about composition dates. For example, he treats six sonnets that he states were written between April and August 1838 as "essentially psychological," "written from the advantage of the inward struggle," which Gittleman believes Very had "seemingly concluded."[87] Three of these sonnets were in fact published in the *Salem Observer* between April and August and were in all likelihood written during that period. One of the remaining three ("The Song") was not published until December 1838, and although it is possible that it was composed several months earlier, between April and August, there is no evidence to indicate that it was. The same is true of "To the pure all things are pure," which was not published until September 1839 in *Essays and Poems.* "Nature" (No. 348), however, could not have been a product of the April–August 1838 period, having appeared in the *Observer* on 29 July 1837. Valuable as Gittleman's study is, it is well to read it with a wary eye for unsubstantiated assumptions.

The publication of Gittleman's biography and of Lyons's edition stimulated the appearance of a number of studies of the poetry in the late 1960s through the 1980s. Ludwig Deringer provided the only extended consideration to date of Very's rhetoric in *Die Rhetorik in der Sonettkunst von Jones Very.*[88] Several of the studies of the last quarter century, including those by Anthony Herbold, Carl Dennis, and David Seed, focused on Very's nature poetry. Herbold searched for but did not find consistency in Very's view of nature:[89] Very, he thought, "held two mutually incompatible concepts simultaneously." The first view was that nature was "finite, contingent, imperfect"; the second, that it was "infinite, self-generating, perfect." Herbold posited as the cause of this inconsistency Very's "double heritage" as both Calvinist and Romantic.[90]

Carl Dennis's consideration of Very's nature poems led him to disagree with Winters's exaggerated contrast of Very and Emerson.[91] He pointed out their similar aesthetic: both see "the poet as receiving direct inspiration from the ultimate source of truth"; both see "the poet's task as awakening man's spiritual life by revealing the moral truths expressed in the material world"; and both see "nature as a source of analogues for the highest laws of the mind, as a language to be read by an inspired interpreter." Very in fact adopts Emerson's theory of correspondence from *Nature*, seeing that nature "bodies forth by analogy spiritual truth." [92]

More recently David Seed has used Very's treatment of nature to argue that he had some beliefs in common with the Transcendentalists,[93] "but ultimately diverged from them." Like Dennis, Seed sees nature as "a source of analogies and parables" for Very that helps relieve the otherwise "constant plainness of expression" of the poems. But he believes that Very had a "wary, defensive" attitude toward nature, seeing it as a secondary means of revelation only if "it did not rival God's primacy or remind him of the profane world he had left behind." [94]

The use of nature as analog is a feature of Very's verse throughout his career but is most obvious (and most simplistic) in the later poetry; in these poems, as Dennis observes, nature to Very is not cryptic (as it is to Emerson) but lucid, and the simplicity of language and form of these poems reflects this view. The ecstatic poetry makes much more subtle symbolic use of images from nature: the unregenerate masses are associated with images of wasteland, winter, night, unfruitfulness; the reborn are identified with day, dawn, morning, fruitfulness; and wind, breath, and rain are connected with the Holy Spirit.[95] The general lack of a critical consensus on Very's view of nature may be attributed to a considerable extent to a failure to distinguish among the various phases of Very's life and poetic career. Indeed, Very did hold conflicting views on nature and on other topics, but he did not hold them simultaneously.

The issue of the voice or persona in many of the ecstatic poems is one of the most intriguing questions raised in recent Very criticism. Lawrence Buell opened this topic with a provocative and insightful discussion of the exploitation of the possibilities of the Transcendentalist idea of the "self" in the poems of Very and Whitman.[96] Buell notes that Very assumes in his poems the identity of various prophets (John the Baptist, Isaiah, Noah, Moses) as well as of God the Father, the Son, and the Holy Ghost, and also "an identity of his own, albeit of a somewhat generalized sort." Buell calls this alternation between divine, prophetic, and human voices "provocatively disorienting" to the reader; he finds it sometimes impossible to resolve the speaker in a particular poem into a single voice. On the whole, Buell judges this manipulation of voices, which he suspects to be more conscious than Very and his friends were willing to admit, to be a "poetic asset." Like William P. Andrews, Harry Jones, and Nathan Lyons before him, Buell finds it tempting to rearrange the poems of the ecstatic period into a sequence; but he concludes, rightly, I believe, that such an ordering of the poems would "impute to [Very] a degree of

calculation which clashes somewhat with one's impression of him as a vision-
ary, and . . . make his work seem more contrived and less spontaneous. . . .
The rich interplay of voices . . . would have been regularized and toned down,
and the prophetic voice would begin to sound like that of the pitchman."[97]

David Robinson responds to Buell's analysis by questioning his assumption
that Very was not consciously exploiting voice for literary purposes.[98] Robin-
son believes the poems were "wrought by a careful strategy of composition,
based not only on the poet's felt inspiration . . . but also on a conscious at-
tempt to create an impact upon his readers." Very carefully manipulated the
voice or person of his poems perhaps not for aesthetic purposes but for his
purpose of conversion. Robinson defines two different techniques by which
Very presents the self: his use of the exemplary self and of the transcendent
self. In certain poems Very creates a persona to be held as an example to his
readers—an example of piety or perception. But in yet other poems Very
uses a voice that has transcended the bounds of selfhood and assumed the
authority of one of the members of the Godhead. These poems of the tran-
scendent self are Very's most daringly transcendental poems, but they often
lose their impact by becoming mundanely biblical. The surrender to biblical
phraseology was "poetically . . . too often a disaster." Some of Very's more
successful poems of this sort, such as "Flee to the mountains," depend on the
poet's "ability to muddy the distinction between man and God as he chal-
lenges the reader, revealing only gradually that the speaker of the poem is no
human agent, but God or Christ."[99]

David Seed too addresses the problem of shifting voices identified by Buell,
linking the phenomenon to Very's literal belief in inspiration. "Once he
achieves sanctification he becomes the efficient receptor of the voices of the
spirit" and "the self becomes destabilized. As the individual submits his will to
God, he loses his singular identity and becomes the locus of different voices"
that "represent the temporary dramatizations of different spiritual forces or
human exempla."[100]

This critical interest in the issue of the voice or persona in many of the
ecstatic poems is well deserved; the assumption of the divine voice and a com-
plex manipulation of voice within certain of these poems is, as Buell notes, a
truly daring poetic pose. The apparent voice of the Holy Spirit proclaims,

> I come the rushing wind that shook the place
> Where those once sat who spake with tongues of fire[.]
>
> ("The Promise," No. 225)

Presumably it is God the Father who announces in "The Message,"

> There is no voice but it is born of Me
> I Am there is no other God beside

and in "The Creation,"

> I said of old when darkness brooded long
> Upon the waste of waters Be thou light
> And forthwith sprang the sun rejoicing strong
> To chase away the mystery of the night[.]

And the Son seems the speaker in "I Am the Bread of Life":

> I am thy life thou shalt upon me feed
> And daily eat my flesh and drink my blood[.]

Buell's observation that it is impossible to resolve the voice in certain poems into a single speaker is striking. He cites as an example "Terror," a poem that seems to begin with the voice of an observer of the apocalypse:

> There is no safety; fear has seized the proud;
> The swift run to and fro but cannot fly;
> Within the streets I hear no voices loud,
> They pass along with low, continuous cry.

But the speaker suddenly shifts in the last two lines to become God himself:

> Repent! why do ye still uncertain stand,
> The kingdom of my son is nigh at hand!

Though he does not quite spell out the idea, Buell implies that Very's poetic practice here reaches beyond the ordinary sense of a single, unified voice or persona.

This notion needs further exploration. An examination of Very's prose epistles "To the Unborn," unpublished in his lifetime, suggests the complexity of Very's vision of himself in his reborn state, a vision that clearly has implications for the nature of his poetic voice. In "An Epistle on Miracles" he writes:

The born are the begetters of the unborn, and those born *again* in their turn the fathers of the born. Who are the *Born* they only know who are so; who are those born *again* they only know who have witnessed the second birth. It is this *second* birth of eternal life of which Jesus said, "*I* am the Resurrection *and* the life, he that believeth on *Me*, though he were dead yet shall he live; and he that liveth and believeth shall never die." So say *I* to you to whom as the unborn I stand in a similar relation. *I* am your Resurrection and life; believe in the *Me* that speaks and you though unborn shall be born yet *again* and shall know the *only Begotten* of the Father. 'He that receives *you*,' said he to his disciples, 'receives Me, and he that receives *Me* receives Him that sent *Me*.' These *Me*'s and *I*'s are the *I's* and *Me's* of persons in the different worlds or states of which I have spoken and which because they are used are confounded by you and you are led to think that the person who speaks is like yourself but gifted in some unaccountable manner with power over you. . . . He who speaks is external to you; he speaks to you from without; but it is *outward from within* and *so* exerts an *external* influence over you. Behold *I* stand without and knock. . . . I was *once* as you *now* are, but I am changed and *as such* exert this power of raising you from the dead; I, this *new I,* stand without *you,* that is the old *you* which I was, and knock. . . . Now *you* see *me,* if sight it may be called, *externally* with an unchanged spirit; then face to face. . . . Then shall you know it was *I* who called you forth from the grave; it was *I* who raised you from the bed of sickness; and *you will* arise and minister unto me.[101]

Here the reborn "I" takes on the role of Christ, standing at the door and knocking, performing miracles of healing and resurrection. The complex mystical concept of self explored in the prose epistles suggests the folly of reducing the voice in certain poems of the ecstatic period to an either/or proposition; such a reduction would at least lessen the poems' suggestiveness.

I would propose that in a number of these poems it is preferable to think in terms of a double or a *layered* voice. A sort of complex voice different from the two unresolved or separate voices in "The Terror" is present in several poems. One of these is "My meat and drink," which reads equally well if the *I* is understood to be that of the reborn or of Christ:

> I do not need thy food, but thou dost mine;
> For this will but the body's wants repair,
> And soon again for meat like this 'twill pine,
> And so be fed by thee with daily care;
> But that which I can give thou needs but eat,   5
> And thou shalt find it in thyself to be;
> Forever formed within a living meat,
> On which to feed will make thy spirit free;
> Thou shalt not hunger more, for freely given
> The bread on which the spirit daily feeds;   10
> This is the bread that cometh down from heaven,
> Of which who eats no other food he needs;
> But this doth grow within him day by day,
> Increasing more the more he takes away.

The poem seems to incorporate two sayings of Jesus in the Gospel of John. The poem's opening statement—"I do not need thy food"—suggests the occasion (recounted in John 4:31–34) when Jesus' disciples urge him to eat

and he responds that he has "meat to eat that ye know not of." The remainder
of the poem seems an allusion to the incident (John 6:31–65) in which Jesus
tells the people, "I am the bread of life: he that cometh to me shall never hun-
ger; and he that believeth on me shall never thirst." Clearly, on one level the
voice in the poem is that of Christ. When it is recalled, however, that Christ
further explains in John 4 that "my meat is to do the will of him that sent me"
and that John 6 includes a similar statement that Jesus came "not to do mine
own will, but the will of him that sent me," the voice in the poem also sounds
very much like that of the regenerated self—the Jones Very of the letter to
Bellows and the "Epistles to the Unborn"—who has lost his own will in the
will of the Father.

A yet more complex layering of voices occurs in the sonnet "I am the Way":

> Thy way is simple for I am the light
> By which thou travelest on to meet thy God
> Brighter and brighter still shall be thy sight
> Till thou hast ended here the path I trod
> Before thee stretches far the thorny way   5
> Yet smoothed for thee by him who went before
> Go on it leads you to the perfect day
> The rest I to the patriarch Abraham swore
> Go on and I will guide you safely through
> For I have walked with suffering feet thy path   10
> Confide in me the Faithful and the True
> And thou shalt flee the approaching day of wrath
> Whose dawn e'en now the horizon's border shows
> And with its kindling fires prophetic glows.

In the first five lines the speaker appears unequivocally to be Christ. In line 6,
which refers to Christ in the third person, the speaker appears to be the voice
of the regenerated preacher. A third voice seems to appear in line 7, that of
God, who swore to Abraham. In this manner, in his mystical state Very uses
poetic voice to mingle his own self with the divine.

Most of the poems of this sort, as Buell notes, did not appear at all either
in Very's lifetime or in the two editions of the 1880s, but were left for Bartlett
to discover and publish in his 1942 biography. Why they did not is matter for
speculation; it is difficult to imagine Very himself during his ecstatic period
practicing self-censorship. It seems likely, however, that these were among the
poems rejected by Emerson for publication in *Essays and Poems*, and possibly
by the *Salem Observer* as well. It is also conceivable that Very's family managed
to suppress these poems during his life as they certainly did after his death:
though they possessed the manuscripts of these sonnets, Very's sisters did not

include them in the so-called "complete" Clarke edition. Neither, fortunately, did they destroy them; but these radical poems were not among the manuscripts that the sisters gave to the Harvard Divinity School and that are now at the Houghton Library. Instead they were left among miscellaneous manuscripts consisting mainly of early drafts and duplicate versions of poems that eventually found their way, after the sisters' deaths, to the Brown University Library.

One question not finally answered by Very's interpreters is whether Very was consciously exploiting the possibilities of voice in these poems. Is he really only a mouthpiece for the divine afflatus, or is he a calculating craftsman, or is he some combination of the two? It is partly our inability to answer such questions definitively that makes the Very of this period intriguing. The early and the late Very as revealed in the poems are both relatively unambiguous and relatively uninteresting.

Toward the end of the ecstatic period, as the chronological arrangement of this edition reveals, Very was exploring verse forms (chiefly quatrains with alternating rhyme) other than the sonnet. The poetry of exaltation continued to be written until early 1840, when it suddenly ceased. Seven or eight months elapse before we can document Very's writing another poem, and that was an occasional poem (No. 351, "The Baker's Island Light"), typical of the kind of verse that he would turn out in greatly diminished quantity and even more greatly diminished quality for the next forty years. Of the 870 or so poems that Very produced during some forty-seven years of writing, approximately one-third belong to an eighteen-month period in 1838–40. (In fact, the prolific period may have been even briefer: since the editor must rely almost entirely on publication dates in order to assign dates to these poems, it is conceivable that Very wrote all or most of them in a considerably shorter period and parceled them out to newspaper publication over the eighteen months. Or perhaps it was not his decision but that of editors to publish only a few poems at a time.)

The poetry of the last forty years is anticlimactic. In 1861 Very responded to the inquiry of a former pupil, the poet Frederick Goddard Tuckerman, concerning his literary activity: "I am not engaged in any literary work. I write occasionally for the Salem Gazette, The Christian Register, and The Monthly Religious Magazine. I have since 1842 been a preacher of the Gospel."[102] Did Very himself not see fit to dignify with the term "literary work" the considerable body of religious, nature, and occasional verse that he was regularly producing? By the time of his death he had written nearly five hundred such poems. The letter does seem to point up what to him was now the focus of his life: his preaching. He was licensed to preach by the Cambridge Association of Ministers (Unitarian) in 1843 but was never ordained, and he never held a regular pulpit. He preached with some regularity throughout eastern Massachusetts and occasionally outside that immediate area—into Maine and Rhode Island. Some 117 of Very's manuscript sermons survive.[103]

The poems that Very wrote for the last forty years of his life include religious, nature, and occasional verse. They generally lack both innovation in style and originality in ideas, reflecting the attitudes of an enlightened, orthodoxly Unitarian New Englander in the mid to late nineteenth century. On several occasions Very took a poem from the ecstatic period and, years later, reworked it into an essentially new poem. A good example is his poem "The First shall be Last," first published on 27 April 1839 in the *Salem Observer*. A comparison with the later version is instructive in delineating the contrast between Very's poetry from the two periods. Though not one of his most successful poems of this period, the first version exemplifies the typical features of his ecstatic sonnets:

> Bring forth, bring forth your silver! it shall be
> But as the dust that meets the passing eye;
> You shall from all your idols break, be free!
> And worship Him whose ear can hear your cry;
> Thou who hast hid within thy learned pelf,   5
> Thou who hast loved another wife than Me,
> Bring forth thine idols, they are born of self;
> And to thy Maker bow the willing knee;
> Each secret thing must now be brought to light,
> Make haste, the day breaks on your hidden spoil;   10
> Go, buy what then will give your soul delight,
> That day can never hurt the wine and oil;
> Make haste, the bridegroom knocks, he's at the door;
> The first must now be last, the last the first before.

The poem bears many of the hallmarks of Very's ecstatic period: the sense of urgency; the suggestion of the divinity of the speaker (the capitalized *Me,* more enigmatic than common even for Very: is the speaker not only divine but female as well?); the reliance on scriptural language; the elliptical nature of the scriptural allusions (there are apparent references at least to Matthew 19:30 [title and line 14], James 5:1–3 [lines 1–2], Revelation 6:6 [line 12], Matthew 25:1–13 [line 13], and possibly Hosea 2:1–8 [lines 1–6, 12]); and the associative rather than logical manner in which the allusions are connected.

More than thirty years later Very recast the poem under a new title for the *Christian Register* (26 February 1870):

Ye have hoarded up treasure in the
last days.—James 5 : 3.

Bring forth your gold and silver! They shall be
But as the dust that meets the passing eye;
You shall from all your idols break; be free!
And worship Him who made earth, sea and sky!
Ye who have hid within your learned pelf,   5
Ye who in gold alone your riches see,
Bring forth your idols! they are born of Self,
Nor longer in their worship bow the knee.
Each secret thing must now be brought to light,
For soon the day breaks on your hidden spoil;   10
Go, buy what then will give your souls delight,
Nor longer for earth's treasures vainly toil;
For each man's work must now be tried by fire,
Which shall consume each selfish, wrong desire.

Some of the sense of urgency is retained, a remnant of the early version, and
the poem continues to rely on scriptural language. But vanished is the pro-
vocative "Me," and the poem is now focused clearly on the message of James
5 : 1–3, a condemnation of the rich. The message is clearer, but the frantic in-
tensity of the early version, in which the speaker alludes to scriptures whose
relevance is not always entirely clear, has been lost. This is typical of the kind
of taming undergone by a number of ecstatic poems as revised by the less
mystical mind of the later Very; and it exemplifies the sorts of differences one
generally finds between the poems of the ecstatic and the later periods.

This is not to say that the later poems are entirely without interest or merit.
There is some historical value in the views of an educated, informed, and
articulate person of Very's place and time on such topics as slavery, war, tech-
nology, and other national and world events. Very expresses in the poems his
strong opposition to slavery as well as to war. Once the Civil War begins, as
much as he wished to see slavery abolished, he never succumbs to the patriotic
fervor, never takes on what would have been the popular role of a propa-
gandist of the war. In the late poems Very is optimistic concerning human
nature and the human condition. He expresses faith in human progress, not
merely in scientific and technological advancement (which he does celebrate
as tokens of that progress), but (despite such temporary setbacks as the war)
in his moral nature as well. In some poems he deplores the materialism of the
age, but without the intensity permeating such searing indictments of man's
lack of spirituality as "The Dead" and "The Graveyard" in the ecstatic period.
In the late poems he continues to use nature, much less cryptically than in

the ecstatic period, as a language in which to read moral and religious truths. He reads lessons in flowers, in trees, in the cycle of the seasons, and regularly observes that the embodiment of such messages is a major function of nature, which can thus be a vital source of truth for man. In keeping with his position as Unitarian preacher, however, he sees the Bible as the definitive source of truth. As he does in his sermons, Very frequently preaches in his poems that man's spiritual existence should begin on earth, not in some future state.

In the late poems there is little if any hint of the Spirit-filled enthusiast of 1838–40. Two of these poems, however, do seem to bear upon his earlier illuminative experience. "The Holy City" presents the view that we are living in two worlds simultaneously, a kind of double environment of the seen and the unseen worlds, the earthly and the heavenly. Though we generally are oblivious to the heavenly realm, it may on occasion be unexpectedly revealed to us—as it was, one imagines, to Very himself:

> Without a warning, save a voice from heaven,
> The holy city doth to earth descend;
> To all alike its light is freely given,
> And men and angels do their voices blend.

In another poem, "On Finding the Truth," Very seems to look back and muse, somewhat wistfully, upon his mystical experience:

> With sweet surprise, as when one finds a flower,
> Which in some lonely spot, unheeded, grows;
> Such were my feelings, in the favored hour,
> When Truth to me her beauty did disclose.
> Quickened I gazed anew on heaven and earth,   5
> For a new glory beamed from earth and sky;
> All things around me shared the second birth,
> Restored with me, and nevermore to die.
> The happy habitants of other spheres,
> As in times past, from heaven to earth came down;   10
> Swift fled in converse sweet the unnumbered years,
> And angel-help did human weakness crown!
> The former things, with Time, had passed away,
> And Man, and Nature lived again for aye.

This poem, dated 1853 in the manuscript but not published in Very's lifetime, is perhaps his most direct poetic statement on this experience. The fact that he did not publish it suggests some reticence on his part in baring his soul on what was perhaps to him now a sensitive subject; but the very fact of his composition of the poem and the attitude which it expresses indicate that, some fifteen years after the event, Very was not renouncing but remembering with feeling the experience that had made him a pariah in Cambridge and Salem and something of a luminary among the Transcendentalists.

If the recent *Columbia Literary History of the United States* is any indication, we may well be on the brink of another renewal of interest in Very: Thomas Wortham there deplores that the nineteenth century "lavished excessive praise on Bryant, Longfellow, Whittier, Holmes and Lowell . . . at the expense of Walt Whitman, Jones Very, and Frederick Goddard Tuckerman," and Lawrence Buell ranks Very and William Ellery Channing the Younger as the most significant Transcendental poets.[104] Very's poetry deserves the fair hearing by scholars, critics, and general readers that has been impossible up to now for the lack of a complete and scholarly edition. It is the goal of the present edition to make possible a full assessment of Very as poet.

NOTES

1. F. O. Matthiessen, *The Oxford Book of American Verse* (New York: Oxford University Press, 1950), p. xix. The two biographies of Very are William Irving Bartlett, *Jones Very: Emerson's "Brave Saint"* (Durham, N.C.: Duke University Press, 1942); and Edwin Gittleman, *Jones Very: The Effective Years, 1833–1840* (New York: Columbia University Press, 1967).

2. David Holmes Conrad, *Memoir of Rev. James Chisholm, A.M.* (New York: Protestant Episcopal Society for the Promotion of Evangelical Knowledge, 1856), pp. 12–13.

3. Helen R. Deese, "A Calendar of the Poems of Jones Very," *Studies in the American Renaissance*, ed. Joel Myerson (Charlottesville: University Press of Virginia, 1986), pp. 305–72.

4. Letter of 29 December 1838 to H. W. Bellows, Bellows Papers, Massachusetts Historical Society; published in Harry L. Jones, "The Very Madness: A New Manuscript," *College Language Association Journal* 10 (March 1967): 196–200; also published as the appendix to this introduction. Hereafter cited as "Letter to Bellows."

5. Samuel G. Ward, Account of interview with Jones Very in 1839, Massachusetts Historical Society; printed in Lyman H. Butterfield, "Come with Me to the Feast; or, Transcendentalism in Action," *Massachusetts Historical Society Miscellany*, No. 6 (December 1960): 3–4. Angle brackets in this edition indicate cancelled material. It is possible to read Very's sonnet "Beauty" and the third paragraph of his "Epistle on Birth" as implying such a sexual crisis.

6. "Records of the Philanthropic Society in the Theological School of Harvard University," p. 105, Harvard University Archives.

7. These poems are now at the Houghton Library of Harvard University.

8. Letter to F. G. Tuckerman, 24 April 1861, Houghton Library, Harvard University.

9. Gittleman, pp. 183–91, 225–26.

10. James Elliot Cabot, *A Memoir of Ralph Waldo Emerson*, 2 vols. (Cambridge, Mass.: Riverside Press, 1887), 1:348–49.

11. *The Journals and Miscellaneous Notebooks of Ralph Waldo Emerson*, ed. William H. Gilman, Ralph H. Orth, et al. (Cambridge: Harvard University Press, 1960–82), 15:340. Hereafter cited as *JMN*.

12. *New Bedford Evening Bulletin*, 5 May 1843.

13. Letter of 18 December 1880, printed in "The Life and Services to Literature of Jones Very: A Memorial Meeting, Dec. 14, 1880," *Bulletin of the Essex Institute* 13 (January–June 1881): 32.

14. Francis B. Dedmond, *Sylvester Judd* (Boston: Twayne, 1980), passim; "The Life and Services to Literature of Jones Very," p. 28.

15. See Helen R. Deese, "Unpublished and Uncollected Poems of Jones Very," *ESQ: A Journal of the American Renaissance* 30 (3d Quarter 1984): 155–57. The tone of the three-line poem "Simmons Mobile Alabama" certainly suggests a relationship of considerable warmth and intensity, at least on Very's part.

16. Gittleman, pp. 158–60; letter of Peabody to William P. Andrews, 12 November 1880, *Letters of Elizabeth Palmer Peabody*, ed. Bruce A. Ronda (Middletown, Conn.: Wesleyan University Press, 1984), pp. 404–5. Hereafter cited as *Letters of E.P.P.*

17. *The Letters of Ralph Waldo Emerson*, ed. Eleanor M. Tilton (New York: Columbia University Press, 1990), 7:302. Volumes 1–6 ed. Ralph L. Rusk (New York: Columbia University Press, 1939). Hereafter cited as *Letters of R.W.E.*

18. Quoted in *Letters of R.W.E.*, 7:302.

19. Joel Myerson, "A Calendar of Transcendental Club Meetings," *American Literature* 44 (May 1972): 197–207.

20. James Boyden, "Manuscript Diary," 6, 9 September 1838, Harvard University Archives.

21. Quoted in Gittleman, pp. 184–86.

22. "George Moore's Diary," 13, 14 September 1838, Moore Family Papers, American Antiquarian Society; printed in Kenneth Walter Cameron, *Transcendental Epilogue* (Hartford: Transcendental Books, 1965), 1:240.

23. "Memoirs of John Pierce," 8:384 (15 September 1838), Massachusetts Historical Society.

24. See *JMN*, 5:463–65.

25. Gittleman, p. 258.

26. Peabody later recalled in a letter to William P. Andrews that Very had brought the poems on the same evening of the day that he had delivered his revelation to her—that is, on September 16 or 17 (*Letters of E.P.P.*, p. 407). If true, it would mean that Very had already composed a large body of this new "inspired" poetry before he entered McLean Asylum. I find Peabody's chronology suspect, however; in the first place, she was writing from a distance of more than forty years; and in the second place, she made no mention of any poems when she wrote Emerson a detailed account of Very's pre-McLean call upon her a week after it had occurred (*Letters of E.P.P.*, pp. 208–10). She does mention the poems in a letter written 3 December 1838 (*Letters of E.P.P.*, p. 220) and her sister Mary mentions them in a letter of November 24 (see

Helen R. Deese, "The Peabody Family and the Jones Very 'Insanity': Two Letters of Mary Peabody," *Harvard Library Bulletin* 35 [Spring 1987]: 218–29).

27. Deese, "The Peabody Family and the Jones Very 'Insanity,'" pp. 223–26.

28. Deese, "The Peabody Family and the Jones Very 'Insanity,'" pp. 218–29. These two letters, both written on 24 November 1838, give one of the few eyewitness accounts of Very's behavior shortly following his release from McLean Asylum.

29. Deese, "The Peabody Family and the Jones Very 'Insanity,'" pp. 223–26. Curiously, as deeply involved as the Peabody family had been with Very, the relationship was short-lived. George Peabody died, the family moved to Boston in 1840, and Sophia and Mary married within a few years. Neither did Elizabeth maintain the relationship. In retrospect she was puzzled herself that the friendship had been allowed to lapse: "He never came to see me in Boston—As the preternatural excitement of his nerves subsided—I was told that he shunned society." After Very's death she speculated that the reason might have been the embarrassment that she assumed Very must have later felt at this period of eccentric behavior: "I marvel that in 40 years I did not do something to <keep> reopen intercourse with a Spirit so rare—I think I got the impression from someone—that it was painful to Mr. Very himself to recur to a season—in which he certainly was in a degree *beside himself*. I was afraid I might wound him by alluding to it or I do think I should have written to him—It is most painful to think he might have pined for intercourse which was so sympathetic and respectful as mine was" (*Letters of E.P.P.*, p. 409). But for another explanation of the rift in the relationship, see below, p. xxiv.

30. Letter of 3 June 1839 is at Wellesley College Library. Elizabeth Witherell and Rich Landers have brought to my attention what was probably Very's copy of volume 3 of the *Dial*, now at the University of California at Santa Barbara, in which Emerson published Very's poems "The World" and "The Evening Choir." Though Very complained to Emerson of changes made in the latter poem (see Textual Notes for this poem, pp. 636–37), in this copy only two alterations are made to the printed text: in line 4 'God,' is altered to 'God;'; in lines 47–48 'Peace be/On this House,' is altered to 'Peace be on/This House.' "The World" was revised by Very for later publication in the *Christian Register*, and some of those revisions are pencilled in on this copy of the *Dial*. The revisions in this copy of the *Dial*, in short, hardly support Very's charges that Emerson edited his works freely, but neither do they prove the negative.

31. Emerson stated that he had chosen sixty-six poems (*Letters of R.W.E.*, 2:209), but only sixty-five were included in the volume. Richard Henry Dana, Sr., sending William Cullen Bryant a copy of *Essays and Poems*, wrote that he understood "that these [poems] were selected from a large number by Ralph Waldo Emerson, & that he has pronounced the others to be unworthy publication" (Letter of 21 May 1840, Dana Papers, Massachusetts Historical Society).

32. Emerson's accompanying note to Margaret Fuller, editor of the *Dial*, suggests that he might have been less than eager to write the review: "Here is a notice of Very's Poems which you demanded for the 16th" (*Letters of R.W.E.*, 2:405).

33. *Dial* 2 (July 1841): 130–31.

34. *The Collected Works of Ralph Waldo Emerson*, ed. Alfred R. Ferguson et al. (Cambridge: Harvard University Press, 1979), 2:119–20.

35. Letters of Very to Emerson, dated 26 March 1840, undated [c. April 1840], 21 November 1841, 23 November 1842 (Wellesley College Library).

36. Manuscript Journals of Caroline H. Dall, 11 June 1880, Massachusetts Historical Society.

37. On 23 November 1842 Very mentions having received the last issue of the *Dial* from Peabody. This is the last direct contact between them that I have been able to document (letter to Emerson, Wellesley College Library).

38. *Letters of R.W.E.*, 2:179, 184; *The Letters of Margaret Fuller*, ed. Robert N. Hudspeth (Ithaca: Cornell University Press, 1983), 2:53.

39. Myerson, "Calendar," pp. 197–207.

40. Gittleman, p. 268.

41. James Freeman Clarke, Introduction to "Religious Sonnets by Jones Very, Salem, Mass.," *Western Messenger* 6 (March 1839): 309–11; letter of Very (8 December 1838) to Bronson Alcott, copied in A. Bronson Alcott, Manuscript Journal, December 1838, pp. 441–45, Houghton Library, Harvard University. Hereafter cited as "Alcott Journal."

42. Walter Harding, *The Days of Henry Thoreau* (New York: Dover, 1982), p. 98; Ellen Sewell is the young woman to whom Thoreau proposed.

43. *Journal. Volume I: 1837–1844*, ed. Elizabeth Hall Witherell et al. (Princeton: Princeton University Press, 1981), p. 459.

44. Manuscript Sermon #1019, first preached 22 May 1841, and Sermon #1040, first preached 1 September 1841, Watertown, Mass., Free Public Library.

45. Letter of 26 June 1839 in Frederick Wagner, "Eighty-six Letters (1814–1882) of A. Bronson Alcott," *Studies in the American Renaissance*, ed. Joel Myerson (Boston: Twayne, 1980), p. 183.

46. Alcott Journal, December 1838, p. 450; *JMN*, 9:339.

47. *Mosses from an Old Manse*, Centenary Edition, ed. William Charvat et al. (Columbus: Ohio State University Press, 1974), p. 638.

48. Letter of 21 May 1840, Massachusetts Historical Society.

49. Letter of 14 January 1865, Massachusetts Historical Society.

50. See letter of Very to Caroline H. Dall, 19 June 1855, Massachusetts Historical Society.

51. Very, letter to Emerson, 21 November 1841, Wellesley College Library.

52. Helen R. Deese, "Selected Sermons of Jones Very," *Studies in the American Renaissance*, ed. Joel Myerson (Charlottesville: University Press of Virginia, 1984), pp. 65–71.

53. Frederick C. Dahlstrand, *Amos Bronson Alcott: An Intellectual Biography* (Rutherford, N.J.: Fairleigh Dickinson Press, 1982), p. 219.

54. F. B. Sanborn and William T. Harris, *A. Bronson Alcott: His Life and Philosophy* (Boston: Roberts, 1893), 1:478; Dahlstrand, p. 219.

55. Sanborn and Harris, 2:438.

56. Sanborn and Harris, 1:297.

57. *Poems and Essays by Jones Very: Complete and Revised Edition*, ed. James Freeman Clarke (Boston: Houghton, Mifflin, 1886), p. 519.

58. "The Life and Services to Literature of Jones Very, pp. 1–35.

59. Letter of 18 November 1838, Essex Institute; quoted in Bartlett, p. 59, and Gittleman, p. 258.

60. Very Papers, Brown University Library.

61. Yvor Winters, "Jones Very: A New England Mystic," *American Review* 7 (May 1936): 159–78; rpt. as "Jones Very and R. W. Emerson: Aspects of New England Mysticism" in *Maule's Curse* (Norfolk, Conn.: New Directions, 1938), pp. 125–36, and in *In Defense of Reason* (Denver: University of Denver Press, 1943), pp. 262–82; James A. Levernier, "Calvinism and Transcendentalism in the Poetry of Jones Very," *ESQ: A Journal of the American Renaissance* 24 (1st Quarter 1978): 30–41; David Robinson, "Jones Very, the Transcendentalists, and the Unitarian Tradition," *Harvard Theological Review* 68 (April 1975): 105–24; Nathan Lyons, Introduction to *Jones Very: Selected Poems* (New Brunswick, N.J.: Rutgers University Press, 1966).

62. Elizabeth Peabody's attempt to distinguish between Emerson's ideas and Very's "insanity" has been noted; Charles Stearns Wheeler similarly argued, "Very does not believe even as Emerson does. Very bases all his insane notion . . . upon the authority of the Bible. Emerson's faith allows no authority" (John Olin Eidson, *Charles Stearns Wheeler: Friend of Emerson* [Athens: University of Georgia Press, 1951], p. 47).

63. Very wrote a letter a few days earlier (December 24) to another former fellow divinity student, Rufus Ellis. Like the letter to Bellows it reveals his religious fixation at this period, but rather than recounting his own mystical experience as Very does in the letter to Bellows, this one urges Ellis to greater spirituality. The letter to Ellis is at the University of Iowa.

64. Harry L. Jones, "Symbolism in the Mystical Poetry of Jones Very," unpub. diss., Catholic University of America, 1967; Evelyn Underhill, *Mysticism: A Study in the Nature and Development of Man's Spiritual Consciousness* (New York: Meridian Books, 1955), pp. 169–70.

65. Manuscripts of these three epistles, "An Epistle on Birth," "An Epistle on Prayer," and "An Epistle on Miracles," are at the Wellesley College Library; they have been published, with analysis, in Phyllis Cole, "Jones Very's 'Epistles to the Unborn,'" *Studies in the American Renaissance* (Boston: Twayne, 1982), pp. 169–83.

66. *Letters of R.W.E.*, 2:165.

67. Cole, p. 176.

68. Cole, pp. 176–77.

69. Cole, pp. 179–80.

70. William James, *The Varieties of Religious Experience: A Study in Human Nature* (New York: Modern Library, 1902), pp. 371–72.

71. James, p. 372.

72. Letter of 10 July 1840 to Sophia Peabody, in Julian Hawthorne, *Nathaniel Hawthorne and His Wife* (Boston: James R. Osgood, 1884), 1:221.

73. Eve LaPlante, "The Riddle of TLE," *Atlantic* 262 (November 1988): 31–35.

74. Warner B. Berthoff, "Jones Very: New England Mystic," *Boston Public Library Quarterly* 2 (1950): 63–76.

75. Lyons, in *Jones Very: Selected Poems*, does include some dating information for the seventy-five poems in his edition.

76. The manuscript version of this poem in the papers of Sylvester Judd (a student at the Divinity School) includes Judd's notation "Cambridge. Sept, 1838./ By My Friend, Jones Very." This notation is the only indication we have that Very was writing his distinctively new sort of poetry as early as September. "The New Birth" appeared in the *Salem Observer* on 27 October 1838. It must have been delivered to the editor by at least October 24, when Very left Salem for a five-day stay with Emerson at Concord.

77. See Carl Dennis, "Correspondence in Very's Nature Poetry," *New England Quarterly* 43 (1970): 272; and Lawrence Buell, *Literary Transcendentalism: Style and Vision in the American Renaissance* (Ithaca: Cornell University Press, 1973), 318–19.

78. Citations are to the 1943 version, in *In Defense of Reason*.

79. Winters, p. 263.

80. Winters, pp. 280–81.

81. Winters, p. 263.

82. Winters, pp. 279, 263.

83. Berthoff, pp. 70, 75.

84. Jones, "Symbolism in the Mystical Poetry of Jones Very," Chapter 2, passim.

85. Jones, "Symbolism in the Mystical Poetry of Jones Very," p. 48.

86. See discussion below, pp. xli–xlii.

87. Gittleman, pp. 170–71.

88. Ludwig Deringer, *Die Rhetorik in der Sonettkunst von Jones Very* (Frankfort Am Main: Peter Lang, 1983).

89. Anthony Herbold, "Nature as Concept and Technique in the Poetry of Jones Very," *New England Quarterly* 40 (1967): 244–59.

90. Herbold, pp. 245–46.

91. Dennis, pp. 250–73.

92. Dennis, pp. 251–52.

93. David Seed, "Alone with God and Nature: The Poetry of Jones Very and Frederick Goddard Tuckerman," in *Nineteenth-Century American Poetry*, ed. A. Robert Lee (London: Vision Press, 1985), pp. 166–93.

94. Seed, pp. 166–68.

95. See Jones, Chapter 2, passim.

96. Buell, pp. 312–30.

97. Buell, pp. 319–24.

98. David Robinson, "The Exemplary Self and the Transcendent Self in the Poetry of Jones Very," *ESQ: A Journal of the American Renaissance* 24 (4th Quarter 1978): 206–14.

99. Robinson, "The Exemplary Self and the Transcendent Self," pp. 206, 213.

100. Seed, pp. 174–76.

101. Cole, pp. 178–80.

102. Letter of 24 April 1861, Houghton Library, Harvard University.

103. See Deese, "Selected Sermons of Jones Very," pp. 1–7.

104. *Columbia Literary History of the United States* (New York: Columbia University Press, 1988), pp. 288, 375.

APPENDIX TO THE

INTRODUCTION

Letter of Jones Very to Henry W. Bellows

Bellows Papers, Massachusetts Historical Society

Salem Dec. 29. 1838

Rev. H. W. Bellows

As I was once acquainted with you and was then a witness that you was [*sic*] struggling on to a better hope, which I hope you have not lost sight of since that time, I now write to you moved by the Spirit of Truth which was promised by Christ to his disciples. You probably heard rumors in relation to my leaving Cambridge the truth of which I am now to testify. From what you knew of me before you are aware that my effort was ever to purify my soul and that I was so led by suffering to make this my constant work. In my senior year in college I experienced what is commonly called a *change of heart*, which tells us that all we have belongs to God and that we ought to have no *will* of our own. It was a great happiness to me to find this change yet I could not rest in it. The temptation I always felt to be in thought and as long as I had a thought of what I ought to banish I felt that some of my will remained. To this I was continually prone and against it I continually strove. During the two years succeeding my senior, in the former of which you saw me at times, I maintained this conflict—it began with the day and was continued into the night—the enemy gradually yielded and I went on rejoicing to the close[.] Towards the end of the second year I felt that I was going about all my engagements without any interest in them of my own and yet I felt very happy for I had so long persevered in this course that it had wrought out for me much peace and content. I began to be happy in simply trying to do and think good. I had nothing more to give up to I had given all I had yet I did not know this then as I do now. I then supposed that this state was to be made permanent by all the future relations of a life I had not yet experienced I had no expectation of another change never having heard of any other. But at the beginning of the third that is this collegiate year I meet with another which I will now relate. I had all along as I have said felt a gradual increase of joy and my life was more and more regularly a sacrifice in all things. After having begun my duties at Cambridge this year about the third week I felt within me a new will something which came some time in the week but I could not tell what day exactly. It seemed like my old will only it was to the good—it was not a feeling of my own but a sensible will that was not my own. Accompanying this was another feeling as it were a consciousness which seemed to say—"That which creates you creates also that which you see or him to whom you speak," as it might be. These two consciousnesses as I may call them continued with me two or three weeks and went as they came imperceptably [*sic*]. While they continued I was moved entirely by the Spirit within me to declare to all that the coming of Christ was at hand, and that which I was led to do caused [me to] be placed contrary to my will at the Asylum. There I remained a month in which under the influence of the Spirit my usual manner retur[n]ed in all things save that I now obey it as my natural impulse. The changes which I there passed through and have since known are such as every one born of God must experience they are within and lead on from glory to glory. I now know by the Spirit of God that my former change and that which is commonly called the new birth, was but the hearing of the voice of John in the wilderness of my heart, and that the purification I experienced, in obeying him, in cutting down the corrupt tree and preparing the way for the One who came after was that of his baptism of water. He, as he said, must *decrease,* he was of the earth;—He whom I now know must *increase,* He is from above. I have been in the heart of the earth obedient to John three days and three nights and am risen in Christ as a witness unto you and all that he comes not by water only but by blood. This blood I daily shed in my sufferings such as he who is born of the Father must suffer; for thereby he is a spirit and to him Christ speaks. All who come before Christ are theves [*sic*] and robbers. Those who apply to themselves his promises from the times of John untill him offer violence to the kingdom of heaven. These are they who rejoice for a season to walk in his light—These are they that go out into the wilderness of [*sic*] see a reed shaken by the wind—and a man clothed in soft raiment. But John comes as I have shown neither [eating (torn off with seal)] nor drinking and wisdom is justified of *her* children. As he is imprisoned now in you believe that this is the Christ that is to come and that you are to expect no other. Behold the blind see, the dumb speak, the dead are raised. Believe and go on rejoicing in Johns *decrease* and you shall find him who comes after who will thouroughly [*sic*] purge your threshing floor and gather you if worthy into his granary. You are ordained to preach Christ beware lest you add to the number of those false prophets who have already come, crying peace, peace when there is no peace, clothed in sheeps clothing but within are ravening wolves. Of such shall men require much. Be you not of these but may you go on unto righteousness and see the coming of your Lord in the flesh. That you may see him with joy and not with grief and soon be a witness of the new birth to others, is ever the prayer of the Spirit. As I hear of the word I publish in the form of sonnets in the Observer a paper in Salem and will send you such copies as I may not otherwise be directed to dispose of if you should so ask in your return. This letter is written that you may make it as public as possible and if you are so disposed communicate it to Mr Dewey and Furniss [*sic*] if you are acquainted with them or to any others whom you may see fitting.

Amen.
Jones Very

TEXTUAL INTRODUCTION

The two major collections of Very's poems in manuscript are at the Houghton Library of Harvard University and the John Hay Library of Brown University. There is a much smaller collection at Wellesley College, and additional manuscripts are scattered in a dozen or so other libraries.[1] The bulk of the Houghton collection was a gift (made originally to the Harvard Divinity School and later transferred to the Houghton Library) from Frances Eliza and Lydia Louisa Ann Very, the poet's sisters, on 22 March 1895. These include almost all of the manuscripts that were used to prepare the 1886 "complete" edition. A separate, much smaller collection of fourteen poems was acquired by the Houghton Library in 1972; these early poems were among the papers of Charles Stearns Wheeler, a classmate of Very's at Harvard. The poems at Brown University were purchased at two different times from bookdealers, the first in 1903 from Goodspeed's, the second in 1929 from Lull.[2] These manuscripts fall into four categories: manuscripts that duplicate those in the large collection at the Houghton Library and presumably were removed from those papers by the Very sisters before giving them to Harvard; early drafts, nearly illegible versions, unfinished poems, and fragments; poems, scattered throughout the collection, by other members of the Very family and by friends, including two copies in an unidentified hand of the poem "Sympathy" by "D. H. Thoreau"; and completed, legible poems that were not published until Bartlett included most of them in his biography. All of these manuscripts were presumably removed from the papers that the Very sisters gave to Harvard, those in the first three categories for obvious reasons; the most likely explanation for the exclusion of the last group from both the gift and the "complete" edition is that they were deliberately suppressed by the sisters.

The manuscript poems exist in various forms: in manuscript books, on loose leaves (lined and unlined) of various sizes, in ink and in pencil. Very's associates spoke of large folio sheets of sonnets that he circulated during the ecstatic period; the only extant manuscript resembling such a description is a large sheet at the Houghton Library covered on both sides with sixteen poems written in pencil.

PUBLICATION HISTORY

Very used a number of different kinds of publication outlets for his poems in his lifetime: (1) newspapers, (2) periodicals, (3) printed programs and broadsides, (4) *Essays and Poems*, the collection of Very's poems and essays edited by Emerson in 1839, (5) poetry anthologies, and (6) hymnbooks.

The two newspapers in which Very published most frequently were Salem-based. The *Salem Observer* was the outlet for his earliest published work, and a large proportion of the poems of his ecstatic period also appeared here. In late 1839 some of Very's poems also began appearing in the *Salem Gazette*, and shortly thereafter that paper became Very's primary vehicle for publication. He continued to publish in the *Gazette* for the remainder of his life. Three poems of the ecstatic period were later published in the *New Bedford Evening Bulletin* by Claudius B. Farnsworth, a student of Very's at Harvard. The only other newspaper in which Very published a significant number of poems was the Unitarian *Christian Register*, which after 1845 became the vehicle for much of his religious poetry, while the *Salem Gazette* typically was publishing his nature verses and poems relating to Salem sites and events.

Very began placing his verse in periodicals while he was a Harvard under-graduate. Several of his pieces appeared in the student publication *Harvard-iana*, and the well-respected New York based *Knickerbocker* published three of his poems. Two Transcendentalist periodicals served as outlets for Very's verse: thirty-four poems of the ecstatic period appeared between 1839 and 1841 in the *Western Messenger*, edited by James Freeman Clarke and others, and Emerson published three poems by Very in the *Dial*. After the period of religious enthusiasm had passed, Very placed one poem in James Russell Lowell's short-lived *Pioneer*, four in the *Christian Examiner*, and scores of poems, over several decades, in the *Monthly Religious Magazine*. The last two were Unitarian organs.

During much of his career Very wrote occasional poetry, and thus a number of his poems were included in various kinds of printed programs and broad-sides. While at Harvard he composed a class song that was published in this fashion. The ecstatic period, however, is devoid of publications of this sort. Then during his later career Very wrote poems that were included in printed programs or broadsides for a number of public and religious events in Salem and Boston. Sometimes these poems were later reprinted in newspapers or periodicals.

Essays and Poems (Boston: Little and Brown, 1839), the only collection of Very's works to be published in his lifetime, contained three essays and sixty-five poems. Some of these were early poems previously published in newspapers and periodicals; approximately three-fourths of them, however, were written during the ecstatic period, some already having appeared in the *Salem Observer* and the *Western Messenger*. Though Emerson selected the poems to be included and prepared them for publication, his name did not appear anywhere in the volume. It was dedicated to Very's professor of rhetoric and oratory at Harvard, E. T. Channing.

Within a short time after the publication of *Essays and Poems* various anthologists began raiding it. William Cullen Bryant included six of these poems in his 1840 anthology *Selections from the American Poets*, Rufus Griswold chose a generous eighteen for *The Poets and Poetry of America* (1842), and numerous anthologies (with such distinguished editors as Henry Wadsworth Longfellow, John Greenleaf Whittier, and Lucy Larcom) continued to draw upon *Essays and Poems* throughout Very's life. With the sole exception of Emerson's late anthology *Parnassus* (1874), which included two poems not in the 1839 volume, all the poems by Very included in these anthologies were taken from *Essays and Poems*. Thus Very's reputation throughout his lifetime was (except in the cases of those who read the periodicals and newspapers in which he published and those close acquaintances who read his unpublished poems in manuscript) for all practical purposes based only on the handful of poems that Emerson had elected to publish in 1839.

Very's poems also appeared during his lifetime in numerous hymnbooks (most often Unitarian collections), beginning with the *Book of Hymns* compiled by Samuel Longfellow and Samuel Johnson (a former student of Very's at Harvard) in 1846. Some of Very's hymns are his own adaptations of earlier poems. Just as almost all the poetry anthologies hearkened back to Emerson's edition, Longfellow and Johnson's hymnbook (which included seven of Very's hymns) is the source for almost all of Very's contributions to compilations of hymns. A significant exception to that rule is *Songs and Hymns of the Liberal Faith* (1875), edited by Alfred P. Putnam, which included several additional hymns at least one of which was written specifically for that hymnbook.

Since Very's death three collections of his poems have been published. Moreover, Bartlett's biography of Very (1942) printed more than a hundred additional poems, and several scholars have since published some other previously unpublished or uncollected poems.

Three years after Very's death William P. Andrews of Salem, who wrote that among Very's papers were "many requests from Mr. Dana and other friends . . . for more copies [of *Essays and Poems*], for which they had searched the bookstores in vain," fulfilled this demand by publishing *Poems by Jones Very* (Boston: Houghton, Mifflin, 1883), a selective edition of 138 poems, including all of those in Emerson's edition. The papers of Houghton Mifflin, the publisher, show that the editor had originally envisioned including the three essays that had appeared in Emerson's edition, but presumably because of printing expenses the decision was made to include only poems. This edition was done with the cooperation of Very's surviving sisters, Frances Eliza and Lydia Louisa Ann Very, who several years later were writing to Houghton Mifflin requesting payment of their fair share of the proceeds from the Andrews edition:

> Will you please send us word if the Edition prepared by William Andrews, with the understanding that it was expressly for our benefit, has by this time, paid for itself. Of course you understood, after our explanation to you, that the profits, after you have taken the usual percentage for selling the book, belong to us, as he was never authorized by us to take, or give the profits to any one. We wish to have a full understanding at this time. Our income is very small, and we need all the profits from both volumes [i.e., both the Andrews edition and the so-called Clarke edition described below]. It was all our brother had to leave us, and he little thought anyone would try to take it from us.[3]

The publisher agreed to pay to the Verys 10 percent of the retail price of all copies sold over and above the book's cost; within a few days they were sent a check for $26.55, and were to receive 10 percent of any future sales. At that time 838 of the 1000 copies printed had been sold.

In the meantime, the Very sisters had arranged with Houghton Mifflin for the printing of a new "complete" edition. James Freeman Clarke acted as sponsor for the edition that appeared in 1886 as *Poems and Essays by Jones Very: Complete and Revised Edition* and, though it has generally been referred to as "Clarke's edition," correspondence with the publisher makes it clear that it was really the Very sisters' edition. The contract between Houghton Mifflin and the Verys specified that for the publication of five hundred copies the Verys were to make two payments of four hundred dollars each, the first on delivery of the manuscript, the second on delivery of the book ready for market. They were also to pay the publisher every six months a commission of 10 percent of the retail price of copies sold. Houghton Mifflin was to send them semi-annual accounting and payments from sales of the book.[4] The finished product included a preface by Cyrus A. Bartol and a biographical sketch by Clarke. The three essays that had appeared in the Emerson edition were included, and the number of poems was greatly expanded from both the previous editions: the table of contents lists 676 poems. However, without constructing a first-line index, the editors were overwhelmed in a quagmire of different poems with identical titles and cases of a single poem that went under more than one title. The result is the duplicate (or in one case, triplicate) printing of twenty-three poems. And despite the title, this was not anywhere near a "complete" collection of Very's poems. Fifteen poems that had appeared in the Andrews edition were omitted, presumably inadvertently; a large number of poems that existed only in manuscript and a smaller number that had appeared in newspapers and periodicals were also missing. It is likely that most of the hitherto unpublished manuscript poems were deliberately suppressed by Very's sisters. Among the most interesting of all his poems to students of Very today, these were written during his "inspired" period and were radical for their time in that the speaker's persona is frequently one of the figures of the Godhead. In 1965 Kenneth Walter Cameron published *Poems by Jones Very: James Freeman Clarke's Enlarged Collection of 1886 Re-edited with a Thematic and Topical Index* (Hartford, Conn.: Transcendental Books); it omitted the essays in the Clarke edition, added two poems and the index, but otherwise reproduced the poems (in reduced size photocopied form) of the 1886 edition.

Many of the poems missing from the 1886 edition were discovered and printed by Bartlett in his 1942 biography. He included eleven previously unpublished poems at Harvard University (then at the Divinity School, now at the Houghton Library) and sixty at the Brown University Library. In addition the book prints sixteen uncollected poems from the *Salem Observer*, twenty from the *Western Messenger*, and one each from the *Dial* and the *National Anti-Slavery Standard*. Two of the poems that Bartlett prints from the collection at Brown University should be removed from the Very canon. That collection contains two manuscript copies of "To an African Bird," one of which is untitled and is printed by Bartlett (pp. 158–59); the other copy of the poem in manuscript is signed by the apparent author, "William Augustus Crafts, Roxbury," a member of the Harvard class of 1840. Another poem, "Lines to the Spout Near My Window" (Bartlett, pp. 159–60), is followed by the word "Huntington." "Huntington" may refer to Frederic Dan Huntington, who studied at the Divinity School from 1839–42, after Very had left Harvard but while he continued his connections with students there; or it is possible that this poem too was written by Crafts, who lived on Huntington Avenue in Roxbury. In either case, it seems clear that these two, like several other poems in the Brown collection, were written by Very's Harvard associates. The untitled poem whose first line is "Haunts of my youth! A while I leave" (No. 160) printed by Bartlett from the Brown collection is likewise suspect; it is unsigned and the manuscript is not in Very's hand. Because it is clearly related to No. 175 (untitled; first line: "Home of my youth! Where first my lot was cast") and could feasibly be a copy of another version of that poem, it is included in the present edition, its uncertain authorship noted. Bartlett prints (p. 152), again from the Brown collection, an untitled poem (first line: "As long as Ceres gives the grain"), which is actually a fragment of a longer poem, No. 418 ("A Song . . . to be Sung at the Class-Supper of the Sophomore Class of 1834"). The entire poem was first printed by Kenneth Walter Cameron (*ESQ* 5 [4th Quarter 1956]: 12–13).

The only translation of Very's works that has appeared to date is a German edition of ninety-two of the poems.[5] The only modern edition of his poems is Nathan Lyons's *Jones Very: Selected Poems* (New Brunswick, N.J.: Rutgers University Press, 1966). Lyons has selected seventy-five poems, all written during the ecstatic period, and has provided useful textual notes. He has arranged the poems thematically under the headings "Obedience," "For the Disobedient," and "Song." Since the publication of Lyons's volume a few additional poems by Very have surfaced in articles by David Robinson and Helen R. Deese.[6]

RELIABILITY OF THE EDITIONS

The reliability of the various editions is a crucial question for the editor of Very. It is well known that Very himself objected to Emerson's editorial changes to his poems. From the first time he saw Very's poems Emerson, while offering the strongest encouragement to the young poet, attempted to effect a change in one of his poems. Referring to line 2 in the sonnet "Enoch" ("Like to the Jewish patriarch of old") Emerson wrote: "Let me suggest the alteration of the word 'Jewish' (patriarch). . . . The country of Enoch I suppose cannot very well be settled though I should think 'Syrian' would not be too great a licence. But Jewish is an alibi, and another whe<re>n."[7] Very evidenced his independence by making a change, but not in the direction that Emerson had suggested: "to the Jewish patriarch" became "the translated patriarch." Very was particularly sensitive to editorial tampering during his ecstatic period. These poems, he told Emerson when the latter was preparing his edition, he valued not because they were his but because they were not his. And though, as Emerson wrote Elizabeth Peabody, "Very forbids all correcting of his verses," Emerson as editor eventually had his own way.[8] A year later, when Emerson was preparing some of Ellery Channing's poems for publication in the *Dial*, he confronted the same problem; in this case Margaret Fuller, Samuel Gray Ward, and possibly Elizabeth Hoar had argued that Channing's "bad grammar & his nonsense" were "consecrated by the true *afflatus*." Emerson's retort underscored the problems posed for an editor by such a theory of composition: "Is the poetic inspiration amber to embalm & enhance flies & spiders? As it fell in the case of Jones Very, cannot the spirit parse and spell?"[9]

A few years later, in perhaps a more rational state, Very once again took to task Emerson as editor, this time for changes that he had made to one of Very's poems which appeared in the *Dial*: "I found my poem the 'Evening Choir' altered considerably from what I had written—I do not know but in one or two cases for the better. Perhaps they were all improvements but I preferred my own lines. I do not know but I ought to submit to such changes as done by the rightful authority of an Editor but I felt a little sad at the aspect of the piece."[10] The statement makes salutary reading for all editors.

The reliability of the Andrews edition was indicted by Lydia L. A. Very in a letter responding to a request for information about her brother. She wrote: "After my brother's death in 1880 a small volume of selections from his writings was published—the memoir written by a Mr Andrews was incorrect in parts, the punctuation in nearly every poem was changed thus altering the sense, words were omitted and even altered. To remedy this my sister and I published a complete edition of his writings."[11] Indeed, a comparison of manuscript versions of poems with those published in the Andrews edition confirms that Andrews freely altered, punctuation in particular. However, a comparison of the Very sisters' 1886 edition with manuscripts indicates some, though far less pervasive, alteration. Pronouns referring to the Deity are regularly capitalized, for example, whether or not they were so in the manuscript. In general, therefore, all of these collections hold little textual authority and are used as copy-texts of last resort.

EDITORIAL PRINCIPLES AND PROCEDURES

Manuscripts of Very's poems have been located through letters of inquiry to libraries, listings in bibliographies and reference works such as *American Literary Manuscripts*, and information provided by other scholars who are aware of the project. The poems that Very published in newspapers and periodicals but that have remained uncollected have been located by searches through Salem and Boston newspapers and issues of literary and religious periodicals during the relevant years and by consulting indexes of such publications. Anthologies that appeared in Very's lifetime have likewise been scanned.

Transcriptions made from manuscript sources have noted all alterations in the manuscript. A transcription of the copy-text version of each poem has been entered into a computer and the printout has been checked twice against the copy-text source.

The following copies of Very's *Essays and Poems* (1839) at the Houghton Library were compared using the Lindstrand Comparator:

*AC85.V6214.839eab	compared with *AC85.V6214.839e(B)
*AC85.V6214.839eaa	compared with *AC85.AL191.zz839v
*AC85.V6214.839ea(B)	compared with *AC85.V6214.839ea(A)
*AC85.V6214.839ea(B)	compared with *AC85.V6214.839eab
*AC85.V6214.839ea(B)	compared with *AC85.L8605.zz839v

No variations were discovered.

This edition presents a critical unmodernized text for each poem. That is, the copy-text chosen for a particular poem on the grounds of being the version nearest the author's latest intention may yet be emended on the basis of other authorities and the editor's knowledge of the author's usual practice, though no emendations are made with a view to simply modernizing the text.

Because the version(s) available and the publication history vary from poem to poem, choice of copy-text has been extraordinarily complex. Since there is no such thing as one master copy-text for the entire collection of Very's poetry, it has been necessary to make a decision on the copy-text for each individual poem. The procedure followed has been to use a fair copy manuscript, when available, as the copy-text; in the case of multiple manuscript versions of a poem, the editor has attempted to determine the latest manuscript version and use it as the copy-text. In most cases there are no more than two surviving manuscript versions of a single poem, and it is generally a simple matter to distinguish original drafts from fair copies. It is sometimes necessary, in the absence of a fair copy manuscript, to rely on contemporary newspaper and periodical versions as copy-texts. The *Salem Observer*, in fact, is often the source for copy-texts of early poems for which there is no extant manuscript and for somewhat later poems which exist only in draft form in manuscript. There is some evidence that the *Observer* may be a more reliable preserver of the author's texts than one might ordinarily imagine, for it is clear that Very himself exercised significant editorial control over poems that were published in this paper. In the 6 January 1838 issue two of his poems ("The Wind-Flower" and "Beauty") were reprinted because, the headnote stated, of "typographical errors" in their original publication. In the absence of either fair copy manuscript or of newspaper or periodical publication (and such occasions are extremely rare), the editor has been forced to rely on a draft manuscript version or on a version published in one of the editions of Very's poems.

The emendation policies of the present edition would presumably come closer to gaining Very's approval than did Emerson's. The general guiding principle has been to determine the author's latest intention. No modernization of spelling or punctuation has been attempted. No attempt, however, has been made to indicate in the case of printed versions of poems such typographical details as capitalization in titles and in first-line text-letters, or the frequent but inconsistent practice of following a title with a period. When the copy-text of a poem is a printed version, this edition regularizes capitalization in the title and omits final periods from the title (unless the title is a quotation of a full sentence). Since Very's printers made his titles conform to their own styles, it is impossible to recover his intentions in such cases. When the copy-text is a manuscript version, the title follows the manuscript in all particulars. Emendations to the copy-text are made only in clear cases of slips of the pen or obvious errors in printing or, rarely, when it seems clear that a later unlocated manuscript version superseded the available manuscript copy-text (as, for example, when entire lines of a newspaper version differ from those of an earlier manuscript version). The most common kinds of emendations are in apostrophe usage and spelling. It is clear from Very's usual practice that he intended to conform to current usage in both areas, as he frequently corrected his own orthography and apostrophe usage, but occasionally he failed to notice his errors.

A number of poems that exist only in a single manuscript version include no punctuation at all, and that is the form in which they appear in this edition. It is certainly arguable that if Very had submitted these poems for publication he would have added punctuation, as he did to much of the ecstatic poetry that was originally unpunctuated. The result of the practice of this edition is an inconsistency between poems from the same period that were published or even simply recopied by Very (and punctuated by him) and those that never went beyond a first unpunctuated draft. Nevertheless, it hardly seems valid editorial practice for an editor at this point to attempt to supply the punctuation that she thinks Very would have used.

On some few occasions Very, years later, took one of his early poems and more or less completely reworked it for newspaper or periodical publication; in such cases these have been treated as two discrete poems. In a few other cases he made relatively minor revisions to early poems that I have not judged sufficient to merit treating the two versions as separate poems. In these latter cases I have made an exception to the general rule of choosing as copy-text the version that embodies Very's latest intention. On the premise that readers will ordinarily have more interest in Very's poems as composed during and immediately after the ecstatic period rather than in revisions of these works made a number of years later, I have used as copy-text the earlier version of poems composed during the 1838–42 period that were afterwards revised. The later revisions are reported of course in the Historical Collation.

Two copies of *Essays and Poems* at the University of Virginia that evidently belonged to the Very household (one of them bears the name of Very's sister, Frances E. Very) present a unique problem for the editor. These copies have been heavily annotated, presumably by Very himself, to indicate revisions of the printed poems in punctuation, single words, and occasionally several entire lines of text. One might speculate at first glance that Very was simply trying to restore the texts of these poems to an original version that Emerson as editor had corrupted. More careful observation shows that this is not the case, for he is here revising some poems for which his own manuscripts are extant. I believe that these revisions were done with a view to republication. The editorial dilemma of what to do with these revisions is intensified by the observation that as often as not the revisions in the two copies do not agree. I have chosen to treat these annotations as abortive attempts at revision and have not reported them in the apparatus. In one case the revision in one of these copies is a precopy-text version of the revised version of No. 518, "The Latter Rain," which I have treated as a separate poem, No. 518a of the same title.

DATING OF POEMS

A number of the manuscripts are dated, and it is possible to date approximately a great many other poems according to the dates on which they appeared in contemporary periodicals. Other poems are dated by their proximity to poems whose date is known. In a number of cases, for example, a few of the large number of poems written on a single sheet can be assigned approximate dates by their newspaper publication; it is usually safe to assume a similar date for all the poems on the sheet, particularly if the manuscript seems to represent the first draft of the poems. In many cases it is possible only to place a poem within a fairly wide range of dates. The poems written between September 1838 and early 1840 show a congruity of style and subject matter, and frequently share certain manuscript characteristics as well (lack of punctuation, crowding of poems on a single sheet or in several pages in a manuscript book that appear to have been composed at the same time). It is clear that such poems belong to the ecstatic period, but frequently the date of composition cannot be fixed more closely. In the chronology of this edition such poems appear grouped together at the end of this period. The Textual Note for each poem indicates the manuscript and publication date(s), if any, and other factors relevant to dating. The probable date of the composition of each poem is indicated following the text of the poem. Poems that cannot be dated appear at the end of the edition.

POEM NUMBERING

The number given each poem in this edition is the poem number assigned in my "Calendar of the Poems of Jones Very,"[12] which cross-references poems by first lines and titles. The calendar may be helpful in conjunction with this edition for use in sorting out different poems with the same titles, single poems that have gone under multiple titles, and poems with identical first lines and titles that differ sufficiently to be treated in this edition as discrete poems. The letter *a* following a poem number (e.g., 160a) indicates that this is one of the few poems that have been added to the list of known Very poems since the publication of the calendar. A poem with a hyphenated double number (e.g., 668-697) indicates that although two different first lines appear in the Calendar, they represent different versions of the same poem.

HISTORICAL NOTES

Nontextual matters such as the identification of quotations or persons mentioned in the poems are treated here. I have identified what appear to be specific scriptural allusions to biblical characters, parables, events, and so forth. Generally, I have not given multiple citations for the same biblical allusion unless Very's wording indicates his borrowing from more than one biblical account. I have made no attempt to identify every scriptural echo—indeed I believe it would be impossible to do so: during his ecstatic period a biblical syntax was Very's natural mode of expression, both oral and written. Allusions to the title or the sense of the entire poem are first given, then allusions that are limited to a specific line or lines.

TEXTUAL NOTES

A separate textual note for each poem names the copy-text, any precopy-text version, and the other versions, if any, collated in the Historical Collation. Any special circumstances influencing the choice of copy-text are described, as well as any other information in the manuscript or printed version relevant to but not a part of the text itself (for example, a date or signature following the text).

ALTERATIONS IN THE MANUSCRIPT

All alterations in manuscript copy-texts and in other manuscripts included in the Historical Collation are registered here. Precopy-text manuscript versions are not included.

The Historical Collation includes all located versions of poems from the period of Very's lifetime except for manuscripts (draft versions) that precede the copy-text version. The reading of this edition (which, except in the case of emendations, is the copy-text version) is given to the left of the bracket; all other variants are then given, with the sources indicated:

10 sear;] ~^ MH; ~,— E, G; sere,— Waif

In this example from No. 399, "A Withered Leaf—seen on a Poet's Table" the tilde (~) indicates the same word that appears to the left of the bracket and the caret (^) indicates punctuation omitted. The entry thus signifies the following variant readings of a portion of line 10:

sear;]   the reading of this edition
~^   MH (Houghton manuscript) reading: sear (no punctuation)
~,—   E (Emerson) and G (Griswold) reading: sear,—
sere,—   the reading of Waif (*The Waif*)

EDITORIAL EMENDATIONS IN THE COPY-TEXT

All emendations in both so-called accidentals and substantives are reported in this section. After the line number the emended reading is first given, to the left of the bracket; any version of the poem that agrees with the emended reading is indicated; then the copy-text reading is indicated, followed by any other variant readings and their sources:

2 wand'rer] MH(1); wandr'er MH(2); wanderer Harv, CR

The above example from Poem No. 47, "The Snow Bird," indicates that the copy-text (Houghton manuscript #2) reading of 'wandr'er' was emended to agree with the Houghton manuscript #1; *Harvardiana* and the *Christian Register* gave yet another reading.

NOTES

1. Among the manuscripts at Brown University are a number of poetic fragments that are not included in this edition. Likewise an apparently unfinished piece at Wellesley entitled "The Spring Bird" is excluded. Yale's Beinecke Rare Books and Manuscript Library holds three manuscripts attributed to Very, one of them ("Spiritual Navigation") probably wrongly so. This poem, which is not included in this edition, is

unsigned, is not in Very's hand, and does not resemble anything that he is known to have written. Though his name appears on the manuscript (verso, where there is a portion of a sermon but no part of the poem), it seems likely that a quotation is simply being attributed to him.

2. William Irving Bartlett, *Jones Very: Emerson's "Brave Saint"* (Durham, N.C.: Duke University Press, 1942), p. 140.

3. Frances E. Very to Houghton, Mifflin, 7 February 1890, Houghton Mifflin Papers, Houghton Library, Harvard University.

4. Houghton Mifflin Papers, Houghton Library, Harvard University.

5. *Jones Very, der Dichter des Christentums*, trans. Albert Ritter (Linz, Vienna, Leipzig: Oesterreichische Verlag Sanstatt, 1903).

6. David Robinson, "Four Early Poems of Jones Very," *Harvard Library Bulletin* 23 (April 1980): 146–51; Helen R. Deese, "Unpublished and Uncollected Poems of Jones Very," *ESQ: A Journal of the American Renaissance* 30 (3d Quarter 1984): 154–62.

7. Letter of 18 November 1838, Essex Institute; *Letters of R.W.E.*, 7:327.

8. Letter of 23 June 1839, *Letters of Elizabeth Palmer Peabody*, ed. Bruce A. Ronda (Middletown, Conn.: Wesleyan University Press, 1984), p. 226.

9. *The Letters of Ralph Waldo Emerson*, ed. Ralph L. Rusk (New York: Columbia University Press, 1939), 2:331.

10. Letter of 23 November 1842, Wellesley College Library; quoted in Edwin Gittleman, *Jones Very: The Effective Years, 1833–1840* (New York: Columbia University Press, 1967), p. 333.

11. Letter of 2 February 1892 to Wm. C. Bamburgh in possession of Helen R. Deese.

12. *Studies in the American Renaissance*, ed. Joel Myerson (Charlottesville: University Press of Virginia, 1986), pp. 305–71.

Jones Very

The Complete Poems

O heaven born muse! inspire my humble lay,
To sing the glories of all charming May!
To wake in all an ardent wish to see
The beauties, which have pleased, delighted me.
Would you with more elastic step than ere you trod, 5
Spring o'er the field and touch the grassy sod;
Would you ere feel your blood with swifter course,
Flow through your veins in all its youthful force;
Would you ere breathe as pure an air as blew,
O'er Eden's garden wet with early dew; 10
Would you ere feel what never you enjoyed,
By other scenes by other pleasures cloyed;
Would you ere feel, what's far above the rest,
Pleasures which sooth and satisfy the breast;
Rise from your couch before the rising sun, 15
Has o'er the plain or lofty hill begun
"To shed his orient beams on herb, fruit, flower,
Glittering with dew," or yet obtained the power
To scatter from before him, far away,
The freshness, beauty of the blushing day. 20
See now the rising sun from ocean's bed,
Has o'er the earth his golden glories shed;
Hear now the birds, as on extended wing
They clear the air, with notes melodious sing,
And raise to him, to him who gave them birth, 25
Gave them besides this green, this lovely earth,
Their morning hymn. And will not these inspire
In man emotions purer far, and higher,
Than ere before he felt, or even thought,
Could with such ease be had, such pleasure sought? 30

Poem No. 375; 9 May 1833

The earth is parched with heat, flowers droop and die,
The clouds of dust fly whirling through the sky;
The cattle lowing seek the friendly shade,
By lofty rock or some dark forest made.
The traveller spent with toil, by heat oppressed, 5
Near some tall oak, exhausted, sinks to rest;

And dreams of home, of all his soul holds dear,
Dreams not, alas! of fatal danger near.
Dark low'ring clouds o'er heaven's bright azure run,
A bloody redness vails the scorching sun.   10
The river's surface, late so green and bright,
Rolls back its waves, dark as the shades of night.
Hushed is the wind, nor e'en a zephyr blows,
All nature sunk in deep profound repose.
The farmer leaves his fields, with terror flies,   15
And often turning views the angry skies.
See now the waves rise higher than before,
In wild commotion lash the sounding shore.
See through the air the leaves and stubble borne,
The slender tree from the thick grove uptorn.   20
Hark through the heavens, with peal of awful sound,
Rolls the deep thunder startling all around.
The lofty hill e'en from its centre shakes,
The bravest heart o'ercome with terror quakes;
See on the ground, by that resistless stroke,   25
The wretched traveller, the blasted oak,
In equal lot, by equal force o'erthrown:
He sunk in death, he uttered not a groan;
He saw no flash, he heard no awful peal,
From life to death insensibly to steal   30
Him God decreed; why then ought man to mourn,
From earthly joys to heavenly he was borne.
The thunder ceased, the gloomy clouds had fled,
Wide o'er the earth, refreshing zephyrs shed
The sweet perfume of many a laughing flower,   35
Or sighed with soothing notes through many a silvan bower.

Poem No. 492; 24 July 1833

Lines,
Written on Reading Stuart's Account of
The Treatment of Slaves in Charleston

Oh slavery! thou bane of human kind;
Thou tyrant o'er the body and the mind;
To all that's just, to all that's right a foe,
Thou fill'st the world with misery and woe.
Ah! many a wretch by thee is caused to mourn;   5
From friend, from relative, from country torn,
From all the joys that e'er his soul held dear,
Beneath thy cruel scourge is doomed to fear.
By curs't desire of gain, by thirst for gold,
The unhappy victim of thy crime is sold.   10
Is sold? to whom? would I could hide the shame!
To man; O traffic base, disgraceful to the name;
To man, with reason and with freedom blest,
O'er all creation placed the first, and best;
Alas! how fallen from that station he,   15
Who, blest with reason, proud in being free,
Can from his proper sphere a being draw,
Deprive of rights, of liberty, and law;
Deprive, (what's far more cruel than the rest,)
Of all the gifts with which himself is blest.   20
Would that my lips the tale could never tell,
The tale of horror, known, alas! too well.
Would that the world had never seen the day,
When man his fellow man should thus betray,
Would rather every ship that sailed the main,   25
For such base traffic, such degrading gain,
Had sunk with all beneath the raging sea,
Where they from slavery ever would be free:
Free from a tyrant's power, who often rends
Parent from children, friend from dearest friend;   30
Free from a life of wretchedness and woe,
Free from all toil and suffering here below.
Ah! who could read the story of that woe?
And who if reading half their sorrow know?
Would that by me their wrongs could half be told,   35
Would that their sufferings I could half unfold.

Before our God and theirs those sufferings rise,
He sees their wrongs, he hears their helpless cries:
Soon may those wrongs and sufferings have an end,
Man be not foe to man, but friend.   40

Poem No. 387; 13 August 1833

Lines on Mount Auburn

Sing, heav'nly Muse, of that fair mountain sing,
Where rest in peace the honoured dead; and where
As the seasons roll around their heads, their
Children oft shall come, and o'er them drop the
Tear of grateful memory; and from their   5
Example learn the better how to live,
The better how to die. Learn from them,
As if the glorious sun his rays still shed
Upon them, and life's swift current still through
Their veins ran warm: as if before them were   10
Those forms so well remember'd, and they stood
Attentive to receive a parent's will
Respected. Hallowed spot! where still the dead
Seem yet to live, yet to give instruction
The more regarded, since from them it comes.   15
Here, as with devious steps we wander through
Thy thickets dark, or near some tomb o'er which
The flowers of spring in beauty wave musing,
We shall from worldly thoughts, and worldly cares
Withdraw ourselves, and deep communion hold   20
With those long since departed; and raise our
Souls to him whose never ceasing goodness
Crowns our life. Here oft let youth retire from
Life's gay scene, from pleasures glittering round, to
Learn that though they live by worldly pleasures   25
Compassed round, and though the flowers of spring are
Breathing there in richest fragrance, and the
Woods are in their greenest verdure crowned, that
As those flowers by winter's cruel blast their
Fragrance and their beauty soon will lose, so   30

They on earth shall flourish but awhile; that
Soon their flowering spring by the chill blast
Of age shall wither; and thus may they be
Led, to place their happiness on things not
Fleeting but eternal in the heavens.   35
Here too let manhood come from restless cares
Of life withdrawn, and learning here, from those
Whose life was most employed in duties to
Their country, and to man most useful, death
Spares not even manhood, life's most active   40
Scene, he shall from this lesson learn to live
A better and thus a happier man.
And here may age, whose silver locks proclaim
Life's winter, learn that their example still
Shall live and generations yet unborn   45
Revere their memory. And let them learn
"The storms of Wintry Time will quickly pass,
And one unbounded Spring encircle all;"
"Where they shall flourish in immortal youth,
Unhurt, amid the war of elements,   50
The wreck of matter and the crush of worlds."

Poem No. 423; 20 December 1833

Lines suggested by hearing the beach, at F. Peabody's Mills, South Salem. December 21. 1833.

The silent moon is rising,
And sheds its light around
The river silent flowing,
In its deep bed below.

The bustle too is dying,   5
Around the noisy mill;
The workmen home are hying,
And every sound is still

Still save the beach's roaring,
Through the shining silent night;   10
Like chariots onward pouring
To mingle in the fight.

Poem No. 562; 21 December 1833

Hast thou ever *heard* the voice of nature,
In the whirlwind's roar, the zephyr's gentle
Breath, in the fierce eagle's cry, when darting
Forth he seeks the spoiler of his nest,
In the soft whispering voice of love with   5
Which the dove salutes his mate? or hast thou
Seen nature put forth her force in various
Forms, the lightning rend the solid oak,
The lofty cedars bend like reeds before
The blast, the madden'd ocean lash the shore   10
With foam, or hast thou seen the rising sun,
When first he looks forth on a summer's day,
Or, when his beams fall fiercer down, the cattle
Seek the cool refreshing shade, slaking their
Thirst in some hoarse-murmuring brook?   15
Hast thou e'er seen such sights or heard such sounds,
And never thought of Him, who rides upon
The whirlwind, who in the gentle zephyr breathes,
Who to the dove, the eagle gave their notes
Of rage or love, who from his awful hand   20
The lightning hurls, the lofty cedars bend,
And with his nostrils heapeth up the waves,
Who made the brook to run to quench the thirst
The cattle feel in summer's sultry reign?
If on thine ear or sight all these have fell   25
Unheeded, and thou hast liv'd unmindful
Of a God, who gave thee sight to see and
Ear to hear, and for these thy senses formed,
Harmonious sounds, and ever varying
Beauties; learn oft as upon thy sight or   30
Ear they fall to think of him who made them.

Poem No. 158; 7 April 1834

"Ambitione inani pectus caret"

Knowest thou what ambition gains,
As reward of all its pain?
Know'st thou what the precious spoils
It receives for all its toils?

See, with what an eager eye,   5
Yon child pursues the butterfly;
Mark his looks of joy and pleasure,
As he strives to seize the treasure.

Now on yonder rose it stands,
Running with extended hands   10
He would grasp the brilliant toy;
Flying from the eager boy

Now within a tulip's cup,
'Tis from sight almost shut up;
Fill'd with joy yet mix'd with fear,   15
Cautiously he's drawing near.

See the prize is now obtain'd,
The long-eluding object's gain'd;
He opes his little hands with joy,
Why that tear? say why? my boy.   20

Ah! its golden splendor's fled,
What thou sought'st, alas! is dead;
Thy rude grasp has crush'd the fair.
See ambition's prize is there.

Poem No. 311; 2 June 1834

What more delightful than to wander forth
In spring, before the sun has chas'd away
The freshness of the morn; or shook the dew
From off the tender grass? Nature seems
As young, as when the morning light first broke   5
On Eden; as calm the river's surface;
And the birds as sweetly tune their morning

Hymn. Beneath the shade of oak reflected
In the sleeping stream, I set me down,
And muse and gaze on the unrival'd scene.   10
Would that my thoughts could speak, my tongue describe
The pleasures, that a scene like this affords!
No—language is too feeble to give them
Utterance. Would to him whose feelings have
Been swallow'd up by love of gold; to him   15
Whom mad ambition drives; to him whose sense
Is cloy'd by luxury's empoison'd cup,
Would that to them the happiness I feel
I could describe! 'twould strike the fetters from
The slave of gold; 'twould stop ambition's mad   20
Career, and dash the bowl from palsied hand
Of luxury. The birds their joy express
In notes of sweetest harmony; without
A wave the peaceful river glides along;
The blue sky without a cloud rejoices;   25
Words fail to give my feelings utterance.
The pleasure within my breast surpasses
Far, that which prompts the sweetest lay
Of bird; more calm my breast than the smooth stream,
With looks more joyful than the azure vault,   30
In silent gratitude, I raise mine eyes
To heaven.

Poem No. 778; 8 June 1834

A Song Composed by Mr J. Very, to be Sung at the Class-Supper of the Sophomore Class of 1834

Shall college suppers be forgot,
And never brought to min'?
The friends we've had remembered not,
And days o' auld lang syne?

Those suppers full o' mirth and glee,   5
Those friends so true and kin';
No better we shall ever see,
Than those o' auld lang syne.

And if those friends we ever meet,
In any foreign clime;   10
We'll take them by the hand and greet,
And speak o' auld lang syne.

If false and hollow all beside,
Shall prove to me and mine;
Then sweetly o'er my mind shall glide,   15
The thoughts o' auld lang syne.

As long as Ceres gives the grain,
And Bacchus yields the wine;
So long shall in my breast remain,
The thoughts o' auld lang syne.   20

Then fill your cups my hearty friends,
We'll have a cheerfull time;
We'll use the gifts that Bacchus sends,
And drink t' auld lang syne.

    Chorus.
For auld lang syne my dear   25
For auld lang syne
We'll tak' a cup of kindness yet,
For auld lang syne.

Poem No. 418; spring 1834

Death of Lafayette

He is gone, loaded with years and honors!
He who before the rich rewards of Kings
Preferred to succor the distressed, and raise
His arm in freedom's holy cause, is gone!
Mourn France a son, who shed around thy name   5
A never-fading splendor! He caus'd no
Widow's tears to flow, he caus'd no orphans
"To demand their sire with tears of artless
Innocence." Heaven hasten'd not to snatch from
Our admiring gaze; but granted riches   10
And honors, length of days to show, that, e'en
Upon earth, virtue is oft rewarded.

Columbia's daughters weep! But for him
Your children, now perhaps in bondage,
Might live to curse the day that gave them birth. 15
And yet her sons lament! lament for him,
Who in his youthful days your fathers' arm
Upheld, reviv'd their drooping hopes, and gave
Them vigor to resist their haughty foe.
Ye mountains veil your heads in clouds and mourn 20
For him, who around your summits cast glory
More bright than noon-day sun! Ye waving pines
Sigh louder in the blast; for he, who gave
You liberty's fair soil, is now no more.
And thou, O boundless ocean, mourn! for ne'er 25
Again thy waves shall bear to freedom's coast,
One more worthy of thy lamentation.
Fairer, Lafayette, than summer's day thy
Latter years, and thou on whom a nation's
Blessings fell, shall now receive a nation's tears. 30

Poem No. 161; 21 June 1834

Old Age

Say not, that in old age,
No joys, no pleasures dwell;
That it is but a page,
Which only sorrows tell.

Say not, in age we find 5
Nought but a wintry shore;
Round which the northern wind,
And raging ocean roar.

Say not, that like the tree
Scorch'd by the light'ning's wing; 10
That thus old age will be,
A sear'd and barren thing.

Say not, 'tis like the sun
Sinking in western skies;
When storm-clouds have begun   15
To shut him from our eyes.

O no, 'tis like the shore
Beneath Italian skies;
T'wards which with moon-lit oar
The joyful boatman plies.   20

O no, 'tis like the tree,
When golden autumn's near;
But with maturity,
It hails its latest year.

It sinks, as sinks the sun   25
From our admiring eyes;
Whose daily course is run,
Fair as we saw him rise.

Poem No. 410; 30 June 1834

Lines
Suggested By Seeing A Butterfly Sculptured
Upon A Tomb

Fit emblem of th' immortal soul! though thou
Art soaring high, thou didst inhabit once
A dark and loathsome mansion. Such is man,
Like to the worm, which once thou wast, he creeps
Encumber'd now by earthly bonds, which check   5
His eager flight, and to a narrower
Sphere confine his untried powers; lest perhaps
The soul ascending premature might fall
Supported by too feeble wing. Attend
O man! and learn thy destiny, which hand   10
Divine has traced on nature's works. Seasons
In their ceaseless round proclaim it; darkness
And light; and ocean's ebb and flow in turn
Succeeding; sun and moon oft veil'd in dim

Eclipse; calm succeeding tempest; nature 15
Through all her works proclaims it, from the orbs,
That wheel their courses through the void immense,
To insect fluttering in the summer's breeze,
All, all proclaim the destiny of man.
Learn then O man! from such unnumber'd signs, 20
Where lies thy happiness, whence thy being
Sprang and whither tends: if with an upward
Flight thou hop'st to soar, when from this earthly
Coil thou'rt freed; plume thy wings while here below;
Cast off what then may clog thy flight, and bear 25
Thee down. Passions fierce attack, attack most
Direful; lust, poisoning the relish
Of the soul for all that's pure; indolence,
With slow yet ceaseless course eating its way,
Like rust, into the mind, and deadening all 30
Its energies: these and thousand nameless foes,
That strive to fix thy thoughts on things below
Thy noble destiny, repel; then, like
The phoenix, thou shalt rise triumphant from
Thine ashes; and, on untiring pinions, 35
Heaven-ward borne shalt seek thy resting place.

Poem No. 127; 6 July 1834

Kind Words

Turn not from him, who asks of thee
  A portion of thy store;
Though thou canst give no charity,
  Thou canst do what is more.

The balm of comfort thou canst pour 5
  Into *his* grieving mind,
Who oft is turn'd from wealth's proud door,
  With many a word unkind.

Does any from the false world find,
  Nought but reproach and scorn; 10
Does any, stung by words unkind,
  Wish that he ne'er was born;

Do thou raise up his drooping heart;
    Restore his wounded mind;
Though nought of wealth thou canst impart,   15
    Yet still thou canst be kind.

Thy kindness, like the summer's shower,
    Shall cheer him on his way
Through the false, hollow world; its power
    Shall reach his latest day: 20

It stays not here, but, as the rain,
    Which ocean's bosom drinks,
Drawn by the sun ascends again,
    To heaven from which it sinks;

So, drawn by thee, thy words shall wing   25
    Backward their course to thee;
And, in thy breast, shall prove a spring
    Of pure felicity.

Poem No. 746; 16 July 1834

Pleasure

Goddess of pleasure, where thy golden car?
Rides it on zephyrs through the unclouded sky?
Or mov'st thou with silken sails and silver
Oars down the smooth river, sported around
By daughters of the sea, fann'd by the wings   5
Of smiling loves; or on its shady bank
Do'st thou repose, lull'd by distant music
Stealing soft o'er its calm bosom? or sit'st
Thou in more cool retreat, some grotto dark
Of living marble hewn by nature's hand,   10
Catching the sound of mighty water-fall
Borne on the wind? Though 'neath unclouded skies
Thy votaries seek thee, where the zephyrs sport
Around, and scatter odors from their wings;
And though down the stream of life, with silken   15
Sails wafted by prosperous winds, they glide;
Thee seeking in ever-varied worldly

Joys; and though from busy scenes of life
Retir'd, some on the shady bank have woo'd thee;
Or in grotto's dark recess, deluded;   20
How oft hast thou, like the false flickering
Light, which leads the weary trav'ller astray,
Danc'd round them in thy golden car, &, when
They sought to enter, fled their eager grasp!
Ask him, who, led astray o'er treach'rous bogs,   25
Is wand'ring; ask of him where shines the light,
Which that he follows seems:—"At home," he says.
There, pleasure, rest thy golden car. The mind
Is its own home. In fair and stormy sky
Alike thou dwell'st, thy bark alike is steer'd   30
Down the calm stream, and through the raging sea.
It is the mind, communing with itself,
That cast a sunshine on the paths of life;
That midst adversity's dark hour can see
Above a clear unclouded sky; that rides   35
As undisturb'd upon the troubl'd waves
Of active life, as in the calm haven
Of retirement. Who seeks thee not within,
In vain he woos thee on the shady bank;
In vain he courts thee in the grotto's dark   40
Recess. Though burst his stores with India's rich
Produce, yet still he will be poor; nations
May bow beneath his sway, yet weaker he
Shall be than those who call him master. Let
His table groan, and let his cup o'erflow;   45
If he neglects the banquet of the mind,
Drinks not from out that inward fount, which he
Who drinks of never thirsts, still he shall live
In want, in want shall die.

Poem No. 150; 22 July 1834

Give me an eye, that manly deeds
Shall kindle up with living fire;
That rolls enraptur'd at the strains
Resounding from the heroic lyre.

An eye, that does on nature's charms,   5
With all a lover's fondness, dwell;
That gazes fixt on mountain height,
And wanders o'er the shady dell.

An eye, that woman's tear will cloud,
And woman's smile light up again;   10
As when the rays of setting sun
Succeed the cool refreshing rain.

An eye, that, at misfortune's tale,
Will shed the sympathetic tear;
Forget its faults and kindly seek   15
The broken, sorrowing heart to cheer.

An eye, that, at a friend's reproof,
Shall bending, mildly own his sway,
Nor kindling rashly at his words
Shall madly turn in wrath away.   20

Is there, who has an eye like this,
To dwell forever next my heart;
To share my joy, to share my grief,
And to my breast his own impart?

Poem No. 146; 9 August 1834

I saw a child, whose eyes had never drank
The cheerful light of heaven; yet they were fair
And beautiful, and oft those mild blue orbs
Would turn, and seem to seek the forms of those
He lov'd. Full well he knew them, for we need   5
Not sight true friends to know. If stranger's voice,
Or stranger's step obtruded on his ear,—
Shrieking, he to his mother closer clung,
And with his fair yet sightless eyes uprais'd
Would seem from her, whom best he knew, to ask   10
Protection. His ear was tun'd to nicest
Harmony. His voice—sweet as nightingale's,
That in some lone vale of Attica,
'Midst ivy dark, sits warbling her plaintive

Notes. Entranc'd the shepherd, as he   15
Hies him home with quicken'd pace, unconscious
Of delay, lingers to hear her evening
Song. Sightless, think not that he was sad, although
The smiles of morn; the blushes of the sun,
When 'neath his crimson canopy of clouds   20
He mildly sinks to rest; the evening star,
Seen from behind dark-rolling clouds smiling
Amid the storm; the moon rising from out
The ocean's bed; the lofty groves bending
To catch the zephyrs, as they come laden   25
With balmy spoils from many a flow'ry field;
The brook leaping from rock to rock, and then
Wand'ring 'mid thickets dark, where scarce the sun
The noon day heat can penetrate, then through
The wide-extended plain, now flowing smooth,   30
Now ruffled, hoarsely murm'ring o'er the rocks,
Until it fades in distance from our view;
And though all the beauties, which with lavish
Hand nature outspreads, all to him were dark;
Think not, although he ne'er was bless'd   35
By sights like these, that he was sorrowful.
O no. He knew not, felt not he had want
Of that he never had. With what delight
O sun, would he have view'd thy morning smiles,
Thy evening blushes, when thou sink'st to rest;   40
If, into those blue eyes, that roll'd in vain
To find thy light, thy piercing beam had gone!
O star of eve, how beautiful wouldst thou
Appear smiling amid the storm! and thou,
Fair groves bending to catch the zephyrs! thou,   45
O brook, flowing through thickets dark, and wide
Extended plain!
But once, ere he departed to the world,
Where all are bless'd with perfect sight, the want
Of vision dimm'd his eyes with tears—but once,   50
For mother's fondest care prevented more.
It was a summer's day cloudless and fair;
Alas! that summer's day he ne'er beheld!
The cooling breezes play'd around his head,
Tossing in sport his auburn locks; as, on   55
A bank cover'd with fairest flowers, mirthful

He sat, near to his paternal mansion.
The rose bent not beneath his airy touch;
The drops of dew, that on it hung, scarce fell,
And falling seem'd to mourn, that he, who on 60
It laid so light a hand, should not behold
Its beauties. Sweeter to him its fragrance,
For loss of one makes other senses more
Acute. Perchance a bee upon his hand
Alighted. He, dreaming nought of harm, held 65
Fast and crush'd it; but ere that was done, its
Sting had deeply pierced, and many a tear
Gush'd from those sightless eyes. Let us from this
A moral draw: though done by him who ne'er
Enjoy'd the light of day, 'twill serve to teach 70
Those, who have always sported in its beams,
A useful lesson. Oft as vice assails,
Rememb'ring that it stings both soul and body,
Let us cast it from us; but if within
Us it has taken root and flourish'd long, 75
Let us, like that sightless boy, though many
A pang we suffer in the attempt, with firm,
Unsparing grasp, crush the dire foe, and be
Forever free.

Poem No. 255; 15 August 1834

The New Year

All hail new year! though clad in storms thou com'st,
To me thou art a welcome guest.
'Tis sweet to struggle with the wintry blast,
And, as the cruel storm is raging round,
To feel within the breast a calm as soft & sweet 5
As summer's eve; to see the snow whirling
In eddies, like the wide world in passion's
Eddies mingled, to see and smile is sweet.
To feel the breast as snow-flake pure, which falls
Upon the cheek; or if within anger 10
Should rise, to know 'twill melt as soon into
The tide of warm and ever-flowing love.

O this is sweet: come let us look where streams
The cheering light, and mark rough winter's gifts,
The social circle round the evening fire.   15
See the fond mother as with looks of love
She turns now here, now there, now her children
Smiles upon, and now their sire; and see him
As the laughing boy he raises, imprint
Upon his lips a father's kiss; and from heart   20
With bliss o'erflowing now to God a prayer
Of silent gratitude he gives. What pomp
Of kings can equal joy afford, or rank
With all her envied state?
Hadst thou a human heart, thou savage blast;   25
'Twould melt at such a sight, and thy rough voice
Would whisper soft in gentle zephyrs round
That dwelling.

Poem No. 31; c. 3 January 1835

Sleigh Ride

Hurra, hurra, away they go
Far over the hills and fields of snow;
Away they go with mirth and glee,
Like the prison'd bird that's just let free.

Away, away, away they fly   5
Swiftly beneath the bright spangled sky;
The mirthful laugh chimes in full well
With the merry gingle of many a bell.

And many an eye is laughing there,
That would with those isles of light compare;   10
That glance from under the brow of night,
And kindle the heart with soft delight.

And there full many a cheek now glows,
That rivals the hues of the fairest rose;
Which spring in its warmest vale could show,   15
But *these* are blushing on hills of snow.

Oh! say not that winter is mirthless, then,
Though the snow lays deep on mountain & glen;
Yet with laughing eyes and hearts of glee
Away we'll fly like a bird let free.   20

Poem No. 206; 5 January 1835

The Snow Drop

Hail early harbinger of Spring!
Thy sight can glad remembrance bring
Of years fled by on swiftest wing,
      Sweet snow-white flower;
I'll spend, thy humble praise to sing,   5
      An idle hour.

Thou boast'st not beauty like the rose,
That ne'er the blasts of winter knows,
And lily-hand-protected glows
      In ladies' bower;   10
Thou hid'st thy head amid the snows,
      My bonny flower.

Yet will I seek the wild retreat,
Where early stray'd my youthful feet,
And with new joy thy presence greet,   15
      Sweet snow-white flower;
Though youth has fled again we meet,
      I feel thy power.

Thou hast not stay'd till warm suns smil'd,
And Spring's soft voice with whispers mild   20
First call'd thee forth; but cradl'd mid the tempest wild
      Thou sprang to birth;
The image, thou, of many a child
      Of modest worth.

Thus in misfortune's rudest storm 25
Will happiness uprear its form,
E'en on the brink of misery born,
    And beauteous grow;
And smile with rosy tints of morn
      O'er night of woe. 30

Poem No. 154; 8 April 1835

Cold cold thy lips my gentle boy
    Thy mother presses now
And closed those eyes that beamed with joy
    And marble white thy brow

I will not mourn—though sad the lot 5
    Life brought to one so young
The grief my child is all forgot
    It from thy bosom rung.

The light of joy that lit thine eye
    Would not be fittened there 10
It sought above a brighter sky
    An earth than this more fair.

Thy lips where dwelt that sweetest smile
    Could not their guest detain
It came to linger there awhile 15
    It could not long remain.

Thy voice—still still its accents sweet
    Are whispering round my heart
And call me to that blissful seat
    Where souls shall never part. 20

Poem No. 87a; spring 1835?

Spring

Look! Winter now in trembling haste
Has snatched his robe from off the hills
And left to run their noisy race
The loud-voiced streams & twinkling rills
And hied him to his sunless cave   5
    Round which the tempest's tongues unceasing rave.

Now to the music of the rills
The Zephyrs circle round the hills
And where the robe of Winter lay
The flowers peep forth to see their play   10
And turn their eyes of various hue
    To catch again heaven's look of mildest blue.

The trees whose stiffened boughs of late
Rattled in Winter's icy blast
Yon free their arms with joy elate   15
To feel their iron bondage past
And stoop towards the river's breast
    To view their limbs from Spring's green wardrobe drest.

Poem No. 320a; spring 1835?

The morn may lend its golden smile
    When age has dimmed the eye
It cannot then of care beguile
    Or check the struggling sigh

Though sweet upon the dulled ear   5
    Life's notes of joy shall fall
They cannot then the spirit cheer
    Within her silent hall.

Yet here shall Friendship's morning beam
    With gladder radiance play   10
The image of Life's brightest dream
    That ever passed away.

Poem No. 528a; spring 1835?

Lines

To ——— On the Death of His Friend

"Then shall the dust *return to the* earth *as it was,*
And the spirit *shall return unto* God *who gave it."*

She sleeps not where the gladsome Earth
Its dark green growth of verdure waves;
And where the wind's low whispering mirth
   Steals o'er the silent graves.

She sleeps not where the wild rose lends   5
Its fragrance to the morning air;
And where thy form at evening bends
   To raise the voice of prayer.

She sleeps not where the wandering wing
Of weary bird will oft repose;   10
And bid Death's lonely dwelling ring
   With joy, at day's still close.

She sleeps not *there*—the wild flower's blush
Would kindle up her closed eye;
She could not hear sweet music's gush   15
   Pass all unheeded by.

Vain, vain would Earth call forth again
Her children from their narrow bed;
The soul that drank her joyous strain
   Has fled, forever fled!   20

The spirit's robe she gave *is* there,
Where leans the wild flower's cheek of bloom,
Where rises oft thy voice of prayer,
   The spirit has no tomb!

Poem No. 419; 10 June 1835

North River

How quiet sleep the silent waves!
As gentle as an infant's breath,
The gales across their slumbers sweep,
Nor wake that sleep as calm as death.

But see, beneath that glassy breast   5
The mingling scenes of life arise;
There spring the leafy groves to meet
The blue expanse of upper skies:

And hills uplift them mid the scene,
And herds beneath the bright wave feed   10
Upon the meadow's mirror'd green,
Or seek repose within the shade.

But look again,—that life has fled,
The breeze has swept too roughly o'er;
The crested wave now rears his head,   15
And frowns indignant on the shore.

So rise within the soul's calm deep
The imag'd smiles of nature's love;
And claim at times their native seat,
And speak of heaven's mild peace above.   20

(Oh! who has known such sacred hours,
And has not felt though all beside,—
Proud wealth's high domes, the pride of power,
All fortune gives,—had been denied;

Yet still beside some stream like this   25
His life would flow as gently on,
And *his* would be far purer bliss
Than sceptr'd monarch on his throne.)

But if upon the soul's calm face
Dash the rough blasts of passion wild,   30
Oh! then how soon is fled each trace
Of all that in that vision smil'd.

Poem No. 199; 20 July 1835

Eheu! fugaces, Posthume, Posthume, Labuntur anni.

Fleeting years are ever bearing
In their silent course away,
All that in our pleasures sharing,
Lent to life a cheering ray.

Beauty's cheek but blooms to wither,   5
Smiling hours but come to fly;
They are gone! Time's but the giver,
Of whate'er is doomed to die.

Thou mayst touch with blighting finger,
All that sense can here enjoy;   10
Yet within my soul shall linger,
That which thou canst not destroy.

Love's sweet voice shall there awaken,
Joys that earth cannot impart;
Joys that live, when thou hast taken   15
All that here may charm the heart.

As the years are gliding by me,
Fancy's pleasing visions rise;
Beauty's cheek, Ah! still I see thee,
Still your glances, *soft blue eyes*.   20

Poem No. 128; c. 1 August 1835

The Humming-Bird

I cannot heal that green gold breast,
Where deep those cruel teeth have prest,
Nor bid thee rear that ruffled crest,
    And seek thy mate,
Who sits alone within his nest,   5
     Nor sees thy fate.

No more with him, in summer hours,
Thou'lt hum amid the leafy bowers,
Nor sip at morn the dewy flowers

To feed thy young,   10
Nor seek, when evening darkly lowers,
    Thy nest high-hung.

No more thou'lt know a mother's care,
The honied spoils at eve to share,
Nor teach thy tender brood to dare   15
    With upward spring
Their path through sunny fields of air,
    On new-fledged wing.

For thy return in vain shall wait
Thy tender young, thy fond, fond mate,   20
Till night's last stars beam forth full late
    On their sad eyes;
Unseen alas! thy cruel fate!
    Unheard thy cries!

Poem No. 220; 1 August 1835

Nature

I love to sit on the green hill's side,
That looks around on a prospect wide;
And send my mind far away to rove
O'er flowery meadow and bending grove,
That looks in the silent depths below   5
At the stranger woods that downward grow;
And fly o'er the face of winding stream
With beach-bird, that starts with sudden scream;
Or skim with the gull the still, calm sea,
Where the white sail sleeps so peacefully;   10
Till I all forget in that waking dream,
But the sky, grove, sea, and winding stream.

And I hie me to the wood's green breast,
On the bird's light wing that seeks her nest,
With swifter flight than she sprang away   15
To meet the bright steps of new-born day;
Hark! from the spot to mother so dear,
Break sweet the cries of young on mine ear.

See! on the sable pine grove a-far
Rains silver light from Dian's bright car;
And stars steal downward with lovely ray,
As if from earth to call me away,
To groves, fields, where flowers of deathless bloom,
Breathe o'er a land unsull'd by a tomb.

Oh! grant me an hour, an hour like this,
To drink from far purer streams of bliss,
Than flow near the dusty paths of life,
Uptost by madd'ning passion and strife;
For my mind comes back with lighter spring,
Than the bird from her weary wand'ring;
With calm more deep than the still bright sea,
Where the white sail sleeps so peacefully;
To join in the world of care again,
And look on the struggles and strife of men,
With an eye that beams with as pure a ray,
As call'd my soul from these scenes away.

Poem No. 247; 15 August 1835

Religion

Gather around thee treasures bright,
   Bid the purple nectar flow;
Will *these* shine with heavenly light
   On thy rayless night of woe?

Snatch the brightest wreath of fame,
   Man has won from fellow worm;
It may prove a wreath of flame
   Round thy brows for aye to burn.

Grasp the monarch's rod of power;
   Seize the warrior's iron spear;
Bid death stay thy coming hour,
   Think ye he *those* arms will fear?

What are *these*—the laurel crown,
   Or the victor's bloody sword,
Or the monarch's darkest frown,   15
   Or the miser's glittering hoard,—

What are *these* to that dread might,
   Which both king and slave obey,
Which can hurl to realms of night
   Yon bright flaming orb of day?   20

What are *these* to soul's calm rest?—
   Diamond's price is paid in vain.
Monarch's might has not possess'd,
   Victor's arm can never gain.

Poem No. 143; 24 August 1835

A Withered Leaf—seen on a Poet's Table

Poet's hand has placed thee there,
Autumn's brown and wither'd scroll!
Though to outward Eye not fair,
Thou hast beauty for the *soul*.

Though no human pen has trac'd   5
On that leaf its learned lore;
Love divine the page has grac'd,
And can *man's* vain words teach more?

Not alone dim Autumn's blast
Echoes from yon tablet sear;   10
Distant music of the Past
Steals upon the poet's ear.

Voices sweet of Summer hours,
Spring's soft whispers murmur by,
Feather'd song from leafy bowers,   15
Draw his listening soul on high.

Far above these realms he soars,
Realms of Death and pale Decay;
And above God's throne adores,
Mid the spirit's native day.   20

Poem No. 399; 14 November 1835

The Stars

Night's wanderers! why hang ye there
    With angel look so bright;
As if ye stooped, bright sons of air!
    From some far distant height?

Ye gaze upon the sleeping earth,   5
    Like mother o'er her child;
And ye too saw its infant birth,
    And looked on it, and smiled.

And come ye now, when day grows dim,
    To bend the listening ear;   10
And meet the heaven-ascending hymn
    From hearts to you so dear?

Why hear I not that seraph voice,
    That woke with earth's first morn;
And do ye not, bright ones, rejoice   15
    As when ye saw it born?

Ah! voiceless now each golden lyre
    Has slumbered many a year;
And each new day ye see expire
    Is numbered by a tear.   20

Yet still ye turn the tearful eye
    Upon earth's wayward course;
For love divine can never die,
    Too deep, too pure its source!

And years shall come—when once again   25
    Your golden lyres shall swell
That sweet, that long forgotten strain,
    For aye on them to dwell.

Poem No. 353; 22 December 1835

The Snow Bird

And hast thou come to gaze on me,
    White wand'rer of the air!
Or dost thou my warm shelter see,
    And ask with me to share?

Thy merry chirp, and rolling eye   5
    Would seem to laugh at fear;
Thou hast but come my lot to spy,
    And see if joy were here.

But thou wast born far, far away,
    Bright bird of snow and storm!   10
And with rude Winter learned to play,
    And love his savage form.

And when he comes, and o'er the land
    Has flung his fleecy shroud;
And on the streams has laid his hand,   15
    And hush'd their voices loud;

And, driven from each hidden nest,
    Thy comrades of the air;
And banished from the wood's green breast
    The music lurking there,—   20

Thou hoverest round his snowy feet,
    And, with his angry howl,
Thy voice of love is heard so sweet,
    We half forget his scowl.

I bless thee bird for He, who lent   25
    Thee love for one so rude,
Has bid thee seek my tenement
    To wake my gratitude;

Thou'rt fled—and gone, perhaps, to find
    Thy playmates of the blast;
I bless thee—for thou'st left behind
    Thine image ere thou'st past.

Poem No. 47; 25 December 1835

Memory

Soon the silver chord is broken,
    Where sweet music lov'd to dwell;
Soon, too soon alas! is spoken
    Love's fond-echo'd word, farewell.

Soon the waves, so lightly bounding,
    All forget the tempest blast;
Soon the pines, so sadly sounding,
    Cease to mourn the storm that's past.

Soon is hush'd the voice of gladness,
    Heard within the green wood's breast;
Yet comes back no notes of sadness,
    No remembrance breaks its rest.

Soon the river, brightly gleaming,
    Rolls its dark forgetful wave;
As if sun were on it beaming,
    And still give the light it gave.

But the *heart* too fond may treasure
    Words it cannot hear again—
Echoes of remember'd pleasure,
    Torturing there for aye remain.

Ling'ring looks around it hover,
    Mock with thoughts of former joy;
Visions it can ne'er recover,
    Looks that time can ne'er destroy.

Poem No. 429; late 1835–early 1836?

Memory

Soon the waves, so lightly bounding,
   All forget the tempest blast;
Soon the pines so sadly sounding,
   Cease to mourn the storm that's past.

Soon is hushed the voice of gladness,   5
   Heard within the green wood's breast;
Yet come back no notes of sadness,
   No remembrance breaks its rest.

Soon the river, brightly gleaming,
   Rolls its dark forgetful wave;   10
As if sun were on it beaming,
   Giving still the light it gave.

But the heart,—how fond 'twill treasure
   Every note of grief and joy!
Oft come back the notes of pleasure,   5
   Grief's sad echoes oft annoy.

There still dwell the looks that vanish,
   Swift as brightness of a dream;
Time in vain earth's smiles may banish,
   There undying still they beam.   20

Poem No. 430; 4 January 1836

King Philip

"Upon the next day, Church, discovering an Indian seated on a fallen tree, made to answer the purpose of a bridge over the river, raised his musket and deliberately aimed at him. "It is one of our own party," whispered a savage, who crept behind him. Church lowered his gun, and the stranger turned his head. It was Philip himself, musing, perhaps, upon the fate that awaited him."–Thatcher's Lives of the Indians

Philip, has the white man's charm
Chilled with fear *thy* kingly breast?
Has his spell unnerved *thy* arm,
Made *thee* woman like the rest?

Say, is *this* the arm, whose shock,
Straight as blazing bolt from heaven,
Sent thy flashing tomahawk,—
And the white man's skull was riven?

Is *this* the hand, whence arrow flew
Winged with eagle's lightning speed?
Did *this* urge thy light canoe,
Quivering like yon wind-struck reed?

Yes—this is still the arm, the hand,—
And there my father's dwelling place;
But like thee, lonely Hope, I stand
Alone amid a stranger race!

My warriors brave, that gathered round
Thy council fires, thou mountain fair!
I hear their distant voices sound,
They call me from the cloudy air.

My wife, my son,—your voices rise
In murmurs soft as summer's stream;
And on my darkened soul those eyes,
Like stars above, in beauty gleam.

But where art thou, my tender wife?
'Tis but your image mocks me now.
Oh! could I snatch thee back to life,
And feel thy lips upon my brow;

That touch would thrill this wasted frame
With all my youth's forgotten fire;
And kindle up to burning flame
The hopes I saw with thee expire.

This is your charm, ye hated race!
No other will my spirit own;
Ye urge me still in deadly chase,
Betrayed, abandoned, and alone.

I scorn your power—could arm avail
To drive you from my native soil;
I should not feel my spirit fail,
This arm would still be nerved for toil.

5

10

15

20

25

30

35

40

I bow not: though I feel your might,—
Though round my head your thunders ring,
And round my heart has gathered night,
Yet know that Philip still is king.

Still will I guard thee, mountain shrine,   45
That looks upon my father's grave;
And thou shalt sadly smile on mine,
And bless the arm that could not save.

And while strange children gather round
Thy base, my father's ancient seat!   50
And thou shalt hear strange voices sound,
And on thee press the stranger's feet;

Thy pine-clad summits still shall wave,
And send their mournful music sweet;—
Above my own, my father's grave,   55
'Twill rising swell our shades to greet.

Poem No. 396; c. late 1835-early 1836

The Painted Columbine

Bright image of my early years!
When glowed my cheek as red as thou,
And life's dark throng of cares and fears
Were swift-winged shadows o'er my sunny brow.

Thou blushest from the painter's page,   5
Robed in the mimic tints of art;
But Nature's hand in youth's green age
With fairer hues first traced thee on my heart.

The morning's blush, she made it thine,
The morn's sweet breath, she gave it thee,   10
And in thy look, my Columbine!
Each fond-remembered spot she bade me see.

I see the hill's far-gazing head,
Where gay thou noddest in the gale;
I hear light-bounding footsteps tread   15
The grassy path that winds along the vale.

I hear the voice of feathered song
  Break from each bush and well-known tree,
  And, on light pinions borne along,
Comes back the laugh from childhood's heart of glee.   20

  O'er the dark rock the dashing brook,
  With look of anger, leaps again;
  And, hastening to each flowery nook,
Its distant voice is heard far down the glen.

  Fair child of art! thy charms decay,   25
  Touched by the withered hand of Time;
  And hushed the music of that day,
When my voice mingled with the streamlet's chime;

  But on my heart thy cheek of bloom
  Shall live when Nature's smile has fled;   30
  And, rich with memory's sweet perfume,
Shall o'er her grave thy tribute incense shed.

  There shalt thou live and wake the glee
  That echoed on thy native hill;
  And when, loved flower! I think of thee,   35
My infant feet will seem to seek thee still.

Poem No. 78; c. early 1836

The Frozen Ship

In 1775 Capt. Warrens, the master of a Greenland whale ship, fell in with an English ship surrounded with icebergs. The last page of her log-book ran thus. 'Nov. 14, 1762. We have now been imprisoned in the ice seventeen days. The fire went out yesterday, and our master has been trying ever since to kindle it, but without success. His wife died this morning. There is no relief.' Capt. Warrens learned on his return to England, that the ship had been missing thirteen years.

Why rings not back the welcome shout
  From yonder ice-bound ship?
Why floats not her glad standard out,
  With bright'ning sunbeams lit?

Why hear we not the hum of life,   5
    Amid that silent throng;
The laugh, the joke, with joyance rife,
    The merry seaman's song?

Ah, mailed in ice their bodies stand!
    Each fixed, and glassy eye   10
Seems gazing on the wondering band,
    That now are gathered nigh.

Each icy hand still grasps the rope,
    It held when life was there;
When round their hearts yet lingered hope,   15
    And wrestled with despair.

Speak, ye cold lips! say what ye lock
    Within that marble breast;
Though deep *our* souls the tale should shock,
    It cannot break *your* rest.   20

Say! what sharp pangs your bosom rent,
    When the low, flickering fire,
Its last warm rays of life had lent,
    And left you vain desire.

Where were your thoughts, when round your frame   25
    Claspt the cold, icy night;
Gathered they round the hearth's warm flame,
    Lighting fond faces bright?

When, to your last loud cries of woe,
    No human accents spoke;   30
And, roaring deep, the waves below
    In fetters o'er you broke;

Did you upraise the trembling prayer
    To Him, who rules the sea;
And triumph o'er your soul's despair   35
    And mortal agony?

Ye answer not: no voice can wake
    That tale within your breast;
Nor human thoughts of suffering break
    Your calm, eternal rest.   40

Beyond this changing, troubled sphere,
    Your spirit rests above;
Where neither death, nor mortal fear,
    Again its peace can move.

Poem No. 825; c. 16 April 1836

My Mother's Voice

My mother's voice! I hear it now,
I feel her hand upon my brow,
    As when, in heart-felt joy,
She raised her evening hymn of praise,
And called down blessings on the days   5
    Of her loved boy.

My mother's voice! I hear it now,
Her hand is on my burning brow,
    As in that early hour;
When fever throbbed through all my veins,   10
And that fond hand first soothed my pains,
    With healing power.

My mother's voice! It sounds as when
She read to me of holy men,
    The Patriarchs of old;   15
And gazing downward on my face,
She seemed each infant thought to trace
    My young eyes told.

It comes, when thoughts unhallowed throng,
Woven in sweet deceptive song,   20
    And whispers round my heart;
As when, at eve, it rose on high;
I hear, and think that she is nigh,
    And they depart.

Though round my heart all, all beside,   25
The voice of Friendship, Love had died;
    That voice would linger there;
As when, soft pillowed on her breast,

Its tones first lulled my infant rest,
　　Or rose in prayer.   30

Poem No. 343; c. spring 1836

The Arab Steed

Amid his foes that slumbered round,
The desert chief lay faint and bound;
And joyless saw the fires of night
Look silent down from their blue height;
For round his heart, as he lay there,   5
Gathered the spectres of despair.

His wife, his home, his children, all
The lonely heart would fain recall
To cheer its darkest hour of gloom,
Seemed phantoms starting from the tomb,   10
That rise when blackening clouds of woe
Their shadows o'er the spirit throw.

He starts—upon him breaks a voice
He ne'er had heard but to rejoice,
The neighing of his sable steed,   15
Whose lion strength and lightning speed
Had been his only, surest trust,
When round him rolled the battle dust.

The captive cord had fettered fast
That swiftness of the winged blast;   20
But still his lion spirit now,
Unchained, is struggling on his brow,
As if there lived a soul of flame,
No chain could hold, no arm could tame.

He starts—though 't were a sight of pain,   25
He still would see that friend again;
Again his noble steed would bless
With his known voice and kind caress;
Wounded and cut by torturing thong
He drew his heavy limbs along,   30

And when he saw his courser nigh,
The tear was starting in his eye.

"I wept not when the thirsty sand
Drank the warm life-blood of my band,
Nor when I heard the Turk's proud voice   35
Loud o'er their fallen foe rejoice;
But when I see *thee,* once so free,
A sharer in my misery,
The tears my pride forbade to flow
Fall now unheeded o'er thy woe.   40

"No more, mid sabres flashing bright,
Thou'lt share the rapture of the fight;
Nor hover round the haughty foe,
With whistling shaft and twanging bow;
Nor, when dark danger's hour is near,   45
Will thy tried strength my courage cheer,
And, swift as dust-cloud in the wind,
Leave far the baffled foe behind.

"No more shall Jordan's limpid tide
With coolness bathe thy reeking side,   50
Nor thy proud chest in triumph brave
The dashings of its angry wave;
No more, when day's bright beams are spent,
Thy feet with joy shall seek the tent,
Where now my children haste to bear   55
The camel's milk, thy wonted share,
And stretch their little hands in vain
To bid thee take the welcome grain.

"And must I see thee then, my brave,
The desert's lord, a Pacha's slave—   60
Shut from the free-trod pastures wide,
The dwellings of thy native pride?
Within the Turk's close-prisoned roof
Shall fetters bind thy swift-winged hoof?
No—though *these* limbs can ne'er be free,   65
His hand shall throw no chain on *thee.*"

He said—and bit the cord that bound
His sable courser's neck around;
And, as his hands so fondly stroke,
His voice in struggling accents broke. 70

"Go—swift as thou wert wont to speed
Along thy oft-trod path, my steed,
Return—and seek the tent, thy home,
Round which thy footsteps loved to roam;
And pass within its folds thy head, 75
Where now my infants sadly tread,
And tell them—they shall hear no more
The voice of love they heard before."

He ceased—but still his steed remained,—
No cord now bound—yet love still chained— 80
He could not leave the voice that blessed,
The hand that had so oft caressed,
But stops, and where his master's belt
Was strongest girt, a moment smelt;
Then seized with firm-set teeth the prize, 85
And homeward o'er the desert flies.

The night's last stars have left the sky,
And day has oped his burning eye;
And now the steed, with labor spent,
Has gained, with morn, the well-known tent, 90
And lifeless sinks upon the sand,
Where round him throng the startled band.
In vain the children strive to raise
The head all silent to their praise,
And call by each endearing name 95
Their hearts' warm sympathy can frame;—
No tongue can now recall the life,
That perished in that noble strife,
The love whose strength was all unknown,
Until with life that love had flown. 100

And loud was heard the voice of grief
For him whose death restored their chief;
And maidens' voice, and minstrels' song
The memory of his deed prolong.

Poem No. 36; c. spring 1836

Hymn,
Sung At The Dedication of The New Stone Church of The North Society In Salem June 22d, 1836.

The weight of years is on the pile
Our fathers raised to Thee, O God;
On this, our temple, rest thy smile,
Till bent with days its tower shall nod.

Thy word awoke, O Power Divine!   5
The hymn of praise in nature's hall;
To man Thou gavst to rear thy shrine,
And on Thee as his Father call:—

To pour in music's solemn strain
The heart's deep tide of grateful love;   10
And kindle in thine earthly fane
A spirit for his home above.

Thou bad'st him on thine altar lay
The holy thought, the pure desire;
That light within a brighter ray   15
Than sunbeam's glance, or vestal fire.

'Twill burn when heaven's high altar flame
On yon blue height, has ceased to glow;
And o'er earth's dark dissolving frame
The sun-light of the spirit throw.   20

Father! within thy courts we bow,
To ask thy blessing, seek thy grace;
O smile upon thy children now!
Look down on this, thy hallowed place!

And when its trembling walls shall feel   25
Time's heavy hand upon them rest;
Thy nearer presence, Lord! reveal,
And make thy children wholly blest.

Poem No. 592; c. 22 June 1836

Song

[For the Valedictory Exercises of the Senior Class of Harvard University, 1836]

No more around the social board
  Shall rise the laugh of glee;
The song that stirred our bosoms once
  Has hushed its melody.

Chorus. Youth's cherished spot! what wreaths of joy   5
  Around thy memory twine!
While throbs the heart's warm beating pulse,
  'Twill tell of "auld lang syne."

The glance of love, the friendly word
  Shall be returned no more;   10
Nor answer when our footsteps tread
  The scenes they loved before.

Chorus. Youth's cherished spot! what wreaths of joy
  Around thy memory twine!
While throbs the heart's warm beating pulse,   15
  'Twill tell of "auld lang syne."

They who upon our pathway shed
  Life's gladdest beams are here,
Upon the shrine where we have knelt
  To shed the parting tear.   20

Chorus. We linger—struggling accents rise
  Each friendly ear to greet;
In one farewell our hearts would breathe
  Whole years of memory sweet.

Adieu! we cannot speak the thoughts   25
  Our swelling breasts would speak,
For feeling's deepest, fullest tide,
  The tongue's vain words are weak.

Chorus. We linger—struggling accents rise
  Each friendly ear to greet;   30
In one farewell our hearts would breathe
  Whole years of memory sweet.

Poem No. 355; c. 19 July 1836

Washington

The Father of his country stood
   And saw awake the glittering plain;
As morn on mountain height and wood
   Returned to look again.

As in his boyhood's earliest hour,   5
   In nature's forest home untrod,
The noblest form of human power
   Kneels childlike to his God.

His sword, that through the battle cloud
   Flashed terror on his country's foe,   10
Its lightening hides beneath the shroud
   Of verdure waving low.

He, who amid the battle's shock
   Spoke calmness to the struggling brave,
And stood like sea-encompassed rock   15
   Unshaken by its wave;

Trusts not the warrior's proudest boasts—
   The thunders of the tented field;—
He kneels before the God of hosts,
   Of all that live the shield!   20

From hence was kindled in thy breast
   That holiest flame of Liberty;
That made thy country's cause *the blest,*
   And gave her sons like thee.

From hence it caught the sacred flame,   25
   That lit with hope her deepest night;
And blazes still around thy name,
   A halo of undying light!

Poem No. 496; c. 20 August 1836

The Autumn Leaf

Thou fair yet lifeless leaf! on whom decay
Seems beautiful, red glowing as thou hangest
Beneath the earliest touch of autumn's hand;
I pluck thee fluttering from thy parent vine,
Before the rude wind tears thee from its fond   5
Embrace to toss thy form, in idle play,
Shrivelled and brown upon the winter air:
For thou art as a tablet to the thoughts
That now are gushing fresh, as if my soul
Had drank new life amid these lofty shades,   10
And felt its being moved by sympathy
With Unseen power.
Brief monitor of frail humanity!
Why has decay that steals from off the cheek
The bloom of health, traces the aged brow   15
With lines of care dimming the burning eye,
And snatching from the form its lofty grace,
Why has it wrought on thee so fair a change;
And why in tints of beauty robed thy form
Brighter than decked before thy vernal prime?   20
Heaven's teachings are not lost on humble heart
Though written on the leaves, and strown upon
The faithless winds, still will its messages
Forever reach the heart that loves its God.
'Twas well to touch thy death with gayest hues   25
Even as the day sinks wrapt in gorgeous clouds,
For thou wert born to live but on the eye,
A thing of outward sense; of whose green youth,
And vigorous noon, and glittering age the child,
In lisping words, recounts. Thou wast not born,   30
Like him who gazes on thy splendor now,
To light a hidden soul with brighter hues
Than wait upon the colored dawn and hang
Upon the dying leaf; and, while decay
Deals rudely with his outward life, and clouds   35
Impatient gather to obscure its glory,
To shape like him, from out a world of change
A spirit into those eternal forms

Of Love, and Majesty, and Beauty, which,
Though here by feeble glance of sense unseen,   40
The all holy eyes of God approve.

Poem No. 673; c. 1 October 1836

The Winter Bird

Thou singest alone on the bare wintery bough
As if Spring with its leaves were around thee now;
And its voice, that was heard in the laughing rill,
And the breeze, as it whispered o'er meadow and hill,
Still fell on thine ear, as it glided along   5
To join the sweet tide of thine own gushing song
Sing on—though its sweetness was lost on the blast
And the storm has not heeded thy song as it passed;
Yet its music awoke in a heart that was near
A thought whose remembrance will ever prove dear—   10
Though the brook may be frozen, though silent its voice
And the gales through the meadows no longer rejoice
Still I felt as my ear caught thy glad note of glee,
That my heart in life's winter might carol like thee.

Poem No. 695; c. 31 December 1836

The Boy's Dream
A Ballad

A youth looked into the running stream,
    And he sighed to be as free;
That he might visit the city's mart,
    And come to the boundless sea.

And on its waters swift be borne   5
    To countries distant, and strange;
Which he read of in books, or heard men tell,
    And over the world to range.

Then he sought for a ship, and left his home,
　　And mother and father dear;　　　　　　　　　　　　10
And he roamed the wide world from land to land,
　　And was gone for many a year.

He sailed where the reefs of coral grow,
　　He sailed by the ice-bergs cold,
He saw the wonders of every clime,　　　　　　　　　15
　　And rich was his ship with gold.

But no place he found, that was so dear,
　　As that he had left behind;
And a weary life he seemed to lead,
　　The sport of the waves and wind.　　　　　　　　　20

He gazed around on the lonely deep,
　　And his heart grew sick, to see
How it stretched forever on, and on,
　　And shoreless seemed to be.

And his thoughts flew back to those early days;　　　25
　　To his home by the river's side;
And his father and mother he there had left,
　　To roam the ocean wide.

It seemed far better to live as they,
　　And see but the sights they saw;　　　　　　　　　30
Than roam as a sailor from land to land,
　　Without a home, or law.

And his mind was changed; he left his ship,
　　And swift sought the pleasant stream;
Where he left his parents to mourn his loss,　　　　35
　　And followed his boyhood's dream.

Poem No. 24; 1834–36?

I murmur not though hard the lot
To see another's that fond smile;
And feel myself all, all forgot,
And left to weep unseen the while.

I murmur not that thou canst give 5
Another joy so dear to me;
Though for that smile alone I live,
Am glad but while I look on thee.

I would not ask those eyes to turn,
And shed their light upon my woe; 10
To cool these throbbing veins that burn
With passion's hottest maddest flow.

I would not cause that gentle heart
A sigh of sorrow, shade of grief;
To bid this mountain weight depart, 15
And give my anguished soul relief.

Still may that bright and sunny brow
No shade of care or sorrow know;
Still beam those eyes as bright as now,
Though not on *me* their smile they throw. 20

I will not mourn though sad the weight,
The weary weight life brings to *me;*
For *thou* shalt live with joy elate,
With cheek all bloom and heart all glee.

Those eyes another's love shall speak, 25
Those lips shall breathe another's name;
Yet vain in other's souls they seek
A purer love, a holier flame.

'Twill burn, when yon bright beaming star
With kindred light has ceased to glow, 30
As pure in yon blue heaven afar,
As in its earthly shrine below.

Poem No. 248; 1836?

The Torn Flower

I tore thee—thou who looked so sweet,
And shed thy fragrance at my feet;
   I tore thee in my wrath;
Scattered thy sweetness to the wind,

Nor left one look of love behind 5
   To smile upon my path.

I mourn too late! Ah! ne'er again
Shall visit thee the small-dropped rain,
   The gently falling dew;
Nor morn, nor noon, nor eve's still hour 10
Shall watch the spot, ill-fated flower!
   Where once thy beauty grew.

The storms that filled the troubled sky
Have lightly passed thy shelter by,
   Pleased with thy sweet perfume; 15
More cruel than the angry blast
I madly crushed thee as I past,
   And robbed thee of thy bloom.

Would that the tears I o'er thee shed
Might raise again thy drooping head 20
   To life and joy once more;
Then would I learn me of the storm
To spare thy bright and tender form,
   My heart's mad passion tore.

Poem No. 278; 1836?

The moon was shining on the deck
The stars looked out upon the sea
The sail had dwindled to a speck
   That was upon our lea.

I crept beside the grey-locked man 5
Whose words I loved to hear so well
He knew my wish and thus began
   His ocean tale to tell.

The ship from Hamburgh held her way
And playing round her stately form 10
The waves curled bright their wreaths of spray
   All heedless of the storm.

The ship seemed glad to feel once more
Around her roll the deep blue main
As onward bounding from the shore   15
    She heard its voice again

And I was young my boy as thou
And all around seemed strange and new
I watched the ocean's deep green brow
    I watched the heaven's so blue   20

I looked behind—my home had fled
And seemed afar like distant cloud
My mother all I loved seemed dead
    I wept and sobbed aloud.

Poem No. 527; 1836?

Home of my youth! Where first my lot was cast
To Thee I dedicate my feeble song
Upon whose hills how swift the moments passed
As linked with flowers the days moved gaily on
Though hills more fair & streams more bright than thine   5
May lure my eye as from thy paths I stray
While memory's ray shall on their summits shine
What spot shall seem more fair to me than they

Home of my youth would that a worthy lay
Might tell my love for thee to distant time   10
Far as thy sons o'er ocean's trackless way
Have borne thy name—to India's sunny clime—
A blessing rest alike on thee & thine
To those whose bark shall rove from strand to strand
Where'er they are whate'er their lot may be   15
Sweet be the name of their own father-land.

Poem No. 175; 1836?

Haunts of my youth farewell! A while I leave
You in your loveliness! A while I go
To visit other scenes, more fair, perhaps, but none
I love so well. Resistless as thy stream,
Fair river, when thou pour'st along swol'n with   5
Autumnal rains, is love of home within
The breast of man. So Afric's wretched son
With eye bent on his fast-receding home,
Has drop'd his scanty fare, heeds not his chains
But with the tear-drops starting in his eye   10
Exclaims—"There I was born"—"There is my home."
The wanderer of ten long years, whom oft
Encounter'd dangers never learn'd to shed
A tear, weeps like a child when he beholds
The smoke of much-lov'd Ithaca. Beauty's   15
Fabl'd Goddess, since on earth no more she
Deigns to dwell, has left with thee, O home, her
All-enchanting Love. Dearer to Lapland's
Sons her new-clad plains, her ice-bound rivers,
Her mountain tops the residence of storms,   20
Than the green sunny plains, the vine-clad hills
The winding streams of favor'd Italy.
And ye my youthful haunts, though some there are
On which my eyes could dwell a summer's day
Nor heed the sun blushing to leave so   25
Fair a scene, nor evening's soft approach warning
My lingering footsteps home, though some there are
Which those who look on fairer scenes would pass
Contemptuous by yet all to me are
Beautiful, round all alike O home thy   30
Charm is thrown I love you all. The yellow
Leaves at my return perhaps will rustle
In the autumnal blast or winter's snows
May hide my winding path still will I trace
It out: for there's no winter in my love   35
For thee no age but death. Amid the snows
Of age 'twill like the ever-green appear
As fresh as in my vernal prime.

Poem No. 160; 1836?

Death Decay and Change

Sounds are ringing on my ear
Sights are floating in my eye
Now those sounds I cannot hear
And those visions too—they fly!

What is this? the tolling bell   5
Mournfully the surges roll
That of the departed tell
He a brother of my soul.

What new note is on the air
That just bore the knell of pain   10
Reaper's voices—home they bear
Autumn's yellow glittering grain.

Where has fled from me the face
That from me this moment past
Ah! Why clothed thee such a grace   15
If thou wast to flee so fast!

See a bud of earliest bloom
Presses now upon my sight
In the distance rolls the gloom
That o'er me had cast its night   20

But though fair as thee 'twill fade
Swift as all that fled before
On its stem Time's hand is laid
There! I see its bloom no more—

Death Decay and Change succeeding   25
Let us live a life of love
Each their silent tokens heeding
As words whispered from above

To the lonely broken hearted
By his kindest nearest Friend   30
Of a love that is not parted
Of a life that cannot end

Poem No. 432; 1836?

The Portrait

Would I might stay those features as they pass,
Where beauty seems as if she loved to dwell;
And chain that smile upon the fickle glass,
That smile whose sweetness words in vain would tell;
Or fix thy glance with all its heaven of blue,   5
The evening star that floats its azure through!
But no—the spot where I would bid them rest
Is all unworthy they should linger there;
The blush of morn on Ocean's slumbering breast,
The star bright-imaged in its depths of air   10
Vanish from off its bosom like thy smile,
That rests but on so frail a thing awhile,
Then seeks a home whence it may ne'er depart,
The faithful mirror of a loving heart.

Poem No. 852; c. late 1836–early 1837

The Canary Bird

I cannot hear thy voice with others' ears,
Who make of thy lost liberty a gain;
And in thy tale of blighted hopes and fears
Feel not that every note is born with pain.
Alas! that with thy music's gentle swell   5
Past days of joy should through thy memory throng,
And each to thee their words of sorrow tell,
While ravished sense forgets thee in thy song.
The heart that on the past and future feeds,
And pours in human words its thoughts divine,   10
Though at each birth the spirit inly bleeds,
Its song may charm the listening ear like thine,
And men with gilded cage and praise will try
To make the bard like thee forget his native sky.

Poem No. 221; c. 15 April 1837

The Tree

I love thee when thy swelling buds appear,
And one by one their tender leaves unfold,
As if they knew that warmer suns were near
Nor longer sought to hide from winter's cold;
And when with darker growth thy leaves are seen   5
To veil from view the early robin's nest,
I love to lie beneath thy waving skreen
With limbs by summer's heat and toil opprest;
And when the autumn winds have stript thee bare,
And round thee lies the smooth untrodden snow,   10
When nought is thine that made thee once so fair,
I love to watch thy shadowy form below,
And through thy leafless arms to look above
On stars that brighter beam when most we need their love.

Poem No. 246; c. 22 April 1837

The Fossil Flower

Dark fossil flower! I see thy leaves unrolled,
With all their lines of beauty freshly marked,
As when the eye of Morn beamed on thee first,
And thou first turn'dst to meet its welcome smile.
And sometimes in the coals' bright rain-bow hues,   5
I dream I see the colors of thy prime,
And for a moment robe thy form again
In splendor not its own. Flower of the past!
Now as I look on thee, life's echoing tread
Falls noiseless on my ear; the present dies;   10
And o'er my soul the thoughts of distant time,
In silent waves, like billows from the sea,
Come rolling on and on, with ceaseless flow,
Innumerable. Thou mayest have sprung unsown
Into thy noon of life, when first earth heard   15
Its Maker's sovereign voice; and laughing flowers
Waved o'er the meadows, hung on the mountain crags,
And nodded in the breeze on every hill.

Thou may'st have bloomed unseen, save by the stars
That sang together o'er thy rosy birth,   20
And came at eve to watch thy folded rest.
None may have sought thee in thy fragrant home,
Save light-voiced winds, that round thy dwelling played,
Or seemed to sigh, oft as their wingéd haste
Compelled their feet to roam. Thou may'st have lived   25
Beneath the light of later days, when man,
With feet free-roving as the homeless wind,
Scaled the thick-mantled height, coursed plains unshorn,
Breaking the solitude of nature's haunts
With voice that seemed to blend, in one sweet strain,   30
The mingled music of the elements.
And when against his infant frame they rose,
Uncurb'd, unawed by his yet feeble hand,
And when the muttering storm, and shouting wave,
And rattling thunder, mated, round him raged,   35
And seemed at times like demon foes to gird,
Thou may'st have won with gentle look his heart,
And stirred the first warm prayer of gratitude,
And been his first, his simplest altar-gift.
For thee, dark flower! the kindling sun can bring   40
No more the colors that it gave, nor morn,
With kindly kiss, restore thy breathing sweets:
Yet may the mind's mysterious touch recall
The bloom and fragrance of thy early prime:
For HE who to the lowly lily gave   45
A glory richer than to proudest king,
He painted not those darkly-shining leaves,
With blushes like the dawn, in vain; nor gave
To thee its sweetly-scented breath, to waste
Upon the barren air. E'en though thou stood   50
Alone in nature's forest-home untrod,
The first-love of the stars and sighing winds,
The mineral holds with faithful trust thy form,
To wake in human hearts sweet thoughts of love,
Now the dark past hangs round thy memory.   55

Poem No. 95; c. early 1837

The April Snow

It will not stay! the robe so pearly white,
Which fell in folds on nature's bosom bare,
And sparkled in the winter moonbeams' light,
A vesture such as sainted spirits wear;
It will not stay! Look, from the open plain,   5
It melts beneath the glance of April's sun;
Nor can the rock's cool shade the snow detain,
It feeds the brooks, which down the hill-side run.
Why should it linger? Many-tinted flowers
And the green grass its place will quickly fill,   10
And, with new life, from sun and kindly showers,
With beauty deck the meadow and the hill;
Till we regret to see the earth resume
This snowy mantle for her robe of bloom.

Poem No. 309; early to mid 1837?

Nature

Nature, my love for thee is deeper far
Than strength of words though spirit-born can tell;
For while I gaze they seem my soul to bar,
That in thy widening streams would onward swell
Bearing thy mirrored beauty on my breast;   5
Now through thy lonely haunts unseen to glide,
A motion that scarce knows itself from rest,
With pictured flowers and branches on its tide;
Then by the noisy city's frowning wall,
Whose armed heights within its waters gleam,   10
To rush with answering voice to ocean's call
And mingle with the deep its swoln stream;
Whose boundless bosom's calm alone can hold
That heaven of glory in thy skies unrolled.

Poem No. 348; c. 29 July 1837

An Evening Walk

I love at quiet eventide,
    Far from the city's noise to stray;
To climb the brow of rocky hill,
    And watch the light of parting day.

To see reflected on the clouds,   5
    In red and gold its colors glow;
Or watch the lengthening shadows fall
    On field and valley, far below.

To hear the quail's low, plaintive call,
    At intervals, the stillness break;   10
Or sprightly sparrow's cheerful note,
    That memory's pleasing fancies wake.

Faint rises on the tranquil air
    The tardy insects' droning song;
Which still, amid the closing flowers,   15
    The busy work of day prolong.

O'er swamp, and meadow stretching far,
    The evening shadows stealthy creep;
Till all the darkening landscape round
    Is wrapt at length in slumber deep.   20

I seem more near to Nature's heart,
    And feel that I her secrets share;
The noisy world forgotten is,
    With all its tumults, toil, and care.

Another, better life I live,   25
    A life to worldly minds unknown;
Which Nature to her votaries gives,
    Enjoyed, and prized by them alone.

Poem No. 244; 25 August 1837

Beauty

I gazed upon thy face—and beating life,
Once stilled its sleepless pulses in my breast,
And every thought whose being was a strife
Each in its silent chamber sank to rest;
I was not, save it were a thought of thee,   5
The world was but a spot where thou hadst trod,
From every star thy glance seemed fixed on me,
Almost I loved thee better than my God.
And still I gaze—but 'tis a holier thought
Than that in which my spirit lived before,   10
Each star a purer ray of love has caught,
Earth wears a lovelier robe than then it wore,
And every lamp that burns around thy shrine
Is fed with fire whose fountain is Divine.

Poem No. 232; 24 September 1837

The Voice of God

They told me—when my heart was glad,
And all around but said rejoice—
They told me, and it made me sad,
The thunder was God's angry voice.

And then I thought that from the sky,   5
Throned monarch o'er a guilty world,
His glance—the lightning flashing by—
His hand the bolts of ruin hurled.

But I have learned a holier creed
Than that my infancy was taught;   10
'Twas, from the words of love I read
And the sweet lips of nature, caught,

Yes—'twas my Father's voice I feared,
It fills the sky, the wide-spread earth;
It called in every tone that cheered   15
Those rosy hours of childhood's mirth.

'Tis only on the heedless ear
It breaks in thunder's pealing wrath
Winging the wanderer's steps with fear
To fly destruction's flaming path. 20

God dwells no more afar from me,
His voice in all that lives is heard;
From the loud shout of rolling sea
To warbled song of morning's bird.

In all that stirs the human breast, 25
That wakes to mirth or draws the tear,
In passion's storm or soul's calm rest,
Alike the voice of God I hear.

Poem No. 650; c. 2 December 1837

The Wind-Flower

Thou lookest up with meek, confiding eye
Upon the clouded smile of April's face,
Unharmed, though Winter stands uncertain by,
Eyeing with jealous glance each opening grace.
Thou trustest wisely! in thy faith arrayed, 5
More glorious thou than Israel's wisest King;
Such faith was his, whom men to death betrayed;
As thine who hear'st the timid voice of Spring,
While other flowers still hide them from her call,
Along the river's brink, and meadow bare; 10
Thee will I seek beside the stony wall,
And in thy trust with childlike heart would share,
O'erjoyed, that in thy early leaves I find
A lesson taught by Him, who loved all human kind.

Poem No. 684; c. 23 December 1837

The Sabbatia

The sweet briar rose has not a form more fair,
Nor are its hues more beauteous than thine own,
Sabbatia, flower most beautiful and rare!
In lonely spots blooming unseen, unknown.
So spiritual thy look, thy stem so light,   5
Thou seemest not from the dark earth to grow;
But to belong to heavenly regions bright,
Where night comes not, nor blasts of winter blow.
To me thou art a pure, ideal flower,
So delicate that mortal touch might mar;   10
Not born, like other flowers, of sun and shower,
But wandering from thy native home afar
To lead our thoughts to some serener clime,
Beyond the shadows and the storms of time.

Poem No. 580; late 1837?

The Passage Bird

Far far o'er city & field thou art flying
While day lends its brightness to shine on thy way
Thou stoopst not though green groves beneath thee are lying
And wave with soft voice their welcome to stay

High high over hill top & mountain thou soarest   5
O'er the wide spreading lake & the still gliding stream
Where Ocean thine anthem in thunders thou pourest
And where on thy bosom the canvass sails gleam

Still onward thou stoopest not though weary thy pinion
Though fair spread the lands that thy wing spreadeth o'er   10
For fairer the climes of the sun's bright dominion
And sweeter the Ocean's loud voice on its shore

Thou hearst though I hear not the rippling waves wander
Beneath where thy nest hangs leaf-sheltered above
Thou seest though unseen in the dark distant yonder 15
The home of thy heart & the mate of thy love—

Poem No. 112; 1837?

A Sonnet

Thy beauty fades and with it too my love,
For 'twas the self-same stalk that bore its flower;
Soft fell the rain, and breaking from above
The sun looked out upon our nuptial hour;
And I had thought forever by thy side 5
With bursting buds of hope in youth to dwell,
But one by one Time strewed thy petals wide,
And every hope's wan look a grief can tell:
For I had thoughtless lived beneath his sway,
Who like a tyrant dealeth with us all, 10
Crowning each rose, though rooted on decay,
With charms that shall the spirit's love enthral,
And for a season turn the soul's pure eyes
From virtue's changeless bloom that time and death defies.

Poem No. 710; c. 21 April 1838

The Columbine

Still, still my eye will gaze long-fixed on thee,
Till I forget that I am called a man,
And at thy side fast-rooted seem to be,
And the breeze comes my cheek with thine to fan;
Upon this craggy hill our life shall pass, 5
A life of summer days and summer joys,
Nodding our honey bells mid pliant grass
In which the bee half hid his time employs;
And here we'll drink with thirsty pores the rain,

And turn dew-sprinkled to the rising sun, 10
And look when in the flaming west again
His orb across the heaven its path has run;
Here, left in darkness on the rocky steep,
My weary eyes shall close like folding flowers in sleep.

Poem No. 441; c. 9 June 1838

The Robin

Thou needst not flutter from thy half-built nest
Whene'er thou hearst man's hurrying feet go by—;
Fearing his eye for harm may on thee rest,
Or he thy young's unfinished cottage spy;
All will not heed thee on that swinging bough, 5
Nor care that round thy shelter spring the leaves,
Nor watch thee on the pool's wet margin now
For clay to plaster straws thy cunning weaves;
All will not hear thy sweet out-pouring joy,
That with morn's stillness blends the voice of song; 10
For over-anxious cares their souls employ,
That else upon thy music borne along
And the light wings of heart-ascending prayer
Had learned that Heaven is pleased thy simple joys to share.

Poem No. 686; c. 9 June 1838

Hymn

Thou who keepst us each together
Who as one in heart may meet;
We are called we know not whither;
Thou wilt guide our wandering feet.

Homes we leave, the world's warm greeting 5
Spoken round the household fire;
We have known in friendship meeting
All the heart can here desire.

Yet Thou givest all we borrow
    From these brightened scenes around,   10
And Thou biddst us rise and follow
    Him who hath acceptance found.

Though through thorny ways his leading,
    And untried the path before;
We as children all things needing   15
    Here a Father's love adore.

He has spoken; Him Thou hearest;
    He descends from heaven to save;
Thou that on the billow fearest,
    'Faith'! 'walk firm the rocking wave'!   20

'Little flock be not ye troubled,
    Thine the kingdom of the Son;
Though earth's weight of woe be doubled,
    He the crown of Light hath won.'

Poem No. 701; 1836–spring 1838?

The Stranger's Gift

I found far culled from fragrant field and grove
Each flower that makes our Spring a welcome guest,
In one sweet bond of brotherhood inwove
An ozier band their leafy stalks compressed;
A stranger's hand had made their bloom my own,   5
And fresh their fragrance rested on the air,
His gift was mine—but he who gave unknown,
And my heart sorrowed though the flowers were fair:
Now oft I grieve to meet them on the lawn,
Scattered along the path I love to go,   10
By One who on their petals paints the dawn,
And gilt with sunset splendors bids them glow,
For I ne'er asked 'who steeps them in perfume?'
Nor anxious sought His love who crowns them all with bloom!

Poem No. 228; c. 18 August 1838

The New Birth

'Tis a new life—thoughts move not as they did
With slow uncertain steps across my mind,
In thronging haste fast pressing on they bid
The portals open to the viewless wind;
That comes not, save when in the dust is laid   5
The crown of pride that gilds each mortal brow,
And from before man's vision melting fade
The heavens and earth—Their walls are falling now—
Fast crowding on each thought claims utterance strong,
Storm-lifted waves swift rushing to the shore   10
On from the sea they send their shouts along,
Back through the cave-worn rocks their thunders roar,
And I a child of God by Christ made free
Start from death's slumbers to eternity.

Poem No. 722; September 1838

The Journey

To tell my journeys where I daily walk,
These words thou hearst me use were given me;
Give heed then, when with thee my soul would talk,
That thou the path of peace it goes may see;—
I know no where to turn, each step is new;   5
No wish before me flies to point the way,
But on I travel with no end in view,
Save that from Him who leads I never stray;
He knows it all; the turning of the road,
Where this man lives, and that, He knows it well;   10
And finds for me at night a safe abode,
Though I all houseless know not where to dwell;
And canst thou tell then where my journeying lies?
If so thou tread'st with me the same blue skies.

Poem No. 741; early to mid-September 1838

"In Him we live, & move, & have our being"

Father! I bless thy name that I do live
And in each motion am made rich with thee
That when a glance is all that I can give
It is a kingdom's wealth, if I but see;
This stately body cannot move, save I   5
Will to its nobleness my little bring,
My voice its measured cadence will not try
Save I with every note consent to sing;
I cannot raise my hands to hurt or bless
But I with every action must conspire;   10
To show me there how little I possess
And yet that little more than I desire;
May each new act my new allegiance prove
Till in thy perfect love I ever live & move.

Poem No. 120; c. 10 November 1838

Enoch

I looked to find a man who walked with God,
Like the translated patriarch of old;—
Though gladdened millions on his footstool trod,
Yet none with him did such sweet converse hold;
I heard the wind in low complaint go by   5
That none his melodies like him could hear;
Day unto day spoke wisdom from on high,
Yet none like David turned a willing ear;
God walked alone unhonored through the earth;
For him no heart-built temple open stood,   10
The soul forgetful of her nobler birth
Had hewn him lofty shrines of stone and wood,
And left unfinished and in ruins still
The only temple he delights to fill.

Poem No. 242; c. 10 November 1838

The Son

Father! I wait thy word—the sun doth stand,
Beneath the mingling line of night and day,
A listening servant waiting thy command
To roll rejoycing on its silent way;
The tongue of time abides the appointed hour,   5
Till on our ear its solemn warnings fall;
The heavy cloud withholds the pelting shower,
Then every drop speeds onward at thy call;
The bird reposes on the yielding bough
With breast unswollen by the tide of song;   10
So does my spirit wait thy presence now
To pour thy praise in quickening life along
Chiding with voice divine man's lengthened sleep,
While round the Unuttered Word and Love their vigils keep.

Poem No. 122; c. 17 November 1838

Love

I asked of Time to tell me where was Love;
He pointed to her foot-steps on the snow,
Where first the angel lighted from above,
And bid me note the way and onward go;
Through populous streets of cities spreading wide,   5
By lonely cottage rising on the moor,
Where bursts from sundered cliff the struggling tide,
To where it hails the sea with answering roar,
She led me on; o'er mountains' frozen head,
Where mile on mile still stretches on the plain,   10
Then homeward whither first my feet she led
I traced her path along the snow again,
But there the sun had melted from the earth
The prints where first she trod, a child of mortal birth.

Poem No. 213; c. 17 November 1838

Day

Day I lament that none can hymn thy praise
In fitting strains, of all thy riches bless;
Though thousands sport them in thy golden rays
Yet none like thee their Maker's name confess;
Great fellow of my being! woke with me   5
Thou dost put on thy dazzling robes of light,
And onward from the east go forth to free
Thy children from the bondage of the night;
I hail thee, pilgrim! on thy lonely way,
Whose looks on all alike benignant shine;   10
A child of light, like thee, I cannot stay,
But on the world I bless must soon decline,
Nor leave one ray to cheer the darkening mind
That will not in the word of God its dayspring find.

Poem No. 98; c. 24 November 1838

Night

I thank thee, Father, that the night is near
When I this conscious being may resign;
Whose only task thy words of love to hear,
And in thy acts to find each act of mine;
A task too great to give a child like me,   5
Thy myriad-handed labors of the day
Too many for my closing eyes to see,
Thy words too frequent for my tongue to say;
Yet when thou see'st me burthened by thy love
Each other gift more lovely then appears,   10
For dark-robed night comes hovering from above
And all thine other gifts to me endears;
And while within her darkened couch I sleep,
Thine eyes untired above will constant vigils keep.

Poem No. 275; c. 24 November 1838

The Coming

The day begins—it comes—the appointed day!
No trumpet sounds, no shouts proclaim its birth;
Yet brighter still, and brighter beams its ray
Upon the mourning tribes that fill the earth.
He comes! The Son of Man is glorified!   5
Crowned with his Father's glory he appears;
And they that scorned, and they that pierced his side,
Before him bow their faces wet with tears.
He comes! *his* peace, his promised peace to give,
In robes of righteousness to clothe the poor;   10
And bid them ever in his presence live,
Heirs of the Kingdom that must aye endure;
Priests, born to lead the long lost tribes of men
Back to the fold of God in joy again.

Poem No. 482; c. 1 December 1838

The Morning Watch

'Tis near the morning watch, the dim lamp burns
But scarcely shows how dark the slumbering street;
No sound of life the silent mart returns;
No friends from house to house their neighbors greet;
It is the sleep of death; a deeper sleep   5
Than e'er before on mortal eyelids fell;
No stars above the gloom their places keep;
No faithful watchmen of the morning tell;
Yet still they slumber on, though rising day
Hath through their windows poured the awakening light;   10
Or, turning in their sluggard trances, say—
"There yet are many hours to fill the night;"
They rise not yet; while on the bridegroom goes
'Till he the day's bright gates forever on them close!

Poem No. 725; c. 1 December 1838

The Weary and Heavy Laden

Rejoice ye weary! ye whose spirits mourn!
There is a rest that shall not be removed;
Press on and reach within the heavenly bourn,
By Christ the king of your salvation proved;
There is a rest! Rejoice ye silent stars,   5
Roll on no more all voiceless on your way;
Thou Sun! no more dark clouds thy triumph mars,
Speak thou to every land the coming day:
It comes! bid every harp and timbrel sound;
Bring forth the fatted calf; make merry all;   10
For this the son was lost, and he is found;
Was dead, and yet has heard his Savior's call;
And comes within to drink the new made wine,
And as a branch abide forever in the Vine.

Poem No. 406; c. 8 December 1838

The Garden

I saw the spot where our first parents dwelt;
And yet it wore to me no face of change,
For while amid its fields and groves I felt
As if I had not sinned, nor thought it strange;
My eye seemed but a part of every sight,   5
My ear heard music in each sound that rose,
Each sense forever found a new delight,
Such as the spirit's vision only knows;
Each act some new and ever-varying joy
Did by my Father's love for me prepare;   10
To dress the spot my ever fresh employ,
And in the glorious whole with Him to share;
No more without the flaming gate to stray,
No more for sin's dark stain the debt of death to pay.

Poem No. 264; c. 8 December 1838

The Song

When I would sing of crooked streams and fields,
On, on from me they stretch too far and wide,
And at their look my song all powerless yields,
And down the river bears me with its tide;
Amid the fields I am a child again,   5
The spots that then I loved I love the more,
My fingers drop the strangely-scrawling pen,
And I remember nought but nature's lore;
I plunge me in the river's cooling wave,
Or on the embroidered bank admiring lean,   10
Now some endangered insect life to save,
Now watch the pictured flowers and grasses green;
Forever playing where a boy I played,
By hill and grove, by field and stream delayed.

Poem No. 789; c. 8 December 1838

The Spirit Land

Father! thy wonders do not singly stand,
Nor far removed where feet have seldom strayed;
Around us ever lies the enchanted land
In marvels rich to thine own sons displayed;
In finding thee are all things round us found;   5
In losing thee are all things lost beside;
Ears have we but in vain strange voices sound,
And to our eyes the vision is denied;
We wander in the country far remote,
Mid tombs and ruined piles in death to dwell;   10
Or on the records of past greatness dote,
And for a buried soul the living sell;
While on our path bewildered falls the night
That ne'er returns us to the fields of light.

Poem No. 126; c. 15 December 1838

The Slave

I saw him forging link by link his chain,
Yet while he felt its length he thought him free,
And sighed for those borne o'er the barren main
To bondage that to his would freedom be;
Yet on he walked with eyes far-gazing still   5
On wrongs that from his own dark bosom flowed,
And while he thought to do his master's will
He but the more his disobedience showed;
I heard a wild rose by the stony wall,
Whose fragrance reached me in the passing gale,   10
A lesson give—it gave alike to all—
And I repeat the moral of its tale,
"That from the spot where deep its dark roots grew
Bloomed forth the fragrant rose that all delight to view."

Poem No. 258; c. 15 December 1838

The Bread from Heaven

Long do we live upon the husks of corn,
While 'neath untasted lie the kernels still,
Heirs of the kingdom, but in Christ unborn,
Fain with swine's food would we our hunger fill;
We eat but 'tis not of the bread from heaven;   5
We drink but 'tis not from the stream of life;
Our swelling actions want the little leaven
To make them with the sighed-for blessing rife;
We wait unhappy on a stranger's board,
While we the master's friend by right should live,   10
Enjoy with him the fruits our labors stored,
And to the poor with him the pittance give;
No more to want, the long expected heir
With Christ the Father's love for evermore to share.

Poem No. 319; c. 15 December 1838

The Latter Rain

The latter rain, it falls in anxious haste
Upon the sun-dried fields and branches bare,
Loosening with searching drops the rigid waste
As if it would each root's lost strength repair;
But not a blade grows green as in the spring,   5
No swelling twig puts forth its thickening leaves;
The robins only mid the harvests sing
Pecking the grain that scatters from the sheaves;
The rain falls still—the fruit all ripened drops,
It pierces chestnut burr and walnut shell,   10
The furrowed fields disclose the yellow crops,
Each bursting pod of talents used can tell,
And all that once received the early rain
Declare to man it was not sent in vain.

Poem No. 518; c. 15 December 1838

The Word

The Word! it cannot fail; it ever speaks;
Unheard by all save by the sons of heaven,
It waits, while time counts on the appointed weeks,
The purpose to fulfill for which 'twas given;
Unchangeable its ever-fixed command;   5
When human feet would from its precepts stray
It points their pathway with its flaming hand,
And bids them keep the strait and narrow way;
And when by its unerring counsels led
The child would seek again his Father's face,   10
Upon its stores of heavenly manna fed
He gains at length through grief his resting place;
And hears its praise from angels' countless throng,
And joins forever in the new-raised song.

Poem No. 598; c. 15 December 1838

Worship

There is no worship now—the idol stands
Within the spirit's holy resting place;
Millions before it bend with upraised hands,
And with their gifts God's purer shrine disgrace;
The prophet walks unhonored mid the crowd   5
That to the idol's temple daily throng;
His voice unheard above their voices loud,
His strength too feeble 'gainst the torrent strong;
But there are bounds that ocean's rage can stay
When wave on wave rush madly to the shore;   10
And soon the prophet's word shall men obey,
And hushed to peace the billows cease to roar;
For he who spoke—and warring winds keep peace,
Commands again—and man's wild passions cease.

Poem No. 630; c. 15 December 1838

The Living God

There is no death with Thee! each plant and tree
In living haste their stems push onward still,
The pointed blade, each rooted trunk we see
In various movement all attest thy will;
The vine must die when its long race is run,   5
The tree must fall when it no more can rise;
The worm has at its root his task begun,
And hour by hour his steady labor plies;
Nor man can pause but in thy will must grow,
And, as his roots within more deep extend,   10
He shall o'er sons of sons his branches throw,
And to the latest born his shadows lend;
Nor know in thee disease nor length of days,
But lift his head forever in thy praise.

Poem No. 619; c. 22 December 1838

Time

There is no moment but whose flight doth bring
Bright clouds and fluttering leaves to deck my bower,
And I within like some sweet bird must sing
To tell the story of the passing hour;
For time has secrets that no bird has sung,   5
Nor changing leaf with changing season told;
But waits the utterance of some nobler tongue,
Like that which spoke in prophet tones of old;
Then day and night and month and year shall tell
The tale that speaks but faint from bird and bough;   10
In spirit songs their praise shall upward swell,
Nor longer pass heaven's gate unheard as now;
But cause e'en angels' ears to catch the strain,
And send it back to earth in joy again.

Poem No. 622; c. 22 December 1838

The Violet

Thou tellest truths unspoken yet by man
By this thy lonely home and modest look;
For he has not the eyes such truths to scan,
Nor learns to read from such a lowly book;
With him it is not life firm-fixed to grow   5
Beneath the outspreading oaks and rising pines,
Content this humble lot of thine to know,
The nearest neighbor of the creeping vines;
Without fixed root he cannot trust like thee
The rain will know the appointed hour to fall,   10
But fears lest sun or shower may hurtful be,
And would delay or speed them with his call;
Nor trust like thee when wintry winds blow cold,
Whose shrinking form the withered leaves enfold.

Poem No. 699; mid-September to mid-December 1838

The Heart

There is a cup of sweet or bitter drink,
Whose waters ever o'er the brim must well,
Whence flow pure thoughts of love as angels think,
Or of its daemon depths the tongue will tell;
That cup can ne'er be cleansed from outward stains   5
While from within the tide forever flows;
And soon it wearies out the fruitless pains
The treacherous hand on such a task bestows;
But ever bright its crystal sides appear,
While runs the current from its outlet pure;   10
And pilgrims hail its sparkling waters near,
And stoop to drink the healing fountain sure,
And bless the cup that cheers their fainting soul
While through this parching waste they seek their heavenly goal.

Poem No. 612; mid-September to mid-December 1838

The Trees of Life

For those who worship Thee there is no death,
For all they do is but with Thee to dwell;
Now while I take from Thee this passing breath,
It is but of thy glorious name to tell;
Nor words nor measured sounds have I to find,   5
But in them both my soul doth ever flow;
They come as viewless as the unseen wind,
And tell thy noiseless steps where'er I go;
The trees that grow along thy living stream,
And from its springs refreshment ever drink,   10
Forever glittering in thy morning beam
They bend them o'er the river's grassy brink,
And as more high and wide their branches grow
They look more fair within the depths below.

Poem No. 132; mid-September to mid-December 1838

The Soldier of the Cross

He was not armed like those of eastern clime,
Whose heavy axes felled their heathen foe;
Nor was he clad like those of later time,
Whose breast-worn cross betrayed no cross below;
Nor was he of the tribe of Levi born,   5
Whose pompous rites proclaim how vain their prayer;
Whose chilling words are heard at night and morn,
Who rend their robes but still their hearts would spare;
But he nor steel nor sacred robe had on,
Yet went he forth in God's almighty power;   10
He spoke the word whose will is ever done
From day's first dawn till earth's remotest hour;
And mountains melted from his presence down,
And hell affrighted fled before his frown.

Poem No. 168; mid-September to mid-December 1838

The Spirit

I would not breathe, when blows thy mighty wind
O'er desolate hill and winter-blasted plain,
But stand in waiting hope if I may find
Each flower recalled to newer life again;
That now unsightly hide themselves from Thee,   5
Amid the leaves or rustling grasses dry,
With ice-cased rock and snowy-mantled tree
Ashamed lest Thou their nakedness should spy;
But Thou shalt breathe and every rattling bough
Shall gather leaves; each rock with rivers flow;   10
And they that hide them from thy presence now
In new found robes along thy path shall glow,
And meadows at thy coming fall and rise,
Their green waves sprinkled with a thousand eyes.

Poem No. 289; mid-September to mid-December 1838

The Serpent

They knew that they were naked, and ashamed
From Him who formed them stole themselves away,
And when He spoke they each the other blamed,
And death speaks living in each word they say;
The serpent grows, a liar born within,   5
Self-slaughter speaks in every uttered word,
And earth is filled with temples built in sin,
Where the foul tempter's praise is sung and heard;
But soon the truth shall gain the listening ear,
And from the lips in sacred utterance speak,   10
And weary souls of Christ's own word shall hear,
And in the living bread salvation seek,
And Satan's reign on earth forever cease,
And the new dawn begin of the eternal peace.

Poem No. 642; mid-September to mid-December 1838

The Dead

I see them crowd on crowd they walk the earth
Dry, leafless trees no Autumn wind laid bare;
And in their nakedness find cause for mirth,
And all unclad would winter's rudeness dare;
No sap doth through their clattering branches flow,   5
Whence springing leaves and blossoms bright appear;
Their hearts the living God have ceased to know,
Who gives the spring time to th'expectant year;
They mimic life, as if from him to steal
His glow of health to paint the livid cheek;   10
They borrow words for thoughts they cannot feel,
That with a seeming heart their tongue may speak;
And in their show of life more dead they live
Than those that to the earth with many tears they give.

Poem No. 266; mid-September to mid-December 1838

The Presence

I sit within my room and joy to find
That Thou who always loves art with me here,
That I am never left by Thee behind,
But by Thyself Thou keepst me ever near;
The fire burns brighter when with Thee I look,   5
And seems a kinder servant sent to me;
With gladder heart I read thy holy book,
Because Thou art the eyes by which I see;
This aged chair, that table, watch, and door
Around in ready service ever wait;   10
Nor can I ask of Thee a menial more
To fill the measure of my large estate,
For Thou Thyself, with all a Father's care,
Where'er I turn, art ever with me there.

Poem No. 269; mid-September to mid-December 1838

The Lost

They wander, straggling sheep without a fold,
Called here and there by falsely-guiding cries;
No hands from them the slaughtering wolves withhold,
But one by one each hireling shepherd flies;
They wander on, but not a blade of green   5
Blesses the sight along the scorching sand;
No spring-fed stream with living voice is seen
Still gliding on companion of their band;
But soon their weary pilgrimage shall close,
And the good shepherd guide their feet in peace;   10
For all its paths his eye experienced knows,
And at each step their joys in him increase,
Till welcomed there where he in honor reigns
He at his Father's board each faithful son sustains.

Poem No. 651; mid-September to mid-December 1838

The Robe

Each naked branch, the yellow leaf or brown,
The rugged rock, and death-deformed plain
Lies white beneath the winter's feathery down,
Nor doth a spot unsightly now remain;
On sheltering roof, on man himself it falls;   5
But him no robe, not spotless snow makes clean;
For 'neath his corse-like spirit ever calls,
That on it too may fall the heavenly screen;
But all in vain, its guilt can never hide
From the quick spirit's heart-deep searching eye,   10
There barren plains, and caverns yawning wide
Must e'er lay naked to the passer by;
Nor can one thought deformed its presence shun,
But to the spirit's gaze stands bright as in the sun.

Poem No. 103; mid-September to mid-December 1838

The Will

Help me in Christ to learn to do Thy will,
That I may have from him eternal life;
And here on earth thy perfect love fulfill,
Then home return victorious from the strife;
This war in heaven must every foe cast down,   5
And bruise the serpent's star-exalted pride;
And gain for me the lyre and martyr-crown
To all who love the praise of men denied;
To do thy will shall bring that day of rest,
When none can work save those who work with Thee;   10
And in thy labors evermore are blest,
From death and sin through Christ forever free;
Beloved by Thee thy children to remain,
Made priests, and kings, and heirs of thy domain.

Poem No. 169; mid-September to mid-December 1838

The War

I saw a war yet none the trumpet blew,
Nor in their hands the steel-wrought weapons bare;
And in that conflict armed there fought but few,
And none that in the world's loud tumults share;
They fought against their wills, the stubborn foe   5
That mail-clad warriors left unfought within;
And wordy champions leave unslain below,
The ravening wolf though drest in fleecy skin;
They fought for peace; not that the world can give,
Whose tongue proclaims the war its hands have ceased;   10
And bids us as each other's neighbour live,
When John within our breasts has not decreased;
They fought for him whose kingdom must increase
Good will to men, on earth forever peace.

Poem No. 256; mid-September to mid-December 1838

Life

It is not life upon Thy gifts to live,
But still with deeper roots grow fixed in Thee;
And when the sun and shower their bounties give
To send out thick-leaved limbs; a fruitful tree,
Whose green head meets the eye for many a mile,   5
Where moss-grown trunks their rigid branches rear,
And full-faced fruit their blushing welcome smile
As to its goodly shade our feet draw near;
Who tastes its gifts shall never hunger more,
For 'tis the Father spreads the pure repast,   10
Who while we eat renews the ready store,
That at his bounteous board must ever last;
For none the bridegroom's supper shall attend,
Who will not hear and make his word their friend.

Poem No. 306; mid-September to mid-December 1838

The Reaper

There are no reapers in the whitening fields,
But many preying on the ripening ears
Forever scatter all the harvest yields,
Planted with toil and wet with many tears;
Eagles they are that on the carcase feed,   5
Not gather with the hand that plants the grain;
With ravening beak they tear the hearts that bleed,
And with their talons aggravate the pain;
But soon the Husbandman his heirs shall send,
Who from the tares shall cull the heavy wheat;   10
Then from the heaven the son too shall descend,
And with his welcome every laborer greet,
And give the weary ones his peace, his rest,
And to the feast invite each ransomed soul, a guest.

Poem No. 608; mid-September to mid-December 1838

Simmons Mobile Alabama

O may I see thy face for without thee
The day returns but round no brightness pours
The light returns I see thy face again—

Poem No. 376; mid-September to mid-December 1838

Winter

There is a winter in the godless heart
More cold than that which creeps upon the year
That will not with the opening spring depart
But freezes on though summer's heats are near
Its blasts are words that chill the loving soul   5
Though heard in pleasing phrase or learned sound
Their killing breath nor thriple folds control
They pierce within though flesh & blood surround

How dead the heart whence drives the arrowy shower
The full blown rose hangs drooping at its breath   10
The bursting buds of promise feel its power
And fixed stand incased in icy death
And e'en the soul which Christ's warm tears fill
Its sleety accents falling thick can chill.

Poem No. 616; mid-September to mid-December 1838

John

What went ye out to see? a shaken reed?
In him whose voice proclaims "prepare the way";
Behold the oak that stormy centuries feed!
Though but the buried acorn of my day;
What went ye out to see? a kingly man?   5
In the soft garments clothed that ye have worn;
Behold a servant whom the hot suns tan,
His raiment from the rough-haired camel torn!
Ye seek ye know not what; blind children all,
Who each his idle fancy will demand;   10
Nor heed my true-sent prophet's warning call,
That you may learn of me the new command;
And see the Light that cometh down from heaven,
Repent! and see, while yet its light is given.

Poem No. 781; late 1838–early 1839

The Flight

Come forth, come forth my people from the place
Where ye have lived so many days secure;
I will destroy within the wicked race,
Their walls of brass and stone shall not endure;
They fall! escape! flee fast! the foe is near!   5
Stop not to take your clothes! escape for life!
Be wise, and of my love-sent message hear!
For swift descends the day with sorrows rife,

Escape! the word is near you in your heart;
Obey within, and make my pathway strait; 10
Hasten! from all your sinful ways depart,
And enter through the strait and narrow gate;
Be warned and flee, the morning watch is spent,
And but a moment for your flight is lent.

Poem No. 90; late 1838–early 1839

The Priest

Grant me forever of thy word to hear,
And live by that which ever speaks from heaven;
That gives the love that knows not of a fear,
For by the gift is every sin forgiven;
Then shall I be, by him who leads me on, 5
A priest to still the people's wave-tost breast;
And when the storm of passion's wrath is gone
Conduct them to the haven of their rest;
Then shall my master hail me as his friend;
The friend of all the weary ones and poor, 10
And when I faint, his promised peace shall send;
In every wound pour oil and wine to cure;
Still beckoning on, till in his Father's peace
He bids my toil and pain forever cease.

Poem No. 153; late 1838–early 1839

The Resurrection

The dead! the dead! they throw their grave clothes by,
And burst the prisons where they long have lain;
I hear them send their shouts of triumph high,
For he the king of terrors now is slain;
I see them; see! the dumb have found a voice; 5
The lame are leaping where they crawled before;
The blind with eyes of wonder see rejoice;
The deaf stand listening to the glad uproar;

Look! each the other as a brother sees;
Hark! each the other welcomes to his home;   10
There are no tones of chilling breath to freeze,
No tears are dropt, no sufferers here can moan;
The joy of love o'er every feature plays,
And every new-born child rejoices in its rays.

Poem No. 488; late 1838–early 1839

My Father's House

My Father's house, I find no entrance there;
But those who buy and sell block up the way,
And that which should be called "the house of prayer,"
Is filled with those whose spirits never pray;
Father! accept my prayer that they may see,   5
Nor in thy presence dwell by Thee unknown;
Open their eyes that they may look on Thee,
And all thy love for disobedience own;
Be this the heaviest scourge to drive them hence,
And may thy word with gentle force persuade;   10
I need no sword but this for my defence,
It speaks; and by the dead shall be obeyed;
And thy new temple from pollution freed
Be filled by those who love in truth and deed.

Poem No. 336; late 1838–early 1839

The Servant

The servant Thou hast called stands ready shod,
Clean through thy holy word, in Christ made free,
To smite the nations with an iron rod,
That haply they may turn and worship Thee;—
Their broken idols own thy spirit's power;   5
The strong men bow, and at its word lie bound;
The lying spirits start to hear the hour
Through all their depths its solemn warning sound;

Nor horse nor chariot now avail for flight,
Thy hand is on the courser's flowing rein;   10
The night unrobed stands guilty in thy sight,
And for a covering pleads, but pleads in vain;—
Through all that waits thy servant bid him stand,
And by thy love supported gain the promised land.

Poem No. 558; late 1838–early 1839

I Was Sick And In Prison

Thou hast not left the rough-barked tree to grow
Without a mate upon the river's bank;
Nor dost Thou on one flower the rain bestow,
But many a cup the glittering drops have drank;
The bird must sing to one who sings again,   5
Else would her note less welcome be to hear;
Nor hast Thou bid thy word descend in vain,
But soon some answering voice shall reach my ear;
Then shall the brotherhood of peace begin,
And the new song be raised that never dies;   10
That shall the soul from death and darkness win,
And burst the prison where the captive lies;
And one by one new-born shall join the strain,
Till earth restores her sons to heaven again.

Poem No. 680; late 1838–early 1839

He Was Acquainted With Grief

I cannot tell the sorrows that I feel
By the night's darkness, by the prison's gloom;
There is no sight that can the death reveal,
The spirit suffers in earth's living tomb;
There is no sound of grief that mourners raise,   5
No moaning of the wind, or dirge-like sea;
Nor hymns though prophet tones inspire the lays,
That can the spirit's grief awake in thee;

Thou too must suffer as it suffers here,
The death in Christ to know the Father's love;
Then in the strains that angels love to hear,
Thou too shalt hear the spirit's song above;
And learn in grief what these can never tell,
A note too deep for earthly voice to swell.

Poem No. 223; c. January 1839

The Fragments

I would weigh out my love with nicest care,
Each moment shall make large the sum I give,
That all who want may find yet some to share;
And bless the crumb of bread that helps them live;
Of thy rich stores how much has wasted been,   5
Of all Thou giv'st me daily to divide;
I will in future count it for my sin,
If e'en a morsel from the poor I hide;
Help me to give them all Thou giv'st to me,
That I a faithful steward may be found;   10
That I may give a good account to Thee,
Of all the seed Thou sowest in my ground;
That nought of all Thou givest may remain,
That can a hungry soul in life sustain.

Poem No. 293; c. January 1839

The Winter Rain

The rain comes down, it comes without our call;
Each pattering drop knows well its destined place,
And soon the fields whereon the blessings fall,
Shall change their frosty look for Spring's sweet face;
So fall the words thy Holy Spirit sends,   5
Upon the heart where Winter's robe is flung;
They shall go forth as certain of their ends,
As the wet drops from out thy vapors wrung;

Spring will not tarry, though more late its rose
Shall bud and bloom upon the sinful heart;   10
Yet when it buds, forever there it blows,
And hears no Winter bid its bloom depart;
It strengthens with his storms, and grows more bright,
When o'er the earth is cast his mantle white.

Poem No. 548; c. January 1839

Forbearance

The senseless drops can feel no pain, as they
In ceaseless measure strike the barren ground;
But o'er its trodden surface constant play,
Without a pang that there no life is found;
Yet oft the word must fall on stony fields,   5
And where the weeds have shot their rankness high;
And nought the seed to him who sows it yields,
But bitter tears and the half-uttered sigh;
But these are rife with precious stores of love,
For him who bears them daily in his breast;   10
For so the Father bids him hence remove,
And so attain His everlasting rest;
For thus He bore with thee when thou wast blind,
And so He bids thee bear wouldst thou his presence find.

Poem No. 557; c. January 1839

The Wolf and the Lamb Shall Feed Together

The wolf, why heeds he not the sportive lamb,
But lies at rest beside him on the plain?
The lion feeds beside the browsing ram,
The tyger's rage is curbed without a chain;
The year of peace has on the earth begun!   5
And see ye not bestowed the promised sign,
The prophets by the spirit moved have sung,
To close the world's long strife with day benign?

Look not abroad, it comes not with the eye;
Nor can the ear its welcome tidings hear;   10
Nor seek ye Christ below, nor yet on high,
Behold the Word to thee is also near;
E'en at thy heart it speaks, Repent! Obey!
And thine eye too shall hail the rising day.

Poem No. 596; c. January 1839

The Rail Road

Thou great proclaimer to the outward eye,
Of what the spirit too would seek to tell,
Onward thou go'st, appointed from on high
The other warnings of the Lord to swell;
Thou art the voice of one that through the world   5
Proclaims in startling tones, "prepare the way;"
The lofty mountain from its seat is hurled,
The flinty rocks thine onward march obey;
The valleys lifted from their lowly bed
O'ertop the hills that on them frowned before,   10
Thou passest where the living seldom tread,
Through forests dark, where tides beneath thee roar,
And bidst man's dwelling from thy track remove,
And would with warning voice his crooked paths reprove.

Poem No. 677; c. January 1839

Behold He Is at Hand That Doth Betray Me

Why come you out to me with clubs and staves,
That you on every side have fenced me so?
In every act you dig for me deep graves;
In which my feet must walk where'er I go;
You speak and in your words my death I find,   5
Pierced through with many sorrows to the core;
And none that will the bleeding spirit bind,
But at each touch still freer flows the gore;

But with my stripes your deep-dyed sins are healed,
For I must show my master's love for you;   10
The cov'nant that he made, forever sealed,
By blood is witnessed to be just and true;
And you in turn must bear the stripes I bear,
And in his sufferings learn alike to share.

Poem No. 818; c. January 1839

The Fruit

Thou ripenest the fruits with warmer air,
That Summer brings around thy goodly trees;
And Thou wilt grant a summer to my prayer,
And fruit shall glisten from these fluttering leaves;
A fruit that shall not with the winter fail,   5
He knows no winter who of it shall eat;
But on it lives though outward storm assail,
Till it becomes in time his daily meat;
Then he shall in the fruit I give abound,
And hungry pilgrims hasten to the bough;   10
Where the true bread of life shall then be found,
Though nought they spy to give upon it now;
But pass it by, with sorrowing hearts that there
But leaves have grown where they the fruit would share.

Poem No. 691; c. January 1839

To Him That Hath Shall Be Given

Why readest thou? thou canst not gain the life
The spirit leads, but by the spirit's toil;
The labor of the body is not strife,
Such as will give to thee the wine and oil;
To him who hath, to him my verse shall give,   5
And he the more from all he does shall gain;
The spirit's life he too shall learn to live,
And share on earth in hope the spirit's pain;

Be taught of God; none else can learn thee aught;
He will thy steps forever lead aright,   10
The life is all that He his sons has taught,
Obey within, and thou shalt see its light;
And gather from its beams a brighter ray,
To cheer thee on along thy doubtful way.

Poem No. 824; c. January 1839

The Thorns

I cannot find thy flowers, they have not blown,
The cruel winter will not let them live;
The seed in every heart thy hand has sown,
Yet none will back to Thee the blossom give;
Their roots without the bosom daily grow,   5
And every branch blooms inward and unseen;
The hidden roots unsightly length they show,
And hide the limbs that thou has clothed with green;
They will not like the plants that own thy care,
The heavy laden boughs extend to all;   10
They will not of the flowers Thou giv'st them share,
But drink the rain that on their bosoms fall,
And nought return but prickly briar and thorn,
That from the enclosed heart thy children warn.

Poem No. 219; c. January 1839

The River

Oh swell my bosom deeper with thy love,
That I some river's widening mouth may be;
And ever on for many a mile above
May flow the floods that enter from thy sea;
And may they not retreat as tides of earth,   5
Save but to show from Thee that they have flown,
Soon may my spirit find that better birth,
Where the retiring wave is never known;

But Thou dost flow through every channel wide,
With all a Father's love in every soul;   10
A stream that knows no ebb, a swelling tide
That rolls forever on and finds no goal,
Till in the hearts of all shall opened be
The Ocean depths of thine Eternity.

Poem No. 388; c. January 1839

The New Jerusalem

I saw the city, 'twas not built by hands,
And nought impure can ever enter in,
'Twas built by those who keep the Lord's commands,
And in his blood have washed away their sin;
Thrice happy those who see the pearly gate   5
Before their earthly vision distant rise;
And keep the path though narrow still and strait
Through many a thorny hedge their journey lies;
Behold within the mansion of thy rest!
Prepared by him who in it went before,   10
Behold the peace that makes the spirit blest!
By him who loved thee kept for thee in store;
Press on, the crown he won shall soon be thine,
And thou amid the just a star in heaven shall shine.

Poem No. 262; c. January 1839

The Cross

I must go on, till in my tearful line
Walks the full spirit's love as I on earth;
Till I can all Thou giv'st again resign,
And he be formed in me who gave me birth;
Wilt Thou within me bruise the serpent's heel,   5
That I through Christ the victory may win;
Then shall the peace the blessed in him must feel,
Within my bosom here on earth begin;

Help me to grasp through him eternal life,
That must by conflict here by me be wrought;   10
With all his faith still aid me in the strife,
Till I through blood like him the prize have bought;
And I shall hang upon the accursed tree,
Pierced through with many spears that all may see.

Poem No. 249; c. January 1839

Nature

Nature would speak through her first master man,
He will not heed her kindly calling voice;
He does not call her name as he began,
For in his Maker he cannot rejoice;
Yet still she woos him back with many a call,   5
That e'en his nature finds it hard to spurn;
And would surrender to his asking all
That now with anxious toil he scarce can earn;
She pleads, but pleads in vain; He will not hear,
But o'er her holds the rod his passions gave;   10
And thinks she will obey through coward fear,
And be like him of her own self the slave;
But ever fresh she rises 'neath his rod,
For she obeys in love her sovereign God.

Poem No. 350; c. January 1839

Ye Gave Me No Meat

My brother, I am hungry, give me food;
Such as my Father gives me at his board;
He has for many years been to thee good,
Thou canst a morsel then to me afford;
I do not ask of thee a grain of that   5
Thou offerest, when I call on thee for bread;
This is not of the wine nor olive fat,
But those who eat of this like thee are dead;

I ask the love the Father has for thee,
That thou should'st give it back to me again;
This shall my soul from pangs of hunger free,
And on my parched spirit fall like rain;
Then thou wilt prove a brother to my need,
For in the cross of Christ thou too canst bleed.

Poem No. 334; c. January 1839

Day Unto Day Uttereth Speech

I would adorn the day and give it voice,
That it should sing with praises meet for Thee;
For none but man can bid it so rejoice,
That it shall seem a joyful day to me;
Break forth ye hearts that frozen winters bind   5
In icy chains more strong than close the year!
Look up! the day, the day, ye suffering blind!
Ye deaf, its notes of welcome come and hear!
Bid it the joy your hearts have long supprest,
Give back to you in new awakening strains;   10
To rouse the sinful from their guilty rest,
And break the captive's more than iron chains;
It shall arise with healing in its beams,
And wake the nations from their lengthened dreams.

Poem No. 286; c. January 1839

Labor and Rest

Thou needst not rest, the shining spheres are thine,
That roll perpetual on their silent way;
And thou dost breathe in me a voice divine,
That tells more sure of thine Eternal sway;
Thine the first starting of the early leaf,   5
The gathering green, the changing autumn hue;
To Thee the world's long years are but as brief,
As the fresh tints the spring will soon renew;

Thou needest not man's little life of years,
Save that he gather wisdom from them all;   10
That in thy fear he lose all other fears,
And in thy calling heed no other call;
Then shall he be thy child to know thy care,
And in thy glorious self the eternal sabbath share.

Poem No. 687; c. January 1839

The Disciple

Thou wilt my hands employ, though others find
No work for those who praise thy name aright;
And in their worldly wisdom call them blind,
Whom Thou hast blest with thine own spirit's sight;
But while they find no work for Thee to do,   5
And blindly on themselves alone rely;
Thy child must suffer what Thou sufferest too,
And learn from him Thou sent e'en so to die;
Thou art my Father, Thou wilt give me aid
To bear the wrong the spirit suffers here;   10
Thou hast thy help upon the mighty laid,
In him I trust, nor know to want or fear;
But ever onward walk secure from sin,
For he has conquered every foe within.

Poem No. 703; c. January 1839

The Mountain

Thou shalt the mountain move; be strong in me,
And I will pluck it from its rocky base,
And cast it headlong in the rolling sea,
And men shall seek but shall not find its place;
Be strong; thou shalt throw down the numerous host,   5
That rises now against thee o'er the earth;
Against thy Father's arm they shall not boast,
In sorrow shall grow dark their day of mirth;

Lift up the banner, bid the trumpets sound,
Gather ye nations on the opposing hill!   10
I will your wisest councils now confound,
And all your ranks with death and slaughter fill;
I come for judgment, and for victory now,
Bow down ye nations! at my footstool bow!

Poem No. 694; c. January 1839

The Mustard Seed

Plant the small seed, the mustard grain within,
And it shall spread its limbs from shore to shore;
But first it must in smallest root begin,
And seem to yield too little for thy store;
But thou hast sparing sown, it cannot grow   5
When thou dost not thy field in order keep;
Wilt thou no rain or sun on it bestow,
And think a plenteous harvest thou shalt reap?
Not so the earth rewards the farmer's toil;
Not so the heart will yield its rich increase;   10
Wouldst thou in time partake the wine and oil,
Wouldst thou within thee find the promised peace,
Sow daily, sow within the precious seed,
And thou shalt find rich crops in time of need.

Poem No. 398; c. January 1839

Eden

Thy service Father! wants not aught beside
The peace and joy it to thy servant brings;
By day in Christ a constant prayer t'abide,
By night to sleep beneath thy outspread wings;
To keep thy ground from thorns and poisonous weeds,   5
That Thou might'st sow in me the fruitful word;
Is all Thou ask'st, is all thy goodness needs,
This the command that Adam from Thee heard;

Oh may I better serve Thee, Lord! than he,
And may my garden be forever clean;   10
From noisome weeds, unsightly branches free,
Within it may thy Presence still be seen;
And wilt Thou speak with me forevermore,
And I forget to sin as I have sinned before.

Poem No. 716; c. January 1839

My meat and drink

I do not need thy food, but thou dost mine;
For this will but the body's wants repair,
And soon again for meat like this 'twill pine,
And so be fed by thee with daily care;
But that which I can give thou needs but eat,   5
And thou shalt find it in thyself to be;
Forever formed within a living meat,
On which to feed will make thy spirit free;
Thou shalt not hunger more, for freely given
The bread on which the spirit daily feeds;   10
This is the bread that cometh down from heaven,
Of which who eats no other food he needs;
But this doth grow within him day by day,
Increasing more the more he takes away.

Poem No. 226; c. January 1839

Forgive me my trespasses

Thy trespasses my heart has not forgiven,
To the full answer that my Lord would ask;
The love in him to me so freely given,
Is for my feeble strength too great a task;
Increase oh Father! swell the narrowing tide,   5
Till the full stream shall reach from shore to shore;
I have not yet each sinful thought denied,
Heal up for me the freshly bleeding sore,

Let me not waste the life my Savior gave,
On the vile lusts that war against the soul;   10
May sin in him forever find its grave,
And all my being own his just controul;
And fixed forever in his perfect law,
May I more freely from thy fountain draw.

Poem No. 718; c. January 1839

The Star

___

Thou mak'st me poor that I enriched by Thee
May tell thy love to those who know it not;
And rise within thy heavens a star to be,
When they thine earthly suns have all forgot;
Grant that my light may through their darkness shine,   5
With increased splendour from the parent source;
A diamond fashioned by the hand divine
To hold forever on its measured course;
But I am dark as yet, but soon the light
Of thy bright morning star on me shall dawn;   10
Sure herald that the curtain of the night,
Forever from my orb shall be withdrawn;
And its pure beams thy rays shall ever boast,
Shining accepted mid the starry host.

Poem No. 685; c. January 1839

The Watchman

___

I place thee as a watchman on a tower,
That thou mayst warn the city of the dead;
The day has come, and come the appointed hour,
When through their streets my herald's feet shall tread;
Prepare ye all my supper to attend!   5
I have prepared it long that you might eat;
Come in, and I will treat you as a friend,
And of the living bread shall be your meat;

Oh come, and tarry not; for yours shall be
The honored seats around your Father's board;   10
And you my sons, your master's face shall see,
And to my love forever be restored;
And you my promises to Abr'am given
Shall find fulfilled to all his seed in heaven.

Poem No. 250; c. January 1839

The Prison

The prison house is full, there is no cell
But hath its prisoner laden with his chains;
And yet they live as though their life was well,
Nor of its burthening sin the soul complains;
Thou dost not see where thou hast lived so long,   5
The place is called the skull where thou dost tread;
Why laugh you then, why sing the sportive song,
As if you lived, and knowest not thou art dead;
Yes thou art dead; the morn breaks o'er thee now,
Where is thy Father, He who gave thee birth?   10
Thou art a severed limb, a barren bough,
Thou sleepest in deep caverns of the earth;
Awake! thou hast a glorious race to run,
Put on thy strength, thou hast not yet begun.

Poem No. 544; c. January 1839

The Prophet

The Prophet speaks, the world attentive stands!
The voice that stirs the people's countless host,
Issues again the Living God's commands;
And who before the King of Kings can boast?
At his rebuke behold a thousand flee,   5
Their hearts the Lord hath smitten with his fear;
Bow to the Christ ye nations! bow the knee!
Repent! the kingdom of the son is near!

Deep on their souls the mighty accents fall,
Like lead that pierces through the walls of clay;   10
Pricked to the heart the guilty spirits call
To know of him the new, the living way;
They bow; for he can loose, and he can bind;
And in his path the promised blessing find.

Poem No. 546; c. January 1839

The Flood

I cannot eat my bread; the people's sins
Call for a day of fasting on my soul;
For the great day of mourning now begins,
The tears of shame adown their faces roll;
Alas, can naught avert the coming gloom,   5
That rises in the east a midnight cloud?
No thunders burst to warn them of their doom,
No faithful watchmen raise their voices loud;
They eat, they drink, they marry still as then,
When o'er the world the flood in fury rolled,   10
Alas, the fire will fall upon the men,
That are to sin and death in bondage sold;
And they nor see, nor heed the coming flame,
But perish all unsuccored in their shame.

Poem No. 218; c. January 1839

The Corrupt Tree

Fast from thine evil growing will within,
Thou hast no other fast than this to keep;
This is the root whence springs all other sin,
This sows the tares while thou art sunk in sleep;
Fast ever here, the voice must be obeyed   5
That bids thee for the Lord prepare the way;
Too long thine inward prayer has been delayed,
Awake, and in thy soul forever pray;

Cut down the tree that good fruit cannot bear,
Why cumbers it for years the fertile ground?   10
Let not a root the axe thou wieldest spare,
Till it no more within thy field be found;
Spare not, and thou shalt reap an hundred fold,
And a new tree shall rise where thou hast felled the old.

Poem No. 117; c. January 1839

The Pure in Heart

Father, Thou wilt accept the pure in heart,
And risest early that Thou mayest them see;
And will not from them e'en at night depart,
But in thy Presence bidst them always be;
I would be holy, for 'tis written so—   5
The pure in heart shall see their Father's face—
So would I journeying through trial go,
And run with patience here the godly race;
That I may see at last thy children pure,
In that blest home where all is peace and love;   10
Where Thou wilt make thy promise to me sure,
That I may dwell with Christ and Thee above;
Where nought impure can ever enter in,
Oh may that peace on earth e'en now begin!

Poem No. 125; c. January 1839

The Complaint

It does my heart with deepest sorrow fill,
That I no more thy praises can proclaim;
To check the mighty tide of human ill,
And bid thine offspring glorify thy name;
By night and day my failings I lament,   5
That draw me back from my full stature high;
I cannot be with this cold love content,
But must in Christ with nobler ardor try

To be whate'er his full command requires;
To show Thee, Father, by my borrowed light,   10
And kindle up, amid the sinking fires,
A sun to fill the darkness of the night;
With rays from thine own glory ever thrown,
That has from age to age on all thy children shone.

Poem No. 305; c. January 1839

Whither shall I go from thy Spirit

Where would I go from Thee? Thou lov'st me here
With love the heaven of heavens cannot contain;
Where can I go where Thou wilt not be near,
Who doth from hour to hour my life sustain?
I cannot leave Thee; Thou dost call me up,   5
When the first blush of morn is on the sky;
Thou mak'st my noon, at even bid'st me sup,
And when I sleep I know that Thou art nigh;
And what then can I want O Lord, but Thee?
Thy word shall be henceforth my daily bread,   10
From every other want it makes me free;
I will for it my heart wide open spread;
Till it shall enter there, and there abide,
And cleanse thy temple with its healing tide.

Poem No. 809; c. January 1839

The First shall be Last

Bring forth, bring forth your silver! it shall be
But as the dust that meets the passing eye;
You shall from all your idols break, be free!
And worship Him whose ear can hear your cry;
Thou who hast hid within thy learned pelf,   5
Thou who hast loved another wife than Me,
Bring forth thine idols, they are born of self;
And to thy Maker bow the willing knee;

Each secret thing must now be brought to light,
Make haste, the day breaks on your hidden spoil;   10
Go, buy what then will give your soul delight,
That day can never hurt the wine and oil;
Make haste, the bridegroom knocks, he's at the door;
The first must now be last, the last the first before.

Poem No. 80; c. January 1839

The Laborer

Father, I thank Thee that the day begins,
And I within thy vineyard too am sent;
That I may struggle on against my sins,
And seek to double what to me is lent;
Thou chast'nest me with false upbraiding word;   5
From many a heart I'm rudely thrust away;
That has not of the man of sorrows heard,
Nor at thy inner temple learned to pray;
Yet so the peace of Christ Thou mak'st me know,
And in his sufferings rise at last to Thee;   10
From glory on to glory still to go,
Till I in him from all that binds me free
Have fought the fight, the life Thou giv'st laid down,
And at his hand received the robe and kingly crown.

Poem No. 121; late 1838–early 1839

Thy Brother's Blood

I have no Brother—they who meet me now
Offer a hand with their own wills defiled,
And while they wear a smooth unwrinkled brow
Know not that Truth can never be beguiled;
Go wash the hand that still betrays thy guilt;   5
Before the spirit's gaze what stain can hide?
Abel's red blood upon the earth is spilt,
And by thy tongue it cannot be denied;

I hear not with the ear—the heart doth tell
Its secret deeds to me untold before;   10
Go, all its hidden plunder quickly sell,
Then shalt thou cleanse thee from thy brother's gore;
Then will I take thy gift—that bloody stain
Shall not be seen upon thy hand again.

Poem No. 234; late 1838–early 1839

The Graveyard

My heart grows sick before the wide-spread death,
That walks and speaks in seeming life around;
And I would love the corse without a breath,
That sleeps forgotten 'neath the cold, cold ground;
For these do tell the story of decay,   5
The worm and rotten flesh hide not nor lie;
But this though dying too from day to day,
With a false show doth cheat the longing eye;
And hide the worm that gnaws the core of life,
With painted cheek and smooth deceitful skin;   10
Covering a grave with sights of darkness rife,
A secret cavern filled with death and sin;
And men walk o'er these graves and know it not,
For in the body's health the soul's forgot.

Poem No. 339; late 1838–early 1839

Sacrifice

Thou dost prefer the song that rises pure
On lips, that speak the words the contrite feel;
To all the hands, without the heart, procure,
And on thine altar lay with soulless zeal;
Thou dost not look to see the uplifted hands,   5
Not hear'st our cry, save when we do thy will;
But, when we keep, within, thy just commands,
Our praises shall thy courts with incense fill.

Ever it rises from the obedient heart,
Hangs clustering from the lips in accents sweet;　　　　　　　10
From which, who taste, unwillingly depart,
Where thorny words with show of verdure cheat;
But sit beneath the vine, and bless its shade,
And Him, who, for their wants, such rich provision made.

Poem No. 672; late 1838–early 1839

The Son of Man

The son of Man, where shall he find repose?
Ever a homeless wanderer o'er the earth,
No brother's there, no sister's love he knows,
A stranger in the land that gave him birth;
Who will receive the pilgrim on his way,　　　　　　　5
The cup of water to his dry lips hold?
A prophet's gift the welcome shall repay,
For he a keeper is of Christ's own fold;
He asks no pittance from your earthly store,
He asks your will, your life to him be given;　　　　　　　10
Give, and the life you lose he will restore,
And lead you onward to the gates of heaven;
Where waits a Father's love to crown your joy,
And banish all the griefs that here annoy.

Poem No. 568; late 1838–early 1839

The Ark

There is no change of time and place with Thee,
Where'er I go with me 'tis still the same;
Within thy presence I rejoice to be,
And always hallow thy most holy name;
The world doth ever change; there is no peace　　　　　　　5
Among the shallows of its storm-vexed breast;
With every breath the frothy waves increase,
They toss up mire and dirt, they cannot rest;

I thank Thee that within thy strong-built ark
My soul across the uncertain sea can sail,   10
And though the night of death be long and dark
My hopes in Christ shall reach within the veil;
And to the promised haven steady steer,
Whose rest to those who love is ever near.

Poem No. 618; late 1838–early 1839

The Father

Thou who first called me from the sleep of death,
Thee may I ever as my Father love;
In Thee my being find, in Thee my breath,
And never from Thyself again remove;
On Thee alone I wait, and Thee I serve;   5
Thou art my morn, my noon, and evening hour;
May I from thy commandments never swerve,
So wilt Thou be to me a heavenly dower;
Friends, brothers, wife, shall all be found in Thee,
Children, whose love for me shall ne'er grow cold;   10
And Thou the Father still o'er all shall be,
In thine embrace thy children ever hold;
In Christ awoke from death's forgotten sleep
Thy hands from harm thy sons shall ever keep.

Poem No. 700; late 1838–early 1839

Rachel

Where are my children, whom from youth I raised
With all a parent's love and gentle care;
That I might be by them forever praised,
And they with Me in all I have might share?
They have not known Me! see them bow the knee   5
To stocks and stones their death has given life;
And while enslaved rejoice that they are free,
Married, yet not to Me their lawful wife;

Turn, turn ye children, why then will ye die?
Why will ye slight the offer of my rest?   10
The day is near when vain will be your cry
With the sharp sword and pestilence opprest;
Turn, turn to Me and I will be your shield,
Before the hour is come that has your slaughter sealed.

Poem No. 801; late 1838–early 1839

Christmas

Awake ye dead! the summons has gone forth,
That bids you leave the dark enclosing grave;
From east to west 'tis heard, from south to north
The word goes forth the imprisoned souls to save;
Though ye have on the garments of the dead,   5
And the fourth day have slept within the earth,
Come forth! you shall partake the living bread,
And be a witness of the spirit's birth;
Awake ye faithful! throw your grave clothes by,
He whom you seek is risen, he bids you rise;   10
The cross again on earth is lifted high,
Turn to its healing sight your closing eyes;
And you shall rise and gird your armor on,
And fight till you a crown in Christ have won.

Poem No. 59; late 1838–early 1839

The Earth

I would lie low, the ground on which men tread,
Swept by thy spirit like the wind of heaven;
An earth where gushing springs and corn for bread
By me at every season should be given;
Yet not the water and the bread that now   5
Supplies their tables with its daily food;
But Thou wouldst give me fruit for every bough,
Such as Thou givest me, and call'st it good;

And water from the stream of life should flow,
By every dwelling that thy love has built;   10
Whose taste the ransomed of thy son shall know,
Whose robes are washed from every stain of guilt;
And men would own it was thy hand that blest,
And from my bosom find a surer rest.

Poem No. 288; late 1838–early 1839

The Hours

The minutes have their trusts as they go by,
To bear His love who wings their viewless flight;
To Him they bear their record as they fly,
Nor from their ceaseless round can they alight;
Rich with the life Thou liv'st they come to me,   5
Oh may I all that life to others show;
That they from strife may rise and rest in Thee,
And all thy peace in Christ by me may know;
Then shall the morning call me from my rest,
With joyful hope that I thy child may live;   10
And when the evening comes 'twill make me blest
To know that I a night to others give;
Such as thy peace does to thy children send,
Will be the night that Thou by me would lend.

Poem No. 526; late 1838–early 1839

The Christ

'Tis not by water only but by blood
Thou comest in the flesh, great Prince of Peace!
John is thy witness in the cleansing flood,
But thou art from above, and must increase;
Thou bidst us suffer on the accursed tree,   5
Where thou wast nailed for sins thou couldst not know;
That by thy blood from death I might be free,
And in thy kingly stature daily grow;

Thou bidst me lose the life that thou hast given,
As thou hast died for me and all before;   10
And win the crown of light from thee in heaven,
By wearing here the thorns thy temples wore;
And loving as thou loved, who sweat within
Great drops of blood unseen for unseen sin.

Poem No. 728; late 1838–early 1839

The Things Before

I would not tarry, Look! the things before
Call me along my path with beckoning love;
The things I gain wear not the hues they wore,
For brighter glories gild the heavens above;
Still on, I seek the peace my master sought,   5
The world cannot disturb his joy within;
It is not with its gold and silver bought,
It is the victory over death and sin;
But those who enter the bright city's gate,
Ride low on one the mocked and scorned of earth;   10
But there the ready mansions open wait,
For those who lived rejected from their birth;
And he who went before them bids all hail!
To those who o'er the world in him prevail.

Poem No. 291; late 1838–early 1839

The Cup

The bitterness of death is on me now,
Before me stands its dark unclosing door;
Yet to thy will submissive still I bow,
And follow him who for me went before;
The tomb cannot contain me though I die,   5
For his strong love awakes its sleeping dead;
And bids them through himself ascend on high,
To Him who is of all the living Head;

I gladly enter through the gloomy walls,
Where they have passed who loved their master here;   10
The voice they heard, to me it onward calls,
And can when faint my sinking spirit cheer;
And from the joy on earth it now has given,
Lead on to joy eternal in the heaven.

Poem No. 467; late 1838–early 1839

Old Things are passed away

The old creation Thou hast formed is dead,
The leaves are fallen from the lifeless tree,
The broken branches at our feet are spread,
And e'en the look of life begins to flee;
Yet while Thou lets the horrid trunk arise,   5
Thy children too can learn to bear with Thee;
Thy love in Christ shall make them truly wise,
And from its death their spirits ever free;
Then shall the world unseen be brought to light,
The starry hosts around thy throne appear,   10
And day on day still open new delight,
As in the eye of faith they shine more clear;
Untill earth's shadows fade for aye away,
And the glad spirit stands in cloudless day.

Poem No. 536; late 1838–early 1839

The Harvest

They love me not, who at my table eat;
They live not on the bread that Thou hast given;
The word Thou giv'st is not their daily meat,
The bread of life that cometh down from heaven;
They drink but from their lips the waters dry,   5
There is no well that gushes up within;
And for the meat that perishes they cry,
When Thou hast vexed their souls because of sin;

Oh send thy laborers! every hill and field
With the ungathered crop is whitened o'er;   10
To those who reap it shall rich harvests yield,
The full eared grain all ripened for thy store;
No danger can they fear who reap with Thee,
Though thick with storms the autumn sky may be.

Poem No. 645; late 1838–early 1839

The City

And Thou hast placed me on a lofty hill,
Where all who pass may mock and pierce me through;
Oh how can I in Christ be humble still,
Save that I learn with him thy will to do;
I cannot now from sight of men be hid,   5
Oh may my life thy heavenly rest proclaim;
That they may see in me the works that bid
The disbelievers glorify thy name;
Oh make them see thy light, thy light from heaven,
That they may be its children too with me;   10
And when, through suffering here, thy peace is given,
Thy nearer presence with me let them see;
And hear from him who but one talent gave,
That they with him shall many cities save.

Poem No. 48; late 1838–early 1839

The Rose

The rose thou showst me has lost all its hue,
For thou dost seem to me than it less fair;
For when I look I turn from it to you,
And feel the flower has been thine only care;
Thou shouldst have grown as freely by its side   5
As springs the bud from out its parent stem,
But thou art from thy Father severed wide,
And turnst from thine own self to look at them;

Thy words do not perfume the summer air,
Nor draw the eye and ear like this thy flower;   10
No bees shall make thy lips their daily care,
And sip the sweets distilled from hour to hour;
Nor shall new plants from out thy scattered seed,
O'er many a field the eye with beauty feed.

Poem No. 554; late 1838–early 1839

Faith

There is no faith; the mountain stands within
Still unrebuked, its summit reaches heaven;
And every action adds its load of sin,
For every action wants the little leaven;
There is no prayer; it is but empty sound,   5
That stirs with frequent breath the yielding air;
With every pulse they are more strongly bound,
Who make the blood of goats the voice of prayer;
Oh heal them, heal them Father with thy word,
Their sins cry out to Thee from every side;   10
From son and sire, from slave and master heard,
Their voices fill the desert country wide;
And bid Thee hasten to relieve and save,
By him who rose triumphant o'er the grave.

Poem No. 620; late 1838–early 1839

The Jew

Thou art more deadly than the Jew of old,
Thou hast his weapons hidden in thy speech;
And though thy hand from me thou dost withhold,
They pierce where sword and spear could never reach;
Thou hast me fenced about with thorny talk,   5
To pierce my soul with anguish while I hear;
And while amid thy populous streets I walk,
I feel at every step the entering spear;

Go, cleanse thy lying mouth of all its guile,
That from the will within thee ever flows;   10
Go, cleanse the temple thou dost now defile,
Then shall I cease to feel thy heavy blows;
And come and tread with me the path of peace,
And from thy brother's harm forever cease.

Poem No. 659; late 1838–early 1839

Spring

The stem that long has borne the wintry blast,
Encased with ice or powdered o'er with snow;
Shall, when its chilling breath has breathed its last,
Its springing leaves and bursting blossoms show;
So ye, on whom the earth's cold wind has blown,   5
While there you suffered for your master's name;
The kindness of the Father soon shall own,
And in the fruit you bear his love proclaim;
Endure, that you the glorious light may see,
That soon will rise upon the perfect soul;   10
Press on, and you accepted soon shall be,
And see the son and he shall make you whole;
And on the Father's name forever call,
And from his perfect wisdom never fall.

Poem No. 574; late 1838–early 1839

The Temple

The temple shall be built, the Holy One,
Such as the earth nor heavens have ever seen;
Nor shall the work by human hands be done,
But from the will of man it shall be clean;
Ages on ages shall the pile be wrought,   5
By Him whose will his children shall obey;
Till every son, by his own Father taught,
The chiseled stone he brought shall cast away;

Slowly the ancient temple is repaired,
While one by one as lively stones we grow;   10
By every son the work is to be shared,
Built on the corner stone in Christ laid low;
That from the eternal shrine might ever rise,
A holy prayer, a living sacrifice.

Poem No. 582; late 1838–early 1839

The White Horse

The Word goes forth! I see its conquering way,
O'er seas and mountains sweeps it mighty on;
The tribes of men are bowing 'neath its sway,
The pomp of kings, the pride of wisdom's gone;
Behold, the poor have raised the victor's shout;   5
The meek are crowned, their triumph too is nigh;
The barren now no more a son can doubt;
The mourner wipes her cheek and glittering eye;
Hark from the lofty places comes a groan,
That they cannot their wealth ill-gotten hide;   10
The midnight darkness from the thief is flown,
The garment's rent of falsely clothed pride;
The veil is drawn; the judgement seat appears;
I see joy mingling with a world in tears.

Poem No. 597; late 1838–early 1839

The Tent

Thou springest from the ground, and may not I
From Him who speeds thy branches high and wide;
And from the scorching sun and stormy sky
May I not too with friendly shelter hide;
There is no shade like thine to shield the poor,   5
From the hot scorching words that meet the ear;
The snowy, frozen flakes they must endure,
Of those whose hearts have never shed a tear;

Yet He who shoots thy leafy fabric high,
Shall in my verse spread wide a tempering skreen,   10
And when oppressed with heat his sons pass by,
With hastening feet they'll seek its arches green;
And bless the Father who has o'er them spread
A tent of verdure for their aching head.

Poem No. 698; late 1838–early 1839

My Sheep

I will not look upon the lands you own,
They are not those my heavenly Father gives;
That with his word of truth forever sown,
Blesses the man that on their bounty lives;
His yoke is easy, and his burthen light;   5
To till his grounds within his only care,
With God to live, his ever new delight,
And with out toil his liberal gifts to share;
He wants no barns, no shelter from the cold,
His Father's love provides for all he needs;   10
One of the flock of his own master's fold,
He hears his voice, and goes where'er he leads;
And pleasant pasture finds where'er he goes,
For all the paths of sin the Shepherd knows.

Poem No. 285; late 1838–early 1839

The Corner Stone

The builders still reject my corner stone,
That I low down in every soul have laid;
Their houses rise and fall; for there are none
That in the building seek its chosen aid;
Why will ye raise upon the shifting sands   5
Houses that every storm must battle down;
Temples and altars reared to Me with hands,
That rain and floods beneath their fury drown?

Clear, clear the ground of all that you have brought,
The corner stone shall now be laid anew;   10
That which the foolish builders set at naught
Shall now be laid where all that pass shall view;
And wonder why men thought them ever wise,
And on their own foundation sought to rise.

Poem No. 474; late 1838–early 1839

The Good Ground

The Word must fall; but where the well-tilled ground
Without a stone or briar to choke the seed;
Where can the deep, black earth it needs be found,
That shall the plant with plenteous juices feed?
Break up your fallow lands! the seed is sown   5
With heaven's own richness in each bosom's field,
Cut down the tares that rankly there have grown,
And heavy crops the word of God shall yield;
Cut down your will that sows the deadly tare,
That bears no fruit but for your own dark breast;   10
Cut down, nor let a root the sharp axe spare,
Then shall my land enjoy its day of rest;
And he that reaps rejoice with Him who sows,
While through the loaded field he daily goes.

Poem No. 599; late 1838–early 1839

The Beginning and The End

Thou art the First and Last, the End of all
The erring spirit seeks of earth to know;
Thee first it left, a Parent at its fall,
To Thee again thy sinful child must go;
With awe I read the lessons of thy grace,   5
To all that disobey so freely given;
The child shall see again his Father's face,
And through thy son return to Thee and heaven;

Ye spirits that around your Maker stand,
Rejoice! the world is ransomed from its weight of woe;   10
Thou earth obey your sovereign's wise command,
Wash, 'twas for you he bade his mercy flow;
It is for you Christ's blood descends like rain,
That you through him might rise to life again.

Poem No. 663; late 1838–early 1839

Nature

The bubbling brook doth leap when I come by,
Because my feet find measure with its call;
The birds know when the friend they love is nigh,
For I am known to them both great and small;
The flowers, which on the lovely hill-side grow,   5
Expect me there, when Spring their bloom has given;
And many a bush and tree my wanderings know,
And e'en the clouds and silent stars of heaven:
For he, who with his Maker walks aright,
Shall be their lord, as Adam was before;   10
His ear shall catch each sound with new delight,
Each object wear the dress that then it wore;
And he, as when erect in soul he stood,
Hear from his Father's lips that all is good.

Poem No. 472; late 1838–early 1839

Morning

The light will never open sightless eyes,
It comes to those who willingly would see;
And every object, hill, and stream, and skies,
Rejoice within th'encircling line to be;
'Tis day—the field is filled with busy hands,   5
The shop resounds with noisy workmen's din,
The traveller with his staff all ready stands
His yet unmeasured journey to begin;

The light breaks gently too within the breast—
Yet there no eye awaits the crimson morn,　　　　　　　　　10
The forge and noisy anvil are at rest,
Nor men nor oxen tread the fields of corn,
Nor pilgrim lifts his staff—it is no day
To those who find on earth a place to stay.

Poem No. 522; late 1838–early 1839

The Temptation

Thou shalt not live e'en by the bread alone,
But by the word from out the mouth of God;
This is the bread by all his children known,
All those who tread the path their Master trod;
For this thou shalt leave all and follow him,　　　　　　　5
The Word of God that has come down from heaven;
For this thou shalt cut off the dearest limb,
That by the Father has to thee been given;
Houses and lands, mother's and father's love,
To this are cheaper than the barren sand;　　　　　　　　10
This is the Life that cometh from above,
To bind the heavens in one eternal band;
And died that us from death he might recall,
And God in us and him be all in all.

Poem No. 693; late 1838–early 1839

Help

Thou wilt be near me Father, when I fail,
For Thou hast called me now to be thy son;
And when the foe within me may assail,
Help me to say in Christ 'Thy will be done';
This ever calms, this ever gives me rest,　　　　　　　　5
There is no fight in which I may not stand,
When Christ doth dwell supreme within my breast,
And Thou upholdst me with thy mighty hand;

To live a servant here on earth I ask,
To be with Thee my ever great reward,   10
To overcome all sin my strengthening task,
Till with Thyself my soul made pure accord;
Then shall my service be in Christ complete,
And I restored in him thy Holyness shall meet.

Poem No. 702; late 1838–early 1839

Change

Father! there is no change to live with Thee,
Save that in Christ I grow from day to day,
In each new word I hear, each thing I see
My feet rejoycing hasten on the way;
The morning comes with blushes overspread,   5
And I new-wakened find a morn within;
And in its modest dawn around me shed,
Thou hearst the prayer and the ascending hymn;
Hour follows hour, the lengthening shades descend;
Yet they could never reach as far as me   10
Did not thy love their kind protection lend,
That I a child might sleep awhile on Thee;
Till to the light restored by gentle sleep
With new-found zeal I might thy precepts keep.

Poem No. 124; late 1838–early 1839

The Poor

I walk the streets and though not meanly drest,
Yet none so poor as can with me compare;
For none though weary call me in to rest,
And though I hunger none their substance share;
I ask not for my stay the broken reed,   5
That fails when most I want a friendly arm;
I cannot on the loaves and fishes feed,
That want the blessing that they may not harm;

I only ask the living word to hear,
From tongues that now but speak to utter death;   10
I thirst for one cool cup of water clear,
But drink the riled stream of lying breath;
And wander on though in my Father land,
Yet hear no welcome voice, and see no beakoning hand.

Poem No. 280; late 1838–early 1839

They Who Hunger

Thou hearst the hungry ravens when they cry,
And to thy children shalt Thou not send bread;
Who on thy aid alone for help rely,
And in the steps of Christ alone would tread?
They shall not cry for righteousness in vain,   5
But bread from heaven thy hand shall soon supply;
When falls in plenteous showers the latter rain,
Thy plants shall push their thrifty branches high;
And untilled lands that now affront the sight
To the strong plough their riches shall lay bare;   10
And like thy fruitful fields the eye delight,
Rejoycing in thy sun and shower to share,
And they who mourn shall sing the harvest song,
And reap the crops that to thy sons belong.

Poem No. 681; late 1838–early 1839

Who Hath Ears To Hear Let Him Hear!

The sun doth not the hidden place reveal,
Whence pours at morn his golden flood of light;
But what the night's dark breast would fain conceal,
In its true colors walks before our sight;
The bird does not betray the secret springs,   5
Whence note on note her music sweetly pours;
Yet turns the ear attentive while she sings,
The willing heart while falls the strain adores;

So shall the spirit tell not whence its birth,
But in its light thine untold deeds lay bare;   10
And while it walks with thee flesh-clothed the earth,
Its words shall of the Father's love declare:
And happy those whose ears shall hail its voice,
And clean within the day it gives rejoice.

Poem No. 577; late 1838–early 1839

The Sign

They clamor for a sign with eyeless zeal,
As if 'twould lift their burthened souls to heaven;
And think the spirit must the body heal,
Not know the want for which alone 'twas given;
They cry; but faithless shall no sign receive,   5
Save that of him who for the sinful died,
That they might on his saving name believe,
And in his promise trustingly confide;
Then from the earth, where buried now they lie,
On the true Sabbath morn shall they arise,   10
And, taught by him, shall then ascend on high
His glory to behold with unsealed eyes,
And in his Father's presence still to live,
The heir of all His perfect love can give.

Poem No. 639; late 1838–early 1839

The Tree

I too will wait with thee returning spring,
When thick the leaves shall cling on every bough,
And birds within their new grown arbor sing,
Unmindful of the storms that tore me now;
For I have stripped me naked to the blast,   5
That now in triumph through my branches rides;
But soon the winter's bondage shall be past,
To him who in the Savior's love abides;

And as his Father to thy limbs returns,
Blossoms and bloom to sprinkle o'er thy dress,   10
So shall Christ call from out their funeral urns,
Those who in patience still their souls possess;
And clothe in raiments never to wax old,
All whom his Father gave him for his fold.

Poem No. 277; late 1838–early 1839

The Meek

I would be meek as He who bore his cross,
And died on earth that I in him might live,
And, while in sin I knew not of my loss,
Suffered with gentle love his hope to give;
May I within the manger too be laid,   5
And mid the thieves his childlike meekness show;
And though by him who kisses me betrayed,
May I no will but his my Master's know;
Thus sheltered by the lonely vale of tears,
My feet shall tread secure the path he trod,   10
Mid lying tongues that pierce my side like spears,
I too shall find within the peace of God;
And though rejected shall possess the earth,
And dead in Christ be witness of his birth.

Poem No. 287; late 1838–early 1839

The Desert

Oh, bid the desert blossom as the rose,
For there is not one flower that meets me now;
On all thy fields lie heaped the wintry snows,
And the rough ice encrusts the fruitful bough;
Oh, breathe upon thy ruined vineyard still,   5
Though like the dead it long unmoved has lain;
Thy breath can with the bloom of Eden fill,
The lifeless clods in verdure clothe again;

Awake, ye slothful! open wide the earth
To the new sun and spirit's quickening rain;   10
They come to bid the furrows heave in birth,
And strew with roses thick the barren plain;
Awake, be early in your untilled field,
And it to you the crop of peace shall yield.

Poem No. 380; late 1838–early 1839

The Clay

Thou shalt do what Thou wilt with thine own hand,
Thou form'st the spirit like the moulded clay;
For those who love Thee keep thy just command,
And in thine image grow as they obey;
New tints and forms with every hour they take,   5
Whose life is fashioned by thy spirit's power;
The crimson dawn is round them when they wake,
And golden triumphs wait the evening hour;
The queenly-sceptred night their souls receive,
And spreads their pillows 'neath her sable tent;   10
And o'er their slumbers unseen angels breathe,
The rest Thou hast to all who labor lent;
That they may rise refreshed to light again,
And with Thee gather in the whitening grain.

Poem No. 692; late 1838–early 1839

The Altar

Oh kindle up thine altar! see the brands
Lie scattered here and there that lit the pile;
Thy priests to other service turn their hands,
And with unhallowed works their souls defile;
No victims bleed, no fire is blazing high,   5
They leave thy shrine to serve another god;
Who will not hear them when to him they cry,
But be to them thine own avenging rod;

The people wait in vain to hear thy voice,
With none to lead them right, with none to feed;   10
No more within thy courts their hearts rejoice,
But at each word the Christ must in them bleed;
Oh kindle up the heart's expiring flame!
Come quickly Lord, and magnify thy name.

Poem No. 385; late 1838–early 1839

Praise

Oh praise the Lord! let every heart be glad!
The day has come when He will be our God;
No fears can come to make his children sad,
His joy is theirs who in his ways have trod;
Oh praise ye hills! praise Him ye rivers wide!   5
Ye people own his love! revere his power!
He makes his peace in one full current glide,
It shall flow on unbroken from this hour;
Shout! shout ye saints! the triumph day is near,
The King goes forth Himself his sons to save;   10
The habitations of the poor to rear,
And bid the palm and myrtle round them wave;
Open your gates ye heaven uplifted walls!
The King of Kings for entrance at them calls.

Poem No. 386; winter–spring 1839

Terror

There is no safety; fear has seized the proud;
The swift run to and fro but cannot fly;
Within the streets I hear no voices loud,
They pass along with low, continuous cry;
Lament! bring forth the mourning garments now,   5
Prepare a solemn fast! for ye must mourn;
Strip every leaf from off the boastful bough,
Let every robe from hidden deeds be torn;

Bewail! bewail! great Babylon must fall!
Her sins have reached to heaven; her doom is sealed;   10
Upon the Father now of mercies call,
For the great day of secrets is revealed!
Repent! why do ye still uncertain stand,
The kingdom of my son is nigh at hand!

Poem No. 625; winter–spring 1839

The Prayer

Father! help them who walk in their own light;
Who think they see, but are before Thee blind;
Give them within thy rest, thy spirit's sight;
And may they in the Christ their healing find;
Father! they have not faith, help Thou their trust;   5
Grant them within thy precepts to fulfill;
Oh bid thy spirit animate their dust,
And bid them once again to know thy will;
Then shall they live with Thee and sin no more;
Then walk with Christ thy well beloved son;   10
And when their earthly pilgrimage is o'er,
And they the martyr's crown in him have won,
Oh take them to thine own eternal rest,
The heaven where he who enters must be blest.

Poem No. 119-123; winter–spring 1839

Humility

Oh humble me! I cannot bide the joy
That in my Savior's presence ever flows;
May I be lowly, lest it may destroy
The peace his childlike spirit ever knows;
I would not speak thy word, but by Thee stand;   5
While Thou dost to thine erring children speak;
Oh help me but to keep his own command,
And in my strength to feel me ever weak;

Then in thy presence shall I humbly stay,
Nor lose the life of love he came to give;   10
And find at last the life, the truth, the way,
To where with him thy blessed servants live;
And walk forever in the path of truth,
A servant yet a son, a sire and yet a youth.

Poem No. 384; winter–spring 1839

Forgiveness

Forgive me Father! for to Thee I stand
Alike with those who have not known thy law;
Oh humble me beneath thy mighty hand,
That I from Christ may every lesson draw;
Thou knowst me needy, naked, blind and poor;   5
Oh help me to buy gold refined by Thee,
May I of Thee the marriage robe procure,
Anoint my eyes that I indeed may see;
May I before thy presence ever kneel,
A suppliant waiting on thy gracious love,   10
That every want before I ask can feel,
And from distress will hasten to remove;
And to my master's joy will me restore,
Where I no want can feel forevermore.

Poem No. 136; winter–spring 1839

The Heavenly Rest

They do not toil in heaven; they live and love,
Their heavenly Father every want supplies;
Nor can they from their blest abode remove,
For nought can enter there, that ever dies.
A life of love! how sweetly pass its hours,   5
No tear, but that of joy, can touch the cheeks;
Their lips distill, like fragrance-breathing flowers,
The truth which each to each forever speaks.

Oh, blessed the Parent, who has bid us know
The joys, which at His own right hand doth dwell;   10
Oh, blessed the children, that His praises show,
And of His love in ceaseless worship tell;
And blessed the Lamb, that for their sins was slain,
That they with Him forevermore might reign.

Poem No. 640; winter–spring 1839

Compassion

He saw them tasked with heavy burthens all,
Bowed down and weary 'neath the heavy load;
With none their faltering footsteps home to call,
Or point them out the strait and narrow road;
His spirit bore their burthens as his own,   5
He healed the sick, restored the sightless eyes;
He heard the mourner for a loved one moan,
And bid the dead from out the grave arise;
In him the spirit ever rests secure,
For there is one to ease its struggling grief;   10
Oh seek the rest that ever shall endure,
And you shall find in him the true relief;
And join with him to succor the distrest,
And be like him forever by them blest.

Poem No. 167; winter–spring 1839

The Rock

Thou art; there is no stay but in Thy love;
Thy strength remains; it built the eternal hills;
It speaks the word forever heard above,
And all creation with its presence fills;
Upon it let me stand and I shall live;   5
Thy strength shall fasten me forever fixed,
And to my soul its sure foundations give,
When earth and sky thy word in one has mixed;

Rooted in Thee no storm my branch shall tear,
But with each day new sap shall upward flow,   10
And for thy vine the clustering fruit shall bear;
That with each rain the lengthening shoots may grow,
Till o'er Thy Rock its leaves spread far and wide,
And in its green embrace its Parent hide.

Poem No. 664; winter–spring 1839

To notice other days were pages given,
That when by former scenes anew we stray,
The leaves of our own growth let fall from heaven
May play in Memory's breath acrost our way.

So these gathered, though strown; by friendly hand,   5
Meet me again as by his door I rove;
Not scattered vainly on his well-tilled land,
So that in Memory's breath they ever move.

Poem No. 739a; winter–spring 1839?

The Crocus

The earliest flower of Spring,
    Thou hast it; it is thine;
The first upon thine unstirred soil,
    To give it thee is mine;

It chose a mild, fair April morn   5
    Its yellow form to show,
When the leaves and grass grew green
    As thou wast here to know.

And its sight had a look like thee,
    Of the early morn and spring;   10
And I've taken it from thy garden bank,
    'Twas left for me to bring.

And upon thy desk it is placed,
    With the water at its root;
That the voice of the spring and early morn   15
    May speak though ever mute.

Poem No. 490a; winter–spring 1839?

The Plant

Thou art my Father Thou dost give me birth
Pleasant thy smile & pleasant e'en thy frown
Thy hand here placed me in the furrowed earth
And sent the rain in plenteous fulness down
Twas Thou who watched when on the spring grain   5
The small dew fell and sunlight daily poured
And when the wind blew fiercely from the main
Thy care each drooping limb has oft restored
Thou art my Father still thy care attend
Support the plant the seed and lofty tree   10
Alike look up to find in Thee their friend
The ear the spring blade draw life from Thee
And Thou the humble fruit I daily yield
Wilt come and view with pleasure in thy field

Poem No. 659a; winter–spring 1839?

I am the Way

Thy way is simple for I am the light
By which thou travelest on to meet thy God
Brighter and brighter still shall be thy sight
Till thou hast ended here the path I trod
Before thee stretches far the thorny way   5
Yet smoothed for thee by him who went before
Go on it leads you to the perfect day
The rest I to the patriarch Abraham swore
Go on and I will guide you safely through
For I have walked with suffering feet thy path   10

Confide in me the Faithful and the True
And thou shalt flee the approaching day of wrath
Whose dawn e'en now the horizon's border shows
And with its kindling fires prophetic glows.

Poem No. 591; fall 1838–summer 1839

The kingdom of God Is within you

My kingdom is within you seek it there
Ye shall not seek in vain who work within
You shall within it find the good and fair
The living spirits freed from death and sin
Thou canst not buy with gold and silver ore   5
The treasures that my kingdom can afford
They are for those who love me kept in store
And they who love me keep my holy word
Repent be quick to do what first thou did
There is but one the strait and narrow way   10
Fear not when thou art faint and must be chid
But only fear lest thou from me should stray
For I am life and they who seek me find
The keys of heaven I hold to loose and bind.

Poem No. 341; fall 1838–summer 1839

My Church

This is the rock where I my church will build
Harder than flint its sure foundations are
Though few now pass the door it shall be filled
The gates of hell shall not my triumph bar
Seek and thou too the door shall find   5
Knock and thou too shall enter in
I hold the keys and who but me can bind?
And who but me can loose the bonds of sin?
Eternal life shall those who worship here
Forevermore receive at my right hand   10

I call thee too my wedding day is near
Haste lest without the bridal hall you stand
And you be found not with the garment on
Which all who live with me on earth have worn.

Poem No. 655; fall 1838–summer 1839

The Charge

I speak in you the word that gave you birth
Fear not I call you to attend my voice
Walk humbly on thy path lies through the earth
But thou shalt in the latter day rejoice
If thou to all hast spoken ever true   5
What thou hast heard from me who send you forth
For every secret thing is brought to view
When I before all men proclaim your worth
Speak boldly then for 'tis not you they hear
But him who in you speaks the living word   10
Nor those who kill the body need you fear
They cannot hear who have not of me heard
My sheep shall hear thee for I bid thee call
And hasten at thy summons one and all.

Poem No. 274; fall 1838–summer 1839

The Sabbath

Thy rest has come thy long expected rest
The spirit sees at last her Maker God
Within His presence ever to be blest
Nor longer feel for sin His chastening rod
The sabbath has begun its sacred hours   5
No more can aught of earthly passions stir
The service of thy shrine demands my powers
And earth no longer can its claim defer
Oh when shall all its service be complete
And I have done thy perfect will on earth   10

That Christ my name before Thee may repeat
And wake me as a witness of his birth?
When shall I wake and know that day of love
That endless Sabbath kept for me above?

Poem No. 715; fall 1838–summer 1839

The Invitation

There is no sound but thou dost hear my voice
And in the silence of thine heart obey
Thou shalt with me before the throne rejoice
When I have led thee in the living way
Follow my steps they lead to God and life   5
Where thou no more shalt fear no more shall fall
For I will give the weary rest from strife
And they with me shall dwell who hear my call
Come then partake the feast for you prepared
I have come down to bid you welcome there   10
For those who have with me the dangers shared
I will with them my Father's blessings share
Come hasten on thy brothers wait within
Strive for in me thou shalt be free from sin.

Poem No. 626; fall 1838–summer 1839

The Preacher

The world has never known me bid them hear
My word it speaks will they but hear its voice
I will uphold thee banish every fear
And in my name alone fore'er rejoice
Thou hast been by my Holy Spirit led   5
And it shall lead you still as gently on
Till thou hast on the word I give you fed
And in my name the crown of life have won
Come hasten on thou shalt not want for I
Will be your guide your rest and your defence   10

Be strong I wipe the tears from every eye
And to my Father's house will lead you hence
Put on thine armor daily fight with me
And you my glory soon in joy shall see.

Poem No. 606; fall 1838–summer 1839

Come unto me

Come all ye weary. I will give you rest
The rest for all my Father's love prepares
Come and in me and him be wholly blest
And I will free you from the world of cares
For I am meek and lowly learn of me   5
And you shall find in me the promised peace
Come learn of me though blind your eyes shall see
And every joy I give shall never cease
The marriage feast is ready hasten in
For those who tarry shall their lateness mourn   10
Come and your robes I'll wash from every sin
And in my arms shall every son be borne
Till freed from every danger he shall be
A child of light and all my glory see.

Poem No. 88; fall 1838–summer 1839

Flee to the mountains

The morn is breaking see the rising sun
Has on your windows cast his burning light
Arise the day is with you onward run
Lest soon you wander lost in murky night
I will be with you 'tis your day of flight   5
Hasten the hour is near you cannot fly
Leave all for he who stops can never fight
The foe that shall assail him from on high
They come the plagues that none can flee
Behold the wrath of God is on you poured   10

Oh hasten find the rest He gives in me
And you shall fear no fear in me restored
They cannot pause oh hasten while you may
For soon shall close around thy little day.

Poem No. 528; fall 1838–summer 1839

Blessed are they that mourn

Blessed are they that mourn my life is theirs
The life I led on earth they too shall lead
Its joy and sorrows and its weight of cares
Shall all be theirs for in my name they bleed
Happy their lot for so I bid them grow   5
And finish here the work my Father gave
And when the weary day its end shall know
They shall through me rejoice them o'er the grave
Happy their death for they shall live again
When I in triumph come to claim the few   10
Who in my name the cross within have worn
And by their toils have found me just and true
Happy thrice happy those who seek my face
They shall not want for they shall find my grace.

Poem No. 70; fall 1838–summer 1839

Faith

Hast thou but faith thou shalt the mountain bid
Remove and it shall walk nor longer stand
Thy weakness to resist and nobly chid
Its giant heights shall nod at thy command
Be strong the word but tries thine infant might   5
And soon thy stature shall resist my rod
Be sober and in wisdom much delight
And thou shalt then be called a child of God
Hasten the way before thee yet extends
Far on where yet thou little dreamst to go   10

Be wise and seek in me who knows its ends
And you no more shall wander to and fro
But onward run till you the race have won
And from my precepts here my Father's will have done.

Poem No. 157; fall 1838–summer 1839

Redeeming the time

Be up betimes there is no need of rest
Save what is given and thou wilt take no more
Thy love will grow and make thee wholly blest
When thou hast drank the streams that freely pour
When nought of sloth nor folly marks the way   5
Thy spirit daily holds for I am there
My path leads onward to the perfect day
Come and thou shalt with me my kingdom share
Come for the needy cry aloud for bread
Do not withhold thy hand but inward pray   10
Give and for you the richest feast they'll spread
When they in me have learnt the better way
Pray always cease not prayer by day or night
Tis so thy course shines brighter and more bright.

Poem No. 61; fall 1838–summer 1839

'Tis Finished

Tis done the world has vanished Christ remains
The only sure the only lasting trust
Look see its smouldering fire the iron chains
Are broke that bound my spirit to the dust
A life of love henceforth my sole employ   5
The Father's love in him so freely shown
Come hasten on and share with me the joy
That only from the cross by blood has flown
The joy I share to all is freely given
Who live the life he led on earth before   10

Come and e'en here thou hast the bliss of heaven
The robe put on the wedding robe he wore
And thou shalt be accepted at his feast
Nor fail of much he loveth e'en the least.

Poem No. 724; fall 1838–summer 1839

Effort

I have not loved thee much my heart is poor
And cannot give like that thou givest me
Oh would with stronger zeal it might endure
And all thy gift in all thy suffering see
Lift up the feeble hands the bending head   5
Come rouse press on the goal is yet before
I will with stronger feet thy pathway tread
And reach while still I may the open door
That thou hast set for me and all who fight
The war with sin thou givest them to wage   10
Oh help me lest upon me fall the night
And I without shall feel the tempest rage
That now is rising in the lowering east
Oh quicken thou my steps to taste thy feast.

Poem No. 236; fall 1838–summer 1839

To the pure all things are pure

The flowers I pass have eyes that look at me
The birds have ears that hear my spirit's voice
And I am glad the leaping brook to see
Because it does at my light step rejoice
Come brothers all who tread the grassy hill   5
Or wander thoughtless o'er the blooming fields
Come learn in sweet obedience of thy will
And every sight and sound new pleasure yields
Nature shall seem another house of thine
Where He who formed thee bid live and play   10

And in thy rambles e'en the creeping vine
Shall keep with thee a jocund holyday
And every plant and bird and insect be
Thine own companions born for harmony.

Poem No. 498; fall 1838–summer 1839

The Task

Thy cross is hard to bear it weighs me down
E'en to the earth where on my feet must tread
Yet I by this must gain the wished for crown
And find the spirit in the body dead
Hard is the lesson patience gives to learn   5
Yet when tis past sweet comfort 'twill bestow
And thou wilt cheer me for I cannot turn
But must in thee to manly stature grow
Oh lift me up with every passing hour
Some higher and still higher sight to gain   10
Till I am raised above temptation's power
And find in thee relief from every pain
For thou wilt give to those who ask aright
To taste thy cup and portion of delight.

Poem No. 711; fall 1838–summer 1839

Spring

I have not lived the flesh has hedged me in
I have not known the joy to be with thee
But I must strive to loose the bonds of sin
That press me round and be forever free
Give me the victory o'er the tyrant death   5
Whose scepter rests now cold upon my heart
Breathe on me and reviving at thy breath
The chills that o'er me steal will quick depart
And I revive like the ice frosted flower
That winter seizes in his rude embrace   10

When spring with kindly sun and loosing shower
Creeps on from southern climes with welcome face
And chides the spoilers of her children fair
And once again restores them to her care.

Poem No. 235; fall 1838–summer 1839

The Day

Break forth in joy my soul the sea retires
Its waters cease to roll across my head
I feel within new kindling of the fires
That seemed but forever lost and dead
Awake give forth thy joy with voice of song   5
There is no death for him who walks with God
Obey and shalt in the land He gives live long
And none shall lay thy head beneath the sod
Awake to sin is sleep death is the night
That round the spirit when it sins   10
The morning comes rise witness the delight
With which the ransomed soul the day begins
Come for the freedom waits thy spirit too
Oh see the day brings all we lost to view.

Poem No. 74; fall 1838–summer 1839

The Strong Man

There is no night I cannot sleep again
For I have learned of patience to obey
And light and darkness cannot now retain
The spirit that has made the life of Christ its day
There is no slumbering when he reigns within   5
Each hand puts forth each foot its vigor shows
Life rules and motion is in every limb
Thou sawst me dead now all within me grows
And strengthens with each pulse all things are small
I can do all things in the spirit strong   10

I will not boast in vain see see them fall
The iron ramparts that withstood so long
Increase my strength Oh Thou who gave me life
That I in Thee may still renew the strife.

Poem No. 623; fall 1838–summer 1839

The Warrior

Where are ye, ye who mocked my arm of late
I triumph now your hour of mirth is past
Bow down I come in strength of Christ elate
Boast not; I breathe; ye fall before the blast.
Ye hills retire! open thou raging sea   5
My steps are onward now; ye cannot stay
The God of battles—lo He fights for me
Submit before His feet prepare the way
Ye iron breasted armies too I scorn
Away how feeble is the spear or sword   10
I am of Him who gives the quicking spirit born
And wield forever wield the conquering word
Its power shall beat in atoms mountain high
And through the parting sea shall lead me dry.

Poem No. 802; fall 1838–summer 1839

The Acorn

The seed has started, who can stay it? see
The leaves are sprouting high above the ground
Already o'er the flowers its head, the tree
That rose beside it and that on it frowned
Behold is but a small bush by its side   5
Still on! it cannot stop; its branches spread;
It looks o'er all the earth in giant pride
The nations find upon its limbs their bread
Its boughs their millions shelter from the heat
Beneath its shade see kindreds tongues and all   10

That the wide world contains they all retreat
Beneath the shelter of that acorn small
That late thou flung away 'twas the best gift
That heaven e'er gave, its head the low shall lift.

Poem No. 556; fall 1838–summer 1839

The Shelter

There is no joy like that in finding Thee
Thou art my shelter from each storm that blows
He walks abroad his way is safe and free
Who loves and in new commandment goes
For him there waits not who can do him harm   5
He knows no fear he sees no covert foe
He carries with him that which rage can charm
And bid the kindled fire of hate burn low
Love turns aside the malar pointed dart
The icy hand it warms and then restores   10
Who feels and knows not of its gentle art
That cures each wound that saddened grief deplores
Come and it healing touch shall give the sight
And borrow for it joy to lend its light.

Poem No. 621; fall 1838–summer 1839

The Harvest

The plant it springs it rears its drooping head
Strengthened with every shower that falls from heaven
See quickly at their touch its branches spread
And soon twill bless with flowers look they are given
The promised blessing cannot be delayed   5
But fast will follow every good intent
Tis not in vain thy mourning spirit prayed
Behold the rich reward in answer sent
Peace from the Father joy a full increase
For all thou sowed in sorrow in the earth   10

Thy joy shall bud and bloom thy new found peace
Grow with each day. Thine is the promised birth
Of all that dies it shall be raised again
See that thou sowest thick the springing grain.

Poem No. 540; fall 1838–summer 1839

The Husbandman

I waited long but now my joy is great
For that which once I sowed begins to appear
Though slow yet sure my harvest tis not late
For Him who guides the oft revolving year
I watch not for the crops that dying earth   5
Yields from her bosom to the tribes of men
I watch for those who come of heavenly birth
A Father's care a Father's love have been
But lightly spent do they repay the toil
My hand upon my vineyard oft bestows   10
Come learn to reap for me the wine and oil
From every field in plenty overflows
I bid thee enter as a laborer now
Go forth and thou shalt pluck from every bough

Poem No. 279; fall 1838–summer 1839

The Last

Why hast thou tarried till the eleventh hour
Yet enter in thou shalt not want for hire
I will repay thou knowest I have power
To give thee all thy spirit can desire
Go in who reap for Me shall find their gain   5
In ever new and ever fresh employ
Thou reapest let no hour thy hand restrain
Be strong fill up the measure of thy joy
It shall o'er flow for He who gives thee meat
Has stores no time nor hunger can exhaust   10

He shall provide thee hasten gain thy seat
At his son's board lest thou from him be lost
And reap not of the full reward he gives
For he that sups with him he ever lives

Poem No. 820; fall 1838–summer 1839

The Call

Come thou and labor with me I will give
To who works abundant work to do
Arise gird on thine armor tis to live
That thou must struggle now and strongly too
There is no pause the conflicts soon begin   5
Arm thee with all thy patience all thy zeal
The gates of vice are open enter in
Nor fear thy foe though armed in thriple steel
I charge thee welcome none who bear the sword
Be true spare not though thou must slay thy nearest friends   10
Remember Him who arms thee with his word
And forth in his own name his servant sends
Be true for He thy crown can take away
And He spirit by his word can slay.

Poem No. 93; fall 1838–summer 1839

The Promise

The words I give thee they are not thine own
Give them as freely as to thee they're given
And thou shalt reap the grain thy hands have sown
When thou hast reached in peace the opening heaven
Come I will give thee kindred friends and wife   5
Such as no earthly lot can have in store
Thou shalt receive them for eternal life
And earth shall yield her many myriads more
My mansion is prepared come enter in
Put on the wedding dress and you shall be   10

A welcome tenant freed from every sin
Henceforth to walk from bondage ever free
In the last day I come it cometh soon
Be wise thy morning hour shall reach its noon.

Poem No. 603; fall 1838–summer 1839

Joy

The joy Thou giv'st no man can take away
For it is born of him who lives within
He comes the power of death o'er all to slay
And cleanse the heart of every secret sin
Thou shalt not see his face and mourn again   5
Save that thy mourning works thee double joy
For he can rich reward thy slightest pain
And give thee hope when sorrows here annoy
Come know with me the riches of his grace
Freely he offers them to all beside   10
And he will show us soon his Father's face
And bid the stream of grief however wide
Its waters here may roll, be dry and we
No more within its waves tossed to and fro shall be

Poem No. 516; fall 1838–summer 1839

Hope

Break forth in joy my soul the waves retire
And the dry land appears the promised land
Awake from sleep and strike the slumbering lyre
That long has lain forsaken by thy hand
Thou hast found grace the peace begins on earth   5
And thou e'en thou art called its joy to share
Awake thy notes are sweet an angel's birth
The trembling strings with joy unknown declare
Go on thy work shall grow with every day
The rising sun shall soon thy wishes greet   10
And thou from all defilement purged array

Thyself with robes the son to meet
And he thy faithful zeal in heaven shall own
And thou shalt strike thy lyre forever near the throne.

Poem No. 75; fall 1838–summer 1839

Relief

Oh give me of thy waters pure and clear
For my soul pants beneath this sultry hour
There is no spring nor running river near
That can assuage the burning fever's power
Oh grant me of thy spirit now to taste   5
Such as it was to me when I obeyed
Then may I walk amid this scorching waste
Nor sink its waters has my thirst allayed
I rise and now can run I now can bear
The heaviest burthen Thou mayst on me place   10
Oh give but of thy rich grace to share
And I no more will wet with tears my face
Nor mourn that hope hast left me but press on
Though mountains rise thy will shall still be done

Poem No. 381; fall 1838–summer 1839

Joy

Thou hast a moon for every cloudy night
And soon the mourner shall rejoice again
Fight well the sun shall come with cheering light
And thou no more thy tearful look retain
The spirit is not slow it comes when thou   5
Hast learnt by chastening of His healing love
Who bade thee for a time 'neath sorrow bow
That gentle peace might visit from above
Oh give the chastener welcome he will bring
Strength and his rod shall guide thy feet aright   10
And though thy tears may fall they are the spring
When gushing joy shall pour thee new delight

And thou shalt bless the hand that gave the pain
For it but fell that thou might joy again.

Poem No. 678; fall 1838–summer 1839

The Creation

I said of old when darkness brooded long
Upon the waste of waters Be thou light
And forthwith sprang the sun rejoicing strong
To chase away the mystery of the night
Behold an earth the heavens are hung above   5
Ascend the sons of men ascend be free
Rise and fulfill my perfect law of love
Believe the Father speaks he calls to thee
Drop every burthen that might clog thy way
Rejoice for thou art called my race to run   10
The oft besetting sin cast far and pray
That you with joy may end what is begun
Rejoice and look on high for thence shall fly
He whom thou hearst to bear thee to the sky.

Poem No. 253; fall 1838–summer 1839

The Snare

My kingdom is within you haste to find
Its glorious dawn bright streaming in the west
Open thine inward eye for thou art blind
Behold the morning waits go cleanse thy breast
For see its herald he who goes before   5
And with his warning voice prepares the way
Quick o'er your hearts his cleansing water pour
And you shall see the rising of my day
Go not from place to place it comes not so
But as the lightning shineth from the east   10
And to the west its forked branches go
E'en so unnoticed has its light increased

Till in its circling brightness all shall stand
And none escape who slight John's true command

Poem No. 340; fall 1838–summer 1839

The Yoke

My yoke is easy and my burthen light
For he who finds me loves and can obey
From him has fled the darkness of the night
He is prepared to cast this life away
And follow me who onward lead the few   5
That have preferred the life I give to gold
They shall not want for glories ever new
Shall on their eyes with every hour unfold
See a new heaven is theirs a rising earth
That shall not from their vision disappear   10
There shall the meek rejoice them in their birth
The troubled be at rest, there shall no fear
Come to disturb the blessed abode I give
But all in joy and peace with me shall live.

Poem No. 345; fall 1838–summer 1839

The Promise

I come the rushing wind that shook the place
Where those once sat who spake with tongues of fire
O'er thee to shed the freely given grace
And bid them speak while I thy verse inspire
The world shall hear and know that thou art sent   5
To preach glad tidings to the needy poor
And witness that by me the power is lent
That wakes the dead, the halt and lame can cure
Thy words shall breathe refreshment to the mind
That long has borne the heavy yoke of pain   10
For thou art to the will of Him who lives resigned
And from thy sorrows reap the promised gain

And gather fruits with Him who with thee sows
Nor can men steal thy goods, for none thy treasure knows

Poem No. 225; fall 1838–summer 1839

The Path of Peace

Turn ye turn ye who tread the wandring path
That leads not to my rest thorn-sprinkled o'er
Why treasure wrath against the day of wrath
And garments buy for burning kept in store
Oh come and I will comfort you indeed   5
With peace no earthly hand can give your soul
Come buy of me against the time of need
Drink drink the wine from out my flowing bowl
Ye shall not want. Your feet shall find again
The flowery path they lost in younger days   10
When every hour but added to your gain
Of pleasant fields and birds' inviting lays
And you were led from hill to streamlet on
Nor knew the day was ended till twas gone.

Poem No. 747; fall 1838–summer 1839

Obedience

My word will teach obedience thou wilt learn
From me the perfect path the living way
Go forward for thy service now shall earn
For thee a sure a never ceasing pay
Thou hast let thee out to one untrue   5
Who will not give thee for thy labor given
Serve me within be inwardly a Jew
And thou shalt reign with me a priest in heaven
Thy way lies onward bright and brighter still
Till thou on earth hast fought the fight for me   10
And done within my Father's perfect will
Then from thy bondage here I'll set you free

And you shall mourn no more no more remove
But ever in me live and in me love.

Poem No. 344; fall 1838–summer 1839

Grief

I bid thee weep but mourn not at thy lot
As though no comfort flowed for those who mourn
Thou shalt not sorrow always tears are not
But that by them thou mayst from sin be torn
Thou canst not weep for when my feet have traced   5
On to the goal whence I first came thy God
There every tear from memory effaced
Thou'lt smile and own as his the chastening rod
What son is he the Father does not strive
By sorrow's porch to bring to me within   10
The plants his hand have raised have learned to thrive
Through much affliction borne to them within
Be wise and He will lead you by the hand
Till you through tears shall see the promised land

Poem No. 215; fall 1838–summer 1839

The Reward

To him who hath to him I love to give
And he each day shall more and more abound
He shall the hidden manna eat and live
That only is in true obedience found
Come and its stores I'll open to your sight   5
They lie concealed save I the treasure show
None find my gold save those restored to light
Where nought of sin the spotless soul can know
There thou shalt live and feast with me in joy
A guest mid many that have owned my name   10
Arise henceforth thine ever blest employ
The praises of the Lamb thy lips shall claim

No more to feed on that which is not bread
No more to mourn and perish with the dead.

Poem No. 738; fall 1838–summer 1839

So is every one who is born of the spirit

It bloweth where it listeth hark the sound
Ye know not whence it comes nor where it goes
Its fruit shall in your borders to be found
Yet know ye not the stalk from which it grows
Go learn whence comes these words of heavenly truth   5
Cleanse ye the fountain whence their murmurs flow
And you though old shall still renew your youth
And of the life the spirit leads shall know
Go count the steps that measure out the path
That leads through John for he must come before   10
Then shall you flee the approaching day of wrath
And enter safely through the accepted door
For I am sure who promise seek my rest
The star the east beheld shines sinking in the west.

Poem No. 304; fall 1838–summer 1839

The Seed

Wouldst thou behold my features cleanse thy heart
Wash out the stains thy will impresses there
And as the clay-stamped images depart
Thou shalt behold my face how wondrous fair
How changed from that thine outward eye must see   5
It wears no form its searching glance can know
From flesh and blood it now has wrought it free
And in the spirit learns from Christ to grow
That which thou sowest is not that which springs
From the dead grain thou givest to the earth   10
Each moment's toil an added lustre brings

To deck the spirit when it springs to birth
From out the seed in Christ that long has lain
Buried beneath the snowy-crusted plain.

Poem No. 853; fall 1838–summer 1839

I am the Light of the World

I am the sun thine eye has seen the light
That lighteneth every man in spirit born
I can restore the blind to perfect sight
I am of heaven the crimson breaking morn
Gird on thy strength thy march will need it all   5
And many round thee hurrying to and fro
Shall stand to hear thy word's prophetic call
The day the day is near proclaim aloud
The day of wrath or joy to all the earth
Behold ^ the ascending cloud (though small appears)   10
'Tis a sure witness of my second birth
I come and every eye their Lord shall see
And those who scorn and pierce shall bow the knee.

Poem No. 208; fall 1838–summer 1839

The Apostle

I am the First and Last declare my Word
For I have sent thee an apostle forth
Thou hast from Me the living gospel heard
Thou shalt proclaim its truth from south to north
The farthest west the early east shall hear   5
My name that by the earth shall hallowed be
And they shall bow before my shrine in fear
And own my truth and it shall make them free
And thou if thou shalt keep my holy name
A priest shall be before the living God   10
And through the world the Father's truth proclaim

Ruling the nations with his chastening rod
And walk from glory on to glory still
Till thou in me has done his perfect will.

Poem No. 207; fall 1838–summer 1839

The Message

There is no voice but it is born of Me
I am there is no other God beside
Before Me all that live shall bow the knee
And be as in a fiery furnace tried
Warn them for I have told thee of my love   5
Bid them prepare my supper to attend
Thou has heard him who cometh from above
Let them receive thee for I am your friend
Though they have scorned the servants that I sent
Year after year within each stubborn breast   10
Let them give back the vineyard I have lent
Them yet another year to find my rest
And sent my son let them thy word receive
And in The Christ that in thee speaks believe.

Poem No. 628; fall 1838–summer 1839

I Am the Bread of Life

I am thy life thou shalt upon me feed
And daily eat my flesh and drink my blood
For nothing else than me canst thou have need
Thou art a spirit I the spirit's food
Come eat and thou shalt ask for bread no more   5
Come drink and thou shalt never thirsting cry again
I shall be in thee an increasing store
A spring forever swollen by the rain
Drink freely thou hast found the stream of life
In deeps where few have sought its healing wave   10
Thou hast fought well with sin the mortal strife

And hath found him who hath the power to save
Abide in me and I will lead you on
Till you the Father's home in me have won.

Poem No. 209; fall 1838–summer 1839

The Foe

There is no pause, the day rolls swiftly on;
Hour adds to hour its distance Lord! from Thee;
And soon the light Thou givest will be gone,
And night be here, and none thy coming see;
O bid them wake! sound ye the trumpets! sound!   5
The foe is on you! haste, he's at the door!
Soon, soon thy limbs will be securely bound,
And you in chains your former sloth deplore;
Wake! wake! there is no time to lose in sleep;
Break from the will that binds you still in sin,   10
A faithful watch o'er every action keep;
And know the foe that spoils thee is within;
Go back, retrace the steps your feet have trod,
That you may find protection in your God.

Poem No. 624; fall 1838–summer 1839

Yet Once More

The heavens are shaken! not the solid earth
But the high heavens, the spirit's own abode;
Through the dark souls whence sin springs armed to birth,
The miracle of miracles is showed!
There mountains shake, there breaks a startling voice   5
Unknown amid its sinful depths before;
The guilty dare not, when it speaks, rejoice;
But fain within its presence would adore;
Fly! fly! it is the spirit's voice you hear,
It is an angel sent to thee from heaven,   10
To tell thee that the marriage feast is near,

And but a moment's warning can be given;
Oh haste! the robe, the robe of white put on,
E'er that for thee that moment shall be gone.

Poem No. 508; fall 1838–summer 1839

The Humble

Thou dost exalt the humble; they shall be
Of thine own sons, and Thou shalt bless their lot;
And make them kings and priests to live with Thee,
Though they before had dwelt in poorest cot;
Over its roof Thou watched with tender care,   5
While they no fear in early childhood knew;
And didst with ready hand each meal prepare,
While they to manlier stature daily grew;
And ever on their steps thine angels wait,
And ever near remain to hear their call;   10
Though with the lowly vine they grew of late,
Thou shalt exalt them like the cedars tall,
That on thy holy mountain lift their heads
Forever wet with dews thy mercy sheds.

Poem No. 670; fall 1838–summer 1839

Comfort

Thou gladst my heart but not with oil and wine,
But that Thou dost forgive me when I sin;
And in thy son would make me wholly thine,
That I may find his peace and love within;
Still may I more and more find peace with Thee,   5
Who hath from infancy my footsteps led;
Till, by his love, from sin and death made free
My feet at length thy heavenly courts shall tread;
Where he a mansion has for me prepared,
With those who trod his thorny path before,   10
Who have with him thy house already shared,

And at his feast the marriage garment wore;
Oh may I see them when my work is done,
Like them a faithful servant of thy son.

Poem No. 676; fall 1838–summer 1839

The Guest

I knock, but knock in vain; there is no call
Comes from within to bid me enter there;
The selfish owner sits within his hall,
And will not open, will not hear my prayer;
Blessed is the man that doth my call attend,   5
And rise with anxious haste to see his guest;
For I to all that hear me am a friend,
And where I enter in that house is blest;
Oh hasten then each mansion to prepare
For him who blesses all that hear his word,   10
He shall with them his Father's mansion share;
Eye hath not seen, nor mortal ear hath heard
That which the heart that loves the Lord shall see,
When they within the veil with him shall be.

Poem No. 240; fall 1838–summer 1839

The Eagles

The eagles gather on the place of death
So thick the ground is spotted with their wings,
The air is tainted with the noisome breath
The wind from off the field of slaughter brings;
Alas! no mourners weep them for the slain,   5
But all unburied lies the naked soul;
The whitening bones of thousands strew the plain,
Yet none can now the pestilence controul;
The eagles gathering on the carcase feed,
In every heart behold their half-formed prey;   10
The battened wills beneath their talons bleed,

Their iron beaks without remorse must slay;
Till by the sun no more the place is seen,
Where they who worshipped idol gods have been.

Poem No. 490; fall 1838–summer 1839

Then shall all the tribes of the earth mourn

The day, the day, 'tis changed to darkest night!
There is no beauty in its morning beams,
But men run to and fro within its light
As haunted by the thought of horrid dreams;
They do not speak of what they spoke before, 5
Nor greet each other now with wonted smile;
Their hearts are pricked within them to the core,
Nor can the sight of aught their pain beguile;
Within their homes they hush the notes of joy,
For like a snare their sorrow has come on; 10
The slightest burthens now their souls annoy,
And in an instant all their mirth is gone;
For he who long has tarried is at hand,
And comes Himself his vineyard to demand.

Poem No. 486; fall 1838–summer 1839

Repent for the kingdom of Heaven is at hand

Repent, repent, the day of wrath is near!
Who shall abide the terror of the hour?
Repent, the sun of righteousness is here,
Thou hast no stay save in his rock-built tower;
The rains descend, the tempest speeds its way; 5
They pour upon the houses built with hands,
That melt before the torrents; walls of clay
Dissolved roll onward with the rolling sands;
Where is the house that stood before secure
With gates and mighty bulwarks lifted high? 10
It stood not on the strong foundation sure

That rain and tempest's shock can still defy,
And, when the storm around has ceased to roar,
Stand still unmoved where once it stood before.

Poem No. 408; fall 1838–summer 1839

Thy Name

The rightful name that thou art called by,
By him who knows thee as thou shouldst be known;
Hast thou e'er learnt it? if not, with me try,
I seek my own and would not be alone;
Though often called, yet I have heard it not,   5
By better name than men can give to me;
For I the one so called have long forgot,
As seen within a glass, yet knew 'twas he;
Come, let us seek ourselves, that they when found
May be at home to him who knocks without;   10
And to our names respond with joyful sound,
Nor longer wander here unknown about,
As those whom none know where their lodgings are,
But sleep in barns or in the open air.

Poem No. 551; fall 1838–summer 1839

The Mourner

How blessed the tears of him who still weeps on,
When he has ceased to feel affliction's rod;
Forgetful that from him the chastening's gone;
His eye beholds in faith his Father, God!
Thy tears are pearls for which the world shall pay;   5
More precious they than India's valued gold,
Go on in humble mind thy kingly way,
Though oft shall scorch the sun and chill the cold;
Faint not; though travellers few shall bid thee cheer,
Thou know'st the road thy well tried feet have found;   10
And soon, be thou but strong, shalt thou draw near

The band that death's strong ties to thee have bound;
And ever onward journey thence with them,
And him who leads, the Prince of Bethlehem.

Poem No. 178; fall 1838–summer 1839

The Giants

The giants, they who walked the earth of old
Are come again to scourge this feeble race;
And weapons long forgot in pride they hold,
To dash to earth your idols in disgrace;
Their armor proof shall be 'gainst sword or spear,   5
Your strength now lifts to smite a feebler foe;
Your cries for help their ears can never hear,
Nor wounded can their eyes your sufferings know;
Arise! gird on the might that now you waste
On harlots, and in feasting night and day;   10
Their coming-on shall be with eagles' haste,
As from the heights they dart upon their prey;
That all-unknowing pass their eyries by,
With idle pace and earthward turning eye.

Poem No. 503; fall 1838–summer 1839

To the Fishermen

Be mending still your nets, and cast not in
While yet they are not strong to hold them all;
For you yourselves will lose some joint or fin,
When one shall draw than you a larger haul;
'Tis not for you as yet to venture far,   5
Thus young upon the shifting shoreless deep;
But guide thee by the highest risen star,
And still thy boat within its cove thou'lt keep;
Behold the wrecks that line the rocky shore,
Of hulks more stout than thine to meet the wave;   10
And hear afar the storm's low-muttered roar,

And learn from me thy feebler bark to save;
Who will not tempt in pride time's wind-tost sea,
Till manned with choicest men my ship shall be.

Poem No. 60; fall 1838–summer 1839

The Sower

To want is there to be where I am not,
Abundance waits for me where'er I tread;
The cares of life in me are all forgot,
I have enough and e'en to spare of bread;
Come, taste, and hunger shall be laid at rest;   5
And thirst once quenched shall never thirst again;
Thou shalt of all I have be long possest,
And long thy life my body shall sustain;
There are who food will give thee, but 'tis theirs;
And hunger rages but the more 'tis fed;   10
'Twas made from out the grains of scattered tares,
That through my field by wicked hands were spread,
But thou shalt have the wheat that's sown by me,
And in thy bosom's field new harvests ever see.

Poem No. 742; fall 1838–summer 1839

Charity

Whate'er thou wouldst receive at others' hands,
Thou first to them must freely give away;
Whether of houses high or spreading lands,
Nought shall be thine till thou hast seen this day;
God gives thee all; but canst thou all receive,   5
When e'en my little thou dost yet refuse?
No longer then thy brother's spirit grieve,
And thou shalt have yet larger gifts to use;
For in my Father's house do many live,
Who, older far, in love have stronger grown,   10
And how to them can'st thou e'er learn to give,

Who all The Father hath can call their own?
Give freely then, for all thou givst away
Shall men with added gifts to thee repay.

Poem No. 783; fall 1838–summer 1839

The Created

There is nought for thee by thy haste to gain;
'Tis not the swift with Me that win the race;
Through long endurance of delaying pain,
Thine opened eye shall see thy Father's face;
Nor here nor there, where now thy feet would turn,   5
Thou wilt find Him who ever seeks for thee;
But let obedience quench desires that burn,
And where thou art, thy Father too will be!
Behold! as day by day the spirit grows,
Thou see'st by inward light things hid before;   10
Till what God is, thyself, his image, shows;
And thou dost wear the robe that first thou wore,
When bright with radiance from his forming hand,
He saw thee Lord of all his creatures stand.

Poem No. 631; fall 1838–summer 1839

To All

Thou know'st not e'er the way to turn or go,
For He whom man would follow turneth not;
Enough for thee that thou thy Lord mayst know,
And canst not for a moment be forgot;
His way is hidden that thine eye may seek,   5
And in the seeking thou thyself may find;
His voice unheard that thou may'st learn to speak,
His eye unseen to show thee thou art blind;
Then haste thee on, his hidden path explore;
And purge thine ear that thou mayst hear his voice;   10

Unseal thine eye to him who walks before,
And that thou hast a friend unseen in me rejoice;
And follow on though now thy feet may tread,
Where clouds still hang above the unnumbered dead.

Poem No. 682; fall 1838–summer 1839

The Unrevealed

Hast thou stolen aught from hunger, or in thirst
Withheld the water-cup from thy parched lips,
That thou mightest speak the blessed words of hope
And joy; thou shalt not lack reward. Loosened
Thy tongue shall with sweet-flowing sounds surprize   5
The ear of sense; another than thyself
Will be seen within to have come, and bringing
Music tones from other spheres to have made
Thee ever the harp of hidden minstrelsy. Forms
Of heaven as seen descending on the eye   10
Shall strike, giving to that men cannot see
A place and name amongst earth's dying sons.

Poem No. 159; fall 1838–summer 1839

Sayings

The world looks not the wider for thy travel,
But stand thou still, and look around; as far
From pole to pole, from east to west it lies,
Stretching with varied rise and fall, as when
With wearied feet thou has found out the utmost   5
Bound of sea and sky. Be wise; travel with
The bright clouds above thee, they are journeying,
Journey too; grow there green trees beside thee
As thou walkest, grow with them; finding one
Common Father on thy way, nor hope an earth   10
Made wider by thy search, nor things more bright

And fair than such as ever like angels
Watch around the steps of one, who in God's
Path begins and ends the journey of each day.

Poem No. 607; fall 1838–summer 1839

The Prisoner

All men around me running to and fro
Are finding life in what to me is death;
I have no limbs that where I please will go,
Nor voice that when I wish will find a breath;
Here, where I stand, my feet take fixed root;   5
This way or that I cannot even move;
A prisoner, ever bound both hand and foot,
While I a slave to mine own choice would prove;
'Tis hard to wait, but grant me thus set free;
And they; how narrow their short bounded lot!   10
My sun the centre of their worlds will be,
In systems moving where they shine forgot;
Their rays too feebly twinkling through the night,
Where I shall shine with all day's lustre bright.

Poem No. 32; fall 1838–summer 1839

Eternal Life

My life as yet is but an infant's walk,
With tottering steps and words half-uttered slow;
But I shall soon in nobler accents talk,
And grown to manlier stature, firmer go;
I shall go out and in and pasture find   5
In him who leads me safe forever on;
The spirit's fetters then shall I unbind,
And sin from me forever shall be gone;
Eternal life will be the gift bestowed,
By him who loved us while yet dead in sin;   10
Such love forever from the Father flowed,

But we were not prepared the crown to win;
Oh bless his name, who calls us on to heaven;
And him in whom the promises are given.

Poem No. 342; fall 1838–summer 1839

Unto you is born a Saviour

Rejoice a child is born a son is given
By Him who giveth all things to the earth
Sing loud ye saints that fill the courts of heaven
Proclaim with welcome sound the infant's birth
The star the wise men saw has led him on   5
Unto the spot where now the babe is lain
Rejoice the darkness from his sight has flown
For he the serpent through the Lamb has slain
He shall not hunger more rejoice ye stars
Nor thirst for he the living brook has found   10
He comes to break of sin the prison bars
And scatter joy and hope his path around
He comes to give the world his promised peace
With joys unknown, that nevermore shall cease.

Poem No. 405; fall 1838–summer 1839

The Redeemed

I bear the prints of my ascended Lord,
Ye cannot part me now, for I am pure;
And hear, forever hear his holy word,
And shall forever in the Truth endure;
Behold the love the Father hath for me,   5
That He should call his son a child of earth;
And from the guilt of sin forever free,
And bid me know in Him a purer birth;
Come, worship with me on the holy hill,
Come, be a brother with a brother's love;   10
He will our hearts with deeper rapture fill,

And we though here shall taste his joy above;
And in our midst, though here, our Lord shall be,
And we, while here on earth, his face shall see.

Poem No. 214; fall 1838–summer 1839

Hallowed be thy Name

Thy name be hallowed, e'en thy Holy name,
That dwells forever on thy children's tongue;
On earth may all thy saints its praise proclaim,
As in thy heavens Thou art forever sung;
Thou art forever worthy! Thou art king!   5
The Great, All Holy, ever righteous Lord!
Let all thy children praise and homage bring,
And in their song let every note accord;
Praise Him! for He is great, his praise prolong
On every harp ye strike around his throne;   10
Join every living voice! come join the song,
What praise can all your Father's goodness own;
Come, throw your crowns and garlands at his feet,
And his new name let every tongue repeat.

Poem No. 714; fall 1838–summer 1839

To him who overcometh

To him who overcometh I will give
The starry crown, the heavenly-sounding lyre;
Within my Father's presence he shall live,
His love shall overflow thy soul's desire;
Come, strip thee of the garments thou hast worn,   5
While on the earth thou wrought for Him in me;
Take off thy raiments, they are soiled and torn,
Behold, the wedding robe prepared for thee;
Come, put it on; thy brothers ready wait,
And ask why tarry still thy feet without;   10
Thou shalt be with them, though thou comest late;

Hark! hear, within they raise the welcome shout,
To hail thee brother born, a son like them,
In mine own Vine a new and fruitful stem.

Poem No. 739; fall 1838–summer 1839

The Children

I saw, strange sight! the children sat at meat,
When they their Parent's face had never known;
Nor rose they when they heard his step to greet,
But feasted there upon his gifts alone;
'Twas morn, and noon, and evening hour the same;   5
They heeded not 'twas He who gave them bread;
For they had not yet learned to call his name,
They had been children, but they now were dead;
Yet still their Father, with a father's care,
Early and late stood waiting by their board;   10
Hoping each hour that they his love would share,
And at his table sit to life restored;
Alas! for many a day and year I stood
And saw them feasting thus yet knew not Him how good.

Poem No. 261; fall 1838–summer 1839

The New Man

The hands must touch and handle many things,
The eyes long waste their glances all in vain;
The feet course still in idle, mazy rings,
E'er man himself, the lost, shall back regain;
The hand that ever moves, the eyes that see,   5
While day holds out his shining lamp on high,
And strait as flies the honey-seeking bee,
Direct the feet to unseen flowers they spy,
These, when they come, the man revealed from heaven,
Shall labor all the day in quiet rest,   10
And find at eve the covert duly given,

Where with the bird they find sweet sleep and rest;
That shall their wasted strength to health restore,
And bid them seek the morn the hills and fields once more.

Poem No. 506; fall 1838–summer 1839

The Veil of the Temple

'Tis rent, the veil that parts the spirit world;
Behold the temple of the Living God!
The Foe who tempted once to earth is hurled,
By him who wields on earth the iron rod;
Rejoice, the peace he gave on earth begins!   5
Hark, from the lowly vale the strains arise,
Rejoice, the Savior comes he frees from sins!
The dumb man speaks, he touches sightless eyes
And Lo the scales fall off, the spirit sees
Within the veil the mysteries of the dead;   10
Bow down ye mighty! bow the stubborn knees!
'Tis on the borders of that land ye tread,
Where you must see the earth's ascended king,
Before whose presence bows each living thing.

Poem No. 732; fall 1838–summer 1839

The Holy of Holies

I cannot show thee that for which I live,
Nor mortal eye hath seen, nor ear hath heard
That which the Christ to those who live will give,
In the rich presence of the Living Word;
Go, cleanse thy soul, blot out the secret sin,   5
Put off thy shoes for this is holy ground;
And thou shalt see the kingdom come within,
And in its holy precincts too be found;
Awake, thou hast long filled the holy place
With idols that thy heart has lifted high,   10
From My pure temple every daemon chase,

Then to thy spirit will My soul draw nigh;
And thou shalt be my son, and I thy God
To lead thee in the way thy Master trod.

Poem No. 222; fall 1838–summer 1839

The Brethren

For we are all His offspring, why deny
The hand of love He bade thee to me give?
Why turn from me, who in the spirit cry,
That thou wouldst share thy Father's love and live?
Let not between us rise the mountain chain,   5
That with its icy cliffs divides the earth;
For we are brothers, let us so remain;
Alike the offspring of a heavenly birth;
Invite me to thy feast, a richer board
Than for thee of the Father I prepare;   10
Thou wilt not in thy breast his treasure hoard,
But send for those who may thy supper share;
If thou hast tasted that the Lord is good,
Thou wilt not hold from me my daily food.

Poem No. 133; fall 1838–summer 1839

The Prodigal

Where hast thou been my brother? thou art torn,
But scarce the rags conceal thy naked soul;
Thou art from desert still to desert borne,
Nor yet hast learned love's yielding, soft controul;
Come, let me o'er thee cast this garment white,   5
Strip off the filthy rags the world has given;
The son has sent me, that I may invite
The weary to his marriage feast in heaven;
Oh come, for there is all thou want'st prepared,
The flowing bowl that cannot ever dry,   10
The bread of life with him who died is shared;

Oh come, thou wilt not my request deny,
And wander on in thorny paths to bleed,
And on the husks thou feedest ever feed.

Poem No. 804; fall 1838–summer 1839

The Fig Tree

Thou wilt not give me aught though I am poor,
And ask with shivering limbs and hungry cry;
And thinkst that I the winter can endure,
And thou dost not my spirit's wants deny;
But thou art poor; for thou hast nought to give   5
Of that which is both meat and drink to me;
Thou bidst me on the husks thou feedest live,
And with the rags thou wear'st in comfort be;
The figs my Father bade me on thee seek,
I taste not from thy thorns and brambles high;   10
He made thee strong, I find thee poor and weak;
He made thee rich, yet thou must of me buy;
Who am but blind, and yet to thee can see;
A servant still, and yet to thee am free.

Poem No. 704; fall 1838–summer 1839

The Branch

Thou bidst me change with every changing hour,
A new formed gift to bless the hungry poor;
For Thou through Christ has blest me with the power
To bear the fruits that shall for them endure;
In him may I grow stronger day by day,   5
A vigorous branch abiding in thy vine;
That men may pluck thereof and eating say,
"These grapes, O Father, these are wholly thine"
Then shall the clusters Thou dost love to see,
With every season changing face the sun;   10
And men rejoice beneath my shade to be,

When day with all the toils it brings is done;
And I in Christ shall be forever blest,
To give them at its close thy holy rest.

Poem No. 665; fall 1838–summer 1839

Not as the World giveth

Thy gifts are not the gifts that others give,
For Thou art kind unto them when they pray;
And giv'st them bread on which their souls can live,
Nor with a serpent sendst them poor away;
The more they eat of all thy hand supplies,   5
The more thy peace within abundant grows,
Till all that is not thine forever dies,
And heaven alone the perfect spirit knows;
Then shall thy children ever find employ,
In acts thy love has taught their hands to do;   10
Each loved by Thee shall swell the other's joy,
And every secret prayer be brought to view;
By Thee who dwellst in secret, and will bring
Into the light of life each hidden thing.

Poem No. 712; fall 1838–summer 1839

The Good Gift

Whate'er I ask I know I have from Thee,
My Father, for Thou lovest me thy child;
And would my spirit from his bondage free,
Who first my infant feet from Thee beguiled;
But Thou hast taught me all his snares to shun,   5
And in thy precepts walk forever sure;
And when thy will on earth in Christ is done
Thou wilt admit me to thy presence pure;
Where he who has betrayed me cannot stand,
For Thou hast placed the gulf of love between;   10
And he who knows not of the new command,

Cannot his robes in water ever clean;
They must within the Lamb's own blood be dyed,
That flows for me and all forever from his side.

Poem No. 782; fall 1838–summer 1839

History

The History that thou hast never known,
That is not on the record lying book;
But by the light thou givest only shown,
Canst thou on this, the truest page yet look?
Then mayst thou leave all others; this the leaf,   5
The healing leaf from off the tree of Life;
It is not numbered by Time's cyphers brief,
It higher dates than counts thy mortal strife;
Its pages are the Scriptures; never read
Till closed the eye that dust-soiled letters pores,   10
And he who saw's forgotten with the dead;
Then opes The Book Divine its heavenly stores,
Its times man's living eras; still the same
While burns within of God the sun-lit flame.

Poem No. 510; fall 1838–summer 1839

The Spirit Land

Open our eyes that we the world may see,
Open our ears that we Thy Voice may hear,
And in the Spirit-Land may ever be,
And feel Thy Presence with us always near.
No more to wander 'mid the things of time,   5
No more to suffer death or earthly change;
But with the Christian's joy & faith sublime
Thro' all Thy vast, eternal scenes to range.
Tho' now against me beats the raging blast,
And o'er my head in scornful triumph rides   10

Soon soon the winter's bondage shall be past,
To him who in the Savior's love confides

Poem No. 393; fall 1838–summer 1839

Thy Father's House

Thou are not yet at home; perhaps thy feet
Are on the threshold of thy father's door,
But still thy journey is not there complete,
If thou canst add to it but one step more;
'Tis not thy house which thou with feet can reach,   5
'Tis where when wearied they will enter not;
But stop beneath an earthly roof, where each
May for a time find comfort in his lot;
Then called to wander soon again must mourn,
That such frail shelter they should call relief;   10
And onward seek again that distant bourne,
The home of all the family of grief,
Whose doors by day and night stand open wide
For all who enter there shall evermore abide.

Poem No. 662; fall 1838–summer 1839

Jacob's Well

Thou prayst not, save when in thy soul thou prayst;
Disrobing of thyself to clothe the poor;
The words thy lips shall utter then, thou sayst,
They are as marble, and they shall endure;
Pray always; for on prayer the hungry feed;   5
Its sound is hidden music to the soul,
From low desires the rising strains shall lead,
And willing captives own thy just controul;
Draw not too often on the gushing spring,
But rather let its own o'erflowings tell,   10
Where the cool waters rise, and thither bring

Those who more gladly then will hail the well;
When gushing from within new streams like thine,
Shall bid them ever drink and own its source divine.

Poem No. 689; fall 1838–summer 1839

The Day of Denial

Are there not twelve whole hours in every day
The sun upon thy dial marks for toil;
How is it some but five, some seven say,
And some among you of the whole make spoil?
Thinkst thou to gain by taking from your life,   5
By dying many hours to live the more?
Dost thou not see the suicidal knife,
Made hour by hour yet redder in thy gore?
The day! the living day! how soon tis night,
With him who rises not till near its noon;   10
His candle lit for many hours to light,
Put out e'er yet he learned to prize the boon;
How dark his darkness, who till latest eve
Still slumbers on nor then his couch will leave!

Poem No. 51; fall 1838–summer 1839

Spiritual Darkness

A darkness, like the middle of the night,
Clouds in the morn, and e'en the mid-day hours;
Men wander round, as if devoid of sight,
Or led astray by false, deluding powers!
The wise knew not its coming, nor can tell   5
Whence fell this darkness, like a plague on all;
In vain they seek by knowledge to dispel
The gloom, that shrouds the earth as with a pall.
So, in eclipse, the sun withdraws his light,
Or sheds a pale, and ineffectual ray;   10
The flowers close up, as at the approach of night,

And men, bewildered, wander from their way;
The stars appear, and with faint lustre burn,
Watching, from their far heights, the sun's return.

Poem No. 5; fall 1838–summer 1839

The New World

The night that has no star lit up by God,
The day that round men shines who still are blind,
The earth their grave-turned feet for ages trod,
And sea swept over by His mighty wind;
All these have passed away; the melting dream   5
That flitted o'er the sleeper's half-shut eye,
When touched by morning's golden-darting beam;
And he beholds around the earth and sky
That ever real stands; the rolling spheres,
And heaving billows of the boundless main,   10
That show though time is past no trace of years,
And earth restored he sees as his again;
The earth that fades not, and the heavens that stand;
Their strong foundations laid by God's right hand!

Poem No. 532; fall 1838–summer 1839

The Word

The voice that speaks when thou art in thy tomb,
And spoke before thou sawst the morning light;
This is the Word! of all that is the womb,
Of all that see the never failing sight;
Speechless yet ever speaking, none can hear   5
The man grown silent in the praise of God;
For they within him live, to hope and fear;
They walk and speak, but he the grass-green sod;
Its presence round them calls them hence to It,
A Voice too great for murmur or reproof;   10
A sun that shines till they are of it lit,

Itself the utterance of Eternal Truth;
Perfect, without a blemish; never found
Save through the veil that wraps thy being round.

Poem No. 588; fall 1838–summer 1839

The Field and Wood

Whence didst thou spring, or art thou yet unborn;
Who treadst with slighting foot so swift along,
Where near thee rises green the bladed corn,
And from the tree pours forth the bird's new song?
Thy heart is ever fluttering, ne'er at rest;   5
A bird that e'er would soar with wily art,
Yet when she seems of what she wished possest,
She feels the strength from out her wings depart;
Learn wisdom from the sweet delaying voice,
And from its melody turn not thine ear;   10
With springing grain in slow decay rejoice,
And thou at one shall be with all things here;
And thy desires that now o'er-top the grain,
Shall with its growth a life like theirs sustain.

Poem No. 800; fall 1838–summer 1839

The Apostles

The words that come unuttered by the breath,
Looks without eyes, these lighten all the globe;
They are the ministering angels, sent where Death
Has walked so long the earth in seraph's robe;
See crowding to their touch the groping blind!   5
And ears long shut to sound are bent to hear,
Quick as they speak the lame new vigor find,
And language to the dumb man's lips is near;
Hail sent to us, ye servants of high heaven!
Unseen save by the humble and the poor;   10
To them glad tidings have your voices given;

For them their faith has wrought the wished for cure;
And ever shall they witness bear of you,
That he who sent you forth to heal was true.

Poem No. 604; fall 1838–summer 1839

The House

I build a house, but in this 'twill appear;
That I have built it not, a shining forth
Of that bright palace that from year to year
New pillars has and domes from my own worth;
The wondrous hand that forms it; in the sea,   5
In crystal depths fashions the coral pile,
The sun-lit roof that o'er our heads we see,
Earth's grassy plain that stretches mile on mile;
'Tis round me like the morning's presence, felt
As that in which apart I live from all;   10
A zone that girds me like Orion's belt,
That I be seen the more on that bright wall,
Where all, as golden constellations, shine
With their own light, yet lit with Light Divine.

Poem No. 216; fall 1838–summer 1839

The Tenant

Trees shall rise around thy dwelling,
   When thy house from heaven appears;
Art thou that thou liv'st in selling,
   As are numbered up thy years?

Thou canst ne'er have leave to enter   5
   That new dwelling's open door;
Where thy hopes and wishes centre,
   Where thy friend has gone before;

Till the hut where now thou livest,
    Low is leveled with the ground;   10
Then thy prayer to Him who givest
    Has at length acceptance found.

Then though poor, yet He will cherish,
    Whose high mansion is the sky;
Houseless left thou shalt not perish   15
    'Neath its wide-spread canopy.

Quick then, leave some poorer dweller
    That wherein thou livest now;
Better far awaits the seller,
    Richer lands his oxen plough.   20

Poem No. 743; June or September 1839

This Morn

Whence came this morn, this glorious morn,
    That hill and valley love so well?
From Thee who gave me voice to sing,
    For they too of thy bounty tell.

Look! how each leaf and grassy blade   5
    Return the glances of the morn;
There is no beauty in the stream
    But of its brightness too is born.

But none can tell how fair they are,
    Who do not with the morning live;   10
And in its light find life with them,
    And like them always praises give.

This morn, this brightly-beaming morn,
    Then shall they know it came from Thee;
For they shall in its light rejoice,
    And own that they thy children be.   15

Poem No. 798; June or September 1839

The Call

Why art thou not awake my son?
The morning breaks I formed for thee;
And I thus early by thee stand,
Thy new-awakening life to see.

Why art thou not awake my son?   5
The birds upon the bough rejoice;
And I thus early by thee stand,
To hear with theirs thy tuneful voice.

Why sleepest thou still? the laborers all
Are in my vineyard, hear them toil;   10
As for the poor with harvest song,
They treasure up the wine and oil.

I come to wake thee; haste, arise,
Or thou no share with me can find;
Thy sandals seize, gird on thy clothes,   15
Or I must leave thee here behind.

Poem No. 816; summer 1839

The Prayer

Wilt Thou not visit me?
The plant beside me feels thy gentle dew;
    And every blade of grass I see,
From thy deep earth its quickening moisture drew.

Wilt Thou not visit me?   5
Thy morning calls on me with cheering tone;
    And every hill and tree
Lend but one voice, the voice of Thee alone.

Come, for I need thy love;
More than the flower the dew, or grass the rain,   10
    Come, gently as thy holy dove;
And let me in thy sight rejoice to live again.

I will not hide from them,
When thy storms come, though fierce may be their wrath;
    But bow with leafy stem,   15
And strengthened follow on thy chosen path.

    Yes, Thou wilt visit me:
Nor plant nor tree thy parent eye delight so well;
    As when from sin set free
My spirit loves with thine in peace to dwell.   20

Poem No. 829; summer 1839

The Bride

I sought of Thee my promised wife,
    She of the golden hair;
But though I toiled with manly strife,
    Thou gave me one less fair.

Again I toiled, and many a day   5
    My hands to labor flew;
But Thou withheld again my pay,
    And gave me one less true.

And still once more my limbs they plied
    Their strength to serve Thee Lord;   10
But Thou wouldst not, though long I tried,
    With her my pains reward.

But still for her I loved in youth,
    My nerves again are strung;
And I will serve Thee still in truth,   15
    As when my limbs were young.

And though the snows fall on my head,
    And lightless grows my eye;
She of my youth I still may wed,
    And dwell with her on high.   20

Poem No. 272; summer 1839

My Garden

The eyes that would my garden see,
Are not that outward objects view;
For this my Father gave to me,
And placed me here my work to do.

At morn, at noon, and evening hour,   5
With Him thou'lt find me at my toil;
And when the night dews wet the flower,
I watch lest thieves my treasures spoil.

Come, see, the rose is budding here,
The rose that blooms without a thorn;   10
No weeds the vale-born lilies fear,
That with their grace the spot adorn.

The lily's cup, the rose is thine,
If thou wilt give the strangers place;
On them thou'lt read in many a line,   15
The love that I have learned to trace.

It grows with every springing blade;
It falls with every evening dew;
'Tis this the light of morning made,
And spangles night's dark curtain too.   20

'Tis this that gives each flower to me,
And bids again each gift restore;
That I may live with Him I see,
And welcome those who pass my door.

Poem No. 494; summer 1839

The Unripe Fruit

I cannot wait, I cannot wait,
   The grapes, though sour, oh give to me:
Or I must pluck them from the vine,
   Before the clusters ripened be.

I cannot wait, I cannot wait, 5
   Shake down the green fruit from the bough:
'Tis hard and bitter to my taste;
   Yet I must eat it, Father, now.

The grapes still cling, they will not give,
   To my unhallowed hasty hand; 10
I know that thus with gentleness,
   Thou dost thy son's desire withstand.

The bough though struck with lustful force,
   Will not the fruit thou gav'st let fall;
I know it hangeth closely there, 15
   My sliding footsteps to recall.

Yes I will wait and learn of Thee,
   Who giv'st each season to the year;
And unto autumn hold'st the fruit,
   For him who walkest in thy fear. 20

Poem No. 224; summer 1839

The Immortal

'Tis not that Thou hast given to me,
   A form which mortals cannot see,
      That I rejoice;
But that I know Thou art around,
   And though there comes to me no sound, 5
      I hear thy voice.

'Tis not that Thou hast given me place,
   Among a new and happy race,
      I serve Thee, Lord;
But that thy mercies never fail, 10
   And shall o'er all my sins prevail,
      Through thine own word.

Its praise has gone abroad; who hears,
   He casts aside all earth-born fears,
      By it he lives; 15
It bids him triumph o'er the grave,

To him o'er death dominion gave,
   Thy joy and peace it gives.

Hear it ye poor! and ye who weep!
   Arise who lie in sin's long sleep!   20
      'Tis strong to free;
Give ear and it shall lead you on,
   'Till you the crown again have won,
      And me and mine can see.

Poem No. 730; summer 1839

The Serving-Man

Lord, thou hast many a serving-man,
   And better far than I;
Yet leave Thee, Lord, I never can,
   Nor Him who bought deny.

Thou brought me out of bondage sore,   5
   When sick and faint of heart;
And can I ask for service more,
   Than never to depart.

A Servant now I'll tend thy sheep,
   Nor know the master's joy;   10
Yet I, if well thy fold I keep,
   Shall find a son's employ.

O hasten, Father, hasten on,
   The days till all are past;
And Thou when all my work is done,   15
   Wilt call me son at last.

Poem No. 322; summer 1839

The Cottage

The house my earthly parent left,
My heavenly Father e'er throws down;
For 'tis of air and sun bereft,
Nor stars its roof in beauty crown.

He gave it me, yet gave it not,   5
As one whose gifts are wise and good:
'Twas but a poor and clay-built cot,
And for a time the storms withstood;

But lengthening years, and frequent rain,
O'ercame its strength, it tottered, fell;   10
And left me homeless here again,
And where to go I could not tell.

But soon the light and open air,
Received me as a wandering child;
And I soon thought their house more fair,   15
And was from all my grief beguiled.

Mine was the grove, the pleasant field,
Where dwelt the flowers I daily trod;
And there beside them too I kneeled,
And called their friend, my Father, God.   20

Poem No. 513; summer 1839

The Still-Born

I saw one born, yet he was of the dead;
   Long since the spirit ceased to give us birth;
For lust to sin, and sin to death had led,
   And now its children people o'er the earth.

And yet he thought he lived, and as he grew   5
   Looked round upon the world and called it fair;
For of the heaven he lost he never knew,
   Though oft he pined in spirit to be there.

And he lived on, the earth became his home,
    Nor learnt he aught of those who came before;   10
For they had ceased to wish from thence to roam;
    And for the better land could not deplore.

Time passed, and he was buried; lo the dust,
    From which he first was taken him received;
Yet in his dying hour ne'er ceased his trust,   15
    And still his soul for something heavenly grieved.

And we will hope that there is One who gave,
    The rest he sighed for, but the world denied;
That yet his voice is heard beyond the grave,
    That he yet lives who to our vision died.   20

Poem No. 260; summer 1839

To-Day

I live but in the present, where art thou?
Hast thou a home in some past future year?
I call to thee from every leafy bough,
But thou art far away and canst not hear.

Each flower lifts up its red or yellow head,   5
And nods to thee as thou art passing by;
Hurry not on, but stay thine anxious tread,
And thou shalt live with me, for there am I.

The stream that murmurs by thee, heed its voice,
Nor stop thine ear, 'tis I that bid it flow;   10
And thou with its glad waters shall rejoice,
And of the life I live within them know.

And hill, and grove, and flowers, and running stream,
When thou dost live with them, shall look more fair;
And thou awake as from a cheating dream,   15
The life to-day with me and mine to share.

Poem No. 241; summer 1839

The Withered Tree

It stands 'mid other trees dry-barked,
  Its limbs with moss are overgrown;
And many a gash its trunk has marked,
  Men sought for fruit but found there none.

I saw them pass, a hungry crowd,   5
  With quickening steps and eager gaze;
Then heard their wailings long and loud,
  Where should have rose the voice of praise.

It stood for many years; the rain
  Fell on it, yet no leaf   10
Came forth when stirs the sprouting grain,
  Nor summer's sun could bring relief.

The roots, whence free the sap ascends,
  Had ceased to drink their rich supply;
Nor sun nor shower the tree befriends,   15
  That does not on the earth rely.

I heard the axe, when winter chills,
  Thick, sturdy blows, in haste it fell,
And soon no more the place it fills,
  Nor smallest root the spot would tell.   20

Poem No. 308; summer 1839

The Hour

I ask not what the bud may be,
  That hangs upon the green-sheathed stem;
But love with every leaf I see,
  To lie unfolded there like them.

I ask not what the tree may bear,   5
  When whitened by the hand of spring;
But with its blossoms on the air,
  Would far around my perfume fling.

The infant's joy is mine, is mine,
    I join its infant sports with glee;   10
And would not for a world resign,
    The look of love it casts on me.

Leave not the bird upon the wing,
    But with her seek her shaded nest,
And then with voice like hers thou'lt sing,   15
    When life's last sun-beam gilds the west.

Poem No. 211; summer–fall 1839

The Old Road

The road is left, that once was trod
    By man and heavy-laden beast;
And new ways opened iron-shod,
    That bind the land from west to east.

I asked of Him, who all things knows,   5
    Why none who lived now passed that way;
Where rose the dust, the grass now grows?
    A still, low voice was heard to say:

"Thou know'st not why I change the course
    Of him who travels, learn to go;—   10
Obey the spirit's gentle force,
    Nor ask thee, where the stream may flow."

"Man shall not walk in his own ways,
    For he is blind and cannot see;
But let him trust, and lengthened days   15
    Shall lead his feet to heaven and Me."

"Then shall the grass the path grow o'er,
    That his own willfulness has trod;
Nor man nor beast shall pass it more,
    But he shall walk with Me, his God."   20

Poem No. 552; summer–fall 1839

The Fair Morning

The clear bright morning, with its scented air,
And gaily waving flowers, is here again;
Man's heart is lifted with the voice of prayer,
And peace descends as falls the gentle rain;
The tuneful birds that all the night have slept,   5
Take up at dawn the evening's dying lay;
When sleep upon their eyelids gently crept,
And stole with stealthy craft their song away;
High overhead the forest's swaying boughs,
Sprinkle with drops of dew the whistling boy;   10
As to the field he early drives his cows
More than content with this his low employ;
And shall not joy uplift me when I lead,
The flocks of Christ by the still streams to feed?

Poem No. 478; summer–fall 1839

The Clouded Morning

The morning comes; and thickening fogs prevail,
Hanging like curtains all the horizon round;
And o'er the head in heavy stillness sad;
So still is day, it seems like night profound;
But see! the mists are stirring, rays of light   5
Pierce through the haze as struggling to be free,
The circle round grows every moment bright,
The sun is breaking forth, 'tis he, 'tis he;
Quick from before him flies each sluggish cloud,
His rays have touched the stream, have climbed the hill;   10
The sounds of life increase, all blending loud;
The hum of men, nor smallest thing is still;
But all have found a voice, and hail their king,
The words of man's high praise, and bird with fluttering wing.

Poem No. 530; summer–fall 1839

The Plagues of Egypt

I see them spreading o'er the land,
   The swarming locust fly;
More numerous than the small-grained sand,
   They speed them from on high.

O'er golden crops that gallant waved,   5
   O'er groves with foliage green;
They march; not e'en the grass is saved,
   Nor hill nor flood can screen.

And lice within men's dwellings creep,
   More small than finest dust;   10
Their kneading troughs, and where they sleep;
   They eat their flesh like rust.

Repent! e'er yet your eldest born,
   Be stricken at your side;
Repent! e'er yet ye see the morn,   15
   The wave with blood be dyed.

For He who lives will Israel call,
   From out their bondage sore;
And Egypt's pride again shall fall,
   And Egypt's sons deplore.   20

Poem No. 267; summer–fall 1839

The Dark Day

A darkness like the middle of the night
Clouds in the morn and e'en the mid-day hours;
Men wander round as if devoid of sight,
Or led astray by false deluding powers;
The wise knew not its coming, nor can tell   5
Whence fell this blackness like a plague on all;
Nor will it yield to e'en their strongest spell;
Nor heed their gods though on their names they call;
The hand that spread the veil alone dispels,
For this alone obeys the all-seeing God;   10

The night that fell where sin in splendor dwells,
Shall flee again when waves the obedient rod;
As mists that from the low, damp earth will fly,
When gains the sun upon the eastern sky.

Poem No. 3; summer–fall 1839

The Removal

When he who owns a house has come to thee,
And begs you move, for he must enter in;
Dost thou not pay, when asked, his little fee,
And for thy journeying hence right quick begin?
But I, when I have come: who own no land,   5
Nor houses built of wood, or wrought of stone;
Why dost thou waiting and uncertain stand,
As if the house I let was not my own?
"I have been here so long it seems like mine,"
Thou sayst; "but still the more ought thou to leave;"   10
"My children here were born; can I resign"
"My all, and thou a stranger too?" "believe"
"And thou canst do it; and I grant yet more"
"A better house for thine I will restore."

Poem No. 786; summer–fall 1839

The Rain

The rain descends; each drop some drooping flowers,
Or parched blade drinks in with grateful haste;
Nor is there from the plenteous falling shower,
A drop that nature will permit to waste;
The river swells beneath the pattering rain,   5
And as a seine its face is dotted o'er;
It falls not on the barren path in vain,
But drunken quick it asks to have yet more;
Nor think that where the pool untasted stands,
As if its life refused the sullen earth;   10

That there the wave is spilt upon the sands,
To-morrow's sun shall see the duck's rude mirth;
As there it sails or drinks with snuffling bill,
Rejoiced that there is spared its thirst with theirs to fill.

Poem No. 550; fall 1839

The Frost

The frost is out amid our open fields,
And late within the woods I marked his track;
The unwary flower his icy fingers feels,
And at their touch the crisped leaf rolls back.
Look, how the maple, o'er a sea of green,   5
Waves in the autumnal wind its flag of red!
First struck of all the forest's spreading screen,
Most beauteous, too, thou earliest of her dead!
Go on; thy task is kindly meant by him,
Whose is each flower, and richly covered bough;   10
And though the leaves hang dead on every limb,
Still will I praise his love; that early now
Has sent before this herald of decay,
To bid me heed the approach of winter's sterner day.

Poem No. 502; fall 1839

Autumn Days

The winds are out with loud increasing shout,
Where late before them walked the biting frost;
Whirling the leaves in their wild sport about,
And strewing twig and limb our path acrost;
But still the sun looks kindly on the year,   5
And days of summer warmth will linger yet;
And still the birds amid the fields we hear,
For the ripe grain and scattered seeds they get;
The shortening days grow slowly less and less,
And winter comes with many a warning on;   10

And still some day with kindly smile will bless,
Till the last hope's deceit is fledged and gone;
Before the deepening snows block up the way,
And the sweet fields are made of howling blasts the prey.

Poem No. 595; fall 1839

Autumn Leaves

The leaves though thick are falling; one by one
Decayed they drop from off their parent tree;
Their work with autumn's latest day is done,
Thou see'st them borne upon its breezes free;
They lie strown here and there, their many dyes   5
That yesterday so caught thy passing eye;
Soiled by the rain each leaf neglected lies,
Upon the path where now thou hurriest by;
Yet think thee not their beauteous tints less fair,
Than when they hung so gaily o'er thy head;   10
But rather find thee eyes, and look thee there
Where now thy feet so heedless o'er them tread;
And thou shalt see where wasting now they lie,
The unseen hues of immortality.

Poem No. 519; fall 1839

The Lost Sheep

Though many, many sheep I have,
   I leave them all to find the one
That high upon the mountain strays;
   And think'st thou not I well have done?

For all are His who gave them me,   5
   And bade with closest watching keep,
Nor suffer one, however poor,
   To wander from his numerous sheep.

Hast thou e'er kept them? then wilt thou
    A brother in affliction know;   10
And if the lost one thou hast seen
    Wilt point him where his feet should go.

And when restored each one shall be,
    With joy our flocks we'll homeward lead;
For He who lent them but a day,   15
    Will give us always them to feed.

Poem No. 707; fall 1839

The Shepherd's Life

My flocks hadst thou e'er seen them, where they feed
    Upon the hills and flowery-vestured plains;
And heard me pipe to them on Shepherd's reed,
    Then would'st thou leave fore'er thy sordid gains;

And haste thee where the streams so gently flow,   5
    Where sounding pines and rocks above me rise;
And seek this quiet life of mine to know,
    And learn its simple joys with me to prize.

How quietly the morning melts away
    Into the noon, while on the grass I lie;   10
And noon fades quickly into evening gray,
    When troop the stars across the o'erhanging sky.

Here day by day I know, nor want, nor care,
    For all I need has love paternal given;
And bid me bounteous all its blessings share,   15
    And know on earth the bliss of those in heaven.

Thine be the Shepherd's life, his cot be thine,
    And may'st thou sit beside him at his board;
Then wilt thou cease to sorrow, or repine,
    And to the peace Christ gave him be restored.   20

Poem No. 337; fall 1839

The Good Samaritan

There journeyed from the south a man,
　　To one whom in the north he'd seen;
And many a river's tide rolled on,
　　And many a city rose between.

At first he travelled hard and strong,　　　　　　　　5
　　For to his friend his heart was bound;
But slow and slower grew his pace,
　　And many a resting place he found.

At last forgot he him he loved,
　　And that he e'er was journeying there;　　　　　10
They called him friend whom he had met,
　　And bade with them their living share.

But soon another journeyed by,
　　To seek the friend that first he sought;
He tarried not, though tempted much,　　　　　　　15
　　Nor could from his first love be bought.

Still on he held his noble way,
　　And he who had forgot his end;
Gained strength as he beheld him walk,
　　And rose and found with him his friend.　　　　20

Poem No. 632; fall 1839

The Birds of Passage

Whence comes those many-colored birds,
　　That fill with songs each field and bower;
When Winter's blasts their force have spent,
　　And spring to summer brings her dower.

I've watched them, but I know not whence　　　　5
　　With voices all-attuned they fly;
'Tis from some distant, unknown land,
　　Some sunnier clime and fairer sky.

And these the notes they bring to tell,
 Of that unseen and distant home;   10
To tempt us who are living here,
 With them when winter comes to roam.

Had I but wings I would not stay,
 When chilling cold I feel him near;
But with them journeying there I'd fly,   15
 That unknown land of which I hear.

Poem No. 799; fall 1839

The Feast

The hour of noon is fully come,
 Yet none of all I ask'd are here;
And now it grows towards the eve,
 Still none arrive to taste my cheer.

I asked them all; the rich, the poor,   5
 For all are welcome to my board;
But none will be my guests to day,
 And eat of what my stores afford.

One, busy, is at home detained;
 Another hies him to his farm;   10
Some other day a third would suit;
 For each there's something else to charm.

But still my house shall be o'erflowed!
 And they who were not honored first
Will come when I my servants send,   15
And at my table quench their thirst.

But they who scorned my offered feast,
 Shall eat of what their hearts now choose;
 'Till they will learn to live with me,
And share the meat that they refuse.   20

Poem No. 512; fall 1839

The Ramble

The plants that careless grow shall flower and bud,
When wilted stands man's nicely tended flower;
E'en on the unsheltered waste, or pool's dark mud,
Spring bells and lilies fit for ladies' bower;
Come with me, I will show you where they grow;   5
The tangled vines and boughs come push aside;
O'er yonder hill top's craggy side we go,
Then by the path beyond we downward slide;
See by yond pond where few but travellers pass,
Each lily opens wide its curious cup;   10
And here where now we track the unmown grass,
The wild-heath bell surprised is looking up,
To view the strangers that thus far have sought
The flowers that in fair nature's robe are wrought.

Poem No. 541; fall 1839

The Barberry Bush

The bush which bears most briars, and bitter fruit,
Wait till the frost has turned its green leaves red,
Its sweetened berries will thy palate suit,
And thou may'st find, e'en there, a homely bread.
Upon the hills of Salem, scattered wide,   5
Their yellow blossoms gain the eye in Spring;
And straggling down upon the turnpike's side,
Their ripened bunches to your hand they bring.
I've plucked them oft in boyhood's early hour,
What then I gave such name, and thought it true;   10
But now I know, that other fruit, as sour,
Grows on what now thou callest *Me,* and *You;*
Yet, wilt thou wait the Autumn that I see,
'Twill sweeter taste than these red berries be.

Poem No. 475; fall 1839

The Hand and the Foot

The hand and foot that stir not, they shall find
Sooner than all the rightful place to go;
Now in their motion free as roving wind,
Though first no snail so limited and slow;
I mark them full of labor all the day,   5
Each active motion made in perfect rest;
They cannot from their path mistaken stray,
Though 'tis not theirs, yet in it they are blest;
The bird has not their hidden track found out,
Nor cunning fox though full of art he be;   10
It is the way unseen, the certain route,
Where ever bound, yet thou art ever free;
The path of Him, whose perfect law of love
Bids spheres and atoms in just order move.

Poem No. 505; fall 1839

The Eye and Ear

Thou readest, but each lettered word can give
Thee but the sound that thou first gave to it;
Thou lookest on the page, things move and live
In light thine eye and thine alone has lit;
Ears are there yet unstopped, and eyes unclosed,   5
That see and hear as in one common day;
When they which present see have long reposed,
And he who hears has mouldered too to clay;
These ever see and hear; they are in Him,
Who speaks, and all is light; how dark before!   10
Each object throws aside its mantle dim,
That hid the starry robe that once it wore;
And shines full-born disclosing all that is,
Itself by all things seen and owned as His.

Poem No. 690; fall 1839

The Sunset

When left the sun the distant west,
   Still lingering there appears his light;
So when a spirit leaves the world,
   Its sunset rays will point its flight.

None leave it now; their suns still stand   5
   Yet high above the horizon's bound;
No rays e'er come from other skies,
   To show another world they've found.

If thou hast seen one die from earth,
   Mark well his path along the sky;   10
And when his orb sinks from thy gaze,
   Still on the west keep fixed thine eye;

And follow on; nor doubt the beams
   That upward shoot shall lead thee on;
To where a sun he'll ever blaze,   15
   Nor light come back to mark him gone.

Poem No. 790; fall 1839

Yourself

'Tis to yourself I speak; you cannot know
Him whom I call in speaking such an one,
For thou beneath the earth liest buried low,
Which he alone as living walks upon;
Thou mayst at times have heard him speak to you,   5
And often wished perchance that you were he;
And I must ever wish that it were true,
For then thou couldst hold fellowship with me;
But now thou hearst us talk as strangers, met
Above the room wherein thou liest abed;   10
A word perhaps loud spoken thou mayst get,
Or hear our feet when heavily they tread;
But he who speaks, or him who's spoken to,
Must both remain as strangers still to you.

Poem No. 733; fall 1839

Thy Better Self

I am thy other self, what thou wilt be,
When thou art I, the one thou seest now;
In finding thy true self thou wilt find me,
The springing blade, where now thou dost but plough.
I am thy neighbor, a new house I've built,   5
Which thou as yet hast never entered in;
I come to call thee; come in when thou wilt,
The feast is always ready to begin.
Thou should'st love me, as thou dost love thyself,
For I am but another self beside;   10
To show thee him thou lov'st in better health,
What thou would'st be, when thou to him hast died;
Then visit me, I make thee many a call;
Nor live I near to thee alone, but all.

Poem No. 210; fall 1839

The Glutton

The bread thou eatest thou canst never know,
That sums untold could never buy thee such;
Or to thy Father's board thou wouldst not go,
With hasty hands his gifts as now to clutch;
The bread thus eaten, it can never feed;   5
Save the lost life that thus in haste is stole;
Thou drinkest, but of more must soon have need;
'Tis not the fount of life that fills the bowl;
Thou art not there where spreads the kind repast,
But thine own will is guest where thou shouldst be;   10
And that which was but born in thee to fast,
Has bid thee serve that should from bonds be free;
And thou a servant wait'st where thou mightst sit,
While sin's foul carrion-bird upon thy dish has lit.

Poem No. 470; fall 1839

The Day not for Gain

When comes the sun to visit thee at morn,
Art thou prepared to give him welcome then?
Or is the day, that with his light is born,
With thee, a day that has already been.
Hast thou filled up its yet unnumbered hours   5
With selfish thoughts, and made them now thine own?
Then not for thee will bloom its budding flowers,
The day, to thee, has past, and onward flown.
The noon may follow with its quickening heat,
The grain grow yellow in its ripening rays;   10
And dusky evening mark the noon's retreat,
Yet thou as dead to them live all thy days;
For thou hast made of God's free gifts a gain,
And would'st the sovereign Day, a slave, in bonds retain.

Poem No. 784; fall 1839

The World

The end of all thou seest is near,
    The world that looks so wide and high,
Shall vanish like the melting cloud,
    Nor smallest spot will meet thine eye.

But thou must bid its vesture change,   5
    And ope another eye within;
The spirit calls thee, haste! arise!
    Awake thee from the death of sin!

Thou sow'st not now what will appear,
    But the bare grain of wrong desire;   10
Soon this shall moulder in decay,
    And then thy new-brought form admire.

Then shall thine eye behold the world,
    From which at first the spirit fell;
And kindred never known before,   15
    In numbers more than words can tell.

Then haste to close that outward eye,
    And stop thee soon thine earthly ear;
And thou shalt walk a child of light,
    And him who breaks thy slumbers hear.   20

Poem No. 493; fall 1839

The House Not Made With Hands, Eternal In The Heavens

There is a house not built with hands,
    Where all who enter shall abide;
Above where eye can reach it stands,
    Whence all depart, who here have died.

Beneath, it rests on many a gem,   5
    Dug from the heart's deep, darkest mine;
Thou who art toiling now for them,
    Shalt see them there in radiance shine.

Of gold the floor, the gold of love,
    Thrice in affliction's fire made pure;   10
There feet of angels ever move,
    There dwell the just in peace secure.

The light is brighter than the day,
    Reflected from its crystal walls;
Thou see'st at times a glimmering ray,   15
    Which to its courts thy spirit calls.

And thou shalt dwell, and worship there,
    When thou hast put thy garment on;
The Savior doth that house prepare,
    There all the pure in heart have gone.   20

Poem No. 613; fall 1839

The Broken Bowl

The fountain flows, but where the bowl
  To catch from heaven the living stream;
That ever shall refresh the soul,
  And make life's ills a passing dream?

'Tis broken at the cistern, broke;   5
  Its waters spilled upon the ground;
The words of old, the preacher spoke,
  I too their truth like him have found.

Prepare, prepare new vessels still,
  Though broken fragments round thee lie;   10
Thou must from hence thy pitcher fill,
  And often drink, or thou wilt die.

Behold the Rock, that smitten gave
  To Israel on the burning sand,
Life, in its cool, refreshing wave;   15
  'Twill flow when smitten by thy hand.

Ho all that thirst! come, drink ye all!
  The fountain pours its waters free;
Come, heed the prophet's early call,
  Fashion new bowls and draw with me.   20

Poem No. 501; late 1839

The Bunch of Flowers

I saw a bunch of flowers, and Time
  With withered hand was plucking one;
I wondering asked him as I passed,
  For what the thing I saw was done.

My gifts are these, the flowers you see;   5
  For her who comes I hold this rose;
I looked; the nurse held out her child,
  Just wakened from its sweet repose.

Its small hand clasped the prize with joy,
　　Each seemed the other to the eye;　　　　　　10
But soon the flowers' bright leaves were strown,
　　And while I gazed a youth came by.

The flower Time gave to him he held,
　　And more admired; and kept awhile;
Yet as I watched him on his way,　　　　　　　15
　　'Twas dropped e'er he had paced a mile.

Man kept it longer; 'twas to him a gift,
　　And with it long was loathe to part;
But as he journeyed on I saw
　　The rose lay withered on his heart.　　　　　20

One aged came; still he received Time's gift;
　　But as he took it heaved a sigh;
It dropt from out his trembling grasp,
　　And at Time's feet his offering lie.

Then knew I none could bear away the flower,　　25
　　That Time on each and all bestows;
Nor would I take his gift when he,
　　To me in turn held out a rose.

Poem No. 254; late 1839

Hymn
Home

I sought my home;—an earthly guide
　　First led me to a house of wood;
And there he told me to abide,
　　Content with shelter, rest, and food.

But He who teaches all the way,　　　　　　　5
　　Oft from my dwelling turned my feet;
And when my heart would backward stray,
　　Did my fond purpose still defeat.

Long time I wandered;—still the voice
    Forbade me, where I wished, to go;   10
Till I would yield to it my choice,
    And only of its leading know.

Then I no longer sought my home,
    For where I was, 'twas there to me;
Nor could I ever wish to roam,   15
    My bonds were broke, and I was free.

Hast thou not found thy dwelling yet,
    Then leave the guide, whose eyes are blind;
And thou shalt earth's frail house forget,
    And God's own habitation find.   20

Poem No. 271; late 1839

The Ghost

There passes by at dead of night,
    When thou in sleep's embrace art lost;
One never seen by mortal sight,
    And whom no mortal may accost.

His hand unheard tries every door,   5
    If he an entrance there can win;
But still asleep he hears men snore,
    And few rise up to let him in.

But if he finds one watching still,
    His door unbarred though late the hour;   10
With untold wealth that house he'll fill,
    For he o'er riches holds the power.

And health and plenty crown his lot,
    Whose board long waits that stranger guest;
Who weary will not seek his cot,   15
    Till he beside him there can rest.

Poem No. 633; late 1839

The Seasons

I will not call it Spring for me
    Till every leaf I've seen,
And every springing blade of grass,
    Has its last touch of green;
Till every blossom I can count,   5
    Upon the budding bough;
Then will I call it spring for me,
    I cannot see it now.

I will not call the Summer come,
    Till every blade shall fall   10
Beneath the mower's swinging scythe,
    The low grass and the tall;
Till where each red and white bud stood,
    Hangs fruit for autumn's hand;
But yet I cannot say 'tis here,   15
    And I will waiting stand.

I will not say that Autumn's hour
    Is come, is come to me,
Till every apple ripened hangs
    Upon the loaded tree;   20
Till every flower that's owned of Spring,
    Where'er my path shall lead,
Shall shake and rattle in the wind
    Its stalk and cherished seed.

Then will I say that Winter's near,   25
    But not that he is found;
Till deep the snows have buried all
    The fields and trees around;
And every rippling brook that runs
    To water grove and flower,   30
I see lie stiffened by his breath,
    And hushed beneath his power.

Poem No. 284; late 1839

The Silent

There is a sighing in the wood,
A murmur in the beating wave,
The heart has never understood
To tell in words the thoughts they gave.

Yet oft it feels an answering tone,   5
When wandering on the lonely shore;
And could the lips its voice make known,
'Twould sound as does the ocean's roar.

And oft beneath the wind swept pine,
Some chord is struck the strain to swell;   10
Nor sounds nor language can define,
'Tis not for words or sounds to tell.

'Tis all unheard; that Silent Voice,
Whose goings forth, unknown to all,
Bids bending reed and bird rejoice,   15
And fills with music nature's hall.

And in the speechless human heart
It speaks, where'er man's feet have trod;
Beyond the lip's deceitful art,
To tell of Him, the Unseen God.   20

Poem No. 614; late 1839

The Way

To good thou ask'st the way—enter the street,
This is the broad high-way that many tread;
Go follow him whom first thine eye shall meet,
Here is his store, go in; behold thy bread;
Thou turn'st away; well, follow him whose ship   5
Has just returned deep-laden from afar;
Look, see his face how gladdened at the trip.
Is there aught here the good thou seek'st to mar?
Still as thou trackest one and all thou find'st it not;
Then learn that *all* are seekers here below;   10

And let the lesson never be forgot,
That none the path to happiness can show,
Save He whose way is hidden; only known
To those who seek his love, and his alone.

Poem No. 737; late 1839

The Sun

Where has the sun a home? didst thou e'er trace
His course when sinking in the distant west,
And see him there begin anew his race,
As if of new-born strength again possest?
Or didst thou leave him in the western skies,   5
Where late his setting glories called thee on;
Nor follow on with still admiring eyes,
Another earth to bless where he has gone?
Stay not where night shuts in on all who sleep,
Faint travellers on the path he onward trod;   10
But on his beams a waking eye still keep,
The daily herald sent to thee from God;
And thou when many suns thy year has known,
Shall rise with him his brightness all thine own.

Poem No. 803; late 1839

The Worm

I saw a worm, with many a fold,
  It spun itself a silken tomb;
And there in winter time enrolled,
  It heeded not the cold or gloom.

Within a small, snug nook it lay,   5
  Nor snow nor sleet could reach it there,
Nor wind was felt in gusty day,
  Nor biting cold of frosty air.

Spring comes with bursting buds and grass,
Around him stirs a warmer breeze;
The chirping insects by him pass,
His hiding place not yet he leaves.

But summer came, its fervid breath,
Was felt within the sleeper's cell;
And waking from his sleep of death,
I saw him crawl from out his shell.

Slow and with pain it first moved on,
And of the dust it seemed to be;
A day passed by; the worm was gone,
It soared on golden pinions free.

Poem No. 257; late 1839

The Watcher

He comes at dead of night, when all asleep
Are sunk in nature's most profound repose;
No eye can then its watchful vigil keep,
Nor hears there one, though loud HIS frequent blows;
I was a Watcher, whom the hours o'ercame,
And heavy slumber weighed my eyelids down;
A sleep like death oppressed my weary frame,
I fell, a traitor to my own renown;
Yet HE who called me, HE was faithful still;
I heard at length HIS knocking loud and long,
And hastened then my dying lamp to fill,
And ope the door with bolts and hinges strong;
That he who bid me wake might enter in,
And I anew with him the watch begin.

Poem No. 160a; late 1839?

The Physician

There is a body, every joint and limb
    Is still, yet moves by God's all-holy law;
The eye turns here and there, yet turns in him,
    The ear no sound but his own words can draw;
Its voice the long-stopped ear obedient hears,   5
    The withered hand outstretched its bidding owns,
And they who mourn the dead dry up their tears,
    The prison walls hear not their captive's groans;
Through the wide world of living death it brings
    A new-born life wherever it walks abroad;   10
Such as beneath the feet of *M*ay up springs
    When forth she steps where Winter late has trod;
And at her coming starts the palsied year,
    That slumbers on though summer months are near.

Poem No. 611a; late 1839?

The Miser

How much there is within this rich abode,
    Thou pass'st uncared for by and call'st it thine;
Forever straying from the narrow road,
    'Mid heaven's own joys, yet still for heaven to pine;
The light that comes to thee thou had'st before;   5
    The gold shines not within the miser's hand,
But he already sighs to have yet more;
    What thou just gave him,—'twas his house and land;
Turn where thou wilt,—alas! where canst thou turn,
    Who goest before as though already there;—   10
Turn where thou wilt, thou dost each blessing spurn;
    Who cares for nought how little feels he care,
Though all the day sweet angels hovering near,
    Are sent his onward path with their glad news to cheer.

Poem No. 194a; late 1839?

The Spheres

The brightness round the rising sun,
   It shall be thine if thou wilt rise;
Thou too hast thine own race to run,
   And pour thy light on waiting eyes.

The expectant millions eager turn,   5
   Oft when thy coming streaks the east;
And ask when shall his glory burn,
   Aloft to mid-day's light increased.

And star on star when thine has lit
   The o'erhanging dome of earth's wide heaven,   10
Shall rise, for as by Him 'tis writ,
   Who to each sun its path has given.

And all with thine, each wheeling sphere
   In ways harmonious on shall move;
Tracing with golden bounds the year   15
   Of the Great Parent's endless love.

Poem No. 471; late 1839–early 1840

The Builders

There are who wish to build their houses strong,
Yet of the earth material they will take;
And hope the brick, within the fire burnt long,
A lasting home for them, and theirs will make.

And one, who thought him wiser than the rest,   5
Of the firm granite hewed his dwelling proud;
And all who passed this eagle's lofty nest
Praised his secure retreat from tempests loud.

They built for Time; and Time reclaimed his own,
Their palaces he toppled to the ground;   10
By grass and moss their ruins were o'ergrown,
I looked for them, but they could not be found.

But one I knew who sought him out no wood,
No brick, nor stone, though as the others born;
And those who passed, where waiting still he stood,   15
Made light of him, and laughed his hopes to scorn.

And Time went by, and he was waiting still;
No house had he, and seemed to need one less;
He felt that waiting yet his master's will
Was the best shelter in this wilderness.   20

And I beheld the rich man, and the wise,
When lapsing years fell heavy on each shed;
As one by one they fled, in lonely guise,
To this poor man for refuge, and for bread.

Poem No. 610; late 1839–early 1840

Give and it shall be given unto you.
Spiritual Debtors

I was heavy-laden, grieving,
    Prest to earth with sense of woe;
When a voice, my grief relieving,
    Sounded thus in accents low:

Every man that's now thy debtor,   5
    Shall his debt to thee repay;
Shall restore e'en to the letter,
    All thy spirit gives away.

Old and young—the man grey-headed,
    And the boy with nimble tread;   10
They that to the world are wedded,
    All that now by thee are fed.

They, how much shall they return thee,
    Crowded measures running o'er;
All that now in spirit owe thee,   15
    Grieve my child, then grieve no more.

Poem No. 283; late 1839–early 1840

The Laborers

The workman shall not always work; who builds,
His house shall finish with the last-raised stone;
The last small measure full the vessel fills;
The last step taken and thy journey's done;
But where is he, who but one hour ago,   5
Lifted with toiling arm the burthen nigh;
And he whose vessel to the brim did flow,
Or he who laid his staff and sandals by?
I see them still at work another way,
From those that late thou sawest thus employed;   10
And heard them each unto the other say,
As to new tasks they bent them overjoyed,
"The sun is rising, haste! that he may see,
When setting, every hand from labor free."

Poem No. 605; late 1839–early 1840

The Unfaithful Servants

Thou hast no other hands than those that toil,
In other tasks than what thou giv'st them now;
For these thou hast the others' work but spoil,
They idly tear the ground that these would plough;
They have been long employed, and learnt them arts,   5
The others know and yet were never taught;
False actors saying to themselves their parts,
Till they the gait and living tone have caught;
'Tis but a show, these buildings that they rear,
Card-fabrics overblown with every breath;   10
Their mightiest labor, things that but appear;
An out-seen world; begat of thee by death,
When first thine eye began to cease to see,
And made; when first thy hand forgot a hand to be.

Poem No. 679; late 1839–early 1840

The Thieves

The night was dark and I alone,
    When midnight's stillest hours begin;
There smote my door a heavy stone,
    And one for plunder broke within.

He took whate'er I valued high,   5
    My books, and often-counted gold;
Nor heeded he my strength or cry,
    For I was young, and he was old.

My neighbors in the morning came,
    Who long had taught me they were mine,   10
And too a better life laid claim;
    And bade me not for them repine.

For they would all restore to me,
    The thief last night had stole away;
And brought these books, this gold you see,   15
    Far more than he had made his prey.

Yet I would not their offerings take,
    For they who learned me so to live,
That I such gifts mine own would make,
    But rob me more the more they give.   20

Poem No. 533; late 1839–early 1840

The Strangers

Each care-worn face is but a book
    To tell of houses bought or sold;
Or filled with words that men have took
    From those who lived and spoke of old.

I see none whom I know, for they   5
    See other things than him they meet;
And though they stop me by the way,
    'Tis still some other one to greet.

There are no words that reach my ear,
   Those speak who tell of other things   10
Than what they mean for me to hear,
   For in their speech the counter rings.

I would be where each word is true,
   Each eye sees what it looks upon;
For here my eye has seen but few,   15
   Who in each act that act have done.

Poem No. 102; late 1839–early 1840

The Light from Within

I saw on earth another light
   Than that which lit my eye;
Come forth as from my soul within,
   And from a higher sky.

Its beams shone still unclouded on,   5
   When in the farthest west
The sun I once had known had sunk
   Forever to his rest.

And on I walked though dark the night
   Nor rose his orb by day,   10
As one who by a surer guide
   Was pointed out the way.

'Twas brighter far than noon-day's beam,
   It shone from God within;
And lit as by a lamp from heaven   15
   The world's dark track of sin.

Poem No. 259; late 1839–early 1840

Thou know'st not what thy Lord will say,
He knows thee and not thou him
And tho' unseen thou wert He
Can still thy every action see

While thou wert busy here and there   5
So He was here and he is gone
Thou oft has time enough to spare
But He thy Lord and Master now.

Then quickly do the thing thou doest
And quickly speak the flying word   10
Nor to thyself a moment trust
For he who trusts himself is weak

Poem No. 683; late 1839–early 1840

The Good

The useful and the sweet the fair and true
    Do grow together the same plant always
From truth, the root, the flower puts forth in view
    With scent and beauty the design to praise.

And good the earth or wave that deep or thin   5
    Gives all to all yet nothing takes away
Itself Itself forever holds within
    The unfolded whole of all that can decay

For Truth and Beauty are but tree or plant
    And that we eat but fruit, and smell but flowers   10
The spirit cannot things of earth of long want
    It dwells not in Time's autumn fading bowers

But there where all in all the hand, the face
    And breath like fragrance mingling with the air
Reveals a form that Perfect Love will trace   15
    The Holy One within the House of Prayer.

Poem No. 586; late 1839–early 1840

The Distant

How far hast thou travelled? Though many thy years,
    And many a day thou hast seen to its close;
Hast thou seen to their end all thy hopes and thy fears,
    Or found where the sun has gone to repose?

The still-growing leaf that thy door springs beside,   5
    Hast thou seen whence it draws all its bright tints of green?
Or found where the rain or the swift wind can hide,
    Or traced to their deep the cloud's colored screen?

Nay, has thy sight followed the fire's warm heat
    That burns on thy hearth on the cold winter's day?   10
Or gone with the flame to its hidden retreat
    When thy lamp in the midnight shoots up its last ray?

Thine eye is but dim if thou hast not found the home
    Of these thy companions in journeying here;
Thy feet to the earth's farthest borders may roam,   15
    Nor thou to the end of life's path be more near.

Poem No. 184; late 1839–early 1840

A Word

The silent history of a word,
    Borne on Time's stream along,
Has never yet been sung or heard,
    It asks the voice of song.

'Twas born from the soul's calm deep,   5
    Smit by the chastening rod;
As Eve, flesh-formed from Adam's sleep,
    Touched by the hand of God.

It wandered o'er the unyielding earth,
    By war and famine worn,   10
A stranger seen, of unknown birth;
    Though night, a child of morn.

'Twas welcomed in the lowly cot,
    'Twas heard in kingly hall;
And men their arms and strife forgot,   15
    In listening to its call.

It told of peace that would not fail,
    Of love that could not die;
'Twas felt beneath the warrior's mail,
    It dried the mourner's eye.   20

I looked along the path it took,
    As told by legends old
Repeated oft from book to book;
    It shone as shining gold.

A furrow through earth's barren field,   25
    Ploughed deep, and sown with care;
But none to notice what it yields,
    Or in its harvest share.

Poem No. 561; early 1840

The Settler

When thou art done thy toil, anew art born;
With hands that never touched the spade or plough,
Nor in the furrows strewed the yellow corn,
Or plucked the ripened fruit from off the bough:
Then shall thou work begin;—thy plough and spade   5
Shall break at early morn the virgin soil;
The swelling hill and thickly wooded glade
With changing aspect own the daily toil;
Thy house shall strike the eye, where none are near,
For thou hast travelled far, where few have trod;   10
And those who journey hence will taste thy cheer,
And bless thee as a favored one of God;
For He it was who in this pathless wild,
Upon thy good intent so richly smiled.

Poem No. 795; early 1840?

The Dwellings of the Just

I saw the dwellings of the Just,
   No sun was in their sky;
Nor candle lit their rooms by night,
   They saw without an eye.

They walked upright as fearing none,   5
   Each step so true they trod;
They moved as those who had been taught
   The perfect law of God.

All day they labored, yet at rest,
   As in His sight who lives;   10
Who to each one his rightful place,
   And rightful portion gives.

And shadowy night was blessed to them,
   As His who gives the day;
And sweet the sleep it brought to these,   15
   Whose joy was to obey.

Poem No. 263; early 1840?

Death

Men live and die in secret; none can see
When going out or lighting up the flame,
Save the all-seeing eye;—frail mortals, we
Call death and life what are but so in name;
Death is that shunning Him who bids thee die,   5
Which thou but disobedience learnst to call;
Words cannot hide thee from the searching eye,
That sees thy corse beneath their sable pall;
And life the lifting up that thou dost feel,
When thy feet follow where he bids thee go;   10
A life beyond disease, or severing steel,
That nought but him who gives it, fears below;
This be thy life, and death shall flee away,
For thou hast learned for ever to obey.

Poem No. 327; early 1840?

The Birth-Day of the Soul

The birth-day of the Soul how sweet its dawn!
It comes to me, and yet for all it is;
Upon the skies its colored form is drawn,
The green earth says 'tis hers, the sea 'tis his;
The voice of feathered tribes thick-swarming tell   5
The day is born to fields and waiting grove,
The meadow's song and forest's rising swell
Are heard by gladsome winds that o'er them rove.
'Tis music all;—but higher song than these
Bears witness also to the day's glad birth;   10
They but the ear of sense a moment please;
The song I hear is not of sense, or earth;
But such as waiting angels joyful sing,
When from its wanderings home a soul they bring.

Poem No. 465; early 1840?

The Bee Hive

The hive the honey-bee has found,
    With loaded wings and heavy sides;
Stands in a garden fenced around,
    Where she called Industry resides.

In and out her menials fly   5
    On their journeys one by one,
As she sends them far and nigh
    Telling each what must be done.

Are there flowers on crag or dell
    Overladen with their sweets,   10
Quick the humming insects tell
    Heard within their wild retreats.

Do they bloom on open field,
    Or the sheltered walks of men;
Not the humblest is concealed,   15
    There her messengers have been.

All the day in quiet haste
　　Thus they do their mistress' will,
Suffering not a drop to waste
　　That may go her hive to fill.

Poem No. 511; early 1840?

Time's House

The stones of time's old house with pelting storms,
That on it long have beat from day to day,
Are loose; the door is gone, and smoke deforms
The boards within and walls of plastered clay;
Long have his children strove to keep it whole;
By many a wile he's taught them to make good,
The waste that creeping years have from it stole,
And long its walls the ruin have withstood;
But now within and out the storms assail.
Its beams rock to and fro with every gust;
And fears o'er cherished hopes at last prevail,
Nor longer to its threatening roof they'll trust;
But cease to patch each rent with jealous care,
And learn at last to live beneath the open air.

Poem No. 575; early 1840?

The Fox and the Bird

The bird that has no nest,
　　The Fox that has no hole;
He's wiser than the rest,
　　Her eggs are never stole.

She builds where none can see,
　　He hides where none can find;
The bird can rest where'er she be,
　　He freely moves as wind.

Thou hast not found her little young,
   E'en though thou'st sought them long;   10
Though from thine earliest day they've sung,
   Thou hast not heard their song.

Thou hast not found that Fox's brood,
   That nestle under ground;
Though through all time his burrow's stood,   15
   His whelps thou'st never found.

Poem No. 463; early 1840?

Faith and Light

The comings on of Faith,
   The goings out of Light;
Are as the brightening of the morn,
   And dying of the night.

Man tells not of the hour,   5
   By Him alone 'tis told;
Who day and night with certain bounds,
   Marked out for him of old!

The singing of the bird,
   And sinking of her strain;   10
The roar of ocean's storm-lashed waves,
   And lull; the date retain.

The fading of the leaf,
   And blending of each hue;
The hour still hold in truth,   15
   When change the old and new.

There's nought in nature's hymn,
   Of earth, or sea, or sky;
But tells, forever tells, the time,
   When birth to death is nigh.   20

Poem No. 480; early 1840?

The Word

The Word where is it? hath it voice,
    That I may hear it and be free;
Hath it a form, that I may know;
    A touch, that I may feel; and see?

Where does it dwell? above, below?   5
    Or is it where e'en now I tread?
I would be near it when it calls,
    And bids awake the slumbering dead.

'Tis near me; yet I hear it not—
    —That voice that cometh down from heaven—   10
And hide myself in shrinking fear,
    When wide above the earth is riven.

Oh strengthen in me faith to rise,
    And go where'er it leads the way;
That I may live with it as one,   15
    And all that it commands obey.

Poem No. 602; early 1840?

The Absent

Thou art not yet at home in thine own house,
But to one room I see thee now confined;
Having one hole like rat or skulking mouse,
And as a mole to all the others blind;
Does the great Day find preference when he shines   5
In at each window lighting every room?
No selfish wish the moon's bright glance confines,
And each in turn the stars' faint rays illume;
Within thy sleeping room thou dost abide,
And thou the social parlor dost prefer;   10
Another thou wilt in the cupboard hide,
And this or that's the room for him or her;
But the same sun, and moon with silver face
Look in on all, and lighten every place.

Poem No. 661; early 1840?

The Pilgrim

'Twas in the winter at the close of day,
The snow fell deep upon the traveller's path,
I saw one journeying on infirm and grey
Yet seemed he not to heed the tempest's wrath;
And oft a citizen would ask him in   5
And sit him down beside him at his board,
Yet soon his weary march would he begin
As if he felt not by the food restored;
I wondering asked him, why he tarried not
To taste the cheer they had so freely given;   10
And why the sheltering roof he had forgot?
He nothing said; but pointed up to heaven;—
And then I knew the food they gave away,
And home they offered were but for a day.

Poem No. 748; early 1840?

The Idler

I idle stand that I may find employ,
Such as my Master when He comes will give;
I cannot find in mine own work my joy,
But wait, although in waiting I must live;
My body shall not turn which way it will,   5
But stand till I the appointed road can find,
And journeying so his messages fulfill,
And do at every step the work designed.
Enough for me, still day by day to wait
Till Thou who form'st me find'st me too a task;   10
A cripple lying at the rich man's gate,
Content for the few crumbs I get to ask;
A laborer but in heart, while bound my hands
Hang idly down still waiting thy commands.

Poem No. 239; late 1838–early 1840

The Lost

The fairest day that ever yet has shone,
Will be when thou the day within shalt see;
The fairest rose that ever yet has blown,
When thou the flower thou lookest on shalt be.
But thou art far away among Time's toys;   5
Thyself the day thou lookest for in them,
Thyself the flower that now thine eye enjoys,
But wilted now thou hang'st upon thy stem.
The bird thou hearest on the budding tree,
Thou hast made sing with thy forgotten voice;   10
But when it swells again to melody,
The song is thine in which thou wilt rejoice;
And thou new risen 'midst these wonders live,
That now to them dost all thy substance give.

Poem No. 495; late 1838–early 1840

The Narrow Way

Where this one dwells and that, thou know'st it well,
Each earthly neighbor and each earthly friend;
But He who calls thee has no place to dwell,
And canst thou then thine all unto Him lend?
Canst thou a stranger be, where now well known;   5
Where now thou oftenest go'st, go nevermore,
But walk the world thenceforth thy way alone,
Broadening the path but little worn before?
Then may'st thou find me, when thou 't faint and weak,
And the strait road seems narrower still to grow;   10
For I will words of comfort to thee speak,
And onward with thee to my home I'll go,
Where thou shalt find a rest in labor sweet,
No friend and yet a friend in all to greet.

Poem No. 807; late 1838–early 1840

The True Light

The morning's brightness cannot make thee glad,
If thou art not more bright than it within;
And nought of evening's peace hast thou e'er had,
If evening first did not with thee begin.
Full many a sun I saw first set and rise,   5
Before my day had found a rising too;
And I with Nature learned to harmonize,
And to her times and seasons made me true.
How fair that new May morning when I rose
Companion of the sun for all the day;   10
O'er every hill and field where now he goes,
With him to pass, nor fear again to stray;
But 'neath the full-orbed moon's reflected light
Still onward keep my way till latest night.

Poem No. 531; late 1838-early 1840

The Invitation

Stay where thou art, thou need'st not further go,
The flower with me is pleading at thy feet;
The clouds, the silken clouds, above me flow,
And fresh the breezes come thy cheek to greet.
Why hasten on;—hast thou a fairer home?   5
Has God more richly blest the world than here,
That thou in haste would'st from thy country roam,
Favored by every month that fills the year?
Sweet showers shall on thee here, as there, descend;
The sun salute thy morn and gild thy eve: 10
Come, tarry here, for Nature is thy friend,
And we an arbor for ourselves will weave;
And many a pilgrim, journeying on as thou,
Will grateful bless its shade, and list the wind-struck bough.

Poem No. 433; late 1838-early 1840

The Sick

Where thou hast been once well received,
There thou shouldst often go again;
That so, of every want relieved,
Joy may find birth in buried pain.
I knew one, but his heart was weak,   5
Who went when keen was sorrow's smart;
And well a moment, would not seek
The hand that touched with healing art;
I knew another; he was wise;
Nor felt he of his wounds made strong,   10
Till he could from his couch arise,
And walk with him who cured along:
Which art thou, friend? for oft the first
Will call the better one the worst.

Poem No. 808; late 1838-early 1840

The Flesh

The Flesh bears early fruit; most eat of it,
And many die who eat e'en that too soon;
They fade like flowers the morning's sunbeam lit,
But wilted fall before the heat of noon;
Behold the friends and children born to be   5
But blossoms overtaken by the frost;
Put forth ere in the limbs the sap ran free,
Or spring gave signs that winter's strength was lost;
See houses fires and creeping age consume,
And fields the weed and thistle boast as theirs;   10
These, blazing up, the night's dark face illume,
And those, the garden whence they reap but tares.
Alas! how soon have vanished those the eye
Looked fondly on; green fields and houses high!

Poem No. 497; late 1838–early 1840

Decay

Disease that on thy body feeds
   Is but decay beneath the ground,
That slowly eats the buried seeds,
   That green above they may be found.

Thou canst not live, save the low earth   5
   Be quickened by the sun and rain,
To give thee everlasting birth,
   And change the form thou wouldst retain.

Wouldst thou rejoice with budding stem,
   When spring anew uncurls the leaf,—   10
When summer comes gain strength like them,
   And laden be with autumn's sheaf:

Then with them bear that slow decay;
   It visits you with mouldering grain;
And thou shalt spring anew as they   15
   To die and find thy life again.

Poem No. 100; late 1838-early 1840

The New Sea

I heard the sound of the wild, heaving sea,
Its billows had rolled on unheard before,
For to some vainly-fancied thing I had given
The name, that gentile nations worship as
A God. But now I heard without deceit   5
Surges that ever roll; the deep below
Answering with awful voice the deep above!
.   .   .   .
The sea was past; the waters met,
And o'er the heads of Pharaoh's hosts; I turned,—
And saw the proud careering waves ride as   10
Reined steeds under some mighty conquerors
Driven on. It was a day when the battle
Had been given unto God's chosen sons;

And I rejoiced as rose its glorious sun
Looking o'er land and sea, the inheritance
Of man new-blessed. And they who beneath its waves
And on its bed as on the dry land walked,
God led, stood on the other bank; and shouts
Louder than from the sea rose up to heaven.

Poem No. 238; late 1838-early 1840

The Baker's Island Light

Near on Salem's rocky shore
   Stands the Baker's Island Light,
Sending o'er the white sea's roar
   Rays that light the darkest night.

Home-bound vessels on their way,
   'Scaped the dangers of the deep,
Hail with joy its far-seen ray
   As to land their course they keep.

On to midnight's hour it shines,
   On from midnight's hour till morn;
Till the east with golden lines
   Marks the day's bright offspring born.

Pale its light before the dawn
   Tells a brighter beacon near,
And the sailor's eyes withdrawn
   To their port in safety steer.

Poem No. 351; c. 21 August 1840

The Gifts of God

The light that fills thy house at morn
   Thou canst not for thyself retain;
But all who with thee here are born
   It bids to share an equal gain.

The wind that blows thy ship along 5
Her swelling sails cannot confine;
Alike to all the gales belong,
Nor canst thou claim a breath as thine.

The earth, the green out-spreading earth;
Why hast thou fenced it off from me? 10
Hadst thou than I a nobler birth,
Who callest thine a gift so free.

The wave, the blue encircling wave;
No chains can bind, no fetters hold!
Its thunders tell of Him who gave 15
What none can ever buy for gold.

Poem No. 521; c. 2 October 1840

The Sepulchre Of The Books

'Tis a high stone pile
It will hold them all;
The books of the great and the books of the small,
They gather to their place of rest,
From the north and the south, and the east and the west. 5

Come gather them in,
Come gather them in,
They cannot repent of their evil & sin
The good & the bad it will hold them all,
They will sleep on forever at rest in Gore Hall. 10

The place of the Skulls!
The place of the Dead!
The dim light will show them as through it we tread!
See here these huge columns! these heavy stones!
'Tis the tomb of the Books, 'tis the high place of Bones! 15

The hemlock and pine
Around it here wave,
They will sleep on in silence they have found here a grave;
Look here on each side what a high massy wall!
They will sleep on forever at rest in Gore Hall. 20

All silent! all silent
    They rest in the pile,
No more to bewilder, no more to beguile;
In silence unbroken their sepulchre be,
No light, save the candle, their resting place see.   25

Poem No. 721; c. January 1841

The Robin's Song

The robin has begun his early song,
   His twitterings on the leafless locust bough;
From hour to hour his notes are loud and long,
   Unheard since autumn's by-gone days till now.

Yet he is there; and calling to his mate;   5
   'The cot is all unbuilded for our young';
At early morn, and into evening late,
   By each to each from tree to tree is sung;—

'The cot is all unbuilded for our young,
   The last year's nest will not our offspring hold;   10
'Tis time for them a new one was begun,
   Where winter's left the relics of the old.'

'Bring willow twigs, and sticks from out the grove,
   And bring the mire, the wet mire from the stream;
These one by one together shall be wove,   15
   And that shall fill and plaster every seam.'

'The soft, soft leaves, and shreds shall line, within,
   The cradle of our tender, infant brood;
Come, hasten love! 'tis time that we begin,
   For now the fields and air all promise food.'   20

Thus morn and eve he sings his twittering song,
   High up upon the slow-leaved locust tree;
And soon their cot new-builded, large and strong,
   And safe from harm, upon its top will be.

Poem No. 553; c. 6 April 1841

The Wounded Pigeon

And thou wast out on yesternight
When the wind blew so high a gale,
And snow and darkness gathered might
Joined with its loud and angry wail!
When rose the storm to smite each roof,   5
And the tree's lofty pride lay low;
And, swift as shuttles through the woof,
To drive the tall ships to and fro;
Thee too, a wanderer from some cot,
Driven up and downward in its whirl,   10
Amid the mightier things it wrought,
Against our porch it came to hurl.
Poor dove! the door man enters oft
Opened not to thee in thy distress,
Thou heardst no welcome voices soft   15
Thou sawest no hands outstretched to bless.
Not so, she who from the waters back
Returning sought the wandering ark,
When yet her foot had left no track,
Was welcomed to the tossing bark.   20
But here thy wounds unheeded flowed,
Nor heard thy moans, nor tapping bill;
Unknown thy pangs, till morning glowed,
And seen thy blood upon the sill.
Perhaps thy wounds by this are healed,   25
And thou hast forgot the unsheltered place;
But I were to instruction steeled
Should I forget thy suffering's trace.
Full oft our eyes are closed in sleep
Too deep to wake at misery's call,   30
Full oft a feeble watch we keep
When, without aid, the weak must fall.
Lord! strengthen me the hour to heed
That brings the sufferer to my door,
That I may to his succour speed,   35
Ere yet the time Thou giv'st be o'er.

Poem No. 49; 26 October 1841

The Swift

Men tell how many blossoms will appear
   On every tree they plant & hope to thrive
How many kernels fill the yellow ear
   How many bees shall swarm in every hive
When Spring's but come, 'tis Autumn here with them   5
   And Summers but of Winter's cold can tell;
And when they see the fruit on laden stem
   With them its early buds begin to swell
'Tis all too slow, fair nature's gentle growth;
   Their hopes are ripe, when hers but bud & bloom;   10
And they accuse her equal pace—of sloth,
   And cast on her the shadow of their gloom.
But she, kind Mother of her children all,
   With voice of dove-like mildness gently chides
"I care for e'en the humble sparrow's fall   15
   Alike with yon bright orb that o'er thee glides!"

Poem No. 329; 1841–42?

The World

'Tis all a great show,
   The world that we're in,
None can tell when 'twas finished,
   None saw it begin;
Men wander and gaze through   5
   Its courts and its halls,
Like children whose love is
   The picture-hung walls.

There are flowers in the meadow,
   There are clouds in the sky,   10
Songs pour from the wood-land,
   The waters glide by;
Too many, too many
   For eye or for ear,

The sights that we see,
  And the sounds that we hear.

A weight as of slumber
  Comes down on the mind,
So swift is Life's train
  To its objects we're blind;   20
I myself am but one
  In the fleet-gliding show,
Like others I walk
  But know not where I go.

One saint to another   25
  I heard say 'How long?'
I listened, but nought more
  I heard of his song;
The shadows are walking
  Through city and plain,   30
How long shall the night
  And its shadow remain!

How long and shall shine
  In this glimmer of things
The Light of which prophet   35
  In prophecy sings;
And the gates of that city
  Be open, whose sun
No more to the west
  Its circuit shall run!   40

Poem No. 723; c. 1 April 1842

The Evening Choir

The organ smites the ear with solemn notes
In the dark pines withdrawn, whose shadows fall
Motionless on the moonlit path which leads
To the house of God, within whose porch I stand.
Behold the stars and larger constellations   5
Of the north hemisphere; glitter more bright
Their ranks, and more harmonious they seem,

As from within swells out the holy song.
The pillars tremble with the waves of sound!
There is in these deep tones a power to abide   10
Within us; when the hand is mouldered
Of him who sweeps its keys, and silent too
Her voice, who with the organ chants so sweet,
We shall hear echoes of a former strain,
Soft soul-like airs coming we know not whence.   15
I would that to the noisy throng below,
Which paces restless through the glimmering street,
Might reach this anthem with its cadence soft,
And its loud rising blasts. Men's ears are closed,
And shut their eyes, when from on high the angels   20
Listen well pleased, and nearer draw to the earth.
Yet here the blind man comes, the only constant
Listener. In the dim-lighted Church, within
Some pew's recess, retired he sits, with face
Upturned as if he saw, as well as heard,   25
And music was to him another sense:
Some thoughtless at the gate a moment stand,
Whom a chance-wandering melody detains,
And then, forgetful, mingle with the tide
That bears them on; perchance to wonder whence   30
It came, or dream from a diviner sphere
'T was heard.
              Tomorrow is the Sabbath-time;
Refreshed by sleep this tired multitude,
Which now by all ways rushes through the city,
Each hurrying to and fro with thoughts of gain,   35
And harried with the business of the world,
Men with children mixed clamorous and rude,
Shall, all at once, quit their accustomed streets,
And to the temples turn with sober pace,
And decent dress composed for prayer and praise.   40
Yon gate, that now is shut upon the crowd,
Shall open to the worshippers; by paths
Where not a foot's now heard, up these high steps
Come arm in arm the mother, father, child,
Brother, and sister, servants and the stranger   45
Tarrying with them, and the stated priest
Who ministers in holy things. Peace be
On this House, on its courts! May the high hymn

Of praise, that now is sung preparative,
Quiet the rough waves that loud are breaking   50
At its base, and threatening its high walls.
I would not, when my heart is bitter grown,
And my thoughts turned against the multitude,
War with their earthly temple; mar its stones;
Or, with both pillars in my grasp, shake down   55
The mighty ruin on their heads. With this
I war not, nor wrestle with the earthly man.
I war with the spiritual temple raised
By pride, whose top is in the heavens, though built
On the earth; whose site and hydra-headed power   60
Is everywhere;—with Principalities,
And them who rule the darkness of this world,
The Spirits of wickedness that highest stand.
'Gainst this and these I fight; nor I alone,
But those bright stars I see that gather round   65
Nightly this sacred spot. Nor will they lay
Their glittering armor by, till from heaven's height
Is cast Satan with all his host headlong!
Falling from sphere to sphere, from earth to earth
Forever;—and God's will is done.   70

Poem No. 537; spring–summer 1842

The Cold Spring
In North Salem

Thou small, yet ever-bubbling spring
    Hid by low hillocks round,
And oaks whose stretching branches fling
    Their shadows on the ground;

I stoop upon thy stony brim   5
    To taste thy waters sweet,
For I am weary and worn of limb,
    And joy thy sight to meet.

I would not from thy free bowl scare
   The birds from the boughs above,   10
But learn with them this fount to share
   As the gift of a Father's love.

Thou hast joy in this thy wilderness,
   In thy still yet constant flow;
Such as one from pure and perfect bliss   15
   Alone with thee can know.

Oh, seldom may the Sea, that near
   Sends up its frequent tide,
Mix with thy cooling waters clear
   And in thy breast abide!   20

And if perchance a lengthened wave
   Should o'er thy margin swell,
Quick may thy bubbling freshness save
   And the salt brine repel.

Poem No. 668-697; October–November 1842

Lines on Reading the Death of Rev. Henry Ware, Jr.

Though thou art dead and gone from mortal sight,
Faith will not let thee go, but follows on;
It sees thee even here beyond the grave,
That farthest limit to the eye of sense!
Blessed is he who puts his trust in him   5
Who came into, and left this earthly sphere,
Yet without sin. Such shall not stay within
The darksome tomb, companion of the dead,
But rise in incorruption with his Lord.
I thought not that so soon thou wouldst depart!   10
It seems but yesterday, and strong thy mind
And vigorous in man's service;—but the day
And hour that calls the faithful servant home
Into his Master's joy we cannot know.
Thou tendest now those "other sheep" which he   15
Has gone to bring. Many have heard thy voice
And known it here, and many learned from thee

The way of peace. Thy words and works shall be
Thy praise, and grateful hearts whom thou hast left
To mourn.
       How many of the great and good   20
Within this fleeting year have passed away!
Alas! it pains me but to tell them o'er.
Names that the world has honored and revered,
And some as worthy that the world ne'er knew.
Much have we cause to mourn, whose lights yet burn,   25
For so much Genius, Wisdom, Goodness gone.
But let us not say "gone;" but see those still
Whom we have lost, in Heaven, their proper home.

Poem No. 709; c. 30 September 1843

Jonathan Huntington Bright

I sit within the room where thou once sat,
When half my age, a curly headed boy;
And live beneath the roof where thou once lived,
And spent life's early hours in peace and joy.
Here by the cheerful hearth and plenteous board,   5
Thou hast known a father's care, a mother's love;
Here was thy soul trained up to know its God,
And taught to prize the Wisdom from above.
And here the School, where many a livelong day
Thou hast pondered o'er the lesson hard and long;   10
And here the fields, the river, and the hills
That first inspired thee with the love of song.
Methinks I see thee with thy many mates
Upon yon sandy bank in healthful play,
Or bathing in the river's cooling tide,   15
Or hastening homeward at the close of day.
Methinks I see thee in the pastures wild,
Seeking the ripening berries far and near;
Breaking through bushy swamps, or on the hill;
Almost thy voice at times I seem to hear;   20
But thou are dead! Fair Salem's earliest bard!
Scarce half accomplished was man's life by thee!
Where rolls the Mississippi's mighty flood

The stranger's eye thy resting place can see!
Though known to few thy name, and few thy song,   25
Of all that now within thy city dwell;
Like thee, a "Traveller"* through earth's passing scenes,
Fain would I of thy worth and wanderings tell.
Fain would I plant with laurel famed thy grave,
Where thou reposest from life's toilsome way;   30
Whose branches ever green, and towering head
Should mark thy rest to those who distant stray:
Still would I love as classic ground the spot,
Where passed in joy thy childhood's early hour;
The quiet roof, the field, the hill, the stream   35
Will from thy memory now have double power.

Poem No. 270; c. 19 January 1844

God's Host

There is an order in our daily life,
Like that the Holy Angels constant keep;
And though its outward form seem but a strife,
There dwells within a calm as the ocean's deep.
The forms that meet you in the house and street   5
Brushing with their rough coats your shining dress,
Did they in their own robes and features greet
Would seem like angels that the world possess:
And thou like Jacob when from Galeed's heap
He journeyed on unto the land of Seir,   10
And sware with Laban vows of peace to keep,
By Abraham's God and by his father's Fear;
Wouldst cry aloud in dread and wonder lost,
"This is the House of God! and these I see God's host!"

Poem No. 617; c. 26 March 1844

*A native of Salem. He was for several years a writer for the public journals and literary magazines under the signature of "Viator."

The Worm

I saw a worm, with many a fold,
    It spun itself a silken tomb;
And there in winter-time enrolled,
    It heeded not the cold or gloom.

The traces of a dry, dead leaf   5
    Were left in lines upon its cone;
The record of its history brief,
    A spring and summer come and gone.

Within a small, snug nook it lay,
    Nor rain nor snow could reach it there;   10
Nor wind was felt in gusty day,
    Nor biting cold of frosty air.

But spring returned; its mild, warm breath
    Was felt within the sleeper's cell;
And waking from its trance of death,   15
    I saw it crawl from out its shell.

And starting where they lay beneath,
    Were eyelet wings spread one by one;
Each perfected as from a sheath,
    And shining in the morning sun.   20

Slow and with pain it first moved on,
    And of the dust still seemed to be;
An hour passed by; the worm was gone;—
    It soared on golden pinions free!

Poem No. 257a; spring 1845

The White Dove And The Snow

The quickly melting snow ran through the street,
The busy street, where man so often treads
Thinking on earthly things, careworn and sad;
And there a milk-white dove drank eagerly,
As if it blessed the heaven-descended stream.   5

Gazing, I thought of Purity and Faith;
How unto these the Lord giveth to drink,
E'en on the crowded city's dusty ways,
Of those clear streams which from His golden throne
Forever flow! Why thoughtless pass we by   10
Those crystal streams, that ever downward flow
To cool our thirsty, feverish spirits
In their daily toil, and make us think of Him?
The world's loud, turbid flood will soon run dry,
And we be left without one cooling draught.   15

Poem No. 547; 16 March 1846

The Latter Rain

The latter rain,—it falls in anxious haste
Upon the sun-dried fields and branches bare,
Loosening with searching drops the rigid waste,
As if it would each root's lost strength repair;
But not a blade grows green as in the spring,   5
No swelling twig puts forth its thickening leaves,
No busy birds, as then, are heard to sing,
Building upon the boughs or 'neath the eaves;
The rain falls still,—yet Nature heeds it not,
She lifeless lies, as lies upon the bier   10
The corse that soon within the ground must rot,
Nor knows that on it falls the scalding tear;
Yet she tho' dead, like man, shall live again,
And bless with smiles and songs the latter rain.

Poem No. 518a; c. 4 April 1846

Moses In Infancy

How! canst thou see the basket, wherein lay
The infant Moses, by the river's side;
And her, who stood and watched it on the tide;
Will Time bring back to thee that early day?

And canst thou to the distant Nile be near,   5
Where lived that mother, tossed with hope and fear,
Yet more than was her infant by the wave?
No: Time will not his dark domain unbar,
Himself he cannot from oblivion save;
Nor canst thou make come nearer what is far;—   10
But thou hast human sympathies to feel
What eye, nor ear, nor sense can e'er reveal;
Hope too is thine, that past the ocean sails,
And Memory, that over Time himself prevails!

Poem No. 182; c. 9 May 1846

Moses at the Bush

'Twas while the bush was burning, Moses saw
The Present God! and heard His voice, I AM!
The God of Jacob, and of Abraham
Spake, in the wild, to him who gave the Law;
Quick as he heard he hid his face in awe!   5
Around him flared the red light on the rocks,
And downward shone upon his sleeping flocks.
He who from Pharaoh hasted to withdraw,
Leaving his palaces, and piles of art
Lit with aye-burning lamps, false idols' seat;   10
Thought not, when in the wilderness he fed
His father's flocks, the great I AM to meet;
From human homes, and man's known ways apart,
Where burned the bush on Horeb's rocky head!

Poem No. 750; c. 30 May 1846

Moses As Leader Of Israel

'Twas not by strength of man, that Moses sought
To guide his people to their promised rest;
Nor his own wisdom, that through deserts brought,
And in a land of plenty made them blest;

Though he was learned in all the hidden lore 5
That Aegypt knew, mighty in word and deed;
'Twas not, by these, he broke their fetters sore,
And Israel's tribes from Pharaoh's bondage freed.
'If Thou wilt not go with us,' was his prayer
Unto the Lord of Hosts, 'let us not go 10
Up to the land, which Thou, before, did'st swear
To give unto our fathers. Thus shall know
All men, that Thou hast chosen us to be
A people called and holy unto Thee.'

Poem No. 749; c. 4 July 1846

The New Jerusalem

There are towers; where they are,
    In the topmost sky;
Thou from here hast never seen,
    With thy clouded eye.

There are houses, temples there, 5
    In that world of bliss;
Yet thou canst not see them here,
    From a place like this.

There I see the Son of Man,
    Of that world the light; 10
Seen by all; their sun by day,
    And their moon by night.

There are beings, they who went
    From thy presence here;
From their mansions looking down 15
    On thine earthly sphere.

Cherubs there, and white-robed men,
    Angels born to love;
High! how high their golden home!
    Dwelling there above. 20

Poem No. 609; c. 15 August 1846

The Autumn Flowers

Though so fair, how soon they perish,
  Few the days, the hours they stay!
Let us then their beauty cherish,
  That so soon must pass away.

Winter waits with icy fingers   5
  Soon to snatch them for his own;
But the Summer's day still lingers,
  Though its months are past and gone.

Every morn I look to see them
  Fallen, shrivelled by the frost;   10
But each morn again restores me,
  What at evening I had lost.

Trees and vines may change their verdure
  Bright with every beauteous hue;
Yet their tints, how fair soever,   15
  Shall not take my love from you.

They will see *another* season,
  Spring will clothe them with its green;
But for you no spring returneth,
  You will here no more be seen!   20

They, with the returning Autumn,
  Bright, as now, will reappear;
And renew their fading glories
  Still for many a coming year.

But within my soul your beauty   25
  Shall, unfading, ever bloom;
There no frosts can blight, or wither,
  There no night conceal with gloom.

Every tint shall memory heighten,
  Seen and loved in these short hours;   30
And, while memory's self continues,
  Still shall bloom the Autumn Flowers.

Poem No. 708; October 1846

The Death Of Man

All Nature dies! wide over hill and plain,
The forests brown and withered meet the eye;
The flowers are gone, the birds will not remain,
The grass, so green of late, is pale and dry.
But what is Nature's death, though, far and wide   5
Thou see'st the emblems of her sure decay,
To Man's; to whom, in soul, thou art allied;
And who but now, unnoticed, passed away!
Daily he passes; in the lowly shed,
In the high palace, 'neath the open sky;   10
No world-wide symbols mark that He is dead,
No gorgeous splendor draws thy wondering eye;
Yet passed there from thee all that Heaven could give,
And more than could within all Nature live!

Poem No. 33; c. 12 December 1846

As ye sow, so shall ye reap.

The bud will soon become a flower,
   The flower become a seed;
Then seize, O youth, the present hour,—
   Of that thou hast most need.

Do thy best always,—do it now,—   5
   For in the present time,
As in the furrows of a plough,
   Fall seeds of good or crime.

The sun and rain will ripen fast
   Each seed that thou hast sown;   10
And every act and word at last
   By its own fruit be known.

And soon the harvest of thy toil
   Rejoicing thou shalt reap;
Or o'er thy wild, neglected soil   15
   Go forth in shame to weep.

Poem No. 473; 1846

God Not Afar Off

Father! Thy wonders do not singly stand,
Nor far removed where feet have seldom strayed;
Around us ever lies the enchanted land,
In marvels rich to Thine own sons displayed.

In finding Thee are all things round us found!   5
In losing Thee are all things lost beside!
Ears have we, but in vain sweet voices sound,
And to our eyes the vision is denied.

Open our eyes that we that world may see!
Open our ears that we Thy voice may hear!   10
And in the spirit-land may ever be,
And feel Thy presence with us always near;

No more to wander 'mid the things of time,
No more to suffer death or earthly change;
But with the Christian's joy and faith sublime,   15
Through all Thy vast, eternal scenes to range.

Poem No. 126a; 1846

The Indian's Retort

The white man's soul, it thirsts for gain,
    He makes himself the slave of gold!
The Indian's free and boundless lands,
    Once all his own, are bought and sold.

An Indian to the forest went,   5
    To strip the birch for his canoe;
His father's fathers' was that wood,
    Before the White his country knew.

A weary journey he must take
    Along a hot, and dusty road;   10
And to his distant wigwam bring,
    Upon his back, the heavy load.

Long searched he for a fitting tree,
    Where once they easy were to find;
The white man's axe had laid them low,   15
    The white man's fire left few behind.

At length 'twas found; he stripped its bark,
    He raised his bundle from the ground;
A white man stood beside him there,
    And on the Indian sternly frowned.   20

"Thou steal'st!" "Thou art a thief!" he cried;—
    The Indian threw his bundle down,
And proudly answered; as he turned
    To meet the white man's angry frown;

"God made the woods, and to his sons,   25
    The Indians, gave them long ago;
The Indian never was a thief,
    I speak the truth, as thou dost know."

"The White man came! he stole the woods,
    The hills, the streams, the fields, the game;   30
The Indian never was a thief!
    The white man steals, his is the name!"

Poem No. 593; c. 9 January 1847

The Widow

A greater tribute than the Temple's height,
Its solid walls, and sounding minstrelsy,
And all that there the senses vain delight,
Is that lone widow's worship, Lord, to Thee.
In her ill-furnished chamber there, alone,   5
She opes the Book, which Thou hast given to all;
And, on her knees, before thy gracious throne,
For light, and strength, in this her need, doth call.
And she shall find them; what the boasting pride
Of minster-service promised her in vain;   10
Though late she seeks, she shall not be denied,
She, through thy Son, Eternal Life shall gain;

When left by crowds, Thou, Father, still art near,
And dost delight the lonely one to hear.

Poem No. 8; c. March 1847

Impatience

Thou chid'st the wind, and snow, and sleet, and ice;
That still delay the Spring, when Spring is near.
Thou see'st the grass as if already green,
And scent'st the flowers, and hear'st the song of birds.
Then why this disappointment of my hopes,   5
You ask? What! would you have the year come forth
To fail, and die? This wind, and snow, and ice,
This second winter was not made in vain.
'Twas sent to retard and check the vital powers,
That else, with fatal haste, might swell the grain,   10
And cause the fruitful trees too soon to bloom.
O'ertook by sudden frosts, and icy blasts,
Nature in all her glow of life would droop,
And famished millions perish!
Scorn not slow Nature's work; chide not her ways,   15
For they are ordered, everywhere, aright;
But from her wisdom learn *thou* to be wise.
There is a Providence in all we see,
Which man should ever study and adore.

Poem No. 667; c. 17 April 1847

Abdolonymus—The Sidonian

The clash of arms, which shook the Persian state,
Did not disturb the peasant at his toil;
In his small garden-plot more truly great,
Than he who stretched his sceptre o'er its soil.
He wanted naught, but what his hands supplied,   5
Content with fruits, the bounty of his field;

There would he, in old age, in peace have died;
But worth and greatness could not be concealed!
O'erlooked were many, who would Sidon rule,
Ambitious princes, seeking kingly sway;   10
Who, trained in arms, had learned from War's proud school,
By fire and sword to win to thrones their way.
The crown and purple robe to him were sent,
Who peaceful lived, with poverty content.

Poem No. 477; c. 31 July 1847

The Arrival

The ship comes up the harbor. Every sail
Is set on every mast. The sun is bright,
And the blue waters 'round seem to rejoice
With her that she has 'scaped all perils now,
And safe returned unto her destined port.   5
Upon the wharf are groups straining their eyes
To tell her signal, and conjecturing
Her name. Some aided by the glass pronounce
More surely. The aged seamen know her
By her spars. Boats put out to welcome her.   10
She's past the Island Light, past yonder head,
And soon she will be here—so swift she sails.
To the wharf's extreme a boy comes running.
He listens to the sounds borne on the breeze.
"That is my father's voice," he cries o'erjoyed,   15
Yet half in doubt as though it might not be.
And then again, "That is my father's voice!"
Nearer the vessel comes. He sees him now,
And points him out there leaning o'er the side.
He's all beside himself with hope and joy.   20
The vessel nears the wharf. The captain speaks,
And swift the sailors fly to every rope.
The yards are dropt, the sails are quickly furled,
And motionless the noble vessel lies
Beside the pier. Joyous greetings follow.   25
But most glad of all the boy. Ere the ship

Had touched the wharf, he from another's side
Had gained her deck, and seized his father's hand.

Poem No. 559; 5 April–23 October 1847

The Soul's Preparation For Adversity

How stript and bare is every bush and tree
Of all the pride of summer, and of spring;
Each of its vain encumbrance shaken free,
While winter's blasts through all their branches ring!
So, when Thou would'st thy children should prepare   5
To meet adversity, and pain, and death;
To suffer all things, every danger dare;
Thou scatterest, Father, with the tempest's breath,
All that they cling to in their hour of pride,
All that the world calls greatness, glory, power;   10
That they in Thee alone may then confide,
And find their proper strength; in that lone hour,
When this world's glory burdens, or is gone;
And they must look to Thee, and Thee alone.

Poem No. 203; c. 4 December 1847

Change In The Seasons

Has Nature a new sympathy with man,
That, in this northern clime, the pansies bloom
To deck the opening year with summer flowers?
In mid December, still the fields were green.
On my walk I found the dandelion   5
Full blown, and bright as when it opes in Spring,
And sprinkles all the mead with yellow gold.
The apple blossoms, early shrubs have leaves,
And Spring seems pressing on in Winter's stead!
These fair signs we see are not deceptive.   10
Experience has shown from year to year,

That Winter grows more mild. Rivers that once
Were frozen, so that heavy wagons crost
Secure as on a bridge, now freeze no more;
And countries, that were buried deep with snow,   15
Through all the year, and uninhabited,
Now yield the olive, and the purple grape.
Astronomers once thought the equator's plane
Approached the ecliptic's, in the lapse of time;
And, should they coincide, perpetual Spring   20
Would come. Changes as great, Geology
Has proved the earth to have seen. That tropic
Plants, and animals have lived, and flourished, here
In our Northern clime. That once the Mammouth
Roamed Siberia's plains, and in the frozen   25
North abundant pasturage found. Here forests
Grew of other leaf, and fruits; here other
Flowers. Pleased with the thought my fancy sees
The tropic's vegetation rise around!
Where now the spreading oak, the palm upsprings;   30
The apple for the olive is exchanged;
The golden orange through the dark leaves glows,
Where now the hardy pine alone will live.
For scraggy briar, the fragrant myrtle
By the roadside blooms. Delicate flowers,   35
That household care alone can now make live,
Bloom wild throughout the year; fearing no blast,
Or cruel frost to nip their tender leaves.
Thus over all the earth, from month to month,
Bland gales shall blow, and birds continual sing;   40
No sudden tempest lash the sea to foam,
Nor shall the earth with sudden tremor shake.
All nature then will be at peace, to which
E'en now by slow degrees she tends. Alas!
When Nature thus improves upon herself,   45
By God's decree, that man should retrograde;
Unfit himself for that new earth and sky,
Which with revolving seasons hastens on.
Now fair his promise, and he seems to tend
Like nature to a new-born, heavenly Spring   50
Of endless happiness, and peace, and love;
But soon his passions like a whirlwind rise,
Fierce hate and wrath hide the mild-beaming sun,

And snatch the pleasing prospect from our view,
And nought is left but hope to light our path.   55

Poem No. 156; January 1848

The Just Shall Live by Faith

'The just shall live by faith' the Prophet cried,
When, sent in judgment on his native land,
He saw the fierce Chaldeans spreading wide,
And Israel's hosts too feeble to withstand;
'The just shall live by faith,' the Apostle said,   5
When Christ delayed his coming on the earth;
And, with these words, his fainting followers staid,
And hope within them had a second birth.
'The just shall live by faith' the Reformer's word,
That roused the Church, when sunk in sin and lust,   10
To turn again unto the Living Lord,
And shake her shining garments from the dust;
Oh may we heed it, when our Lord delays,
And tarries long, that He may prove our ways!

Poem No. 517; c. 26 February 1848

Salem

Boast not, my native spot, thy sons were first
To shed their blood in Freedom's noble cause;
Nor glory when thou hear'st the tale rehearst,
Though all the world should greet thee with applause.
Another day has come, another age,   5
And rights by blood and strife no more are won;
Awake! and write thee on a holier page,
Nor boast with warriors what thy sword has done.
*Scorn, as thou ever hast, to build thy walls

*See the answer of the citizens of Salem to Gov. Gage in 1774, when he proposed to remove the
General Court to that place; Boston being a closed port.

Upon a suffering neighbor's hapless lot;   10
Heed Peace, Humanity, and Justice's calls;
And, when in coming ages are forgot
The strife of war and every blood-stained field,
Thy Name alone undying fame shall yield!

Poem No. 72; 25 March 1848

Spring in the Soul

The bough which long has borne the winter's blast,
Enclosed with ice, or heavy with the snow;
Does, when its cold and stormy months are past,
The springing leaves and bursting blossoms show.
So ye, on whom the world's cold breath has blown,   5
While here you suffer for your Master's name;
The kindness of the Father soon shall own,
And, in the fruit you bear, His love proclaim.
Its storms are sent by the same Father's love,
Who, with the seasons, marks the varied year,   10
That you may thus your full obedience prove;—
Then courage take, and calm each rising fear;
Endure! For Spring will quickly come again,
Come in your hearts, as now on hill and plain.

Poem No. 469-573; March 1848

Nature's Invitation

Pine not, my child, to distant lands to go;
The flower with me is pleading at thy feet,
The clouds delaying through the azure flow,
And soft the breezes come thy cheek to greet.
Why hasten on, hast thou a fairer home?   5
Has God more richly blessed the world than here,
That thou in haste wouldst from thy country roam,
Favored by every month that fills the year?
What though in other climes rise loftier piles,

And Art with fairer colors decks her halls;   10
No fairer there than here are Nature's smiles,
No sweeter there than here her music calls;
Attune thy mind, open thine inward eye,
And thou wilt seek no more a distant sky.

Poem No. 397; c. 27 May 1848

Christ's Compassion

Matt. IX. 35–38.

He saw them tasked with heavy burthens all,
Bowed down and weary 'neath the heavy load;
With none their faltering footsteps home to call,
Or point them out the strait and narrow road;
His spirit bore their burthens, as his own,   5
He healed the sick, restored the sightless eyes;
He heard the mourner for a loved one moan,
And bade the dead from out the grave arise!
Truly on him the Spirit did descend,
For he, by works divine, its influence proved;   10
Of all our race Consoler, Guide, and Friend,
By heavenly Love, divine Compassion moved;
Oh, that his spirit might on us abide,
And flow in healing streams on every side!

Poem No. 166; c. 17 June 1848

Hymn
Nevertheless, when the Son of Man cometh, shall he find faith on the earth? Luke XVIII:8.

Alas, that faith is wanting now,
   As when the Savior came of old;
The wreaths still deck the warrior's brow,
   And love in Christians' hearts grows cold.

A faith in better things is dead,   5
    Than what the world before has seen;
Men still in their own ways will tread,
    And ask no more, than what has been.

They trust in carnal weapons still,
    The warrior's spear, the warrior's sword,   10
And deeds of blood that history fill,
    And ask, "Where is the coming Lord?"

They want a deeper faith in man,
    That looks beneath the outward show
Of difference in wealth, or clan,   15
    And man in every form doth know.

A deeper faith in God they need,
    That they in him can all things do;
A faith from every weakness freed,
    And finding still his promise true.   20

Lord! let us not with those appear,
    Who faithless shall thy Coming see;
But may we view that Coming near,
    And, in thy likeness, come with thee.

Poem No. 29; c. 19 August 1848

The Man of Science

A man, whom Science had made wise,
    Above the multitude around;
Till he could tread the starry skies,
    As other mortals tread the ground;
Conceived that he could grasp the thought,   5
    How Nature into being sprang;
When worlds were called from empty naught,
    And morning's stars together sang!
That he the mystery could tell,
    How man himself at first began;   10

And trace from microscopic cell,
    Through lower forms, the noblest, Man!
At last he rose to such a height,
    That even human feeling fled;
And he could look without affright,   15
    On what would fill the world with dread;—
In abstract musing, he could see
    The earth return to naught again;
And man and Nature cease to be,
    Yet heave no sigh, and feel no pain!   20

But once, in midnight's solemn hour,
    His natural feelings all awoke;
And gifted with diviner power,
    Thus to his trembling spirit spoke.
"Where wast thou, when the world was made?"   25
    "Where wilt thou be, when it shall end?"
He heard, and he was sore afraid,
    Nor would his voice an answer lend.
Unwonted thoughts and feelings thronged
    His awe-struck soul, and it possessed;   30
For his own nature he had wronged,
    And all his nobler wants suppressed.
That which before unreal seemed,
    And but a distant, shadowy thought,
When he, in abstruse studies dreamed;   35
    Was to his soul all real brought.
He sympathized with Nature's fate,
    Nor saw unfeeling her decay;
Beheld far back her ancient date,
    And joyed to see her earliest day.   40
Nor felt for worlds' vast change alone,
    But for the little short-lived flower;
Whose beauteous morn is scarcely known,
    Before it sees its evening hour.
And though as earnest still to scan   45
    The wonders of creation o'er;
He was a wiser, better man,
    And mingled Love with Science' lore.

Poem No. 12; c. 21 October 1848

The Congress Of Peace At Brussels

From out the midst of Europe in alarms,
A voice is heard persuading men to peace;
A voice whose power with heavenly music charms,
And bids the tumult of the world to cease.

The nations, blessed with thirty years repose,   5
Seemed on the borders of the promised land;
The land that war's fierce conflicts never knows,
Where all who live are one united band.

And even now they stand on Jordan's stream;
But unbelief still sways the human mind;   10
And all the glorious prospect seems a dream,
For to its near approach their souls are blind.

Not by the sword, or violence shall rights,
Long lost to nations, be at once regained;
Not by the prowess shown in deadly fights,   15
Shall Freedom, once achieved, be still maintained.

God of one blood has all the nations made
To dwell, in peace, together on the earth;
That none should be of others' power afraid,
And none should boast them of a nobler birth.   20

We are all One. Boast not of rights, if won
By conquering hosts upon the gory plain;
But mourn for what thine own right hand hath done,
Nor think thy brother's blood thy Country's gain.

Humanity laments, and still will weep   .   25
Her slaughtered sons of every age, and clime;
And hourly does her fasts and vigils keep
For millions perished since the birth of time!

And shall she never from the dust arise,
And put her robe of fleecy whiteness on;   30
And dry her swoln, and ever-flowing eyes
For wrongs, that man his brother man has done?

Yes: for though passing clouds may dim her sight,
They shall not long prevent the approaching day;

Already are the hill-tops glad with light,   35
And man's proud tyrants starting with dismay.

Soon shall she see her children dwell in peace
On all the earth, of every name and clime;
Their friendly intercourse of love increase,
Unfettered by the bonds of space and time!   40

A deep abiding joy her soul shall fill,
Beholding thus her countless children blest;
Secure from rude alarms, from every ill,
And entering here on their eternal rest!

Poem No. 141; 24 November 1848

'Tis A Great Thing to Live

'Tis a great thing to live. Not small the task
Our Heavenly Father gives us here below;
And we have need continually to ask,
That light, and strength may through our being flow.
Not on the trifles of the passing hour,   5
With those who squander life, fix thou thy mind;
(For these may rob thy spirit of a power
Which was for greater, nobler things designed;)
But on some mighty work, some worthy plan,
Requiring e'en an angel's strength to do;   10
For scarce below the angel is the man,
And both may, here, one great design pursue;
The same on earth, the same in heaven above,
A holy ministry of peace and love.

Poem No. 720; 30 December 1848

The Indian's Petition

The Indian calls! Grant him a place of rest,
From wrong, and violence forever free;
Grant him a portion of the boundless West,
Where he may dwell, and learn to live like thee.

There let him learn to till the fruitful soil,   5
Subdue his passions fierce by reason's sway;
And find how vast the gains of patient toil,
And all his nobler energies display.
There let him learn it was not all a dream,
His fathers taught him of the Indian's heaven;   10
That there, beyond the mighty western stream,
That home of rest may yet to him be given;
Where he shall know His love, who died for all,
And on his Heavenly Father learn to call.

Poem No. 515; 23 March 1849

The Struggle

A mighty struggle in the world goes on,
A struggle, not for wealth, or Time's vain toys;
But one, in which the crown of Life is won,
And man inherits here eternal joys!
Not those who slumber, or who trifle here,   5
Can win the prize, which crowns that mighty strife;
But they, whom active love doth onward cheer
To fill with noble deeds their fleeting life;—
Who oft through suffering, oft through shades of death
Are called to pass, that they their crowns may win;   10
Oft only victors, with their dying breath,
Against the world-destroying power of Sin;
Which still disputes Christ's triumph on the earth,
And claims, as hers, each soul of heavenly birth.

Poem No. 13; June 1849

The Things Before

I would not tarry, Look! the things before
Call me along my path, with beckoning love;
The things I gain wear not the hues they wore,
For brighter glories now my spirit move.

Still on; I seek the peace my master sought,   5
The world cannot disturb his joy within;
It is not with its gold and silver bought,
They give not victory over death and sin.
Awake, ye sensual, from your sleep of shame!
Shake off the slumbers of the earthly mind;   10
For higher objects now your spirits claim,
To which the soul, that slumbers here, is blind;
Objects, which, like the soul itself, endure;
Things that are true, and lovely, just, and pure.

Poem No. 292; c. 21 July 1849

The Dying Leaf

'Tis not a natural law alone,
  By which the dying leaf
Falls whirling, when its work is done,
  Unto the ground beneath.

Before the rising autumn blast   5
  Commissioned was to bear
The little leaf, once bound so fast,
  And whirl it through the air;

The Lord of Life had checked the tide,
  Which through its fibres flowed;   10
And, to its being, had denied
  The gift He once bestowed.

The gift of life, mysterious thing!
  That form and substance gave;
Which filled its tender veins in spring,   15
  And made it gladsome wave:

But now, recalled, leaves hard and dry,
  The sport of lightest wind,
The leaf, which once could storms defy,
  Though all their blasts combined.   20

Poem No. 727; 25 October 1849

The New Body

God careth for the smallest seed,
   Which falls into the ground;
It springeth up a noble tree,
   And spreads its branches round.

He careth for the feeble worm,   5
   Which spins its shroud to die;
He gives it many-colored wings,
   And bids it soar on high.

Through all the realms of God below,
   Through all his realms above;   10
A differing glory still proclaims
   The same great Father's love.

So is the rising from the dead!
   'Tis not what thou hast sown;
But, in the body God shall give,   15
   Will each to each be known.

A mortal body here thou see'st
   Unto dishonor given;
But that no pain, nor death shall know,
   A glorious house from heaven!   20

God's various power, which cares for all,
   E'en for the smallest seed;
And gives to each its different form,
   According to its need;

Will for thy body, Man, provide,   25
   Which now thou see'st decay;
And crown it with a glory too,
   Which shall not fade away.

Poem No. 148; c. 29 December 1849

The Clock

The slowly-moving fingers minutes find,
And hours and days, and e'en the lengthening years;
As much before them still as is behind,
No want their circling movement ever fears.
How different Man! By sudden impulse driven,   5
Now in the distant past he seeks for rest;
Now in the far-off future is his heaven;
"He never is, but always to be blest."
His morn is with his noon, his noon with night,
His hand can never point to one true hour;   10
But marks one past, or future in its flight,
For o'er the present he has lost all power;
Unlike the clock, whose ready tongue can all
The hours, and days of Time find voice to call.

Poem No. 565; c. 19 January 1850

On The Sudden Snow

How beautiful the sight,
    This robe of spotless white,
        O'er nature flung!
On every bush, and tree,
    Its pearly folds we see,   5
        In beauty hung.

To bless this sacred day,
    And clothe in fit array,
        It fell from heaven;
To make men think of God,   10
    And his own blest abode,
        The sight was given.

God doth in Nature show
    His love, e'en here below,
        Each passing hour;   15
And with his children plead,

Oh, may we ever heed,
 And feel its power.

Soon will He change the scene,
 And, with a sudden green,   20
  The earth surprise!
Earth too his dwelling is,
 All that we see is his,
  The Good, and Wise.

Poem No. 176; 24 March 1850

On the late Disgraceful Scene in Congress

Fools! That when things of high import concern
Their country's glory, and the human race;
They will not from the times a lesson learn,
But bring dishonor on their name and place.
When millions stand expectant to be free,   5
Is it the time for brawling and for strife;
For men on trifles still to disagree,
And waste the hour with highest duties rife?
The statesman's words are few, and full of grace,
The babbler's loud, and vulgar in their tone;   10
Ever unworthy of the time and place,
And now by folly, now by madness known;
They fill the world with tumult, and with shame,
And bring a foul reproach upon his country's name.

Poem No. 129; 27 April 1850

The Funerals

I sit and watch the winding way,
 Where, o'er the bridge, and through the grove,
The sorrowing mourners, day by day,
 Follow the forms of those they love.

In Winter's snows, and Summer's heat,   5
   When leaves spring forth, and when they fall;
They follow on, with weary feet,
   The mournful hearse with sable pall.

How many there, who mourn a friend,
   Such as can never be supplied;   10
Who loved them e'en unto the end,
   And gladly would for them have died.

Unnoticed passed they on through life,
   Forgotten in their humble spheres;
The parent, child, the husband, wife;   15
   The early lost, the bowed with years.

What though their lives, as now their death,
   Passed like yon quiet stream along;
Unheralded by public breath,
   Unhonored by the poet's song?   20

Not less their deeds, because unknown,
   Their daily toils, domestic care;
Than such as Fame's loud trump has blown,
   Than such as widest glory share.

Nor less their joy's calm, peaceful flow,   25
   Than theirs, whose breasts with tumults swell;
Who with the pride of victory glow,
   Or of a nation's honors tell.

Yon *Grove, whose name describes their life,
   Should best receive their honored dust;   30
They perished not in war's fierce strife,
   But died in peace, and holy trust.

There oft Affection's feet shall turn,
   To dwell upon their memory dear;
To wreath with flowers the funeral urn,   35
   Or shed the sympathetic tear.

*Harmony Grove in Salem.

There, purified by grief, she views,
    (The vail withdrawn,) their blest abode;
And, quickened by the sight, pursues
    With joyful hope her heaven-ward road.   40

Poem No. 268; April 1850

The New Aqueduct

Those old wooden logs
    The water has flown through,
These many, many years;
    'Tis time that we had new;
Improvement is the cry,   5
    And we throw them useless by.

Iron take their place,
    More permanent and sure;
Through which the stream will run
    Abundantly, and pure;   10
And all shall drink their fill
From the sweet, unfailing rill.

Through its hollow way
    The stream runs under ground;
No eye beholds its course,   15
    No ear can catch its sound;
Till it sparkles forth again,
In the glad abodes of men.

Like it is to deeds,
    Unconscious Worth doth hide;   20
In secret silence done,
    Without a throb of pride;
They too shall one day shine,
With a radiance all divine.

Patriarchs and kings   25
    Have gained their noblest fame,
In peaceful works like these;
    And left enduring name;

Tradition still can tell,
Who dug old Sichem's well. 30

Ever may it flow!
    Within our homes, 'twill prove
An ever-during type
    Of Purity and Love,
'Twill give to sickness health, 35
And raise poverty to wealth.

Poem No. 657; c. 7 June 1850

The Soul's Freedom

The green grass grows where'er it wills,
    On earth's wide-peopled floor;
In valleys low, and on the hills
    Which look the valleys o'er.

The river flows, nor feeble man 5
    Its tide directs, nor stays;
But Him from whom the current ran
    Forever it obeys.

There is no wind, which man can guide,
    Nor tell its certain bound; 10
Restless the airy currents glide
    The earth's wide surface round.

Thou shalt not mark with narrow walls
    Thine own vast being's scope;
'Tis farther back than memory calls, 15
    Nor bounded is by hope.

Then fetter not with human creed,
    The symbol of an hour,
The mind; which God's own Word has freed,
    And his own Spirit's power. 20

The wind, the tide, the growing grass,
   Thy will cannot controul;
Then fix no bounds, it shall not pass,
   To the free, living soul.

Poem No. 504; c. 6 July 1850

Looking Before And After

How oft by passion, or by interest led,
Men see not that they purpose, till 'tis done!
The string is snapt, the fatal arrow sped,
And to its mark it flies unerring on.
Look not before thee merely, but behind;   5
See how thy deed, when finished, will appear;
Like him who some fair temple has designed,
And views complete; ere men a column rear.
And see thy work, as it shall one day stand
Before thy spirit's pure, unclouded sight;   10
No longer subject to thy mortal hand,
But in Eternity's unchanging light!
Say, doth it then with added glory shine?
Then boldly act, thy deed is all divine.

Poem No. 195; c. 14 September 1850

The Succory

I ask not what the learned name,
   Thou hast in College book*;
I feel thou would'st the question blame,
   Blue Flower! with thy bright look.

I'll ask then of yon playful child,   5
   That stooped to pluck thee there;
What name she gave thee, when she smiled,
   And placed thee in her hair.

*This flower grows in great abundance around the Colleges, at Cambridge, Mass.

Her prattling tongue shall frame for me
   A name of sweeter tone,   10
Than Science ever gave to thee,
   To mark thee for her own.

A name a mother's lips have taught
   To call the way-side flower;
A name with thoughts and feelings fraught   15
   Of childhood's happy hour.

Still may it wake sweet child, as now,
   That smile, when years have fled;
And left their wrinkles on thy brow,
   Their silver on thy head.   20

Still may that name in memory dwell,
   Loved guardian of thy heart;
And be through life a holy spell,
   Recalling what thou art.

Poem No. 212; c. 28 September 1850

The Reapers Are The Angels

How few the reapers in life's whitening fields!
How many, preying on the ripening ears,
Forever scatter all the harvest yields,
Planted with toil, and wet with many tears!
Ah, little know they at what price was sown   5
The seed field of the world, a waste before;
When He, who sowed the seed, went forth alone,
And all the toil, and all the suffering bore.
But soon the Husbandman his heirs shall send,
Who, from the tares, shall cull the precious wheat;   10
And, from the heavens, the Son himself descend,
And with his welcome every laborer greet;
And give the weary ones his peace, his rest,
And to the feast invite each ransomed guest.

Poem No. 185; c. 12 October 1850

The Sumach Leaves

Some autumn leaves a painter took,
And with his colors caught their hues;
So true to nature did they look,
That none to praise them could refuse.

The yellow, mingling with the red,   5
Shone beauteous in their bright decay;
And round a golden radiance shed,
Like that which hangs o'er parting day.

Their sister leaves that, fair as these,
This far had shared a common lot;   10
All soiled, and scattered by the breeze,
Are now by every one forgot.

Soon trodden under foot of men,
Their very forms will cease to be;
Nor they remembered be again,   15
Till Autumn decks once more the tree.

But these shall still their beauty boast,
To praise the painter's wondrous art;
When Autumn's glories all are lost,
And with the fading year depart.   20

And through the wintry months so pale
The Sumach's brilliant hues recall;
Where, waving over hill and vale,
They gave its splendor to our Fall.

Poem No. 427; c. 9 November 1850

The Just

Do all thy acts with strictest justice square,
Lov'st thou thy neighbor, as thou lov'st thyself;
Refusing in unrighteousness to share,
Loving Christ's Kingdom, more than worldly pelf?
Does morning find thee, with its earliest beam,   5

Seeking each selfish purpose to control;
And, when the stars upon thy labors gleam,
Is there no stain, no burden on thy soul?
Then mayst thou rest in peace: for thee the sun
Does from his ocean-bed each morning rise;   10
And, when across the heavens his course is run,
For thee the dusky night his place supplies;
That thou with quiet conscience still may sleep,
While watchful stars above their vigils keep.

Poem No. 101; c. 28 December 1850

Slavery

Not by the railing tongues of angry men,
Who have not learned their passions to control;
Not by the scornful words of press and pen,
That now ill-omened fly from pole to pole;
Not by fierce party cries; nor e'en by blood,   5
Can this our Country's guilt be washed away;
In vain for this would flow the crimson flood,
In vain for this would man his brother slay.
Not by such means; but by the power of prayer;
Of faith in God, joined with a sense of sin;   10
These, these alone can save us from despair,
And o'er the mighty wrong a victory win;
These, these alone can make us free from all
That doth ourselves, our Country still inthral.

Poem No. 362; c. 4 January 1851

The Fugitive Slaves

Ye sorrowing people! who from bondage fly,
And cruel laws, that men against you make;
Think not that none there are who hear your cry,
And for yourselves, and children thought will take.
Though now bowed down with sorrow and with fear,   5

Lift up your heads! for you are not alone;
Some Christian hearts are left your flight to cheer,
Some human hearts not wholly turned to stone.
God to his angels shall give strictest charge,
And in their hands they'll bear you safe from harm;   10
Where, in a freer land, you'll roam at large,
Nor dread pursuit, nor start at each alarm;
Till in His time you shall return again,
No more to feel man's wrath, or dread his chain.

Poem No. 854; 3 March 1851

The Lost Sheep
Suggested by an Engraving

Beneath the wild thorn stretched upon the ground,
Lo, Christ the wanderer from his fold has found;
Pierced by the thorns it torn and bleeding lies,
And fills the desert with its piteous cries.
Neglected by its shepherd, it had strayed,   5
And left the murmuring brook, and sunny glade;
To wander, parched and hungry, o'er the plain,
No more its happy pastures to regain.
And he, who should have searched, with anxious fear,
On every hill and valley, far and near;   10
And, when he found, upon his shoulder laid,
And with his friends a great rejoicing made;
Cared not to leave his ease the lost to find,
To give it food, its bleeding wounds to bind;
He heeded not its fate, nor piteous cry,   15
But left it suffering, there alone to die.
But Christ, who careth for the lost and poor,
His Father's mansions left to seek and cure;
He from its foot plucked out the festering thorn,
Smoothed its soft fleece, by cruel branches torn;   20
And bore it, in his arms, beside the brink
Of cooling stream, and gave it there to drink;
There washed the crimson from its bleeding side,
And with the tender grass its wants supplied;

Then, calling it by name, he homeward led,   25
And as his own the lost and wandering fed.

Poem No. 67; April 1851

Thoughts and Desires

How, in the inmost soul,
   Do thoughts, desires have birth?
Own they no just controul,
   Are they of heaven, or earth;

As chance, or outward things   5
   Do bid them come and go?
Can none controul the springs
   Of his own joy, or woe?

Yes: ours the power of prayer
   To Him, who rules within;   10
Whose sway extends e'en there,
   Where thoughts, desires begin.

God's eye doth there behold
   The thoughts of every mind;
The heart's desire untold,   15
   The purpose, but designed.

And He can cleanse the heart
   From every guilty stain;
And Peace and Power impart,
   That ever will remain.   20

Lord, give us strength to pray,
   To fix the wandering thought;
Till we have learned thy perfect way,
   And unto Thee are brought.

Poem No. 188; April 1851

Hymn

Tune,—"Arlington."

As by the quickening breath of Spring,
The flowers and buds unfold,
And on the air their perfume fling,
And deck the fields with gold;

So, by the life Instruction gives 5
Do minds their powers expand;
And man a nobler being lives,
Nobler in heart and hand.

No more with dull and grovelling thought,
He idle roves the earth; 10
With busy hands the works are wrought
To which his mind gives birth.

He builds the city's dwellings fair,
He sails across the sea;
And doth in nature's secrets share, 15
Her might and mystery.

The factory huge, the tapering spire,
Alike proclaim his skill;
The steam-drawn car, the electric fire,
Are subject to his will. 20

He bows not now in mental night
To idols like the clod;
But in his soul receives the Light,
And worships only God.

Poem No. 52; c. 15 May 1851

The Soul's Rest

Rejoice ye weary! ye whose spirits mourn,
There is a rest which shall not be removed;
Press on and reach within the heavenly bourne,
By Christ, the King of your Salvation, proved.

There is a rest! Rejoice ye silent stars,   5
Roll on no more all voiceless on your way;
Thou Sun! no more dark cloud thy triumph bars,
Speak thou to every land the coming day.
And thou, my soul, that feel'st the rest within,
That greater art than star, or burning sun;   10
Rejoice! for thou hast known the rest from sin, ·
And hast the eternal life in God begun:
Praise thou the Lord, with every living thing,
And for his grace with saints, and angels sing.

Poem No. 407; c. 21 June 1851

The Sliding Rock

*Passing up the turnpike a few evenings since, I saw the workmen just finishing a drill in
the centre of the beautiful Sliding Rock, which, ever since Salem was settled, has been the
play-place of the children, in the upper part of the city. By the feet of many generations it was
worn as smooth as polished marble. I felt a pang, as the blast shivered it into pieces, and
echoed from the hills around. I have endeavored to commemorate the pleasant associations
connected with it by a few lines.*

The Sliding Rock! that pleasant spot,
    So dear in childhood's hour;
Say, can it ever be forgot,
    While memory holds her power?
How smooth 'twas worn! Like glass, or steel,   5
    Its polished surface shone;
No hobbly place the foot could feel,
    Upon that slippery stone.
For boys and girls, with busy feet,
    Its face kept ever bright;   10
There oft for play they loved to meet,
    At morn, and noon, and night.
I see them now, at even-tide,
    A merry, happy band;
I see them ready for a slide,   15
    Upon its top they stand.
Now as the oldest takes the lead,
    And glides across its face;

They, one by one, in turn succeed,—
   And then renew the race. 20
They seem as if with wings possest,
   As up and down they go;
Without a pause, or moment's rest,
   Above, and now below.
When hot and weary down they sit, 25
   And watch the passers by;
With pleasant smiles their faces lit,
   And pleasure in each eye;
They sit and watch the pasture gate,
   Till it shall open wide 30
For yonder herd, that stand and wait,
   Upon the green hill's side;
They count their number as they crowd
   The path beneath their feet;
And hear their lowings, long and loud, 35
   Far down the busy street.
The dusty traveller with his staff
   There stops to watch their play;
Pleased with their sport and merry laugh;
   Then passes on his way. 40
The loaded stage, with quickening speed,
   Comes rumbling down the hill;
While every panting, smoking steed
   New ardor seems to fill.
But now the travellers all are gone, 45
   The shadows darker grow;
They leave, 'till morn, the sliding stone,
   And to their homes they go.
The fire-flies gleam among the hay,
   The stars are in the sky; 50
And, wearied with their pleasant play,
   In slumbers sweet they lie.

Poem No. 564; July 1851

The Potato Blight

Nature has her sickly years,
   'Tis to show she's not divine;
In the failure it appears
   Of an humble, blighted vine.

Says vain man, with plenty blest,   5
   'Thus to-morrow too shall be;'
But who knows what will be best?
   Who the morrow can foresee?

On the morrow, in his sight,
   Droops his harvest far and wide;   10
Touched by some mysterious blight,
   Sent to humble human pride.

' 'Tis the effect of natural laws,'
   Says proud Science, blinded still;
'I will show mankind its cause,   15
   And remove it by my skill.'

'God no miracle has wrought,
   Since creation's early hour;
When from chaos, or from naught,
   Worlds were fashioned by his power.'   20

But the human heart, more wise,
   Sees in this His present hand;
And in lowly wisdom, tries
   All He does to understand.

Asks, 'why, with a blighted vine,   25
   Nations' fate should be entwined?'
'How all nature doth combine
   To fulfill what God's designed?'

Learns whate'er the Lord may give,
   Or whate'er he takes away;   30
Trusting in His love to live,
   That doth feed us day by day.

With new sympathy it glows
　　For its hapless neighbor's lot;
And its love to others shows,
　　Who to like distress are brought. 35

Feels that all mankind are one,
　　Not in knowledge, but in love;
And, wherever shines the sun,
　　Should their common kindred prove. 40

Poem No. 347; c. 4 October 1851

Congregational Singing

With the spirit Christians sung,
　　In the church's early days;
Every heart, and every tongue
　　Joined the soul-inspiring praise.

Gathered in an upper room, 5
　　In the desert lone and drear,
In the cavern's midnight gloom,
　　Rose their voices loud and clear.

Giving thanks for every gift,
　　Asking wisdom, asking grace; 10
Thus they sought their souls to lift,
　　When they met in every place.

Now, though mighty temples stand
　　Rearing their high walls to heaven,
Filling every Christian land, 15
　　No such praise to God is given.

Silent is the people's voice
　　In the temples of the Lord;
Never do their hearts rejoice,
　　Singing hymns in sweet accord. 20

Like the sounding ocean's waves,
　　When they break along our coast;
Should arise, to Him who saves,
　　Praises from his countless host.

Vain the labored strains of art,   25
    That but please the nicer ear;
'Tis the music from the heart,
    That the common heart doth cheer.

Simple tunes, that lingering dwell
    In the temple of the mind;   30
And with secret, holy spell
    Soul to soul forever bind.

Strains that lift our thoughts above
    Earthly toil, and earthly care;
Filling all our souls with love   35
    Every grief and joy to share.

Poem No. 849; c. 6 December 1851

Kossuth

Illustrious man! who doth to heaven appeal
Against the tyrant's might, and tyrant's wrong;
And, as thine own, thy Country's wounds doth feel,
Forget not in whose strength vain man is strong:
Not in the mighty winds that mountains shake,   5
Not in the earthquake, nor the avenging fire;
But in the still small voice Jehovah spake,
Rebuking thus his warlike prophet's ire.
'Tis ours for Truth to suffer, and to speak;
But not to fight, or warlike trumpet blow;   10
The strength of armies in her cause is weak,
And Freedom finds in these her deadliest foe;
For never can the Truth, or Right prevail,
Till rust consume the sword, and warrior's mail.

Poem No. 295; January 1852

John Woolman

Friend of the slave, and friend of all mankind;
He felt for all that suffering man doth feel;
And labored through his life, with humble mind,
The cause of all his suffering to reveal.
He preached deliverance to the captive slave,   5
Justice and mercy to his cruel lord;
Strong in his faith and love, who came to save,
And bring fulfilment to the prophet's word;—
Thou sowd'st not seed in vain; in want and tears
Oft journeying from place to place alone;   10
The rich reward of all thy toils appears,
A glorious harvest waves, where it was sown;
And countless reapers, with their sickles stand,
Reaping what thou didst sow with single hand.

Poem No. 139; c. 6 March 1852

Hymn
Waiting For Christ

Thou for Christ hast waited long,
    Art thou weary, art thou faint?
Still have patience, and be strong,
    Such his charge to every saint.

Hast thou suffered, for his name,   5
    Persecution, scorn, and loss?
Count not suffering, want, nor shame,
    Ever glory in the cross.

Mind not scoffers, when they say,
    'Where's the Coming of the Lord?'   10
'Who shall see his glorious day?'
    He is faithful to his word.

He, too, waited long for thee;
   Called thee, but thou still delayed;
Longed from sin to set thee free,   15
   And for thee his Father prayed.

With compassion, from on high,
   Still he views thy sufferings here;
By the Spirit still is nigh,
   What can then his follower fear?   20

Fainting, suffering, still abide
   Constant in thy Savior's love;
In his promises confide,
   He can never faithless prove.

"Lo!" he says, "I quickly come,   25
   Thou my Glory too shalt see;
That which fills my Father's home,
   That which He has given me."

Poem No. 674; c. 26 June 1852

The Wild Rose of Plymouth

Upon the Plymouth shore the wild rose blooms
As when the Pilgrims lived beside the bay
And scents the morning air with sweet perfumes,
Though new this hour more ancient far than they;
More ancient than the wild, yet friendly race,   5
That roved the land before the Pilgrims came;
And here for ages found a dwelling-place
Of whom our histories tell us but the name!
Though new this hour out from the Past it springs
Telling this summer morning of earth's prime;   10
And happy visions of the Future brings
That reach beyond, e'en to the verge of time;
Wreathing earth's children in one flowery chain
Of Love and Beauty ever to remain.

Poem No. 754; 28 June 1852

Voting In The Old North Church

No unfit place is this wherein to vote,
That once a Temple was to the Most High.
Though some may deem it as a thing of chance,
That it for such a purpose should be used;
I see in this a sign of deep import   5
Unto my Country, and her future weal:
A sign it is, that with no foolish haste,
No ignorance of what our duty is,
No base or sordid purpose in our souls,
We on this *Table now should lay our votes,   10
And exercise a freeman's holy trust.
Hence ye profane! who would these courts invade
With consciences defiled, and passions fierce;
Who scorn all bounds, and, in the sacred name
Of Liberty; indulge in foul excess,   15
Shouting her name to violate her rights.
Hence too ye ignorant! who know not yet
The value of the rights, which you enjoy.
Neglecting your own minds, in vain you strive
To serve your Country in her hour of need.   20
The ends of Government, its righteous ends,
Peace, Order, Industry, and steady growth
In Knowledge, and in Virtue, are forgot
By ignorant, deluded multitudes;
For mad Ambition's warlike, wasteful schemes.   25
The industrious citizen and peaceful man,
Who for long years has served his country well,
And understands her history, and her laws;
Is set aside for heroes of an hour;
Who nothing know, but to excell in arms,   30
And nothing but a victory recommends.
In vain does Freedom, with her gifts, endow
A people; that neglect to know their worth,
Or satisfy the claims on which they are held.
Ye sordid hence! if such, in such a land,   35
There live; who, though in deepest poverty,
Could so forget a freeman's holy trust,

*The Communion Table, on which the Ballot box is placed.

As for the heaviest purse to sell their votes!
Hence all, who have not in their heart of hearts
Their Country's good! who bring not here to lay   40
Upon her altar sincere gifts, and free.
Who, by whatever name they may be called,
Seek not her highest welfare as their own.
Oft as I tread these courts, I seem to hear
A voice, still lingering round their walls, which says,   45
'Ye who would serve your Country, serve your God.
Choose ye this day, if ye will serve the Lord.
Do justice, and love mercy. Let not pride
Of country blind you to your country's sins.
Uphold not by your votes her wickedness,   50
Her love of war, the oppression of the slave,
Or any wrong, that man inflicts on man.
Give the law's sanction only to what's just,
To precepts such as reason doth approve,
And Christ has taught. Obedient to these truths,   55
Americans! your Country's safe. The will
Of the majority will prove the reign of right,
Of reason, and self-government mature.
And He who rules the nations shall sustain,
And cherish your Republic; till it grow   60
To be a blessing, lasting and unmixed,
To all the human race.'

Poem No. 358; c. 10 July 1852

The Day Lily

Learn O man! the worth of time,
    By the lily's humble flowers;
Not alone the stars sublime
    Mark for thee the rolling hours.

See below thee, at thy feet,   5
    Where it lifts its purple bell;
Hear it hour by hour repeat,
    'Day is passing, use it well.'

Flower by flower blooms forth to die,
    With the course of every sun;   10
On the rod they drooping lie,
    Telling each of duty done.

Waste not then a single day,
    That both heaven and earth record;
But, in cheerful haste, obey   15
    Their harmonious-spoken word.

Rouse thee, ere thy life has flown,
    Speak thy word, and do thy deed;
In the field of Time is sown,
    Precious, and immortal seed.   20

Every seed thou sowest now
    Shall a future harvest bear;
In the furrows of thy plough
    Wave the wheat, or useless tare!

Poem No. 315; July 1852

The Solitary Worshipper

A single member of the Society of Friends, in Boston, is said to have gone to their place of worship for some years after all his fellow-worshippers were dead.

Alone and silent there he sat
    Within the house of prayer;
Where, once with him, his brethren met,
    In silent worship there.
They all had gone; the young and old   5
    Were gathered to the dead;
He saw no more their friendly looks,
    He heard no more their tread.
Yet still he loved, as came the day,
    When they were wont to meet,   10
To tread the old familiar way,
    And take his 'customed seat.
Plain was the place, an humble hall,
    In which he sat alone;
The show of forms, the pride of art   15
    To him were all unknown.

No organ pealed its solemn notes,
  No choir the stillness broke,
No preacher read the sacred page,
  Or to his hearers spoke.   20
He needed not those outward things
  To wake the reverent mind;
For other ends than such as this,
  They seemed to him designed.
In silence, gathered to himself,   25
  The Spirit he implored;
And without speech, or outward sign,
  The Father he adored.
And to his mind was opened then
  The meaning of the word,   30
"Ask and receive," "seek ye and find"
  The Spirit of the Lord.
That Spirit strengthened and consoled,
  And gave him inward sight;
And round the lonely worshipper   35
  There shone a marvellous light!
No more alone! For he had come
  To Zion's holy hill,
The city of the Living God,
  Which saints and angels fill.   40
The elders there with silver locks,
  The sisters' modest grace,
The young, in all their innocence,
  With glory filled the place.
No cloud of sorrow, or of care   45
  A soul had ever known,
That in that happy band he saw,
  Nor felt it e'er alone.
Their looks of peace and love unchanged
  Assured his trembling soul;   50
And bade him banish every fear,
  And every doubt controul.
With them again, as when on earth,
  He held communion sweet;
And by their sympathy was made   55
  For heaven's own worship meet.

Poem No. 34; c. 30 October 1852

Sonnet,
To the Rev. James Flint, D. D.,
On reading his Collection of Poems.

The Poet often strives, on eagle's wings,
Above the earth, and all it holds to soar;
Forgetting humble, and familiar things,
Which touch the heart, and thus improve us more.
Not such thy Verse, beloved, and honored Friend!   5
Which loves our earthly griefs, and joys to share;
And doth amusement with instruction blend,
Dwelling on every object grand and fair.
Of Change it tells, propitious, or adverse,
That, in Time's flight, our own New England's known;   10
And doth, in pensive, pleasing strains, rehearse
The changes which Old Harvard's halls have shown.
Thine too are Hymns; that elevate and cheer,
And all our homes, and temples more endear.

Poem No. 542; October 1852

The Mind The Greatest Mystery

I threw a stone into a cavern deep,
And listening heard it from the floor rebound;
It could not from my thought its secret keep,
Though hidden from the sight its depth I found;
I dropped a lead into the ocean brine,   5
That silent sank; I sought its depth to know;
And the swift running of the deep sea line
Told me how far was ocean's bed below;
By geometric skill I spanned the sky,
And found how far from earth the fixed star;   10
Through widening spaces glanced my wondering eye,
Where the last sun lights up the heavens afar;
But when, from these, I turned to explore the mind,
In vain or height, or depth I sought to find.

Poem No. 276; December 1852

The Conspiracy

Nations and kings conspire against the Lord,
Exulting in their numbers, and their might;
And in their pride reject His holy word,
Proclaiming to the world that Power is Right.
The prophets in the dungeons pine and die,   5
The patriots from their country far are driven;
The captives toiling in their bondage cry,
And raise their eyes, and fettered hands to heaven.
Cast down, O Lord, the proud! Uphold the weak!
For Thou art God of heaven, and earth, and sea;   10
Make bold thy servants, Lord, thy truth to speak;
Our country save, and set the captives free;
Rule Thou in righteousness through Christ thy Son,
And, as in heaven, on earth thy will be done.

Poem No. 346; 8 February 1853

The Horsemen on the Sands

Upon the treacherous sands the horsemen ride,
And careless pass the bright and happy day;
Unmindful of the swift returning tide,
That long has warned them of their mad delay.
The winds arise, and sudden falls the night,   5
On every side the hungry billows roar;
With breathless haste they urge their rapid flight,
And, with their utmost speed, scarce gain the shore.
So, on the sands of Time we careless live,
Forgetting oft, how short life's little day;   10
And scarce a serious thought to duty give,
Till all its golden hours have fled away;
And but a few short moments yet remain,
In which we may the Shore in safety gain.

Poem No. 756; 24 March 1853

My Dear Brother Washington

He passed away with morning light,
    Released from every pain;
For him, the weary hours of night
    No longer could remain.

O holy Light! that blessed his eyes,   5
    Before they closed in peace;
Symbol of that, which doth arise,
    When earthly sorrows cease.

The sun arose; with faith possest,
    He felt his Father near;   10
And sunk in peaceful, childlike rest,
    Without a doubt, or fear.

In that last hour, with parting breath,
    His sorrowing friends he cheered;
And, as in life, so in his death,   15
    He was to all endeared.

Still, with the eye of faith, I see
    His form to us so dear;
Though dimmed my earthly sight may be,
    With many a falling tear.   20

Poem No. 163; 30 April 1853

On Seeing The Victoria Regia In Bloom, At The Garden of J. Fisk Allen Esq. July 22ᵈ, 1853.

Thou wondrous Flower! in which, on grander scale
Than in our northern clime, we see displayed
Creative Power, and Skill, that never fail;
By which the world and all therein were made;
With reverence on thy beauty would I gaze,   5
Inhale thy fragrance, and admire thy Leaf;
Whose wondrous size, and structure claim our praise,
Surpassing our conception and belief.

Yet on our ponds & streams, O Tropic Queen!
The *type of thee in stem, and leaf, and flower,   10
In beauty, and in fragrance too is seen;
Displaying here the same Creative Power,
As where, on Amazon's gigantic stream,
Thou lift'st thy head to greet the morning beam.

Poem No. 705; c. 22 July 1853

On Finding the Truth

With sweet surprise, as when one finds a flower,
Which in some lonely spot, unheeded, grows;
Such were my feelings, in the favored hour,
When Truth to me her beauty did disclose.
Quickened I gazed anew on heaven and earth,   5
For a new glory beamed from earth and sky;
All things around me shared the second birth,
Restored with me, and nevermore to die.
The happy habitants of other spheres,
As in times past, from heaven to earth came down;   10
Swift fled in converse sweet the unnumbered years,
And angel-help did human weakness crown!
The former things, with Time, had passed away,
And Man, and Nature lived again for aye.

Poem No. 846; July 1853

Goliath

With bold, unblushing front the Giant Wrong
Stalks forth, with helmet armed, and sword, and spear;
In its own strength, and brazen armor strong,
Inspiring e'en the hosts of God with fear!
Thus War amidst the nations rears its head,   5

*The Pond-Lily

Thus Slavery defies its banded foes;
They fill the world with tumults and with dread,
And to the present add prophetic woes.
But oft, by feeblest arm, God shows his might,
When e'en the numerous host with terror quails;   10
Some stripling David dares the unequal fight,
And in the name of Israel's God prevails;
To show the earth the Lord is God alone,
And Strength, and Skill, and Victory are his own.

Poem No. 833; October 1853

A Sunset In Haverhill

To a high hill, that overlooks
    The Merrimac, and Haverhill town;
I climbed one pleasant afternoon
    To see the setting sun go down.

The summit gained, I gazed around   5
    On farm, and forest, town, and stream;
Each formed for each, a beauteous whole,
    Bathed in the Autumn's yellow beam.

Asleep upon the river lay
    A fertile island fair, and large;   10
With elm, and oak, and maple fringed,
    Blending their hues around its marge.

I could not tell, which fairer seemed,
    The heavens above, or earth below;
The woods in richest colors drest,   15
    Or gorgeous sunset's purple glow.

Upon the horizon's utmost rim,
    Inspiring thoughts and feelings high,
Wachusett and Monadnock stood,
    Like pillars of the vaulted sky!   20

Still larger grew the orb of day,
    Still brighter, till it passed from sight;
And on the distant hill-top left
    A golden diadem of light.

Why haste to other lands, I said?   25
    Why leave so fair a scene behind?
In western, or in eastern clime,
    Canst thou a fairer prospect find?

Poem No. 735; October 1853

The Past

Thou Past! What art thou? whither dost thou lead
Through countless generations fled away;
Empires, and races, that have left no trace,
Save in the nameless mound, or city's site,
Disputed oft, and called by different names.   5
Thou point'st to Nineveh, and storied Thebes,
To Aegypt's pyramids, and Paestum's fanes;
And say'st, with solemn, awe-inspiring voice,
"These are of yesterday, compared with Me."
And still thou beckon'st on, with shadowy hand,   10
Through hoary epochs before man was made,
And at the head of the creation placed.
I pass gigantic forms, unknown to man,
Save by their impress, left upon the rock;
Or their huge bones dug from the miry clay;   15
Mammoth and Mastodon, and, stranger still,
The monsters of the Oolitic age.
And still beyond, amidst gigantic ferns,
And towering reeds, I pass; whose thick rank growth,
O'erwhelmed by fire and flood, was changed to coal;   20
Before the lofty mountains were upheaved.
Not there, nor in the central depths beneath,
I reach the boundaries of thy mighty realm.
Leaving the earth, I soar amidst the stars,
And far beyond the solar system range;   25
Where light, the swiftest messenger of God,

Has winged its arrowy flight for countless years,
Yet never reached the world to which 'twas sent!
Lost and bewildered, by the amazing thought,
In vain I seek above, as on the earth,   30
Thy origin; or what thou art, O Past!
Wearied with outward search, I turn within;
And, of my soul, I ask thy origin.
But vainly there would I explore thy depths.
For deeper mysteries within us lie,   35
Than in the world of time and sense without.
Of spirit's hidden essence, who can tell,
Or mark, by years, the time when it began?
The mind within its mighty thought can grasp
The laws, that bind the planets in their course,   40
Measure the stars' vast distance from the earth,
Predict the wandering comet's sure return,
Compel the elements to do its will.
In vain Philosophy would seek to read
The dark inscriptions on the human soul,   45
More ancient, and obscure than print of beast,
Or bird, or tree, left on the solid rock,
When the foundations of the earth were laid.
In God alone my wandering mind can rest,
In Him the Present, Past, and Future meet.   50
Though, to our weak view, succession marks
The history of man, and all we see;
And e'en our language echoes with the past;
Yet this is but our feeble, finite thought,
That sees not from beginning to the end.   55
He who, in the Beginning, formed the earth,
And woke the soul to conscious life and joy;
He fixed thy boundaries, O mysterious Past!
And crowned Thee monarch of thy mighty realm.
And He determined, when thy reign shall end,   60
And in our thought Eternity begin.

Poem No. 688; c. 26 November 1853

Hymn,

Sung at the Thompson Jubilee, at Barre, Jany. 12, 1854

We hail our Jubilee to-day,
    The Christian's Jubilee comes round!
We come our grateful vows to pay,
    For this we bid the trumpet sound.

Its welcome notes our bosoms thrill,   5
    For earthly blessings long enjoyed;
How large a space their memories fill,
    With pleasures sweet and unalloyed!

The Lord has blessed each fruitful field,
    And we would of his goodness tell;   10
Our Fathers' farms abundance yield,
    And here their sons in safety dwell.

With Health, and Liberty, and Peace,
    For fifty years He's crowned our lot;
O, may these blessings never cease,   15
    Or be in coming time forgot.

For fifty years thy servant, Lord,
    Has preached the Gospel of thy love;
We thank Thee for thy saving Word,
    All other gifts how far above!   20

Behold, as in a fruitful land,
    The precious seed he here has sown;
Still prosper, Lord, thy servant's hand,
    And still, as Thine, the Vineyard own.

Till, resting from his earthly care,   25
    He join thy saints in courts above;
In higher joys, and duties share,
    And feel new measures of thy love.

Poem No. 761; c. 12 January 1854

On The Nebraska Bill

An Eden land, an Eden in the west,
Where once the Indians roamed erect and free;
Where now their few and weary tribes find rest,
Shall it be blasted, cursed by Slavery?
Our plighted faith to the red man was given,   5
That there should be the asylum of his race;
Our vow to Afric's sons is writ in heaven,
And shall we thus fair Freedom's name disgrace?
O plant not then the poisonous upas there,
Nor heed the subtle serpent's guileful speech;   10
But rather bid all races come and share,
And Freedom's Gospel to the nations teach;
That unborn millions there may learn its name,
And the glad tidings through the world proclaim.

Poem No. 46; 27 February 1854

On An Ear Of Wheat
Brought, By My Brother, From The Field Of Waterloo

Sign of Plenty, Peace, and Joy,
    From a field once desolate;
Where conflicting armies met,
    Filled with pride, revenge, and hate;

Where all Europe was in arms,   5
    And its mightiest captains led;
And the promise of the year
    Trampled was by soldiers' tread;

Welcome! for thou tell'st of Him,
    Who in trouble is our Friend;   10
Upon whom, though earth shall shake,
    We unmoved may still depend.

Sign art thou, that on the earth
    God will cause all wars to cease;
And the hostile tribes of men   15
    All to dwell in Love and Peace.

Sign, that still his word is sure;
    That, while earth itself remains,
Seed-time, harvest, shall not fail
    Whitening all her fruitful plains.   20

Hasten, Lord, the coming years,
    By thy Prophets long foretold;
And may we the promise find,
    That Thou mad'st to them of old.

Poem No. 422; March 1854

The Dead Elm

It stands amidst the beauty of the Spring,
Its graceful outline stretched against the sky;
Warm suns, and rains, which life to others bring,
Blossoms, and leaves to it alone deny.
A subtle gas has been its fatal foe,   5
Through all the ground the noxious fumes have spread;
Its roots have drunk the poisoned stream below,
The noble elm roots, trunk, and limbs, is dead!
So, without sign of aught the soul can harm,
Amidst a sinful world, it droops and dies;   10
Concealed, the evil gives it no alarm,
When, from gross vice, with wings of fear, it flies;
Its subtle foe is in the air it breathes,
Mixed with the very food on which it lives.

Poem No. 307; 30 May 1854

Hymn

Sung at the Celebration of the Fourth of July, in Salem, 1854.

Hail, Love of Country! noble flame,
 That never can expire;
In every age and clime the same,
 Alike in son and sire.

Light in our souls a holy zeal,   5
 As one united band,
Our growing Country's wounds to heal,
 And all her foes to withstand.

No more to battle would we go
 To fight against our kind;   10
Through human veins one blood doth flow,
 And one the heart and mind.

But forth we go to break the chain
 Of error and of sin,
To free our land from every stain,   15
 And rights for all to win.

To triumph in the Gospel's might,
 And Christian patriots be;
To battle for the Truth and Right,
 And every bondsman free.   20

Poem No. 155; c. 4 July 1854

The Camphene Lamp

Fatal Lamp! whose brilliant ray
 Shines in homes of rich, and poor;
Yet more false than leads astray
 Traveler o'er the midnight moor.

Thou dost in man's dwelling come,   5
   Promising to aid, and bless;
But has filled his peaceful home
   With keen anguish, and distress.

Gathered round the social board,
   At the happy evening hour,   10
Each to each in love restored,
   What for evil can have power?

Naught but Thee, thou baleful light!
   *Author of so many woes;
Better far primeval night,   15
   Than the day thy beam bestows.

Like the box, that artful Jove
   Sent the first of human kind;
Thou a curse to man dost prove,
   Every plague in one combined.   20

Wise Prometheus did reject
   E'en the gift of heaven's high king;—
We should treat, with like neglect,
   Gifts, that death and suffering bring.

Let the Press its warning sound,   25
   Till no more sad tales we hear;
And thy light no more be found
   In the home to us so dear.

Poem No. 118; c. 18 July 1854

The Homeless Wind

Where hast thou been roaming,
Thou houseless, homeless wind?
Thy voice is sad and moaning,
Thou hast none of thy kind.

*Since 1850 from the use of camphene and kindred articles for the purpose of illumination, there have been 169 persons killed, and 279 wounded. J.V.

Wind

"I've been in lone places,   5
Upon the wild sea shore;
Where billow billow chases,
And listened to their roar.

I've been on the high hill-top,
And on the lonely plain;   10
Where'er I roamed, I could not stay
Contented to remain.

Now, around man's dwelling,
From places lone and drear,
My story I've been telling,   15
But found I none to hear.

For none there had feeling
For the houseless, homeless wind;
To receive its sad revealing,
In sympathy of mind."   20

Poem No. 805; c. 13 January 1855

What Of The Night?

What of the night? O watchman! tell,
    Who on the watchtower high doth stand;
What of the night? I hear it swell
    In every tongue, from every land.

Lo! half the earth in darkness lies,   5
    Millions to idols bend the knee;
When shall the day-spring bless their eyes,
    And the deep gloom before it flee?

Nations that boast the Christian name,
    Still meet as foes in bloody fight;   10
When shall they own their deeds with shame,
    And in the ways of Peace delight?

When shall they use the talents lent,
   To elevate and bless mankind;
Each with its own domain content,   15
   Each to its proper sphere confined?

When shall the Church the risen Lord
   Own as the Way, the Truth, the Life?
Walk in obedience to his Word,
   And cease from every angry strife?   20

When shall the year of Jubilee
   Return to bless Columbia's soil;
And all her captive sons be free,
   Who now in cruel bondage toil?

The watchman saith, "The morning's nigh,   25
   Awake, ye dwellers in the land!
The redd'ning dawn is in the sky,
   And the Lord's kingdom is at hand."

"I watched of old when Babylon fell,
   And heard afar her mighty fall;—   30
But greater tidings now I tell
   To all who shall for tidings call."

Poem No. 780; c. 3 February 1855

To the Memory of the Rev. James Flint, D.D.

Much-loved Pastor! thou hast gone
   To thy longed-for home of rest;
Suffering past, and duties done,
   Thou with heavenly peace art blest.

With the Sabbath's closing hour,   5
   Peaceful passed thy life away;
Fell disease had lost its power,
   Naught thine upward flight could stay.

We would follow, but in vain,
   With our feeble, earthly sight;   10
Faith alone those heights can gain,
   See thee midst the dazzling light.

Where thou dost communion hold
   With loved spirits gone before;
And in thine embrace enfold 15
   Near and dear, to part no more.

Let thy Holy Spirit, Lord,
   Comfort to the mourners bring;
Such the promise of thy Word,
   To that promise, Lord, we cling. 20

May it in our hearts renew
   Holy zeal, and fervent love;
Till again his face we view
   In our Father's house above.

Poem No. 333; 9 March 1855

McLean Asylum, Somerville

Oh! House of Refuge; for those weary souls,
   Trembling on dizzy heights, mid gloom and shade,
While Reason from their path her light withholds,
   Oh! House of Refuge! thou for them wast made.

Oh! House of Refuge! ever stand thou there— 5
   A Refuge thou from fiery Passion's sway—
A shelter from the scorching heat of care—
   A Holy Refuge, in grief's wintry day.

The hand of kindness reared thy stately pile,
   A goodness kinder keeps thee fair within; 10
Thy gates are open, and a welcome smile
   Here greets the weary wanderer—enter in.

Oh! House of Refuge; thou receivest all,
   The young, the old, the innocent, the gay;
The sighs, the groans, the burning tears that fall, 15
   Oh! Holy Refuge! thou wilt chase away.

Oh! House of blissful Hope! The orb of day
   First robes thy lofty domes with morning light
So the first dawn of orient Reason's ray
   Beneath thy walls lights up the soul's dark night. 20

A House of Refuge, and a home of love,
    A blest retreat, to me, thou wast for years,
When discord, doubt and fear for mastery strove—
    There, first, His bow of Peace shone amid falling tears.

Poem No. 383; March 1855

The Age Changeful and Worldly

Amidst a changeful, worldly age like ours,
How hard to keep a fixed, aspiring mind!
The Present with its sights and sounds o'erpowers,
And makes us to the Past and Future blind.
In vain does History tell, with faithful page,   5
Of mighty realms by luxury o'erthrown;
Men heed not, in an over-anxious age,
Their ruined capitals with grass o'ergrown.
In vain the prophets of a coming time
Proclaim for earth a bright, millennial day;   10
But few, responsive to their call sublime,
With a high purpose live, and toil, and pray;
Lord, from our hearts, pluck up each noxious weed,
And, in their places, sow the heavenly seed!

Poem No. 40; c. 26 May 1855

Hymn
So also will God, through Jesus, bring with him them
who sleep.

They, that in the Savior sleep,
    Are not perished, are not dead;
Christ his own doth faithful keep,
    All for whom on earth he bled.

Sleeping, waking, we are one,   5
    In the one, and risen Lord;
They, who from our sight have gone,
    Soon with Him shall be restored!

Naught created can divide
    Soul from soul and heart from heart;   10
We in Him do still abide,
    Though from earthly scenes we part.

Weep not then, as others weep,
    Who nor hope, nor peace have found;
Nor the soul in pleasures steep,   15
    Which amid the world abound.

Keep their memories bright and fair,
    Who, in Christ, have passed away;
Give not way to dark despair,
    Rather strive, and watch, and pray.   20

Faith will take from death its sting;
    And the friends, whom we deplore,
God, through Jesus, too will bring,
    And with Him again restore.

Poem No. 649; June 1855

"Blessed are they that mourn: for they shall be comforted." Math. 5:4.

How blessed the tears of those, who still weep on,
When they have ceased to feel Affliction's rod;
Forgetful that from them the chastening's gone,
Their eyes behold in faith their Father, God!
No more their tears for pain, and suffering flow,   5
They weep, for joy, to know their sins forgiven;
That God, e'en on the sinful, doth bestow,
Through his dear Son, the peace, and bliss of heaven.
Thus, when the storm is o'er, and, in the west,
The sun breaks forth amid the falling shower;   10
In heavenly hues the far-off clouds are drest,

And songs are heard within the sparkling bower;
And Nature weeps; though, midst her falling tears,
The bow of Promise in the clouds appears.

Poem No. 179; c. 14 July 1855

To The Memory Of The Rev. James Chisholm

Amidst the sick and dying, falling round,
He stood the faithful Pastor, and the friend;
In every call of duty ready found,
And loving his own charge unto the end.
Chisholm! thy memory long shall cherished be   5
In every state of this our country wide,
Both South and North in one, the bond and free
Shall speak of thee with patriotic pride!
Thy gentle manners and thy loving heart
Thy friends and classmates long shall cherish here;   10
Called, in mid-life, from one they loved to part;
They drop, in sympathy, the falling tear,
With sorrowing kindred, that for thee shall weep,
Who now hath gone reward in heaven to reap.

Poem No. 44; 21 September 1855

The Woodwax

Laughing, midst its yellow blooms,
    At the fire, that it consumes;
Springs the woodwax every year,
    It has naught from man to fear.

From the turnpike's grassy side,   5
    See it flourish far and wide,
On the steep and rocky hills;
    Naught the woodwax hurts, or kills.

Over all the pastures spread,
    Where the humblest feet may tread;   10
Richer carpet never king
    For his palace flower could bring.

Glorious sight, in summer time,
    'Tis, to see it in its prime;
With its spikes of flowers untold,   15
    Covering all the hills with gold!

Though a plant of stranger race,
    It with us has found a place;
Vain the farmer's art, or toil,
    That would drive it from the soil.   20

Vain in winter is the fire,
    Which he kindles in his ire;
Still it laughs amidst its blooms,
    At the flame, that it consumes.

Poem No. 314; October 1855

The First Telegraphic Message

What hath God wrought? What hath God wrought?
    Along the iron wires,
The electric current, swift as thought,
    Of this our Age enquires.

What marvel in these latter days,   5
    His purpose to fulfil;
Has God, to whom be all the praise,
    Wrought with sublimest skill.

From land to land, from shore to shore,
    He stretches wide the chain;   10
Which shall in one forevermore
    Link all earth's broad domain.

The wandering Indian of the west
    Shall see it stretching on,
To where the setting sun finds rest,   15
    And hear what God hath done.

And where again, from ocean's bed,
    On eastern lands he shines;
By millions shall the words be read,
    Transmitted o'er its lines. 20

The North and South shall hear the word,
    O'er all their frozen plains;
And nations with new thought be stirred,
    Where Winter ever reigns.

And each in his own tongue shall hear 25
    The Message it has brought,
And all shall say, with love and fear,
    Behold What God Hath Wrought.

Poem No. 772; 24 November 1855

The Mission Of The Friends To The Emperor Nicholas

Bold in their cause they stood before the Czar,
Careless alike of splendor and of power;
To bear their witness 'gainst the coming war,
Which over Europe darkly 'gan to lower:
Of Love, Forgiveness, and of Peace they spoke, 5
The laws which Christ unto the nations gave;
Which king, nor people never can revoke,
And which alone can king, or people save.
They pleaded, in behalf of suffering man,
The countless evils, which from war must flow; 10
Moved, deeply moved, ere yet the strife began,
By thought of human agony and woe;
And fearless spake the threatening of the Lord,
"Who take the sword shall perish by the sword!"

Poem No. 73; January 1856

Be of Good Courage

Ye who against the evils of our lot
Alone, and single-handed do contend;
Faint not! though you to greatest straits are brought,
And earthly succor fail, and earthly friend.
Near you in sympathy the angels stand,   5
Their unseen hosts encompass you around;
Strong, and unconquerable the glorious band,
And loud their songs, and hymns of victory sound.
And near you, though invisible, are those,
The good and just of every age, and clime;   10
Who, while on earth, have fought the self-same foes,
And won the fight, through faith and love sublime;
Let not the hosts of sin inspire a fear,
For lo! far mightier hosts are ever near!

Poem No. 856; c. 21 June 1856

To An Ancient Locust-Tree, Opposite Carltonville

Why stand'st thou here alone, when all thy mates,
That crowded by the river's bank are gone?
From near a century thy history dates,
Amidst new scenes thou standest now alone!
How changed yon fields! how changed the river too,   5
When on its bank thy tiny form upsprung!
Swift cars and streets and work shops now we view,
Where once were groves and fields, when thou wast young.
On Nature's wild, yet beautiful domain,
Man by his arts encroaches more and more;   10
Acrost the river broad he throws his chain,
And builds the solid bridge from shore to shore;
Yet still thy top with milk-white flowers is crowned,
And summer breezes waft thy fragrance round.

Poem No. 828; July 1856

A Walk In The Pastures

A free breath breathes in Nature,
   That maketh all things grow;
The breath of the Creator,
   From whom all things do flow.

It warms and gladdens all things,   5
   The flower and creeping vine,
The grass which in the meadow springs,
   The oak and lofty pine.

And every beast, and every bird,
   Its quickening influence feels;   10
And tiny insect's note is heard,
   Whose form the leaf conceals.

I feel it on our rocky hills,
   And lightly bound along;
My languid frame new vigor fills,   15
   My voice breaks forth in song;

I praise and bless the Being great,
   Who made this world so fair;
And did for joy each thing create,
   And doth for all things care.   20

Poem No. 7; August 1856

O, cleave not to the things of earth,
   For they must pass away;
But for the better, heavenly birth,
   With earnest longings pray.

Is it a time to lust for gain,   5
   To dig for golden ore;
Or to relieve disease and pain,
   From out thine ample store?

Is it a time thy wealth to spend
   On garments rich and rare,
And naught of it to others lend,
   Who've not a robe to wear?

Is it a time thy house to build,
   In grandeur all alone;
With every costly luxury filled,
   When many a man hath none?

Is it a time for thee to live
   For self, to earth confined;
And not a thought to others give,
   Or to the immortal mind?

Oh, cleave not to the things of earth,
   For they must pass away;
But for the better, heavenly birth,
   With earnest longings pray.

Poem No. 373; c. 8 November 1856

Nature Intelligible

Thou art not, as the Hindoos say,
   A vain illusion to the sight;
That doth the mind of man betray,
   Whilst thou his senses dost delight.

No wildering maze, without a plan,
   In Nature doth her votary find;
But glorious mansion built for man,
   The work of One, Eternal Mind!

Floor above floor, thy strata rise,
   Height above height, thy mountains stand;
Like pillars of the vaulted sky,
   O'erlooking far the sea and land.

In smallest thing, in leaf, or fly,
   How finished, perfect every part!
And, hidden from the curious eye,
   Are forms and hues of wondrous art.

From lowest fossil in its bed,
    Onward Creative Thought proceeds,
Through beast and bird, to man their head,
    And upward to his Maker leads.   20

Summer and Autumn, Winter, Spring,
    Each season of the varied year,
Doth each for us a lesson bring,
    If we but turn the listening ear.

Awake, O man! and face to face   25
    With Nature stand, a living soul;
And every word and letter trace,
    Written on her mysterious scroll.

And humbly rise, from earthly things,
    To Revelation's truth sublime;   30
Which from the same Great Being springs,
    Who built the world of space and time.

Poem No. 660; c. 3 January 1857

The Great Facts Of Christ's History

The traveller sees afar the mountain rise,
And thinks that soon he'll reach, and scale its height;
He hastens on, but finds to his surprise,
No nearer grows the object to his sight.
So the great facts of Jesus' history stand,   5
While onward still we journey day by day;
In youth we see them seeming near at hand,
And think to master them without delay:
But, in the soul's horizon, high they tower
Above our common thoughts, and common ways,   10
And a long life will scarcely lend the power,
(So full is life of trifles and delays,)
To reach at last the glorious mount of God,
And climb the heights, on which the Savior trod.

Poem No. 585; c. 14 February 1857

Freedom National, Slavery Sectional

'Tis written by God's finger on our land,
On mountains, prairies, lakes, and mighty streams,
'Tis thundered by the ocean on the strand,
From sun and stars in quenchless light it beams,
This land to Freedom is for aye ordained!   5
'Twas this inspired the roving Indian's breast,
'Twas this our fathers by the sword maintained,
'Tis this which bids us feel for the oppressed.
Then what are human laws, on parchment writ,
Fastening on man's free limbs the heavy chain;   10
Interpreted by learned jurists' wit,
Laws born of pride of birth, and lust of gain;
To those eternal laws, of God's decree,
Forever sounding forth, That Man Is Free?

Poem No. 734; 13 March 1857

Christ Abiding Forever

I followed Christ, and vainly hoped on earth
That he would stay, and in the flesh would dwell;
I knew not that He came of heavenly birth,
As doth the loved disciple of Him tell.
Sudden He left me here! and much I grieved,   5
And wandered on in sorrow and alone,
Till in his Resurrection I believed;
Then He appeared again, who just had gone;
Spake of his kingdom, which must soon prevail
O'er all the earth, and evermore remain;   10
The foes which for a time would it assail;
Then He ascended up to heaven again,
Sending the Spirit, that the heart doth fill
With joy and peace and power to do his will.

Poem No. 227; c. 27 June 1857

The South River At Sunset

Mirrored in the waters lie
   Hill and grove, and cloud and sky;
Each with form distinct, and clear,
   As they to the eye appear.

Moss-grown rocks, and grasses green,   5
   In the river's depths are seen,
Ferns, and flowers with colors bright,
   All are pictured to the sight.

See the cattle far below,
   Where the mimic grasses grow;   10
Cropping still the grassy sod,
   As if on the earth they trod!

When did painter's beauteous art
   Sight so fair as this impart?
Vain is human skill to line,   15
   Paint with colors so divine.

Thus the calm, and peaceful soul
   Doth reflect the mighty whole;
Every object bright and fair,
   Heaven and earth are mirrored there.   20

Poem No. 330; c. 8 August 1857

On Receiving A Flower
From the Rev. C. H. A. Dall, in India.

Fair flower! from one who toils in distant land,
Preaching a Gospel sent the world to save;
Welcome! for thou wast plucked by his own hand,
And safe hast reached me here o'er land and wave.
Why need I ask, "what tidings dost thou bear?"   5
When in thy form a Father's love I see,
Who for the grass, and tender flower doth care;
Much more for us, wherever we may be.

Dear friend! though now with dangers compassed round,
And far from home, and all the heart holds dear;
Still mayest thou be as ever faithful found,
Trusting in God without one anxious fear;
Whose Word will hush all strife, and bring the day,
When wars from the whole earth shall pass away.

Poem No. 107; 21 August 1857

Hymn

Sung at the Dedication of Plummer Hall, Salem, Oct. 6, 1857.

This building, graced with Plummer's name,
   We dedicate to day;
Long may its influence and fame
   Our service here repay.

To Science, and to Learning's aid
   We dedicate its halls;
From out their calm, and peaceful shade
   The voice of Wisdom calls.

'Come! learn what ancient sages taught,
   Come! list the poet's strain;
Scorn pleasure's lure, and raise your thought
   Above the lust of gain.'

'Here learn the history of your race,
   The mind's wide fields explore;
And in the works of Nature trace
   A Mind to love, adore.'

'For every star that gems the night,
   The world's majestic plan,
And things too small for human sight,
   A study are for man.'

'From morn till eve, from youth till age,
    Delight in study find;
And gain from books, and Nature's page,
    Food for the immortal mind;'

'Which gropes, like base and purblind things   25
    Along its darksome way;
Or soars on high, with sun-bright wings,
    To realms of lasting day.'

Poem No. 654; c. 6 October 1857

Philosophy And Religion

A stern philosophy it is, which says,
Bear with thy lot, O man! thou canst not change
The will of God, nor alter aught his ways;
For this would be all nature to derange;
'Tis the fixed law of nature men should die,   5
And thou must, in thy turn, that law obey;
To view thy fate with calm indifference try,
And naught of sorrow, nor of fear betray.
Not so Religion, with its heavenly voice,
Speaks to the suffering, dying sons of men!   10
It bids their sinking hearts in hope rejoice,
Declares that man, though dead, shall live again;
Points to the Savior, who, e'en from the grave,
Has power, above all nature's might, to save.

Poem No. 21; c. 28 November 1857

The Day Begins To Dawn

The Day begins to dawn, O blessed word!
That doth our darkness with its light illume;
In the long, cheerless night of sorrow heard,
It comes to banish from the mind its gloom;
Bidding it wake again to life, and joy,   5

In faith, and hope its daily tasks pursue;
Wisely for good each day on earth employ,
With brighter worlds than this still kept in view.
Though vanished from our sight, our friends still live,
Starlike and pure in Hope's immortal sphere;   10
And to our souls a heavenly peace they give,
While, subject to life's cares, we linger here;
Till the pale dawn become the glorious day,
And sorrow, pain, and death shall flee away.

Poem No. 483; c. 22 January 1858

On The Late Mild Winter

With spring-like mildness passeth, day by day,
The winter months; the wild flowers bloom,
And careless of the cold their charms display;
Why on our faces rests a cloud of gloom?
Do we not see in this mild season, sent   5
For man's relief, a providential care?
Shall we not learn a lesson of content,
And with less favored ones our blessings share?
All things are providential. Yet more plain
We see God's hand, when tempered is the wind   10
To the shorn lamb, and want and pain
Are ministered unto by angels kind;
Than when in Nature's course there is no change,
And naught occurs, which we, like this, call "strange!"

Poem No. 844; 15 February 1858

The Evergreen

If here the imaginative Greek had lived,
And seen thy lively green, through the dead grass
And leafless shrubs threading its devious way;
He might have fancied thee, fair Color's self,
And called thee Evergreen! And fabled thus.   5

That, when the winter's cold had killed the grass,
And robbed the forest of its emerald hue;
Thou didst escape; and, hiding in the swamp,
Wast there transformed into this beauteous vine;
Which still preserves, unchanged, the summer's green,   10
When it has vanished from the hill and plain.

Poem No. 294; c. 27 February 1858

Hindoo Converts
On the Domestic Trials of Hindoo Converts.
Report of Unitarian Mission in India.

"I came to cast a fire into the earth,"
The Savior said, that error shall consume,
The false beliefs, which in the mind have birth,
And with the Truth its inmost depths illume.
And what will I, if now it kindled be,   5
And natural kindred for a time divide?
The end of all their trials I foresee,
And heavenly mansions for their rest provide.
"Endure unto the end!" That cheering word
Doth still encourage all his chosen saints;   10
They look to Him, their Master, and their Lord,
Whene'er in trials sore the spirit faints;
Patient endure the danger, and the strife,
And tried, receive at length the Crown of Life!

Poem No. 217; c. 27 March 1858

The Soul's Invitation

Come, and enter Heaven, O soul!
   Bring the riches thou hast gained,
Wealth and honors, bring the whole
   For which thou such toils sustained;
Thou hast titles, houses, lands;   5

Costly robes the body wore;
All the busy, toiling hands
    Have laid up for thee in store.

        The Soul's Answer
What are all these things to me,
    Now that I would upward soar?   10
Boundless wealth on land and sea,
    I can never need it more.
What are honors, what is power
    Man on man doth here bestow?
They are his but for an hour,   15
    He must leave them here below.

Not with these can I ascend,
    And amidst heaven's light appear;
They nor joy, nor grace can lend
    In that higher, holier sphere.   20
Nay, they ever draw me down
    To the dark and sinful earth;
I forget the glorious crown,
    And my higher, heavenly birth.

Not in these I put my trust,   25
    But in Him who died to save;
They are now but glittering dust,
    Spoils and trophies of the grave!
In the knowledge of my Lord,
    In the love that He has shown,   30
In the keeping of His word,
    In these things, and these alone
Trusting, I am not ashamed;
    And in heaven may enter in;
For the Lord my name has named,   35
    And has made me free from sin.

Poem No. 89; c. 24 April 1858

Morning Hymn for a little Child

Glad I wake with morning light.
   Thou hast kept me through the night.
Lord! with grateful heart I pray,
   Keep me through another day.

Poem No. 147; c. 4 May 1858

Nature Teaches only Love

Well reason they, who from the birds, and flowers
Would prove that God is all a God of Love;
For feelings, that transcend e'en reason's powers,
To all mankind the same great doctrine prove.
'Tis true the fire, and tempest work his will,   5
Yet not in wrath, but for the good of man;
What seems to us with tear-dimmed eyes but ill,
Is still a part of one all-perfect plan!
The good of man, this is the gracious end,
For which all things were made on earth, in heaven;   10
To this alone forever do they tend,
For this alone to man were all things given;
Thus Nature with the Scriptures doth accord,
For God is Love declares the Sacred Word.

Poem No. 771; c. 5 June 1858

The First Atlantic Telegraph

With outward signs, as well as inward life,
The world is hastening onward to its end!
With higher purposes our Age is rife,
Than those to which with grovelling minds we tend.
For lo! beneath the Atlantic's stormy breast   5
Is laid, from shore to shore, the Electric Wire;
And words, with speed of thought, from east to west

Dart to and fro on wings that never tire.
May never man, to higher objects blind,
Forget by whom this miracle was wrought;   10
But worship and adore the Eternal Mind,
Which gave at length to man the wondrous thought;
And on wise-hearted men bestowed the skill
His Providential Purpose to fulfill.

Poem No. 841; c. 28 August 1858

Life and Death

Men live and die in secret; none can see
　　When lighting up, or going out the flame,
Save the All-Seeing eye; frail mortals, we
　　Call death and life, what are but so in name.
Death is the living to thyself in sin,   5
　　Which thou dost pleasure, ease, or grandeur call;
Nor even now death may for thee begin,
　　Before the shadows of the funeral pall;
Life is the lifting up which thou dost feel,
　　When thy feet follow where love bids thee go;   10
A life beyond disease, or severing steel,
　　Which naught but Him who gives it fears below;
Such be thy life! and thou in heaven shalt live,
When men unto the earth thy body give.

Poem No. 328; c. 11 December 1858

Lines On The Old Danvers Burying Ground

Above the ancient Burying place
　　Looks calmly down the full-orbed moon;
Each well known grave I plainly trace,
　　As in the effulgent light of noon.

And through the cold, transparent air,   5
    The stars and planets brightly glow;
As if they listened to the prayer
    Of dwellers on this sphere below.

And is there not some secret tie,
    Some influence from yon shining spheres;   10
Which lifts the sorrowing soul on high,
    Above this lowly vale of tears?

There is. For gazing on this spot
    My tearful eyes are upward turned,
And mortal feelings are forgot,   15
    A higher lesson I have learned.

For He who formed the wondrous whole,
    And doth each planet's motions guide;
Will clothe again the immortal soul,
    And for his children still provide.   20

For as the earthly form we wear,
    The fading emblem of decay;
The heavenly image we shall share,
    Which fadeth not, like that, away.

All live to God! Though earth may hide   25
    The forms of loved ones from our sight;
Our friends still live, with Him abide,
    Who on the grave sheds holy light.

Poem No. 25; c. 28 December 1858

On Seeing The Portrait of Helen Ruthven Waterston

Gazing on some higher sphere,
    Far, far off, and yet so near!
Thou dost join, with mortal's sight,
    Angel's vision clear and bright.
Not with vain and curious eye   5
    Dost thou gaze beyond the sky;
But with warm admiring look,
    As if thou its life partook;

And to thee were here foreshown
    Scenes to earthly minds unknown.   10
Yet, as mortal, thou dost gaze
    Far beyond the solar blaze;
And with love, unmixed with fear,
    Dost behold heaven's portals near!
Who would thee on earth detain?   15
    Our sad loss, thy happy gain;
In the many mansions fair,
    Which the Savior doth prepare;
Parents, child, again shall meet,
    Joy unclouded, bliss complete!   20

Poem No. 145; late 1858

Hymn

The Promise of The Spirit

When from their sight the Savior went,
    To dwell no more upon the earth;
The Spirit to his own he sent,
    And souls were born of heavenly birth.

He left them not as orphans here,   5
    To mourn their sad and bitter fate;
But gave them promises to cheer,
    While in the world, their lonely state.

"My Father greater is than I,
    I will not leave you here alone;   10
But send the Spirit from on high,
    And you, in Me, shall still be one."

Sweet promise to the mourning Bride,
    The Church, that mourns her absent Lord!
While in his love we still abide,   15
    He will fulfil his parting word.

Henceforth no more let Christians mourn;
   They hear again the bridegroom's voice,
From heavenly heights of glory borne,
   Which bids them with Himself rejoice.   20

So faith, and joy, and peace, and love,
   Became our heritage below;
Descending, with the holy dove,
   On all, who Christ's obedience know.

Poem No. 785; c. 19 February 1859

The Moss and Its Teachings

How often pass we by the works of God
Unnoticed, and forget his presence too!
The sea, the sky, the plain, and mountain top,
All these attract our gaze, and make us feel
That mighty Being's Presence, who first formed,   5
And still sustains the world in which we live.
And yet the tiny moss, which the child's found,
And so admires, to the reflecting tells
The same great truth, too oft by man forgot!
That God is everywhere, his power the same.   10
Gaze at the moss' varied tints, and arm
Thine eye with microscopic power. Behold
With what a wondrous skill each leaf is made,
Each stalk, a tree, rises above the mould;
Forming, with countless more, a beauteous grove.   15
Like mightier forests, wilted by the sun,
And covered black with dust, it droops and dies.
Refreshed and washed by showers it lifts its head,
Expands its shrunken boughs, puts on fresh hues,
As grateful for the timely-falling rain.   20
Think you God's presence here is less displayed,
Than in the forest of high towering oaks;
Which have, for centuries, withstood the storms?
That less than they, it needs the Maker's care?
Who scattered on the rock its dust-like seed,   25
Preparing thus the way for giant pines,

And mighty oaks to lift their forms on high?
Who hid the mosses 'neath the polar snow,
To feed the reindeer through the winter months,
Or save the life of far-adventuring man?   30
To humblest things the highest are allied;
And the low moss, on which man careless treads,
Hath with the noblest forms a unity;
And like them, too, an end for which twas made.
Scattered o'er all the earth the mosses grow,   35
On loftiest mountain and in deepest glen,
In gloomy forest and in open plain;
That no where man may come, and look around,
Without a witness of God's care and love.

Poem No. 197; c. 8 March 1859

On the Bunyan Tableau

Behold, O Christian! to the life displayed
The pilgrim's progress through this evil world;
The many foes by which he is delayed,
Apollyon's fiery darts against him hurled,
The vain allurements of the city spread   5
Like fowler's net to take him in their snare,
Its riches and its pomps, to which are wed
The souls of men; the castle of Despair
With dungeon deep, and Error's fatal hill.
And friends behold, who help the pilgrim here,   10
And arm him 'gainst his foes with heavenly skill;
Fair visions too his fainting spirit cheer,
The land of Beulah, and the city bright
To which he goes, revealed to human sight!

Poem No. 65; c. March 1859

The Lament Of The Flowers

I looked to find Spring's early flowers,
   In spots where they were wont to bloom;
But they had perished in their bowers,
   The haunts they loved had proved their tomb!

The alder and the laurel green,   5
   Which sheltered them, had shared their fate;
And but the blackened ground was seen,
   Where hid their swelling buds of late.

From the bewildered, homeless bird,
   Whose half-built nest the flame destroys;   10
A low complaint of wrong I heard,
   Against the thoughtless, ruthless boys.

Sadly I heard its notes complain,
   And ask the young its haunts to spare;
Prophetic seemed the sorrowing strain,   15
   Sung o'er its home, but late so fair!

"No more, with hues like ocean shell,
   The delicate wind-flower here shall blow;
The spot that loved its form so well
   Shall ne'er again its beauty know."   20

"Or, if it bloom, like some pale ghost,
   Twill haunt the black and shadeless dell,
Where once it bloomed a numerous host,
   Of its once pleasant bowers to tell."

"And coming years no more shall find   25
   The laurel green upon the hills;
The frequent fire leaves naught behind,
   But e'en the very roots it kills."

"No more, upon the turnpike's side,
   The rose shall shed its sweet perfume;   30
The traveller's joy, the summer's pride,
   Will share with them a common doom."

"No more shall these, returning, fling
    Round Childhood's home a heavenly charm;
With song of bird, in early Spring,   35
    To glad the heart, and save from harm."

Poem No. 243; May 1859

The Voice In The Poplars

A spirit in the tree top breathes,
    Familiar to my ear;
I hear a sound amid'st its leaves,
    My childhood loved to hear;

A rustling in the poplar tall,   5
    Which bends with every blast;
So to my soul its murmurings call,
    From out the silent past!

They tell in many an answering tone,
    As in my childhood's hour,   10
Of things, to gross, dull minds unknown,
    Of a mysterious Power;

That with the soul, by speechless things,
    Doth often converse hold;
And lessons to the spirit brings,   15
    Which books have never told.

For, written on each tree that grows,
    The story of its birth;
When perfect from God's hand it rose
    Upon the new made earth.   20

And when the stormy wind doth move,
    Or gentle zephyr fan;
It telleth still of Eden's grove
    To listening ear of man.

Poem No. 20; c. 13 August 1859

How Faith Comes

Faith in the Lord how can I find?
I hear you say. Alas so blind!
Dost thou not see the works He's made,
And all the glory there displayed;
The glory of the morning hour,5
And that which decks the lowly flower?
Dost thou not of the Savior read,
His wondrous words, His every deed,
An act of pure and holy love,
To lift the earth-bound soul above.10
And see'st thou not the heavenly light,
That's risen on the ancient night;
Which banishes from death its gloom,
And shows the world beyond the tomb?
Faith comes from sight, when clear and true,15
It comes, says Paul, from hearing too,
It comes from doing too the Word,
Obeying what we've seen and heard;
From humble toil, self-sacrifice,
When man his lower self denies;20
And follows Him, who died to save,
And his own life for others gave.

Poem No. 110; c. 22 October 1859

The Poet

As one who 'midst a choir alone doth sing,
When voices harsh fill all his soul with pain,
So that from even a note he would refrain,
And flee away as with a dove's swift wing,
Yet for Religion's sake you see him stay,5
And try to raise her service what he may;—
So doth the Poet live amidst his age!
Though at the first his lyre he scarce can hear,
He does not drown its discords in his rage,
Nor fly where they will not offend his ear;10

But for their very sakes who spoil his songs,
His heaven-taught strain he more and more prolongs;
Till one by one they with his paean blend,
And all in one harmonious concert end.

Poem No. 55; c. December 1859

The Set Times, And The Boundaries of Nations, Appointed By God

Not of self-will are States & Nations born;
Their times & bounds are fixed by God's decree;
Thus were these States from parent Country torn,
And, at his Word, became forever free.
To seek the Lord, to do his righteous will,   5
For this He prospered them in low estate;
And, that He might his purposes fulfil,
Amidst earth's mightiest Kingdoms made them great.
But hidden oft His purpose from our eyes,
As to the people & the kings of old,   10
To whom He sent his teachers, prophets wise
By whom their righteous downfall He foretold;
Would, O my Country! thou their fate might'st read,
And even now their prophets' warnings heed!

Poem No. 366; February 1860 or 1861

The Cemetery of Harmony Grove

Well is this place a cemetery called;
For here do we unto the earth commit,
With hope in Christ, the forms of those we love;
And say our friends have fallen asleep in Him,
To wait, with us, his Coming, long foretold.   5
So named they first the spot where martyrs slept,
And saints whose faith had overcome the world;
To show that death o'er them had lost his power.

Here once the sower came, and sowed his seed,
And watched the springing of the new green blade,   10
So different from the mouldering form below,
And pondered on the lesson Nature taught.
For she, with faithful trust, restores the grain,
Which man unto her bosom doth commit;
Yet tells him not, that he shall live again;   15
Or only in dim type obscurely speaks.
She makes but credible, what God reveals.
By revelation taught we clearly see
The hidden meaning of her countless forms,
Differing in glory on the earth, in heaven;   20
And, by analogy, the springing grain
Doth teach us of the body that shall be,
The spiritual body, that shall this succeed;
For reason's powers are limited and weak,
Nor fully can the mystery comprehend.   25
Earth can restore but that which is her own,
Give back the grain again an hundred fold,
Perpetuate her kinds, beasts, insects, birds,
The individual in the species lost.
Christ is the Resurrection, and the Life;   30
And, at his Coming, them who sleep shall bring.
With the same beauty do the flowers return,
And with like foliage is the tree new clothed;
But with more glorious bodies shall they come,
Whose life on earth was hid with Christ in God;   35
When He, who is our Life and Hope, appears.
E'en now are earth and man, though mortal, touched
With foregleams of the bright, immortal dawn.
They followed not myths cunningly devised,
Who have proclaimed the Coming of the Lord;   40
For they beheld his glory on the mount,
And heard the voice, which came to him from heaven.
No more, as once, neglected and forgot,
A source of superstitious fears to all,
The resting place of those we mourn remains.   45
Planted with trees, vocal with songs of birds,
Whose music morn and eve fills all the grove;
Adorned with flowers of every hue and kind,
With cheerful hopes we consecrate the grave.
Engraved on humble stone, or splendid tomb,   50

The holy texts of scripture meet the eye;
Or words of poet speaking heart to heart,
That tell men of a higher life to come.
While thus I tread these much frequented paths,
And hold communion with the loved and mourned;   55
The mystic veil between us thinner grows,
And nearer seems the time, when Christ shall come
To abolish death, and triumph o'er the grave.

Poem No. 770; c. February 1860

Preparation for Life's Voyage

Prepared, the sailor o'er the ocean sails;
His ship is strong, and skillful are the crew;
Watchful his glance to see what wind prevails,
When to the breeze he spreads his canvass new;
With chart and compass he no danger fears   5
From rock, or reef, or treacherous current strong;
From clime to clime, and port to port he steers
In his stout ship borne by the waves along.
Why thoughtless then, O man, wilt thou embark
Upon Life's sea, no chart or compass thine?   10
There tempests oft prevail, and dangers dark
Lie hid like rocks that lurk beneath the brine;
And oft man's bark, with all its swelling pride,
Sinks in the waves, or drives o'er ocean wide.

Poem No. 402; c. 17 March 1860

The Slowness of Belief in a Spiritual World

The astronomer with patient, searching gaze
Doth with his tube the depths of space explore;
Shows Neptune's orb, or, 'neath the solar blaze,
Reveals a world by man unseen before.
Justly the world rewards his arduous toil,   5
And claims to share the glory of his fame;

Beyond the boundaries of his native soil
From land to land the breezes bear his name.
But he who doth a Spirit-world reveal,
Not far in space, but near to every soul;   10
Which naught but mists of sense and sin conceal,
(Would from men's sight those mists at length might roll!)
He is with incredulity received,
Or with a slow, reluctant faith believed.

Poem No. 460; c. April 1860

Hymn
The Dew

'Tis not the copious rains alone,
   Which bless the parched soil;
The gentle dews that nightly fall
   Reward the sower's toil.

Unseen, unheard the dews descend,   5
   Like slumber on the mind;
And on the thirsty hills, and fields
   A blessing leave behind.

In the cool stillness of the night
   The drooping plants revive,   10
The grass and every tender herb
   With their sweet influence thrive.

See, gathered on each pointed blade
   How bright the dew-drops shine!
And learn in humble trusting faith   15
   To trace the Hand Divine.

That, though no clouds their fulness drop
   In answer to our prayer;
Still we may own that day by day
   Our God for us doth care.   20

Poem No. 731; c. July 1860

The Triennial

He reads in a book, he reads in a book,
  Many years have swiftly passed,
Since the August morn, that saw him look
  For the page, where he was classed;
He was then a youth, and his clear eye beamed,   5
  As he paused on each comrade's name;
And visions arose, as he thought and dreamed
  Of their pathways to virtue and fame.

This one shall soon win a poet's bays,
  And this in the senate be heard;   10
And this one will walk in his own quiet ways,
  That as now he has always preferred;
A fourth be a teacher and guide to the young,
  Another the priest of our God;
Around each beloved name a glory was flung,   15
  That illumined the paths which they trod.

But now he *turns back* on the Catalogue's page,
  Which shakes in his trembling hand,
As he slowly reads, with the helps of age,
  The names of that youthful band;   20
Not fifty years have come and gone,
  Since first the long column he read;
Now, on the starred page, he stands almost alone,
  As he reads and communes with the dead.

With those who remain he is walking there,   25
  Through the scene of their early days;
Recalling the joys, in which each had a share,
  As they brighten in memory's rays;
Though more of the dead, than the living, they know,
  As they sit in Old Harvard's high hall;   30
Or muse through its shadowy precincts below,
  They sit and they talk with them all.

Nor small is their pleasure, though saddened the while,
  This remnant from Time's tossing wave;
Like mariners cast on some sea-beaten isle,   35
  Who see every where round them a grave;

Each joys as he tells of his own favored lot,
    Points the rock, where he clung for his life;
While their tears fall for those, who can ne'er be forgot,
    Who there entered with them on the strife.   40

Still meet here, ye few, while the lamp of life burns,
    Where ye met at life's early hour;
Where often so fondly the memory turns,
    As the spot of her strongest power;
Here gladly she'll soothe your swift-flying days,   45
    With past thoughts of Friendship and Love;
Till no more ye are found in the world's busy ways,
    But have joined your companions above.

Poem No. 165; August 1860

Welcome
Written for the Essex Institute Fair, Held at Salem Sept. 4th, 1860.

We welcome to our Hall and Fair
    All who would aid in Learning's cause!
The noble work we fain would share,
    Which man to clearer knowledge draws.

With still increasing light it beams,   5
    As we the world around explore;
From earth and sky its radiance streams,
    That all may see, believe, adore.

The beast, the bird, the fish, the shell,
    The flower, the crystal from the mine,   10
Have each some word of truth to tell
    Of the Creator's vast design.

But oft, with uninstructed eye,
    And soul unmoved, on these we gaze;
And e'en the glories of the sky   15
    No knowledge show, call forth no praise.

From Learning's hall to Nature's page
  With more enlightened minds we turn;
Delighted still, from youth to age,
  New charms to see, new truths to learn.   20

As Nature, to her children all,
  Opens her realms of wonder wide;
Aid us that Learning's sun-lit hall,
  To none who seek, may be denied.

Poem No. 766; c. 4 September 1860

The Child's Answer

Who made these flowers, I asked a child,
  So many and so fair?
"God," she replied, "He made them all,
  And for them all doth care."

But man, than child, less wise may be,   5
  Who proudly seeks to know
The truths, which Faith, by humblest flower,
  To infant minds can show.

Him doubts perplex. And oft he seeks
  By reasonings long to prove;   10
What to the child so plain appears,
  God's being, and his love.

It is not that all outward things
  Do not his power proclaim;
But in ourselves the darkness is,   15
  Who cannot read his Name.

There's not a star in heaven above,
  Nor flower beneath our feet;
But doth to all men, everywhere,
  That glorious Name repeat.   20

Oh may we have a humble mind,
    Their teachings to receive;
And may we, like the little child,
    In God, in Christ believe!

Poem No. 814; c. 15 September 1860

Freedom And Union

By deeds not words we prove our inmost mind,
For things, not names, we labor and contend;
In noble souls the two are still combined,
And each to each a nobleness they lend!
Freedom and Union are not names, but things,   5
By deeds our fathers proved for them their love;
In vain with words like these the country rings,
If to the things themselves we recreant prove.
In this alone all patriots agree,
To labor for their country's highest good;   10
And, by the fruit it bears, to judge the tree,
However party names are understood.
'Tis not the title that makes good the claim,
But nobler deeds, which justify the name.

Poem No. 85; September 1860

The Cross

Raised on high, above the city,
    Oft I see the sacred cross;
Telling of the Savior's sufferings,
    Borne for men with shame and loss!

When amidst its streets I wander,   5
    And its tempting pleasures seek;
From the cross a strength there cometh,
    And no longer I am weak.

When I covet others' honors,
    Wish their wealth, or homes were mine;   10
Then the cross uplifts my spirit,
    And no longer I repine.

When I murmur faint, and weary,
    Grow impatient at my lot;
Then I look upon the symbol,   15
    And my sufferings are forgot.

When for good of men I labor,
    Yet for this I suffer wrong;
Then the cross its lesson teaches,
    Then, though weak, I yet am strong.   20

Then, the outward cross doth vanish,
    From my eye and from my thought;
And, all glorified, my Savior
    To my mind again is brought!

Not as when he bore his anguish,   25
    Hanging on the accursed tree;
But, as raised above all passion,
    Doth the Savior come to me;

And another life I enter,
    With its peace before unknown;   30
And, with countless tribes and nations,
    Stand confessed before the throne.

Poem No. 404; c. September 1860

On reading the Memorial of John White Browne

Forgetful thou to manhood's years had'st grown,
Thou knelt'st in Spring upon the grassy sod
To greet the early *Flower in fragrance blown,
And own the presence of its Maker, God.
Forgetful? No! but mindful rather thou   5
Of what true manhood must forever be;

*The houstonia.

Before each beauteous thing it loves to bow,
With a child's faith, and child's humility;
But, joined with these, a courage too was thine,
In Freedom's cause, boldly to do and dare;   10
Each worldly honor, for her sake, to resign,
And with her humblest follower all things share;
Nature, with early flower and falling leaf,
Doth mourn a life, like thine, should be so brief!

Poem No. 135; 25 October 1860

Hymn

And God shall wipe away every tear from their eyes. Rev. xxi.4.

Not tears alone for natural grief
   Our God shall wipe away;
To sinners too He sends relief,
   When unto Him they pray.

We mourn the loss of dearest friends,   5
   For want, and woe, and pain;
But still our God some comfort sends,
   And we rejoice again.

But most we weep and mourn for Sin,
   Will God, our God, forgive;   10
And purify the heart within,
   That we to Him may live?

Shall we as sinners ever know,
   That we are all-forgiven?
Shall Memory's page no record show,   15
   'Gainst such as dwell in heaven?

God wipes away the sinner's tears,
   Reveals a Father's love;
And all our doubts and all our fears,
   But passing shadows prove.   20

E'en Memory's self at length shall cease
    To bear one guilty stain,
And naught but joy, and heavenly peace
    Within the soul remain.

Poem No. 368; c. November 1860

One generation passeth away, and another generation cometh: but the earth abideth for ever. Ecclesiastes 1:4.

As is the sand upon the ocean's shore,
    So without number seems the human race;
And to that number still are added more,
    As wave on wave each other onward chase.

As are the drops of rain, that countless fall   5
    Upon the earth, or on the briny sea;
So seem man's generations great and small,
    Those that have been, and those who yet shall be.

As are the snow flakes fluttering on the air,
    Succeeded still by others thick and fast;   10
So many souls the mortal image bear,
    That stand within the present, or the past.

More than the ancient Preacher now we know,
    Though wiser he than all the sons of men;
God, through his Son, the promise doth bestow,   15
    That all the sons of earth shall live again.

Nor countless forms alone the earth doth hold,
    Which on it move, or in its bosom lie;
As numberless the stars, which we behold,
    Which fill the spaces of the azure sky,   20

So, we believe, unnumbered still in heaven
    Will be the forms, that meet our new-born sight;
When to each soul a spotless robe is given
    To dwell forever in its cloudless light.

Poem No. 54; c. 26 January 1861

What of Our Country?

What of our Country? is the word,
   The word from all we meet;
From young and old the question's heard,
   At home and in the street.

What of our Country? War or peace?   5
   The question comes to all;
Shall this our glorious Union cease,
   And into fragments fall?

What of our country? Has the plan
   Of God been here achieved?   10
Have we obtained the rights of Man,
   In which our sires believed?

What of our Country? Shall her name,
   Glorious in every clime,
Dishonored be? Or grow in fame   15
   Till the last hour of time?

In vain we ask, in vain we peer
   Into the future dim;
To God alone the vision's clear,
   We trust alone in Him!   20

For us the present only is,
   Be strong, be true to-day;
The future, the event is His,
   Whom worlds on worlds obey.

Poem No. 779; c. 29 January 1861

The Hour Before The Dawn

The darkest hour that falls upon the earth,
Is that before the coming of the dawn;
When light with darkness struggles for its birth,
And help Divine for man seems oft withdrawn!
In vain the eye would penetrate the gloom,   5

And look beyond the darkness of the hour;
To see of Wickedness the fated doom,
Of Virtue's Kingdom come with mightier power.
Thus when, amidst convulsive throes of old,
Christ's Kingdom in its glory should appear; 10
He the dark hour before the day foretold,
In signs and wonders to his followers clear;
And bade them earnest watch, and earnest pray,
Until in splendor rose his peaceful day.

Poem No. 481; February 1861

State Rights

Wisely each state for its own rights contends;
And jealous is of the whole Country's sway;
From arbitrary power those rights defends,
Nor tamely would a tyrant's will obey.
But to itself, meanwhile, it false may prove, 5
Seeking its own, its ease, its wealth, its power;
Acknowledging no more the bond of love,
Its Country's good, which was its nuptial dower.
Our Country's good! Ah, here we all have erred,
Unmindful of her good and noble fame; 10
Each state its separate interest has preferred,
And gloried even in the Nation's shame;
Nor seen, that what its greatness each may deem,
Without the general good, is but a dream!

Poem No. 830; c. 1 March 1861

The Rights of Man

With narrow view each state its own would claim,
Forgetful of the greater common good;
Forgetful of its heritage of fame,
When they the mightiest foe on earth withstood.
The Rights of Man seem now a short-lived dream, 5

An abstract good, an unsubstantial thing;
Of boastful orators the annual theme,
Or glory of which poets vainly sing.
Thus we our selfish ends too oft pursue,
Blinded by avarice, or lust of power;   10
Seeking our own, yet to ourselves untrue,
Unfaithful to our Country, and the hour;
Nor know that in the nation's good each state,
Whate'er it boasts, alone is truly great.

Poem No. 838; c. 15 March 1861

A Longing For The Spring

A longing for the Spring,
   Amidst the deepening snows;
To hear again the sweet birds sing,
   My spirit often knows.

For freedom and the joy   5
   That fill its happy hours;
When pleasant thoughts the mind employ,
   And pleasant sights are ours.

I see the pastures green,
   Where I am wont to stray;   10
Where flowers of every hue are seen
   To bloom along my way.

I follow on the brook,
   That prattles down the vale;
And tells, to many a leafy nook,   15
   Its short and gladsome tale.

The flower-crowned hill I see,
   Thick swamp and shady grove;
And welcome hear from bush and tree,
   Where'er my footsteps rove.   20

These haunt my memory still,
    With pictures of the past;
And longings for the spring-time fill
    My soul at every blast.

Poem No. 11; c. 29 March 1861

The Abolition Of Serfdom In Russia

From the great, imperial city
    Has gone forth the fixed decree,
That the Russian serf forever
    From oppression shall be free!

Through a long, long night of bondage,   5
    He has felt the oppressor's rod;
Bought and sold by haughty boyars,
    Held for life to till the sod.

The increasing light of knowledge
    Still denied to heart and mind;   10
He for ages has toiled onward
    To its cheering radiance blind.

With a nature thus degraded,
    His own good he scarce has known;
While, in lands by Freedom favored,   15
    Man to manhood's height has grown.

But the day at length is dawning
    O'er the dark and frozen North;
Now the trumpet's voice proclaimeth
    Man's true dignity and worth.   20

That to all the right belongeth,
    To the strong and to the weak,
To the noble, and the peasant,
    Knowledge, happiness to seek.

Unto Russia's Czar be honor,   25
    For his brows the laurel twine;
His a nobler crown and kingdom,
    Than the greatest of his line.

Poem No. 142; c. 6 April 1861

Fear not: for they that are with us are more than they that are with them. 2 Kings 6:16.

The wicked and the base do compass round
The meek and humble in their righteous way,
And, with fierce onset and the trumpet's sound,
They seek the servants of the Lord to slay;
They trust in wealth, or in the cruel sword,   5
Vain idols that cannot defend, or save!
They fear no threatenings of God's holy Word,
But, trusting in themselves alone, are brave.
But though no human help the righteous know,
They fear not in the last, the trying hour;   10
God, through his gracious love, to them doth show
The unseen hosts and ensigns of his power;
Who compass them about on every side,
In whose protection they may safe confide.

Poem No. 594; c. April 1861

Hymn
Nature's Sympathy with Freedom

A sadder aspect wears the spring,
    Less beauteous bloom its early flowers,
Less cheerily the gay birds sing,
    Within its fragrant budding bowers.

The hills and fields are still the same,   5
    But o'er their green a cloud has past;
From Southern skies swift-winged it came,
    And all the heavens were overcast!

The tempest's wrath, the ocean's rage,
    Though terrible, are quickly o'er;   10
Shall man a fiercer conflict wage,
    And Nature's short-lived strife deplore?

Ah no! Though fierce his passions rise,
    To desolate her fair domain;
Soon may the peaceful, cloudless skies   15
    Smile on our favored land again.

More favored still;—for Freedom then
    From Slavery's curse our land shall save,
Acknowledged be the Rights of men,
    Where'er our Country's flag shall wave.   20

Poem No. 19; 12 April–7 May 1861

Christ's Capture In The Garden
A Paraphrase

When shrouded by the darkness of the earth,
And soon to pass away from human sight;
Thus spake the Wisdom, born of heavenly birth,
Which was before the world, of men the Light.

"Why come ye forth as 'gainst a thief, with swords,   5
When daily in the Temple I have taught?
Have ye not listened to God's gracious words,
Which to a sinful world salvation brought?

"Why stretched ye forth no hands against me then,
When, in your sight and hearing, there I stood?   10
Was it because ye stood in fear of men?
But thus it was to prove the Scriptures good.

"This is your hour! The covert gloom of night
Is the fit time for violence and wrong;
The evil hide them from the morning light,   15
And, leagued with Darkness, only are they strong.

"The children of the Light do wisdom love,
And gladly listen to her holy word;
The evil hate the light, which doth reprove,
And 'gainst the righteous draw the bloody sword."   20

Poem No. 793; c. May 1861

Song
Words Of Love To A Parent

Each word of love a child doth speak,
    It sows a flower, to bloom
Along its aged parent's path,
    Descending to the tomb!

No more may blush the summer's rose   5
    To glad their failing sight;
Nor to the ravished sense, as once,
    Its fragrance give delight.

But every word of love they hear
    Is treasured in the heart;   10
A bloom, a fragrance there to shed,
    Which never can depart!

Poem No. 104; c. 29 June 1861

The Comet

Strange visitant! that burst'st upon our sight,
And with thy meteor-splendors fill'st the sky;
From what far distant bourn, what starless night,
Com'st thou, in terror clad, to every eye!
Amidst the stars' unquenched, eternal fires,   5

I see thee like some mighty warrior burn;
Who, with his flaming sword upraised, aspires
A seat among their peaceful spheres to earn.
But vain the strife! Soon in the depths of space
Thou'lt vanish, and thy place no more be found!   10
The astronomer thy path may never trace,
Nor know the years of thine appointed round;
While moving on, in its benignant sphere,
Nightly each star the heart of man doth cheer.

Poem No. 445; c. 13 July 1861

Each Day a Prophecy

What image of a higher, holier day
Does each returning sun earth's children bring?
Bright as o'er land and sea he takes his way,
He seems the herald of the heavenly King;
Before him fly the murky shades of night,   5
That veil from sight earth's plains and mountains high;
The sea's thick rolling vapors take their flight,
And vanish upward in the kindling sky.
I gaze upon the scene, and from within
A light too streams upon the suffering earth;   10
I see the promised day of God begin,
And all earth's children share the second birth;
And to my mind the image doth unfold
Of Life and Joy and Peace so long foretold.

Poem No. 773; c. July 1861

The Influence Of The Night on Faith And Imagination

The day with well-known duties now is o'er;
No more, by its clear light, each thing I see
Distinct and plain to sight, or reason's power.
As fade familiar objects on my sight,

And on my ear the sounds of labor cease,   5
The higher faculties assert their power,
Imagination and adoring faith.
And now the night has come, mysterious night!
To call away my spirit from the earth,
That faith may quickened be in things unseen.   10
With mind no longer bent on daily tasks,
Or fixed on earth with its brief term of years;
Upward I gaze, and feel my soul expand,
And to its native height majestic tower.
Akin to mystery is the soul of man,   15
And in the stars he feels that mystery solved.
Not in the narrow space, which we call life,
I feel the boundaries of my being end;
To those vast cycles is my soul allied,
Which yonder orbs in mystic circles trace.   20
To me is given to call them each by name,
And, in the time to come, familiar grow
With all their hosts, as now with flowers of earth.
No more my mind, to one small orb confined,
Narrows its view; but flies from world to world,   25
From sun to sun, swifter than morning light.
Lift up your eyes, ye denizens of earth!
And raise your thoughts above its narrow sphere.
Let yonder countless stars a lesson teach.
Think not to earth, and earth alone, confined   30
This mortal race, with its attendant forms;
But, worthier thought, to each revolving sphere
Its own peculiar habitants assigned,
With varying life, to suit each changing scene.
Perhaps in yon fair planet-world there dwells   35
A happier race, though mortal, than on earth;
Where death is but a change to higher life,
Without its sufferings and without its fears.
There war may be unknown, and men in peace
And friendly intercourse united live.   40
To them may come, as once to men on earth,
Angels from higher spheres to bring them gifts;
To mingle freely in their peaceful homes,
And teach them of the Father's boundless love.
Thus as I muse, my faith doth stronger grow;   45

Imagination soars with loftier flight;
And, as the parched plant beneath the dews,
So is my spirit by the night restored.

Poem No. 487; c. August 1861

Sunset in Derby's Woods

This a fitting scene would prove
   For the Painter's beauteous art,
Scenes like this the Poets love,
   Speaking to the eye and heart.

Winding river here I see,   5
   Fields and woods on either hand;
From all noise the place is free,
   As for quiet musings planned.

Nature here asserts her power
   O'er the freed and grateful soul!   10
Swiftly flies the sunset hour,
   'Neath her gentle, sweet control.

Not alone I seem to be,
   While she ministers around;
Though no human form I see,   15
   Hear no voice of mortal sound.

As I turn to leave the spot,
   Still it doth my vision fill;
It can never be forgot,
   Woods, and stream, and lofty hill.   20

Lighted oft by Memory's ray,
   They no more can fade from sight;
Like the hues of dying day,
   Quickly changing into night.

Poem No. 653; c. 6 September 1861

My People are destroyed for lack of Knowledge.
—Hosea 4:6.

For lack of Knowledge do my people die!
No fell diseases in our land abound,
No pestilential vapors fill the sky,
No drought, or barrenness has cursed the ground;
The harvest-fields are white on every side,   5
For God has given to all with liberal hand;
To none His sun and rain has He denied,
But with abundance blessed our fruitful land.
But Him, who gives to all, they have not known!
His truth, his mercy, and unfailing love;   10
Who sends not on one favored race alone,
His gifts and mercies from the heavens above;
Therefore the land doth mourn, and, day by day,
War wastes our fields, and doth the people slay!

Poem No. 131; c. 21 September 1861

Autumn Flowers

Still blooming on, when Summer-flowers all fade,
    The golden rods and asters fill the glade;
The tokens they of an Exhaustless Love,
    That ever to the end doth constant prove.

To one fair tribe another still succeeds,   5
    As still the heart new forms of beauty needs;
Till these, bright children of the waning year!
    Its latest born have come our souls to cheer.

They glance upon us from their fringed eyes,
    And to their look our own in love replies;   10
Within our hearts we find for them a place,
    As for the flowers, which early Spring-time grace.

Despond not traveller! on life's lengthened way,
  When all thy early friends have passed away;
Say not, "No more the beautiful doth live,   15
  And to the earth a bloom and fragrance give."

To every season has our Father given
  Some tokens of his love to us from heaven;
Nor leaves us here, uncheered, to walk alone,
  When all we loved and prized, in youth, has gone.   20

Let but thy heart go forth to all around,
  Still by thy side the beautiful is found;
Along thy path the Autumn flowers shall smile,
  And to its close life's pilgrimage beguile.

Poem No. 437; 26 September 1861

Hymn

From out its large estate,
  Little the world will give;
The rich, the powerful, and the great,
  Care not that thou shouldst live.

The world doth love its own,   5
  Its ways, its wealth, its pride;
'Twill leave thee weak and poor alone,
  Nor care though thou hadst died.

Then look unto the Lord,
  And trust his gracious care;   10
Believe the promise of his Word,
  He, pitying, hears thy prayer.

He shall thy wants supply,
  Who gives to all their food;
Nor, to the thankless, doth deny   15
  Each needed earthly good.

Poem No. 140; c. 26 September 1861

The Poet's Plea

Why sing, amidst the strife which reigns around?
Will men the poet's heart-felt music hear?
Or will they heed the Gospel's peaceful sound,
And sheathe the sword, and break the threatening spear?
Ah no, yet unsubdued men's passions rage!   5
The never-ceasing conflict born within,
Or outward foes, their energies engage,
O'er which they strive the victory to win.
But still the poet midst the tumult sings,
Hoping from war and strife men's thoughts to gain;   10
He touches with diviner skill the strings,
And from his harp there breathes a holier strain;
Such as the watchful shepherds wondering heard,
When the still night by angels' lyres was stirred!

Continued

That strain harmonious through the war-worn earth   15
Shall yet be heard, and every nation move;
It tells the glories of the heavenly birth,
Heroic deeds of Faith and Christian Love.
O'er the wild tumults of the world it steals,
Calming the fury of its outward strife;   20
A higher, holier conflict it reveals;
The victory and the crown, Eternal Life!
The warrior hears, and drops his blood-stained sword,
No more with war's fierce flames his bosom burns;
Man in God's image is once more restored,   25
The golden age of Peace and Love returns;
And Nature with new beauty decks her bowers,
Scattering with lavish hand her fruits and flowers.

Poem No. 826; October 1861

On The Completion Of The Pacific Telegraph

Swift to the western bounds of this wide land,
Swifter than light, the Electric Message flies;
The continent is in a moment spanned,
And furthest West to furthest East replies.
While War asunder drives the nearest states,   5
And doth to them all intercourse deny,
Science new bonds of Union still creates,
And the most distant brings forever nigh!
I hail this omen for our Country's cause;
For it the stars do in their courses fight!   10
In vain men strive against the eternal laws
Of Peace, and Liberty, and Social Right;
Rebel against the light; and hope to stay
The dawn on earth of Freedom's perfect day.

Poem No. 454; c. 5 November 1861

On the First Church
Built by the Puritans in 1634.*

Still may it stand! For Time himself has spared,
As if by miracle, the humble fane,
In which our fathers worshipped; when they dared
To seek Religious Freedom o'er the main.
Though poor and perishing unto the sight,   5
A glory seems to rest upon the place;
Its walls and roof are lit with heavenly light,
While we its history and purpose trace.
Their simple worship seems again restored,
Again we hear the hymn, the heart-felt prayer,   10
With them we listen to the preached Word,
And in each hallowed rite and service share;
Long as a sacred Relic, may we hold
The Church our fathers built to God of old.

Poem No. 439; c. 26 November 1861

*Standing on the estate of David Nichols, Esq, in the rear of Boston street.

The Barque Aurelia
of Boston

The old Barque's picture we took from the wall,
    In which I sailed over the sea;
Which our sailor-boy days did so brightly recall
    To my boyhood's *companion, and me.

With our fathers once more we sailed over the main,   5
    From country to country to roam;
New knowledge of earth, and its nations to gain,
    Yet never forgetful of home.

The ocean, so grand in its aspect & form,
    Seemed again on our vision to rise;   10
By night and by day, in calm and in storm,
    As its wonders first greeted our eyes.

The sailors' quaint speech, and their strange dress, and ways,
    Again to my fancy appeared;
Yet their honest, kind hearts I remember to praise,   15
    For to them was the ship's boy endeared.

And the *port where we lay, and the winter time spent,
    Where first our acquaintance began;
What pleasure has time to those early days lent,
    Since each has become a grown man!   20

The river, the shipping, the flat boats we view,
    Slaves, and Indians we ne'er saw before;
At every turn we see something new,
    As the city again we explore.

And with us was one, whom our hearts loved so well,   25
    Long since from the earth passed away;
How oft of his looks does memory tell,
    Board the barque, or at school, or at play!

*Rev. William Hooper

*New Orleans.

With him too have gone, to the fair world above,
    Our fathers, the seamen we knew;   30
Where cherished for aye are friendships, and love,
    Which on earth have proved faithful and true.

Poem No. 535; 1861?

The Traveller At The Depot

The traveller at the depot waiting stands,
Impatient for the coming of the train;
The night is hastening on, the hour demands
That he the shelter of his home shall gain.
We, too, are travellers here! But short our stay,   5
And swiftly flies for each the allotted hour;
Swift as declines the sun of winter's day,
Or fades the petals of the summer's flower!
Why do we then our short probation spend,
Unmindful of the night which hastens on;   10
Unmindful of the soul's true goal, and end;
Until our days and years are fled and gone;
And we no nearer to our heavenly home,
Though the last hour for us on earth has come?

Poem No. 584; c. 11 January 1862

Salvation Is Of The Lord
The Book of Jonah ii.9.

"Sleeper, arise and call upon thy God!"
The master to the sleeping prophet cried;
As to and fro with anxious fear he trod,
And vainly every art for safety tried.
E'en Superstition owns a Higher Power,   5
And doth upon its gods in trouble call;
When mighty tempests rise, in danger's hour,
It doth before its idols prostrate fall.

And shall not we, whom Faith's bright beams illume,
Who to the One True God our worship pay,   10
Call on his Name, amid the deepening gloom,
Bow at his altars, at his footstool pray?
Christians, arise, and call upon *your* God,
Who o'er the nation lifts his chastening rod!

Poem No. 424; c. January 1862

The Newspaper

In this one sheet, how much for thought profound,
How much for feeling deep doth meet the eye!
Here man's decease, here empire's fate is found,
And yet, with careless glance, we pass them by!
Perchance, upon one page enough we find,   5
On which through a long life we well might muse;
But oft with husks we fill the hungry mind,
When men the gifts of speech, and thought abuse.
Not in the many words, or books we read,
Is knowledge gained of Nature, or of man;   10
Oft, in a single word, lies wrapt the seed
Of changes vast, would we its meaning scan;
But lacking still the wisdom to be wise,
The Truth we seek is hidden from our eyes.

Poem No. 301; c. 22 February 1862

E Pluribus Unum

A higher thought than fills the narrow mind
Of selfish States, that seek some private end;
Did once these States with us together bind,
And to the Union power and glory lend.
'Twas Liberty which made us great and free,   5
A nation midst the nations of the earth;
A higher hope, a nobler unity,
Gave to each State a new, diviner birth!

That thought still lives, and still asserts its power
O'er selfish pride, and every hateful foe;   10
It guards our country in its evil hour,
And doth new life and energy bestow;
Will with a higher Freedom lead us on,
And as of old, of Many make us One.

Poem No. 9; c. 12 April 1862

Song

I sought the flowers, but o'er them lay
    Piled deep the frozen snow;
They felt not there the warm sun's ray,
    Nor heard the soft winds blow.

Again I came; the snow-bank then   5
    Had melted from the earth;
But vainly still I sought the glen,
    To hail the flower's new birth.

With faithless heart did I repeat
    My visit to their bowers;   10
When lo! in beauty at my feet,
    Bloomed bright Spring's earliest flowers!

Poem No. 273; c. 2 May 1862

This Mortal Shall put on Immortality

The mortal body quickly dies,
    Struck by disease and pain;
In vain we gaze, our longing eyes
    Behold it not again.

'Tis but a tent, a house of clay,   5
    Where for a time we dwell;
For years, or for a single day
    No one of us can tell.

Mysterious union of the soul,
   Of spirit with the clod;
One being, Man, a perfect whole   10
   The image of his God!

O keep that image pure and bright
   Of body and of mind,
And keep the glory still in sight,
   For which it was designed.   15

Since not for suffering, or disease,
   God formed us of the dust;
But that we might our Maker please,
   And place in Him our trust.   20

Who through his Son the promise gave,
   That man shall never die;
But triumph o'er the opening grave
   In immortality!

Poem No. 656; c. 24 May 1862

Hymn

The Spirit Itself Maketh Intercession For Us

The Spirit doth our weakness aid,
   When thought, and utterance fail;
When all our words can say is said,
   Its sighs and groans avail.

They reach the ear of God on high,   5
   Who doth the heart discern;
He hears the feeblest sufferer's cry,
   And swift to him doth turn.

Oh faint not, then, when all thy might
   Of thought, and word is gone;
God's help shall make thy burden light,   10
   Thou art not, then, alone.

His Spirit doth within thee dwell,
    To comfort, and console;
No tongue the love, and peace can tell,   15
    It brings unto the soul!

And though no voice of man makes known
    The prayer, which then we pray;
Yet God doth hear each sigh and groan,
    And knows what we would say.   20

Poem No. 571; c. May 1862

The Elm Seed

Scattered, with every breeze, I see them fly
This way and that upon the Summer air;
Trodden to dust beneath our feet they lie,
Yet not without the great Creator's care!
Some single seed his Providence directs,   5
That Providence, which guards & governs all;
The tiny germ through Winter it protects,
And, in the Spring-time, from its grave will call.
No more a seed; but now a growing tree,
Though scarce its slender form at first is seen;   10
Still, nourished & sustained, in time 'twill be
A mighty elm; from Summer's suns a screen
To man and beast, that seek its friendly shade;
And birds, that, in its boughs, their nests have made.

Poem No. 411; c. 17 June 1862

The Cause

The body sick, the cause we seek to find,
In head, or limb, or ever-beating heart;
Or in the secret workings of the mind,
Nor rest till we have found the suffering part.
Once found, we use our utmost power and skill   5

The cause itself of suffering to remove;
Nor do we bear a single pain, or ill,
Till every healing remedy we prove.
And why should Nations mighty ills endure,
War's horrid scourge, and Slavery's ancient wrong,   10
Nor seek to find their cause? or found, to cure?
But still from age to age their guilt prolong;
Till by some sudden shock, or slow decay,
Their greatness, like a shadow, pass away!

Poem No. 468; June 1862

Outward Conquests Not Enough

'Tis not enough to overcome with arms,—
These may the body, not the mind subdue;
A mightier foe, within, the spirit harms,
Than that the armed warrior ever knew.
Here Ignorance and Error still prolong   5
Their ancient rule, and dread the coming light;
And, joined with them, Ambition, Pride, and Wrong
Muster their hosts, and, leagued with darkness, fight.
These not by carnal weapons are o'erthrown,
But by the power of light, and truth, and love;   10
Weapons the warrior's hands have never known,
Sent from the armory of God above;
Boldness to speak, the quick and powerful Word,
That sharper is than his two-edged sword!

Poem No. 729; c. July 1862

Ship Rock

With a sudden, sweet surprise
   Burst the prospect on our eyes;
Far the city's spires are seen,
   Hills, and fields, and woods between.

Farther still, the ocean blue   5
    Fitly bounds the charming view;
Where, on the horizon clear,
    Noble ships their courses steer.

By the pond, beneath the hill,
    Silent stands the noisy mill;   10
While the brook with laugh and song
    Through the meadow glides along.

Science may thy birth explore,
    On the far-off Arctic shore;
And thy various wanderings show,   15
    In the ages long ago;—

With more interest here I trace
    Backward my own name and race;
From thy top the scene behold,
    Where they lived and toiled of old.   20

Here the wooded fields they cleared,
    And their humble homesteads reared;
Here they planted, gathered here
    Harvests ripe from year to year.

Here they worshipped Him, whose word,   25
    In their father-land, they heard;
Him, who, o'er the ocean wide,
    Was their Hope, their Strength, their Guide.

Here, in sweet and holy trust,
    They committed dust to dust;   30
Minding where the soul's conveyed,
    More than where the body's laid.

Still their orchard-lot I see,
    Here and there a moss-grown tree;
Here their dwelling's site is known,   35
    Now by shrubs and vines o'ergrown.

Sacred is this spot to me,
    Rock, and brook, and lofty tree;
For, amid the scenes I tread,
    Rests the dust of kindred dead!   40

Poem No. 831; c. 15 July 1862

The Light Of Freedom Necessary To National Progress

When sets the sun, the traveller waits for light,
Ere he his dangerous journey shall renew;
Vain in the forest dark his sharpest sight,
Where moon and stars alike are hid from view.
The sun returns; again he onward goes,   5
Its light reveals all objects to his eyes;
He fears no danger now, nor lurking foes,
His path all plain and bright before him lies.
Frail Freedom's sun for us has hid its beams,
The moon and stars have e'en their light withdrawn;   10
Then let us wait, till once again it gleams
Upon the mountain tops, and its bright dawn
Shall the dark valleys fill with cheerful day;
Then like the traveller safe pursue our way.

Poem No. 792; September 1862

Ode to Freedom

Freedom a fortress firm shall stand,
    No foes combined can take;
Though cannon roar by sea and land,
    Its walls no power can shake;

For it is founded on the rock,   5
    On which our fathers stood;
Firm as the cliffs, that meet the shock
    Of ocean's angry flood.

Proud Slavery's hosts inspire no fear,
    Though state on state conspire,   10
To compass her with sword and spear,
    And hurl their bolts of fire;

Though 'gainst her Capital are led
    Confederate armies on,
Dishonoring the glorious dead,   15
    The name of Washington!

Once honored men, now traitors grown,
    Found faithless at their post;
No more their fathers' virtues known,
    Lead on the rebel host.   20

In vain; for Washington still lives,
    Though sleeps his noble form;
And to his sons the courage gives
    To meet the battle's storm.

And once again, through all the land,   25
    Freedom her trumpet blows;
To call her sons, on every hand,
    To meet their Country's foes.

Poem No. 138; 19 September 1862

Philanthropy Before Nationality

Upon the Rights of Man, at first, was built
This free Republic, which our fathers planned;
For these, at first, their precious blood they spilt,
Though they its meaning failed to understand.
But wider still expands their mighty thought,   5
Raising from bondage e'en a subject race;
What to themselves, at first, but freedom brought,
Gives to the slave at length a name, and place!
But still through blood and strife the boon we gain
Against Ambition, Pride, and lust of Power;   10
Which on man's limbs would rivet still the chain,
When long ago has struck the appointed hour;
And Liberty proclaims throughout the earth,
That all are free and equal in their birth.

Poem No. 755; c. 20 September 1862

The King's Arm Chair

Steep cliff, round which a child I played,
   Or climbed to view the prospect o'er;
Where hour by hour I frequent stayed;
   Thou wear'st not now thy look of yore!

For man, by many a blast, has torn   5
   Thy hoary moss-grown front away;
And at thy feet the fragments borne,
   Like some vast ruin strew the way.

But still, as in that day, I see
   Thy bold steep forehead gainst the sky;   10
When round thy base I climbed in glee,
   Till gained the lofty summit high.

There, seated in the King's arm chair,
   I loved the landscape round to view;
The busy streets and houses fair,   15
   The harbor with its waters blue.

Before me spread the pastures green,
   With hills and meadows far away;
Seaward the white-winged ships were seen,
   Bound to their ports along the bay.   20

Beneath, I watched the living tide,
   Swift hurrying on with ceaseless flow,
Along the smooth-worn turnpike wide,
   And round thy jutting base below.

The wagon, chaise, or crowded stage,   25
   By turns I watched as they came by,
The weary traveller bent with age,
   Glad from the hill the town to spy.

Each hastening on with various mind,
   Some far o'er land and sea to roam,   30
Sad for the friends they'd left behind;
   While others joyed to reach their home.

By day, by night, the stream flowed on,
    Like a full river to the sea;
Long since the lengthening train has gone,   35
    A picture now of Memory!

Whose power restores the past again,
    The summer days, the golden flowers;
To soothe stern manhood's toil, or pain,
    Or deck for age its leafless bowers.   40

In vain would man thy form destroy,
    Or level thee e'en with the ground;
I see thee still, as when a boy,
    And from the Arm Chair gaze around.

Poem No. 409-434; October 1862

The Falling Leaf

Fall, yellow leaf, for thy brief work is done!
    The work for which thy beauteous form was made;
No more thou'lt glisten in the morning sun,
    No more thou'lt darken with the evening shade.

Thy work is done! No more the parent tree   5
    Shall need thy aid, for winter-time is near;
No more upon its boughs thy form we'll see,
    Through the long winter months to charm and cheer.

But though thy work is done, to outward sight,
    And thou art trodden 'neath the feet of men;   10
Still to the memory thou shalt bring delight,
    And in thy beauty seem to live again.

Thy work can never cease, while thought shall bring
    Some pleasant memories of days gone by;
When wandering in the woods, in early spring,   15
    Thy brilliant green first caught the admiring eye.

Or when, in Summer, from the glare and heat
    We've sought the shelter of the quiet grove;
And found, beneath its shade, a cool retreat,
    To pass the sultry hours with friends we love.   20

Or when, in Autumn, midst her changing bowers,
    I mused upon the lessons, which they taught;
Forgetful of the swiftly passing hours,
    Lost in a dream of sweet, yet solemn thought.

Thy work shall never cease, while thou shalt be   25
    A thought the springs of memory to controul,
A power the mind of man from sense to free,
    A joy and teaching to the deathless soul!

Poem No. 111; c. 8 November 1862

National Unity

A nobler unity, than that which came
    From out the conflict of our sires of old,
Which gave to us throughout the world a name
    Shall we, our trials past, at length behold;
A unity of Justice and of Power,   5
    As theirs of Freedom from a foreign foe;
Through the dark clouds, that o'er the nation lower,
    We see its rising sun, its morning glow.
No more shall party spirit rule the land,
    But One Great Thought inspire each freeman's breast,   10
The rock on which alone our cause can stand,
    The Love of Man and Justice for the oppressed.
Arise, O sun of Freedom to restore
Their rights to all! Arise! and set no more!

Poem No. 16; c. 15 November 1862

Faith In Time Of War

I read of battles, and my faith grows weak;
Does God look down on us with pitying eye?
With loving care each day his children seek?
I ask, but hear no voice to mine reply!
When tens and hundreds dying strew the plain,   5

What thought, I ask, is there for one alone?
Heeds He the single sufferer's short, sharp pain?
Hears He amidst the shouts his dying groan?
Ah faithless heart! No one forsaken is,
Each soul of man is his perpetual care;   10
Living, or dying we are ever His,
Whose tender mercies all his creatures share;
Who, though the sword may slay, has power to save;
And gives to man the victory o'er the grave!

Poem No. 252; c. 22 November 1862

Hymn
The Light of Life

The Light of Life! O blessed words,
    To him, who midst the darkness lives;
To every son of Adam's race,
    What joy, what hope, the promise gives!

As to the man of old, born blind,   5
    But whom the Savior made to see;
So do the precious words he spake
    Bring life, and light, and hope to me.

No doubt obscures his meaning clear,
    Who miracles of healing wrought;   10
To show, e'en to the earthly mind,
    From whence the doctrine he had brought.

They speak of Him, who came from God;
    To tell men of the Father's love;
To lead them through earth's sin, and strife,   15
    To their bright home in heaven above.

Who follows Him, no more shall walk
    In Error's maze, or Death's dark night;
But, e'en amidst their gloomy shades,
    Shall have within the Life, the Light.   20

And when no more the paths he treads
    Of suffering, and of trial here;
The Light of Life, on earth he saw,
    Shall greet him in a higher sphere.

Poem No. 520; c. November 1862

Man's Heart Prophesieth Of Peace

A sad confession from the heart of man
It is, that War, dark hateful War, must be;
That ever thus, e'en since the world began,
Has been on earth the dire necessity!
Behold, he says, the truth on History's page,   5
Written in blood upon her lengthening scroll;
The warrior's wreaths still green from age to age,
And warlike glory still man's highest goal.
But deeper look, O man, into thy heart,
And Peace, a mightier need thou there shalt see;   10
As yet thou know'st thy nature but in part,
What thou hast been, but not what thou shalt be!
And read the promise of God's holy Word,
That nations shall no more lift up the sword.

Poem No. 17; c. January 1863

Hymn
The New Life of Humanity

What Life is that, which, like the Spring,
    Now breathes o'er land and sea?
Which doth new life to nations bring,
    To all humanity?

Is it the life which, year by year,   5
    Calls forth the same fair flowers;
So soon, alas, to disappear
    From out their summer bowers?

The same bright birds calls forth again,
　　With songs to cheer the grove;
So soon, alas, to cease their strain,
　　And distant far to rove?

No: 'tis a life yet more divine,
　　To humbler things unknown;
Which nature, time cannot confine,
　　'Tis felt by man alone.

More quickening than the vernal wind,
　　Like mighty poets' lyre;
That stirs the hearts of all his kind
　　To something nobler higher;

To nobler Freedom, purer Love,
　　To perfect lasting Peace;
Till to these thoughts men faithful prove,
　　And wars forever cease.

Poem No. 777; c. 4 April 1863

The Statue of Flora, On the grounds of R. Brookhouse Esq, Washington Street.

Still gazing on thy wreath of carved flowers,
A sight of beauty to the passing throng!
Thou tellest of the Summer's blooming bowers,
As to the mart, or court they haste along.
And though perchance absorbed in thoughts of gain,
But few admire thy flowers, or form of grace;
Yet not upon the street thou standst in vain!
Still on some heart thou may'st thine image trace,
Recalling to the mind youth's early day;
When hills and fields so oft he wandered o'er,
When Nature o'er his soul acquired her sway,
And every scene bright hues of beauty wore;
And the stern man was once a playful boy,
Whom e'en the smallest flower could thrill with joy!

Poem No. 438; c. 28 April 1863

Hymn

Sung At the Unitarian Festival, in Faneuil Hall, May 26th 1863

Amidst the memories of the past,
   And cherished hopes sublime;
Whose glorious record shall outlast
   The fading scroll of time;

We meet each other's hearts to cheer,   5
   Sweet friendships to renew;
To serve the Faith we hold so dear,
   Faith of the brave and true!

The faith, that doth the power control
   Of foes without, within;   10
And gives the victory to the soul
   O'er evil, death, and sin:

Which, to the wounded, brings relief,
   And soothes the sufferer's pain;
And doth the mourner's secret grief,   15
   With heavenly hopes, sustain.

The faith that, on the cloud of War,
   Beholds the bow of Peace;
Which sees Christ's triumph from afar,
   When Wrong and War shall cease.   20

Poem No. 37-42; c. 26 May 1863

The Tree of Liberty

As to the fruitful tree, which, in the Spring,
Puts forth its fresh, green leaves, and blossoms red,
The canker-worm doth desolation bring,
And, like a fire, o'er all its branches spread;—
E'en thus, fair Liberty, thy tree doth stand!   5
Which at the first, did leaves and blossoms hold,
And with its boughs o'ershadowed all the land;

No more with verdure clad, as seen of old!
But from neglect, from want of care and toil,
When now the harvest time was drawing near,   10
Become of basest men the prey and spoil;
Who blighted have the promise of the year;
And would the tree, which filled the earth with joy,
As well as its fair fruits, at once destroy!

Poem No. 58; c. 4 July 1863

Hymn
Our Country's Dead

They live to God, they live to God,
   Though gone from human sight!
The good and brave, who left their homes
   To battle for the right.

To Thee, O God, they still live on,   5
   Though ceased their mortal strife;
And wait the triumph of the Cause,
   More dear to them than life.

In sight of men they seem to die,
   And perish from the earth;   10
But Thou dost give them even here,
   A new, immortal birth.

Though chastened for a little time,
   Thou dost reward their pain;
To die, to suffer for the right,   15
   Is e'en on earth to gain.

For to their Country still they live,
   And, on her roll of fame,
Recorded shall forever stand
   Each brave, and honored name!   20

Poem No. 644; c. 1 August 1863

The Intuitions Of The Soul

In every soul is born some thought of God,
Of Beauty, or of Wisdom, Power, or Love;
No one so grovelling on the earth has trod,
But sought on sun-bright wings to soar above.
For man in God's own image first was made,   5
And dimly in himself these thoughts beholds;
The same in Nature too he sees displayed,
As she to him her glorious book unfolds.
Thus ever upward doth our being tend,
As we more clearly these great thoughts discern;   10
And ask of God his heavenly grace to lend,
That we as children all the truth may learn;
That in our souls, unclouded and divine,
The Life, the Light of men, may ever shine!

Poem No. 298; c. August 1863

Still a Day To Live

Still a day to live, still a day to live,
The thought to my mind doth wisdom give;
For what, in a day, may not be done?
What may not be lost? what may not be won?

In a day we may turn from the evil away,   5
Resist the temptations, that lead us astray;
In a day we may goodness forever secure,
And thus our high calling of God may make sure.

As bright from the east upriseth the sun,
Let the morning with prayer and with praise be begun;   10
Commune with thy Maker, and ask for his care,
He hears, and will bless thy heart-spoken prayer.

In the hours of thy business, thy pleasure, thy rest,
Let the thought of his Presence on all be impressed;
'Twill strengthen for toil and thy pleasures make pure,   15
And give thee the riches that ever endure.

Each hour heed the voice that to duty may call,
Though that duty to thee seem but trivial, or small;
Each deed, timely done, to remembrance how sweet!
Be quick, for the moment of action is fleet.   20

For the night quickly cometh, when labor is o'er,
And the sun at his rising shall see us no more;
When fruitful, or faithless, no more we can say,
"I have still, I have still yet to live for a day!"

Poem No. 436; c. 19 September 1863

The Vagrant at the Church Door

For years he had not seen his native place—
For years he had not spoken to a friend—
For years he had not stood within a church;
And now he linger'd in the dusky porch,
And watch'd the congregation, one by one,   5
Cheerfully enter, and devoutly bend
In silent adoration. Many a face,
Familiar long ago, glanced toward his own—
Perhaps with wonder, for they knew him not,
And he was sadly changed, since in this spot   10
His happy boyhood swiftly pass'd away.

Strange fascination! Now he needs must stay;
For, in the echoes of the choir, he hears
A melody familiar to long past years
And sweet associations. Soon his tears   15
Tell how the vagrant's spirit has been moved.
All that he dreamt, all that he ever loved,
All that youth's prophecy said "might have been,"
All the grim shadows of the wasted past,
In dim procession moved before him now.   20

The vagrant pass'd his fingers o'er his brow,
And seemed bewilder'd—crazed—until at last
The dawning of a hopeful smile was seen
Upon his face. The music of the psalm
Died out in whispering echoes; and the voice,   25

In earnest accents, of the village priest,
Was heard in prayer. Once more the vagrant glanced
Within the church, and then he entered in.
Beneath a column's shadow sat entranced
The poor world-weary man. A holy calm   30
Encompass'd him, and made his heart rejoice—
The past dissolved as though it had not been.

The service ends. The rolling organ ceased.
The verger came to where the vagrant sat
Mute as a statue. "Come, my man," said he,   35
"The church is closing; take your stick and hat,
And let me shut the doors." Then wonderingly
The verger look'd again, and muttered low,
"Poor soul! I knew him thirty years ago—
I little thought he would come here to die."   40

Poem No. 134; c. 26 September 1863

Health of Body dependent on the Soul

Not from the earth, or skies,
    Or seasons as they roll,
Come health and vigor to the frame;
    But from the living soul.

Is this alive to God,   5
    And not the slave of sin?
Then will the body, too, receive
    Health from the soul within.

But, if disease has touched
    The spirit's inmost part;   10
In vain we seek, from outward things,
    To heal the deadly smart.

The mind, the heart unchanged,
    Which clouded e'en our home;
Will make the outward world the same,   15
    Where'er our feet may roam.

The fairest scenes on earth,
　The mildest, purest sky
Will bring no vigor to the step,
　No lustre to the eye.　　　　　　　　　　　　　　　　20

For He, who formed our frame,
　Made man a perfect whole;
And made the body's health depend
　Upon the living soul.

Poem No. 364; c. 17 October 1863

The Crisis

With the great thought, thy Country's cause, its life,
Mix not the selfish end of party gain;
The Patriot knows no party in the strife,
When called his Country's freedom to maintain.
Against the principles, which make us free,　　　　　　5
Against the rights of Man, our foes contend;
And at the root of Liberty's fair tree
The axe is laid, by such as these befriend.
Choose ye this day, whose service ye prefer,
For Freedom, or for Bondage, will ye fight?　　　　　10
No more the duty of the hour defer,
To follow Truth, to vindicate the Right;
But give thyself to Freedom's holy cause,
Thy Country's honor, and thy Country's laws.

Poem No. 847; c. 23 October 1863

The Forsaken Harvest Field

When the farmer, from his fields,
　Home has borne the ripened grain;
Where his hands no more can reap,
　Harvests yet for me remain.

Autumn flowers, of every hue,   5
    Brightly bloom along my way;
Golden rods and asters fair
    Make the fields and pastures gay.

Then the bitter-sweet I seek,
    Draping rock and leafy tree;   10
And its berries homeward bear,
    Ripened harvest left for me.

Then the gentian, trustful flower!
    In the meadow low I find;
Last of Autumn's brilliant train,   15
    Fearless of the chilling wind!

Scattered o'er his stubble ground,
    Each some lesson can impart;
Wisdom for the thoughtful mind,
    Pleasure for the feeling heart.   20

Oft your lessons, on my walks,
    Autumn flowers! I ponder o'er;
But how little have I learned
    Of your sweet and sacred lore!

Poem No. 794; c. 24 November 1863

The Freedmen of the Mississippi Valley

Wakeful I think upon the suffering race,
That, fled from bondage, claim our fostering care;
What tongue their want can tell, or pen can trace,
Or who the story of their woes could bear?
The mother with her child, the aged one,   5
Now unprotected from the wintry blast;
Soon, soon for them the winter will be gone,
Soon, without aid, their sufferings here be past!
Help, till the storms of winter shall be o'er,
When their own hands abundance will supply;   10
Give all thou canst, food, raiment, from thy store,
Nor aught thou hast these suffering ones deny;

Lest they, escaped from Slavery's hateful chain,
Should find but graves in Freedom's fair domain.

Poem No. 757; c. 26 December 1863

Dying Words of John Foster
"I Can Pray, And That's a Glorious Thing."

The dying Christian peaceful lay,
   No more his hands could do;
No more his feet the earthly paths
   Of duty could pursue.

No more the Gospel's joyful sound   5
   Could he to men proclaim;
To warn them of the strength of sin,
   Make known a Savior's name!

That all at length should hear his voice,
   The dead should hear & live;   10
That God was love, a Father still,
   And ready to forgive.

His earnest mind, so strong and clear
   The realms of thought to scan,
No more, with steadfast will, could toil   15
   To serve his fellow man.

Where once was strength, was weakness now;
   Weakness unknown before;
Yet with a spirit calm, resigned,
   The change he meekly bore.   20

For in that Master's steps he trod,
   Whom he so long had loved;
And faith in him sustained his soul,
   And all-sufficient proved.

"Still I can pray," he cheerful said,   25
   "And that's a glorious thing;"
"O Grave, where is thy victory?
   O Death, where is thy sting?"

Poem No. 489; 1863

Home and Heaven

With the same letter heaven and home begin,
And the words dwell together in the mind;
For they who would a home in heaven win,
Must first a heaven in home begin to find.
Be happy here, yet with a humble soul,   5
That looks for perfect happiness in heaven;
For what thou hast is earnest of the whole,
Which to the faithful shall at last be given.
As once the patriarch, in vision blest,
Saw the swift angels hastening to and fro;   10
And the lone spot, whereon he lay to rest,
Became to him the gate of heaven below;
So may to thee, when life itself is done,
Thy home on earth and heaven above be one.

Poem No. 848; January 1864

The Search For The Truth Not Vain

Is that Philosophy, which doth declare,
That man the Truth may seek, but never find?
Do all its teachings end but in despair?
Knows it but this, that Wisdom's self is blind?
Such might the ancient sages have confessed,   5
On whom the Truth, undimmed, had never shone;
Not he, whose mind its noon-day beams have blessed,
And who, from earliest years, its words have known.
Those words to Him who spake them ever lead,
To Christ, to God, who doth the truth inspire;   10
Not vain the search, if in his Word we read,
And of the Sacred Oracles inquire;
Where he, who seeks the Truth, will surely find
The world's True Light, which lightens every mind.

Poem No. 303; c. 20 February 1864

On The Three Hundredth Anniversary
of Shakespeare's Birthday

Shakespeare, whose life once filled an English home,
With childhood's mirth and manhood's noble cheer,
What time our fathers to these wilds did roam;
We hail thee, mighty Bard! without a peer!
To thee did Nature's countless forms unfold   5
Their meaning, hidden from the common eye;
The earth, the sea, the sky, their secrets told,
And man's deep spirit did to thine reply.
By Avon's banks we tread; thy home we see,
The church, where still in peace thy bones repose;   10
Join with the throng, that holds thy Jubilee,
And guards thy fame, that, with each century, grows;
No longer to thy native land confined,
For the whole world may claim thy glorious mind.

Poem No. 417; April 1864

Hymn
The Way of the Righteous Easy

Thou dost make the pathway easy
    For thy saints to travel in;
Though it seem but steep and tiresome,
    When the journey they begin.

Not the path of ease and pleasure   5
    Have they chosen here to go;
But the way that upward leadeth,
    From the flowery vale below.

Thou dost tax their powers of action,
    Powers of body and of mind;   10
Till the world they have forsaken,
    Left each pleasing lure behind.

Then the way Thou makest easy
  To their worn and weary feet;
And doth cheer their spirit's fainting, 15
  Showing them thy glorious seat!

Far below they see the cities
  Of the low and darksome plain;
Where the sons of earth-born pleasure,
  In their bondage, still remain. 20

Noble forms appear around them,
  Heavenly voices cheer them on;
And thy holy mountain's summit,
  By their feet is quickly won.

Poem No. 671; c. 7 May 1864

Untimely Arguments

Thou arguest wisely, with profoundest skill,
Forgetful that the world doth onward move;
That, swifter than thy thought, the active will
Doth all thy arguments but useless prove.
He, who on shipboard has outsailed his foe, 5
Cares not for lessons in the sailing art;
The other may the science better know,
But he has gained, e'en at the first, the start.
'Tis not the time for speech, or calm debate,
When, like the waves, event event succeeds; 10
Thy reasonings may be good, but come too late,
To serve man's good, or check his evil deeds;
Already doth the event the case decide,
And faithful from the faithless too divide.

Poem No. 658; c. 11 June 1864

Hymn

Ps. XLVI. 10: "Be still, and know that I am God."

In the shock of mighty armies,
    Which the land with tumults fill;
Learn, my soul, the lesson taught thee,
    And, in waiting trust, be still.

Though the solid earth be shaken,   5
    And the mountains tottering fall;
Yet, if God be our protection,
    Naught can harm, and naught appall.

He, in every time of trouble,
    Is a present help indeed;   10
And will to his children hearken,
    In their darkest hour of need.

He our country will deliver,
    If we call upon his name;
And the foes of Truth, and Justice,   15
    He will put to open shame.

Come, behold what works he doeth!
    Making wars at length to cease;
Sending to earth's farthest borders
    Messengers of love, and peace;   20

Calling on the sinful nations
    To forsake their sins, and pride;
And believe the Savior's message,
    Who, for all who live, has died.

He in earth will be exalted,   25
    And his purposes fulfil;
Know my soul his power, and goodness,
    And, in waiting trust, be still!

Poem No. 300; c. June 1864

The Voice of Nature In Youth And Age

With sights of beauty rare,
   In earth, and sea, and air,
Nature invites her children aye to roam;
   "Come, live", she says, "with me,
   A life unchecked and free,   5
     And leave your home."

"Come, o'er the ocean rove,
   Through flower-decked field and grove;
Come walk with me, nor longer idly pine;
   With you my gifts I'll share   10
   Of earth, and sea, and air;
     For all are mine."

Listening, youth leaves behind
   His home, his parents kind;
And with a sense of freedom onward goes;   15
   Long seems the summer's day,
   And blooms along his way
     The blushing rose.

And days and years pass by;
   All things, in earth and sky,   20
To him are known. He nature's lord doth stand!
   Her powers obey his will,
   He flies, with magic skill,
     O'er sea and land.

But o'er him comes a change!   25
   No more he loves to range;
Nor power, nor knowledge will his soul suffice;
   He backward turns his gaze,
   And thoughts of other days
     Bedew his eyes.   30

Although with freedom blest,
   His spirit longs for rest;
Longs for the friendships of life's early morn;
   And memory brings to mind
   The home of parents kind,   35
     Where he was born.

There age shall soothe his grief,
    And bring his soul relief
From care, and toil, and pain, that downward bend;
    There Nature's voice doth seem,   40
    As in his early dream,
        Like human friend.

Poem No. 843; c. 15 July 1864

Hymn
Christ's Invitation in the Apocalypse

You, who confess that you are poor,
    And blind, and sinful, come to me!
For I have riches that endure,
    The sick I heal, the blind make see.

Yes, you will come! For well you know,   5
    That you are poor and all things need;
And I have treasures to bestow,
    That can the soul make rich indeed.

And you, who say that rich you are,
    And needing nothing I can give;   10
O stand not in your pride afar!
    But come to me, and you shall live.

For you are naked, poor, and blind,
    And wretched, though you know it not;
While you the gold of earth may find,   15
    The heavenly treasures are forgot.

I counsel you to buy of me
    The gold that has been tried by fire,
Anoint your eyes that you may see,
    And buy of me the saints' attire.   20

You will not come! For still your sight
    Is blinded by the world's bright glare;
In earthly things you take delight,
    And naught for things of mine you care.

Poem No. 858; c. 23 July 1864

Hymn In Drought

Not without thee, our God, the skies
    Pour down the plenteous rain;
To thee our prayers in faith arise,
    Nor shall we ask in vain.

Scorched are the hills on every side,   5
    And e'en the meadows dry,
And dry the brooks, that through them glide,
    And verdure fresh supply.

The birds are hushed, the cattle stand
    Beside the empty pool;   10
Or wander far on every hand,
    Their raging thirst to cool.

In vain to Science would we look,
    To teach, of this, the cause;
She finds in nature's wondrous book,   15
    But fixed and general laws.

Through Nature's laws, we look to Thee,
    On whom those laws depend;
And, in the suffering that we see,
    Would own some gracious end.   20

Teach us the lesson we should learn,
    To look to Thee in prayer;
From sin and every idol turn,
    And daily own thy care.

Poem No. 371; July 1864

The Rain

The rain descends; each drop some drooping flower,
Or parched blade drinks in with grateful haste;
Nor is there, from the plenteous falling shower,
A drop that nature will permit to waste.
Upon the river falls the pattering rain   5

In countless drops, that soon are seen no more;
The river swells, and overflows the plain,
And richer harvests wave than e'er before.
Nor think, that on the surface of the rock
The rain drop falls in vain, a useless thing;   10
From out the crevice of the granite block
The savin grows, and lichens to it cling;
And there, when all around is parched and dry,
The thirsty birds will come and find a full supply.

Poem No. 549; c. 20 August 1864

The Fair Morning

The clear bright morning, with its scented air,
And gaily waving flowers, is here again;
Man's heart is lifted with the voice of prayer,
And peace descends, as falls the gentle rain;
The tuneful birds, that all the night have slept,   5
Take up, at dawn, the evening's dying lay;
When sleep upon their eyelids gently crept,
And stole, with stealthy craft, their song away.
High overhead the forest's swaying boughs
Sprinkle with drops the traveller on his way   10
He hears afar the bells of tinkling cows,
Driven to pasture at the break of day;
With vigorous step he passes swift along,
Making the woods reecho with his song.

Poem No. 478a; c. 3 September 1864

The Clouded Morning

The morning comes, and thickening clouds prevail,
Hanging like curtains all the horizon round,
Or overhead in heavy stillness sail,
So still is day, it seems like night profound!
Scarce by the city's din the air is stirred,   5

And dull and deadened comes its every sound;
The cock's shrill, piercing voice subdued is heard,
By the thick folds of muffling vapors drowned.
Dissolved in mists the hills and trees appear,
Their outlines lost and blended with the sky;   10
And well-known objects, that to all are near,
No longer seem familiar to the eye;
But with fantastic forms they mock the sight,
As when we grope amid the gloom of night.

Poem No. 529; c. 1 October 1864

Nature Repeats Her Lessons

Nature repeats her lessons; day and night,
With the same solemn words, to all return;
To all the morning comes with cheering light,
And over all the stars of evening burn.
The seasons, to their coming ever true,   5
Repeat the lesson of the varied year;
The early flower, the fading leaf we view,
But their oft-spoken words we fail to hear.
For thoughts of pleasure, or of sordid gain,
Possess the heart and cloud the seeing eyes;   10
Nature in youth and manhood speaks in vain,
For trifles light her wisdom we despise;
And e'en in age at last, when wiser grown,
But half her meaning to our minds is known.

Poem No. 349; c. 5 November 1864

What Is A Word?

What is a word? A spirit-birth,
   Born of the living soul;
Which, uttered by the voice of man,
   Time's power cannot controul.

A gift thou art to man alone,   5
    To bird and beast denied;
To show that to the heavenly race
    His nature is allied.

Mysterious Essence! Birth and death
    Are in one instant thine;   10
Yet, born and dying with a breath,
    Thy being is divine.

The outward world thou dost ally
    To things by man unseen;
And, like an angel, ever pass   15
    The heavens and earth between.

Thou dost to childhood's feeble powers
    A help to knowledge lend;
And aid the race, from age to age,
    Its wisdom to transcend.   20

Thou tellest of the distant Past,
    And bid'st it live again;
And can, with mystic key, unlock
    The Future's dim domain.

Still lingering in our common tongue   25
    We hear the elder speech;
And words, which fell from Adam's lips,
    His latest offspring reach.

The world and all it holds shall fade,
    And man himself shall die;   30
But thou, unchanged, shalt live the same,
    Through God's eternity.

Poem No. 774; c. November 1864

To Charles W. Felt Esq.
On His New Type-Setting Machine

While men, in War's dread service, tax their powers
New weapons to invent to harm and slay;
A new invention, Charles, thou hast made ours,
And one prophetic of a brighter day;
When man with man no longer shall contend,   5
Save with the nobler weapons of the mind;
When War on earth forevermore shall end,
And Peace all nations shall forever bind;
The Press with mightier power the truth diffuse,
And like the sun each darkened land illume;   10
And none the light of Knowledge shall refuse
To those who sit in ignorance and gloom;
But all shall Liberty & Knowledge share,
Who see the sun, or breathe the vital air!

Poem No. 810; 12 December 1864

The Young Drummer Boy of Libby Prison
An Incident Related by Capt. James Hussey.

The slumberer wakes! "Are these the walls,
The prison walls around, I see?"
His voice unto his comrades calls,
The sharers of his misery.
"Thou hast been dreaming," one replied.   5
He answered;—"Was it then a dream?
I stood beside the river wide,
My native Hudson's noble stream:
My mother dear was with me there,
And in her arms did me embrace;   10
I gazed upon the prospect fair,
And on her happy, smiling face.
We talked of all our sufferings here,
As if they all were passed and o'er;

I wake to shed the bitter tear,   15
For I shall see her face no more!"
   A few short hours, and death had broke
The starving captive's galling chain;
To life, immortal life he woke,
That knows no tears, nor death, nor pain.   20
O dream, which closed his earthly life!
Be thou fulfilled in happier clime,
Where hushed, forever hushed the strife,
Which saddens oft the years of time.
Still visit those, who sink and pine   25
In prison's gloom, from friends afar;
And o'er the dying prisoner shine,
With radiance bright as evening's star!

Poem No. 566; c. 30 December 1864

Inward Direction

With outward impulse, running to and fro,
How many men with restless minds we meet,
(Who but an outward impulse only know)
In the swift cars, or in the busy street!
By man they're sent, and man's behests fulfil,   5
They hear no other voice within their souls;
Nor have they learned to obey a higher will,
Which earthly hopes, and earthly fears controls:
They know not whence they came, nor whither tend;
In trifling, vain pursuits their lives are spent;   10
Unmindful of life's highest, holiest end,
For which its days and years to us were lent;
To learn the Father's will, his words to hear,
And find his Presence with us always near!

Poem No. 840; c. 7 January 1865

The Cherry Birds

God maketh the birds his care,
    When the ground lies buried with snow,
They speed through the cold, wintry air,
    He teacheth them where to go.

In flocks to the city they speed,   5
    The ash tree's red berries to find;
And perched on its branches they feed,
    Till they leave scarce a cluster behind.

They come to the cottage door,
    Where the woodbine's berries remain;   10
And the white snow is sprinkled o'er,
    With the berries' crimson stain.

Strange visitants to us they seem,
    As they seek for their daily food;
Forsaking the hard-frozen stream,   15
    The meadow and leafless wood;

To visit the homes of men,
    Their lessons of trust to bring;
And then to their wild haunts again,
    Their joyful flight to wing.   20

Poem No. 149; c. 17 February 1865

The Soul's Questioning Of The Universe, And Its Beginning

The simple rustic's soul
    Will question, Whence is man?
And whence has come this perfect whole,
    The world's majestic plan?

The plant, the grass, the tree,   5
    The forms 'mid which we dwell;
Whence are they? When began to be?
    He asks; but none can tell;

And the deep musing sage
   Doth the same questions ask;   10
And spends his manhood and his age
   To solve the mighty task.

But, without light from heaven,
   In vain we seek to find
The answer; that, by faith, is given   15
   To man's bewildered mind.

Not timeless Nature's date,
   As men believed of old;
But God did all things first create,
   As in his Word is told.   20

The forms of earth and air,
   The stars, the sun's bright flame,
Alike his majesty declare,
   And magnify his name.

And man himself he made   25
   Godlike erect and free,
Made in the image it is said
   Of his own deity!

Not all things now to know
   Our Maker placed us here,   30
But to walk humbly here below,
   Walk in his love and fear.

And these shall pass away,
   Wax old and fade with age;
Created things must know decay,   35
   Declares the sacred page.

Poem No. 563; c. 11 March 1865

Hymn

Sung at the Eulogy on Abraham Lincoln June 1st 1865.

O God! who dost the nations lead,
  Though oft in ways to them unknown;
To thee we look, in this our need,
  A supplicant people seek thy throne.

For he, whom thou didst raise to guide,   5
  Has fallen, by the assassin's hand;
In thee alone would we confide,
  To guide, to guard, to save our land.

Through perils great, from year to year,
  Thou hast thus far our nation brought;   10
And given the victory to cheer,
  And, by our Chief, deliverance wrought.

With earnest prayer he sought thy will,
  In all the great events of life;
And nobly did his work fulfil,   15
  Through four long years of bloody strife.

O, lift us up in this sad hour,
  Let not our Country's foes prevail;
Sustain us by thy mighty power,
  Let not to us thy promise fail.   20

May Justice, Liberty, and Peace,
  For which his life he freely gave,
Bless all our land; and never cease
  To shed their glory round his grave.

Poem No. 374; c. 1 June 1865

Soul-Sickness

How many of the body's health complain,
When they some deeper malady conceal;
Some unrest of the soul, some secret pain,
Which thus its presence doth to them reveal.

Vain would we seek, by the physician's aid, 5
A name for this soul-sickness e'er to find;
A remedy for health and strength decayed,
Whose cause and cure are wholly of the mind.
To higher nature is the soul allied,
And restless seeks its being's Source to know; 10
Finding nor health, nor strength in aught beside;
How often vainly sought in things below!
Whether in sunny clime, or sacred stream,
Or plant of wondrous powers of which we dream.

Poem No. 193; c. 3 June 1865

Song
of The Early Spring

The clouds across the azure sky
    Fly swift, with changing forms;
To tell that Winter's reign is o'er,
    Its snow, and cold, and storms.

A warmer wind now breathes around, 5
    And in the balmy air
It seems as if new life there came,
    A life for all to share.

And welcome signs, on every hand,
    Of Spring's return I see; 10
The sparrow by the roadside sings,
    How sweet its note to me!

The grass along the turnpike's edge
    Grows green with sun, and showers;
And soon will May, fair May be here, 15
    To scatter wide her flowers.

Shall I, with dull, and thoughtless mind,
    Behold returning Spring;
And to the gracious God above
    No thanks, no offering bring? 20

With birds, and every living thing,
　　My grateful hymn I raise;
To thank the Giver of all good,
　　And celebrate his praise.

Poem No. 479; c. 17 June 1865

Sensibility to the Beauty and Fragrance of Flowers

How freely do the flowers their wealth bestow
Of beauteous tints on every passer by!
How freely, too, their fragrance round them throw!
To none, who pass, their gifts do they deny.
But though for all their beauty they dispense,　　　　　　5
Alike for all their fragrance round them fling,
Yet is there wanting oft a finer sense,
Than to their blooming bowers we thoughtless bring.
So, when I meet them in the vale, or wood,
Or, on the hill, their varied charms survey;　　　　　　10
Blest with some purer thought, some happier mood,
They to my soul a new delight convey;
And, to their well-known haunts, as I draw near,
More fair they seem, more fragrant they appear.

Poem No. 186; c. 28 July 1865

What Is The Word?

What is the word? I often hear men say,
Greeting each other in the mart or street;
Seeking for something new, from day to day,
Of friend, or neighbor, whom they chance to meet.
The question wakes in me the thoughtful mind,　　　　　5
Do they receive the word they ask to hear?
Or is it only like the passing wind,
Or empty echo dying on the ear?
The word, O man, is not some idle sound,
Lost on the ear almost as soon as heard;　　　　　　10

Unto the wise *life-giving* it is found.
And by its voice the inmost soul is stirred;
It falls not on the mind a barren seed,
But springeth up in fruitful thought, or deed.

Poem No. 776; c. 12 August 1865

The Sight of the Ocean

I gazed afar from the rocky hill,
   As if I never could drink my fill
Of the prospect fair, the ocean wide,
   The blue, bright ocean on every side.

For, with the prospect, grew my mind;   5
   And seemed, in the vast expanse, to find
A space for its flight, without shore, or bound,
   Save the sky above, and the sea around.

But soon o'er my spirit a feeling stole,
   A sad, lonely feeling I could not control;   10
Which the sight of the ocean doth ever bring,
   As if, like the soul, 'twere a lonely thing.

The plaintive wave, as it broke on the shore,
   Seemed sighing for rest forevermore;
And glad at length the land to reach,   15
   And tell its tale to the silent beach.

So seemed it then to my wandering thought,
   That in the vast prospect a home had sought;
The ship o'er the waters a port may find,
   But never the longing and restless mind.   20

As night o'er the ocean its shadow threw,
   And homeward the weary sea-bird flew;
I turned from the dark and rocky height,
   With grateful heart, to my hearth-stone bright.

Poem No. 230; c. 8 September 1865

Prayer For Rain

Pray, pray for rain; thou may'st not know,
    How man's weak prayer avails;
But pray, with earnest, trusting soul,
    The prayer of faith prevails.

Pray, pray for rain; each morning lift   5
    Thy prayer with humble mind,
That thou the longed-for gift may'st have,
    The promised blessing find.

And pray, with earnest, humble prayer,
    For every perfect gift;   10
To God in every time of need,
    Thy trusting spirit lift.

He knows our needs before we ask,
    Yet bids us toil and pray,
And ask of Him our daily bread   15
    To give us day by day.

And when the blessing He shall send,
    Of rain, or daily food;
O, let thy heartfelt prayer ascend,
    In loving gratitude!   20

Poem No. 401; c. 15 September 1865

Hymn On The Logos
The Light Still Shining In The Darkness

Once I musing was in spirit,
    Why the Light in darkness shone;
Why, amidst the early ages,
    It by man was never known.

Though Essential, Uncreated,   5
    Though within the mind it beamed;
Yet the Light none comprehended,
    Prophets mused and sages dreamed.

Then to me a voice there answered,
    "Why thy wonder thus express?   10
In the world that Light still shineth,
    All mankind to save and bless.

But how few behold its glory,
    Shining in the Savior's face!
And how few his life have copied,   15
    Full of heavenly truth and grace.

And though everywhere it shineth,
    Brighter than the orb of day;
Men and nations still reject it,
    Walking not in wisdom's way.   20

But to all who love, receive it,
    They the sons of God become;
Dwelling with the Lord forever,
    In his bright, eternal home."

Poem No. 390; c. 23 September 1865

Hath The Rain A Father? Or Who Hath Begotten The Drops of Dew? Job 38:28

We say, "It rains." Slow of belief the Age;
Its very words its unbelief doth show;
Forgot the lessons of the sacred page,
Spoken by men of faith so long ago!
No farther than they see, men's faith extends;   5
The mighty changes of the earth and sky
To them are causeless all, where Science ends;
An Unseen Cause they know not, or deny.
They hear not in the whirlwind, or the storm,
The mighty Voice, which spake to man of old;   10
They see not in the clouds of heaven his form,
Nor in his ceaseless works his power behold;
Who maketh small the countless drops of rain,
And sends soft showers upon the springing grain.

Poem No. 764; October 1865

"It is vain to say, that this is the country of the 'white man.'
It is the country of man." Charles Sumner.

True, noble words, which thrill the very soul,—
This country is for man, the human race;
Words, too, that should our policy control,
If we would not our fatherland disgrace.
This country is for all, of every name,   5
Reserved by Providence' all-gracious plan,
That each his proper dignity might claim,—
The right to be, and feel himself a man.
Here may the oppressed of foreign nations come,
And find, in our wide country, peace and rest;   10
The roving Indian reach a settled home,
In the broad prairies of the fertile West;
And here the slave, to manhood born at last,
Forget the wrongs and miseries of the past.

Poem No. 744; c. November 1865

The East India Marine Museum

A noble company, that early band,
Who left their homes to sail across the sea;
And distant voyages to the Orient planned,
The land of wealth, and dark Idolatry.
Behold their Monument! the rich and rare,   5
Gathered, with cost and pains, from every clime;
And, in this spacious hall, preserved with care,
To interest and instruct the future time;
To cherish in their sons the spirit brave,
Which gave to Salem its world-wide renown;   10
That thus their exploits, on the ocean wave,
From age to age might still be handed down;
And distant generations might behold,
And guard the trust, more precious far than gold.

Poem No. 14; c. 15 December 1865

Finishing The Work

"Let us strive to finish the work we are in; to bind up the nation's wounds; to do all which may achieve and cherish a just, and a lasting peace among ourselves, and with all nations."
Second Inaugural Address of PRESIDENT LINCOLN.

While men with ceaseless strife, in Church and State,
About the means of doing good contend;
The wounded man is left unto his fate,
And, in the means, forgotten is the end.
Lo, for a thousand years, the Church has striven   5
To guide the nations in their heavenward way;
But, by conflicting sects and dogmas riven,
Too oft, alas! her light has led astray.
And lo the State, still struggling to be free,
Oft wastes the precious years in wordy strife;   10
Forgetting the great end of Liberty,
And the great work of every nation's life;
To raise the low, instruct the darkened mind,
And live in lasting peace with all mankind.

Poem No. 811; c. December 1865

'O Lord, How Long?'

One saint to another I heard say, 'How long?'
I listened, but naught more I heard of the song;
The shadows are gliding through city and plain;
How long shall the night with its shadows remain?

How long ere shall shine, in this glimmer of things,   5
The light of which prophet in prophecy sings;
And the gates of that city be open, whose sun
No more to the west in its circuit shall run?

Poem No. 392; c. 1865

Our Soldiers' Graves

Strew all their graves with flowers,
   They for their country died;
And freely gave their lives for ours,
   Their country's hope and pride.

Bring flowers to deck each sod,   5
   Where rests their sacred dust;
Though gone from earth, they live to God,
   Their everlasting trust!

Fearless in Freedom's cause
   They suffered, toiled, and bled;   10
And died obedient to her laws,
   By truth, and conscience led.

Oft as the year returns,
   She o'er their graves shall weep;
And wreath with flowers their funeral urns,   15
   Their memory dear to keep.

Bring flowers of early Spring
   To deck each soldier's grave,
And Summer's fragrant roses bring;
   They died our land to save.   20

Poem No. 447; 1861–65?

The Still Small Voice

The Lord passed by! A mighty wind
   The lofty mountains rent
The ancient trees, by the strong blast,
   Like pliant reeds were bent.

But in the wind the Lord was not;   5
   Nor in the earthquake dire,
Which shook the solid mountain's base,
   Nor in the flaming fire.

But, after these, a still, small voice
    The listening prophet heard;
And in his mantle wrapt his face,
    He knew it was the Lord.   10

The War is past, with earthquake shock
    That shook our native land;
And quenched the fierce, consuming flame,
    By his divine command.   15

And now the still small voice we hear,
    Unheard amidst its strife;
That bids the sons of men return
    Unto the paths of life.

O, may we know that pardoning voice,   20
    That speaketh from above!
And to its words of Peace and Love
    Forever faithful prove.

Poem No. 523; 1865?

Indian Relics

In making the excavations for the moat, at Fort Pickering, on Winter Island, the grave of an Indian was found; in which were many curious relics. These are now in the possession of the Essex Institute.

A touching sight, these relics rude,
    Again exposed to day!
Where once, in nature's solitude,
    They first were laid away.

An Indian's bones, and dust are here,   5
    His arms for war and chase;
The arrow-heads, and pointed spear,
    The weapons of his race.

And various implements of stone,
    Which for his use he made;   10
The well-wrought bowl, and tools unknown
    Are with his weapons laid.

Was it, that, in another life,
 Again these things he'd need?
Again renew his savage strife,   15
 Or through the forest speed?

'Twas thus he pictured life again,
 No higher vision knew;
And from the natural, earthly plane,
 His highest wisdom drew.   20

And who are they who stand around,
 And view his narrow bed?
What nobler knowledge have they found,
 Who in God's Book have read?

Have they learned there, what Nature wise   25
 Doth in dim figure teach;
That man in nobler form shall rise,
 And his perfection reach?

Have they learned there the life of love,
 To live in lasting peace?   30
For such alone can soar above,
 When earthly life shall cease!

Then why this lofty fort uprear,
 Or dig this fosse deep,
To leave war's sad memorials here,   35
 Their memory long to keep?

To prove that, in the Gospel's light,
 Dark hate the soul can fill;
And nations with each other fight,
 And boast their warlike skill.   40

Poem No. 22; c. 12 January 1866

The Veil upon the Heart

Why cannot I make plain, to sinful men,
The heavenly kingdom that within me lies?
That kingdom lies not far beyond their ken,
Although its glory's hidden from their eyes.

A veil there is! a veil, like that of old,   5
Which hid the Christ from Jewish, Gentile mind;
That they could not his wondrous life behold,
But to his wisdom and his grace were blind!
That veil is on the heart; unfelt, unseen
By worldly men, who will not truth receive;   10
In vain heaven's light would penetrate the screen,
That they might on the truth of God believe;
His glorious kingdom to their souls is near,
They see it not! nor can its welcome hear!

Poem No. 817; c. 27 January 1866

True Knowledge Necessary for the Voyage of Life

Ships on the ocean meet, each other hail,
"Where from?" they say? and, "Whither art thou bound?"
Response is given; then on their voyage they sail,
Cheered by the cry, though dangers still surround.
Whither, O man! and whence, o'er life's dark sea,   5
Dost thou thy frail and tossing vessel steer?
Knowest thou that ocean's depth and mystery?
And canst thou to those questions answer clear,
Then mayst thou cheerful on Life's voyage proceed,
Nor dread its storms, nor fear its currents strong;   10
The soul, from darkling doubt and error freed,
By favoring gales is swiftly borne along;
While driven by adverse winds, by tempests tost,
The skeptic's bark, on unknown shores, is lost!

Poem No. 420; c. 26 May 1866

Sonnet

There is a natural body, and there is a spiritual body. – I Cor. xv. 44.

I gazed upon the silent burial-ground,
Where many forms lay mingling with the dust;
The gloomy shades of night had veiled it round,
And nought I saw to inspire a Christian's trust.
"Where are the forms," I said, "that once I knew,—.   5
Of friends and kindred, whom I love so well?
Have they for ever vanished from my view?
Ah! who will come their blessed abode to tell?"
But, as I spake, I turned my tear-dimmed eyes
Upwards, where countless stars and planets roll,   10
Filling with splendors bright the wintry skies;
And, like a revelation to my soul,
Came, from their shining orbs, a voice that said,
"So come, in glorious forms, with Christ, the dead!"

Poem No. 231; c. June 1866

Nature's Help for the Soul

When, wrapt in self, the soul grows dull,
   And thought doth lose its power,
Open thy window, gaze abroad,
   Go forth and walk an hour.

Commune with things, which God has made,   5
   The earth, the sea, the sky;
Let every object grand and fair
   Allure thy languid eye.

These shall from self the spirit free,
   Restore its healthy tone;   10
And banish doubt and care, that cloud
   The mind too much alone.

For this the earth, the sea, the sky,
    In beauty were arrayed;
In flower, and shell, and star, and sun,   15
    God's glory is displayed.

For flower and sun alike are parts
    Of one majestic plan,
The smallest object he beholds
    A study is for man.   20

That, drawn by each, the soul may leave
    Its doubts and cares behind;
And, in fair Nature's boundless realm,
    New health and vigor find.

Poem No. 797; c. 14 July 1866

Nature a Living Teacher

I would not study Nature's lore
    In books, or cabinets displayed;
But hill, and wood, and beach explore,
    Where lessons ne'er from memory fade.

In the dry leaf, and scentless flower   5
    I scarce the rose, or violet know;
But in the field, or leafy bower,
    How sweet they smell! how bright they glow!

The pearly shell no longer shines,
    From the sea-shore borne far away;   10
The crystals of the deep, dark mine
    No more their sparkling light display.

The butterflies on rainbow wings
    I watch as here and there they rove,
Or listen as some songster sings,   15
    And fills with music all the grove.

Their stiff, dead forms with pain I see,
    The beauteous bird's unruffled breast;
The butterflies, once roving free,
    With wings forevermore at rest!   20

No longer now they lessons teach,
   Such as from Nature's self I learn;
So to the fields, and pebbly beach
   From Science' joyless halls I turn.

Poem No. 290; c. 10 August 1866

Primitive Worship

God's worship to no temple is confined,
Amid the scenes of Nature it may be;
The song of praise borne on the summer wind,
Beneath the shelter of the forest tree.
So mused I, as I walked beside the lake,   5
Where Peters preached unto the listening throng;
The low-voiced waves that on its borders break,
With whispering pines all joined the sacred song.
So mused I, as amid the Camp I strayed,
Where Christians yearly meet for praise and prayer;   10
Beneath the hemlock's shade the people prayed,
And sweet their voices rose upon the air;
As when our fathers mid these forests trod,
And, without temples, worshipped here their God.

Poem No. 151; 24 August 1866

The Holy Land

I go not on a pilgrimage,
   As those, who went of old;
The holy land around us lies,
   Of which we have been told.

'Tis everywhere. The pure in heart   5
   Alone can enter in,
And those, whom grace and love have made
   Forever free from sin.

I see it, when the morning sun
    Doth rise o'er land and sea;   10
The moon's mild beams, the silent stars,
    Reveal it unto me.

In all that's good, in all that's fair,
    I see its glory shine;
As in the holy land of old,   15
    The ancient Palestine.

Wherever Freedom, Truth prevail,
    Wherever God is known;
That land is still Jehovah's land
    He calls it still his own.   20

And brighter yet, in days to come,
    Shall shine its wondrous light;
Till all the earth is holy land,
    With heavenly radiance bright.

I go not on a pilgrimage,   25
    As those, who went of old;
The holy land around us lies,
    Of which we have been told.

Poem No. 233; c. 1 September 1866

Standley's Grove

How quick upon the eye and mind,
    Flashes the prospect on the sight;
Like a surprise, which Nature planned,
    For those who climb this lofty height.

With patient steps we upward wind,   5
    Till on its rocky brow we stand;
Where, at one glance, we see outspread
    A picture fair of sea and land!

The harbor with its islands green,
    The rocks o'er which the breakers foam,   10
And, inland far, the city's spires,
    The factory's towers, and many a home;

From which a merry band has come
　　Of sportive children, bright and fair,
To swing and dance and rove and sing,　　　　　　　　　15
　　And breathe a while a purer air.

Their elders, too, their sports enjoy,
　　For once they all were children too;
Mid scenes like this their years forget,
　　And with the young their youth renew.　　　　　　　20

The music and the social feast
　　Add to the pleasures of the hour,
And swift the winged moments fly,
　　Beneath the pine grove's sheltering bower.

For see aglow the western sky,　　　　　　　　　　　25
　　With the last rays of parting day;
We bid farewell to hill and grove,
　　And to our homes we speed away.

Poem No. 198; c. 28 September 1866

October

All day, amidst the forests' splendor bright,
Spread o'er the landscape far as eye could see,
We journeyed on; and every vale and height
Transfigured in the glory seemed to be.
What colors of the earth, or e'en the sky,　　　　　　　5
Can paint the hues, which decked each hill and plain;
That, with their richness, tired the gazing eye?
What canvass can those wondrous tints retain?
Yet, as the seasons of the year return,
Again o'er all the land will they be cast;　　　　　　　10
Again each height and plain with glory burn,
And shall as long as Nature's self shall last;
Crowning with beauty e'en her latest day,
When all that we behold shall pass away!

Poem No. 30; October 1866

The Soldier and the Statesman

The soldier to preserve his Country dies,
When'er in peril hangs its very life;
With ardent courage to the field he flies,
And mingles fearless in the fatal strife.
That Country safe; the ends, for which it lives,   5
Become the patriot statesman's highest goal;
To these his life and all he has he gives,
He lives not for a party, but the whole:
That all the rights of men may there enjoy,
That liberty of speech and thought may spread,   10
And every foe to freedom thus destroy;
Towards those great ends, with steadfast mind he's led,
For which the nation sprang at first to birth,
And gained a name and glory through the earth.

Poem No. 567; c. 27 November 1866

The Triumphs of Science, And of Faith

Beneath the ocean's ever-tossing breast,
Now ruffled only by the summer wind,
Sinks the vast cable to its final rest,
Which shall two continents together bind.
Triumph of Science over space and time,   5
That kindred nations long have kept apart!
When shall our Faith, with triumphs as sublime,
Bind realm to realm and kindred heart to heart?
Yet still, in faith, man's triumph we behold,
Subduing nature to his lofty will;   10
And wait the day, in prophecy foretold,
Which, tarrying long, Oh may our age fulfil!
When nations shall from strife forever cease,
And the whole earth shall dwell in sacred peace.

Poem No. 66; November 1866

Christian Influence

And wouldst thou hasten, in another soul,
God's Kingdom on the earth of love and peace;
Learn first thyself, thy spirit to control,
From all that's false and evil in thee cease.
Nor think, that suddenly the reign shall come,
With pomp and glory for the outward eye;
Within, around thee, in thine earthly home,
The Kingdom of the Lord is drawing nigh!
As shines the light, with still increasing ray,
Till from the earth the brooding night has fled;
So, in man's spirit, comes the eternal day;
As gently as the dawn its beams have spread;
Till all within, and all around is bright,
And the whole world rejoices in its light.

Poem No. 50; c. 2 February 1867

The Reconciling Power

O Power! that waits not on man's feeble will,
Though granted still to faith, and hope, and prayer;
Thy gracious purposes in us fulfil,
And may we in thy favor ever share.
Vain is the people's strength, the ruler's power;
The statesman's wisdom and his arts are vain;
They hasten not on earth the blessed hour,
Which thou, in thine own keeping, doth retain.
The world, with its vain shows, doth souls divide,
Renew in all the simple heart of youth;
That friend from friend, by passion sundered wide,
May live again the life of love and truth.
Still mightier energies thou hast in store,
Than those with which the world has yet been blest;
Enduring peace, ne'er known on earth before,
The nations' Sabbath, the Millennial Rest.
O'er our wide land thy quickening influence send,
That, as one people, we may soon rejoice;

That party strife and pride may have an end,
Subdued and healed by thine all-powerful voice!   20

Poem No. 378; February 1867

The Heralds of the Spring

My ear is listening for the sound
　　Of earliest bird upon the tree,
Or sparrow, flitting o'er the ground,
　　Whose note so welcome is to me.

How long the trees have silent stood,   5
　　Through the cold, cheerless, winter days!
How lone the fields, the turnpike's road,
　　While hushed so long the sparrow's lays!

They tell of Spring's returning reign,
　　With its warm sun and milder sky: 10
That every stream has burst its chain,
　　And the green grass and flowers are nigh.

When man with Nature too awakes,
　　And feels with it the quickening breath;
And of the general joy partakes   15
　　Of earth's return from sleep and death,

Come quickly then, with welcome song,
　　Ye heralds of the early Spring;
Why tarry on your way so long,
　　Nor haste your joyful notes to sing?   20

Poem No. 335; c. 4 April 1867

The Bridge of Time

High o'er a flood, which boils and foams below,
　　Upon a bridge, with musing steps, I tread;
Who built its ancient piers we cannot know,
　　Long since their names were numbered with the dead.

Scarcely a thought the hurrying travellers give 5
    To those old builders, long since passed away;
Contented in the present time to live,
    To enjoy the pleasures of the passing day.

Yet on their memory I grateful dwell,
    As on I walk amid the thoughtless throng; 10
And of their toils for others fain would tell,
    And celebrate their virtues in my song.

For who can say, how many nameless ones,
    With busy hands, have toiled from year to year;
To gather, one by one, these moss-grown stones, 15
    To raise the arch and build the massive pier.

Who fashioned first the spade, the axe, the knife,
    The tools man needs where'er his feet may roam?
Who taught mankind the arts that cherish life,
    And fill with comforts many a happy home? 20

Who laid the State's foundations firm and deep,
    That winds and waves might not its strength o'erthrow;
That the full river might its channel keep,
    And man's strong passions still their bounds might know?

Forgotten mid the conquerors of old, 25
    Whose deeds have filled the annals of our race;
Their names proud History has never told,
    Nor midst its heroes found for them a place.

For peaceful ends they lived, and toiled, and died,
    For ends unto themselves perhaps unknown; 30
But to the future is the past allied,
    Nor without purpose raised the smallest stone.

If high and safe o'er Time's deep, swelling flood,
    They have prepared a pathway for mankind;
Which has its current and its rage withstood, 35
    How great the work which they have left behind!

And shall not we, as o'er Time's bridge we move,
    The builders' skill, and strength, and toil admire;
And, moved alike by gratitude and love,
    To nobler deeds and nobler lives aspire? 40

Poem No. 173; c. 6 April 1867

Our Dear Mother

No more our mother meets our sight,
   As here she moved from day to day,
Our constant solace and delight;—
   She from our home is called away!

Her books, her work are laid aside,   5
   No more the household is her care;
And to our hearts the joy's denied,
   At times her daily toils to share.

Her plants, her study and her joy,
   With their bright verdure and their bloom,   10
No more her leisure hours employ,
   Nor give to her their sweet perfume.

Long did she labor for our good,
   To inform the mind, improve the heart;
Cared for our raiment, health, and food,   15
   With all a mother's love and art.

Far into night her busy hand,
   Or thoughtful care our comfort sought;
With morning's light again she planned,
   And with untiring patience wrought.   20

To her we came in every ill,
   Whether of body, or of mind;
Sure in her sympathy and skill,
   Healing and balm for each to find.

And still, though now we see her not,   25
   I know her thoughts must on us dwell;
That we can never be forgot,
   Whom here she loved, and loved so well.

Clothed in immortal form of light,
   E'en now, perchance, she hovers round;   30
Though unperceived by mortal sight,
   Nor known by words of mortal sound;

A messenger, by night, by day,
    Sent by our heavenly Father's love;
Unseen, to guide us on our way   35
    Unto her blessed home above!

Poem No. 356; May 1867

Hymn
The Word Before All Things

Not first the things, which we behold;
    Though they, since time began,
E'en from Creation's dawn of old,
    Have been beheld by man.

Not first the grove, the hill, the stream,   5
    Though beauteous to the sight;
Nor first the sun's bright, golden beam,
    Nor stars with silvery light.

Nor first were beasts, nor creeping things,
    Nor insects' glittering throng,   10
Nor birds, that soar on sun-bright wings,
    And fill the groves with song:

But first the Word, which gave them birth,
    Eternal and divine;
Which built the heavens, and spread the earth,   15
    And bade the stars to shine.

By it, each thing that is was made,
    Beast, insect, bird, and man;
Ere earth's foundations first were laid,
    God saw the wondrous plan.   20

In it is light forever pure,
    Brighter than man can see;
That must eternally endure,
    When these shall cease to be.

Within the darkened human mind   25
    It shines, though dimmed its ray;
To lead the soul, which sin makes blind,
    To realms of endless day;

Where fairer things, and more sublime,
    That Word shall then reveal;   30
Which, now, the world of sense and time
    Doth from man's sight conceal.

Poem No. 363; c. June 1867

The Whiteweed

Swept by every passing breeze,
    See the meadow fall and rise!
See its green waves, sprinkled o'er
    With the whiteweed's starry eyes!

Gay they bend as in a dance,   5
    Up and down a thousand ways;
So I've watched them many an hour,
    In my bygone childhood's days.

Still I watch them, as of old,
    With an ever new delight;   10
Following still their mazy dance,
    Ever changing to the sight.

For of grace and beauty still
    Do they now as ever teach;
Vain are fancy's feeble powers   15
    Nature's perfect forms to reach.

Poem No. 451; June 1867

The Teachings of the Spirit

Not of the earth, nor sense are we,
  Though here on earth we dwell;
But higher things than these we see,
  Of higher things can tell.

The Spirit doth our spirits teach,   5
  Though dull, and slow to hear;
And messages it brings to each,
  Had each the listening ear.

It speaks of God, it speaks of heaven,
  Of Christ, who from it came;   10
And of eternal life, that's given
  To those who love his name.

Of faith and hope, and peace and joy,
  Unknown to worldly mind;
Which time, and sense cannot destroy,   15
  Which they who seek shall find.

Come, Holy Spirit, from above,
  And of thy gifts impart;
Come with thy light, thy truth, thy love,
  And dwell in every heart.   20

Poem No. 367; c. 3 July 1867

Hymn

Amidst the pastures green,
  Beside the rivers still;
Thou leadest those, O Lord, in peace,
  Who seek to do thy will.

They rest 'neath shady rock,   5
  Or trees beside the way;
Nor more they thirst, no more they feel
  The sun's hot, scorching ray.

No more the world disturbs,
    Or fills them with alarm;   10
For where thou givest peace, and rest,
    Vain is man's power to harm.

And near those pastures green,
    Those peaceful rivers near;
To all who seek to do thy will,   15
    Thy voice of love to hear.

Thou teachest them the way,
    Unseen by other eyes;
And, e'en amidst the desert waste,
    Prepar'st a glad surprise.   20

Poem No. 43; July–October 1867

The Help of the Spirit

How can we upward go,
    Without thy help, O Lord?
The way of life indeed we know,
    For thou hast taught us in thy blessed word.

Still upward doth it lead,   5
    But we grow faint, and weak;
A strength above our own we need,
    That strength from thee we seek.

For thou art present still,
    Though not sense and sight;   10
Thy word of promise to fulfil
    Of strength, and peace, and light.

Thou hast not left alone
    Thy followers here below;
To thee their trials all are known,   15
    And help thou dost bestow.

The Spirit thou dost send,
    To cheer the mind, and heart;
To guide them to their journey's end,
    And nevermore depart!   20

Poem No. 181; c. 3 August 1867

The Birthright Church

The birthright church; where shall we find its door,
For every new-born soul to enter in;
And, once within, never to leave it more,
To wander in the paths of doubt, and sin?
In churches of the past with crumbling walls,   5
To which the moss, and climbing ivy cling?
No; from the coming future still it calls,
And to the present doth its promise bring.
City of God, descending out of heaven,
Beheld by seer of old in vision bright!   10
O may it to our eyes, like his, be given
To see on earth thy mild, and peaceful light;
Shining, with steadfast beams, on childhood's way,
That it from out thy gates no more may stray.

Poem No. 466; c. 26 October 1867

Midas

Turn all I touch to gold,
    King Midas said.
His wish was granted, and behold!
    His very meat was gold, gold his bread.

And liquid gold the drink   5
    He raised on high;
When o'er the golden goblet's brink,
    The water to his eager lips came nigh.

Ah fatal gift! that balked
 His greedy soul;   10
Which in its very richness mocked;
 For gold is but one thing, and not the whole.

So they, who money seek,
 Gold, only gold;
Are childish, disappointed, weak,   15
 Though gained their end; like that famed king of old.

Poem No. 745; c. 29 October 1867

Revelation

Addressing reason, yet above it still,
The True Religion speaks unto the soul;
It bids the conflicts of the mind be still,
And doth each motive of the will controul.
From low to higher still is nature's law,   5
Written on stony tablets of the earth;
And things we see upward the spirit draw
To things, and beings of a nobler birth.
Nor man alone aspires; but God descends,
And to our faculties doth lend his aid;   10
That we, amidst our doubts, may see the ends,
For which the world, and all therein were made;
See too his gracious love for sinful man,
More wondrous far than e'en Creation's plan.

Poem No. 26; c. 7 December 1867

How come the Dead?

How come the dead? we anxious ask,
 When, parting from our sight,
The spirit leaves its earthly home,
 To dwell in realms of light.

How come the dead? Shall we no more 5
    The friends we love behold;
Nor clasp again within our arms,
    Their forms so still, and cold?

The very question that we ask,
    May its own answer give; 10
Is it the mortal that we mourn?
    Our friends immortal live.

They come, though unperceived by sense,
    Through memory's open door;
We see their looks, their voices hear, 15
    Familiar as before.

They come; for hope will whisper still,
    Undying in the heart;
That friends who love shall meet again,
    Meet nevermore to part. 20

And faith, with heaven-directed gaze,
    As seeing things concealed;
Declares the dead, with Christ, shall come,
    When he shall be revealed!

Poem No. 183; c. January 1868

The Hacker School House

Swift fly the years! Men call thee mean and old,
But I behold thee still as in thy prime;
The scroll of memory quickly is unrolled,
Wherein I read of childhood's early time;
Of that first morn, when finished, bright, and new, 5
We took our seats within thy well-built walls;
The master's voice I hear, his form I view,
As to his place, in order, each he calls.
Again I see, 'twas a beauteous sight!
Adorned with evergreen, and summer flowers; 10
The parents sharing in their sons' delight,
And gay the school room looked as garden bowers.

Thus ever stand, flower-wreathed and fair and new,
A picture bright for memory to view!

Poem No. 452; c. 27 March 1868

The Houstonia

Welcome sweet flower, that scent'st the morn,
    From the moist earth so newly born,
Sprinkling afar the grassy sod,
    Where'er I look for many a rod!

In families thou lov'st to grow,   5
    Sweet, social bands, a beauteous show;
As if some secret tie did bind
    Each floweret, like the human kind.

Companion of the little child,
    With eye so blue, and look so mild,   10
To me as welcome is thy bloom,
    As welcome too thy sweet perfume.

He calls thee, Innocent, a name
    Unknown to science, or to fame;
A name that he from Nature took,   15
    Expressive of thy form and look.

Thou dost return, with early spring,
    Thy fragrance and thy bloom to bring;
To call the young with willing feet,
    To seek thee in thy wild retreat.   20

With them do I, in early May,
    Rejoice to greet thee on my way;
And e'en when summer's heats have come,
    To find thee still where'er I roam.

In thy slight form, and mild blue eye,   25
    To feel some bond of sympathy;
And learn again the lesson mild,
    Thou taught'st me, when a little child.

Poem No. 768; c. 12 May 1868

To The Salem Gazette,
On The Completion Of Its First Century

One hundred years with their events have fled,
Since first thy sheet was sent from door to door;
How many have thy pleasant pages read,
Now known amid life's busy scenes no more!
How vast the changes, since those years have flown;   5
Our Country's growth in commerce, wealth, and power;
The rule of haughty King long since o'erthrown,
And Freedom's triumph in the present hour!
And chronicled upon thy welcome page
The news from country round, and o'er the sea;   10
Domestic scenes endeared to youth and age,
Instructive tale, or gem of poesy.
For many a century may thy page record
Each noble deed, and fitly-spoken word.

Poem No. 391; c. early August 1868

Ocean's Treasures

I walked on the ocean beach,
   I saw a beautiful shell;
But 'twas carried beyond my reach,
   As the billows rose and fell.

A sun-fish I sought to take,   5
   But the waves rolled strong and high,
And bade me the prize forsake,
   And back from the breakers fly.

Then a pebble, round and white,
   I sought of the ocean to steal;   10
But the wave returned, and, far from sight,
   Did the stone in its bosom conceal.

'Twas as if it loved its own,
    The ocean so vast and drear;
The shell and fish and round white stone   15
    To its mighty heart were dear.

And a stranger sought to bear
    Its treasures far, far away;
Where no more they'd shine forever fair,
    And bright with the dashing spray.   20

Poem No. 281; c. 21 August 1868

SONNETS ON RECONSTRUCTION

I.

A Nation's Life Of Slow Growth

Slowly a Nation doth unfold its life,
A life, perhaps, in violence began;
Unfolding still through years of peace, or strife,
According to some high and noble plan.
It seeks Perfection in the social state;   5
Though oft astray by kings and conquerors led,
Or party leaders, skilful in debate;
To party, more than to their Country wed.
Yet still the People, as by instinct taught,
Or higher impulse moving every soul;   10
By various fortunes on their way are brought,
Till they shall reach at length the appointed goal;
When all in social harmony shall dwell,
And state 'gainst state no more again rebel.

Poem No. 425; c. 18 September 1868

II.

The Ends For Which A Nation Exists

Was it for mere existence, that we fought,
Contending only that the state might be?
Through war's dread scenes the higher ends we sought
Of Social Progress, civil Liberty;
For which, at first, our fathers did contend;   5
That here a true foundation might be laid,
That far and wide the mighty tree might send
Its roots into our soil, and spread its shade;
For Education, free alike for all,
For Temperance, Justice, Virtue, Order, Peace;   10
That ancient wrongs and errors here might fall,
And war on earth at length forever cease.
What is a nation, if for party ends,
Or for a mere existence it contends?

Poem No. 759; c. 18 September 1868

III.

Political Ambition

Again doth lust of Power lift up its head,
Seeking our Country for its ends to rule;
Feeding the flame, which it so long has fed,
Before war's lava torrents yet are cool.
What are the ends for which it power would seek?   5
To educate, to civilize, refine,
To raise the lowly and uphold the weak,
Develop, cherish every art benign?
To make our land, by Providence so blest,
Still onward in the path of progress move;   10
That here the heavy laden might find rest,
And nations dwell in brotherhood and love?
Ah no;—it strives not thus mankind to bless,
But only power to gain, and to possess.

Poem No. 28; c. 25 September 1868

IV.

National Unity

A unity complete, assured, and high,
Is that for which our Country still contends;
Fulfilling thus a nation's destiny;
For this its mighty energies it lends.
No more for party purposes it lives,   5
For it has entered on a nobler strife;
A higher motive higher objects gives,
Long years of progress, and of peaceful life;
In which it may its vast domain explore,
And with its commerce whiten every sea;   10
Stretch the strong iron bands from shore to shore,
Encourage Science, Art, and Industry;
That thus established firm on Nature's plan,
Might rise secure at length the work of man!

Poem No. 23; c. 29 September 1868

Reflections on the History of Nations

When I consider mighty nations' fate,
Their rise, their growth, their grandeur, and decline;
And all their varied history contemplate,
I see and own in each the Hand divine!
Not of themselves they rose to wealth and power,   5
And gained on earth a glory and a name;
Alike, to God, the nation of an hour,
And that which stands a thousand years the same.
To such as walk in righteousness and truth,
He gives long years of steady, sure increase;   10
They, like the eagle, shall renew their youth,
Their honor and their glory never cease;
While such as from his just commandments stray,
Shall sudden fall; or waste by slow decay.

Poem No. 788; 2 October 1868

Scepticism With Regard To The Gospels

Strange words are these, that little now we know
Of Him, who lived in ancient Palestine;
And mighty works performed so long ago,
Which all the ages since have called divine.
That all is legend, mystery, which we read   5
Of Him, who died mankind from death to save;
He, who man from death, and error freed,
Himself became the trophy of the grave.
Ah faithless age! which cannot see the light,
E'en though it does with noon-day brightness beam;   10
Which boasts its Science and its clearer sight,
Yet calls the Gospel histories but a dream.
It is not that the Light has never shined,
Nor shineth still; but we to it are blind!

Poem No. 446; c. 31 October 1868

The Tide

With daily ebb and flow
   The waters by us glide,
They tell us of the mighty Power,
   That rules their constant tide.

Yet, thoughtless still we gaze,
   Untaught from day to day;   5
Unheeded still the unseen Hand,
   That doth their motions sway.

As if thus, of itself,
   The river's tide might flow;   10
Now fill its empty channels high,
   Then back to ocean go.

As if attraction's force
   Could be the only law;
And moon and sun could, of themselves,   15
   The bulk of ocean draw.

Ah, who shall give us sight
    This miracle to see?
In ocean's constant ebb and flow,
    The work of Deity! 20

In Nature's constant law,
    To own God's ceaseless power;
Who makes the sea to know its bounds,
    And keep the appointed hour.

Poem No. 835; c. October 1868

The Spiritual Birth

Thy knowledge cannot reach
    Unto the heavenly birth;
Thou knowest only what is done
    Below, upon the earth.

Believe, and thou shalt know 5
    Things holy and divine;
Things unperceived by mortal sense,
    By faith alone are thine.

To naught the Lord compares
    The Spirit, but the wind; 10
Whose voice indeed we listening hear,
    But none its way can find.

It calls thee to repent,
    Christ's kingdom enter in;
And while thou dwellest here below, 15
    The heavenly life begin.

Obey the Spirit's call,
    And by its voice be led;
And thou within the heavenly courts,
    At length shall surely tread. 20

Poem No. 713; c. November 1868

The Youth and the Stream

The Youth.
Why so swift thou hurrying tide,
Why unto the ocean glide?
Why not here prolong your stay,
Through the long, bright summer's day?
Here are flowers of every hue,   5
Here are groves and fields to view;
Stay, and let them ever rest
Imaged on thy peaceful breast.

The Stream.
Why O mortal! thus replied,
To my quest, the rushing tide.   10
Why art thou, too, hurrying on,
And so soon from earth art gone?
All things here one law obey,
Naught in time can rest, or stay;
Use these moments as they fly,   15
Time well-spent can never die;
It but goes to fill the sea
Of a blessed eternity.
Mortal! raise your thoughts sublime,
Find eternity in time!   20
In the Christian's life is rest,
He alone in time is blest;
Living, in the passing hour,
With a life beyond its power.
Souls, made pure, do still retain   25
Earth's fair flowers on hill, and plain;
In their depths reflected are
Groves, and fields, and evening star;
Lit by Memory's golden ray
There they never fade away.   30

Poem No. 827; 1859–68?

The Daily News

As one who, standing safe upon the land,
Beholds a vessel tossing on the wave,
Or by the tempest driven on the strand,
Without the power the mariner to save;
So do I read, from danger's path afar,   5
Of many a sad event on field, and flood;
Of the fierce ravages of cruel war,
Of people perishing from want of food;
Of single sufferers, whom no help of mine
Can ever reach, whom I can never see;—   10
Why read the harrowing page, the mournful line,
If I can only give my sympathy?
Ah, say not so. Believe the Sacred Word,
Pray for all men, the prayer of faith is heard!

Poem No. 56; c. 9 January 1869

On A Hyacinth From Georgia

Fair flower! that, from the southern skies,
    Hast reached us with thy bloom;
Thou dost our hearts with joy surprise,
    And banish winter's gloom!
For oft, we know not, how or why,   5
    Its gloom steals o'er the heart;
Earth's frozen breast, the stormy sky,
    Seem of ourselves part.

Thou break'st the spell; as when the Spring
    Returns to cheer our sight;   10
And, in her train, doth with her bring
    The flowers, our chief delight;
She calls them, with her gentle voice,
    And bids their tribes appear;
With southern fields our own rejoice,   15
    For Spring again is here!

A bond thou art 'twixt state and state,
   A link in Nature's chain;
That doth man's written laws out date,
   That ever shall remain;   20
To tell us of God's boundless love
   To all of human kind;
And, like the Gospel from above,
   Their hearts in one to bind.

Poem No. 108; 20 January 1869

Things Unseen

With higher thoughts, O God, uplift
   My sinking, feeble mind;
And let it, in the things unseen,
   Its rest and portion find.

For these are real;—though the world   5
   Doth not in them believe;
Can worldly, carnal-minded men
   The things of God receive?

Such things the Spirit doth reveal,
   Things, like Itself, divine;   10
Oh that they might more real grow,
   And be forever mine.

Around my spirit ever breathe
   A calm, and holy joy;
Which earthly cares might not disturb,   15
   Nor human power destroy.

Into my darkened spirit shine,
   With ever brightening ray;
Till gone each cloud, which dims my sight,
   And come the perfect day.   20

That thus I might, with truth and power,
   To others too declare,
How great, how vast eternal things!
   How wondrous and how fair!

Poem No. 836; c. 30 January 1869

The Oak And The Poplar

There grew upon a sandy hill
    An oak and poplar tree;
The oak seemed almost to stand still,
    Its growth you scarce could see;
For years its strong, and stubborn roots   5
    Were burrowing 'neath the ground,
While on its trunk no lofty shoots,
    Nor spreading limbs were found.
The poplar shot up tall and fast,
    And looked around with pride;   10
And o'er the oak its shadow cast,
    As 'twould its neighbor hide;
Its bright leaves glittered in the sun,
    And danced in every breeze;
From all it admiration won;   15
    While none the oak could please.
A century passed.—The tardy oak
    Had reared *its* head on high,
And praise, and reverence bespoke
    From every passer by;   20
A hundred arms it had outspread,
    Its thick, and gnarled form
Seemed not the lightning's bolt to dread,
    Nor fear the wildest storm!
Fit for man's use, it waiting stood   25
    To rib the stout ship's side;
And bear him safely o'er the flood,
    Without its aid denied;
Or form, with timbers tough and strong,
    His dwelling's massive frame;   30
That should protect the builder long,
    And still hand down his name.
And there, around the parent tree,
    A thousand younger stood;
That, age on age, for man should be   35
    A magazine of wood;
And, on its boughs, the acorns still
    In countless numbers hung,

The falling forest's place to fill,
  And keep it ever young.   40

The quick-grown poplar long had ceased
  To be remembered there,
The old men told, "how it increased,
  And flourished once so fair;
That many nurseries were made,   45
  'Twas planted through the town,
And much admired for growth and shade,
  But short-lived its renown!
For soon", they said, "its tender frame
  The blustering winds o'erthrew;"   50
And now 'tis scarcely known by name,
  Where once in pride it grew.

Poem No. 611; 6 March 1869

The Yellow Violets

In a broad, grassy field,
  By the old turnpike's side;
Once grew a bed of fairest flowers,
  Of early Spring the pride.

Close to the craggy hill,   5
  And near a walnut tree;
Those lilies fair, though years have fled,
  I seem again to see!

Amidst green, speckled leaves,
  The graceful flowers were found;   10
Each, pendant on a slender stem,
  Bent gazing on the ground.

With playmates there I strayed,
  When April days had come;
To search for buds, or opening flowers,   15
  And bear my treasures home.

But, like my childhood's hours,
    Their beauty now is fled;
Their flowers no more the field adorn,
    And hid their lowly bed.   20

The grassy field's destroyed,
    Where they so long had grown;
And the yellow violet now no more
    By the children there is known!

Poem No. 297; c. 4 May 1869

The City of God

How strange the thought, that in the very light
Of God's own city we may walking be;
That holy city, where there is no night,
Nor yet the light, nor those about us see!
Its music, too, may fall upon the ear,   5
Celestial strains from the angelic choirs;
No soul-entrancing melody we hear,
For naught divine the heavenly strain inspires.
Without a warning, save a voice from heaven,
The holy city doth to earth descend;   10
To all alike its light is freely given,
And men and angels do their voices blend;
But oft, alas, within its streets we tread,
Nor know that to its scenes our souls are dead!

Poem No. 202; c. 5 June 1869

The Scholar Dreaming

Gazing, listless, from his book
    Doth the scholar outward look,
Through the window, far away,
    At the close of summer day.

Objects bright and fair he sees,
   Feels the cool, refreshing breeze;
Which doth from the meadow blow,
   Bending all its surface low.

Sees the rocky hills so steep,
   Where he longs to climb and leap;
Hears the songs of birds so free,
   As they sport from tree to tree.

Strange the words upon the page,
   They no more his mind engage;
School and books unreal seem,
   They have vanished like a dream!

Chide not, Teacher, chide him not,
   Though his lesson be forgot;
Nature takes him by the hand,
   He her words can understand. 20

Follow too her wiser plan,
   Let the child instruct the man;
All his nature learn to train,
   Or thy toil may prove in vain.

Through long years, the mind will grow 25
   Ere its stature it shall know;
Soon the body's height is gained,
   And its fullest powers attained.

Give him motives pure and high,
   Point to earth, and sea, and sky; 30
Let him far and wide explore
   Hill, and field, and rocky shore.

Give the body health and strength,
   That it may not fail at length;
That the ever-active mind 35
   May a fit companion find.

Poem No. 144; c. 29 June 1869

Hymn

Sung at the Dedication of the Peabody Academy of Science, Salem, Aug. 18, 1869.

The noble hall our fathers planned,
  Where gathered were the rich and rare;
From every clime, and every land,
  And long preserved with faithful care;

To Science now we dedicate,   5
  That doth all Nature's realms explore;
New ways through continents create,
  And cables stretch from shore to shore.

And higher still, on soaring wing,
  The great Creative Thought would find;   10
And study, in each living thing,
  The end for which it was designed.

That it may serve the lot of man,
  And to the race a blessing prove;
Unfold the universal plan   15
  Of God's beneficence, and love.

Honor to him, who, far and wide,
  For these high ends his wealth bestows;
Which, like some mighty river's tide,
  Through all our land exhaustless flows.   20

Poem No. 534; c. 18 August 1869

Spiritual Darkness

A darkness, like the middle of the night,
Clouds in the morn, and e'en the mid day hours;
Men wander round, as if devoid of sight,
Or led astray by false deluding powers.
The wise knew not its coming, nor can tell   5
Whence fell this darkness, like a plague, on all;
In vain they seek by knowledge to dispel

The gloom, that shrouds the earth as with a pall!
The astronomer the sun's eclipse foretells,
The day and hour, when quenched his glorious ray;   10
The moment, when his arrowy beam dispels
The sudden night, and brings returning day;
But who the dark eclipses of the mind
Can thus predict? by calculation find?

Poem No. 4; c. 9 October 1869

Friendship

How sweet the memory of a friend,
    Whom now we meet no more!
How oft his looks do we recall,
    Repeat his sayings o'er.

The places where with him we strayed,   5
    The meadow, grove, and hill;
How oft we picture them to view,
    And with fond memories fill!

Sad are our hearts, that now no more
    His face, his form we see;   10
When we frequent the much-loved spots,
    Where he was wont to be.

As wandering there the things we see
    All seem to us more fair
Each thing he loved each flower & tree   15
    When he was with us there.

Each well-remembered object makes
    His image more complete;
Till earthly trials, sorrows past,
    With him again we meet.   20

Poem No. 204; c. 1 January 1870

The Sparrows And The Crop of Weeds

Think not yon tall, rank growth of weeds
 A useless crop is found;
Though man himself has sowed no seeds,
 Nor tilled the fertile ground.

Though he neglect, as here we see,   5
 The primal, great command;
Nor grain, nor plant, nor bush, nor tree,
 Is witness of his hand.

For He, who all things, small and great,
 Includes in one vast plan;   10
Did humble sparrows too create,
 As well as nobler man.

He shelters them through winter's night,
 So long, and drear, and cold;
In swamp, or wood, till morning light;   15
 As shepherd keeps his fold.

And still the earth brings forth the weed,
 Man's idleness to shame;
The birds in wintry time to feed,
 Who naught from him can claim.   20

Thus doth the Lord for these provide,
 Who neither sow nor reap;
Nor to the smallest is denied
 His care, who all doth keep.

Poem No. 652; 15 February 1870

Ye have hoarded up treasure in the last days.—James 5 : 3.

Bring forth your gold and silver! They shall be
But as the dust that meets the passing eye;
You shall from all your idols break; be free!
And worship Him who made earth, sea and sky!
Ye who have hid within your learned pelf,   5

Ye who in gold alone your riches see,
Bring forth your idols! they are born of Self,
Nor longer in their worship bow the knee.
Each secret thing must now be brought to light,
For soon the day breaks on your hidden spoil;   10
Go, buy what then will give your souls delight,
Nor longer for earth's treasures vainly toil;
For each man's work must now be tried by fire,
Which shall consume each selfish, wrong desire.

Poem No. 81; c. 26 February 1870

Hymn
The Spiritual Body

Clothed upon with house from heaven,
    See each bush and naked tree;
Unto us an image given
    Of man's immortality!

Still the spirit needs a covering,   5
    When the fleshly garment fails;
Like the snow flakes downward hovering,
    It the new-born spirit veils.

Many a soiled, and time-worn raiment
    Suddenly is laid aside;   10
And the humble, earthly claimant
    With new body glorified!

Clothed is the weary spirit
    With immortal vigor strong,
Angels' nature doth inherit,   15
    Powers that unto them belong.

Not in vain the Resurrection
    Doth the Church forever preach;
Nature doth to our reflection
    The same wondrous lesson teach.   20

In the insect's new-found pinions,
    Breaking from its sealéd tomb;
Heir of Summer's bright dominions,
    Freed from winter's death and gloom;

In the grain of wheat, which springeth   25
    With new beauty from the ground;
In the pure, white robe, that clingeth
    Unto shrub, and tree around.

Poem No. 87; c. 9 April 1870

Hymn

The Efficacy of a Mother's Prayer

Pray, mother, for thy prayer may keep
    Thy child in virtue's way;
A blessed harvest he shall reap,
    For whom thou oft dost pray.

'Twill bless him in his early days,   5
    And consecrate his home;
'Twill bless him mid the world's rough ways,
    And wheresoe'er he roam.

Through manhood e'en to life's last close,
    Thy prayers shall council, guide;   10
Keep pure his heart from deadly foes,
    From hatred, lust, and pride.

Pray, mother, for thy prayer has power
    To help, to save thy child;
To give him strength in evil hour,   15
    By pleasure's voice beguiled.

And pray, O pray, when erring, frail,
    Thy feeble child may fall;
Thy prayer, thy faith may still prevail,
    And back to life recall!   20

For God the prayer of faith doth hear,
    And answer from on high;
To those who seek Him, He is near,
    Nor will their quest deny.

Poem No. 400; c. 9 July 1870

The Fireflies

The Summer's day has reached its close,
    The darkness settles round;
The weary mower seeks repose,
    And sinks in sleep profound.

But o'er the field of new-mown hay,   5
    Behold a wondrous sight!
Though gone the brightness of the day,
    The air is full of light.

Like sparkles, glancing to and fro
    Among the new-mown grass,   10
The fireflies gleam; how strange the show!
    As back and forth they pass;

Each with a lamp, like human kind;
    They seek perchance their food;
Or, by its light, each other find,   15
    As suits their varying mood.

Or, hiding them from dangerous foe,
    They darken now its ray;
That none their secret path may know,
    And seize them for their prey.   20

How marvelous the works of God,
    His wisdom, skill, and power!
In starry hosts or glittering sod,
    In insect, plant, or flower.

Oh may I not, whereere I turn,
    Careless his works behold;
But from each thing some lesson learn,
    Which He to man has told.

Poem No. 576; c. 19 July 1870

Be Not Many Teachers

James 3:1.

"Be ye not many teachers; for we all,"
The Apostle wrote, "in many things offend;"
His admonition let us oft recall,
As words of wisest teacher, and of friend.
"Be ye not many teachers". First receive   5
The gift of Wisdom, ere ye claim to teach;
And first the Gospel's glorious truths believe,
Before that Gospel ye to others preach.
We all offend. Confession humble, meek,
To those who would instruct their fellow men;   10
That they may ever grace, and wisdom seek
To guide their speech; whether of tongue, or pen;
Lest they, as teachers, labor but in vain,
And but the greater condemnation gain!

Poem No. 62; c. 6 August 1870

Military surprises and the capture of capitals, are the events of a by-gone age. D'Israeli.

A by-gone age appears again,
    Though gone its weapons, spear and shield;
Men's baser passions still the same,
    Will the same fatal harvest yield.

Yea, deadlier weapons they contrive,   5
    As aided by Satanic skill;
More wide destruction's bolts to hurl,
    And with a surer aim to kill.

The march of armies trampling down
    The harvests raised by care and toil,   10
The works of noblest skill destroyed,
    And cities burnt, or given to spoil;

Homes made forever sad and lone,
    For children in the battle slain;
These are the scenes of which we read,   15
    A by-gone age appears again!

Ambition grasping wider power,
    Involving nations in its plan,
Musters its hosts; appeals to arms;
    Regarding neither God nor man.   20

The pomp and circumstance of war
    No more the statesman's thoughts engage;
He views them but as idle shows,
    The relics of a barbarous age;

Restored to deck despotic rule,   25
    With semblance of its ancient power;
Its prestige and its name prolong
    Beyond the fixed, allotted hour.

Poem No. 1; c. 9 September 1870

The Bible Does Not Sanction Polygamy

I.

The Word of God doth sanction nothing ill,
Nor low, nor base; whatever men may find
Written of old. The letter oft doth kill,
Or to the grovelling Past the spirit bind.
So they, who once did Slavery uphold,   5
Found in the Bible sanction for their deed;
Their hearts more hardened like the King of old,

When Israel was from Egypt's bondage freed.
So War, twin-relic of a barbarous age,
Claims too the sanction of the Holy Word;   10
And nations still in hostile strife engage,
And call themselves the followers of the Lord!
The Spirit only quickens; gives the light,
That we may read the Word of God aright.

II.

A loftier state of purity and bliss,   15
Than this man's mortal lot doth yet unfold;
In the new life, which shall succeed to this,
Was by the Savior to mankind foretold;
The Resurrection;—when no more we die,
Nor parted are by time, or cruel fate;   20
But as the angels are, who dwell on high;
And, made immortal, share their deathless state!
There soul meets soul, and heart to heart is known,
Nor sundered are the ties, which spirits bind;
There none is ere compelled to walk alone,   25
Or lacks the fellowship of kindred mind;
Would that such purity we now might share,
And for that blissful state might here prepare!

Poem No. 600; c. 16 September 1870

Bitter-Sweet Rocks

There is no spot so lonely, rough, and wild,
But Nature doth, with careful fingers, deck
With flowers, or vines, or ferns, or soft green moss,
To give to those, who to such haunts may stray,
A sweet surprise, a pleasure all their own.   5
To such a spot, an unfrequented dell,
When Autumn comes, some warm October day,
I love to wander, and in silence muse.
O'er rocky hills, where cattle roam and feed,
Cropping the meadows and the pastures green,   10

My way I take; pausing at times to view
The city's spires, or ocean's blue expanse;
Then down the narrow glen, shady and still,
Save when some startled bird has taken to flight,
Or cricket's song amid the grass is heard.   15
Here from the cliff whose vast rocks have fallen,
Thrown down by some convulsion, or by frost;
And at its base lie in confusion piled.
But not neglected doth this ruin lie,
For here a beauteous show hath Nature wrought   20
For those, who to this lonely spot have come.
Among these broken rocks the bitter-sweet
Has taken root, and clasped the fragments round
In close embrace, covering the mossy rocks
With leafy screen; where clustering bunches hang   25
Of purest gold. And, sight most beautiful!
As Nature sought yet more to please and charm;
Up to the very top of a high tree,
Which rooted grows amid'st the fallen crags,
A vine has clomb; and every bough and twig   30
Is laden with its golden berries ripe,
And from the top in gay festoons they hang;
Giving a wondrous beauty to the place.

Poem No. 627; c. 31 October 1870

Humanity Mourning
For Her Children Slain In War

Humanity laments, and still will weep
   Her slaughtered sons of every age and clime;
And hourly doth her fasts and vigils keep,
   For millions perished since the birth of time!

And shall she never from the dust arise,   5
   And put her robe of fleecy whiteness on;
And dry her swollen and ever flowing eyes
   For wrongs, that man his brother man has done?

Yes; for though passing clouds now dim her sight,
    They shall not long prevent the approaching day;   10
Already are the hill-tops glad with light,
    And man's proud tyrants starting with dismay.

Soon shall she see her children dwell in peace
    On all the earth, of every name and clime;
Their friendly intercourse of love increase,   15
    Unfettered by the bonds of space and time.

A deep, abiding joy her soul shall fill,
    Beholding thus her countless children blest;
Secure from rude alarms, and every ill,
    And entering here on their eternal rest!   20

Poem No. 205; c. 15 November 1870

The Poor Clergyman

Long had Christ's servant preached the word of truth,
And labored in the vineyard of his Lord;
But gone his strength, his manhood, and his youth,
And age had come;—but what was his reward?
Men had forgot the laborer; rich had grown,   5
And added house to house, and land to land;
The truth he preached forgot, or never known;
Like those who heard, but did not understand.
Perhaps, neglected, in some poorhouse he
Might linger out his days, they never knew;   10
Or homeless roam in bitter poverty,
While they each day, and year the richer grew;
The riches of this world to them were given,
To him the treasure that's laid up in heaven!

Poem No. 320; c. 13 December 1870

The Teaching Of History Confirmed

Why look we to the distant past to learn
Lessons of wisdom from the days gone by?
When to the living present we may turn,
And read the teaching of all History.
Behold a mighty city, boasting all   5
That wealth, or splendor, or renown can give,
Encompassed now by armies, soon to fall;
No more the glory of the world to live!
One moment on the pinnacle of fame,
Another humbled to the very dust;   10
How vain the prestige of a Conqueror's name!
In arm of flesh how vain to place our trust!
And not in arts, whose glory shall endure,
By which great nations dwell in peace secure.

Poem No. 822; c. 7 January 1871

Childhood's Songs

"All the songs of my childhood float back to me, and I wander in far off realms."
– William E. Clark.

I hear again my childhood's songs,
    When life was bright and fair;
Their melodies my spirit hears,
    They float upon the air.

In far off realms I seem to stray,   5
    Mid childhood's early flowers;
And all my weariness forget,
    Amid its happy bowers.

My mother's voice, it comes again
    So clear, and pure, and sweet;   10
I seem a child again to be,
    And listening at her feet!

They cheer and soothe my sinking heart,
 As if from heaven they came;
In manhood, as in youthful hours,   15
 Their power is still the same.

A power to purify and bless,
 And thus my soul prepare;
With those I loved in early days,
 The life of heaven to share.   20

Poem No. 237; c. 18 March 1871

Hymn,
Sung at the Fiftieth Anniversary of the Essex Historical Society, Salem. April 21, 1871.

Amid the swift onrushing years,
 We hear a voice that bids us stay;
Back to the storied Past we turn,
 And reverently its call obey.

For not dissevered, weak, alone,   5
 Do we amid the Present live;
But to our lives the by-gone days
 Their knowledge, and their virtues give.

Made wise by wisdom of the Past,
 We for the Future shall prepare;   10
Sharing our Fathers' noble aims,
 We shall their fame, and glory share.

But soon forgotten, or destroyed,
 The records of that early age;
Had not their sons with loving care,   15
 Memorials left for History's page.

Honor we give to those, who here
 Recorded for our use their lore;
Whose names, and virtues we revere,
 Though seen with us their forms no more!   20

Inspired by their example high,
    May we their chosen path pursue;
Alike to Present, and to Past,
    In all our thoughts, and acts be true.

Poem No. 38; c. 21 April 1871

The Lessons of History Unlearned

Again doth France, unhappy France, behold
    Renewed the scenes of terror and of crime;
Still unprepared for Freedom, as of old,
    Though passed almost a century of time.
Of her long history how sad the end,   5
    Freedom by King and People both betrayed!
While faction doth the boastful city rend,
    And for another age is Peace delayed.
So doth a noble river, that should bless
    And fertilize its banks on either side,   10
Bursting its bounds, bring ruin and distress,
    And desolate a happy region wide!
Ah, when shall man, if not by reason taught,
    Learn from the wondrous works in Nature wrought?

Poem No. 27; c. 16 June 1871

The Fulness of The Gentiles

Swift speeds the time, the time long since foretold,
When all the nations shall be gathered in;
The scroll of Prophecy be all unrolled,
And a new Age, a grander Age begin.
By signs the day its coming doth portend,   5
In swifter intercourse the nations meet,
Old dynasties are hastening to their end,
The electric wire its circuits doth complete.
O Love, that did the Apostle's bosom swell,
And gave him knowledge of the mystery high,   10

And fitting words, that mystery to tell;
Would that like him, we saw Christ's Kingdom nigh!
Come, Church Triumphant! in thy glory come;
And gather all earth's weary children home!

Poem No. 453; c. 8 July 1871

To a Cloud

Whither, O Cloud! with richest treasures fraught,
From some unseen, and distant regions brought;
Whither so swiftly dost thou wing thy way,
And why not o'er this dusty city stay?
The grass is withered, and the flowers are dead,   5
From our fair gardens all their beauty fled;
And e'en the lofty trees, with foliage dry,
Imploring look as thou art passing by.
We know not why so swift thou passest on,
For, while we gaze, thou from our sight art gone!   10
Like glorious angel hastening to fulfil,
On pinions swift the great Creator's will.
How small our knowledge of the mighty plan
Controuling nature, since the world began!
Vainly would Science search the hidden cause,   15
Which wings thy flight, obedient to His laws;
Who fillest all things, and dost all contain,
Who sendeth, or withholds alike the rain.
Perhaps, beyond our own horizon's bound,
More needing thee, more dry and parched the ground;   20
And, with more earnest prayers, more anxious eyes,
Men turn their gaze unto the cloudless skies.
O'er the proud city thou wilt not remain,
Where dwell the sons of pleasure, and of gain;
But, where the toiling husbandman doth stand,   25
And mourning views his crops, his parched land,
Thou hastenest on; and drop'st thy fulness down,
And dost his toil, and prayers with plenty crown.

Poem No. 813; c. 1 September 1871

The Child's Dream of Reaching the Horizon

A child beheld the o'er arching heaven,
    Where earth blends with the sky;
And longed to reach the blissful spot,
    It seemed to him so nigh.

All night he could not sleep a wink,
    As on his bed he lay;   5
And a bright day in June beheld
    The dreamer on his way.

Not e'en his parents did he tell
    For what, and where he went;   10
Lest they should laugh his thoughts to scorn,
    And his fond hopes prevent.

Thus onward, on a summer's morn,
    To earth's fair bound he sped;
And yet whene'er he reached the spot,   15
    The blissful vision fled.

It was not where the hill he climbed,
    Nor on the meadow green;
Nor where on the horizon's line,
    The silver brook was seen.   20

Nor where the forest's branches waved,
    And the birds sang so sweet;
He came; but reached not there the place,
    Where heaven and earth did meet.

Ah, many a weary mile he went   25
    To reach the bending sky,
But found at last 'twas still afar,
    What he had dreamed so nigh.

Some laborers found the wandering child,
    And homeward turned his face;   30
With slow, and toilsome steps once more
    His path did he retrace.

Glad were his parents, when at eve,
 He safely reached his home;
But sad the child; the dream had fled,   35
 Which called his feet to roam!

Poem No. 2; c. 2 September 1871

Lead Me To The Rock That Is Higher Than I

In a barren land I wander,
 And no tree, nor house I spy;
Lead me to a Rock for refuge,
 Rock that higher is than I.

Fierce the sun has beat upon me   5
 From a burning, cloudless sky;
Friendly shadow now I long for,
 Rock that higher is than I.

Strange and wild the scenes around me,
 And no help from man is nigh;   10
But a shelter Thou canst show me,
 Rock that higher is than I.

Treacherous guides have me forsaken,
 Many paths deceive my eye;
Thou alone canst guide, and show me   15
 Rock that higher is than I.

Night is falling dark & dreary,
 Help me, or I sink and die!
Show me, ere the light shall fail me,
 Rock that higher is than I.   20

Then my soul shall sing thy praises,
 And extol thy mercies high;
Praise and bless, through endless ages,
 Rock that higher is than I.

Poem No. 296; c. 18 November 1871

Forevermore

A sad refrain I heard, from poet sad,
Which on my soul with deadening weight did fall;
But quick another word, which made me glad,
Did from the heavens above me seem to call.
The first was Nevermore: which, like a knell,   5
Struck on my ear with dull, funereal sound;
The last was Evermore; which like a bell,
In waves of music filled the air around.
Forevermore with loved and lost to be,
No more to suffer change, nor grief, nor pain,   10
From partings sad to be forever free,—
Such was that sweet bell's music; its refrain
Blended with voices from the heavenly shore,
Each whispering to my heart Forevermore.

Poem No. 18; c. 24 November 1871

Man's First Experience of Winter

When man, born 'mid luxuriant Tropic bowers,
   Beheld, 'neath northern skies, all Nature change;
The falling leaves, the dying grass and flowers,—
   How desolate the sight! the scene how strange!
And when the sun declined, and Winter's breath   5
   Had frozen hard the river's rapid tide,
And spread o'er hills and fields the pall of death,—
   Feared he not then, that Nature's self had died?
Yet in his heart a faith and trust did spring,
   Faith conquering doubt, and trust in Power Divine;   10
That from this seeming death new life would bring,
   And clothe again the tree, the grass, the vine;
And banish from the earth dark Winter's gloom,
   And bid her hills and fields with beauty bloom.

Poem No. 791; c. 6 February 1872

Interpreting God's Ways

Interpret not God's ways, unless his light
Has shone upon thy dark, beclouded mind,
Making earth's scenes of sin and suffering bright,
That thou his way, his perfect way, may'st find.
Boast not thy knowledge of old Nature's laws,   5
Though thou may'st something of her secrets know;
Canst thou explain her being, or her cause?
Tell how a single blade of grass doth grow?
Or knowest thou how thine eye, or cunning hand,
Doth execute its work with nicest skill?   10
Canst thou the mind's swift motions understand,
Make all its movements subject to thy will?
Boast not thy knowledge, though, with angel's sight,
Thine eye could pierce the darkness as the light.

Poem No. 302; c. 10 February 1872

I Prayed, Thy Kingdom Come

I prayed, Thy kingdom come! For Winter long
Had held the frozen earth in fetters bound;
And wretchedness, and misery, war, and wrong,
Age after age, did in the world abound.
I prayed, Thy kingdom come! And lo, the Spring   5
Came with its warmth and joy to glad the earth;
New hope the sight did to my spirit bring,
That Man at length should share the quickening birth.
For He who worketh thus great Nature's change,
Works in the heart his miracles of power;   10
Than those we see more marvellous and strange!
Have faith in God, and wait his promised hour;
For He who doth the quickening Spring-time send,
Will sin destroy, bring suffering to an end.

Poem No. 251; c. 20 April 1872

Justification By Faith

Strongly did Luther seize the mighty thought,
Which the Apostle's mind had first conceived,
And which in him so mightily had wrought,
That he is Justified, who hath believed;
Freed from the observance of the Jewish law,   5
Which sought by fear man's nature to controul;
From higher motives did his thoughts withdraw,
And bound to forms and rites the aspiring soul.
By faith, and not by works, man lives; he said;
And, by his word, the nation's bondage broke!   10
From land to land quickly the tidings spread,
To life and thought the slumbering people woke!
From slavish forms, and slavish errors free,
And standing firm in Christian liberty.

Poem No. 448; c. 4 May 1872

The First of May

May has come, but flowers are rare,
    Blooming only here and there,
In some sheltered, sunny spot,
    Where the bleak winds reach them not.
Still the pastures pale and dry   5
    With no verdure greet the eye,
Only on the turnpike seen
    Narrow borders touched with green.
E'en the savins, hardy band,
    Winter-killed and blasted stand;   10
And their green has yellow turned,
    As by fire their boughs were burned.
But the children, on the hill
    Love to keep the May-day still;
Love to search the fields around,   15
    Though no flowers by them are found.
In vain they ask of passer-by,
    Where is the anemony?

Where the violet's deep blue?
    None can show them, but the few,
Who their favorite haunts may know,
    And can tell them where to go.
There, though Spring elsewhere delays,
    Each their beauteous tints displays;
And upon the breeze their bloom   25
    Sheds its delicate perfume.
Call not then the custom vain,
    For to seek is still to gain:
Though we find not that we prize,
    In the seeking pleasure lies.   30
They who seek shall ever find
    Health of body and of mind;
They who will not ask, nor seek,
    Live in mind and body weak.

Poem No. 325; 1–7 May 1872

On the Great Divisions of the Christian Church, The Catholic, the Protestant, and the Greek

Still other sheep Thou hast, O Shepherd fair,
Than that one flock to which we may belong;
For all alike Thou dost provide and care,
And call them by thy voice, and tuneful song.
Though they, estranged, may not each other know,   5
And deem their fold, and theirs alone, is thine;
Thou dost to all the heavenly pastures show,
And watch and guard them all with love divine.
O that thy Church again might be but one,
One Shepherd and one flock, as once of old!   10
That Thou the wanderers who astray have gone,
And all the lost, might gather to thy fold;
That they, with thine, might in green pastures feed,
From want, and fear, and every danger freed.

Poem No. 440; c. 8 June 1872

The Nine O'Clock Bell

'Tis "nine o'clock;" but few the summons heed;
   The street is full of passers to and fro;
No homes they seek, no homes they seem to need;
   And some, alas! a home may never know.
They hear no voice of father, mother dear,   5
   To bid them "sure return, when rings the bell;"
In its loud tones no friendly signal hear
   Of household cares, and loving hearts to tell.
Trained in a different school the people now
   No steady habits, nor obedience gain.   10
To keep good hours, when duty calls to go,
   Are all forgot for pleasure, feasting, gain.
Ring on Old Bell! and from their ways recall
   Gay, thoughtless youth, and warn them lest they fall!

Poem No. 726; c. 12 July 1872

"Are there Few that be Saved?"
Luke 13 : 23.

So questioned one of old, as we
   Do often anxious ask;
And from our work we look around,
   Forgetting our own task.

We see the busy multitudes,   5
   That throng the world's highway;
We see the multitudes that meet
   To worship and to pray.

Shall few, or shall all men be saved?
   We question, too, the Lord;   10
But the same answer we receive,
   As he who heard his word.

Strive earnestly to enter in
    God's kingdom, given to all;
And while thou hear'st the Gospel preached,   15
    Obey its gracious call.

Look not around, nor curious be
    To learn another's fate;
But rather strive thyself to gain
    An entrance ere too late.   20

When once the Master of the House
    Has risen, and shut the door,
In vain they seek to enter in
    Who welcomed were before.

For many then shall stand without,   25
    And wait, and knock in vain;
Who, if they strove to enter now,
    Might easy entrance gain.

Poem No. 426; c. 24 August 1872

On Seeing the White Mountains from Cook's Hill, in West Peabody

Far off I see, like a dim cloud, the hills,
    Which, in my youth, I climbed with daring feet;
Whose memory still my mind with grandeur fills,
    And pleasant thoughts of love and friendship sweet.
But nearer do the humble hill-tops rise,   5
    On which my childhood loved to sit and stray;
Gazing on pastures wide, on sea and skies,
    Lit by the sun's bright beams, or moon's soft ray.
And many a merry voice and sunny face
    Of early playmates round my happy home   10
    Come back to me, as the green paths I trace,
And craggy cliffs, 'mid which we loved to roam;
    Nor long I now yon distant hills to climb,
Though grand their scenes, their summits more sublime.

Poem No. 115; c. 30 August 1872

Signs in the Natural World

The earth doth with the heavens sympathise!
When, by the civil war, our land was rent,
Scorched was the ground, and from the cloudless skies
The sun blazed fierce, no rain from heaven was sent:
Now, filled with vapor is the summer sky,   5
And drenched with frequent rains the needy ground;
On their dread errands oft the lightnings fly,
And echoes through heaven's vault the thunder's sound.
But dull the eye of sense, and dull its ear
Unto these signs; that wake the listening soul;   10
That doth in Nature more than Nature hear,
That sees the Hand that doth her powers controul;
And feels that earth and man, and sea and sky
Are bound in one by hidden sympathy.

Poem No. 491; c. 5 October 1872

A Walk in Harmony Grove

I walked the grove where rest the mortal forms
   Of those we love, and still with tears deplore;
Unheard as yet the blasts of Winter's storms,
   And still the trees their thickest foliage wore;
But through the forest came a soft, sad sound,   5
   As Nature were attuned to human grief;
And, fluttering from the trees unto the ground,
   In frequent showers fell many a dying leaf.
How oft does Nature speak unto the soul,
   But we, alas! have not the listening ear;   10
In falling leaf, as in the mighty whole,
   She speaks to man, would he her voices hear;
In sober Autumn, as in joyous spring,
   To souls attuned she doth instruction bring.

Poem No. 282; c. 22 October 1872

The Prayer of Jabez

The prayer of Jabez, too, should be our prayer:
"Keep me from evil, that it may not grieve."
How hard the sight of wrong and ill to bear,
When we cannot the sufferers relieve!
The child of sorrow, he for others' woe,   5
As if it were his own, did deeply feel;
Though he had naught of riches to bestow,
Nor power their wrongs and miseries to heal.
God heard his prayer, and answered his request;
And by his sympathy, did help impart   10
Unto the poor, the suffering, and opprest,
That healed their wounds and robbed them of their smart;
Nor suffered cruel deeds, nor words unkind
To grieve his heart, or rankle in his mind.

Poem No. 543; c. 9 November 1872

The Life of the Flower

Know'st thou the life of a single flower,
    How it blooms from out the earth?
Whence came its beauty? and what the Power,
    That gave its beauty birth?

How long has the seed of that flower been sown,   5
    In the ages past away;
Since first on the earth its form was known,
    And it oped to the light of day?

In the hardened rock its form is found,
    Ere man the earth had trod;   10
Ere his toiling hands had tilled the ground,
    Or sowed with its seed the sod.

Before the bird, or the beast was made,
    The desolate earth still in gloom;
Ere a tree o'er the dry land had spread its shade,   15
    Did the flower in its beauty bloom.

Thou may'st trace its life to the single cell,
　　By the aid which Science gives;
But can'st thou by searching the secret tell,
　　Whence the seed, or how it lives?　　　　　　　　　　　　20

Oh no: for the secret is hid from thee,
　　Known to none save the Perfect Mind;
Whom thou in his works alone can see,
　　But not to perfection find.

For the life of the flower, like the life of the soul,　　　　　25
　　Is hid in God above;
And the humblest flower, like the mighty Whole,
　　Sprang forth from his boundless love.

Poem No. 313; c. 28 December 1872

The Old Danvers Burying-Ground

Above the ancient burying place
　　Looks calmly down the full orbed moon;
Each well known grave I plainly trace,
　　As in the effulgent light of noon.

And through the cold, transparent air,　　　　　　　　　　5
　　The stars and planets brightly glow,
As if they listened to the prayer
　　Of dweller on this sphere below.

And is there not some secret spell,
　　Some influence from yon shining spheres;　　　　　　　10
Of the Immortal Life to tell
　　Beyond Time's few and fleeting years?

There is; for though no voice nor speech
　　May reach the mourner's listening ear,
The Resurrection's truth they teach,　　　　　　　　　　　15
　　By revelation's words made clear.

That though the mortal body die,
　　A nobler, fairer, shall succeed;
As stars in differing glory vie,
　　As springs the stalk from buried seed.　　　　　　　　　20

That as the earthly now we wear,
    Subject to suffering, change, decay;
The heavenly image we shall bear,
    That fadeth not, like that, away.

There is no death in scene like this,   25
    Though mortal forms repose around;
My thoughts mount upward to the bliss
    The immortal soul with God has found.

All live to Him! Though earth may hide
    The forms of loved ones from our sight;   30
Our friends still live, with Him abide,
    Who on the grave sheds holy light.

Poem No. 25a; c. 18 February 1873

Hymn

"He that loveth not, knoweth not God."

He loveth not! he knows not God!
    For God himself is love;
And dwelleth with his children here,
    And in the heavens above.

To Him they pray to cleanse their hearts   5
    From every guilty stain;
Nor is a single cry unheard,
    Nor prayer breathed forth in vain.

His Spirit too doth in us dwell,
    And teaches us to pray;   10
Though we from fear, or doubt, or sin,
    May know not what to say.

It teaches others to forgive,
    As we would be forgiven;
That we God's children here may be,   15
    And dwell with Him in heaven.

It strengthens in temptation's hour,
   When worldly foes assail;
And gives us courage strong to stand,
   And o'er them all prevail.   20

Pray, pray for those who know not God,
   Nor ask his help in prayer;
That they may know the Father's love,
   And in his kingdom share.

Poem No. 162; c. 8 March 1873

Norman's Rocks

Along the base of Norman's Rocks
   I stroll, as when a boy;
Or climb their steep and craggy sides
   The prospect to enjoy;

Or feel the cool, refreshing breeze,   5
   Which round their summit plays;
And makes this hill a favorite haunt,
   In the warm Summer days.

This pleasant height a prospect gives
   O'er fields, and pastures green;   10
While, on the far horizon's line,
   The ocean's blue is seen.

Below, the city stretches far,
   With many a shady street;
And all its homes, and gardens fair   15
   Lie smiling at its feet.

More beautiful to me the scene,
   Than painter's canvass shows;
For this in memory's brightest hues,
   And fancy's colors glows.   20

Here did I climb, when Spring returned,
   To pluck her earliest flowers;
Or mid the golden woodwax play,
   In Summer's sultry hours.

Here picked the barberry's bunches red,   25
    When Autumn time had come;
Or sought the bitter-sweet to deck
    With gay festoons my home.

Though to the scene the musing mind
    Doth its own coloring give;   30
Yet doth the prospect charm the more,
    The longer still I live.

The lichens clinging to the rocks,
    The moss forever green,
The saxifrage, with milk-white flowers,   35
    The first in childhood seen;

Still many a pleasing lesson have,
    As on their leaves I pore;
New beauties charm in manhood's prime,
    Ne'er seen in years before.   40

For Science opens wide her book,
    And bids her children read,
With wonder filled the hidden life
    In flower and plant and seed.

And still the varying seasons bring   45
    An ever new delight;
As from these cliffs I look around
    On each familiar sight;

A picture that can never fade,
    While life and memory last;   50
Made soft and fair by loveliest hues,
    Reflected from the past.

Poem No. 35; c. 20 June 1873

On visiting the beautiful estate of H. H. Hunnewell, Esq., at Wellesley.

We wandered hours amid a lovely scene,
   Which every moment brought a fresh surprise;
So beautiful the flowers, the grass so green,
   It seemed like Paradise unto our eyes.
Is this all nature's work? or has man's art,   5
   By nature taught, but perfected her plan?
So blended are they each in every part,
   We know not nature's work from work of man.
What level lawns! what vistas opening fine
   Through shady groves! with forest-fringed lake;   10
Which, in one whole, do every charm combine,
   And soul and sense, as willing captives, take;
Which a new sense of nature's beauty give,
   That in the grateful mind will ever live.

Poem No. 765; c. 1 July 1873

The Revelation of The Spirit Through The Material World

We call material this fair world of ours,
And so it seems to gross, material eyes;
That see no beauty in earth's fairest flowers,
No heavenly splendors in her sunset skies.
But are there not, in yonder gorgeous scene,   5
A beauty and a grandeur not of earth;
A glory breaking from yon cloudy screen
Revealing to the soul its nobler birth?
Can things material such fair forms assume,
And thus delight and charm the human mind;   10
Or doth the Spirit with its rays illume
Their inmost depths, from matter now refined;
That man may thus with it communion hold,
And learn of higher things than sense has told?

Poem No. 760; c. 26 July 1873

And a little child shall lead them. Isaiah XI. 6.

Thou call'st me, little child,
   With thy voice sweet and mild,
     To go with thee;
I take thy guiding hand,
   For thou the happy land   5
     Dost clearly see.

The land, where heard no more
   The lion's angry roar;
     Nor beast of prey
Doth ravage and devour;   10
   And gone the tyrant's power,
     To hurt, and slay.

The fields and pastures green
   Through all the year are seen,
     No drought they know;   15
There flowers of beauty rare,
   Without man's fostering care,
     Abundant grow.

There in a peaceful life,
   Forgotten war's rude strife,   20
     All men shall live;
No enemy shall spoil,
   Earth without painful toil,
     Shall plenty give.

There nevermore is heard   25
   Harsh speech, nor angry word;
     No more we hear
Of deeds of shame and crime,
   Darkening the page of time;
     Nor dwell in fear.   30

No sorrow there shall be,
   New heavens and earth we'll see,
     Where dwelleth Love;

There, there, O gentle guide,
    May I with thee abide,   35
        Blest land above.

Poem No. 666; c. 16 August 1873

The Blessing of Rain

How, like a blessing, falls the rain
    On thirsty field, and parched hill,
And on the dry, and dusty plain,
    Low swamp and pool the rain drops fill.

They wash the tall tree's withering leaves   5
    And fresh the forest's branches wave;
The dying shrub the gift receives,
    That comes its feeble life to save.

The birds their painful silence break,
    And fill with joyful notes the grove;   10
The cattle now their thirst can slake,
    Nor for a spring they vainly rove.

A pleasant smell the moist earth sends
    To heaven for the reviving shower;
Which with unnumbered odors blends,   15
    The incense sweet of many a flower.

And man, with every living thing,
    With grateful heart his voice doth lift
In praise to God; and thanks doth bring
    For every good and perfect gift.   20

Poem No. 189; c. 26 August 1873

On the Mountain Ash Tree
In front of the house of the late Capt. Robert W. Gould

He planted, years ago, before his door,
A mountain ash; which now a tree has grown,
And year by year its golden berries bore.
Could it to him who planted have been known,
How much more beautiful his home would be   5
In years to come! How much of joy and grace
The leaves, and flowers, and fruit of this one tree,
Would give to passers-by, and to the place?
Well I remember, passing through the street,
When but a boy, its beauty caught my eye;   10
And often now I pause the tree to greet,
As on my daily walk I pass it by;
Nor doth it fail, in winter cold, and drear,
With clustering berries red the eye to cheer.

Poem No. 164; c. 21 October 1873

October

How beautiful the sight of woods still fair,
That yet no heavy frost, nor rain has harmed;
And warm as summer is the autumn air,
As by some spell its chilly winds were charmed!
Still blooms the golden rod in many a glade,   5
And asters open still their mild blue eyes;
The Spring beyond its season long delayed,
The added warmth of Autumn well supplies.
'Tis pleasant, 'mid the grove's rich colored light,
Along its paths with musing mind to stray;   10
And meditate on Autumn's glories bright,
Which fully compensate the Spring's delay;
Learning a lesson of the varied year
Of patience, trust, and hope the heart to cheer.

Poem No. 177; October 1873

The Mound Builders.
On Reading the work of the late J. W. Foster

Strange record of a people past away,
Once numerous as the leaves the forests shed,
As mindful of man's frailty, and decay,
Upon their mounds, and grave-hills of their dead.
Here lived, and planned, and toiled another race,   5
A pre-historic race, forgotten long;
Who in the speech of men have left no trace,
Unknown alike to history, and to song.
Yet were they to ourselves, as men, allied,
In God's own image made, though of the earth;   10
And, though the help of Learning's stores denied,
Destined with us to an immortal birth.
With reverence may we ope their graves, and tread
With thoughtful minds the cities of the dead.

Poem No. 444; c. 1 November 1873

Blessed are they that mourn: for they shall be comforted.

How hard the truth of words like these to feel,
To realize a promise such as this!
Yet have they balm the heart's deep wounds to heal,
That mourns the loss of friends, and earthly bliss.
For they were spoke by him, who knew our lot,   5
A sorrowing man, who felt, and shared our grief;
Who ne'er the lowliest sufferer forgot,
To whom his mighty power could bring relief.
Still, from on high, the Comforter he sends,
That fills with joy and peace the lonely heart;   10
As once he gave unto his dearest friends,
That should abide with them, and ne'er depart.
Oh that earth's sorrowing children all might know
The Heavenly Gift the Savior doth bestow!

Poem No. 187; c. 12 December 1873

There shall be one Flock, one Shepherd

Prophetic thought of Unity, and Peace,
That ever filled the blessed Saviour's mind!
When men from cruel wars and strife should cease,
And friendly intercourse the nations bind.
One Shepherd, and one Flock there then shall be,   5
By the good Shepherd guided, watched, and fed;
Dwelling in peace, or wandering safe and free
In pastures green, and by still waters led.
Not to exalt one nation did he come,
But all to gather in one sacred fold;   10
To make of earth, as heaven, a peaceful home,
By prophets long in prophecy foretold.
Hasten ye Ages, till the world fulfil
The word of Christ, and learn the Father's will.

Poem No. 403; c. 17 January 1874

Old Houses of Salem
Illustrated by George M. White

These humble dwellings, old, and quaint,
    The artist bids us view,
A history have; which often shames
    The modern, grand and new.

For here the wealthy, and the poor,   5
    The high-born, and the low
Contented dwelt; nor cared for gain,
    For grandeur, and for show.

Honest and true, and pure, and kind,
    Their homes and hearths they loved;   10
And to each other in their need
    They firm and faithful proved.

The wilderness they here subdued,
   By manly toil, and pain;
Or on the ocean bravely strove   15
   A livelihood to gain.

They worshipped God in purity,
   In spirit, and in love;
And sought on earth a church to be,
   Like to the church above.   20

They sought a Commonwealth to found,
   A free and Christian State;
Now, through their toil and suffering,
   Grown strong, and rich, and great.

A lesson may their children learn,   25
   As here their homes they see;
That not in wealth or outward good
   Is man's nobility.

To keep, improve the heritage,
   Which they have handed down;   30
By virtuous lives, and noble deeds,
   Our fathers' work to crown.

Poem No. 635; c. 23 January 1874

Columbines and Anemones

Prang's American chromos,—"Wild Flowers, after water-color by Miss Ellen Robbins, have been much admired, and are well suited to the decoration of boudoirs."

Before the early flowers have faded quite,
   That breathed their fragrance over vale and lea;
The Columbines, in scarlet vesture bright,
   Quickly succeed the pale Anemone;

Crowning our rocky hills in gay attire,   5
   Or nodding on the steep and craggy rock;
They bid us climb for that which we desire,
   Or, far beyond our reach, with beauty mock.

In fancy groups of children there I see,
　　Gathering large bunches for their distant home;　　　10
And hear again their shouts, and merry glee,
　　As through the fields, and o'er the hills they roam.

Fair Flowers! my boyhood's love, and still so dear;
　　Thanks to the Artist, who has made you bloom,
When Winter's storms, and Winter's snows are here,　　　15
　　To cheer us through its months of cold, and gloom.

Poem No. 64; c. 14 February 1874

The Hepatica in Winter

Underneath its snowy bed,
The hepatica lies dead!
All its beauteous colors fled!

No, not dead, but sleeping; Spring
Shall again its beauty bring,　　　　5
And its beauty poets sing.

There, protected from the cold,
Doth the plant its life still hold,
Woolly leaves the germ infold.

In the bud a flower survives,　　　　10
Hidden from man's searching eyes;
'Tis not Beauty's self that dies!

Beauty still is born anew,
We again its tints shall view,
Rosy purple, deepest blue.　　　　15

Poem No. 751; c. 24 February 1874

Reverence

We need more reverence in this froward age,
That doth forget the teachings of the past;
The wisdom of the old, the Sacred Page,
Whose truth shall fleeting time itself outlast.
Not by the light alone the present sheds,   5
Nor by the sun's bright beams alone we see;
Upon the path, in which man darkling treads,
Fall glimmering rays from far antiquity.
And all are needed, lest we go astray;
In our own wisdom confident and bold;   10
Careless to learn, too proud to ask the way,
Doubting, perhaps, when often plainly told;
Unwilling to confess the truth, whose light
Shone in the darkness of the ancient night.

Poem No. 762; c. 21 March 1874

Inward Phenomena

More strange than wonders of the earth, or skies,
The earthquake's shock, the fiery comet's train,
On which men gaze with terror and surprise,
Are those within; which scarce a thought may gain.
There sudden passion oft doth shake the soul,   5
Banishing reason from her kingly throne;
Owning no more her just and wise control,
Obedient to its own behests alone.
And there the dark eclipse, that clouds the mind,
When doubt at length doth over faith prevail;   10
And, in the light of truth, men wander blind,
Powerless to draw aside the murky veil!
Why should these outward wonders draw man's eye,
When in himself far mightier wonders lie?

Poem No. 331; c. 18 April 1874

To the Memory of Alpheus Crosby

A noble life, well spent in learning's cause,
  And public good, has passed from earth away!
With saddened thoughts, in its swift round, we pause,
  A heart-felt tribute to its worth to pay.
E'en from his youth, to studious lore inclined,   5
  By day, by night, he turned the classic page,
And, by his studies cultured and refined,
  He gave new grace and culture to the age.
Nor less he labored for the public good,
  In every noble work an earnest man;   10
Boldly the power of Slavery, War, withstood,
  A true reformer, ever in the van.
Our loss it is, not his, that we deplore,
That we on earth shall see his face no more!

Poem No. 15; c. April 1874

The Birds

The birds are singing still their songs
  In vale, and leafy wood;
As when the earth itself was made,
  And all was fair and good.

They sing as if no death were here,   5
  No suffering, pain, disease;
And sweet their notes at morning's hour
  Are borne upon the breeze.

No want they know, like suffering man,
  Whom famine vexes sore;   10
For God doth for their wants provide,
  From out his liberal store.

Ye heralds of the early Spring!
  Would I your joy might share;
And learn, though evil still abounds,   15
  That all is good and fair.

That every thing, which God has made,
    E'en sinful, suffering man;
Is part, though dimly now perceived,
    Of one all gracious plan.   20

For faith a future doth reveal,
    To which all beings tend;
A future on the earth, in heaven,
    And sin and suffering end.

Poem No. 464; c. 19 May 1874

Superfluities

How many things there are in common life
That needful seem, because they always lie
About us everywhere; we ask not why.
We were born with them, and in vain our strife;
For heavier grow the burdens we must bear,   5
Till childhood even has a look of care.
And, growing with our growth, the things of sense
Like to an army gather daily round;
Till scarce they have left a passage to us hence
Big as a needle's eye, so close they have bound.   10
Thus custom, luxury, do man's life control,
Pamper the body, starve the immortal soul;
Till we forget our high and heavenly birth,
And deem ourselves at length but sons of earth.

             Continued
And what's the remedy? All at once to break   15
The thousand cords of this connected life,
And by one step, a hermit, end the strife?
Will selfish solitude man nobler make?
Or shall we leave our home the world to rove,
And to our social duties faithless prove?   20
Nay, let not rashness, haste, the burden try;
Nor pleasure-seeking mind, that loves to stray;
These are the very things we should deny,
For more than all our other evils they.

Rather be patience, suffering long the road,   25
On which we learn to bear life's 'customed load;
Perhaps, while through its darkling paths we tread,
A light shall beam, and prove its guiding thread.

Poem No. 194; c. 23 May 1874

Arethusa Meadow

Far off, among the distant hills,
    A lonely meadow lies;
Where grows a flower of beauty rare,
    But hid from careless eyes.

Though all around the woodwax spreads   5
    Its brilliant cloth of gold,
More dazzling than was ever seen
    By knights and kings of old;

And the azalea in the swamp,
    Its fragrance sheds around;   10
Yet not for these my feet have sought
    This unfrequented ground.

But for the Arethusa rare,
    That in the meadow grows;
With petals blushing like the dawn,   15
    Or like the summer's rose.

With down-cast look it bends its head,
    As shunning human gaze;
Nor asking, like yon gorgeous flowers,
    For words of human praise.   20

Like her, who gave to it its name,
    From man's pursuit it hides;
And where his feet but seldom come
    Midst blue eyed grass abides.

Sprinkling the low wet meadow o'er,   25
    With flowers of loveliest bloom;
That shed upon the passing breeze
    Their delicate perfume.

Poem No. 114; c. 3 July 1874

The Night Blooming Cereus

Strange flower, to ope when day is o'er,
    Beneath the stars' faint light;
Shunning the sun's bright, cheering rays,
    That other flowers delight.

The lily now has closed its leaves,   5
    The pansy shut its eye;
While thy fair petals open wide
    Beneath the evening sky.

And strange, that such an ugly stem
    So fair a flower should bear;   10
That thus the contrast too should make
    So fair a flower more fair.

A miracle thou truly art,
    Waking when others sleep;
In thee we see the law reversed,   15
    Which others faithful keep.

I watch the eager wondering throng,
    As on thy form they look;
Half conscious of the lesson taught
    In Nature's pictured book.   20

On which, as we more deeply pore,
    New wonders still we find;
To raise our thoughts and hearts in love
    To the All-perfect Mind.

Poem No. 442; c. 24 July 1874

On The Wild Flowers of the Art Exhibition

While Nature still delays her flowers to bring,
And all the fields around are white with snow,
With not a token of the coming Spring,
On Art's fair page we see their beauties glow.
The snowdrop with its slender stem is seen,   5
The houstonia with its pale blue flower,
Scattered by myriads o'er our pastures green,
When Spring returns to deck her faded bower.
And Summer's gorgeous colored flowers are here,
Lobelia with its brilliant, dazzling hue,   10
The lily red, and painted cup appear,
With the fair rose; and each to Nature true.
Art waits not for the tardy months of time;
All seasons are her own, and every clime.

Poem No. 812; c. 24 July 1874

Interpreting Nature

The sights we see, the sounds we hear,
Are fitted to the eye and ear;
They're not a dumb, unmeaning show,
But speak a language all men know.

The flower, the rock, the bush, the tree,   5
Have each some message unto me;
They give direction to my way,
And lead me on from day to day.

The storm-tost wave, the moaning wind,
Have meaning to the listening mind;   10
Oft the forgetful soul is stirred
By insect's hum, or song of bird.

We need not rove o'er land and sea
Ere we shall find this mystery;
Close to ourselves the wonder lies,   15
In things perhaps we little prize.

We wander on as in a dream,
O'er lofty hill, by wandering stream;
Yet in the scene no beauty find,
With heart untouched, or worldly mind.   20

Daily the sights and sounds return,
Till we the lesson taught shall learn
That Nature everywhere doth teach,
Though not in words of human speech.

Poem No. 560; c. 25 July 1874

The Incarnation

Time's greatest Mystery, the Word made man,
That took our nature, suffered on the tree;
Existing ere the world of sense began,
That was before all time, O God, with Thee!
To that mysterious moment would we soar,   5
When by the Word the heavens and earth were made;
And with a reverent, childlike faith adore
The glorious power in all thy works displayed.
But deeper reverence would our spirits feel
For Him, who in our human nature came,   10
The glory of the Father to reveal;
A glory that outshines the sun's bright flame,
Which shines into our hearts, where all was night,
With splendors that make dim the morning's light.

Poem No. 719; c. 8 August 1874

On a Lichen from North Cape
Gathered by Mr. J. M. Richards, July 3d, 1874

Where no tree nor grass can grow,
    On a far northern hill,
This humble lichen brought to me,
    Doth their place in Nature fill.

Food for the reindeer fleet,   5
    And e'en for human kind,
Do such as live in that region cold
    In thy tiny leaflets find.

There all is strange and new;
    For there, there is no night;   10
On thy native hill the midnight sun,
    Unquenched, shines warm and bright.

Long, long is the Winter time,
    With no returning day;
But instead the moon, or stars' faint light,   15
    And the red auroral ray.

And the ocean, like the land,
    Doth its mystery retain;
No ship has sailed to the farther shore,
    And returned o'er the trackless main.   20

Yet still, o'er that pathless sea,
    Doth man's spirit restless go;
Seeking to reach its farthest bounds,
    And its secrets all to know.

And thou, from that far-off Cape,   25
    Hast come a new bond to be,
'Twixt this our land and the frozen North,
    With its mysterious sea.

Poem No. 806; 3 July–18 August 1874

For we Walk by Faith, not by Sight

Not as beholding with our mortal sight
The things unseen, not yet to sense revealed;
Nor yet as those, who in the world delight,
From whom the glorious gospel is concealed;
We walk by faith; while many a vision sweet   5
Doth cheer us on our path from day to day:
And many a worldly show with grandeur cheat,
And seek to draw us from the narrow way.

The world doth walk by sight; its kingdom here,
To outward view, is builded high, and strong;   10
It knows not that the Lord is drawing near!
To whom the world and all therein belong;
Before whose face its towers shall melt away,
As swift dissolving clouds in morning's ray.

Poem No. 360; c. 22 August 1874

On the Neglect of Public Worship

"The interruption of public worship may consummate, in the period of a few years, the important work of a national revolution." – Gibbon.

I.

Worship declines; nor hidden is the cause;
'Tis found in pride, and in the greed for gold,
That larger crowds the voice of pleasure draws
Than does the Preacher gather in Christ's fold.
In pleasure's cup would men their sorrows drown.   5
"Come, let us eat and drink, for soon we die,"
We hear them say; "our heads with roses crown,
Enjoy the present moments as they fly."
'Twas thus, as history tells, the nations spake
That in their pride have long since passed away;   10
May we in time its solemn warning take
That pride and luxury go before decay;
Where these prevail pure worship soon must end,
And noblest nations swift to ruin tend.

Worship we need, true worship, not the name;   15
Within the temples, 'neath the open sky;
Together, or alone, it is the same,
To the lone wanderer his God is nigh.
He heareth not our words, though 'neath the domes
Of costly temples we our voices raise;   20
Or worship Him apart within our homes,
If we are not his own; and love his praise.
Amid the scenes of Nature we may rove,

Nor see his Power, nor own his guiding Hand;
All Nature teaches of a Father's love,   25
But oft we fail to know and understand.
Lord, grant thy Spirit, hear our earnest prayer,
That we may praise and worship everywhere.

Poem No. 851; c. 5 September 1874

The Solitary Gentian

I searched the meadow far around,
   Where once the Gentian grew;
And but a single flower I found,
   With its dark, purple hue.

Nor summer suns, nor latter rain   5
   Can now their life restore;
Beside the brook I search in vain,
   There they are seen no more!

Man gathered, with unsparing hand,
   Their beauty, and their bloom;   10
Nor dreamed he robbed the generous land,
   And sealed the fair flowers' doom.

Nor seed, nor even roots, were left,
   New flowers again to yield;
Of all its beauty was bereft   15
   The lovely meadow field.

A single, solitary flower
   Yet lingered in the place;
The last to deck bright Autumn's bower,
   The last of all its race!   20

The meadow mourns its darlings' fate,
   And I, in plaintive song,
Would still to years of distant date
   Their memory prolong.

Poem No. 265; c. 13 October 1874

Indian Remains

With ocean shell clasped to his breast,
  The chief doth on the hillside rest;
As if he still could hear the roar
  Of waves upon the rocky shore.

Or sign it was of high estate,
  And buried only with the great;
His royal power and rule to show,
  That all in death a king might know.

His bear skin robe is changed to dust,
  Its ornaments consumed by rust;
And from the tiny, tinkling bell,
  No sound is heard his name to tell.

Oft have the redmen's bones been found
  On sloping hill, or field around;
No more the forest shade they rove,
  Or feast beside yon sheltered cove!

We ponder on their strange, sad fate;
  Whence was their origin? and date?
From rising, or from setting sun,
  Was their long pilgrimage begun?

No record tells;—but as the shell
  Doth of the distant ocean tell,
Far inland from its native beach,
  These relics meaning have, and speech.

They show that sympathy can bind
  In one all tribes of human kind;
That e'en their forms one image bear,
  Their Maker's image, noble, fair.

Though through long ages soiled, debased,
  In all one lineage may be traced;
As when from the Creative Hand
  Man stood, the lord of sea and land.

And raised again, by Power Divine,
    Their forms shall with new glory shine;
One destiny with them we share,   35
    As they with us God's image bear.

Poem No. 839; c. 1 December 1874

English Sparrows

Here, where our fathers homeless came,
    Nor rudest shelter found,
The English sparrows find a home,
    And chirp and flit around.

They felt the blasts of wintry winds,   5
    Ere they their cots could rear:
And deep the snows around them fell
    O'er hills, and forest drear.

And oft in hunger here they pined,
    And sickness wasting sore;   10
And yet with faith and courage strong,
    They every trial bore.

But thoughtful minds and feeling hearts
    Do for your wants provide;
And shelter from the winter's storms,   15
    Where you may safe abide.

The sparrow-house we grateful place,
    Where it can build its nest;
And, through the winter's cold, and storms,
    Find shelter, food, and rest.   20

In token of that Providence,
    That here our fathers led;
And gave them here a quiet home,
    And with its bounty fed.

Poem No. 172; c. 25 December 1874

The Home

Love builds for us a bower,
    As bird its nest;
E'en from life's earliest hour
    A home, a rest.

There order dwells, and joys   5
    That never cease;
Calm that no storm destroys,
    And lasting peace.

It may be poor and spare,
    A clay-built cot;   10
Or palace wondrous fair;
    We heed it not.

For there each helping hand,
    And loving heart,
And thoughtful mind that planned,   15
    Have borne their part.

Father and mother dear,
    And brothers kind,
And sisters' love are here,
    Our souls to bind.   20

Shelter in youth and age,
    To man 'tis given
To be his heritage
    On earth, in heaven.

Poem No. 323; c. 2 January 1875

Behold, I Make All Things New

There's nothing new the Preacher cries,
    With saddened heart, and weary mind;
That which hath been is that which is,
    And nothing new on earth we find.

Night follows day, and day the night,   5
    As the earth circles round the sun;
The rivers from the ocean rise,
    And back into the ocean run.

Man cannot rise above himself,
    And reason's calm behests obey;   10
Though for a time he heed her laws,
    Soon will he yield to passion's sway.

The order of our daily life
    May wild confusion yet succeed;
We see not yet those happy years,   15
    Of which in prophecy we read.

For in a circle all things move,
    They different seem, yet are the same;
That which the future now we call,
    Is still the present but in name.   20

Not so the Spirit teaching saith,
    New heavens and earth shall we behold;
A brighter, fairer, happier scene
    Shall, even here, succeed the old.

The same, yet changed, improved, adorned   25
    By skill of man, and Power Divine;
Coworking here to our great end,
    Far-seeing, healthful, and benign.

No more disease, nor pain, nor death
    Shall in that blessed world be known;   30
Nor sin can enter, and defile,
    And make that paradise its own.

The former things have passed away,
    Like the dark shadows of the night;
And God himself shall dwell with men,   35
    And be their Everlasting Light.

Within, the spirit, quickened, sees
    New power and love in all around;
And heavenly music greets the ear
    In every voice, and every sound.   40

Behold, He maketh all things new,
   It hears from angel harps above;
Come quickly Lord! on earth fulfil
   Thy prophecy of joy and love.

Poem No. 634; c. 16 January 1875

Oliver C. Felton, Esq., of Brookfield

Far from his early charge, at four score years,
The aged Teacher passed from earth away;
With saddened heart each distant pupil hears,
Who knew so well his worth in life's young day.
Faithful, and earnest; to his calling true,   5
With knowledge he the gift of teaching brought;
For not the lore of books alone he knew,
But by his life, and friendly guidance taught.
With honor passed his peaceful, happy age,
Serving, in after years, his town, and state;   10
In rural labors loved he to engage,
Till gathered, like a shock of corn, full late!
Long will his pupils cherish here his fame,
In love and honor hold their teacher's name.

Poem No. 113; c. 29 January 1875

On the Increase of Crime since the Late Civil War

War brings increase of crime; itself a sin,
Unnumbered evils follow in its train;
With war at first did Slavery begin,
And, in the end, by war was Slavery slain.
For though a nation struggle to be free,   5
And conquer in the fratricidal strife,
Still unto sin in bondage it may be,
Nor gain a nobler, purer, higher life.
Intemperance, lust, and greed of gold may still
Follow war's triumph with their deadly blight;   10

More fatal far than arms the body kill,
Threatening our future with disastrous night;
Till ignorance, vice and crime fill all the land,
That else might Freedom's bulwark ever stand!

Poem No. 758; c. 20 February 1875

The Meteorologists

Ye watch the appearance of the earth and sky,
And oft with certainty predict a change;
Fair weather now, and now a storm is nigh,
As o'er our mighty continent they range.
And this is well; to study Nature's laws,   5
And all her hidden mysteries make known;
But if in these the immortal mind shall pause,
Content to know phaenomena alone;
If, with no grateful heart, no reverent mind,
The sunshine and the rain we shall receive;   10
To higher truths, to nobler knowledge blind,
In Nature and her laws alone believe;
What profits it? Wiser were men of old,
Who could each change with wonder, faith behold.

Poem No. 855; c. 6 March 1875

The Origin of Man

I.

Man has forgot his Origin; in vain
He searches for the record of his race
In ancient books, or seeks with toil to gain
From the deep cave, or rocks some primal trace.
And some have fancied, from a higher sphere,   5
Forgetful of his origin he came;
To dwell awhile a wandering exile here
Subject to sense, another, yet the same.

With mind bewildered, weak how should he know
The Source Divine from whom his being springs?   10
The darkened spirit does its shadow throw
On written record, and on outward things;
That else might plainly to his thought reveal
The wondrous truths, which now they but conceal.

II.

Not suffering for their sins in former state,   15
As some have taught, their system to explain;
Nor hither sent, as by the sport of fate,
Souls that nor memory, nor love retain,
Do men into this world of nature come;
But born of God; though earthy, frail and weak;   20
Not all unconscious of a heavenly home,
Which they through trial, suffering, here must seek.
A heavenly Guide has come the way to show,
To lead us to the Father's house above;
From Him he came, to Him, he said, I go;   25
Oh may we heed the message of his love!
That we no more in darkness, doubt, may roam,
But find while here we dwell our heavenly home.

Poem No. 324; c. 20 March 1875

Sailing on Cakes of Ice in the North River

The thick ice breaks, it floats away,
  It sails towards the sea;
No longer on the shore 'twill stay,
  Spring's breath has set it free.

For three long months, beneath, the tide   5
  Has daily ebbed and flowed;
While fixed its frozen surface wide
  Nor life nor motion showed.

Now all is changed! the river's face
   Reflects the azure sky;
In fleets the cakes each other chase
   To ocean hurrying by.

Methinks I see on many a cake
   My schoolmates boldly sail;
Swiftly, or slow, their course they take,
   As winds or calms prevail.

With various fates they onward steer,
   Some stranded, broken, lost;
Some down the stream are sailing clear,
   Some in mid current tost.

The merry laugh, the shout, the name,
   Still echo from the shore;
All for a moment seems the same,
   As long, long years before.

The scene my fancy doth recall,
   With pleasing, fresh delight;
A picture hung in memory's hall,
   Forever fair and bright.

Poem No. 583; c. 8 April 1875

Original Hymn

Not unto men alone has come
   The Saviour's earnest call,
"Go, feed my sheep, that homeless roam;"
   It comes alike to all.

It finds response in childhood's heart,
   That, moved with others' need,
Would gladly do its humble part
   Christ's suffering lambs to feed.

In many a city's streets they rove,
   With none to shelter, bless,
With none to guide, instruct, and love,
   As in a wilderness.

"Lov'st thou me?" the Saviour said
　　To him who had denied;
"Then feed my sheep, the feeblest aid;　　　　　　　　　　　15
　　To thee I them confide."

That blessed mission may we all
　　Like Peter, too, fulfil;
So shall we heed the Saviour's call,
　　And do our Father's will.　　　　　　　　　　　　　　　20

Poem No. 369; c. 16 May 1875

The Faith of the First Christians

Blessed were they, who in the early time,
In Jesus saw the Christ, the Son of God;
Followed his footsteps with a faith sublime,
And the same path of duty, suffering trod.
They saw what prophets, kings desired to see,　　　　　　　5
And heard what they had longed to hear in vain;
The parable's deep truth, the mystery,
Hid from the multitude, to them was plain.
In him they saw the world redeemed, forgiven,
Suffering no more the blight and curse of sin;　　　　　　　10
And, still beyond, the encircling walls of heaven,
Whose radiant light bids all to enter in.
Would that like faith were ours, that we might be
Thus born of God, and thus his kingdom see!

Poem No. 71; c. 16 June 1875

On the Great Earthquake in New Grenada

For when Thy Judgments are in the earth, the inhabitants of the world will learn
Righteousness Isa. 26:9.

Thy sudden terrors strike the world with dread,
Whole cities by the earthquake's shock laid low!
The maimed, and suffering buried with the dead,

The living stunned, bewildered by the blow!
Fair was the day, and joyously the throng   5
Filled all the streets, on gain, or pleasure bent;
The city full of revelry and song;
When by the shock the solid earth was rent!
So dost Thou teach the nations, Lord of heaven
And earth, to own Thy righteous sway;   10
Not unto them alone the lesson given,
But that all men might Thy commands obey.
Nor dost Thou teach them only by Thy Word,
But earth, too, trembles at Thy voice, O Lord!

Poem No. 717; c. 29 June 1875

The Woodwax in Bloom

We roam afar, o'er sea and land,
    The grand and beautiful to see;
But things that near us lie, at hand,
    See not; though grand and fair they be.

We have no sense to feel their power;   5
    The ocean's grandeur and its might,
The beauty of the sunset hour,
    How oft they fail to give delight!

Spread with a lavish wealth around,
    The golden woodwax, see in bloom!   10
O'er hills and pastures wide 'tis found,
    In rocky clefts its roots find room.

The rugged rocks a beauty wear,
    That else we never should behold;
The barren hills grow wondrous fair,   15
    Each covered with its cloth of gold!

A scene surpassing all that kings,
    With all their riches, can display;
A glory every summer brings,
    Effulgent pomp of summer's day!   20

Yet vainly is that glory shown
  To careless eyes, and grovelling mind;
That dull to Nature's charms have grown,
  And to her beauty, grandeur, blind.

Why do we roam, with discontent,   25
  Afar; when Nature meets us here?
Such glory to our hills has lent,
  Such grandeur in the ocean near?

Poem No. 763; c. 20 July 1875

On Visiting the Graves of Hawthorne and Thoreau

Beneath these shades, beside yon winding stream,
Lies Hawthorne's manly form, the mortal part!
The soul, that loved to meditate and dream,
Might linger here unwilling to depart,
But that a higher life has called away   5
To fairer scenes, to nobler work and thought.
Why should the spirit then on earth delay,
That has a glimpse of such bright regions caught
And near another, Nature's child, doth rest?
Thoreau, who loved each woodland path to tread;   10
So gently sleeping on his mother's breast!
Living, though numbered with the numerous dead.
We mourn! But hope will whisper in the heart,
We meet again! and meet no more to part.

Poem No. 68; c. 6 August 1875

On Viewing the Falls of Niagara, as Photographed by George Barker

Amidst those scenes of wonder do I stand,
Though not in bodily presence, but in thought;
Stupendous works of the Almighty's hand!
By artist's skill before my vision brought.

The deep, strong floods, that downward ever pour,   5
The mists, that from their bosom ever rise,
I see; and almost seem to hear the roar
Of many waters, sounding to the skies.
The littleness of man, the power of God,
Doth to the sight as visible appear!   10
So felt the Indian, as these scenes he trod;
'Twas the Great Spirit's voice he seemed to hear,
That the deep silence of the forests broke,
And to his children in its thunders spoke.

Poem No. 45; c. 3 September 1875

Knowledge and Truth

Knowledge is not like truth, of heavenly birth,
It partial is, and may be done away;
Too often proud, and selfish, born of earth,
Its light grows dim before truth's purer ray.
One we acquire with eager, thirsting mind,   5
Curious to search, and prove possess and hold;
The other is a gift; who seek shall find;
Truth's ever young, but knowledge groweth old.
Increase of knowledge oft doth sorrow bring,
For it can never fill the human soul;   10
That longs to drink of a diviner spring,
To know the truth; man's rest, and highest goal.
While here we knowledge seek with restless mind,
May we not fail the heaven-born truth to find.

Poem No. 312; c. 9 October 1875

Mt. Shasta.
A Painting, by H. O. Young.

How, like a spiritual Presence, dost thou rise,
O lonely mountain, spotless, pure, and white!
While far beneath, in shade, the prairie lies,

Thy snowy peak reflects the morning light!
Thy base is hidden from our searching gaze,   5
As if no earthly mountain thou might'st be;
But a creation of the sun's bright rays,
A spiritual mount, a mystery.
So have I seen a cloud, in summer's day,
Piercing with its white peak the azure sky;   10
Calling men's thoughts from earth and sense away,
Teaching man's spirit, through the outward eye,
To hold communion with the Mind, that made
Nature's forms, alike in all displayed.

Poem No. 190; c. 19 November 1875

Song
I Love the Light

I love the light, when first its beams
    Steal o'er the earth and sky;
And gently wake the slumbering world,
    And bid the shadows fly.

I love the light of noon-day sun,   5
    Its full, effulgent ray;
That floods the earth, and sea, and sky,
    And brings the perfect day.

I love the light of sunset hour,
    Which lingers in the west;   10
Which soothes the weary heart and mind,
    And gives the laborer rest.

I love the moon's soft, silvery light,
    The light of stars, that keep
Their watches o'er a weary world,   15
    When wrapt in slumbers deep.

Poem No. 245; c. 27 November 1875

Nature Teaches Us of Time and its Duration

To show us time, its passing and its change,
Was Nature made; in which we all do live;
And all its mighty panorama strange
Doth the same lesson to earth's children give.
The seasons come and go, the flower, the leaf,   5
Teach us how quickly it has taken flight;
And setting suns, with golden splendors brief,
Warn us how soon to day succeeds the night.
And the bright stars that glitter in the sky,
And seem to mock our lives' short, busy round,   10
And, in their orbits, time itself defy,
Have yet, like man, their date, and certain bound.
What Nature teaches heed; no lesson miss;
And fleeting years shall bring eternal bliss.

Poem No. 740; c. 18 December 1875

Take ye heed, watch and pray: for ye know not when the time is. Mark 13 : 33.

Come suddenly, O Lord, or slowly come,
    I wait thy will, thy servant ready is;
Thou hast prepared thy follower a home;
    The heaven in which thou dwellest too is his.

Come in the morn, at noon, or midnight deep,   5
    Come, for thy servant still doth watch and pray;
E'en when the world around is sunk in sleep,
    I wake, and long to see thy glorious day.

I would not fix the time, the day, nor hour,
    When Thou with all thine angels shall appear;   10
When in thy kingdom Thou shalt come with power,
    E'en now, perhaps, the promised day is near!

For though, in slumber deep, the world may lie,
   And e'en thy Church forget thy great command;
Still year by year thy Coming draweth nigh, 15
   And in its power thy kingdom is at hand.

Not in some future world alone 'twill be,
   Beyond the grave, beyond the bounds of time;
But on the earth thy glory we shall see,
   And share thy triumph, peaceful, pure, sublime. 20

Lord! help me that I faint not, weary grow,
   Nor at thy Coming slumber too, and sleep;
For Thou hast promised, and full well I know
   Thou wilt to us thy word of promise keep.

Poem No. 92; 1875

The Ancient Burial Places in Peabody

It was the custom in Danvers, now Peabody, for many families to bury their dead on their own farms; a custom not wholly discontinued. There are many such ancient burial places in this town.

They lie by the roadside, where they lived,
   In the fields they loved to till;
And the landscape round a fitness lends,
   Which the musing mind doth fill

With a peace and rest, in sweet accord 5
   With the lives, which here they led;
As with honest toil, and frugal ways,
   They toiled for their daily bread.

In sight of the homes to them so dear,
   Of the woods, and hills they lie; 10
And the plaintive brook, with its soft, low voice,
   Is heard as it glideth by.

With simple rites, by their neighbors' hands
   They were laid in the kindly earth;
With heavenly words for the sorrowing heart, 15
   That told of a higher birth.

Though no costly tomb, nor e'en a stone,
    May tell where their bodies rest;
Yet not less sacred the cherished spots,
    Which are by their memory blest.   20

In the faith of their fathers they lived and died;
    That the spirit survives the dust,
That the righteous shall wear a heavenly crown,
    And receive the reward of the just.

Poem No. 643; c. 4 January 1876

Man's Need of a Spiritual Birth

How sayest thou we must be born again,
The Jewish teacher to Messias said;
Hast thou a message to the sons of men,
So different from what we have taught, and read?
Yet is it true; another birth we need,   5
Ere we the kingdom of our God shall see;
The heavenly plant is born of heavenly seed,
Its birth and growth to man a mystery.
The Spirit send, O Lord, and thus renew
Our feeble powers, make pure our hearts within,   10
As falls the quickening rain, or silent dew,
That we the heavenly life may here begin;
And, while we tread the sorrowing, sinful earth,
Be born of God, and know a higher birth.

Poem No. 200; c. 5 February 1876

On some Eternals from a friend's garden

Gone are the flowers, which bloomed so sweet and fair,
Where late I walked in Summer with delight;
Of all their beauties, Winter none would spare
Save these Eternals, that still charm the sight.
When fair Petunias lose their varied bloom,   5

And Pansies rich are buried 'neath the snow;
With fadeless colors these adorn our room,
And oft recall thy garden's beauteous show.
Thus do they love, and friendship symbolize,
As well as Summer's fair and fragrant flowers;   10
Amid the winter's gloom, and stormy skies,
To fancy picture still her blooming bowers;
And in their fadeless colors we may find
Emblems of feelings lasting as the mind.

Poem No. 152; c. 11 February 1876

Hymn
The Rest of the Righteous

Sweet is the rest the righteous gain!
    They to a higher life
Have come, through weariness and pain,
    Through earthly toil and strife.

They rest in peace! no foes can harm,   5
    Nor persecution kill;
No terrors strike them with alarm;
    No power can work them ill.

No inward conflicts now they wage,
    Their strife with self is o'er;   10
No doubts disturb, and passion's rage
    Shall shake their souls no more.

They gaze, as from some hill serene,
    Upon the world below;
Calmly they view the troubled scene,   15
    And all its trials know.

Another, higher life is theirs;
    Thus from their toils they rest;
For each the heavenly life now shares,
    And in its work is blest.   20

Their works bear witness to their faith,
    And have a sure reward;
They follow them, the Spirit saith,
    Their Judge, the risen Lord.

Poem No. 450; c. 4 March 1876

"Tuesday night, the schooner Weaver, of Glen Creek, N.J.,
went to pieces near Sandy Hook, and her entire crew were
lost."–*Transcript, March 22d.*

"For God's sake, help!" the drowning seaman cries,
But vain man's help! the shoremen cannot save!
The driving snow clouds blind their gazing eyes,
Vessel and crew are whelmed beneath the wave!
But trust in God still filled his fainting soul,   5
Whose power he witnessed on the raging deep;
May the same trust the mourners' hearts control,
And comfort those, who for their loved ones weep.
Have faith in God. Man's help, at times, is vain,
To reach the sufferers on life's dangerous coast;   10
His power alone can then their souls sustain;
In mortal aid, or skill how vain our boast!
But they who trust in Him, shall find him near,
To calm their minds, and banish every fear.

Poem No. 130; 22–31 March 1876

The Purification of the Temple

Lord! cleanse thine inner temple, as of old
Thou didst thy holy place of traffic vile;
Of those who in its precincts bought and sold;
With sheep and oxen did thy courts defile.
Purge Thou the inner temple of the mind,   5
The heart itself of man, O Lord, make pure,
That he may Thee and thy true worship find,

Which through eternal ages shall endure.
Then will the offerings accepted be
Which he unto thy holy mount shall bear;   10
Fulfilled the word the prophet spake of Thee,
"My temple shall be called the House of Prayer";
For every nation then shall hear thy Word,
And all the people know and serve the Lord.

Poem No. 321; c. 22 April 1876

The May Flower

I found upon our neighboring hills
   A flower, there growing thick as dropping rain;
And from its friends removed it far,
   And in strange company did it detain.

And far I took it from the old grey rocks,   5
   And from the dark green wood wax spreading round,
From barberry bush with its prickly stems,
   And placed it in the distant garden's ground.

Then I thought that it would quickly die,
   When removed so far from the rocky hills;   10
Where the sun shines bright the live-long day,
   And the bird's sweet song every covert fills.

For not lightly sundered frailest thread,
   Which binds to its haunt the sweet May flower;
Mid the garden's bloom it droops and fades,   15
   And pineth still in the fairest bower.

The floweret lived; but an exile seemed
   That pined for his country far away;
In summer it seeded, in autumn
   Grew sere; and it bloomed, once again, in May.   20

And I marked, as its little white flowers
   Appeared, that still to its friends it was true;
Though afar from the spot of its birth,
   They came forth as when by their side it grew.

So we, though we roam to far distant lands,   25
    Through the grandest and fairest of earth;
Can never forget mountain, river, and vale,
    Trees, and flowers in the place of our birth.

For something there is in every place,
    Where kind Providence places his lot;   30
Binds man to his home, like the humblest flower,
    Which heralds the Spring in his natal spot.

Poem No. 229; c. 2 May 1876

The International Exhibition at Philadelphia

A joyful spirit to the world
    The welcome poet brings,
And from the music in his heart
    He to the people sings.

No more of war his numbers tell,   5
    But of abiding peace;
When the whole world shall be renewed,
    And nations' strife shall cease.

Their passions that ungoverned were
    Shall yield to reason's sway;   10
Kings' hearts be, like the rivers, turned;
    The law of love obey.

In friendly intercourse they meet,
    From every land and clime;
In peaceful arts alone to vie,   15
    A brotherhood sublime.

From Europe, Asia, Africa,
    And islands of the sea,
They meet upon Columbia's soil,
    The land of liberty.   20

Whate'er is useful, grand or fair,
    The gifts of prince or king,
The people's workmanship and art,
    They o'er the ocean bring.

And to the city famed for peace   25
   And love to man of old,
They come, this great Centennial year,
   Their festival to hold.

Poem No. 10; c. 6 May 1876

Evolution

I.

Because the gradual growth of things we see,
And naught at once mature and perfect made;
From tiny seed the lofty branching tree,
Yielding at length its fruit and thick-leaved shade;
Or, from the egg, we see the bird, or beast,   5
By gradual growth to perfect stature grow;
Tracing all forms the mightiest from the least;
We think the origin of things we know.
In the same order we ourselves do live,
Nor aught immediate see, nor understand;   10
But to phenomena a meaning give,
As if man's narrow thought had Nature planned;
Nor rise with reverent mind and faith sublime,
Above the encircling bounds of space and time.

II.

Man's thoughts turn on himself; and whence is Man?   15
He asks. What countless forms, and changes vast,
Since first his life upon the earth began!
In vain do we interrogate the past;
The torch of knowledge doth but dimly show
His path from land to land, from clime to clime;   20
And who, by natural descent, can know
His origin, or era date in time?
Yet is he one, where'er his feet have trod;
Though changed in mind, as well as outward frame,
Created in the image of his God,   25

Though lost by some the knowledge of his Name;
Our brother still, and destined too, as we,
To show the ages of eternity.

Poem No. 63; c. 3 April 1875 (ll. 1–14); c. 12 May 1876 (ll. 15–28)

Capt. Samuel Cook

Well I remember him long years ago,
　As on our vessel's deck I saw him stand;
When yet, the Crescent City far below,
　He came to take my *father by the hand.
And with him Noble, Felt, and Hooper there,　　　　　　5
　Brave captains then, like him, and in their prime,
Yet none more ruddy, and erect, and fair;
　Remembered well through fifty years of time.
But all are gone! himself the last to leave
　This changing scene for higher, nobler life!　　　　　10
Why for the aged seaman should we grieve,
　Who bore so well life's storms, and ocean's strife?
Safe in the harbor of an endless rest,
　With those he mourned and loved on earth the best.

Poem No. 769; c. 30 May 1876

On the Beautiful Roses,
In front of the Mansion of John Hodges, Esq.

Fair damask roses! that, from year to year,
　Blush in your beauty on the busy street;
Thanks to the unknown hand that placed you here,
　And made the spot with bloom and fragrance sweet.
The sun's hot rays upon the pavement beat,　　　　　5
　Where not a blade of grass, or flower, can grow;

*Capt. Jones Very of the barque Aurelia, of Boston. Seeing signal, Capt. Cook of the ship Delphos, came down the river in his boat to meet us, before we arrived at the city.

But you, within your pleasant, green retreat,
     More pleasure give than garden's beauteous show.
How many from the sight have borne away
     Some glad remembrance of your gorgeous bloom,   10
How many, in the sultry summer's day,
     Borne on the air, have caught your sweet perfume!
Through coming years may still your beauties last,
     And fragrant make the future as the past.

Poem No. 106; c. 23 June 1876

The Cows waiting at the Pasture Gate

The herd is standing on the hill,
     Or lying on the ground;
Their number now is all complete,
     The last stray wanderer found.

They wait the opening of the gate,   5
     How peaceful their repose!
It soothes the mind, and o'er the scene
     A quiet beauty throws.

O'er the wide pastures they have roamed
     Through all the summer day,   10
Grazing at will o'er hill and vale,
     Where'er they chanced to stray.

At some cool spring they quench their thirst,
     Whose source is never dry;
The water trickling from the rock   15
     Yields still a full supply.

O'er rocky hills their pathway winds,
     Through swamps and meadows green;
Till resting 'neath the distant pines,
     The herd at noon is seen.   20

When in the west the sun declines,
     The cowherd's voice they hear,
And homeward turn; his barking dog
     Still hanging on their rear.

And, winding slowly o'er the hills,   25
    The deep worn path is trod;
Till on the last they waiting stand,
    Or rest upon the sod.

The keeper opens wide the gate,
    For now the hour is come;   30
And lowing down the busy street
    The cows are driven home.

Poem No. 509; c. 4 August 1876

Song
The Summer Day

The day has gone, the summer day,
Fled on its golden wings away;
Why will it not yet longer stay?

'Tis gone to make still others blest,
Gone to its goal in the far west,   5
Leaving us here to quiet rest.

If we its hours have well employed,
The gifts it brought improved, enjoyed,
Our pleasure will be unalloyed.

No vain regrets will fill the mind,   10
The day has left us here behind;
But we from toil sweet rest shall find.

Poem No. 485; 5 August 1876

On some blue and golden Columbines
from Pike's Peak, Colorado

O new-born State, what lovely flowers are thine!
Differing in color, but, in form, the same,
From mountain heights has come thy Columbine,

Which shares with ours in beauty and in name.
Our youngest State may grander scenes disclose,   5
Far loftier mountains, parks and vales more fair;
Yet where the Columbine on hillside grows,
Strange tho' the scene, one heritage we share.
The lonely emigrant beholds the flower,
Which in his boyhood's haunts far off he knew;   10
And, at the sight, imagination's power
Brings absent friends, and early home to view;
And he forgets, in thoughts and visions dear,
The mountain heights, which rise so grand and near.

Poem No. 377; c. 1 September 1876

The Stony Desert of Life

In far Australia's middle region lies
   A stony desert, treeless, hot and bare;
All hope to pass it in the traveler dies;
   No brook, nor stream, nor native well is there.
So do we in our lives some desert meet   5
   Which seems impassable, so wild and drear,
Untrodden yet, perchance, by human feet;
   Where naught is found the sinking heart to cheer.
Yet He who to such pass our steps may bring,
   When human help shall fail, will grant his own;   10
E'en in the wild will show some cooling spring,
   Nor leave us there to perish, weak, alone;
But guide our steps, if we but trust His care,
   Beyond its bounds to pastures green and fair.

Poem No. 299; c. 2 September 1876

Cadmus

The ancient Greeks a fable had, that he
Who brought them letters sowed a dragon's teeth,
And armed men sprang up; some wisdom we

Perhaps may find the fable's form beneath.
No gift so great but may be turned to ill;   5
Thus e'en with letters may be born fierce strife,
And armed men spring up to fight and kill,
And that bring death which should have brought us life.
The Press may grow corrupt, deceitful words,
The seeds of war, scatter in every land;   10
Till men shall beat their ploughshares into swords,
And armed men spring up on every hand!
Ah, when will God's great gift of human speech
Naught but his love to all his children teach?

Poem No. 459; c. 16 September 1876

The True Worshipers

No outward service doth the Lord require,
So much as inward service of the mind;
The carnal mind doth carnal things desire,
In forms and ritual doth religion find.
The Temple service could not save, of old,   5
Though none so grand, imposing, in man's sight;
While the plain worship of the Christian fold
Accepted was, and did the Lord delight.
The Spirit doth a temple, forms, prepare,
The lowliest worship it doth choose and bless;   10
How blest are they who in its service share,
In spirit and in truth the Lord confess!
They in their worship shall accepted be,
And, born of God, e'en now his kingdom see.

Poem No. 357; c. 7 October 1876

Song
We Have No Ship at Sea

When thoughtlessly two lamps were burned,
    'Twas in our poverty,
"We need but one," we oft were told,
    "We have no ship at sea."

"For oil is dear, it will not do   5
    To use it thus so free;
Two lamps we cannot now afford,
    We have no ship at sea."

How oft this proverb comes to mind,
    As, looking round, I see   10
The idle, wasteful, ignorant,
    Who have no ships at sea.

They will not work, they will not save,
    That prosperous they may be;
That, when to manhood they have come,   15
    They may have ships at sea.

In youth they will not knowledge seek,
    Of wealth and power the key;
They learn no trades to live at home,
    Nor how to sail the sea.   20

'Tis knowledge, thrift, and honest toil,
    That brings prosperity;
These make men prosper on the land,
    And have their ships at sea.

Poem No. 796; c. 10 October 1876

The Gospel the Reconciling Power

The word the Gospel brought was love and peace,
A reconciling word to sinful men;
That they from enmity and strife should cease,
And as one family should dwell again.

But, still estranged, behold the nations stand! 5
While over Europe hangs the cloud of war,
Which but of late made desolate our land,
But now, in mercy driven from us afar.
But still do enmity and hate remain.
One nation still we are, but not one race; 10
From human limbs have fallen Slavery's chain;
When from the mind shall vanish, too, its trace,
And in our hearts the Gospel's power be known,
And self, and sin, and hate be overthrown?

Poem No. 601; c. 4 November 1876

Every Day a Day of Freedom

A day of Freedom is each dawning day,
And day of Grace to sinful erring men;
While shines its sun they all may find their way
Back to the path of virtue truth again.
Its beauty all may love, its light all see, 5
Its noon-day glory fills the heaven and earth;
From night's dark bondage it the soul would free,
And make it heir of an immortal birth.
In it the Psalmist saw God's law made clear,
The law of freedom, purity, and right; 10
But Christ taught unto God all men were dear,
And called to be the children of the light;
In its warm beams, and rains that plenteous fall,
He saw a Father's love, that cares for all.

Poem No. 6; c. 25 November 1876

Hymn
Reflections at the Close of the Year

The flowers of Spring have faded fast,
The Summer's glories did not last,
Autumn is gone, and Winter near;
End of the varied, changeful year.

Deep in thy mind consider well   5
The lessons, which these changes tell,
Of birth, growth, ripeness, and decay,
How short man's life, how brief his stay.

'Tis His appointment here below,
Who doth our state, and nature know;   10
That we may thus submissive be
To His all-wise, and just decree.

Still may we own a Father's care
In every suffering, grief, we bear;
And through His works and Word, discern   15
His righteous will, His wisdom learn.

Oh, that some fruit we here may bear,
That shall our souls for heaven prepare;
Where days, and years, and seasons round,
And change, and death, no more are found.   20

Poem No. 500; c. 19 December 1876

On Hearing the Clock Strike, in Harmony Grove

Why heard, amidst these shades, the tongue of time,
Telling the number of the passing hours?
For other thoughts, and feelings more sublime,
Than those of earth, amidst these scenes are ours.
What thoughts are theirs of time, whose mortal part   5
Alone is subject to its stern controul;
Who in this life can have no more a part,
Living the life of the immortal soul?

Say, do they mourn their days, and years misspent,
Neglected opportunities recall;   10
Or joy, that they improved the talents lent,
Nor lived as though this earthly life were all?
Ah, who can tell what are their thoughts, but he,
Who with them shares their own eternity?

Poem No. 821; c. 29 December 1876

The Indians' Belief in a Future State

Beyond the river, they believe
  A happy country still is found,
When their wild, roving life is o'er,
  Where forests, streams and game abound.

Beyond the cañons' gloomy sides,   5
  Where scarce can pierce the light of day,
A happy hunting-ground there is,
  Though men know not the trackless way.

Beyond the mountains' distant heights
  There is a fairer earth and sky,   10
Where, unmolested, they shall dwell
  As warriors, hunters, when they die.

Beyond the ocean, where the sun
  Sinks in his journey to the west,
They say their weary, wandering tribes   15
  Shall find at length a home, a rest.

Thus dream they of the spirit-land,
  Nor higher rest they hope to find;
They know no country of the soul,
  No home for the immortal mind.   20

Beyond, and still beyond *we* gaze,
  For the green earth is not our home;
A heavenly country, too, we seek,
  Where we, like them, no more shall roam.

Poem No. 69; c. 27 January 1877

The Telephone

The marvel of our age, the Telephone!
What is the Telephone, do you inquire?
The marvel of our time, before unknown,
The human voice speaks through the electric wire!
The distant city hears the spoken word,   5
In waves of sound, transmitted o'er the line;
The notes of music in sweet strains are heard;
From Boston comes the song of "Auld Lang Syne."
These triumphs o'er the world of space and time
The Telegraph and Telephone can show;   10
And Science now, with joy and faith sublime,
Doth a new gift upon the race bestow.
Beneath the ocean soon man's voice may reach,
And a new power be given to human speech.

Poem No. 524; c. 23 February 1877

Love Needing a Visible Object

How love whom we see not, and cannot see
With mortal sight, the Invisible, Unknown?
To highest angel still a mystery,
Who nearest stands before his awful throne.
Yet by the worlds we see is God revealed,   5
On earth below and in the starry sky;
The Invisible Spirit, else from man concealed,
Reveals his goodness, power, to every eye.
And by his son, who did his image bear,
The image of his mercy and his grace,   10
He doth his love, a Father's love declare,
That we, though sinful, yet might see his face.
Yea, our own hearts do tell us of his love,
And, though invisible, his presence prove.

Poem No. 191; c. 10 March 1877

The Perfect Love that Casts out Fear

There is a state that all may know,
   No fear, no shame we feel;
For God doth all his mercy show,
   And all his love reveal.

His goodness manifested is,   5
   And all his ways are clear;
The Spirit seals our souls as his,
   For we to him are dear.

A Father's love, in our past years,
   By us is clearly known;   10
For he has wiped away our tears,
   And as his sons doth own.

And he has called us by his Son
   To know a higher life,
With them forever to be one,   15
   No more with sin at strife.

The darkness of the world has fled,
   That dimmed our mortal sight;
We dwell no more in bondage, fear,
   But walk in heavenly light.   20

Poem No. 615; c. 31 March 1877

The Glacial Marks on our Hills

Here on our rocks the marks we see,
   Where once the glaciers moved on;
Man shares in Nature's mystery,
   And lives in ages past and gone.

In these smooth lines we trace their course   5
   From north to south across the land,
A steady, but resistless force,
   That e'en the hills could not withstand.

Up their rough slopes they onward go,
  To where the hills abruptly end;   10
Then at their feet the fragments throw,
  And onward to the ocean tend.

The boulders, which we see around,
  Like pebbles on their surface borne,
Were in far distant regions found,   15
  From craggy hills, and mountains torn.

The long moraine, which, like a road,
  Stretches through forests, fields afar;
Tells where dissolved the icy flood,
  With warmer suns and skies at war.   20

Imagination backward flies,
  And views with wonder, and with fear,
The prospect which around her lies,
  Where naught is seen the mind to cheer!

Yet in that scene man's thought can live,   25
  Though wild, and desolate, and bare;
Can to these marks a meaning give,
  And the long life of Nature share.

The present, like a fleeting dream,
  Does from his musing spirit fade!   30
He gazes down Time's darkling stream,
  When mountains and the hills were made!

Poem No. 171; c. 10 April 1877

The Future State of the Wicked and its Duration

Seek not with mortal sight to pierce the gloom
Which shrouds the wicked in a future state;
Foretell the nature of their righteous doom,
Nor seek to know how long or short its date.
In the few years which thou on earth dost spend,   5
Use well the time which God to thee has given;
Known unto him alone can be the end,
Make of thy home on earth a present heaven.

Trust in a father's love; no gloomy fear
Nor chilling doubts can then disturb thy mind;   10
But thou shalt find his presence with thee near;
Unto his will in patient hope resigned,
That what Time's shadows from our eyes conceal,
The eternal ages clearly will reveal.

Poem No. 415; c. 14 April 1877

Faith in the Resurrection Confirmed

That friends we loved, in dying did not die,
We do believe; but oft our faith is weak,
For error, doubt and fear our minds will try,
And for our faith we confirmation seek.
Imagination promises its aid,   5
And pictures them to us as still alive;
And brighter scenes than earth by it are made,
By which our souls do strength and hope derive.
But most the Word of God new hope doth bring,
And with its light our spirits' depths illume;   10
For Christ is risen! Death's conqueror and king!
And banished from the earth its night of gloom,
Which with its terrors did the soul assail,
And even o'er our faith at times prevail.

Poem No. 457; c. 5 May 1877

Spring and Summer Flowers

The mingling scent of flowers is in the air,
Gathered from piny wood and rocky dell;
Of roses, callas, that the fostering care
Of man through winter's stormy months can tell.
The seasons' differing hues together meet;   5
The gorgeous colors of the summer's flowers
The delicate tints of early spring-time greet,
That tell of wild wood haunts, and budding bowers.

Scarce can the mind such contrasts fair retain,
From each to each it turns with new delight;   10
The blushing roses now the thoughts detain,
And now the May flowers' beauties charm the sight;
Now, the glad Present bids us here to stay,
And now, the Future beckons us away.

Poem No. 525; c. 11 May 1877

The Return of the Columbine

Thou comest again, in bright scarlet drest,
    To cheer the heart, and to please the eye;
To nod o'er the ground sparrow's lowly nest,
    And lure the bee as he wanders by.

And the beauteous sight the prospect fills,   5
    For wherever we turn we admire;
Thou comest again to our rocky hills,
    Blushing deep with their summer attire.

In every crevice thou findest a place,
    With thy beauty the rocks to adorn;   10
The dark, craggy hillside thou lovest to grace
    With bright hues like the colors of morn.

And the children come o'er the hills to roam,
    And gather in bunches thy flowers;
Sweetest tokens they are, in many a home,   15
    Of their walks, and the glad summer hours.

Thou comest again; and oft hast returned,
    With thy beauty and fragrance so sweet;
But we other lessons than Nature's have learned,
    Nor hastened thy coming to greet.   20

Oh, would that the beauty, so lavish and free,
    And that doth with each season return;
We might, with the glad heart of childhood see,
    And the lesson it brings for us learn.

Poem No. 669; c. 25 May 1877

Man's Accountability

How shalt thou give account to God, O man,
For all that in the body thou hast done,
Since first thy life upon the earth began,
Recalling every action, one by one?
We cannot, save the memory quickened be,   5
And every deed shall in God's light appear;
And each the record of his life shall see,
The evil to condemn, the good to cheer.
Yet must thou give account, though weak and frail,
And memory to its trust unfaithful prove;   10
Say, shall the good, or evil then prevail?
Unrighteous deeds, or works of mercy, love?
For memory cannot die, but quickened lives,
And in heaven's light a perfect record gives.

Poem No. 201; c. 2 June 1877

Hymn
The Cause of Peace

The Ages pass;—yet still delayed
    The Cause of Peace on earth;
The Cause for which the Savior prayed,
    Proclaimed e'en at his birth.

The time of which the Angels sang   5
    In sweet, prophetic strains;
When 'neath the stars, their voices rang
    O'er Judah's favored plains.

Yes, still delayed; for passion, pride
    Usurp calm reason's throne;   10
And nations in their power confide,
    And not in God alone.

Yes, still delayed; but signs we see
  The fainting soul to cheer;
That that blessed day is yet to be,   15
  That it may still be near.

May we its glorious light behold
  Of Peace, and Truth, and Love;
By Prophet-bards so long foretold,
  And Angel-hosts above.   20

Poem No. 458; c. 16 June 1877

The Nodding Meadow Lily

How came this modest lily fair,
  In this lone meadow here to grow;
When other meadows far around
  Can no such beauteous treasure show?

Has it from some far centre come,   5
  Where such fair flowers do most abound;
Brought by the winds, or flowing streams,
  And here a soil congenial found?

Or did it spring spontaneous here,
  When earth brought forth each plant and tree?   10
Was this the Eden of its race?
  Can Science solve the mystery?

He who the soil could ready make,
  And for each seed a place prepare,
Could here transplant from far thy germ,   15
  Or here create, and for it care.

Here, or in meadow like to this,
  Though far away, thy golden flowers
First opened to the light of day,
  The pride of summer's sultry hours.   20

Enough for me thy flowers to find,
    Admire their form and matchless grace;
And own His love, who thus has given
    Peculiar beauty to the place.

Poem No. 180; c. 20 July 1877

The Destruction of Public Property by Mobs

With madness seized men their own works destroy,
Nay their own lives; they know not what they do;
Destruction for a time is their employ;
In peace they would the scenes of war renew.
'Tis their own work their maddened hands pull down!   5
For, in his Country, each one has his part,
And each is sharer too in her renown;
His are her works of skill, of use, of art.
For, sadder than the ruins, is the thought,
That men should lose their Patriotic Pride: 10
Nor feel the stain, which their own deeds have brought
On Liberty's fair name, they have denied;
In one short hour of riot and of spoil
Wasting the fruits of years of peaceful toil.

Poem No. 837; c. 10 August 1877

The Barberry-Pickers

The barberry's red with ripened fruit;
    The merry children come,
And fill their baskets from its boughs,
    And bear their burdens home.

What if their fingers oft are pricked   5
    With the sharp-pointed thorn;
Or e'en a dress, by the thick briars,
    Is rent and sadly torn?

A pleasant day among the hills
  The barberry-pickers spend;
Nor passed in vain the happy hours,
  That work with pleasure blend.

For many a lesson they shall learn
  From this fair Autumn day;
Which, in the distant after years,
  Their toil shall well repay.

New strength and health from labor come,
  They breathe a purer air,
And in the bounty Nature yields
  They feel that all may share.

Though learning of the school be lost,
  Forgot the printed page,
The lessons Nature taught in youth
  They'll treasure still in age.

Poem No. 461; c. 9 October 1877

Pompeii

Amidst the dwellings of a distant age,
As by the enchanter's wand we seem to stand!
Science and Art illume the historic page,
And far-off scenes we view as near at hand.
Pompeii's daily life again appears,
The noble Roman sunk in pleasure, ease;
Forgot the virtues of his earlier years,
When manly toil and deeds alone could please.
So slumbered they; till, on their midnight sleep,
Vesuvius showered its dense and murky rain,
Burying their city 'neath its ashes deep,
Like the doomed cities of Gomorrah's plain!
Like them, still warning, in a voice sublime,
Proud cities filled with luxury and crime.

Poem No. 41; c. 16 October 1877

The Communion

Why forms discuss, if that the soul is fled?
Is the communion in the wine and bread;
Or in the loving hearts, that would draw near
A dying Savior's last command to hear?
Ah, still have met again that little band,   5
And in their midst the Savior still doth stand:
Where Love doth break the bread and pour the wine,
And they are one in fellowship divine.
How few this fellowship of love profess!
How few a dying Savior's name confess!   10
For what are rites and forms? an empty show,
If we their meaning, life, have ceased to know.
Quicken in us, O Lord, the dying love,
Fit us on earth for fellowship above;
Where holy friendships shall be made complete,   15
And all who love on earth again shall meet.

Poem No. 819; c. 23 November 1877

The Winter Night

Brief is the day, and soon the hastening sun
Sinks in the west, its narrow circuit run.
How much there is, through the long winter night,
To cheer the mind, instruct us, and delight.
When darkness hides earth's beauty from our eyes,   5
We still may gaze upon the starry skies;
And own the mighty Maker's hand divine,
In suns and worlds, that with new lustre shine.
The glittering constellations, o'er our head,
Fill the deep musing mind with wonder, dread.   10
What secrets there have been from man concealed,
To angels' high intelligence revealed!
To sister planets oft our gaze we turn;
From each the thoughtful may some lesson learn.
Each has some different history of its own,   15
As each by its own color, form, is known.

Now in conjunction Mars and Saturn see,
As if almost one planet they might be;
Then ruddy Mars moves on with swifter pace,
And leaves behind slow Saturn in the race.   20
But beautiful and bright beyond compare,
Look, where the evening star shines silvery, fair,
The near companion of the crescent moon,
Again to part with her, alas, how soon!
Each onward moving in its diverse way,   25
While each doth still one heavenly law obey.
How many gaze, with unobservant eyes,
On all this beauty of the winter skies;
On stars and systems, that in glory burn
Yet from the sight no word of wisdom learn!   30
Seeing they see, and yet not understand
The works, and wonders of the Almighty's hand;
Who launched in space this vast terrestrial ball,
Yet notes the insect's flight, the sparrow's fall;
Who bids unnumbered worlds their courses run,   35
Yet guides the motes, that glitter in the sun.
The wise, the musing, meditative mind
More wisdom in the night, than day, may find;
Heaven's gifts are not alone to labor given:
E'en, in the hours of sleep, descend from heaven   40
High thoughts and feelings, visions too sublime,
That link eternity with fleeting time.

Poem No. 76; c. 25 December 1877

The Coasters

Upon the coasters' spreading sails
    December's sun is shining bright;
And to their port, with favoring gales,
    They'll safely come ere falls the night;
Secure from harm has been their way,   5
    No wintry storms have swept the bay.

From yon high hill I saw their fleet,
    By many a gallant crew 'twas manned;

A pleasant company they meet,
 And steer their courses near the land;   10
Joyous, for now all danger's past,
 The rocky shore, the icy blast.

But a few days; and others, tost,
 Strive manfully their port to reach;
In storm and darkness they are lost,   15
 Their spars and rigging strew the beach;
And frozen, stretched upon the sand,
 Lie some of that brave sailor band!

In nobler fight they did contend
 Than that, in which war's heroes fall;   20
In peaceful toil they found their end;
 War's strife the world doth glory call;
But these should have a nobler name,
 Than heroes, on the roll of fame.

Not with their fellow men they strove,   25
 To waste the earth, destroy and kill;
But o'er the ocean loved to rove,
 To toil with courage, strength, and skill;
And, midst the elements' fierce strife,
 To conquer, or to yield their life.   30

Varied and strange life's shifting scene!
 Like ocean's ever changing form;
To-day, all peaceful and serene,
 To-morrow, dark with clouds and storm;
Oh, that we might in Him confide,   35
 Who to blest ends doth all things guide.

Poem No. 753; c. 1 February 1878

The Message

On the bare alder bough,
 I heard the sparrow sing;
To me a message it had brought
 Of the returning Spring.

No leaf had yet unrolled
   Its fresh and tender green,
No flower, in all its loveliness,
   On hill or plain was seen.

Its sweet out-pouring joy
   The winter's silence broke;
Of the green trees, and vernal flowers,
   In plainest language spoke.

Not by man's voice alone,
   God's messages are brought;
The birds' sweet strain, the opening flower,
   Convey to us his thought.

The sparrows' welcome song
   Will tell us of his love,
And, though the Maker is unseen,
   His Presence with us prove.

Its notes of joy and praise
   Proclaim his love, and care;
And far and wide through all our land,
   Spring's joyful message bear.

Poem No. 389; c. 11 April 1878

Do Nations Ever Become Insane?

May not whole nations, as the single man,
Become insane; and know not what they do:
Deep-reasoning Butler asked. Past history scan,
How oft its page proves his suggestion true.
Founded on force, they their own law obey;
The slaves of passion, and the lust of power;
With no strong love for peace, or reason's sway,
They folly serve, the madness of the hour!
When will the law of Peace by all be known,
Discord and war be banished from the earth;
His lower nature be by man outgrown,
And men assert their higher, nobler birth;

And Arbitration rule, and not the sword,
And history cease war's madness to record?

Poem No. 326; c. 30 April 1878

Know Thyself
Suggested by hearing Dr. A. E. Miller's Lectures on the Human Body.

Who, with dull mind, can view man's wondrous frame;
And not with deepest reverence and awe?
For from the hand of God at first it came,
And from his breath did life and motion draw.
The bones, which show such marvellous strength and skill,   5
The blood, which circulates through every vein,
The ever-moving lungs the air doth fill,
The pulsing heart, the all-directing brain.
What higher knowledge than thyself to know?
Though countless objects gain our time, and thought,   10
On our own frame we scarce a thought bestow,
The body thus so marvellously wrought;
The type of that, which shall immortal be,
From pain, disease, and death forever free.

Poem No. 815; c. 3 May 1878

The Blueberry Blossoms

Why pluck their flowers? Each might have been
   A ripe and luscious fruit,
When summer months had fully come,
   And well the palate suit.

The birds might there have found a meal;   5
   The children love their taste;
Why pluck and bring the useless flowers,
   And thus God's bounty waste?

Thus sense doth plead; nor for a flower
   A higher use can see,   10
Than that it may become a seed,
   Or ripened berry be.

The poet, in its blossoms fair,
   A nobler use can find;
Of which, who love the fruit alone   15
   Are ignorant, and blind.

In their sweet fragrance he delights,
   Their beauty fills his heart;
And he on others would bestow
   What they to him impart.   20

Nor deems it loss to sacrifice
   The low to higher need,
That thus what might but please the sense,
   The mind and heart may feed.

Man's life is not for bread alone,   25
   Nor worldly toil and gain;
For beauty doth the soul inspire
   To reach a higher plane.

Enough God's bounty too has given
   For all alike to share;
Nor only for our earthly wants,   30
   But higher needs doth care.

Poem No. 823; c. 28 May 1878

William Cullen Bryant

No gloom o'er Nature's face is spread,
   Though to his rest her son is gone;
He who her choir in song has led,
   And her bright crown, and laurel won.

She comes in all her beauty bloom,   5
   To deck the forest, field, and hill;
Her roses breathe their sweet perfume,
   Her songs the groves with music fill.

Why should we mourn? with honors crowned,
    And length of days, he passed away;   10
A nobler life than this has found,
    Why on the earth prolong his stay?

Why mourn the Patriot, and the Man,
    Lover of Country, and his race;
Who, in his broad, far reaching plan,   15
    Could all mankind as one embrace?

Why do we mourn? for still shall live
    The strains, which Nature's self inspired;
To other minds his genius give,
    And other hearts by his be fired.   20

Poem No. 354; 12–21 June 1878

"Agriculture the Source of Individual and of National Prosperity."–Anne Pratt.

The husbandman doth still go out to hire
Men for his vineyard, which doth labor need;
And of the idlers in the land to inquire,
"Why stand ye idle?" "Up, and sow the seed,
That in the Autumn shall rich harvests yield;   5
Plant fruitful trees, and vines on every side,
On every hill, and in each fertile field;
Like a fair garden make your Country wide."
But idle in the market place they stand,
With folded hands, and discontented mind;   10
While all untilled, unpeopled lies the land!
Murmuring, that none can now employment find;
Or of the goodman of the house complain,
That others for their labor more should gain.

II.

Where spring the cornfields in their tender green,   15
Or bend and rustle in the summer breeze,

Where in the Autumn, year by year, are seen
The reapers gathering in their golden sheaves,
There dwell domestic happiness and peace;
No more wild savage wanderers men rove;   20
From their fierce strifes, and idleness they cease,
And in the peaceful arts of life improve.
Dwellings are reared, beneath their roofs are born
Children, with beauty, strength the home to grace;
The virtues, which humanity adorn,   25
Can find on earth no more congenial place;
The love of kindred, neighbors, country, friends,
Unto the spot a heavenly glory lends.

Poem No. 514; c. 26 July 1878

Pleasure

With business haste, or with a worldly mind
Men Pleasure seek, as they some work would do;
But in the beaten track they fail to find
The rest they need, or prize that they pursue.
In some by-path, or quiet nook she hides,   5
Away from public haunts, and worldly eyes;
With those who love her truly there abides,
And with her choicest gifts doth them surprise.
The tired laborer doth find her there,
At home returning from his daily toil;   10
The city dweller doth her visits share,
Fleeing the city's dust, and loud turmoil;
While crowds, that speed in haste o'er land and sea,
But seldom meet, or share her company.

Poem No. 834; c. 16 August 1878

On The Late Tornado, At Wallingford, Conn.

With aimless fury hurries on its path,
For so it seems unto man's narrow mind,
The dread tornado, messenger of wrath!
Like to some maddened giant strong and blind.
Yet Mercy guides its course, confines its sway,   5
From the beginning to the appointed end;
For Nature's forces all One law obey,
And none can its allotted bounds transcend.
The stormy winds, O God, thy word fulfil,
As doth the gentle breeze, that whispers peace;   10
All are obedient to thy holy will;
Thou dost command, and fiercest tempests cease;
And men, with grateful hearts, again rejoice;
Awed, chastened, humbled, by thy Sovereign Voice.

Poem No. 832; c. 30 August 1878

Hymn

Though few, with noble purpose came
    Our fathers to this distant wild;
A Commonwealth they sought to frame,
    From country, and from friends exiled.

Religious freedom here they sought,   5
    In their own land to them denied;
With courage, and with faith they wrought,
    Nor monarch feared, nor prelate's pride.

That Commonwealth to power has grown,
    Religious liberty is ours;   10
What now we reap their hands have sown,
    And changed the wild to garden bowers.

The trees they planted year by year
    Still yield their precious fruit, and shade;
Fair Learning's gifts still flourish here,   15
    And Law man's rights has sacred made.

They from their labors long have ceased,
  On the green hill-sides saintly rest;
Their sons, in wealth, and power increased,
  Have by their fathers' God been blest.   20

Their noble deeds our souls inspire,
  Be ours their faith, and courage still;
Keep pure the home, the altar's fire,
  And thus their cherished hopes fulfil.

Poem No. 94-706; c. 18 September 1878

On the Neglect of the Study of History

History repeats her lessons; oft in vain!
For we to profit by her page are slow;
She shows how States may eminence attain,
How ignorance and vice their power o'erthrow;
How Government was formed for noble ends,   5
To establish order, vice and crime remove;
But these, neglected, it to ruin tends,
And what was made for good doth evil prove.
So doth a noble river, that should bless
And fertilize its banks on either side,   10
Bursting its bounds, bring ruin and distress,
And desolate a happy region wide!
Ah, when shall man, if not by History taught,
Learn from the wondrous works in Nature wrought?

Poem No. 174; c. 29 October 1878

Christ's Final Victory

Over men's graves we lightly tread!
  Ah, soon forgotten are the dead!
"Christ is not risen," we hear men say,
  "There is no Resurrection Day."

"Death over us will soon have power, 5
    To pleasure give life's little hour;
Like leaves the generations fall,
    Death still is sovereign over all."

Ah thoughtless men, ah faithless Age,
    Not to believe the Sacred Page; 10
That Christ at length o'er death shall reign,
    The final victory shall gain.

That to the dead, who in Him sleep,
    He will his faithful promise keep;
That, at his coming, they shall rise, 15
    Welcomed by angels to the skies.

That e'en mortality shall be
    A sharer in his victory;
Changed to immortal, it shall wear
    The heavenly image, wondrous fair. 20

Let these high thoughts our souls inspire,
    Fill us with earnest, pure desire,
That we the prize in Christ may win,
    His victory over death and sin.

Poem No. 395; 26 November 1878

Thanksgiving Flowers

Bright flowers! November's frosts and cold have spared,
To greet us on this late Thanksgiving morn;
A tender love for you, as us, has cared;
The pansies still our garden plot adorn,
Chrysanthemums, that, with the waning year, 5
Round many homes in golden clusters bloom;
And e'en December's stormy month can cheer,
Stealing from many a clouded day its gloom.
While grateful for the harvest we would be,
Which with abundance fills our wide domain; 10
In these bright flowers new tokens, too, we see
Of the same Love, which gives the fruits and grain;

And makes November's bare and cheerless bowers
Bright with the hues of Memory's fadeless flowers.

Poem No. 77; c. 6 December 1878

Original Hymn

We welcome, with the opening year,
   Our Pastor, to this ancient fold;
With words of love, and hope to cheer,
   The gracious Gospel, never old.

In cultured ground the seed is sown,   5
   As in a good and fruitful soil;
Long has this field the blessing known
   Of faithful laborers' care and toil.

As come the swift returning years,
   May nobler aims our spirits raise;   10
Faith triumph over doubts and fears,
   Move grateful hearts, inspire our praise.

Our Father, may thy gracious word
   Quicken in all the life divine;
'Till we from error, sin, restored,   15
   Through Christ, thy Son, are wholly thine.

Poem No. 767; c. 2 January 1879

Our Lighthouses

The sun has set; but lit the Light,
   Which guides the vessels on their way;
Far o'er the ocean's gathering gloom
   It sends its bright and cheering ray.

Nor this alone; but many a lamp   5
   Along our coast and lakes will burn;
Each, through the night, a guiding star,
   Till day's o'erpowering beams return.

And faithful men their watches keep
    Through the cold, stormy, winter nights;   10
They slumber not when duty calls,
    But rise, and trim their warning lights.

Were one, before the morning dawns,
    To dim, or quench its guiding ray,
How many souls might meet their doom!   15
    How many wrecks might strew the bay!

Returning from a distant land,
    Joyful the Light the sailor hails;
And guided by its friendly beams,
    Soon, safe in port, he furls his sails.   20

Poem No. 578; c. 4 February 1879

The African's First Sight of the Ocean

Dr. Livingstone's Travels.

Without an end the world had seemed,
    A boundless plain, where they were born;
Stretching beyond the setting sun,
    And where again it rose at morn.

And so the ancients them had taught,   5
    Their fathers' fathers all believed;
Nor of an end they ere had dreamed,
    But as the truth their words received.

But when they saw the ocean wide,
    And all its grandeur on them broke;   10
With wonder and amazement filled,
    The voice of Nature in them spoke.

The world itself they seemed to hear
    Say, "I am finished! I am no more!"
The world your fathers boundless thought,   15
    Is ended at the ocean's shore.

The end! Oh thought beyond our grasp,
 Which earth, and sky, and ocean teach;
To which all Nature witness bears,
 Though not in transient human speech.   20

Poem No. 850; 4 March 1879

The Zodiacal Light

Strange light, long lingering in the west,
 With its pale saffron glow!
In vain thy origin we seek,
 Or mystery strive to know.

Unlike the noonday's dazzling beams,   5
 Or sunset's colors bright,
Or the moon's faint, reflected rays,
 Or the stars' silvery light;

Art thou a radiance from the earth?
 Corona of the sun?   10
Or light of meteor's golden band,
 Which round the globe doth run?

We know not whence the radiant glow,
 That fills us with delight;
On which, admiring, oft we gaze   15
 Till fading into night!

A light, whose mystery allures
 The thoughtful, musing mind;
And leads it on in wonder, awe,
 The hidden cause to find.   20

Poem No. 443; c. 28 March 1879

Education

What is it to educate a human soul?
Is it to teach it how to read, and write,
Grammar, Arithmetic; is this the whole?
Can these alone teach it to live aright?
Such knowledge is but means unto an end,   5
Too oft to earth's brief, narrow sphere confined;
But higher thoughts there are, that these transcend,
Motives enduring as the human mind;
The love of knowledge, human and divine,
The love of goodness, purity, and truth;   10
Happy the teacher, who can souls incline
To virtuous ends, in early days of youth;
And, while he useful knowledge doth impart,
Inspires the soul, the teacher's noblest art.

Poem No. 775; c. 11 April 1879

The Kingdom of Heaven
In Its Growth and Coming a Mystery

As swift the changing seasons come and go,
That Summer comes before we are aware;
And we are living midst its beauteous show,
A new creation wonderful and fair;
So, unperceived, God's kingdom cometh too!   5
Hid from the slothful and the worldly wise;
The heavenly seed is to its nature true,
And in the harvest will thy soul surprise.
By night, by day, there is an Unseen Power,
That to perfection brings each word, and deed;   10
Surely as buried grain or blooming flower
Become in Autumn the perfected seed.
We sleep, and rise; they grow we know not how,
And soon the harvest waves, where went the plough.

Poem No. 57; c. 6 June 1879

Azalea Swamp

Just o'er the stony wall,
   And near the travelled way,
The wild Azalea's fragrant flowers
   Their richest bloom display.

The travellers, as they pass,   5
   Stop to admire their bloom;
Or, wafted on the summer breeze,
   To catch the sweet perfume.

Why seek in distant lands
   Azaleas costly, rare;   10
When by the roadside bloom, for all,
   These, not less fragrant, fair?

Here too the woodwax spreads
   Its brilliant cloth of gold,
Richer by far than princes' halls   15
   Or palaces behold.

Nor can their artists show,
   With e'en their highest skill,
Such colors as are lavished here
   On swamp and rocky hill.   20

Renewed from year to year,
   The picture never tires;
Awakening thoughts and feelings deep
   No artist's work inspires.

Poem No. 310; c. 27 June 1879

Guido's Aurora

Not with bright forms alone, that please the eye,
Aurora comes encircled by the Hours;
Whose feet, in measure, tread the purple sky,
Such forms as love to sport in Summer's bowers;
But nobler forms, for duty's calls sublime,   5

With garments fitted for life's daily toil;
Knowing the worth to man of fleeting time,
Nor fearing lest their shining robes they soil.
Their earnest looks are on their business bent,
To finish every task ere day shall fade;   10
To use each moment for the purpose lent,
Till falls on earth again the evening's shade;
When the day's labors and its noises cease,
And the night brings its gifts of rest and peace.

Poem No. 370; c. July 1879

The Humming Bird

Like thoughts that flit across the mind,
   Leaving no lasting trace behind;
The humming bird darts to and fro,
   Comes, vanishes before we know.

While thoughts may be but airy things,   5
   That come and go on viewless wings,
Nor form, nor substance e'en possess,
   Nor number know, or more, or less;

This leaves an image, well defined,
   To be a picture of the mind;   10
Its tiny form and colors bright
   In memory live, when lost to sight.

There oft it comes at evening's hour,
   To flutter still from flower to flower;
Then vanish midst the gathering shade,   15
   Its momentary visit paid.

Poem No. 317; c. 8 August 1879

Jupiter as the Evening Star

Calm o'er the hills the evening star
   Majestic rises on the sight,
Sending its brilliant rays afar
   To wake our wonder and delight.

The evening shadows gently fall 5
   On all the varied landscape round,
And a deep silence broods o'er all,
   As Nature sinks in sleep profound.

And stilled the tumults in the breast,
   As on the lovely scene I gaze; 10
For every feeling is at rest,
   Save that which fills the heart with praise.

The hills are touched by the soft beams;
   As Memory lights the gathering shade,
Where youth's bright hopes and golden dreams, 15
   In years long past, grow dim and fade.

Shine lonely Star! the heart to cheer
   With feelings pure, serene, and high,
Above this dark and earthly sphere,
   Where youth's fair visions never die. 20

Poem No. 86; c. 16 September 1879

The National Thanksgiving

The harvests with abundance fill the land,
And call for gratitude and festive song;
And industry revives on every hand,
Which from war's wasteful scourge has suffered long.
And fell disease, that wasted day by day, 5
Is checked and staid, confined to narrow bound;
That else might thousands and ten thousands slay,
And desolate a fertile region round!
Our fathers' God! who, in their sore distress,
Did'st save from famine and from dangers dire, 10

And gav'st them shelter in the wilderness;
Our hearts with praise and gratitude inspire,
For all thy mercies to our fathers shown,
And for unnumbered blessings all our own.

Poem No. 507; c. 27 November 1879

The Stock-Gilly Flowers

When hides the sun behind the hills,
    And shortest days are seen;
How beautiful are Christmas flowers,
    Or wreaths of Christmas green!

All else has faded from my mind,   5
    That dark December day;
Save that full wagon load of flowers,
    That stood beside the way.

Stock-Gilly plants in bloom, for sale,
    Sprinkled with falling snow;   10
That made the chill and wintry scene
    With warmest colors glow.

And many a home those flowers made bright,
    When earth was brown and sere,
Or buried deep beneath the snows,   15
    And naught around to cheer.

And there, as in the open air,
    They shed their sweet perfume;
Long years have passed, but linger still
    Their fragrance and their bloom.   20

Poem No. 787; c. 23 December 1879

Spiritual Intercourse

They cannot come to us though we
    May long for them to come;
And leave, with us on earth to be,
    Their blest, eternal home;
The parents we have loved so well,   5
    The children that we mourn,
They cannot come, with us to dwell,
    From that mysterious bourn.

They cannot come to dwell on earth,
    And leave their heavenly sphere;   10
A life there is of higher birth,
    As earthly life is here;
A life of holy service, love,
    Which here we but begin,
Employs them in that home above,   15
    Which they have entered in!

Yet in the brightness of the day,
    And in the shades of night,
We are with them, with us are they
    Though not revealed to sight;   20
For memory's bright unbroken chain
    Doth bind us heart to heart,
Hope whispers we shall meet again,
    Meet nevermore to part.

Ah, who would have them here again,   25
    To suffer and to die;
To leave, for the abodes of men,
    Their happy homes on high?
Better that we should patience learn,
    And strive like them to be;   30
Than vainly sigh for their return,
    That we our friends may see.

Cold winter's blasts they feel no more,
    Nor summer's burning rage,
Disease, and pain, and death are o'er,   35
    The want and ills of age;

And, in that peaceful, happy clime,
  War cannot hurt, nor kill;
For past the fleeting years of time,
  Their mingled good and ill.   40

No more with doubts they struggle on,
  Nor walk in Error's night;
Their doubts and errors all are gone
  In heaven's unclouded light;
For God their light and glory is,   45
  His truth their minds doth fill;
And Christ doth own them now as his,
  Who did his Father's will.

They come not; but to them we go,
  That higher life to share;   50
The life begun by them below
  Midst earthly toil, and care;
Whate'er of good, or ill we've sown,
  We then with them shall reap;
We then shall know as we are known,   55
  No soul its secret keep.

And, in our Heavenly Father's time,
  We shall united be;
To share that intercourse sublime
  Of joy and purity;   60
Oh, let us then for this prepare,
  While yet the light is given;
That we the life and bliss may share
  Of those we love in heaven.

Poem No. 638; c. 3 February 1880

Invitation to the Robin

Come, Robin, come, and sing to me,
  —The winter time has gone—
Upon the ancient locust tree,
  That silent stands, and lone.

For pleasant now the spring-like days,   5
    I long thy voice to hear,
And listen to thy morning lays,
    So full of joy and cheer.

Thou art a Messenger of love,
    And dost glad tidings bring;   10
Thy prophecy our hearts doth move,
    True Herald of the Spring!

That soon the pastures will be green,
    The early flowers appear,
The blossoms and the leaves be seen,   15
    And May's fair month be here.

In thy glad message we rejoice,
    No longer then delay!
We long to hear thy cheerful voice,
    And list thy morning lay.   20

Poem No. 91; c. 12 March 1880

The Influence of Channing

Stern creeds and outward forms must pass away,
Their purpose served to guard the Life within;
We hail the Advent of a milder Day,
Whose dawn on earth at length we see begin!
Channing, though thy frail form no more we see,   5
Nor hear, as once, thy calm persuasive voice,
Thou livest still! we hail thy Jubilee,
And in thy growing influence would rejoice.
The love of God and man thy simple creed;
The love of man as an immortal soul,   10
That has the slave from cruel bondage freed,
And shall War's desolating wrath controul.
Still may thy influence spread from clime to clime,
And win new victories with the years of time.

Poem No. 435; c. 8 April 1880

The Calling

The Voice that spake to Abraham of old,
Go, leave thy Country, to our fathers spake;
And made them, with like faith and courage bold,
The ties of kindred and of home to break.
Austere and strict were they, yet kind and pure;   5
Above the common level they had risen,
And, taught by Persecution to endure,
Their faith and hopes were fixed on God and heaven.
Why name, among those worthies bold and true,
Brave-hearted Endicott, who led the van;   10
Or Higginson, who, midst the suffering few,
Lent glory to the name of Puritan?
Beyond the western ocean's farthest bound
New homes they sought, a Commonwealth to found.

Poem No. 587; c. 1878–80

Endecott

Amidst a band of worthies bold and true
The noble Endecott was in the van,
The gallant leader of the suffering few,
Who gloried in the name of Puritan.
Austere and strict was he, yet kind and pure,   5
Above the common level he had risen;
And, taught by Persecution to endure,
His hopes, like theirs, were fixed on God, and heaven.
His wife and children with him too embark,
His firm attachment to the cause to prove;   10
What precious freight was trusted to that ark!
Of Faith and Hope, of Purity and Love;
When were such treasures on the ocean cast
The sport of the wild waves, and stormy blast?

Poem No. 39; c. 1878–80

Farewell

"Farewell dear England, and thy Church farewell!
Farewell all Christian friends abiding there!"
Such were the words from Puritans that fell;
A holy benediction, and a prayer,
As from old England's coast our fathers sailed;   5
Sweet memories and tender filled each heart,
And o'er the sense of loss & wrongs prevailed,
How hard from homes and dearest friends to part!
What gave them courage, o'er the ocean wide,
To seek upon this wild, and unknown shore,   10
Freedom to worship God, at home denied?
And what sustained them in the toils they bore?
Conscience, that doth self-sacrifice approve,
And trust in God's protecting care and love.

Poem No. 116; c. 1878–80

The Departure

The tall white cliffs of England fade away,
They leave with tears their father land behind;
The monsters of the deep around them play,
And onward swift they speed before the wind.
Backward they gaze, alas! how soon have fled   5
Their happy homes, green fields, and village spires;
While all around the waves of ocean spread,
As if the grave of all their heart's desires!
Seaward they turn; but lonely, dim, and drear,
The ocean stretches on as without end;   10
And fancy peoples it with shapes of fear,
And trials hard, with which they must contend;
With many an anxious thought they seek their rest,
Dreaming of home, though tossed on ocean's breast.

Poem No. 476-581; c. 1878–80

The Petrels

Day dawns again, with wondering gaze they see
The stormy petrels skim the waves' rough crests,
Or, lighting in the hollows of the sea,
Securely sit as on their shore-built nests.
And shall not He, who doth for these provide,   5
Without a shelter and without a home,
His children keep, and guard whate'er betide,
Whate'er their straits, or wheresoe'er they roam?
Such thoughts sustain;—for oft, by humble means,
The Lord instructs the lowly, trusting mind;   10
Who on his arm alone for safety leans,
Shall, in his Word and works, direction find;
Whether on land, or sea, afar they rove,
His guardian care and love alike, they prove.

Poem No. 96; c. 1878–80

At Sea

Day follows day, and week succeeds to week,
And still they sail across the boundless main;
New homes in distant regions far to seek,
And civil and religious freedom gain.
How little do the timid landsmen know   5
Of sailors' toils, and watches on the sea;
When night returns, when loud the tempests blow,
What hardships, and what perils there may be!
While safe beneath the sheltering roof they sleep,
Nor heed the rising blast, nor dashing wave;   10
The seamen must their watchful vigils keep,
Lest ocean, at each moment, prove their grave;
Or, driven by tempests on some desert shore,
They see their native land and friends no more.

Poem No. 97; c. 1878–80

At Sea

Frail woman there and childhood's tender years
Endure the hardships of the seaman's life;
Yielding at times, unto their natural fears,
While gazing on the ocean's fearful strife;
How strange on the wide ocean thus to be!   5
Where naught is seen around but sea and skies;
Shall they again the shore in safety see,
They ask? and westward gaze with longing eyes.
The gorgeous clouds at sunset mock their sight
With mountains, valleys, forests, harbors near;   10
But, as they fade away, with fading light,
Their high-raised hopes as often disappear;
And farther e'en than ever seems the land,
Which but an hour before, looked close at hand.

Poem No. 137; c. 1878–80

The Sabbath

Bright is the morn, and hushed is every sound,—
For e'en the sea has stilled its tossing breast;—
With reverent looks the seamen gather round,
And, with the passengers, from labor rest.
Hark, rising on the still, bright morning air,   5
Their blended voices charm the listening deep;
Succeeded by the solemn words of prayer,
As, on the ocean, they the sabbath keep:
The preacher then his lesson doth impart,
Drawn from God's Word, and works, which they behold;   10
His simple teachings touch and cheer the heart,
As he the text of Scripture doth unfold,
Of Trust in God; on sea, as on the land;
Who holds us ever in his mighty hand.

Poem No. 79; c. 1878–80

Land

They near the coast; the land-birds hover round,
Far out upon the ocean sent before;
With flowers and leaves the rippling waves abound,
Washed by the tide from off their native shore;
The air with fragrant odors too is filled,   5
Borne o'er the sea, from unseen, flowery fields,
Forerunning signals to the seamen skilled,
To whom each trifling thing some knowledge yields.
No Lights on island, cape, or rock they see,
By which to steer their courses through the night,   10
They shorten sail, lest danger there may be,
And anxious wait for morning's cheerful light;
Day dawns at length, the land! the land! they cry,
And the New World is seen by every eye.

Poem No. 646; c. 1878–80

Salem

They reach a harbor spacious and secure,
With wooded islands at its entrance found;
And fair, green pastures, springs of water pure,
And pleasant groves of different wood abound;
The rocky hills, that round about it stand,   5
O'erlook the sea and country far and wide;
Like the stern chieftains of their native land,
They wear a look of freedom, and of pride:
Salem they call the spot. Here peace and rest
From prelates proud and kings they hope to find,   10
With civil and religious Freedom blest;
Such blessings God will give to all mankind;
And break the double yoke and heavy chain,
Which tyrants, for their race, have forged in vain.

Poem No. 647; c. 1878–80

The Landing

With flag unfurled along the shore they sail
By pleasant cove and by the rippling beach,
Till heard from land the joyous Planters' hail,
As they a fitting place for anchorage search.
These Planters welcome them with homely cheer,   5
In their log cabins, on the rising ground;
O'erjoyed from distant friends again to hear,
That with success at length their prayers are crowned!
Their joy how full how deep they only know,
Who, sick with hope deferred, have waited long;   10
What solitude was theirs, who here had dwelt
Through two long winters in this forest wild,
And many a storm and sad privation felt,
By hope of aid from father-land beguiled!

Poem No. 428-835a; c. 1878–80

The Old Planters

Nor slightly pass those early planters by,
Whose names and fortunes are less known to fame;
Who can the nobleness and worth deny,
Which ever must adorn a Conant's name?
Or who o'erlook the few, brave pioneers,   5
Who with him to this spot in duty clung,
With none to help, through two, long, trying years.
Would that by worthier verse their praise were sung!
The Christian love that seeketh not her own,
That envieth not another's gifts, was theirs;   10
And while the name of Salem shall be known,
Or one descendant in her glory shares,
The memory of their virtues shall remain
A theme for history and the poet's strain.

Poem No. 359; c. 1878–80

Paradise

How lovely in the warm September days,
The hills, and groves, and winding rivers clear;
Across the stream, where now I love to gaze,
They named it Paradise, who first came here;
And such, when Autumn changed the forests' hue,   5
Dying their leaves a thousand varied dies,
Did Salem seem unto the pilgrims' view,
Bathed in the golden light of Autumn's skies!
The grapes hung clustering from the lofty trees,
The nut groves showered their ripened fruit around,   10
'Twas all their own to settle where they please,
The scattered Planters only here they found;
Or Indians roving still from place to place,
As seasons came for fishing, or the chase.

Poem No. 192; c. 1878–80

Naumkeck River

Up Naumkeck they sail, and far explore,
Upon each side, the unknown region round;
Upon the left, the locusts line the shore,
Where on the sandy bank they still are found;
Upon the right, the oak and walnut grow,   5
Towards the west, high rocky hills arise,
Where pines and savins dark their shadows throw;
While, at their feet, the grassy meadow lies;
Within the woods strange birds unnumbered sing,
The lively squirrels leap from tree to tree,   10
The sun-bright brooks their crystal tribute bring
To swell the tide that's hastening to the sea;
On every side, where'er they turn their eyes,
New sights and sounds the voyagers surprise.

Poem No. 752; c. 1878–80

The Same

Much they admire the wild flowers scattered wide,
Their gorgeous asters, purple, white, and blue,
The golden rod that fringed the river's side,
And the wild rose on every side that grew.
To each new object, bird, or flower, or tree,   5
They give the old and fond-remembered name;
And, though but slight resemblance there may be,
Called by the self-same word, they seem the same.
Another robin-red breast here they find,
Their morn and evening meals with them to share,   10
They teach their children to it to be kind,
And oft, in winter, crumbs for it to spare;
For not mere creatures of the earth we live,
But to each scene ideal life we give.

Poem No. 332; c. 1878–80

Winter

The perils of the ocean safely o'er,
Their hearts with glad emotions free expand;
Ah, little think they of the trials sore,
That wait them inexperienced on the land;
Swift fly the warm and pleasant Autumn days,   5
And Winter comes before they are aware;
The falling leaf its near approach betrays,
And morn and eve the keen and frosty air;
The rudest dwellings they can scarcely rear,
Before the blasts of Winter howl around;   10
With their cold breath glassing the waters clear,
And burying deep with snow the frozen ground,
Making the unknown wilderness more wild,
That late with such a pleasant welcome smiled.

Poem No. 539; c. 1878–80

Location

With sturdy blows the echoing woods resound,
Startling their tenants from their leafy lairs;
The lofty oaks and pines soon strew the ground,
Where each a shelter for himself prepares.
Between the rivers, on the highest land,   5
They build their cabins to each other near;
That they may thus the savage foe withstand;
Though brave of heart, his cunning wiles they fear.
Soon curls the smoke above the forest trees,
Marking amidst the wild their chosen spot;   10
Think not that palaces alone can please;
Contentment loves to dwell in humble cot,
Where Piety and Industry reside;
But shuns the gilded domes and halls of pride.

Poem No. 845; c. 1878–80

The Home

See! from yon low-roofed cottage shines a light,
To guide the absent homeward on his way;
On mantled bush, and tree, and meadow white,
It throws its ruddy glare and cheerful ray.
There, sheltered from the cold, the aged sire,   5
And mother with their children gather round;
Beside the hearthstone and the blazing fire,
When day is o'er, their chief delights are found.
The absent one they welcome from his toil,
And for them all is spread the frugal board;   10
Perhaps from sea he brings the fisher's spoil,
Or home returns with what the woods afford;
The sire doth bless, with grateful heart, the food,
Sent from the bounteous Source of every good.

Poem No. 412; c. 1878–80

The Home

The supper o'er, with books, or converse sweet,
Or lightsome tasks the happy hours they spend;
Perhaps some tale of olden time repeat,
Or welcome give to neighbor, and to friend;
Of the new Country and its sights they tell,   5
Of Indian wiles and savage beasts of prey;
And now their voices loud in concert swell,
As pleased they sing some simple, household lay.
Dear Social Joys! that, on our journey here,
Reflect the hues of heaven's serener clime;   10
Through the dark vista seen of many a year,
How brightly shines your lamp, undimmed by time,
To guide the wanderer, wheresoe'er he roam,
Till he shall gain his sure, eternal home!

Poem No. 579; c. 1878–80

Sickness

With sickness and with famine they contend,
No help can reach them till another year;
The dreary Winter seems to have no end,
And oft the savage foe awakes their fear;
From want, exposure, and attendant ills,   5
Full eighty of their number sink and die;
Grave after grave Death unrelenting fills,
And side by side the strong and feeble lie!
How dear is sympathy in our distress,
As did the Puritans in trouble prove;   10
A kind physician comes to heal and bless,
The messenger of Plymouth's early love;
Such help as sufferers can to sufferers send,
The Plymouth pilgrims to their brethren lend.

Poem No. 842; c. 1878–80

Longing

How oft, with homesick hearts, their fancy flies
Back to Old England o'er the wintry main;
And thoughts of distant friends bedew their eyes,
Whom they on earth may never see again;
Musing they start! amid the deepening gloom,   5
And think the forms of distant friends they see;
And e'en at times, within the darkened room,
The buried dead with them would seem to be!
Sickly and weak how oft, with anxious gaze,
From yonder hills they searched the ocean o'er?   10
Spring slowly comes, with many backward days,
Before the longed-for fleet has reached the shore;
When scarce provisions for a week remain,
Their failing strength and courage to sustain.

Poem No. 196; c. 1878–80

Winthrop's Fleet

But help arrives! The welcome fleet appears!
From the high hill-top first by one perceived
Far out at sea; then up the harbor steers;
Scarcely for joy the tidings are believed;
Soon friend clasps friend in heartfelt warm embrace,   5
Awhile their mutual sufferings are forgot;
Mindful alone they see each other's face,
And share again for life each other's lot.
And welcome too the comforts, and supplies,
Which, in their strait, the timely vessels bring;   10
From house to house the message quickly flies,
To each how precious then the smallest thing;
Taught by stern want, and hard necessity,
In things we little prize their wealth to see.

Poem No. 83; c. 1878–80

Arabella Johnson

As fades the delicate flower of Southern skies,
Transplanted to our cold New England shore,
At the first chilling touch of Winter dies,
And we behold its beauteous tints no more;
So did the Lady Arabella fade!   5
The fairest flower of Winthrop's numerous band;
Near yonder shore her fragile form is laid,
Mourned by each plaintive wave that beats the strand!
A courtly splendor and a life of ease
She left for one of trial, want, and pain;   10
Seeking her conscience, and her God to please,
And counting loss for Christ eternal gain!
A ministering angel to his suffering fold,
She shared the hardships of the strong and bold.

Poem No. 53; c. 1878–80

Spring

The Spring returns, and, with fresh ardor filled,
Their interrupted labors they renew;
The land is cleared, the virgin soil is tilled,
Some the stout oaks for houses fell and hew,
Some build a fort against their savage foe,   5
Some guard from beasts and birds the springing grain,
While some in boats to sea a fishing go,
To dare the perils of the stormy main;
With energy and zeal the work proceeds,
No one is idle, and they all unite   10
In common cause, as each assistance needs,
By which the heaviest labors are made light;
For the same ardor every bosom fires,
And one great object here on earth inspires.

Poem No. 572; c. 1878–80

Motive

They came not from afar from lust of gain,
Which lures adventurers to a distant shore;
Nor followed they some mighty conqueror's train,
Whose track through earth is red with human gore;
No common purpose did their souls inspire,   5
No earthly object did their vision fill;
God's Kingdom here to found their sole desire,
And, unmolested, here to do his will;
For this He called them from their native land,
For this He led them through the pathless sea,   10
For this upheld them by his mighty hand,
In sickness, death, and bitter poverty;
Causing e'en savage hearts to melt, and share
With them, in their distress, their scanty fare.

Poem No. 637; c. 1878–80

The Church

Soon to his Name they rear a temple rude,
Where they may worship God, the Lord of all;
First Church of Christ, in this vast solitude,
Gathered and formed obedient to his call.
With simple forms, they, for themselves, ordain   5
A pastor, and a teacher them to lead;
Their minds in their great trials to sustain,
And with the bread of Life their hunger feed.
Amidst the service, lo! a pilgrim band,
By adverse winds and waves, till then delayed,   10
From Plymouth comes; to offer the right hand,
With messages of love, and cheer conveyed;
May sacred bonds, thus formed in early day,
Endure when temples built with hands decay.

Poem No. 431; c. 1878–80

Worship

But, still preserved by pious care behold,
As if too sacred for Time's ruthless hand,
The house our fathers built to God of old,
Its ancient form unchanged as once they planned!
Assembling there they meet for praise and prayer,   5
And reverent listen to the preachéd word;
As Higginson, with eloquence, declares
The truths of God with which his soul is stirred.
In psalms and hymns together too they raise
Their notes of gratitude and holy joy,   10
No tremblings mingle with their tuneful lays,
For none there are their worship to annoy;
Inspired with Christian liberty they sing,
And with their songs the desert places ring!

Poem No. 84; c. 1878–80

Song

They sing of Zion, city built of old,
Jerusalem compacted, high, and fair;
Whither the tribes went up their feasts to hold,
And where established thrones of judgement were.
They sing how God, in ancient times, had led   5
His chosen people through a desert way,
How He by miracle their hunger fed,
And mighty acts by Moses did display;
How He drove out the heathen from their place,
And gave his people in their land to dwell;   10
That they might ever stand before His face,
And of his deeds to children's children tell;
And while they kept his holy just command,
Inherit still, as theirs, the promised land.

Poem No. 648; c. 1878–80

Here let the Church her holy mission prove
Of Truth and Liberty of Love and Joy
The image of that heavenly House above
Which naught again shall threaten or destroy
Within her walls wide as the social state   5
Through countless years may all the people throng
With joyful hearts and countenances sedate
To bow in worship and to join in song
No more without her fold may Childhood stray
To wander in the desert parched and wild   10
Forgetful of the strait and narrow way
By Pleasure's voice from virtue's path beguiled
But happy in her sacred courts remain
Its heart still young its robe without a stain.

Poem No. 170; c. 1878–80

The Puritan Church and State

I.

They envied not the vast Cathedral's pile,
Its high-hung roof filled with the organ's sound,
Its pictured windows, and the long-drawn aisle,
With dim religious light o'er all around;
Its ceremonial forms seemed stiff and cold,   5
No more the vesture of Immortal Truth;
But rather like her cast off garments old,
Which once she wore in infancy and youth.
In manhood's form to them did she appear,
From childish rites and childish errors free,   10
In virtue and in discipline severe,
And beckoned them across an unknown sea;
In a new world, with worship free and pure,
To found a Church which ever should endure.

Poem No. 641; c. 1878–80

The Puritan Church and State

II.

New depths of truth within God's holy Word,
They saw from age to age would be revealed;
As men, to Revelation's light restored,
Pondered the Book by Priestcraft long concealed.
By this the Reformation of the Church they sought,   5
That pure and perfect it might rise again;
Built on the Corner Stone, that brings to naught
The creeds and systems formed by erring men:
The right to search the Scriptures they maintained,
Each for himself, unbiassed and alone;   10
Such was the right, which Christ himself proclaimed,
Who would to every soul his truth make known;
That each from human bondage might be free,
And all in one great family agree.

Poem No. 352; c. 1878–80

The Puritan Church and State

III.

Not bound by slavish bondage to the Past,
They a new form of Government unfold;
Which shall the mighty monarchies outlast,
Founded by kings and conquerors of old;
For this was founded on the Rights of man,   5
And all alike might in its freedom share;
No worldly scheme, no narrow, selfish plan
Did they for this vast continent prepare.
Self government their high and noble aim,
Events their teacher, Providence their guide,   10
Their Polity a gradual growth became;
Oft was the State by error, conflict tried;
Yet still advancing towards the perfect goal,
The highest good and welfare of the whole.

Poem No. 361; c. 1878–80

Appeal

Ye who behold the State in grandeur rise,
By Industry and Virtue still sustained;
Learn, from the page of History, to be wise!
By the same arts it rose a state's maintained.
Remember too your fathers' early toil,   5
When first adventuring to this distant shore;
How slowly they subdued the stubborn soil,
And every want and every suffering bore,
For Conscience' sake, that doth uphold the just;
From their example learn ye to endure,   10
And in your fathers' God, still place your trust;
So shall you find his word of promise sure,
And, when you hear of Massachusetts' name,
Blush with an honest pride to own her fame.

Poem No. 857; c. 1878–80

Influence of Puritanism

See, gentle as the light, their Influence spread
From state to state, from east to western shore;
Till, like the night, the shadows all are fled,
And Ignorance shall cloud our land no more.
The Indian tribes, far wandering shall behold   5
The beams of knowledge on their pathway shine;
And of the Gospel's sacred truths be told,
And own their power and influence all divine.
The African, with new awakened mind,
Rejoice in Freedom's full and perfect day;   10
And blessings, in the coming ages, find,
Far more than shall for all his wrongs repay;
And universal as the race of man,
Shall be the name and praise of Puritan.

Poem No. 413; c. 1878–80

The Bible

That Church they founded on the Word of God,
Thy Word is Truth, their single, only creed;
Obeying this they feared not princes' nod,
And this from prelates' iron yoke had freed.
As the One Spirit did its words reveal,   5
They strove its holy precepts to obey;
From this in Church and State was no appeal,
For none God's just commandments could gainsay.
Within the family, and in the school,
That Word was morn and eve devoutly read;   10
Ye, their descendants still observe the rule,
Not by the letter, but the Spirit led;
So shall our social fabric stand secure,
Long as the sun, and moon, and stars endure!

Poem No. 456; c. 1878–80

The Common School

The School-house next they build, a structure small,
Near to the Meeting House, upon the green;
A noble structure built, like that, for all,
Noble, though in appearance rough, and mean;
But judge not by the sight, the purpose scan;   5
An angel guest oft comes in lowly guise;
And, on some narrow scale, the mightiest plan
Works unperceived, at first, by human eyes:
Here all the young were taught to read and write,
The rich, and poor the same great boon enjoyed;   10
So long withheld in Superstition's night,
Who would the mind's fair Temple have destroyed;
And those, who sought to instruct, and bless mankind,
Within her dungeons' rayless depths confined.

Poem No. 555; c. 1878–80

A Christian Commonwealth

Seeking a Christian Commonwealth to found,
Our fathers deep its true foundations laid
In pure Religion and in Learning sound,
By wise instructors to the young conveyed;
They sought no harvest, where they had not sown   5
Broad cast the seeds of Christian knowledge pure,
They knew that by its fruit the tree is known,
By Virtue only can a State endure.
In vain did they unto the red men preach
The truths, revealed by God mankind to save;   10
In vain the arts of life they sought to teach,
And Learning's lore upon their minds engrave;
Heedless of knowledge, they must soon decay,
Before a wiser race they melt away!

Poem No. 416; c. 1878–80

Discontent

Sigh not for richer lands, nor milder skies,
Ye whom these hills and ocean's prospect bound;
Within the mind itself man's fortune lies,
And where men are, are power and riches found.
Sigh not for California's golden strand,   5
Nor covet the broad prairies' richer soil;
By steady industry on sea and land,
Your frugal wants supply by honest toil;
And richer harvests in the virtues reap
Of those, who made these rocky shores their home,   10
And here on sunny hill-sides saintly sleep;
Than they, who to earth's farthest borders roam;
For these have left to earth, and sea, and sky,
A beauty of the soul that cannot die!

Poem No. 421; c. 1878–80

Conclusion

Descendants of the Puritans! whose fame
Shall brighter grow with every coming age,
See that ye tarnish not their honest name,
But add new lustre to the historic page;
Yours are the Church and State for which they fled   5
Their father land, and sought this distant shore;
For which in after times they fought and bled,
And every want and every suffering bore;
In their free spirit still your rights maintain
'Gainst every secret, every open foe;   10
The laws of God above all laws sustain,
And in your minds and hearts His precepts know;
Till earth, restored from error and from sin,
Her great Millennial Day of Love and Peace begin!

Poem No. 99; c. 1878–80

The Old Organ
Of The East Society Salem

Burdened with precious memories of the past,
How oft again thy mighty voice I hear;
Now rising, like the solemn swelling blast,
Now falling sweet and plaintive on the ear!
Expressing all the heart unuttered feels,   5
Its longing for another, higher life;
The grief and sorrow that no word reveals,
The outward conflict, and the inward strife.
And as the organist, with ready skill,
Touches the keys; again the School I see   10
Gathered around, and all the choir they fill;
Still lingers in my heart the melody
Of youthful voices, joined in concert sweet,
Within the choir, where we were wont to meet.

Poem No. 82; date unknown

On Some Beautiful Crocuses
In Front of the House of B. H. Silsbee, Esq.

Fair flowers! that open to the April sun
Your beauteous petals, purple, white, and gold,—
We joy with you that winter's race is run,
And gone its months of barrenness and cold.
There breathes around us now a softer air;   5
In frequent showers descends the quickening rain,
That doth the frozen earth for man prepare,
That he may sow for food the fruitful grain.
Not vain your beauty, though no outward good
You minister to man, and quickly die;   10
You fill his soul with hope, with heavenly food,
And higher wants than those of earth supply,
Long may you bloom, with each returning year,
The passer-by with pleasant looks to cheer!

Poem No. 109; date unknown

The Return of the Savior

Lo Christ returns! But where is love,
    The love he showed for men;
Does he behold it, here on earth,
    Returned to earth again?

Lo Christ returns! But where the faith,   5
    Which here on earth he sought;
The faith which overcomes the world,
    And mighty works has wrought?

And where is hope, which cheers the soul,
    The Spirit's fruit and joy;   10
Which doth like faith, and hope abide,
    And naught can ere destroy?

Ah, where are these? we see them not;
 But, Lord, we still believe;
Increase our faith, increase our love,   15
 That we may thee receive.

Poem No. 318; date unknown

The Kingdom of the Truth

Not of one sect thy kingdom is,
 O Savior, Guide of man;
'Tis his whoever loves the truth;
 E'en since the world began.

A kingdom 'tis of Righteousness,   5
 Of Purity, and Love;
Which all on earth, who seek, may find;
 As in the heavens above.

Whoever does confess thy name,
 Whoever hears thy voice;   10
Shall in that kingdom have a part,
 And in its light rejoice.

It shall destroy the works of sin,
 Which in the world abound;
The lofty towers of error, pride,   15
 Shall level with the ground.

Great is the truth, omnipotent;
 It cannot faint, nor fail;
O'er all the earth, in every land
 It shall at last prevail.   20

May each a faithful witness bear,
 Truth's kingdom enter in;
And, while on the earth we dwell,
 Its heavenly life begin.

Poem No. 365; date unknown

Sunset after a Clouded Day in April

O'er all the city comes a glow
  From the red setting sun;
Clouded since morn, it doth bestow
  A smile when day is done.

Its dwellings and their chimneys blaze   5
  With the red crimson light;
The lofty steeples catch the rays,
  And draw the admiring sight.

The leafless elms a glory wear;
  Their buds of golden brown,   10
Touched by the parting sunbeams fair,
  Become a beauteous crown.

The busy streets the radiance fills,
  We walk on heavenly ground;
The sudden glow lights up the hills,   15
  And all the prospect round.

Too bright, too beautiful to last,
  This light o'er Nature spread;
A few short moments, and 'tis past!
  The golden gleam has fled!   20

Poem No. 379; date unknown

Hymn
Prayer for the Gift of the Holy Spirit

Oh, heavenly gift of Love Divine,
  The Spirit's grace and power;
Come, in our hearts abide, and shine;
  How long delayed thine hour!

"Ask and receive," the Savior said,   5
  "And seek, and ye shall find;"
For we are weak without thine aid,
  Without thy light are blind.

Our heavenly Father loves us all;
   More ready He to give,   10
Than we upon his name to call,
   To turn to Him and live.

Lord, for thy coming us prepare,
   As Spring's soft showers the earth;
That we may, in the harvest, share,   15
   The soul's new life, and birth.

Oh, make us worthy of thy love,
   May we thy words believe;
Thy faithfulness now these shall prove
   And thy best gift receive.   20

Poem No. 382; date unknown

Hymn

Our voices with our hearts we lift
   To thee, O God, in grateful praise;
For every good, and perfect gift
   A song of gratitude we raise.

Thine is the seed in Spring we sow,   5
   And thine the harvests that we see;
Sunshine, and rain Thou dost bestow,
   And strength to labor comes from Thee.

Thine is the fragrance of the flowers,
   And beauty, that delights the eye;   10
And thine the hues of Autumn's bowers,
   Which in transfigured glory die.

O God, with all thy gifts still give
   The grateful, and the trusting heart;
So shall our souls have learned to live,   15
   When called from earthly scenes to part.

Poem No. 394; date unknown

Hymn
The Forms of Nature, and the Unity of their Origin

Seek not, in outward things,
   The origin and birth
Of animal, and plant, and seed,
   In air, or sea, or earth;
In vain their history we trace   5
   Through ages vast, through time and space.

From One Eternal Mind
   Have come the forms we see;
Those countless forms, whose difference make
   Nature's variety;   10
Each stamped with impress of its kind,
   And each to its own sphere confined.

No atom but obeys
   The One Creative Will;
Whose Word, beneficent and good,   15
   The universe doth fill;
Without which naught was made, or born,
   Which was before Creation's morn.

Globule and secret cell
   A history contain;   20
Which Science, with its marvellous powers,
   Still seeks to read in vain;
To the All Perfect Mind alone
   Their origin, and types are known.

In Nature's primal plan   25
   Prophetic types we see;
Which lead us onward up to Man,
   Their end, and destiny;
A unity of mind and thought
   Through every form and being wrought.   30

But, in her labyrinth lost,
   Too oft we miss the clue;
Which, midst her ever varying forms,
   Runs through the old, and new;

And in phenomena we rest,   35
    As of the truth itself possest.

Rest not, O Soul, till thou
    That clue, that thread shall find;
Without whose constant, guiding help,
    We wander dark and blind;   40
In endless mazes led astray,
    Missing the strait and narrow way.

For this still upward leads;
    Steep is the mount of Thought;
Which we, aspiring still, must climb,   45
    Till to the summit brought;
Where, with clear vision, we discern
    Nature's vast realm, her mysteries learn.

Poem No. 414; date unknown

Friendship
To J. M. S.

Sweet as it is for seamen, who have sailed
Long weeks with naught but sea and sky in view;
When they some friendly barque at length have hailed,
And the same course with her awhile pursue.
With gently-wafting wind they onward glide,   5
In pleasant converse pass the favored hour;
They part; but on the lonely ocean wide,
Midst other scenes, how oft they feel its power!
So sweet it is upon the voyage of life,
Midst heartless intercourse to meet a friend;   10
And for a time forget its cares and strife,
While mind with mind and soul with soul doth blend!
Would thus my friend that we might often meet
To enjoy the hours, alas, how few and fleet!

Poem No. 449; date unknown

Hymn
The Good Fight

The battle is within,
    And not on outward plain;
'Tis there the conflicts first begin
    And longest shall remain.

Our word, our thought, our deed,   5
    That battle still makes known;
We are not from the conflict freed,
    Till sin be overthrown.

The world doth claim the soul,
    As well as outward things;   10
It seeks the spirit to controul,
    Its hidden, vital springs.

The motive thou must scan,
    Which doth thy spirit move;
For 'tis the motive makes the man,   15
    And doth his virtue prove.

Thou needst a heavenly power,
    A mightier strength than thine,
To guard thee in temptation's hour;
    O, seek for strength divine.   20

Not with an outward foe
    Must thou the battle wage,
A mightier contest thou must know,
    Than warriors' martial rage.

Watch, pray, that thou mayst be   25
    A victor in the strife;
And God from sin shall set thee free,
    And give eternal life.

Poem No. 462; date unknown

The Day calling us to a New Life

The day goes on, but we are left behind,
Bright with its robes it travels o'er the earth,
Seeking its sons, in every land, to find,
And tells earth's children of a heavenly birth.
From early dawn to eve it travels on,   5
But few its beauty see, or hear its voice;
When, in the west, its glorious form is gone,
How few are they, who in its light rejoice!
'Tis but the natural day, that we perceive,
Its spiritual beauty's hidden from our sight;   10
The gifts of sense full gladly we receive
But fail in higher gifts to find delight;
We live but as the children of the earth,
When the day calls us to a nobler birth.

Poem No. 484; date unknown

To the Misses Williams,
On seeing their beautiful Paintings of Wild Flowers

The flowers of Spring had faded from my sight,
The summer flowers had come, and quickly gone;
Autumn was here; of Flora's children bright
Asters and goldenrods were left alone.
But, in thy pleasant room, their beauteous hues   5
And forms we saw restored by hand of Art,
That Nature's vanished scenes again renews,
To charm the mind, and cheer the saddened heart.
There violets and houstonia sweet,
Bloodroot and blue hepatica still bloom,   10
And blushing roses, from their wild retreat,
Make Spring and Summer inmates of thy room;
Why roam, O Artist, to a distant land,
With lovely scenes, and flowers so near at hand?

Poem No. 499; date unknown

Jacob wrestling with the Angel

The Patriarch wrestled with the angel long,
For though of mortal race, yet he was strong;
Nor would release him at the break of day,
That he might take his upward, heavenly way.
Bless me, he cried, ere I shall let thee go,   5
Thou art an angel, and no mortal foe;
Who, through the night's dark hours, couldst thus maintain
With me a contest on the starry plain.
What is thy name? the angel asked again,
For thou hast power alike with God, and men.   10
Jacob, he said. The angel blessed him there,
Henceforth the name of Israel thou shalt bear;
Thou hast prevailed, thou art a Prince indeed,
A blessing rest on thee, and on thy seed.
Deem not that to those ancient times belong   15
The wonders told in history, and in song;
Men may with angels now, as then, prevail;
Too oft, alas! they in the contest fail.
Their blessed help is not from man withdrawn,
Contend thou with the angel till the dawn;   20
A blessing he to earth for thee doth bring,
Then back to heaven again his flight will wing.

Poem No. 538; date unknown

Rain Clouds

The promises they give, alas, to fail!
   They bring not to our hills and fields relief;
To distant regions onward still they sail,
   Leaving the hopeful husbandman to grief.

Perhaps less earnest for the gift he prays   5
   Than others where the rain clouds hastening go
Thus to our coast the blessing God delays
   Who freely doth on all his gifts bestow.

Perhaps more needed than with us the rain,
   More dry and parched than ours some distant shore,   10
Without its aid man's labors prove in vain,
   And he his blighted harvest sad deplore.

How little still of what we need we know,
   How soon we yield to doubt, or dark despair,
How are our minds engrossed with things below,   15
   How weak our faith in God, our trust in prayer!

To us, perhaps, upon its humid wings
   Already doth the wind commissioned speed
To swell the rivers, fill the falling springs
   Relieve distress provide for future need.   20

Poem No. 545; date unknown

The Soul in Dreams

The soul heeds not, though darkest night
   Each object doth conceal;
In dreams it sees the noonday light,
   Which all things doth reveal.

Nor doth it heed the Winter's snow,   5
   That deep around it lies,
Nor wintry winds that piercing blow;
   But in sweet dreams it flies

Where Summer clothes each vale and hill,
   And plucks its fruits and flowers;   10
And wanders freely at its will
   Amid its blooming bowers.

To gardens ever green and fair,
   Where blooms the deathless rose,
Where deathless lilies scent the air,   15
   It oft in slumber goes.

'Tis not to sense, nor Nature kin,
   Nor grows it ever old;
Though dim the eye, and mind within,
   It can its youth behold.   20

For 'tis of a celestial birth,
    And casts around it here
A glory, that is not of earth,
    But of its native sphere.

Poem No. 569; date unknown

Our Native Sparrows

The sparrows still are lingering here,
    Though winter-time has come;
Within the swamp, or piny wood,
    They find a sheltering home.

They flit along the turnpike's side,   5
    As in the early Spring;
Though they no songs of pleasant cheer
    May to the passer bring.

Nor are they left, when Autumn's past,
    To perish in their need;   10
They still find every want supplied
    With berries, grain and seed.

They need no care of man to feed,
    Nor for them to provide
A shelter, in the wintry storm,   15
    Where they may safe abide.

Our heavenly Father cares for them,
    Who cares alike for all;
He made their shelter from the cold,
    And hears their feeble call.   20

Poem No. 570; date unknown

Hymn
I Am The Way

The way! ah, who could tell, as well as thou,
   The way to God, the way no man had found;
Wherein who walk shall never go astray,
   Where joy, and peace forevermore abound?

The narrow way of suffering, pain, and death,   5
   Thou didst pursue enduring mortal ill;
That thou might'st teach mankind the way of life,
   Obedient to thy Heavenly Father's will.

Thus plainly didst thou show that way to men,
   Thou wast the way, the way and thou were one;   10
And, when thy course was finished, thou didst say,
   The work thou gavest me, O God, is done.

Then to the Father, thou didst upward soar,
   To strengthen fainting souls with gift divine;
The Spirit thou didst send to guide, and help,   15
   And make thy feeble followers wholly thine.

Ah, why should men that perfect way neglect,
   Or having found, still from it go astray?
Is there another path than this more plain,
   Is there another guide than Christ, the Way?   20

To whom, O Savior, may his followers say,
   To whom, but thee, for guidance shall we go,
Thou art the Christ, the anointed Son of God,
   And dost to all the Heavenly Father show.

Poem No. 590; date unknown

Early Companions

They are not dead, but gone before!
   Their love doth still remain;
Another life will them restore,
   Unite the broken chain.

They loved the things, which here we love,
    Their hearts were kind and true;
And in the glorious world above,
    Their friendship shall renew.

But here we wander sad and lone,
    As in a foreign clime;
Till we again shall meet our own,
    Beyond the shore of time.

They wait us in that happy land,
    As we are waiting here;
With warm embrace with clasping hand,
    For each they love so dear.

There death no more can friends divide,
    Nor sorrow grieve the heart;
Beyond time's bounds, death's narrow tide,
    They meet no more to part.

Poem No. 636; date unknown

The Gift

Thou gav'st me many a fragrant flower,
    But I have given them all away;
To restore thy gifts I have no power,
    And when Thou ask'st;—what shall I say?

I'll say Thou taught'st me too to give,
    And I but did what Thou hast done;
By doing what Thou do'st I live;—
    And then Thou'lt call me, Lord, thy son.

'Twas Thou who gav'st them all their bloom,
    Each colored leaf its differing hue;
And could I selfishly presume
    What Thou hast made for all to view?

Their sweet perfume they caught from Thee,
    That scented hill and lonely vale;
And could there dwell aught good in me,
    And not for others too avail?

'Tis not thy gift; but that thy love
   Is infinite in great & small
For even the humblest flower can prove
   And show Thee Father all in all.   20

Poem No. 675; date unknown

The Soul's Opportunities

To every soul, howe'er obscure its birth,
A boundless heritage is freely given;
The wealth, and beauty of the spacious earth,
And the bright glories of the starry heaven.
This goodly world, and all which it doth hold   5
Were for man's use, and pleasure too designed;
A school, in which he might his powers unfold,
His various faculties of heart and mind.
From such a school shall man go forth in vain,
Squandered in foolish play its precious hours?   10
Or from its lessons higher wisdom gain,
And nobler use of his immortal powers;
Till for an endless state he shall prepare,
And in an angel's bliss, and knowledge share.

Poem No. 736; date unknown

The Book of Life

My hands have long been busy cutting from each
Day's paper the short tale or verse, that told
To many that around me dwell the shade of grief,
Or note of joy; as to my opening eye
They flitted half-seen by. These pasted in   5
The blank pages of my unfilled book stand as
Life's true memorial. There every word
The heart unconscious uttered, finding wings,
Has flown to sing of its sweet birth. As birds
From out some thicket scaped to tell to the open   10

Fields and travelled ways the secrets of their
Bower. There live! the record of the Past!
To tell of him who from his labors ceased
Enjoys the goodman's rest forevermore.

Poem No. 338; date unknown

For the Sailors' Fair

Like gallant barque, with canvas spread,
    And streamers fluttering in the wind;
The youthful sailor leaves his home,
    And all he loves on earth behind.

His Country calls;—he hears her voice,   5
    And boldly o'er the ocean sails;
He cares not for its fiercest storms,
    Nor for an armed foe he fears.

Nor, when, in port, disease has laid
    Its hand upon his manly frame,   10
And far from home and friends he dies,
    Is he forgetful of her fame.

His Country's flag, his chief delight,
    As bright it waved above his head;
Is folded round his lifeless form,   15
    In honor of the noble dead!

And shall the living back return
    Aged and sick, infirm and poor;
Without a shelter, or a home,
    Begging their bread from door to door?   20

No! Let them, conflicts wanderings o'er,
    In their last years find peace and rest;
The comforts which the body needs
    The hopes with which the soul is blest.

Here Christian Love's kind voice and hand   25
    Shall for their wants a Home prepare,
And bid each friendless seaman come,
    And freely all her blessings share.

Poem No. 316; date unknown

Parting Hymn

Air—"Auld Lang Syne."

I.

Now, parting from the festive board,
    A grateful hymn we raise;
For all our favored fields afford,
    To God be all the praise.
'Tis He who gives each cloudless sun,   5
    'Tis He who sends the rain;
He blesses, when man's work is done,
    The fields of ripening grain.

II.

'Tis He who gives us home and friends,
    All that we here receive;   10
And gifts of Grace from Heaven He sends,
    By which our souls may live.
Then, parting from the festive board,
    A grateful hymn we raise;
For all the joys our lives afford,   15
    To God be all the praise.

Poem No. 372; date unknown

The Peace Congress the Promise of a Higher Civilization

Thanks for the omen, that War's rule is spent,
   And Europe from a barbarous custom free!
Too long her statesmen have their influence lent,
   And to the idol bowed a willing knee;
A thousand voices heralded its fame, 5
   And History adorned each bloody strife;
The nations gloried in their deeds of shame,
   And not in saving, but destroying life.
In peaceful arbitration we behold
   The dawn of a new era for the race, 10
That milder day, by prophets long foretold,
   When Reason's sway shall violence displace,
Nations in peaceful arts alone contend,
And War's dread conflicts shall forever end.

Poem No. 455; date unknown

Hymn to the Living

The voiceless spirits, they who have given up
The being that God gave; till hand, foot, and voice,
Apart from him whom once they honored,
Find their tasks without forethought or wish,
These ever give thee back unto thyself, 5
When wandering thou wouldst stray, a new-born man.
I sing of them, for they have fallen asleep;
And no voice comes back, nor motion shows them
Living amid the dead, yet living still.
Where are they? in your midst; the forms that night 10
Radiant with fires discloses o'er your head,
And day walks forth with, when bright-girt he comes;
And thou but findst a lamp for thine own task,
A moon and stars that still may light thee on
Till finished the short race thy day begun. 15
Motionless yet moving roll on their orbs,
Measuring in shining planes thy little life
Of days, and months, and years unnoticed save

For them.
Hail Forms, the eye sees not; and Tones, that speak   20
But in the silent hymn of nature's praise!
Hail ye, who touch no lyre, but that low harp
That man can never hear till woke in God!
Come forth, ye whom the tombs have held so long!
Though but the shadows of your greatness fall   25
Upon the sight, and echoes reach the ear;
'Twill strengthen us to rise, who now are dead,
And follow on, where you have led the way.
Long have we sought you, and in distant worlds;
When ye were here amongst us; on your lives   30
We live, yet ask we who you are, as men
Forgotten. With the bud and leaf comes forth
Daily the record of your excellence,
In words that will not die upon our ear,
Ye hidden all; as is the current sap,   35
That weaves Spring's robe, or light that gives it hue.
In you as her we lose our little selves,
Forgetting in your bounties they who give.
Great Teachers! born to be with God, and teach
The letters of His wisdom; may we all   40
Count costless till with you we live as brothers;
Of the same Father, born to hear His word.
Come! we will sit as children at your feet,
And throw away the pride, that made us call
They who were sent from Him, the Good, our equals.   45
Pour, pour the rain from out your burial urns,
Scatter the sun-beams on our wasted fields,
Till blossoms, flowers, and fruit scent hill and plain;
Yet will we shut our eyes on all, to see
The Giver, and who teach to give like Him.   50
Ye stand not on the numbered page of Time;
But have withdrawn yourselves beyond the praise,
The short-lived praise of men, to hear of God.
The day on which you speak is called his own;
The hour on which He calls us children bids   55
Wait on you to learn our Father's acts;
Whom first He honored with the name of sons.
The world that is has vanished from your sight;
Its journeys with your last-day's march complete:
Teach us to walk the road that you have been,   60

Made plain at every step by what you were;
Invisible; still be to us as seen;
Fresh breathing on us with each gale that blows,
Our way still lighting with each sun that shines.
Ye Unseen Messengers! Apostles sent   65
By Christ, moving and finding voice in words!
Forms! that visit human hearts as dwellings;
Be near us ever, ever be our guests!
The night is dying out; and ye begin
To walk among us, Gigantic Shadows   70
Flung before the rising sun; in early
Morning's pale light seen, noticing the Day.
And Thou, who givest all, whose children these;
Ever Invisible! The Day in which all see!
Amid thy gifts may we walk fearfully;   75
Lest, lost in their profession, we find them
Instead of Thee. Straying amid thy works
We know Thee not; best seen in these thy sons;
In whom Thine Image shines to light our way.

Poem No. 589; date unknown

ABBREVIATIONS AND SYMBOLS

A	*Poems by Jones Very*. Ed. William P. Andrews. Boston: Houghton, Mifflin, 1883.
Bartlett	William Irving Bartlett, *Jones Very: Emerson's "Brave Saint."* Durham, N.C.: Duke University Press, 1942.
BH	*Book of Hymns for Public and Private Devotion*. Ed. Samuel Longfellow and Samuel Johnson. Cambridge: Metcalf, 1846.
BS	*The Book of the Sonnet*. Ed. Leigh Hunt and S. Adams Lee. Boston: Roberts, 1867.
BW	*Book of Worship: For the Congregation and the Home. Church of the Disciples*. Boston: Walker, Wise, and Co., 1852.
CAL	*Cyclopaedia of American Literature*. Ed. Evert A. and George L. Duyckinck. New York: C. Scribner, 1855.
CE	*Christian Examiner*.
CG	*The Crystal Gem*. Ed. J. A. Adams. Boston: Buffum, 1853.
Cl	*Poems and Essays by Jones Very: Complete and Revised Edition*. Ed. James Freeman Clarke. Boston: Houghton, Mifflin, 1886.
CP	*Children's Praise: A Book of Prayers and Hymns for the Children of the Church*. Boston: Ticknor and Fields, 1858.
CR	*Christian Register*.
CtY	Yale University Library.
DHB	*The Disciples' Hymn Book: A Collection of Hymns for Public and Private Devotion*. Boston: Walker, Wise, and Co., 1855.
E	*Essays and Poems: By Jones Very*. Ed. Ralph Waldo Emerson. Boston: Little and Brown, 1839.
FU	Parkman Dexter Howe Library, University of Florida.
G	*The Poets and Poetry of America*. Ed. Rufus W. Griswold. Philadelphia: Carey and Hart, 1842.
Gittleman	Edwin Gittleman, *Jones Very: The Effective Years, 1833–1840*. New York: Columbia University Press, 1967.
HA	*Hymns of the Ages: Being Selections from Lyra Catholica, Germanica, Apostolica, and Other Sources*. Comp. C.S.W. and A.E.G. Boston: Phillips, Sampson, 1859.
HBP	*The Household Book of Poetry*. Ed. Charles A. Dana. New York: Appleton, 1858.

HC	*The Harp and the Cross.* Comp. Stephen G. Bulfinch. Boston: American Unitarian Association, 1857.
HCC	*Hymns for the Christian Church, for the Use of the First Church of Christ in Boston.* Boston: Little, Brown, 1869.
HFS	*Hymns for the Sanctuary.* Comp. Cyrus A. Bartol. Boston: Crosby and Nichols, 1849.
HS	*Hymns of the Spirit.* Comp. Samuel Longfellow and Samuel Johnson. Boston: Ticknor and Fields, 1864.
HTB	*Hymn and Tune Book, for the Church and the Home.* Boston: American Unitarian Association, 1868.
I.	Signature of Jones Very on many earlier poems.
Knick	*Knickerbocker.*
LA	*Lyra Americana; or, Verses of Praise and Faith, from American Poets.* Ed. George T. Rider. New York: Appleton, 1865.
LG	*Ladies' Gems; or, Poems on the Love of Flowers, Kindness to Animals, and the Domestic Affections.* New York: n.p., 1855.
LSA	*Lyra Sacra Americana; or, Gems from American Sacred Poetry.* Ed. Charles Dexter Cleveland. New York: Scribner, 1868.
LWP	*Library of World Poetry.* Ed. William Cullen Bryant. New York: Avenel Books, 1870.
MB	Boston Public Library.
MH	Jones Very Papers, Houghton Library, Harvard University.
MH-Ar	Harvard University Archives.
MH(E)	Emerson Papers, Houghton Library, Harvard University.
MH(J)	Sylvester Judd Papers, Houghton Library, Harvard University.
MH(OP)	Notebook "OP," Emerson Papers, Houghton Library, Harvard University.
MHi	Massachusetts Historical Society.
MLi	Lincoln (Massachusetts) Public Library.
MRM	*Monthly Religious Magazine.*
MSaE	Essex Institute, Salem, Massachusetts.
MWelC	Wellesley College Library.
Myerson	Collection of Joel Myerson.
NASS	*The National Anti-Slavery Standard.*
NBEB	*New Bedford Evening Bulletin.*
NN	New York Public Library.
NNPM	Pierpont Morgan Library.
Parnassus	*Parnassus.* Ed. Ralph Waldo Emerson. Boston and New York: 1874.
PA	*The Poets of America: Illustrated by One of Her Painters.* Vol. 2. Ed. John Keese. New York: S. Colman, 1842.
PG	*The Poet's Gift: Illustrated by One of Her Painters.* Ed. John Keese. Boston: Carter, 1845.
PF	*The Poetry of Flowers.* Ed. Rufus W. Griswold. Philadelphia: J. Locken, 1844.
PHC	Haverford College Library.
PHi	Pennsylvania Historical Society.
PL	*The Psalm of Life.* Comp. John S. Adams. Boston: Oliver Ditson, 1857.
Rosary	*The Rosary of Illustrations of the Bible.* Ed. Edward E. Hale. Boston: Phillips, Sampson, and Co., 1848.

RPB	Jones Very Papers, Brown University Library.
RPST	*Roadside Poems for Summer Travellers*. Ed. Lucy Larcom. Boston: Osgood, 1876.
SAP	*Selections from American Poets*. Ed. William Cullen Bryant. Harpers Family Library, No. III. New York: Harper, 1840.
SO	*Salem Observer*.
SG	*Salem Gazette*.
SSLF	*Singers and Songs of the Liberal Faith*. Ed. Alfred P. Putnam. Boston: Roberts Brothers, 1875.
STC	*Songs of Three Centuries*. Ed. John Greenleaf Whittier. Boston: Osgood, 1875.
TU	University of Tennessee Library.
ViU	University of Virginia Library.
VTH	*Voices of the True Hearted*. Philadelphia: n.p., 1846.
Waif	*The Waif: A Collection of Poems*. Ed. Henry Wadsworth Longfellow. Cambridge: John Owen, 1845.
WM	*Western Messenger*.
^	Punctuation omitted.
~	Same word.
<>	Material inside angle brackets cancelled.
⇅	Material between arrows inserted.

Poem numbers are keyed to Helen R. Deese, "A Calendar of the Poems of Jones Very," *Studies in the American Renaissance*, ed. Joel Myerson (Charlottesville: University Press of Virginia, 1986).

375. [Untitled] (O heaven born muse! inspire my humble lay)
   17–18 Inexact quotation of *Paradise Lost*, IV.643–45.

387. Lines, Written on Reading Stuart's Account of the Treatment of Slaves in Charleston
Title: James Stuart, an Englishman, had published his two-volume *Three Years in North America* in 1833.

423. Lines on Mount Auburn
Mount Auburn Cemetery in Cambridge, begun in 1831, and by 1834 already a major point of interest in the Boston area, became a prototype for the "rural cemetery" movement in this country (Stanley French, "The Cemetery as Cultural Institution: The Establishment of Mount Auburn and the 'Rural Cemetery' Movement," *American Quarterly* 26 [March 1974]: 37–59).
   47–48 Quotation from James Thomson, *The Seasons: Winter*, 11. 1068–69.
   49–51 Quotation (slightly altered) from Joseph Addison, *Cato*, V.i.29–31.

562. Lines suggested by hearing the beach, at F. Peabody's Mills, South Salem. December 21. 1833.
Colonel Francis Peabody (1801–68) was a prominent Salem industrialist (Salem History Class 1957, *Colonel Francis Peabody, 1801–1868: Mechanic, Merchant, Teacher and Patriot* [Salem: Printed by Deschamps Bros. for the Salem Books Co., 1957]).

311. "Ambitione inani pectus caret"
Title translation: "There is no empty ambition in my breath."

161. Death of Lafayette
The Marquis de Lafayette died 20 May 1834.

128. Eheu! fugaces, Posthume, Posthume, Labuntur anni. Title is from Horace's *Odes*, II.xiv.i: "Alas, Posthumus, Posthumus, the fleeting years glide by."
The ms. inscription "To S.T.H." refers to Samuel Tenney Hildreth (1817–39). Both he and Charles Stearns Wheeler (1816–43), among whose papers this ms. was found, were fellow students with Very at Harvard; all three were aspiring poets.

396. King Philip
Headnote: Quotation from B. B. Thatcher, *Indian Biography* (New York: Harper,

1832), 1:166. Philip, son of Massasoit, led the Pokanoket Indians against the New England settlers in King Philip's War (1675–76).

684. The Wind-Flower
    5–6 Solomon was "Israel's wisest king"; see Matthew 6:28–29.

701. Hymn
    19–20 Matthew 14:25–33
    21–22 Luke 12:32

242. Enoch
Genesis 5:18–24
    7–8 Psalms 19:1–3

725. The Morning Watch
    13–14 Matthew 25:1–13

406. The Weary and Heavy Laden
Matthew 11:28–30

264. The Garden
Genesis, Chapters 2–3

319. The Bread from Heaven
John 6:31–58
    1–4 Luke 15:11–32
    6 John 4:14, 7:37–38

518. The Latter Rain
Zechariah 10:1

630. Worship
    13–14 Mark 4:36–41

168. The Soldier of the Cross
    5 The tribe of Levi was the Jewish priestly tribe.

642. The Serpent
Genesis, Chapter 3

651. The Lost
John 10:11–14

169. The Will
    5–6 Revelation 12:7–11
    7–12 Revelation 14:13
    14 Revelation 5:10

256. The War
    12 For John, cf. Very's letter to Bellows, Appendix to the Introduction.

608. The Reaper
Luke 10:2, John 4:35
    5 Matthew 24:28
    9–10 Matthew 13:24–30

376. Simmons Mobile Alabama
George F. Simmons, a student with Very at the Divinity School, had recently left New England for a pulpit at Mobile, Alabama. See Helen R. Deese, "Unpublished and Uncollected Poems of Jones Very," *ESQ* 30 (3d Quarter 1984): 157.

781. John
Matthew, Chapter 3; Mark 1:2–9; Luke 3:1–22; John 1:6–36
   12 The new command is to love one another (John 13:34).

90. The Flight
Matthew 24:2, 15–18

488. The Resurrection
   1 Cf. John 11:44.

336. My Father's House
Matthew 21:12–13, John 2:13–17

558. The Servant
Revelation 19:11–15

680. I Was Sick And In Prison
Matthew 25:36

223. He Was Acquainted With Grief
Isaiah 53:3

557. Forbearance
   5–8 Matthew 13:3–23

596. The Wolf and the Lamb Shall Feed Together
Isaiah 65:25

677. The Rail Road
   5–14 Isaiah 40:3–4

818. Behold He Is at Hand That Doth Betray Me
Matthew 26:46
   1–2 Matthew 26:55

824. To Him That Hath Shall Be Given
Matthew 13:12

262. The New Jerusalem
Revelation, Chapter 21

249. The Cross
   5 Genesis 3:15

334. Ye Gave Me No Meat
Matthew 25:42

286. Day Unto Day Uttereth Speech
Psalms 19:2

694. The Mountain
   1–3 Matthew 21:21

398. The Mustard Seed
Matthew 13:31–32

716. Eden
Genesis, Chapters 2–3

226. My meat and drink
John 6:31–58

718. Forgive me my trespasses
Matthew 6:12–15

250. The Watchman
Habakkuk 2:1
    13–14 Genesis 12:1–3, Galatians 3:8–29

544. The Prison
    6 The place called the skull is Calvary or Golgotha, where Jesus was crucified
(Matthew 27:33, Luke 23:33).

117. The Corrupt Tree
Luke 13:6–7; Matthew 3:10, 7:18–19
    4 Matthew 13:24–30

125. The Pure in Heart
Matthew 5:8

809. Whither shall I go from thy Spirit
Psalms 139:7

80. The First shall be Last
Matthew 19:30; cf. Hosea 2:1–8.
    1–2 James 5:1–3
    12 Revelation 6:6
    13 Matthew 25:1–13

121. The Laborer
Matthew 20:1–16
    4 Matthew 25:14–30

234. Thy Brother's Blood
Genesis 4:1–15

672. Sacrifice
Isaiah 1:11–17

568. The Son of Man
Matthew 8:20

801. Rachel
Matthew 2:18

59. Christmas
    5–9 Cf. Jesus' raising of the dead Lazarus (John 11:39–44).

728. The Christ
    11 John 5:6

2 Isaiah 9:6
3–4 John 3:22–30
9 Matthew 10:39
13–14 Luke 22:44

291. The Things Before
Philippians 3:13–14

467. The Cup
Matthew 26:36–46

536. Old Things are passed away
2 Corinthians 5:17

645. The Harvest
Luke 10:2, John 4:35

48. The City
Matthew 5:14

620. Faith
Matthew 17:20
  4 1 Corinthians 5:6

582. The Temple
  10–14 1 Peter 2:4–7

597. The White Horse
Revelation, Chapter 6, 19:11–16

474. The Corner Stone
Matthew 21:42, 1 Peter 2:6–7
  5–8 Matthew 7:24–27

599. The Good Ground
Matthew 13:3–23
  9–11 Matthew 3:10

663. The Beginning and The End
Revelation 1:8

693. The Temptation
Matthew 4:1–11
  5 Matthew 19:21
  7–8 Matthew 5:30
  9–10 Matthew 19:29

280. The Poor
  7 Matthew 14:15–21

681. They Who Hunger
Matthew 5:6
  7 Zechariah 10:1

577. Who Hath Ears To Hear Let Him Hear!
Matthew 13:9

639. The Sign
Matthew 12:38–40

692. The Clay
Isaiah 64:8, Romans 9:20–21

625. Terror
Revelation, Chapter 18

167. Compassion
Matthew 11:28–30
   7–8 John 11:1–46

591. I am the Way
John 14:6
   8 Hebrews 11:8–13

341. The kingdom of God Is within you
Luke 17:21
   13–14 Matthew 16:19

655. My Church
Matthew 16:13–19
   11–14 Matthew 22:1–14

274. The Charge
Matthew 10:5–28

626. The Invitation
Matthew 11:28–30, 22:1–10

88. Come unto me
Matthew 11:28–30
   9–10 Matthew 22:1–14, 25:1–13

528. Flee to the mountains
Matthew 24:16–18

70. Blessed are they that mourn
Matthew 5:4

157. Faith
Matthew 17:20

61. Redeeming the time
Ephesians 5:16
   13 1 Thessalonians 5:17

724. 'Tis Finished
Revelation 21:1–6

498. To the pure all things are pure
Titus 1:15

711. The Task
Matthew 16:24

623. The Strong Man
   10 Philippians 4:13

621. The Shelter
   4 John 13:34

540. The Harvest
   10–11 Psalms 126:5–6

820. The Last
Matthew 20:1–16

603. The Promise
   2 Matthew 10:8
   5 Luke 18:29–30
   9 John 14:2–3

253. The Creation
Genesis 1:1–8
   10–11 Hebrews 12:1

340. The Snare
   1 Luke 17:21
   5–8, 14 Matthew, Chapter 3

345. The Yoke
Matthew 11:28–30

225. The Promise
Acts 2:1–4

738. The Reward
   1–2 Matthew 13:12

304. So is every one who is born of the spirit
John 3:8
   10 Matthew 11:7–11

208. I am the Light of the World
John 8:12

207. The Apostle
   1 Revelation 22:13

628. The Message
   2 Exodus 3:14
   8–14 Matthew 21:33–46

209. I Am the Bread of Life
John 6:30–58

508. Yet Once More
Joel 2:10–11, Matthew 24:29–31, Revelation 6:12–17
   10–14 Revelation 19:7–9

670. The Humble
Matthew 23:12

676. Comfort
    1 Psalms 104:15

240. The Guest
Revelation 3:20
    12–14 1 Corinthians 2:9

490. The Eagles
Matthew 24:28

486. Then shall all the tribes of the earth mourn
Matthew 24:30

408. Repent for the kingdom of Heaven is at hand
Matthew 3:2
    2 Malachi 3:2
    4–14 Matthew 7:24–27

178. The Mourner
Matthew 5:4

503. The Giants
Genesis 6:4

60. To the Fishermen
Matthew 4:21

742. The Sower
Matthew 13:24–30
    5–10 John 6:35
    11–12 Matthew 13:24–30

783. Charity
Matthew 7:12, 10:8

631. The Created
Genesis 1:26–28
    2 Ecclesiastes 9:11

405. Unto you is born a Saviour
Luke 2:11–14, Matthew 2:1–10

214. The Redeemed
Cf. John 20:24–28

714. Hallowed be thy Name
Matthew 6:9

739. To him who overcometh
Revelation 2:7, 10–11, 17, 26; 3:5, 12, 21
    5–8 Revelation 6:9–11
    14 John 15:1–8

732. The Veil of the Temple
Matthew 27:50–53; Revelation, Chapter 12

222. The Holy of Holies
Hebrews 9:3
  2–3 1 Corinthians 2:9
  6 Exodus 3:5

133. The Brethren
  1 Acts 17:28

804. The Prodigal
Luke 15:11–32

704. The Fig Tree
Matthew 7:16–20

665. The Branch
John 15:1–8

712. Not as the World giveth
John 14:27, Matthew 7:7–11

782. The Good Gift
Matthew 7:7–11
  11–14 John 13:34, Revelation 7:14

662. Thy Father's House
John 14:2

689. Jacob's Well
John 4:5–15

5. Spiritual Darkness
Cf. Exodus 10:21–23.

532. The New World
Revelation, Chapter 21

588. The Word
John 1:1–14

604. The Apostles
Matthew, Chapter 10

272. The Bride
  1–4 Cf. Genesis 29:1–30.

308. The Withered Tree
Matthew 21:18–20

267. The Plagues of Egypt
Exodus 7:8–12:31

3. The Dark Day
Exodus 10:21–23

707. The Lost Sheep
Matthew 18:12–13

632. The Good Samaritan
Luke 10:29–37

512. The Feast
Matthew 22:1–14

613. The House Not Made With Hands, Eternal In The Heavens
2 Corinthians 5:1

501. The Broken Bowl
Ecclesiastes 12:6
    13–16 Exodus 17:6, 1 Corinthians 10:4

160a. The Watcher
Cf. Matthew 25:1–13, 26:36–46.

283. Give and it shall be given unto you. Spiritual Debtors
Luke 6:38

239. The Idler
    11–12 Luke 16:19–22

807. The Narrow Way
Matthew 7:13–14

531. The True Light
Cf. John 1:9.

238. The New Sea
Cf. Exodus 14:13–31.

721. The Sepulchre Of The Books
Cl prints the following headnote:
    It appears that Gore Hall, which was finished for the library of Harvard College in the year 1841, is "unsuitable and inconvenient," that "it will never be what is wanted for a library." The objections are: "the bad light, the discomfort in winter, the entire want of private rooms for any of the officers of the library, or for *strangers* visiting it to make investigations, or for any of the persons employed in it, and . . . the slow but certain ruin of the books by dampness." This account of the library building is taken from the last printed report [1867?] which we have at hand of the Librarian. There is something suggestive in the fact that he speaks of such occasional persons who look in to make investigations, as "strangers."
    This description gives the merit of prophecy to the striking verses with which Mr. Jones Very, in January, 1841, heralded the completion of this building.

709. Lines on Reading the Death of Rev. Henry Ware, Jr.
Henry Ware, Jr. (1794–1843), was Professor of Pulpit Eloquence and the Pastoral Care at the Harvard Divinity School, 1828–42.
    15 John 10:16
    20–24 Dr. William Ellery Channing (1770–1842) was one of "the great and good" whose recent loss Very was lamenting. Cf. No. 435, "The Influence of Channing."

270. Jonathan Huntington Bright
Bright (1802–37), a Salem native who left there in 1825, published poetry in such periodicals as *Atlantic Souvenir* and *Knickerbocker*. He died of a fever in Manchester,

Mississippi (Sidney Perley, *The Poets of Essex County, Massachusetts* [Salem, Mass.: Sidney Perley, 1889], pp. 25–26).

617. God's Host
Genesis 31:43–55, 32:1–3

518a. The Latter Rain
Zechariah 10:1

182. Moses In Infancy
Exodus 2:1–10

750. Moses at the Bush
Exodus, Chapter 3

749. Moses As Leader Of Israel
   5–6 Acts 7:22
   9–14 Exodus 33:15–16

609. The New Jerusalem
Revelation 3:12, Chapter 21

473. As ye sow, so shall ye reap.
Galatians 6:7

559. The Arrival
The poem is based on the arrival in Salem Harbor of the brig *Cherokee* on 5 April 1847 (see Textual Note) with William B. Bates (1809–94) as captain.

517. The Just Shall Live by Faith
   1–4 The Prophet is Habakkuk; see Habakkuk, Chapter 1 and 2:4.
   5–8 Paul is the Apostle (Romans 1:17, Galatians 3:11).
   9 The Reformer is Martin Luther.

72. Salem
Very has probably been reading Joseph B. Felt's *Annals of Salem*, 2 vols. (Salem: W. and S. B. Ives, 1849), where the following account of Salem's support of Boston is given:

> The port of Boston having been closed on this day [June 1, 1774], Salem becomes the rendezvous of the custom-house officers who had resided there. In an address of our townsmen to General Gage [the British military governor], on the 11th, they uttered the noble sentiment, 'By shutting up the port of Boston, some imagine that the course of trade might be turned hither, and to our benefit; but nature and the formation of our harbor forbid our becoming rivals in commerce to that convenient mart. And were it otherwise, we must be dead to every idea of justice, lost to all feelings of humanity, could we indulge one thought to seize on wealth and raise our fortunes on the ruin of our suffering neighbors.'

(2:266)

141. The Congress Of Peace At Brussels
This Congress held in September 1848 was sponsored by advocates of nonviolence, primarily the Quakers.

292. The Things Before
Philippians 3:13–14

565. The Clock
8 Quotation slightly altered from Alexander Pope, *An Essay on Man*, Epistle 1, line 96.

129. On the late Disgraceful Scene in Congress
On 17 April 1850 a near brawl occurred in the Senate chambers when Senators Henry Stuart Foote of Mississippi and Thomas Hart Benton of Missouri had to be restrained from violence against each other, Foote actually drawing a pistol.

657. The New Aqueduct
The wooden aqueduct had supplied water to Salem since 1799.
30 old Sichem's well] Abraham built an altar at Sichem after his arrival in Canaan (Genesis 12:6–7), but there is no mention of any well. Perhaps Very had in mind Shibah, the name of a well that Isaac's servants dug (Genesis 26:32–33).

185. The Reapers Are The Angels
Matthew 13:24–30, 36–43

854. The Fugitive Slaves
The Fugitive Slave Law, passed in 1850, required all citizens to aid in the return of runaway slaves.

67. The Lost Sheep: Suggested by an Engraving
Matthew 18:12–14

407. The Soul's Rest
Matthew 11:28–30

295. Kossuth
Louis Kossuth (1802–94), a Hungarian revolutionary, made an American tour beginning in December 1851 and was enthusiastically received. He spoke at Mechanic Hall in Salem on 7 May 1852.

139. John Woolman
Woolman (1720–72), famous for his *Journal* (published in 1774), was a Quaker leader and early advocate of the abolition of slavery.

674. Hymn: Waiting For Christ
25–28 Revelation 22:12, John 14:2–3

34. The Solitary Worshipper
31 Matthew 7:7

542. Sonnet, To the Rev. James Flint, D. D., On reading his Collection of Poems.
Flint (1779–1855) was pastor of the East Church, Salem; his *Verses on Many Occasions, with Others for Which It May Be Thought There Was No Occasion* was printed in 1851 (Lynn, Mass.: Press of H. J. Butterfield).

163. My Dear Brother Washington
Washington Very (b. 1815), who was briefly a minister and then a teacher in Salem, died after being ill a "little more than a week" of "an enlargement of the heart" on 18 April 1853 (copy of letter of Jones Very to William A. Richardson, secretary of the Class of 1843, in the Class Book of 1843, Harvard Archives).

705. On Seeing The Victoria Regia In Bloom, At The Garden of J. Fisk Allen Esq.
July 22d, 1853.

John Fisk Allen (1807–76) of Salem, a noted horticulturist, grew at his home the Victoria regia, an Amazonian water lily remarkable for the rapidity of its growth. Its leaves often expanded by eight inches daily, up to a length of seventy-one inches. Allen published, soon after the composition of this poem, his illustrated *Victoria Regia; or, The Great Water Lily of America* (Boston: privately printed, 1854).

833. Goliath
1 Samuel, Chapter 17

761. Hymn, Sung at the Thompson Jubilee, at Barre, Jany. 12, 1854
James Thompson (1805–81), a native of Barre, Massachusetts, was preacher for the Barton Square Church in Salem.

46. On The Nebraska Bill
The Kansas-Nebraska Bill, passed by Congress in 1854, repealed the Missouri Compromise and left the question of slavery in these territories to the inhabitants.

422. On An Ear of Wheat Brought, By My Brother, From The Field Of Waterloo
Washington Very (1815–53), the poet's brother, had interrupted his studies at the Harvard Divinity School by travel in Europe, 1844–45.

333. To the Memory of the Rev. James Flint, D.D.
For Flint, see Historical Note on No. 542, "Sonnet, To the Rev. James Flint, D.D., on Reading His Collection of Poems."

649. Hymn: So also will God, through Jesus, bring with him them who sleep.
1 Thessalonians 4:14

44. To The Memory Of The Rev. James Chisholm
Chisholm (1815–55), a Salem native and friend and classmate of Very at Harvard, was an Episcopal clergyman. He died while ministering to the people of Portsmouth, Virginia, during an outbreak of the "pestilence" (David Holmes Conrad, *Memoir of Rev. James Chisholm* [New York: Protestant Episcopal Society, 1856]).

772. The First Telegraphic Message
Samuel F. B. Morse had sent this message between Baltimore and Washington, D.C., on 24 May 1844.

73. The Mission Of The Friends To The Emperor Nicholas
In January–February 1854 a delegation of three English Quakers journeyed to St. Petersburg, where they were politely received by the czar but unsuccessful in their attempt to dissuade him from a course of action that soon resulted in the Crimean War. See John Cunningham, *The Quakers from Their Origin Till the Present Time*, 2d ed. (London: Friends Tract Society, 1897), pp. 336–42.

227. Christ Abiding Forever
3–4 John 1:1–14

107. On Receiving A Flower From the Rev. C. H. A. Dall, in India.
Charles Henry Appleton Dall (1816–86), a fellow divinity student at Harvard with Very, was a Unitarian missionary in Calcutta.

654. Hymn: Sung at the Dedication of Plummer Hall, Salem, Oct. 6, 1857.
The building of the Salem Athenaeum's newly completed Plummer Hall, dedicated

to "literature, art, science, and improvement," was supported by a bequest from Caroline Plummer (SG, 9 October 1857).

217. Hindoo Converts: On the Domestic Trials of Hindoo Converts. Report of Unitarian Mission in India. The title refers to *Fifth Report, by the Missionary* [C. H. A. Dall] *and Treasurer* [Richard Lewis] *for the Half-Year (Beginning on the 1st of July and Ending on the 31st Dec. 1857,) showing the progress of the Mission to India, Commenced by British and Indian Unitarians in 1821, and Re-opened by the American Unitarian Association in February 1855* (Calcutta: Military Orphan Press, 1858). The report mentions that "some of the most constant visitors [to the Mission Room], young men of good promise, say that they are jealously watched by relatives and friends, lest they should come in contact with the hated name of Christ," adding that "their clothes are locked from them so that they cannot come to us on Sunday" (p. 7). For C. H. A. Dall, see Historical Note for No. 107, "On Receiving a Flower from the Rev. C. H. A. Dall, in India."

841. The First Atlantic Telegraph
The first successful transatlantic cable was completed on 5 August 1858.

145. On Seeing The Portrait of Helen Ruthven Waterston
Helen Ruthven Waterston, who died on 25 July 1858 in Naples at the age of seventeen, was the daughter of R. C. Waterston, Unitarian minister and friend of Very's since their student days at Harvard, and the granddaughter of Josiah Quincy. For a memorial of her see MRM 20 (October 1858): 260–63.

785. Hymn: The Promise of The Spirit
John 14:16–20, 26

65. On the Bunyan Tableau
In 1852 a number of New York artists, the best known of whom was Frederick Church, completed a panorama depicting *Pilgrim's Progress* (*A Descriptive Catalogue of the Bunyan Tableaux* [Albany, N.Y.: J. Munsell, 1856]). This work, with its "sixty magnificent scenes," then toured the country, showing in Salem from 7 to 26 March 1859 (SG, 4 March 1859).

110. How Faith Comes
16 Romans 10:17

770. The Cemetery of Harmony Grove
Harmony Grove Cemetery was established in Salem in 1840 as a "rural cemetery"; see Henry Wheatland, *Harmony Grove Cemetery, Salem, Mass.* (Salem: G. M. Whipple and A. A. Smith, 1866).

165. The Triennial
This poem was no doubt inspired by the Triennial Convention of the Salem Normal School, held on 27 July 1860 (SG, 31 July 1860).

766. Welcome: Written for the Essex Institute Fair, Held at Salem Sept. 4th, 1860
The Essex Institute resulted from the union in 1848 of the Essex Historical Society (founded in 1821) with the Essex County Natural History Society.

135. On reading the Memorial of John White Browne
In Memoriam J.W.B., ed. A. G. Browne, Jr. (Boston: Crosby, Nichols, Lee, 1860) included eulogies by Wendell Phillips, Charles Sumner, Charles C. Shackford, and

others. Browne (1810–60), a Salem native, was a Boston lawyer who had early taken an antislavery stand (p. 55). When he died from a fall from a moving train, he was carrying a copy of Very's poem No. 829, "The Prayer," attributed to *Essays and Poems* (p. 23).

142. The Abolition Of Serfdom In Russia
Russian serfdom was abolished by order of Czar Alexander II on 3 March 1861.

793. Christ's Capture In The Garden: A Paraphrase
Matthew 26:47–56

445. The Comet
This "magnificent" comet appeared on 2 July 1861 in the northern skies, taking "astronomy, with the rest of the world, entirely by surprise" (SG, 5 July 1861).

454. On The Completion Of The Pacific Telegraph
The first transcontinental telegram was sent on 24 October 1861 from Stephen J. Field, chief justice of California, to President Lincoln.

535. The Barque Aurelia of Boston
This poem recounts Very's own boyhood experience of sailing to New Orleans aboard the *Aurelia*, of which his father was captain. Captain Samuel Cook of the *Delphos*, to whom RPB(1) is inscribed, was in the city at the same time. William Hooper (1812–87), son of the Marblehead sea captain Joseph Hooper (1775–1837) was, like Very, a cabin boy. Cf. No. 769, "Capt. Samuel Cook."

571. Hymn: The Spirit Itself Maketh Intercession For Us
Romans 8:26

831. Ship Rock
An anonymous article entitled "A Genealogical Ramble" in SG, 23 August 1859, associates the area near Ship Rock with the earliest Very settlers.

520. Hymn: The Light of Life
John 8:12
    5–8 Mark 8:22–26

438. The Statue of Flora, On the grounds of R. Brookhouse Esq, Washington Street.
Robert Brookhouse (1779–1866) was a Salem merchant.

489. Dying Words of John Foster: "I Can Pray, And That's a Glorious Thing."
John Foster (1770–1843), English preacher and religious writer, is reported to have uttered these words in *The Life and Correspondence of John Foster*, 2 vols. (Boston: Gould and Lincoln, 1850), 2:231.

858. Hymn: Christ's Invitation in the Apocalypse
Revelation 22:17–20

810. To Charles W. Felt Esq.: On His New Type-Setting Machine
Felt, of Salem, with the support of Salem capital, was perfecting a type-setting machine that would justify lines (SG, 16 August 1867).

566. The Young Drummer Boy of Libby Prison: An Incident Related by Capt. James Hussey.
Libby Prison was a converted warehouse in Richmond, Virginia, used to house

Union prisoners. A James Hussey of Gloucester enlisted in the U.S. Navy on 11 November 1863 and served on the receiving ship *Ohio* and on the *USS Niagara*, from which he deserted on 9 January 1864 as Captain of the Maintop (Adjutant General, *Massachusetts Soldiers, Sailors, and Marines in the Civil War* [Brookline: Riverside Press, 1935], 8:205).

563. The Soul's Questioning Of The Universe, And Its Beginning
  33–35 Isaiah 51:6

374. Hymn: Sung at the Eulogy on Abraham Lincoln June 1st 1865.
The eulogy was delivered by George W. Briggs in Salem on the day of the National Fast.

401. Prayer For Rain
  13–15 Matthew 6:8–13

390. Hymn On The Logos: The Light Still Shining In The Darkness
  John 1:1–4

744. "It is vain to say, that this is the country of the 'white man.' It is the country of man." Charles Sumner.
Sumner (1811–74) was a U.S. senator from Massachusetts. Quotation is unlocated.

14. The East India Marine Museum
The East India Marine Society was founded in 1799 by Salem mariners. One of its purposes was the collection, preservation, and display in a museum of artifacts gathered from around the globe by Salem seamen. In 1867 the museum was renamed the Peabody Museum in honor of its benefactor, George Peabody.

151. Primitive Worship
This poem appears at end of an article in SG, 24 August 1866, describing a journey on foot to Asbury Grove, a Methodist camp meeting site. The anonymous author of the article was accompanied by Very, who wrote this poem about the experience.
  5–8 Hugh Peters (1599–1660) was an early Puritan clergyman in Salem who preached a sermon to the few original settlers in 1638 at Wenham (then a part of Salem) on a hill overlooking Wenham Lake. Peters later returned to England, became active in the Commonwealth, and was executed as a regicide.

66. The Triumphs of Science, And of Faith
  1–4 The transatlantic cable was completed on 5 August 1858.

356. Our Dear Mother
Lydia Very died on 3 May 1867 at the age of seventy-three.

363. Hymn: The Word Before All Things
John 1:1–14

367. The Teachings of the Spirit
John 14:26

452. The Hacker School House
Very himself attended the Hacker Grammar School on Dean Street in Salem.

827. The Youth and the Stream
This poem may have been inspired by a poem by Goethe appearing as "The Youth

and the Mill Stream" in J. S. Dwight's translation of Goethe and Schiller's *Select Minor Poems* (Boston: Hillard Gray, 1839). The poem was printed in a review of this work in WM 6 (February 1839): 262–63, where Very would almost certainly have seen it.

534. Hymn: Sung at the Dedication of the Peabody Academy of Science, Salem, Aug. 18, 1869.
The Peabody Academy of Science was established by a gift of the philanthropist George Peabody to promote the study and dissemination of knowledge of the natural and physical sciences. The trustees were empowered to purchase the Museum of the East India Marine Society and to arrange there both the collections of the East India Marine Society and the scientific collections of the Essex Institute. After a two-year period of classifying and arranging these collections, the Academy dedicated its hall.

822. The Teaching Of History Confirmed
  5 The "mighty city" is Paris, under siege by the German army.

27. The Lessons of History Unlearned
In late May 1871 France was thrown into a brief but bloody civil war involving the suppression of the Commune of Paris, with twenty thousand casualties.

453. The Fulness of The Gentiles
Romans 11:25

18. Forevermore
  5 Nevermore] The obvious allusion is to Edgar Allan Poe's "The Raven."

115. On Seeing the White Mountains from Cook's Hill, in West Peabody
  2 In August of 1837 Very and several friends spent two weeks in the White Mountains.

543. The Prayer of Jabez
1 Chronicles 4:10

765. *On visiting the beautiful estate of* H. H. Hunnewell, Esq., *at Wellesley.*
Horatio Hollis Hunnewell owned a large estate in Wellesley, Massachusetts, inherited from his father-in-law John Welles, an advocate of agricultural improvements (*Proceedings of the Massachusetts Historical Society* [Oct. 1886]: 99–100).

164. On the Mountain Ash Tree: In front of the house of the late Capt. Robert W. Gould
Gould, a Salem ship's captain, died in April 1873 at the age of eighty-nine.

444. The Mound Builders: On Reading the work of the late J. W. Foster
John Wells Foster (1815–73) wrote several articles on the mound builders, as well as a book published in 1873: *Pre-historic Races of the United States of America* (Chicago: Griggs).

403. There shall be one Flock, one Shepherd
John 10:16

635. Old Houses of Salem: Illustrated by George M. White
White was a Salem artist who had reproduced the drawings for this work (n.p., n.d.) by "the new process of the Heliotype" (Preface).

64. Columbines and Anemones
Louis Prang, a Boston lithographer, was selling "chromos" (chromolithographs, or colored lithographs) of famous (and, apparently, less than famous) works of art.

15. To the Memory of Alpheus Crosby
Crosby (1810–74) taught Latin and Greek at Dartmouth, acted as an agent for the Massachusetts Board of Education, served as principal of the state normal school at Salem (1857–65), wrote textbooks, and edited the reform paper *The Right Way* (1865–67).

812. On The Wild Flowers of the Art Exhibition
An art exhibit was under way in Plummer Hall in Salem (SG, 24 July 1874).

360. For we Walk by Faith, not by Sight
2 Corinthians 5:7

634. Behold, I Make All Things New
Revelation 21:1–5, Ecclesiastes 1:1–11

113. Oliver C. Felton, Esq., of Brookfield
Felton (1795–1875) taught Very himself in grammar school (Bartlett, p. 18), was the author of a grammar textbook (1842), and later became a state legislator.

324. The Origin of Man
  23–25 John 14:2–3

369. Original Hymn
John 21:15–17

717. On the Great Earthquake in New Grenada
The Boston *Daily Evening Transcript* of 12 June 1875 reported that a terrible earthquake in New Grenada, near the Venezuelan border, had claimed an estimated sixteen thousand lives.

68. On Visiting the Graves of Hawthorne and Thoreau
Both Hawthorne and Thoreau are buried in Sleepy Hollow Cemetery, Concord.

45. On Viewing the Falls of Niagara, as Photographed by George Barker
Barker (active early 1860s to late 1890s) was a major producer of views of the falls from his studio in Niagara Falls (John S. Waldsmith, *Stereo Views* [Radnor, Penn.: Wallace-Homestead Book Co., 1991], p. 31).

190. Mt. Shasta. A Painting, by H. O. Young.
Harvey Otis Young (1840–1901), a Vermont native influenced by the Hudson River School, was known for his western landscapes.

200. Man's Need of a Spiritual Birth
John 3:1–13
2 Nicodemas is the Jewish teacher.

321. The Purification of the Temple
Matthew 21:12–13

10. The International Exhibition at Philadelphia
The Centennial Exposition, the first world's fair held in the United States, opened on

10 May 1876. It stressed achievements in the arts, agriculture, manufacturing, and technology.

769. Capt. Samuel Cook
All of the sea captains remembered by Very from his youth were long since gone. Cook, the last survivor, was supposedly the oldest of the Salem sea captains at his death in 1861 at the age of ninety-two (SG, 13 December 1861). The other captains mentioned are probably Joseph Noble (1798–1834), Jonathan P. Felt (1785–1860), and Joseph Hooper (1775–1837) (Salem Marine Society, *By-Laws, Acts of General Court, List of Members* [Salem: Milo A. Newhall, 1936]; and *Portraits of the Marine Society at Salem in New-England* [Salem: Marine Society, 1972]). Cf. Very's poem No. 535, "The Barque Aurelia of Boston."

106. On the Beautiful Roses, In front of the Mansion of John Hodges, Esq.
This is probably the Salem sea captain John Hodges (1802–82).

357. The True Worshipers
John 4:19–26

821. On Hearing the Clock Strike, in Harmony Grove
For Harmony Grove, see Historical Notes for No. 770, "The Cemetery of Harmony Grove."

615. The Perfect Love that Casts out Fear
1 John 4:18

201. Man's Accountability
Cf. 2 Corinthians 5:10.

458. Hymn: The Cause of Peace
Luke 2:8–14

837. The Destruction of Public Property by Mobs
July 1877 had been a month of strikes and riots in the United States requiring in some cases the intervention of troops. On 22 July President Hayes issued a proclamation against turbulent gatherings in Maryland, and on 23 July against domestic violence in Pennsylvania.

819. The Communion
Luke 22:15–20

815. Know Thyself: Suggested by hearing Dr. A. E. Miller's Lectures on the Human Body.
Albert Eber Miller, physician of Needham and Boston, lectured on public health throughout the country, using skeletons, models, and drawings as illustrations.

354. William Cullen Bryant
Bryant died on 12 June 1878.

514. *"Agriculture the Source of Individual and of National Prosperity."*—Anne Pratt.
Anne Pratt (1806–93) was an English botanist best known for her *Flowering Plants and Ferns of Great Britain* (London, 1855). This quotation has not been located.
1–14 Matthew 20:1–16

832. On The Late Tornado, At Wallingford, Conn. Reports in the Boston *Daily Evening Transcript* (10 August 1878) estimated that the tornado on the previous day had killed twenty, injured forty, and destroyed one hundred buildings in Wallingford.

395. Christ's Final Victory
1 Corinthians 15:1–28; Revelation, Chapter 20

767. Original Hymn
The incoming pastor George Herbert Hosmer (1839–99), a native of New York and a graduate of the Meadville Theological School, preached for Salem's East Church until January 1886 (*Sermons and Records of the East Church* [Salem, 1898]).

850. The African's First Sight of the Ocean
Dr. David Livingstone (1813–73), an African missionary and explorer, published *Travels and Researches in South Africa* in 1860.

370. Guido's Aurora
The acknowledged masterpiece of Guido (1575–1642), Bolognese painter, was the fresco *Phoebus and the Hours Preceded by Aurora*.

435. The Influence of Channing
The date 7 April 1880 was the one hundredth anniversary of the birth of William Ellery Channing (1780–1842), the eminent Unitarian clergyman. Celebrations of his life were held in Boston, Newport, Rhode Island (his birthplace), and throughout New England, as well as in Brooklyn, Chicago, Cincinnati, Washington, London, and elsewhere (CR, 17 April 1880).

587. The Calling
1–2 Genesis 12:1
10 John Endicott (or Endecott) sailed from England with a group of about fifty settlers in June 1828 and reached Naumkeag (Salem) on 6 September. He became the governor of the settlement.
11 Francis Higginson arrived in 1629 to become minister to the settlers at Salem; he died in August 1630.

39. Endecott
For Endecott, see note on No. 587, "The Calling," l. 10.

359. The Old Planters
Roger Conant had been governor of a group of settlers at Cape Ann that disbanded; Conant and a few others moved to what is now Salem in 1626 and were known as the "old planters."

752. Naumkeck River
Although "Naumkeag" eventually became the standard spelling for this river, there are numerous early spellings, the earliest of which is probably John Smith's "Naimkeck" (James Duncan Phillips, *Salem in the Seventeenth Century* [Boston: Houghton Mifflin, 1933], p. 15).

83. Winthrop's Fleet
John Winthrop, who was the first governor of Massachusetts Bay, arrived at Salem in June 1630 with a contingent of settlers and supplies.

53. Arabella Johnson
Arabella Johnson, daughter of the third earl of Lincoln and Lord High Admiral of England, became ill on the voyage and died in August 1630.

352. The Puritan Church and State: II.
    11–13 John 8:32

109. On Some Beautiful Crocuses In Front of the House of B. H. Silsbee, Esq.
Benjamin Hodges Silsbee (1811–80) was a prominent East India merchant and civic leader in Salem.

382. Hymn: Prayer for the Gift of the Holy Spirit
John 14:16–17, Acts 2:38
    5–6 Matthew 7:7

462. Hymn: The Good Fight
2 Timothy 4:7

538. Jacob wrestling with the Angel
Genesis 32:24–32

590. Hymn: I Am The Way
John 14:6

375. [Untitled] (O heaven born muse! inspire my humble lay)
Copy-text: SO, 18 May 1833
Following the poem is printed: Salem, May 9, 1833   I.

492. [Untitled] (The earth is parched with heat, flowers droop and die)
Copy-text: SO, 10 August 1833
Precopy-text version: RPB
SO is dated and signed: July 24, 1833   I.

387. Lines, Written on Reading Stuart's Account of The Treatment of Slaves in Charleston
Copy-text: SO, 24 August 1833
SO is dated and signed: *August* 13, 1833.   I.

423. Lines on Mount Auburn
Copy-text: SO, 4 January 1834
Precopy-text version: RPB
Following SO is printed: Salem, Dec. 20th, 1833.   I.
RPB version entitled: Lines on Mount Auburn December 1833.

562. Lines suggested by hearing the beach, at F. Peabody's Mills, South Salem. December 21. 1833.
Copy-text: RPB
Bartlett first printed a version of this poem (p. 150) and erroneously gave the date in the title as 1883. Bartlett ignored Very's revisions and omitted the third stanza. The poem is probably an unfinished draft; note in Alterations in the Manuscript that a fourth stanza was written and cancelled, and another begun and aborted. The title in the ms. appears garbled.

158. [Untitled] (Hast thou ever *heard* the voice of nature)
Copy-text: SO, 20 April 1834
SO is dated and signed: *April* 7, 1834.   I.

311. "Ambitione inani pectus caret"
Copy-text: RPB
Other version collated: SO, 7 June 1834

Following RPB is written: Salem. June 2. 1834   I.
Following SO is printed: *Salem, June 2,* 1834.   I.

778. [Untitled] (What more delightful than to wander forth)
Copy-text: RPB
Other version collated: SO, 14 June 1834
RPB is dated: June 8, 1834
Following SO is printed: *Salem, June 8,* 1834.   I.

418. A Song Composed by Mr J. Very, to be Sung at the Class-Supper of the Sopho-
more Class of 1834
Copy-text: RPB
Other version collated: MH-Ar (in unidentified hand)
Bartlett (p. 152) printed stanzas 5–6 as a separate poem; the entire poem was first
published by Kenneth W. Cameron (*Emerson Society Quarterly* 5 [4th Quarter 1956]:
12–13).

161. Death of Lafayette
Copy-text: SO, 28 June 1834
Following the poem is printed: Salem, June 21, 1834   I.

410. Old Age
Copy-text: SO, 5 July 1834
Following the poem is printed: *Salem, June 30.*   I.

127. Lines Suggested By Seeing A Butterfly Sculptured Upon A Tomb
Copy-text: SO, 12 July 1834
Following the poem is printed: *Salem, July 6th.*   I.

746. Kind Words
Copy-text: SO, 19 July 1834
Other version collated: BH
Following SO is printed: Salem, July 16, 1834   I.

150. Pleasure
Copy-text: SO, 2 August 1834
Following the poem is printed: *Salem, July 22,* 1834.   I.

146. [Untitled] (Give me an eye, that manly deeds)
Copy-text: SO, 16 August 1834
Following the poem is printed: *Salem, Aug. 9th.*   I.
This is the earliest of Very's poems included in Clarke's "complete" edition. In
Clarke's version it is entitled "Stanzas."

255. [Untitled] (I saw a child, whose eyes had never drank)
Copy-text: SO, 30 August 1834
Following the poem is printed: *Salem, August* 15, 1834.   I.
Though untitled in SO, in Clarke's edition this poem is entitled "My Brother
Franklin." Very's brother Franklin (1818–22) was blind from birth. Another substan-
tive change made in the Clarke edition is the alteration of the color of the child's hair
from "auburn" (l. 55) to "golden."

31. The New Year
Copy-text: SO, 3 January 1835

Following the poem is printed: Salem.   I.

206. Sleigh Ride
Copy-text: SO, 10 January 1835
SO is dated and signed: *Jan. 5th*.   I.

154. The Snow Drop
Copy-text: SO, 11 April 1835
Following the poem is printed: *Salem, April* 8.   I.

87a. [Untitled] (Cold cold thy lips my gentle boy)
Copy-text: RPB
Probable date: spring 1835 (based on poems with which it is in proximity at RPB)

320a. Spring
Copy-text: RPB
Probable date: spring 1835 (based on poems with which it is in proximity at RPB)

528a. [Untitled] (The morn may lend its golden smile)
Copy-text: RPB
Probable date: spring 1835 (based on poems with which it is in proximity at RPB)

419. Lines: To ——— On the Death of His Friend
Copy-text: MH
Other version collated: Harv, 2 (July–August 1836): 377
Precopy-text version: RPB
RPB is dated: June 10, 1835
Harv is signed: I.
See David Robinson, "Four Early Poems of Jones Very," *Harvard Library Bulletin*
28 (April 1980): 149–50, for a discussion of this poem as well as No. 248 (untitled),
No. 278 ("The Torn Flower"), and No. 852 ("The Portrait").

199. North River
Copy-text: SO, 25 July 1835
SO is dated and signed: July 20.   I.

128. Eheu! fugaces, Posthume, Posthume, Labuntur anni.
Copy-text: MLi
Other versions collated: SO, 1 August 1835; E
Written in Very's hand beneath title in MLi: To S.T.H. [See Historical Notes.]
MLi is signed: J.V.

220. The Humming-Bird
Copy-text: Harv, 2 (June 1836): 326
Other versions collated: SO, 8 August 1835; E
Harv is signed: I.
SO is dated and signed: *August* 1.   I.

247. Nature
Copy-text: SO, 22 August 1835
Precopy-text version: MH-Ar
SO is dated and signed: *August* 15.   I.

143. Religion
Copy-text: SO, 29 August 1835

SO is dated and signed: *Aug. 24th*   I.

399. A Withered Leaf—seen on a Poet's Table
Copy-text: SO, 5 December 1835
Other versions collated: MH, E, G, Waif
SO is dated and signed: Nov. 24th   I.
MH is inscribed: Nov. 14. JV. to STH. [See Historical Notes for No. 128, "Eheu!
fugaces . . . ."]
SO was chosen as copy-text over MH because of its later date and the fact that,
as indicated by substantive revisions, it is clearly based on a later ms. that has not
survived.

353. The Stars
Copy-text: Harv, 2 (February 1836): 199
Other versions collated: MH; SO, 26 December 1835
MH is inscribed: S.T.H. [See Historical Notes for No. 128, "Eheu! fugaces . . . ."]
SO is dated and signed: Dec. 22   I.
Harv is signed: I.
Judging from variants in the various versions of the poem, it is probable that there
existed at least three ms. versions. The sequence of these versions is uncertain, though
it is likely that MH is the earliest of the three, with its marginal addition of a stanza
that appears in the other two versions (see Alterations in the Manuscript). The fact
that it was presented to Samuel Tenney Hildreth, one of the student editors of *Har-
vardiana*, also suggests that MH precedes the poem's appearance in that publication.
But it also appears likely, in view of variants between MH and Harv versions in lines
9 and 23, that the Harv version was based on yet another ms., presumably later than
the one on which SO, with its earlier publication date, was based.

47. The Snow Bird
Copy-text: MH(2)
Other versions collated: MH(1); SO, 2 January 1836; Harv, 2 (February 1836): 200;
CR, 25 February 1854
Written at end of MH(1): S.T.H. [See Historical Notes for No. 128, "Eheu!
fugaces . . . ."]
Written at end of MH(2): Cambridge 1836
SO is dated and signed: Dec. 25   I.
Harv is signed: I.
It is likely though not certain that MH(2) is the later ms. version. The presentation of
MH(1) to Samuel Tenney Hildreth, one of the student editors of *Harvardiana*, sug-
gests that it precedes the poem's appearance in that publication, and the later printed
versions all follow MH(2) more closely than they do MH(1).

429. Memory
Copy-text: MH
This poem is perhaps a slightly earlier version of a poem (No. 430) with the same
title. Because three of the six stanzas (in 429) or five stanzas (in 430) differ in the two
versions, they are treated here as two separate poems. MH is inscribed: JV to STH.
[See Historical Notes for No. 128, "Eheu! fugaces . . . ."]

430. Memory
Copy-text: SO, 9 January 1836
Other version collated: E

SO is dated and signed: Jan. 4   I.
See Textual Notes on No. 429, of the same title, for the probable relationship of these two poems.

396. King Philip
Copy-text: CtY
Other versions collated: MH; Harv, 2 (January 1836): 137–39
CtY and MH are both signed: I.

78. The Painted Columbine
Copy-text: SO, 23 April 1836
Other versions collated: Harv, 2 (March 1836): 231–32; E; G; PF; PA; PG; LG; CAL; STC
SO and Harv are both signed: I.

825. The Frozen Ship
Copy-text: MH(1)
Other versions collated: MH(2); SO, 16 April 1836; CR, 1 February 1851
SG, 7 February 1851, prints the poem, attributing it to CR. MH(2) is inscribed: JV to S.T.H. [For S.T.H. see Historical Notes for No. 128, "Eheu! fugaces . . . ."]
SO is signed: I.

343. My Mother's Voice
Copy-text: MH
Other versions collated: TU; Harv, 2 (April–May 1836): 248; SO, 4 June 1836; CR, 14 February 1846; SG, 12 June 1868
TU is signed: Jones Very
Harv and SO are signed: I.
Written at end of MH: Cambridge. 1836.
CR does not give the author.
Headnote in SO:

> The following beautiful Stanzas were written in a Lady's Album, a few weeks since, by Jones Very, of Salem, a young poet, who has occasionally furnished articles of the same description for one of the papers published in this city. It is sufficient to say, that Mr. Very, in *this,* as well as in all his other productions gives evidence that he possesses a fine poetical talent—a spirit alive to whatever is beautiful in nature, or lovely and attractive in the human heart. There is a music in the numbers, and an eloquence in the tone of "My Mother's Voice," which will make every bosom thrill.
>
> [*Landmark*

Headnote in SG:

> *Editors of the Gazette.*—The following lines from the pen of our mutual friend and fellow-townman [*sic*], Rev. Jones Very, first appeared in 1835 [*sic*], in the "Harvardiana," a magazine conducted by members of the Senior and Junior classes of Harvard College. It was reproduced in many of the newspapers of that time, and, if we mistake not, was set to appropriate music by Mr. Luther O. Emerson, a well known composer, who, for several years was a resident of our city. By some strange oversight they were omitted in a collection of "Essays and Poems" by Mr. Very which was given to the public in 1839, by the appreciative kindness of Ralph Waldo Emerson, Esq. and whose sterling merits were soon after endorsed by critics no less responsible than the elder Dana and the author of "Thanatopsis." Their insertion in your columns will gratify one at least who regards them as a "gem," and who

recalls no effort on a kindred theme so successful since the appearance of Cowper's beautiful lines "On the Receipt of my Mother's Picture."

J.F.W.

36. The Arab Steed
Copy-text: Harv, 2 (April–May 1836): 262–64
Precopy-text version: RPB
Harv is signed: I.

592. Hymn, Sung At The Dedication of The New Stone Church of The North Society In Salem June 22d, 1836.
Copy-text: MH(1)
Other versions collated: MH(2); MSaE; SO, 25 June 1836
Precopy-text version: RPB
Following MH(2) is written: To .S.T.H. / "O mihi tam longae / maneat pars ultima vitae, / Spiritus et, Quantum sat erit tua dicere facta!" ["I hope that I have enough life left, and breath, to sing of your deeds."] [For S.T.H., see Historical Notes for No. 128, "Eheu! fugaces . . . ."]
SO appears in an article entitled "New Stone Church" and is introduced as follows:
The following Dedication Hymn, composed by Mr Jones Very, a member of the North Society, was sung on the occasion:—

355. Song [For the Valedictory Exercises of the Senior Class of Harvard University, 1836]
Copy-text: Printed program (copies at MH and MH-Ar): *Harvard University / Valedictory Exercises of the Senior Class of / 1836. / Tuesday, July 19, 1836. / Song. By Jones Very.—Salem. / Tune—"Auld Lang Syne"*
Precopy-text versions: RPB(1), RPB(2)
MH-Ar copy is inscribed on verso: To William Allen from Jones Very July 19th 1836

496. Washington
Copy-text: SO, 20 August 1836
Precopy-text version: RPB
SO is signed: I.

673. The Autumn Leaf
Copy-text: SO, 1 October 1836
SO is signed: I.

695. The Winter Bird
Copy-text: RPB
Other version collated: SO, 31 December 1836

24. The Boy's Dream: A Ballad
Copy-text: MH
Precopy-text version: MH-Ar
Probable date: 1834–36 (based on the fact that other poems at MH-Ar date from Very's undergraduate years)

248. [Untitled] (I murmur not though hard the lot)
Copy-text: MH
See Textual Notes on No. 419, "Lines to ——— on the Death of His Friend."

Probable date: c. 1836 (based on dates of manuscripts with which it is in proximity at MH)

278. The Torn Flower
Copy-text: MH
Written at end of poem: JV. to STH. [See Historical Notes for No. 128, "Eheu! fugaces . . . ."]
See Textual Notes for No. 419, "Lines to ——— on the Death of His Friend."
Probable date: c. 1836 (based on dates of manuscripts with which it is in proximity at MH)

527. [Untitled] (The moon was shining on the deck)
Copy-text: RPB
Probable date: c. 1836 (based on dates of manuscripts with which it is in proximity at RPB)

175. [Untitled] (Home of my youth! Where first my lot was cast)
Copy-text: RPB
Probable date: c. 1836 (based on dates of manuscripts with which it is in proximity at RPB)

160. [Untitled] (Haunts of my youth farewell! A while I leave)
Copy-text: RPB
It is uncertain that the ms. is in Very's hand and the authorship is thus likewise uncertain. Bartlett printed it as one of Very's poems.
Probable date: c. 1836 (based on its relationship to No. 175)

432. Death Decay and Change
Copy-text: RPB
Probable date: c. 1836 (based upon style and its location at RPB)

852. The Portrait
Copy-text: MH
Other version collated: Knick, 9 (February 1837): 176
Following Knick is printed: Cambridge, (Mass.,) 1837.
Poem is unattributed in Knick.
See Textual Notes for No. 419, "Lines to ——— on the Death of His Friend."

221. The Canary Bird
Copy-text: SO, 15 April 1837
Other versions collated: E, SAP, G, LG

246. The Tree
Copy-text: SO, 22 April 1837
Other versions collated: E; SAP; G; SG, 6 September 1878
Precopy-text version: RPB
SO is signed: I.

95. The Fossil Flower
Copy-text: Knick, 9 (April 1837): 371
Other version collated: E
Precopy-text versions: RPB, MH
Following Knick is printed: Salem, (Mass.,) 1837.

Poem is unattributed in Knick.

SO, 2 March 1839, prints the poem, attributing it to Knick and to Very.

Although MH is a complete and a relatively clean version, it is clear from substantive differences between the MH and the Knick and E versions that a later (now lost) ms. version intervened between MH and the printed versions.

309. The April Snow
Copy-text: MH(1)
Other versions collated: MH(2); Knick, 9 (June 1837): 553; CE, 36 (May 1844): 389
Precopy-text version: RPB
MH(1) is dated: 1844.
MH(2) was sent to E. S. Gannett, editor of CE, on 6 March 1844.
Knick is unattributed but is followed by: Salem, (Mass.) The copy-text MH(1) (which is generally followed by Knick) represents Very's 1837 conception of the poem; seven years later he changed the title (from "The April Snow" to "The Snow") and revised it slightly (MH[2]) for publication in CE. The earlier version is represented here with the later revisions recorded in the Historical Collation.

348. Nature
Copy-text: MH(OP)
Other versions collated: SO, 29 July 1837; E

244. An Evening Walk
Copy-text: ViU
Other version collated: SG, 18 July 1871
Precopy-text version: MH
Following ViU is written: Jones Very / Salem Aug 25, 1837

232. Beauty
Copy-text: SO, 6 January 1838
Other versions collated: SO, 30 December 1837; E; SSLF
Precopy-text version: RPB
RPB is entitled "Love" and is dated: Sept 24th 1837.
SO is signed: I.
This sonnet and "The Wind-Flower" were reprinted in SO to correct typographical errors; see Textual Notes for No. 684, "The Wind-Flower."

650. The Voice of God
Copy-text: RPB(2)
Other versions collated: MH; SO, 2 December 1837
Precopy-text version: RPB(1)
MH is inscribed: JV. to STH [See p. 577 for notes on No. 128, "Eheu! fugaces . . ."]

684. The Wind-Flower
Copy-text: ViU
Other versions collated: MH(OP); SO, 23 December 1837; SO, 6 January 1838; E; SAP; G; LG; CAL
Precopy-text version: RPB
Headnote for SO, 6 January 1838:
     [Owing to some typographical errors in the two following original Sonnets {"The Wind-Flower" and "Beauty"}, (from an extremely poetical correspondent,) which have appeared in the Observer, we republish them corrected.]

580. The Sabbatia
Copy-text: ViU
Other version collated: CR, 18 August 1877
Precopy-text version: MH
Probable date: Late 1837; the poem is at ViU together with No. 244, "An Evening Walk," and No. 684, "The Wind-Flower."

112. The Passage Bird
Copy-text: RPB
Probable date: 1837 (based on dates of manuscripts with which it is in proximity at RPB)

710. A Sonnet
Copy-text: SO, 21 April 1838
Other versions collated: E, G, BS

441. The Columbine
Copy-text: SO, 9 June 1838
Other version collated: E
Precopy-text version: MH(OP)

686. The Robin
Copy-text: FU
Other versions collated: MH(OP); SO, 9 June 1838; E; G; PA; PG; SG, 20 May 1859; SG, 19 April 1861; BS
CR, 15 June 1838, also prints the poem, attributing it to SO.
FU is signed: J.V.

701. Hymn
Copy-text: RPB(1)
Other versions collated: RPB(2), MH(J)
RPB(2) is not in Very's hand.
Probable date: 1836–spring 1838 (based on style and location at RPB and MH(J)).

228. The Stranger's Gift
Copy-text: SO, 18 August 1838
Other version collated: E

722. The New Birth
Copy-text: MH(OP)
Other versions collated: MH(J); SO, 27 October 1838; E; Rosary; CAL; SSLF
A note in Sylvester Judd's hand following the MH(J) ms. reads: Cambridge. Sept, 1838. / By My Friend Jones Very.

741. The Journey
Copy-text: Myerson
On the back of the manuscript are Greek exercises, followed by "Cushing 2d Division." This inscription suggests that the poem was written before Very was forced to leave his tutoring position at Harvard (14 September 1838), but after his ecstatic period had begun. Approximate date is thus early to mid-September 1838.

120. "In Him we live, & move, & have our being"
Copy-text: MH(OP)
Other versions collated: SO, 10 November 1838; E

A copy of the poem is in Caroline S. Tappan's hand in the Tappan Papers at MH (bMS Am 1221 [288A]). Henry David Thoreau transcribed from SO this poem and No. 242 ("Enoch"), No. 213 ("Love"), No. 122 ("The Son"), No. 98 ("Day"), and No. 275 ("Night") (Notebook MA.594, Pierpont Morgan Library).

242. Enoch
Copy-text: NN
Other versions collated: MH(OP); SO, 10 November 1838; E; SAP; G; Rosary
A copy of the poem is in Caroline S. Tappan's hand in the Tappan Papers at MH (bMS Am 1221 [288A]).
See also Textual Notes for No. 120, "In Him we live, & move, & have our being."
MH(OP) is signed: J. Very
SO is signed: I.

122. The Son
Copy-text: MH(OP)
Other versions collated: SO, 17 November 1838; E; SAP; G; BH; HS; DHB; LSA; HTB; SSLF
SSLF includes this paragraph in the introduction to its selection of poems by Very:
    In copying some of the hymns and sonnets contained in his "Essays and Poems," we first present three of them ["The Son," "The Spirit-Land," and "Change"] in the altered form which the writer himself authorized or approved to adapt them to church use, without any other omission or change which compilers may have since made and perpetuated. In this form they first appeared, we believe, in the "Book of Hymns," except that the headings are here given as they are found in "Essays and Poems."
See also Textual Notes for No. 120, "In Him we live, & move, & have our being."

213. Love
Copy-text: SO, 17 November 1838
Other version collated: E
See also Textual Notes for No. 120, "In Him we live, & move, & have our being."

98. Day
Copy-text: SO, 24 November 1838
Other versions collated: E, G, PA, PG, CAL
Precopy-text version: MH
See also Textual Notes for No. 120, "In Him we live, & move, & have our being."

275. Night
Copy-text: SO, 24 November 1838
Other versions collated: E, G, PA, PG, CAL
Precopy-text version: MH
See also Textual Notes for No. 120, "In Him we live, & move, & have our being."

482. The Coming
Copy-text: MH(1)
Other version collated: SO, 1 December 1838
Precopy-text version: MH(2)

725. The Morning Watch
Copy-text: SO, 1 December 1838

Other version collated: E
Precopy-text version: MH

406. The Weary and Heavy Laden
Copy-text: SO, 19 January 1839
Very included a copy of this poem in a letter dated 8 December 1838 to A. Bronson
Alcott; though the original letter and poem are missing, Alcott copied them into his
journal for 10 December 1838 (journal at MH).

264. The Garden
Copy-text: MH(1)
Other versions collated: SO, 8 December 1838; E; Rosary
Precopy-text version: MH(2)

789. The Song
Copy-text: MH(1)
Other versions collated: SO, 8 December 1838; E
Precopy-text version: MH(2)

126. The Spirit Land
Copy-text: MH(1)
Other versions collated: SO, 15 December 1838; SO offprint (in A. Bronson Alcott's
Journal, MH); E; G; Rosary; HBP; BS; LWP
Precopy-text version: MH(2)
MH(1) is signed: I.
This poem was altered by Very to produce a hymn, No. 126a; see Textual Notes for
No. 122, "The Son," for headnote in SSLF that refers to this alteration.

258. The Slave
Copy-text: MH(1)
Other versions collated: SO, 15 December 1838; SO offprint (in A. Bronson Alcott's
Journal, MH); E
Precopy-text version: MH(2)
MH(1) is signed: I.

319. The Bread from Heaven
Copy-text: MH(1)
Other versions collated: SO, 15 December 1838; SO offprint (in A. Bronson Alcott's
Journal, MH); E
Precopy-text version: MH(2)
MH(1) is signed: I.

518. The Latter Rain
Copy-text: MH(1)
Other versions collated: PHi; SO, 15 December 1838; SO offprint (in A. Bronson
Alcott's Journal, MH); E; G; CG; CAL; HBP; LWP
Precopy-text version: MH(2)
MH(1) is signed: I.
PHi is addressed: Mr. J. Eastman Chase / Box 89 Present
Following the text in PHi is written: Salem Nov. 23d 1860 Jones Very
This poem was altered by Very to produce a substantially different poem of the same
title, No. 518a.

598. The Word
Copy-text: MH(1)
Other versions collated: SO, 15 December 1838; SO offprint (in A. Bronson Alcott's Journal, MH)
Precopy-text version: MH(2)
MH(1) is signed: I.

630. Worship
Copy-text: MH(1)
Other versions collated: SO, 15 December 1838; SO offprint (in A. Bronson Alcott's Journal, MH); E; Rosary
Precopy-text version: MH(2)
MH(1) is signed: I.

619. The Living God
Copy-text: NN
Other versions collated: SO, 22 December 1838; E; SAP
Precopy-text version: MH

622. Time
Copy-text: MH(1)
Other versions collated: SO, 22 December 1838; E
Precopy-text version: MH(2)
MH(1) (entire poem) marked through with large *X*
MH(1) is signed: I.

699. The Violet
Copy-text: SO, 22 December 1838
Other version collated: E
Precopy-text version: MH
This is one of sixteen poems closely written in pencil on one sheet. It is probable that all of these were composed at about the same time (between Very's crisis in mid-September and mid-December), though publication dates range from 22 December 1838 to 30 March 1839 and two of the poems (No. 376, "Simmons Mobile Alabama" and No. 616, "Winter") remained unpublished in Very's lifetime.

612. The Heart
Copy-text: SO, 22 December 1838
Other versions collated: E, G
Precopy-text version: MH
See Textual Notes for No. 699, "The Violet."

132. The Trees of Life
Copy-text: SO, 29 December 1838
Other versions collated: E, G
Precopy-text version: MH
See Textual Notes for No. 699, "The Violet."

168. The Soldier of the Cross
Copy-text: SO, 29 December 1838
Other versions collated: E, VTH
Precopy-text version: MH
See Textual Notes for No. 699, "The Violet."

289. The Spirit
Copy-text: SO, 29 December 1838
Other version collated: E
Precopy-text version: MH (entitled "The Breath")
See Textual Notes for No. 699, "The Violet."

642. The Serpent
Copy-text: SO, 29 December 1838
Precopy-text version: MH
See Textual Notes for No. 699, "The Violet."

266. The Dead
Copy-text: MH(1)
Other versions collated: SO, 5 January 1839; E; VTH
Precopy-text version: MH(2)
MH(1) signed: I.
See Textual Notes for No. 699, "The Violet."

269. The Presence
Copy-text: MH(1)
Other versions collated: SO, 5 January 1839; E; SSLF
Precopy-text version: MH(2)
MH(1) signed: I.
See Textual Notes for No. 699, "The Violet."

651. The Lost
Copy-text: MH(1)
Other version collated: SO, 5 January 1839
Precopy-text version: MH(2)
MH(1) signed: I.
See Textual Notes for No. 699, "The Violet."

103. The Robe
Copy-text: MH(1)
Other versions collated: SO, 12 January 1839; E
Precopy-text version: MH(2)
MH(1) signed: I.
See Textual Notes for No. 699, "The Violet."

169. The Will
Copy-text: MH(1)
Other version collated: SO, 12 January 1839
Precopy-text version: MH(2)
MH(1) signed: I.
See Textual Notes for No. 699, "The Violet."

256. The War
Copy-text: MH(1)
Other versions collated: SO, 12 January 1839; E
Precopy-text version: MH(2)
MH(1) and SO signed: I.
See Textual Notes for No. 699, "The Violet."

306. Life
Copy-text: MH(1)
Other versions collated: SO, 12 January 1839; E; HA
Precopy-text version: MH(2)
MH(1) signed: I.
See Textual Notes for No. 699, "The Violet."

608. The Reaper
Copy-text: MH(1)
Other version collated: SO, 30 March 1839
Precopy-text version: MH(2)
See Textual Notes for No. 699, "The Violet."

376. Simmons Mobile Alabama
Copy-text: MH
See Textual Notes for No. 699, "The Violet."

616. Winter
Copy-text: MH
See Textual Notes for No. 699, "The Violet."

781. John
Copy-text: MH
Other version collated: SO, 5 January 1839

90. The Flight
Copy-text: SO, 19 January 1839

153. The Priest
Copy-text: SO, 19 January 1839

488. The Resurrection
Copy-text: SO, 19 January 1839

336. My Father's House
Copy-text: SO, 26 January 1839

558. The Servant
Copy-text: SO, 26 January 1839

680. I Was Sick And In Prison
Copy-text: SO, 26 January 1839
Other versions collated: E, VTH

223. He Was Acquainted With Grief
Copy-text: WM, 6 (March 1839): 312
Other version collated: E
Precopy-text version: MH
Probable date: c. January 1839. This is one of the twenty-seven sonnets that Very sent in February 1839 to James Freeman Clarke, editor of the *Western Messenger* in Louisville, along with this note:

Hearing of your want of matter for your Messenger, I was moved to send you the above sonnets; that they may help those in affliction for Christ's name is ever the prayer of me his disciple, called to be a witness of his sufferings and an expectant of his glory. If you should ask for more as I have them so will they be communicated freely. Amen. The hope of Jesus be with you when you are called to be a partaker of his temptations.

(Quoted in WM, 6 [March 1839], 308)

293. The Fragments
Copy-text: WM, 6 (March 1839): 313
Precopy-text version: MH
See Textual Notes for No. 223, "He Was Acquainted With Grief."

548. The Winter Rain
Copy-text: WM, 6 (March 1839): 312
Precopy-text version: MH
See Textual Notes for No. 223, "He Was Acquainted With Grief."

557. Forbearance
Copy-text: WM, 6 (March 1839): 312–13
Precopy-text version: MH
See Textual Notes for No. 223, "He Was Acquainted With Grief."

596. The Wolf and the Lamb Shall Feed Together
Copy-text: WM, 6 (March 1839): 311
Precopy-text version: MH
See Textual Notes for No. 223, "He Was Acquainted With Grief."

677. The Rail Road
Copy-text: WM, 6 (March 1839): 310–11
Other versions collated: E, G
Precopy-text version: MH
See Textual Notes for No. 223, "He Was Acquainted With Grief."

818. Behold He Is at Hand That Doth Betray Me
Copy-text: WM, 6 (March 1839): 311–12
Precopy-text version: MH
See Textual Notes for No. 223, "He Was Acquainted With Grief."

691. The Fruit
Copy-text: WM, 6 (March 1839): 313–14
Precopy-text version: MH
See Textual Notes for No. 223, "He Was Acquainted With Grief."

824. To Him That Hath Shall Be Given
Copy-text: WM, 6 (March 1839): 314
Precopy-text version: MH
See Textual Notes for No. 223, "He Was Acquainted With Grief."

219. The Thorns
Copy-text: WM, 6 (April 1839): 370–71
Precopy-text version: MH
See Textual Notes for No. 223, "He Was Acquainted With Grief."

388. The River
Copy-text: WM, 6 (April 1839): 366
Precopy-text version: MH
See Textual Notes for No. 223, "He Was Acquainted With Grief."

262. The New Jerusalem
Copy-text: WM, 6 (April 1839): 366
Precopy-text version: MH
See Textual Notes for No. 223, "He Was Acquainted With Grief."

249. The Cross
Copy-text: WM, 6 (April 1839): 367
Precopy-text version: MH
See Textual Notes for No. 223, "He Was Acquainted With Grief."

350. Nature
Copy-text: WM, 6 (April 1839): 367
Precopy-text version: MH
See Textual Notes for No. 223, "He Was Acquainted With Grief."

334. Ye Gave Me No Meat
Copy-text: WM, 6 (April 1839): 367–68
Other version collated: E
Precopy-text version: MH
See Textual Notes for No. 223, "He Was Acquainted With Grief."

286. Day Unto Day Uttereth Speech
Copy-text: WM, 6 (April 1839): 368
Precopy-text version: MH
See Textual Notes for No. 223, "He Was Acquainted With Grief."

687. Labor and Rest
Copy-text: WM, 6 (April 1839): 368–69
Precopy-text version: MH
See Textual Notes for No. 223, "He Was Acquainted With Grief."

703. The Disciple
Copy-text: WM, 6 (April 1839): 369
Other version collated: E
Precopy-text version: MH
See Textual Notes for No. 223, "He Was Acquainted With Grief."

694. The Mountain
Copy-text: WM, 6 (April 1839): 369
Precopy-text version: MH
See Textual Notes for No. 223, "He Was Acquainted With Grief."

398. The Mustard Seed
Copy-text: WM, 6 (April 1839): 369–70
See Textual Notes for No. 223, "He Was Acquainted With Grief."

716. Eden
Copy-text: WM, 6 (April 1839): 370
Precopy-text version: MH
See Textual Notes for No. 223, "He Was Acquainted With Grief."

226. My meat and drink
Copy-text: WM, 6 (April 1839): 371
Precopy-text version: MH

See Textual Notes for No. 223, "He Was Acquainted With Grief."

718. Forgive me my trespasses
Copy-text: WM, 6 (April 1839): 371
Precopy-text version: MH
See Textual Notes for No. 223, "He Was Acquainted With Grief."

685. The Star
Copy-text: WM, 6 (April 1839): 372
Precopy-text version: MH
See Textual Notes for No. 223, "He Was Acquainted With Grief."

250. The Watchman
Copy-text: WM, 6 (April 1839): 372
Precopy-text version: MH
See Textual Notes for No. 223, "He Was Acquainted With Grief."

544. The Prison
Copy-text: WM, 6 (April 1839): 372–73
Precopy-text version: MH
See Textual Notes for No. 223, "He Was Acquainted With Grief."

546. The Prophet
Copy-text: WM, 6 (April 1839): 373
Precopy-text version: MH
See Textual Notes for No. 223, "He Was Acquainted With Grief."

218. The Flood
Copy-text: MH(1)
Precopy-text version: MH(2)
This poem, along with the five that follow, appears on a single sheet at MH that is crowded front and back with thirty-two poems, most of which were sent to James Freeman Clarke in Louisville in February 1839 for publication in the *Western Messenger* of March and April 1839.

117. The Corrupt Tree
Copy-text: MH(1)
Precopy-text version: MH(2)
See Textual Notes for No. 218, "The Flood."

125. The Pure in Heart
Copy-text: MH(1)
Precopy-text version: MH(2)
See Textual Notes for No. 218, "The Flood."

305. The Complaint
Copy-text: MH(1)
Precopy-text version: MH(2)
See Textual Notes for No. 218, "The Flood."

809. Whither shall I go from thy Spirit
Copy-text: MH(1)
Precopy-text version: MH(2)
See Textual Notes for No. 218, "The Flood."

80. The First shall be Last
Copy-text: MH(1)
Other version collated: SO, 27 April 1839
Precopy-text version: MH(2)
See Textual Notes for No. 218, "The Flood."

121. The Laborer
Copy-text: SO, 2 February 1839

234. Thy Brother's Blood
Copy-text: SO, 2 February 1839
Other version collated: E

339. The Graveyard
Copy-text: SO, 2 February 1839
Other versions collated: E, VTH

672. Sacrifice
Copy-text: MH
Other version collated: SO, 2 February 1839
Though it is a finished version, MH clearly precedes SO (see Alterations in the Manuscript). MH is used as copy-text but is emended in line 10 to reflect a presumed later substantive revision.

568. The Son of Man
Copy-text: MH
Other version collated: SO, 9 February 1839

618. The Ark
Copy-text: MH
Other versions collated: SO, 9 February 1839; E; G; LSA

700. The Father
Copy-text: MH
Other version collated: SO, 9 February 1839

801. Rachel
Copy-text: MH
Other version collated: SO, 9 February 1839

59. Christmas
Copy-text: MH
Other version collated: SO, 16 February 1839

288. The Earth
Copy-text: MH
Other versions collated: SO, 16 February 1839; E

526. The Hours
Copy-text: MH(1)
Other versions collated: MH(2); SO, 16 February 1839; CR, 3 November 1849; HC
MH(1) and MH(2) differ significantly at lines 12–14; MH(1) appears to be the 1839 version on which SO is based, while MH(2) is a revised version written a decade later for publication in CR.
SSLF also prints the poem, attributing it to HC.

728. The Christ
Copy-text: MH
Other version collated: SO, 16 February 1839

291. The Things Before
Copy-text: MH
Other version collated: SO, 23 February 1839

467. The Cup
Copy-text: MH
Other version collated: SO, 23 February 1839

536. Old Things are passed away
Copy-text: MH
Other version collated: SO, 23 February 1839

645. The Harvest
Copy-text: MH
Other version collated: SO, 23 February 1839

48. The City
Copy-text: MH
Other version collated: SO, 2 March 1839

554. The Rose
Copy-text: MH
Other versions collated: SO, 2 March 1839; E

620. Faith
Copy-text: MH
Other versions collated: SO, 2 March 1839; E; SG, 19 May 1871
SG, 30 May 1871, prints the poem, attributing it to *Poems by Jones Very* (apparently a reference to *Essays and Poems* [E]).

659. The Jew
Copy-text: MH
Other versions collated: SO, 2 March 1839; E

574. Spring
Copy-text: MH
Other version collated: SO, 9 March 1839

582. The Temple
Copy-text: MH(1)
Other versions collated: MH(2); SO, 9 March 1839; CR, 13 November 1858
SO is signed: I.
MH(2) is dated: 1858.
MH(1) and MH(2) differ significantly at lines 9–11; MH(1) appears to be the 1839 version on which SO is based, while MH(2) is a revised version written nineteen years later for publication in CR.

597. The White Horse
Copy-text: MH
Other version collated: SO, 9 March 1839

698. The Tent
Copy-text: MH
Other version collated: SO, 9 March 1839

285. My Sheep
Copy-text: MH
Other version collated: SO, 16 March 1839

474. The Corner Stone
Copy-text: MH(1)
Other versions collated: MH(2); SO, 16 March 1839; CR, 2 March 1850

599. The Good Ground
Copy-text: MH
Other version collated: SO, 16 March 1839
CR, 23 March 1839, prints the poem (unsigned), attributing it to SO.

663. The Beginning and The End
Copy-text: MH
Other version collated: SO, 16 March 1839

472. Nature
Copy-text: NNPM
Other versions collated: MH; SO, 23 March 1839; E; G; CAL; HBP; LWP; RPST
NNPM is signed: Jones Very.

522. Morning
Copy-text: MH
Other versions collated: SO, 23 March 1839; E; G; Rosary; BS

693. The Temptation
Copy-text: MH
Other version collated: SO, 23 March 1839

702. Help
Copy-text: MH
Other version collated: SO, 23 March 1839
Poem also appears in CR, 30 March 1839, signed "I.," with this headnote:
    The following Sonnet is copied from the Salem Observer, in which paper a Salem
    Poet has of late published many similar effusions. We have no doubt as to their
    author's name. There is a peculiar tone, pervading all these Sonnets, that indicate
    [sic] them as the productions of a gentleman of rare genius and purity of character,
    who was not long since a Tutor in Harvard University.

124. Change
Copy-text: MH
Other versions collated: SO, 30 March 1839; E; BH; HFS; DHB; CP; HS; LSA;
HTB; HCC; SSLF
For headnote in SSLF, see Textual Notes for No. 122, "The Son."

280. The Poor
Copy-text: MH
Other versions collated: SO, 30 March 1839; E

681. They Who Hunger

Copy-text: MH
Other version collated: SO, 30 March 1839

577. Who Hath Ears To Hear Let Him Hear!
Copy-text: SO, 6 April 1839
Other versions collated: E; SG, 19 July 1878

639. The Sign
Copy-text: SO, 6 April 1839
Other version collated: MH
It is uncertain which of these versions is later; SO has been chosen as copy-text on the basis of a few alterations in MH that might indicate that the poem was still in flux at that point.

277. The Tree
Copy-text: SO, 13 April 1839
Other version collated: MH
MH (dated "Dec.ᵐ 1849." and entitled "The Leafless Tree") is a revised version of the 1839 poem.

287. The Meek
Copy-text: SO, 13 April 1839

380. The Desert
Copy-text: MH
Other versions collated: RPB; SO, 20 April 1839
It is uncertain whether MH or RPB is the later version.

692. The Clay
Copy-text: MH
Other versions collated: SO, 20 April 1839; E

385. The Altar
Copy-text: MH(1)
Other versions collated: MH(2); SO, 27 April 1839

386. Praise
Copy-text: MH
Other version collated: SO, 4 May 1839

625. Terror
Copy-text: MH
Other version collated: SO, 4 May 1839

119-123. The Prayer
Copy-text: MH
Other version collated: SO, 11 May 1839

384. Humility
Copy-text: MH
Other version collated: SO, 11 May 1839

136. Forgiveness
Copy-text: MH
Other version collated: SO, 18 May 1839

640. The Heavenly Rest
Copy-text: MH(1)
Other versions collated: MH(2); SO, 18 May 1839; CR, 15 January 1848

167. Compassion
Copy-text: MH
Other version collated: SO, 25 May 1839

664. The Rock
Copy-text: MH
Other version collated: SO, 25 May 1839

739a. [Untitled] (To notice other days were pages given)
Copy-text: MH(OP)
Date is probably winter–spring 1839, judging from dates of other poems in Emerson's Notebook "OP" and the likelihood that these poems were given to Emerson while he was preparing *Essays and Poems*, which appeared in September 1839.

490a. The Crocus
Copy-text: MH(OP)
For dating, see Textual Notes for No. 739a, [untitled] "To notice other days were pages given."

659a. The Plant
Copy-text: MH(OP)
For dating, see Textual Notes for No. 739a, [untitled] "To notice other days were pages given."

591. I am the Way
Copy-text: RPB
Probable date: fall 1838–summer 1839. This poem, along with thirty-eight other complete poems and a few abortive fragments, appears in a manuscript book marked "MSS Book 1" at RPB. The only two of these poems to have been published in Very's lifetime (No. 498, "To the pure all things are pure," and No. 556, "The Acorn") were included in Emerson's edition, which appeared in September 1839.

341. The kingdom of God Is within you
Copy-text: RPB
For dating, see Textual Notes for No. 591, "I am the Way."

655. My Church
Copy-text: RPB
For dating, see Textual Notes for No. 591, "I am the Way."

274. The Charge
Copy-text: RPB
For dating, see Textual Notes for No. 591, "I am the Way."

715. The Sabbath
Copy-text: RPB
For dating, see Textual Notes for No. 591, "I am the Way."

626. The Invitation
Copy-text: RPB
For dating, see Textual Notes for No. 591, "I am the Way."

606. The Preacher
Copy-text: RPB
For dating, see Textual Notes for No. 591, "I am the Way."

88. Come unto me
Copy-text: RPB
For dating, see Textual Notes for No. 591, "I am the Way."

528. Flee to the mountains
Copy-text: RPB
For dating, see Textual Notes for No. 591, "I am the Way."

70. Blessed are they that mourn
Copy-text: RPB
For dating, see Textual Notes for No. 591, "I am the Way."

157. Faith
Copy-text: RPB
For dating, see Textual Notes for No. 591, "I am the Way."

61. Redeeming the time
Copy-text: RPB
For dating, see Textual Notes for No. 591, "I am the Way."

724. 'Tis Finished
Copy-text: RPB
For dating, see Textual Notes for No. 591, "I am the Way."

236. Effort
Copy-text: RPB
For dating, see Textual Notes for No. 591, "I am the Way."

498. To the pure all things are pure
Copy-text: RPB
Other versions collated: E, VTH
For dating, see Textual Notes for No. 591, "I am the Way."

711. The Task
Copy-text: RPB
For dating, see Textual Notes for No. 591, "I am the Way."

235. Spring
Copy-text: RPB
For dating, see Textual Notes for No. 591, "I am the Way."

74. The Day
Copy-text: RPB
For dating, see Textual Notes for No. 591, "I am the Way."

623. The Strong Man
Copy-text: RPB
For dating, see Textual Notes for No. 591, "I am the Way."

802. The Warrior
Copy-text: RPB
For dating, see Textual Notes for No. 591, "I am the Way."

556. The Acorn
Copy-text: RPB
Other version collated: E
For dating, see Textual Notes for No. 591, "I am the Way."

621. The Shelter
Copy-text: RPB
For dating, see Textual Notes for No. 591, "I am the Way."

540. The Harvest
Copy-text: RPB
For dating, see Textual Notes for No. 591, "I am the Way."

279. The Husbandman
Copy-text: RPB
For dating, see Textual Notes for No. 591, "I am the Way."

820. The Last
Copy-text: RPB
For dating, see Textual Notes for No. 591, "I am the Way."

93. The Call
Copy-text: RPB
For dating, see Textual Notes for No. 591, "I am the Way."

603. The Promise
Copy-text: RPB
For dating, see Textual Notes for No. 591, "I am the Way."

516. Joy
Copy-text: RPB
For dating, see Textual Notes for No. 591, "I am the Way."

75. Hope
Copy-text: RPB
For dating, see Textual Notes for No. 591, "I am the Way."

381. Relief
Copy-text: RPB
For dating, see Textual Notes for No. 591, "I am the Way."

678. Joy
Copy-text: RPB
For dating, see Textual Notes for No. 591, "I am the Way."

253. The Creation
Copy-text: RPB
For dating, see Textual Notes for No. 591, "I am the Way."

340. The Snare
Copy-text: RPB
For dating, see Textual Notes for No. 591, "I am the Way."

345. The Yoke
Copy-text: RPB
For dating, see Textual Notes for No. 591, "I am the Way."

225. The Promise
Copy-text: RPB
For dating, see Textual Notes for No. 591, "I am the Way."

747. The Path of Peace
Copy-text: RPB
For dating, see Textual Notes for No. 591, "I am the Way."

344. Obedience
Copy-text: RPB
For dating, see Textual Notes for No. 591, "I am the Way."

215. Grief
Copy-text: RPB
For dating, see Textual Notes for No. 591, "I am the Way."

738. The Reward
Copy-text: RPB
For dating, see Textual Notes for No. 591, "I am the Way."

304. So is every one who is born of the spirit
Copy-text: RPB
Style, content, and location suggest a date of fall 1838–summer 1839.

853. The Seed
Copy-text: RPB
Style, content, and location suggest a date of fall 1838–summer 1839.

208. I am the Light of the World
Copy-text: RPB
Style, content, and location suggest a date of fall 1838–summer 1839.

207. The Apostle
Copy-text: RPB
Style, content, and location suggest a date of fall 1838–summer 1839.

628. The Message
Copy-text: RPB
Style, content, and location suggest a date of fall 1838–summer 1839.

209. I Am the Bread of Life
Copy-text: RPB
Style, content, and location suggest a date of fall 1838–summer 1839.

624. The Foe
Copy-text: MH
Style, content, and location suggest a date of fall 1838–summer 1839.

508. Yet Once More
Copy-text: MH
Style, content, and location suggest a date of fall 1838–summer 1839.

670. The Humble
Copy-text: MH
Style, content, and location suggest a date of fall 1838–summer 1839.

676. Comfort
Copy-text: MH
Style, content, and location suggest a date of fall 1838–summer 1839.

240. The Guest
Copy-text: MH
Style, content, and location suggest a date of fall 1838–summer 1839.

490. The Eagles
Copy-text: MH
Style, content, and location suggest a date of fall 1838–summer 1839.

486. Then shall all the tribes of the earth mourn
Copy-text: MH
Style, content, and location suggest a date of fall 1838–summer 1839.

408. Repent for the kingdom of Heaven is at hand
Copy-text: MH
Style, content, and location suggest a date of fall 1838–summer 1839.

551. Thy Name
Copy-text: MH
Style, content, and location suggest a date of fall 1838–summer 1839.

178. The Mourner
Copy-text: MH
Other version collated: RPB
RPB is probably not in Very's hand.
Style, content, and location suggest a date of fall 1838–summer 1839.

503. The Giants
Copy-text: MH
Style, content, and location suggest a date of fall 1838–summer 1839.

60. To the Fishermen
Copy-text: MH
Style, content, and location suggest a date of fall 1838–summer 1839.

742. The Sower
Copy-text: MH
Style, content, and location suggest a date of fall 1838–summer 1839.

783. Charity
Copy-text: MH
Style, content, and location suggest a date of fall 1838–summer 1839.

631. The Created
Copy-text: MH
Style, content, and location suggest a date of fall 1838–summer 1839.

682. To All
Copy-text: MH
Style, content, and location suggest a date of fall 1838–summer 1839.

159. The Unrevealed
Copy-text: MH(1)

Precopy-text version: MH(2)
Style, content, and location suggest a date of fall 1838–summer 1839.

607. Sayings
Copy-text: MH
Style, content, and location suggest a date of fall 1838–summer 1839.

32. The Prisoner
Copy-text: MH
Style, content, and location suggest a date of fall 1838–summer 1839.

342. Eternal Life
Copy-text: MH
Style, content, and location suggest a date of fall 1838–summer 1839.

405. Unto you is born a Saviour
Copy-text: MH
Style, content, and location suggest a date of fall 1838–summer 1839.
More than half of the page on which this poem is written has been cut off, including line 14 of this poem and probably the whole of another, as well as an entire poem on the reverse. Line 14 in this edition follows Cl.

214. The Redeemed
Copy-text: MH
Style, content, and location suggest a date of fall 1838–summer 1839.

714. Hallowed be thy Name
Copy-text: MH
Style, content, and location suggest a date of fall 1838–summer 1839.

739. To him who overcometh
Copy-text: MH
Style, content, and location suggest a date of fall 1838–summer 1839.

261. The Children
Copy-text: MH
Style, content, and location suggest a date of fall 1838–summer 1839.

506. The New Man
Copy-text: MH
Style, content, and location suggest a date of fall 1838–summer 1839.

732. The Veil of the Temple
Copy-text: MH
Style, content, and location suggest a date of fall 1838–summer 1839.

222. The Holy of Holies
Copy-text: MH
Style, content, and location suggest a date of fall 1838–summer 1839.

133. The Brethren
Copy-text: MH
Style, content, and location suggest a date of fall 1838–summer 1839.

804. The Prodigal
Copy-text: MH

Style, content, and location suggest a date of fall 1838–summer 1839.

704. The Fig Tree
Copy-text: MH
Style, content, and location suggest a date of fall 1838–summer 1839.

665. The Branch
Copy-text: MH
Style, content, and location suggest a date of fall 1838–summer 1839.

712. Not as the World giveth
Copy-text: MH
Style, content, and location suggest a date of fall 1838–summer 1839.

782. The Good Gift
Copy-text: MH
Style, content, and location suggest a date of fall 1838–summer 1839.

510. History
Copy-text: MH
Style, content, and location suggest a date of fall 1838–summer 1839.

393. The Spirit Land
Copy-text: MH(1)
Precopy-text version: MH(2)
This twelve-line poem may be an uncompleted sonnet.
Style, content, and location suggest a date of fall 1838–summer 1839.

662. Thy Father's House
Copy-text: MH
Style, content, and location suggest a date of fall 1838–summer 1839.

689. Jacob's Well
Copy-text: MH
Other version collated: RPB
RPB is probably not in Very's hand.
Style, content, and location suggest a date of fall 1838–summer 1839.

51. The Day of Denial
Copy-text: MH
Style, content, and location suggest a date of fall 1838–summer 1839.

5. Spiritual Darkness
Copy-text: MH
Lines 1–6 are essentially the same as those of No. 3, "The Dark Day"; lines 1–8 are essentially the same as those of No. 4, also entitled "Spiritual Darkness."
Style, content, and location suggest a date of fall 1838–summer 1839.

532. The New World
Copy-text: MH
Style, content, and location suggest a date of fall 1838–summer 1839.

588. The Word
Copy-text: MH
Style, content, and location suggest a date of fall 1838–summer 1839.

800. The Field and Wood
Copy-text: MH
Style, content, and location suggest a date of fall 1838–summer 1839.

604. The Apostles
Copy-text: MH
Style, content, and location suggest a date of fall 1838–summer 1839.

216. The House
Copy-text: MH
Style, content, and location suggest a date of fall 1838–summer 1839.

743. The Tenant
Copy-text: MWelC
Very included this poem and No. 798, "This Morn," in an undated letter to Lidian Emerson apparently written shortly after his September 1839 visit to the Emersons. He mentioned that they were "formerly written" at her house and that she had requested copies of them. His language seems to suggest an earlier visit than his most recent—probably his extended stay on 14–17 June 1839—though it is possible that he was referring to the September visit (letter at MWelC).

798. This Morn
Copy-text: MWelC
See Textual Notes for No. 743, "The Tenant." Gittleman's discussion of this episode (pp. 342–43) confuses this poem with No. 784, "The Day not for Gain," which has a similar first line.

816. The Call
Copy-text: SO, 13 July 1839
Other version collated: E

829. The Prayer
Copy-text: SO, 20 July 1839
Other versions collated: SG, 10 September 1839; E; WM, 7 (May 1840): 43; BH; HC; HFS; DHB; PL; CAL; BW; HS; LA; LSA; HTB; HCC; SSLF
Precopy-text version: RPB
Headnote in SSLF:
    The next four pieces are also from the "Essays and Poems." The first one of these ["The Prayer"], with the exception of the fourth stanza, appeared in the "Book of Hymns," and has since passed into various other Collections, and has become a favorite with many of our churches. We present this exquisitely beautiful hymn in its entire form.

272. The Bride
Copy-text: SO, 27 July 1839

494. My Garden
Copy-text: MH
Other version collated: SO, 3 August 1839

224. The Unripe Fruit
Copy-text: SO, 10 August 1839

730. The Immortal

Copy-text: MWelC
Other version collated: SO, 5 October 1839
This poem, along with "The Serving Man" and "The Cottage," was sent to Emerson with the following note, dated 13[?] August 1839:

> I send you these by letter that they may come earlier to hand—I hardly dared to write them and that will excuse me from a letter. They are the true letter as I am true. There is more joy and freedom as I advance yet still I long to be clothed upon with my house from heaven. In you too may more of the old pass away and the new and abiding be more & more felt, this I pray for ever as I am.
>
> J. Very

Emerson was to include only one of the three ("The Cottage") in *Essays and Poems*. After the first word of line 4 in the manuscript of "The Immortal," the handwriting changes and from that point on and throughout "The Serving-Man" and "The Cottage" does not seem to be Very's; yet it seems clear from the note above that Very authorized these versions. It is possible that the second hand is Very's as well, perhaps in a changed mental state from when he began the poem. For both this poem and "The Serving-Man," SO gives the author as "Jones Very" rather than the usual "I."

322. The Serving-Man
Copy-text: MWelC
Other version collated: SO, 26 October 1839
See Textual Notes for No. 730, "The Immortal."

513. The Cottage
Copy-text: MWelC
Other version collated: E
Precopy-text version: MH
See Textual Notes for No. 730, "The Immortal."

260. The Still-Born
Copy-text: SO, 17 August 1839

241. To-Day
Copy-text: SO, 24 August 1839
Other versions collated: RPB; MH; CR, 24 June 1871
MH is a later revision of the original poem, including an extra stanza (see Historical Collation), which was published in CR in 1871. It is probable (in view of the substantive differences between the RPB and SO versions in the title and lines 14 and 16) that SO is based on a later ms. than RPB; SO was thus chosen as copy-text. SO is signed: I.

308. The Withered Tree
Copy-text: SO, 31 August 1839
Other version collated: CR, 22 December 1849
CR is a later revised version of the original poem.

211. The Hour
Copy-text: SO, 7 September 1839
Precopy-text version: MH (entitled "The Life of the Hour")

552. The Old Road
Copy-text: SO, 14 September 1839
Other version collated: SG, 20 July 1849

478. The Fair Morning
Copy-text: SO, 21 September 1839
This poem was significantly revised for publication in 1864.
The revised version is here treated as a separate poem, No. 478a of the same title.

530. The Clouded Morning
Copy-text: SO, 21 September 1839
This poem was significantly revised for publication in 1864.
The revised version is here treated as a separate poem, No. 529 of the same title.

267. The Plagues of Egypt
Copy-text: SO, 28 September 1839
Other version collated: MH (copy in unidentified hand)

3. The Dark Day
Copy-text: SO, 12 October 1839
Two other poems (Nos. 4 and 5, both entitled "Spiritual Darkness") are essentially
the same as this one for the first six lines only.

786. The Removal
Copy-text: SO, 12 October 1839

550. The Rain
Copy-text: SO, 19 October 1839

502. The Frost
Copy-text: MH
Other versions collated: SO, 19 October 1839; CE, 39 (November 1845): 331
The *Boston Courier* (5 November 1845), in an article reviewing the *Christian Exam-
iner*, reprinted this poem from CE with this introduction: "Of the poetical Con-
tributions . . . the following we presume from the signature to be from the pen of
an accomplished scholar, who seems for a long time to have retired from the world,
but whose renewed contributions will be welcome to the friends of American litera-
ture." SG (11 November 1845) then reprinted the above introduction and the poem
from CE.

595. Autumn Days
Copy-text: SO, 2 November 1839
Other version collated: MH
The substantive differences between MH and SO suggest that SO is based on a later
ms. than MH.

519. Autumn Leaves
Copy-text: SO, 2 November 1839
Other version collated: RPB
The substantive differences between RPB and SO suggest that SO is based on a later
ms. than RPB.

707. The Lost Sheep
Copy-text: SG, 5 November 1839
Other version collated: MH
The substantive differences between MH and SG suggest that SG is based on a later
ms. than MH.

337. The Shepherd's Life
Copy-text: SG, 8 November 1839
Other version collated: CR, 12 August 1871

632. The Good Samaritan
Copy-text: SO, 9 November 1839

799. The Birds of Passage
Copy-text: SO, 9 November 1839

512. The Feast
Copy-text: SG, 12 November 1839

541. The Ramble
Copy-text: SO, 16 November 1839

475. The Barberry Bush
Copy-text: MH
Other versions collated: SO, 16 November 1839; Dial, 2 (July 1841): 131; Parnassus, p. 32
The poem appears in the *Dial* in Emerson's review of Very's *Essays and Poems*, taken, Emerson writes, from a newspaper (presumably SO) published after *Essays and Poems* appeared.

505. The Hand and the Foot
Copy-text: SG, 19 November 1839

690. The Eye and Ear
Copy-text: SG, 19 November 1839
Other version collated: RPB (copy in unidentified hand)

790. The Sunset
Copy-text: SG, 22 November 1839

733. Yourself
Copy-text: SO, 23 November 1839

210. Thy Better Self
Copy-text: MH
Other version collated: SO, 23 November 1839

470. The Glutton
Copy-text: MH
Other versions collated: RPB; SG, 26 November 1839
RPB is in an unidentified hand.

784. The Day not for Gain
Copy-text: MH
Other versions collated: RPB; SG, 26 November 1839
RPB is in an unidentified hand.

493. The World
Copy-text: SG, 29 November 1839

613. The House Not Made With Hands, Eternal In The Heavens
Copy-text: MH

Other versions collated: SO, 30 November 1839; CR, 13 May 1871

501. The Broken Bowl
Copy-text: SG, 3 December 1839
Other version collated: MH

254. The Bunch of Flowers
Copy-text: SO, 7 December 1839

271. Hymn: Home
Copy-text: MH(1)
Other versions collated: MH(2); SG, 10 December 1839

633. The Ghost
Copy-text: MH
This poem and No. 284, "The Seasons," were sent by Very on 10 December 1839 to
C. B. Farnsworth, Scituate Harbor, Massachusetts, along with the following note:
"If you will copy these two poems in the form of a letter and direct it in my name to
R. W. Emerson of Concord." Claudius Buchanan Farnsworth was at the time a junior
at Harvard and one of several former students with whom Very seems to have kept in
touch after his dismissal in September 1838. See Helen R. Deese, "Unpublished and
Uncollected Poems of Jones Very," *ESQ* 30 (3d Quarter 1984): 159, for further dis-
cussion of the circumstances of the transmission of the manuscript. See also Textual
Notes for No. 160a, "The Watcher."

284. The Seasons
Copy-text: MH(1)
Other versions collated: MH(2); SO, 28 December 1839; CR, 29 April 1854
MH(1) is inscribed above the title: Mr. C. B. Farnsworth and others
MH(1) is signed: By Jones Very
MH(1) is followed by a note by J. M. Keyes indicating that he has taken a copy of the
poems and will deliver the manuscript to Emerson at his next lecture.
See Textual Notes for No. 633, "The Ghost."
MH(1) and SO are the 1839 versions; MH(2) is apparently a much later revision on
which CR is based.

614. The Silent
Copy-text: SG, 17 December 1839
Other versions collated: MH; CR, 24 February 1849
MH (entitled "Man's Sympathy with Nature") is a revision of the 1839 version of the
poem (represented in SG) for publication in 1849 in CR.

737. The Way
Copy-text: SG, 20 December 1839
Other version collated: RPB (copy in an unidentified hand)

803. The Sun
Copy-text: SG, 20 December 1839
Other version collated: RPB (copy in an unidentified hand)

257. The Worm
Copy-text: SO, 21 December 1839
No. 257a of the same title is a later, considerably altered version treated here as a
separate poem.

160a. The Watcher
Copy-text: NBEB, 5 May 1843
This headnote in NBEB introduces the three poems "The Watcher," "The Physician,"
and "The Miser":

> The following sonnets are by one of the most remarkable, though perhaps one of
> the least known poets in this country. The greatness of the thoughts in them, con-
> taining the germs of a whole system of philosophy, will perhaps, not be generally
> appreciated. But the architectural propriety and beauty, particularly in *The Physician*
> and *The Watcher*, must be obvious to the most casual reader of poetry. —They were
> given me some three years ago, with others, by the author, with leave to do what
> I pleased with them, and it seems to me that I cannot do people of taste a better
> service than by giving them to the public.
>
> F.

"F." is probably C. B. Farnsworth (see Textual Notes for No. 633, "The Ghost"),
to whom Very sent two other poems on 10 December 1839. Farnsworth was in
New Bedford, Massachusetts, in 1843. The probable date of composition of "The
Watcher," "The Physician," and "The Miser" is sometime during 1839, about the
time when the other poems were sent to Farnsworth; the style and subject matter
are consistent with that date, and it is only a few months removed from Farnsworth's
estimate of "some three years ago."

611a. The Physician
Copy-text: NBEB, 5 May 1843
See Textual Notes for No. 160a, "The Watcher."

194a. The Miser
Copy-text: NBEB, 5 May 1843
See Textual Notes for No. 160a, "The Watcher."

471. The Spheres
Copy-text: SG, 3 January 1840

610. The Builders
Copy-text: RPB
Other version collated: SG, 7 January 1840

283. Give and it shall be given unto you. Spiritual Debtors
Copy-text: MH(1)
Other versions collated: MH(J); SG, 17 January 1840
MH(J), in the Sylvester Judd papers, is in Judd's hand. It is copied at the end of a
conversation, which Judd records with Very, that apparently took place on 22 Sep-
tember 1839.

605. The Laborers
Copy-text: SO, 18 January 1840

679. The Unfaithful Servants
Copy-text: SO, 18 January 1840
Precopy-text version: MH

533. The Thieves
Copy-text: SO, 1 February 1840

102. The Strangers

Copy-text: SO, 15 February 1840
Other versions collated: MH(E); Parnassus, p. 159; CR, 25 January 1879
MH(E) is in Emerson's hand.

259. The Light from Within
Copy-text: MB
Other versions collated: SO, 22 February 1840; BH; HS; HTB; HCC; SSLF
Above title in MB is written: Rev. J. S. Dwight and others

683. [Untitled] (Thou know'st not what thy lord will say)
Copy-text: RPB
Probable date: late 1839–early 1840 (based on style, content, and location)

586. The Good
Copy-text: RPB
Probable date: late 1839–early 1840 (based on style, content, and location)

184. The Distant
Copy-text: MH
Probable date: late 1839–early 1840 (based on style and content)

561. A Word
Copy-text: WM, 8 (April 1841): 550
Other versions collated: CR, 15 May 1847; MH-Ar; MH(1); RPB; SG, 30 May 1848
Precopy-text version: MH(2)
This poem perhaps underwent more revisions than any other of Very's works. The probable order of the versions is MH(2), a draft; WM, which generally follows MH(2); CR, which includes some substantial changes; MH-Ar, a draft revision of CR incorporating more changes; MH(1) (dated 1847), which follows MH-Ar; RPB, a draft revision of MH(1), which essentially restores the poem to its original finished form (represented by WM); and SG, which follows RPB. Both MH-Ar and RPB incorporate layers of revisions that are not reported in Alterations in the Manuscript; it is the final revisions of these versions that are represented in the Historical Collation. This poem is copied in the back of William P. Andrews's copy of *Essays and Poems* now in the collection of Joel Myerson. It is followed by this note:

> The above was sent to Mr. [Caleb] Stetson of Medford, enclosed with a letter which commenced thus—Rev Sir In a discourse preached by you in the College Chapel several years ago you asked this question "'who can describe the orbit of a word?' I send you these lines to help you in this course."
> The poem was given to me by the author April 21st 1840.

This version of the poem is nearly identical to WM. Following the poem in WM is this paragraph, apparently by Very:

> The words of God are affirmations of life and immortality, thus and thus only made known. Let him that hath an ear, hear. They tell of conditions of existence made permanent by long conflict, and thus outshining upon men; in words, whose height and depth have never been measured. He who "*loves*," is of God. Loves what? not this or that;—still that mighty word continues sounding in our ears until all things have fled away from before it; and this remains but as the condition of being, which says, of such is the kingdom of heaven. "*Ask*," and it shall be "*given*" you. What? Ask not this or that.—Ask *always*, ask *everything*, this word is of the spirit; it quickens until all vain petitions have ceased from your lips, and that which it is Itself abides with you, as the true state of your soul. "*Stand*," not here or there; for these

are but temporal, but be such as I whose position in life is expressed by that one word, and that alone. He that reads, may he love, may he ask, may he stand; until these great watch-words uttered of old, become the daily expressions of his being; then will I call him one with us, the brotherhood without number, the friends who have come together, and of whom Jesus is the midst.

795. The Settler
Copy-text: WM, 8 (January 1841): 424
Though this poem and the following ten poems were not published until early 1841 in WM, it is reasonable to assume that they were sent to WM at the same time as No. 561, "A Word," which also appeared there. Since "A Word" was written before 21 April 1840 (see Textual Notes on "A Word"), it is likely that all of these poems date from early 1840, a supposition supported by their similarities in form and tone with other poems from the late 1839–early 1840 period.

263. The Dwellings of the Just
Copy-text: MH
Other version collated: WM, 8 (February 1841): 467
See Textual Notes for No. 795, "The Settler."

327. Death
Copy-text: WM, 8 (February 1841): 462
See Textual Notes for No. 795, "The Settler."

465. The Birth-Day of the Soul
Copy-text: MH(1)
Other versions collated: MH(2); WM, 8 (February 1841): 462; MRM, 28 (August 1862): 126
See Textual Notes for No. 795, "The Settler."

511. The Bee Hive
Copy-text: MH
Other version collated: WM, 8 (February 1841): 472
See Textual Notes for No. 795, "The Settler."

575. Time's House
Copy-text: WM, 8 (February 1841): 449
See Textual Notes for No. 795, "The Settler."

463. The Fox and the Bird
Copy-text: WM, 8 (April 1841): 551
See Textual Notes for No. 795, "The Settler."

480. Faith and Light
Copy-text: WM, 8 (April 1841): 552
Other version collated: CR, 8 December 1855
Precopy-text version: MH
See Textual Notes for No. 795, "The Settler."

602. The Word
Copy-text: WM, 8 (April 1841): 551
See Textual Notes for No. 795, "The Settler."

661. The Absent

Copy-text: MH
Other version collated: WM, 8 (April 1841): 549
See Textual Notes for No. 795, "The Settler."

748. The Pilgrim
Copy-text: RPB
Other versions collated: MH; WM, 8 (April 1841): 549–50; CR, 13 February 1847
At end of MH is written: (Feby,) 1847 [parenthesis in pencil]
RPB is the ms. on which the WM (1841) version of the poem is based; Very revised
it slightly in MH for publication in CR in 1847.
See Textual Notes for No. 795, "The Settler."

239. The Idler
Copy-text: A, pp. 41–42
Other version collated: Cl
This is one of nine poems that do not exist in manuscript versions but were printed in
either A or Cl and that, because of subject matter and form, I have judged to belong
to the late 1838–early 1840 period. The other poems are Nos. 495 ("The Lost"), 807
("The Narrow Way"), 531 ("The True Light"), 433 ("The Invitation"), 808 ("The
Sick"), 497 ("The Flesh"), 100 ("Decay"), and 238 ("The New Sea").

495. The Lost
Copy-text: A, p. 62
Other version collated: Cl
See Textual Notes for No. 239, "The Idler."

807. The Narrow Way
Copy-text: A, p. 63
Other version collated: Cl
See Textual Notes for No. 239, "The Idler."

531. The True Light
Copy-text: A, p. 91
Other version collated: Cl
See Textual Notes for No. 239, "The Idler."

433. The Invitation
Copy-text: A, pp. 101–2
Other version collated: Cl
See Textual Notes for No. 239, "The Idler."

808. The Sick
Copy-text: Cl, p. 125
See Textual Notes for No. 239, "The Idler."

497. The Flesh
Copy-text: Cl, p. 142
See Textual Notes for No. 239, "The Idler."

100. Decay
Copy-text: Cl, pp. 199–200
See Textual Notes for No. 239, "The Idler."

238. The New Sea

Copy-text: Cl, p. 167
See Textual Notes for No. 239, "The Idler."

351. The Baker's Island Light
Copy-text: MH(OP)
Other versions collated: MH(1); SG, 21 August 1840; SG, 7 February 1871
Precopy-text version: MH(2)
Other uncollated version: RPB (a draft version of SG 1871)
SG 1840 bears the unusual signature "J."

521. The Gifts of God
Copy-text: SG, 2 October 1840

721. The Sepulchre Of The Books
Copy-text: MH
MH is dated: January, 1841.

553. The Robin's Song
Copy-text: MH
Other versions collated: SG, 6 April 1841; CR, 10 May 1851
Very mentions (in an undated letter at MWelC that must have been written in April 1841) having sent this poem "last week" to Emerson.
SG is unsigned.
MH is dated (at the end in different ink): May, 1851.

49. The Wounded Pigeon
Copy-text: MH
Other versions collated: SG, 26 October 1841; CR, 2 March 1857
Precopy-text version: RPB
MH is dated: Oct. 26th 1841
SG is unsigned.

329. The Swift
Copy-text: MWelC
MWelC is not in Very's hand, though it is followed by the pencilled notation "Jones Very." It is a copy, probably in the hand of Lydia Louisa Ann Very (presumably from a now lost original in her brother's hand), in the notebook of clippings, letters, and poems, that William P. Andrews used in preparing his edition of Very's poems in 1883. Conjectural date is based on style and subject matter.

723. The World
Copy-text: SG, 1 April 1842
Other versions collated: MH; Dial, 3 (July 1842): 99–100; CR, 16 May 1846; HBP
The poem also appears in the *Harbinger* 2 (6 June 1846): 404, attributed to CR.
SG is unsigned. MH is a slightly revised version done for CR; see p. lii, 30n.

537. The Evening Choir
Copy-text: Dial, 3 (July 1842): 97–98
See p. lii, 30n. It is unfortunate that no ms. version of this poem has survived. Very complained to Emerson of his editing of this poem for the *Dial*:

I found my poem the "Evening Choir" altered considerably from what I had written—I do not know but in one or two cases for the better. Perhaps they were all improvements but I preferred my own lines. I do not know but I ought to submit to such changes as done by the rightful authority of an Editor but I felt a little sad at the aspect of the piece.

(Letter, Very to Emerson, 23 November 1842, MWelC)

668-697. The Cold Spring In North Salem
Copy-text: MH(1)
Other versions collated: MH(OP); MH(2); MH-Ar; Pioneer, 1 (January 1843): 12; SG, 15 August 1851; CR, 15 July 1854
MH(1) was sent to James Russell Lowell [editor of the new periodical *Pioneer*], Boston, Mass., on November 5, 1842[?].
(The notation of the year on the back of the ms. is almost illegible, but has been read by MH as 1843; the publication date of the poem in the *Pioneer* would seem to argue 1842 as the correct date.)
MH(1) is signed: By Jones Very
MH-Ar is dated: Oct 5. '42.
MH(2) is dated: 1854.
MH(OP) is signed: J. Very
SG is signed: I.
The probable order of the versions is as follows: MH(OP) (undated, but included in a notebook with other poems of 1838–39); MH-Ar (5 October 1842); MH(1), sent to Lowell on 5 November 1842; the publication in the *Pioneer*, based on MH(1); SG, based on MH(OP); MH(2) (1854); CR, based on MH(2). MH(1) was chosen as copy-text because it represents the final version of the poem until Very took it up again twelve years later.

709. Lines on Reading the Death of Rev. Henry Ware, Jr.
Copy-text: SG, 30 September 1843

270. Jonathan Huntington Bright
Copy-text: SG, 19 January 1844

617. God's Host
Copy-text: MH(1)
Other versions collated: MH(2); CE, 36 (May 1844): 389
Precopy-text version: RPB
MH(1) was sent to E. S. Gannett, editor of the *Christian Examiner*, on 26 March 1844.

257a. The Worm
Copy-text: CE, 38 (May 1845): 349–50
This is a much altered version of No. 257 of the same title, here treated as a separate poem.

547. The White Dove And The Snow
Copy-text: MH
Other version collated: CR, 11 April 1846
Precopy-text version: MH-Ar
MH-Ar is followed by two dates: March 16, 1846, and April 4th 1845.

518a. The Latter Rain
Copy-text: CR, 4 April 1846
Precopy-text version: in Frances E. Very's copy of *Essays and Poems* at ViU

This poem is a much altered version of No. 518 of the same title, here treated as a separate poem. The poem is preceded by the following headnote:

> If any man, save Shakespeare, Milton and Wordsworth, has written, in the English language, better sonnets than Jones Very, we know not where to find them. What can be more exquisitely beautiful than the following, which has been furnished to us with corrections by the author? His poems need to be read in still and quiet hours, and then they come over us like the sound of distant bells on a Sabbath morning, chiming in with what is purest and most sacred in our own thoughts and in the hour.

SG, 7 April 1846, prints the poem (with the headnote), attributing it to CR.

182. Moses In Infancy
Copy-text: MH
Other version collated: CR, 9 May 1846

750. Moses at the Bush
Copy-text: MH
Other version collated: CR, 30 May 1846

749. Moses As Leader Of Israel
Copy-text: MH
Other version collated: CR, 4 July 1846

609. The New Jerusalem
Copy-text: MH
Other version collated: CR, 15 August 1846

708. The Autumn Flowers
Copy-text: MWelC
Following the poem is written: Eastport, Me; Oct⁰, 1846.

33. The Death of Man
Copy-text: MH
Other versions collated: CR, 12 December 1846; CR, 8 June 1850
Precopy-text version: MH-Ar
MH-Ar is dated: Oct⁰ 26, 1845
MH is dated: 1846.

473. As ye sow, so shall ye reap.
Copy-text: BH

126a. God Not Afar Off
Copy-text: BH
Other versions collated: PL; DHB; HS; LSA; HTB; STC; SSLF
The first eight lines are identical to those of No. 126, "The Spirit Land," which Very has here rewritten into what was to become a popular hymn.
Headnote to SSLF reads (in part):

> In copying some of the hymns and sonnets contained in his [Very's] "Essays and Poems," we first present three of them in the altered form which the writer himself authorized or approved to adapt them to church use, without any other omission or change which compilers may have since made and perpetuated. In this form they first appeared, we believe, in the "Book of Hymns," except that the headings are here given as they are found in "Essays and Poems."

593. The Indian's Retort
Copy-text: MH
Other versions collated: CR, 9 January 1847; SG, 22 May 1860
MH is dated: 1847.

8. The Widow
Copy-text: MH
Other version collated: CE, 42 (March 1847): 282–83
CE is signed: V.

667. Impatience
Copy-text: MH
Other versions collated: CR, 17 April 1847; CR, 8 May 1869

477. Abdolonymus—The Sidonian
Copy-text: MH
Other version collated: CR, 31 July 1847

559. The Arrival
Copy-text: CR, 23 October 1847
Precopy-text version: MH-Ar
Following MH-Ar is written: The Cherokee, Salem, April 5th 1847

203. The Soul's Preparation For Adversity
Copy-text: MH
Other version collated: CR, 4 December 1847
The *Boston Transcript* (1 February 1848) and SG (8 February 1848) both reprinted the poem, changing the title to "Preparation for Adversity" and attributing the poem to CR. Both publications included the following headnote, which SG attributed to the *Transcript*:

> We find the following lines on the "soul's preparation for adversity" in the Christian Register. They are signed with the initials J.V., which, we will venture to say, stand for Jones Very. The lines would have done credit to Wordsworth in his best days:—

156. Change In The Seasons
Copy-text: MH
Other versions collated: CR, 12 February 1848; SG, 6 December 1853
MH, CR, and SG are dated: January 1848
Headnote to SG:

> Mr. Editor,—A correspondent, of the 29th ult., has gratified your readers by an account of his ramble on Thanksgiving week, and by a notice of the many autumnal flowers then in bloom. The mildness of the present season is certainly remarkable; but he will find, by reference to your columns in November and December, of 1847, that that season was still more so. The following poem was written at that time. It may serve as a description of the present season, while it marks, at the same time, the sad contrast which exists between Nature and Man.
>
>   Nov. 30th, 1853.
>
> J.V.

517. The Just Shall Live by Faith
Copy-text: MH
Other version collated: CR, 26 February 1848

72. Salem
Copy-text: NN
Other versions collated: MH; CR, 25 March 1848
SG (31 March 1848) reprints the poem, attributing it to CR. NN is pasted on page 522 of a copy of Duykinck's *Cyclopaedia of American Literature* (New York: Charles Scribner, 1855).
Following NN is written:
   Salem, March 1848.
      Copied for Mr Henry M. Brooks by his

                                                            Friend, Jones Very
   (December 1848)

469-573. Spring in the Soul
Copy-text: MH
Other version collated: CR, 15 April 1848
MH is dated: March, 1848.
This is a greatly revised version of No. 574, "Spring," here treated as a separate poem.

397. Nature's Invitation
Copy-text: CR, 27 May 1848

166. Christ's Compassion: Matt. IX. 35–38.
Copy-text: MH
Other version collated: CR, 17 June 1848
This is a greatly revised version of No. 167, "Compassion," here treated as a separate poem.

29. Hymn: Nevertheless, when the Son of Man cometh, shall he find faith on the earth? Luke XVIII:8.
Copy-text: MH
Other version collated: CR, 19 August 1848

12. The Man of Science
Copy-text: MH(1)
Other version collated: CR, 21 October 1848
Precopy-text version: MH(2)

141. The Congress Of Peace At Brussels
Copy-text: MH
Other version collated: CR, 9 December 1848
MH is dated: Nov. 24. 1848
Following CR is written: Salem, Nov. 24th, 1848. / J.V.

720. 'Tis A Great Thing to Live
Copy-text: MH
Other version collated: CR, 13 January 1849
MH is dated and signed: Dec. 30th, 1848. J.V.

515. The Indian's Petition
Copy-text: MH
Other version collated: CR, 7 April 1849
MH is dated: April, 1849. ["April" interlined above cancelled "Jany 1."]
CR is dated: March 23d, 1849.

13. The Struggle
Copy-text: MH
Other version collated: CR, 23 June 1849
Following CR is printed: Salem, June 1849.

292. The Things Before
Copy-text: MH
Other version collated: CR, 21 July 1849
This is a greatly revised version of No. 291, of the same title, treated here as a separate poem.

727. The Dying Leaf
Copy-text: MH
Other version collated: CR, 10 November 1849
CR is dated: Oct. 25th, 1849.

148. The New Body
Copy-text: MH(1)
Other version collated: CR, 29 December 1849
Precopy-text versions: MH-Ar, MH(1)

565. The Clock
Copy-text: MH
Other version collated: CR, 19 January 1850

176. On The Sudden Snow
Copy-text: MH
Other version collated: CR, 6 April 1850
MH is dated: March 24th, 1850.

129. On the late Disgraceful Scene in Congress
Copy-text: MH
Other version collated: CR, 27 April 1850
MH is dated: April 27th, 1850.

268. The Funerals
Copy-text: MH
Other version collated: SG, 7 June 1850
MH is dated in pencil: 1851
Following CR is printed: Salem, April, 1850.

657. The New Aqueduct
Copy-text: MH
Other version collated: SG, 7 June 1850
MH is dated in pencil: 1851

504. The Soul's Freedom
Copy-text: MH(1)
Other versions collated: CR, 6 July 1850; MRM, 36 (July 1866): 52–53; MRM, 38 (August 1867): 100
Precopy-text version: MH(2)
SG, 6 August 1867, prints the poem without naming the author and attributes it to MRM 1867.

195. Looking Before And After
Copy-text: MH
Other version collated: CR, 14 September 1850
Precopy-text version: RPB

212. The Succory
Copy-text: MH
Other version collated: CR, 28 September 1850
Precopy-text version: RPB
RPB is entitled "The Roadside Flower."

185. The Reapers Are The Angels
Copy-text: MH
Other version collated: CR, 12 October 1850
MH is signed, then signature cancelled: J.V.

427. The Sumach Leaves
Copy-text: MH
Other version collated: CR, 9 November 1850
Precopy-text version: RPB

101. The Just
Copy-text: MH
Other version collated: CR, 28 December 1850

362. Slavery
Copy-text: CR, 4 January 1851

854. The Fugitive Slaves
Copy-text: MH
Other versions collated: SG, 4 April 1851; CR, 5 April 1851
MH is dated: <March 3ᵈ> April, 1851.
SG and CR are dated and signed: March 3d, 1851. J.V.

67. The Lost Sheep: Suggested by an Engraving
Copy-text: MH
Other version collated: CR, 21 October 1854
MH is dated: April, 1851

188. Thoughts and Desires
Copy-text: MH
Other version collated: CR, 25 April 1857
MH is dated: April, 1851.

52. Hymn
Copy-text: broadside, *Order of Exercises, at the Fourth Anniversary of the Evening Free School at Franklin Hall, Thursday Evening, May 15th, 1851.*
Precopy-text version: MH

407. The Soul's Rest
Copy-text: MH
Other version collated: CR, 21 June 1851
This is a greatly revised version of No. 406, "The Weary and Heavy Laden," here treated as a separate poem.

564. The Sliding Rock
Copy-text: MH
Other version collated: SG, 15 July 1851
MH is dated: July, 1851.
SG is dated: July 1851.

347. The Potato Blight
Copy-text: MH
Other version collated: CR, 4 October 1851
Precopy-text version: RPB
MH is dated: 1851.

849. Congregational Singing
Copy-text: MH
Other version collated: CR, 6 December 1851
MH is dated: 1851.

295. Kossuth
Copy-text: MH
Other version collated: CR, 10 January 1852
MH is dated: Jan^y, 1852.

139. John Woolman
Copy-text: MH
Other version collated: CR, 6 March 1852
MH is dated: 1852

674. Hymn: Waiting For Christ
Copy-text: MH
Other version collated: CR, 26 June 1852
MH is dated: 1852.

754. The Wild Rose of Plymouth
Copy-text: MH
Other version collated: CR, 10 March 1855
Precopy-text version: RPB
RPB and CR are dated: June 28th 1852.

358. Voting In The Old North Church
Copy-text: RPB
Other version collated: CR, 10 July 1852

315. The Day Lily
Copy-text: MH
Other version collated: CR, 29 September 1855
MH is dated (between two cancelled stanzas): July 1852

34. The Solitary Worshipper
Copy-text: MH
Other versions collated: CR, 30 October 1852; SG, 24 December 1852
MH is dated: 1852.

542. Sonnet, To the Rev. James Flint, D. D., On reading his Collection of Poems.
Copy-text: MH

Following MH is written: <Salem> Oct^{o.ber} 1852.

276. The Mind The Greatest Mystery
Copy-text: MH
Other version collated: CR, 29 August 1857
MH is dated: Dec^m, 1852.

346. The Conspiracy
Copy-text: MH
MH is dated: Feb. 8th, 1853.

756. The Horsemen on the Sands
Copy-text: MH
Other version collated: CR, 19 July 1856
MH is dated: March 24th, 1853.

163. My Dear Brother Washington
Copy-text: MH
MH is dated: April 30th, 1853.

705. On Seeing The Victoria Regia In Bloom, At The Garden of J. Fisk Allen Esq.
July 22^d, 1853.
Copy-text: MH

846. On Finding the Truth
Copy-text: MH(1)
Precopy-text version: MH(2)
MH(2) is dated: July 1853
MH(1) is dated: 1853.

833. Goliath
Copy-text: MH
Other version collated: CR, 22 October 1853
MH is dated: Oct^{o.}, 1853.

735. A Sunset In Haverhill
Copy-text: MH(1)
Other version collated: CR, 16 September 1854
Precopy-text version: MH(2)
MH(1) is dated: Oct^o— 1853 J.V.
MH(2) is dated: Oct^o 1853
CR is dated: October, 1853.

688. The Past
Copy-text: MH
Other version collated: CR, 26 November 1853
MH is dated: 1853.

761. Hymn, Sung at the Thompson Jubilee, at Barre, Jany. 12, 1854
Copy-text: MH
Other versions collated: broadside, *Hymn for the Jubilee at Barre / By Rev. Jones Very*;
CR, 28 January 1854; untitled in James Thompson, *A Discourse Preached at Barre
Jan. 11, 1854 at the End of a Ministry of Fifty Years in That Town* (Boston: Crosby,
Nichols, 1854), pp. 74–75.

46. On The Nebraska Bill
Copy-text: MH
MH is dated: Feb. 27th, 1854.

422. On An Ear of Wheat Brought, By My Brother, From The Field of Waterloo
Copy-text: MH
Other version collated: CR, 25 March 1854
MH is dated: March, 1854.

307. The Dead Elm
Copy-text: MH
Other versions collated: CR, 1 July 1854; SG, 4 July 1854
MH, CR, and SG are dated: May 30th, 1854.

155. Hymn: Sung at the Celebration of the Fourth of July, in Salem, 1854.
Copy-text: MH
Other versions collated: printed program (at MSaE), *Order of Exercises at Mechanic Hall, July 4, 1854*; PL

118. The Camphene Lamp
Copy-text: CR, 30 August 1856
Other version collated: SG, 18 July 1854

805. The Homeless Wind
Copy-text: MH
Other version collated: CR, 13 January 1855
CR includes three stanzas omitted from MH; alterations in the manuscript, however, make it likely that MH is the later version.

780. What Of The Night?
Copy-text: CR, 3 February 1855

333. To the Memory of the Rev. James Flint, D.D.
Copy-text: CR, 24 March 1855
Following CR is printed: Salem, March 9th, 1855

383. McLean Asylum, Somerville
Copy-text: CR, 21 April 1855
Printed at end of CR: Salem, March, 1855.
The poem is unattributed in CR. I have attributed it to Very on the basis of its topic, the institution where Very was confined for a month in 1838; its place of composition; the compatibility of its diction and style with Very's; its appearance in CR, where Very was regularly publishing poems; and the close resemblance between its final image with that of No. 179, "'Blessed are they that mourn . . . ,'" lines 13–14, a poem signed by Very that appeared in CR three months later (14 July 1855).

40. The Age Changeful and Worldly
Copy-text: MH
Other version collated: CR, 26 May 1855
MH is dated: 1855.

649. Hymn: So also will God, through Jesus, bring with him them who sleep.
Copy-text: MH
Other version collated: CR, 8 March 1856

MH is dated: June, 1855.

179. "Blessed are they that mourn: for they shall be comforted." Math. 5:4.
Copy-text: MH
Other versions collated: MSaE; CR, 14 July 1855
Though it is unclear whether MH or MSaE is the later version, an alteration in line
10 of MH suggests that it may be a revision of MSaE.
Lines 1–4 are similar to those of No. 178, "The Mourner."

44. To The Memory Of The Rev. James Chisholm
Copy-text: MH
Other version collated: CR, 20 October 1855
SG, 26 October 1855, prints the poem, attributing it to SG.
Following CR is printed: Salem, September 21, 1855.

314. The Woodwax
Copy-text: MH
Other version collated: SG, 30 October 1855
Following SG is printed: Salem, Oct. 1855.

772. The First Telegraphic Message
Copy-text: MH
Other version collated: SG, 7 December 1855
Following SG is printed: Salem Nov. 24th, 1855.

73. The Mission Of The Friends To The Emperor Nicholas
Copy-text: MH
Other version collated: CR, 19 January 1856
MH is dated: Jan^y, 1856.
CR is dated: January, 1856

856. Be of Good Courage
Copy-text: MH
Other version collated: CR, 21 June 1856

828. To An Ancient Locust-Tree, Opposite Carltonville
Copy-text: MH
Other version collated: SG, 3 July 1857
MH is dated: July, 1856.
SG is dated: July, 1857

7. A Walk In The Pastures
Copy-text: MH
Other versions collated: SG, 13 July 1858; CR, 12 July 1873
MH is dated: August, 1856.

373. [Untitled] (O, cleave not to the things of earth)
Copy-text: MH
Other version collated: CR, 8 November 1856
MH is dated in ink over pencil: 1856

660. Nature Intelligible
Copy-text: MH
Other version collated: CR, 3 January 1857

585. The Great Facts Of Christ's History
Copy-text: MH
Other version collated: CR, 14 February 1857
MH is dated in pencil, then date is cancelled: 1855

734. Freedom National, Slavery Sectional
Copy-text: MH
Other version collated: CR, 20 March 1857
MH is dated in pencil over ink: March 1857.
Following CR is printed: Salem, Mar. 13. J.V.

227. Christ Abiding Forever
Copy-text: MH
Other version collated: CR, 27 June 1857

330. The South River At Sunset
Copy-text: MH
Other version collated: CR, 8 August 1857
Precopy-text version: RPB
Following MH is written: [illeg. date] J.V.

107. On Receiving A Flower From the Rev. C. H. A. Dall, in India.
Copy-text: MH
Other version collated: CR, 5 September 1857
MH is dated: September, 1857.
CR is dated: August 21, 1857.

654. Hymn: Sung at the Dedication of Plummer Hall, Salem, Oct. 6, 1857.
Copy-text: MH
Other versions collated: printed program, *Dedication of Plummer Hall / Oct. 6, 1857*;
SG, 9 October 1857

21. Philosophy and Religion
Copy-text: MH
Other version collated: CR, 28 November 1857

483. The Day Begins To Dawn
Copy-text: MH
Other version collated: SG, 22 January 1858

844. On The Late Mild Winter
Copy-text: MH
Other versions collated: SG, 26 February 1858; CR, 18 March 1876
MH is dated: Feby 15, 1858.
SG is dated: Feb. 15, 1858.

294. The Evergreen
Copy-text: MH
Other version collated: CR, 27 February 1858

217. Hindoo Converts: On the Domestic Trials of Hindoo Converts. Report of
Unitarian Mission in India.
Copy-text: MH
Other version collated: CR, 27 March 1858

MH is dated: 1858.

89. The Soul's Invitation
Copy-text: CR, 24 April 1858
SG, 30 April 1858, reprints the poem, attributing it to CR.

147. Morning Hymn for a little Child
Copy-text: SG, 4 May 1858

771. Nature Teaches only Love
Copy-text: MH
Other version collated: CR, 5 June 1858

841. The First Atlantic Telegraph
Copy-text: MH
Other version collated: CR, 28 August 1858

328. Life and Death
Copy-text: CR, 11 December 1858
The first four lines are similar to those of No. 327, "Death."

25. Lines On The Old Danvers Burying Ground
Copy-text: MH
Other version collated: SG, 28 December 1858
SG, 18 February 1873, prints a greatly revised version, No. 25a, "The Old Danvers Burying-Ground," here treated as a separate poem.

145. On Seeing The Portrait of Helen Ruthven Waterston
Copy-text: MH

785. Hymn: The Promise of The Spirit
Copy-text: MH
Other versions collated: MSaE; CR, 19 February 1859

197. The Moss and Its Teachings
Copy-text: MH
Other version collated: SG, 8 March 1859

65. On the Bunyan Tableau
Copy-text: Cl, p. 280

243. The Lament Of The Flowers
Copy-text: MH
Other version collated: SG, 10 May 1859
SG is dated: May, 1859.

20. The Voice In The Poplars
Copy-text: MH
Other version collated: CR, 13 August 1859
Precopy-text version: RPB

110. How Faith Comes
Copy-text: MH
Other versions collated: CR, 22 October 1859; SG, 12 November 1875

55. The Poet

Copy-text: MRM, 22 (December 1859): 412
SG, 20 December 1859, reprints the poem, attributing it to MRM.

366. The Set Times, And The Boundaries of Nations, Appointed By God
Copy-text: MH
Other version collated: SG, 19 February 1861
MH is dated: Feby. 1860. [Possibly MH is misdated, 1860 for 1861.]

770. The Cemetery of Harmony Grove
Copy-text: MH(1)
Other versions collated: MRM, 23 (February 1860): 123–24; CR, 31 July 1869; SG,
19 June 1874
Precopy-text versions: RPB, MH(2)
After line 25 the handwriting in MH(1) changes and is not Very's. I have nevertheless
chosen MH(1) as the copy-text on the theory that the second hand was presumably
preparing a clean copy from the same source that Very used in the first twenty-five
lines. The other two manuscripts are heavily revised.

402. Preparation for Life's Voyage
Copy-text: CR, 17 March 1860

460. The Slowness of Belief in a Spiritual World
Copy-text: MRM, 23 (April 1860): 268

731. Hymn: The Dew
Copy-text: MH(1)
Other versions collated: MRM, 24 (July 1860): 41; SSLF
Precopy-text version: MH(2)
SG, 28 August 1863, prints the poem, attributing it to MRM.
MH(1) is dated: Aug 15th 1860

165. The Triennial
Copy-text: MH
Other version collated: SG, 7 August 1860
MH is dated: August, 1860.

766. Welcome: Written for the Essex Institute Fair, Held at Salem, Sept. 4th, 1860.
Copy-text: MH
Other version collated: *The Weal-Reaf: A Record of the Essex Institute Fair, Held at
Salem, Sept. 4, 5, 6, 7, 8, with Two Supplements*. Sept. 10, 11, 1860.
Poem is unattributed in *Weal-Reaf*.

814. The Child's Answer
Copy-text: MH(1)
Other version collated: CR, 15 September 1860
Precopy-text version: MH(2)

85. Freedom And Union
Copy-text: MH(1)
Other version collated: SG, 21 September 1860
Precopy-text version: MH(2)
MH(1) is dated: Sept. 1860.

404. The Cross
Copy-text: MH
Other version collated: MRM, 24 (September 1860): 178
SG, 11 September 1860, prints the poem, attributing it to MRM.

135. On reading the Memorial of John White Browne
Copy-text: MH
MH is dated: Oct° 25, 1860.

368. Hymn: And God shall wipe away every tear from their eyes. Rev. xxi.4.
Copy-text: MH
Other version collated: MRM, 24 (November 1860): 327

54. One generation passeth away, and another generation cometh: but the earth
abideth for ever. Ecclesiastes 1:4.
Copy-text: MH
Other version collated: CR, 26 January 1861

779. What of Our Country?
Copy-text: SG, 29 January 1861

481. The Hour Before The Dawn
Copy-text: MH
Other version collated: MRM, 25 (February 1861): 104
SG, 12 February 1861, prints the poem, attributing it to MRM.
MH is dated: Feb^y, 1861.

830. State Rights
Copy-text: MH(1)
Other version collated: SG, 1 March 1861
Precopy-text version: MH(2)

838. The Rights of Man
Copy-text: MH
Other version collated: SG, 15 March 1861

11. A Longing For The Spring
Copy-text: MH
Other version collated: SG, 29 March 1861

142. The Abolition Of Serfdom In Russia
Copy-text: MH
Other version collated: CR, 6 April 1861

594. Fear not: for they that are with us are more than they that are with them.
2 Kings 6:16.
Copy-text: MH
Other version collated: MRM, 25 (April 1861): 260
SG, 2 August 1861, prints the poem, attributing it to MRM.
MH is dated: 1861

19. Hymn: Nature's Sympathy with Freedom
Copy-text: MH
Other version collated: SG, 7 May 1861
MH is dated: 1860.

The ms. date must be erroneous: the content of the poem indicates that it was written between the beginning of the Civil War with the firing on Fort Sumter (12 April 1861) and the poem's publication in SG.

793. Christ's Capture In The Garden: A Paraphrase
Copy-text: MH
Other version collated: MRM, 25 (May 1861): 355
CR, 20 July 1861, prints the poem, attributing it to MRM.
MH is dated: 1861.

104. Song: Words Of Love To A Parent
Copy-text: MH
Other version collated: CR, 29 June 1861

445. The Comet
Copy-text: MH
Other version collated: CR, 13 July 1861

773. Each Day a Prophecy
Copy-text: MH
Other version collated: MRM, 26 (July 1861): 54
SG, 16 July 1861, prints the poem, attributing it to MRM.

487. The Influence Of The Night on Faith And Imagination
Copy-text: MH
Other version collated: MRM, 26 (August 1861): 123–24

653. Sunset in Derby's Woods
Copy-text: MH
Other version collated: SG, 6 September 1861

131. My People are destroyed for lack of Knowledge.—Hosea 4:6.
Copy-text: RPB
Other version collated: CR, 21 September 1861

437. Autumn Flowers
Copy-text: MH(1)
Other versions collated: CR, 12 October 1861; CR, 20 October 1866
Precopy-text version: MH(2)
MH(1) is dated: Sept, 26th, 1861.

140. Hymn
Copy-text: MH
Though undated, the poem appears on the same sheet with No. 437, "Autumn Flowers," dated 26 September 1861.

826. The Poet's Plea
Copy-text: MH
Other version collated: MRM, 26 (October 1861): 233
MH is dated: Oct°., 1861.

454. On The Completion Of The Pacific Telegraph
Copy-text: MH
Other version collated: SG, 5 November 1861
MH is dated: 1862

439. On the First Church, Built by the Puritans in 1634.
Copy-text: MH
Other version collated: SG, 26 November 1861

535. The Barque Aurelia of Boston
Copy-text: RPB(1)
Other version collated: RPB(2)
Inscription at end of RPB(1): Capt. Samuel Cook, / With the respects of / Jones Very.
RPB(2) is dated: 1871
Despite the date on RPB(2), the poem must have been composed no later than 10 December 1861, when Samuel Cook died.
RPB(1) is actually addressed to send to Cook, but was apparently never mailed.

584. The Traveller At The Depot
Copy-text: MH
Other version collated: CR, 11 January 1862

424. Salvation Is Of The Lord: The Book of Jonah ii.9.
Copy-text: MH
Other version collated: MRM, 27 (January 1862): 47
MH is dated: 1862

301. The Newspaper
Copy-text: MH
Other versions collated: CR, 22 February 1862; MRM, 27 (May 1862): 330

9. E Pluribus Unum
Copy-text: MH
Other version collated: CR, 12 April 1862

273. Song
Copy-text: MH
Other version collated: SG, 2 May 1862

656. This Mortal Shall put on Immortality
Copy-text: MH
Other version collated: CR, 24 May 1862

571. Hymn: The Spirit Itself Maketh Intercession For Us
Copy-text: MH
Other version collated: MRM, 27 (May 1862): 278
MH is dated: 1862.

411. The Elm Seed
Copy-text: MH
Other version collated: SG, 17 June 1862

468. The Cause
Copy-text: MH
Other version collated: CR, 21 June 1862
MH is dated: June, 1862.

729. Outward Conquests Not Enough
Copy-text: MH

Other versions collated: MRM, 27 (July 1862): 14; CR, 12 July 1862
SG, 18 July 1862, prints the poem, attributing it to MRM.

831. Ship Rock
Copy-text: MH
Other version collated: SG, 15 July 1862
Precopy-text version: RPB

792. The Light Of Freedom Necessary To National Progress
Copy-text: MH
Other version collated: CR, 6 September 1862
MH is dated: Sept. 1862

138. Ode to Freedom
Copy-text: MH
Other version collated: SG, 19 September 1862
MH is dated: Sept. 19, 1862

755. Philanthropy Before Nationality
Copy-text: MH
Other version collated: CR, 20 September 1862

409-434. The King's Arm Chair
Copy-text: MH(1)
Other versions collated: SG, 21 October 1862; SG, 12 July 1870
Precopy-text version: MH(2)
MH(1) is dated: Oct°, 1862.
SG 1862 is dated: October, 1862

111. The Falling Leaf
Copy-text: MH
Other version collated: CR, 8 November 1862

16. National Unity
Copy-text: CR, 15 November 1862

252. Faith In Time Of War
Copy-text: MH
Other version collated: CR, 22 November 1862

520. Hymn: The Light of Life
Copy-text: MH
Other version collated: MRM, 28 (November 1862): 315

17. Man's Heart Prophesieth Of Peace
Copy-text: MH
Other versions collated: MRM, 29 (January 1863): 20; CR, 18 January 1873
SG, 16 January 1863, prints the poem, attributing it to MRM.
MH is dated: 1863.

777. Hymn: The New Life of Humanity
Copy-text: MH
Other version collated: CR, 4 April 1863

438. The Statue of Flora, On the grounds of R. Brookhouse Esq, Washington Street.

Copy-text: MH
Other version collated: SG, 28 April 1863
Precopy-text version: RPB

37-42. Hymn: Sung At the Unitarian Festival, in Faneuil Hall, May 26th 1863
Copy-text: MH(1)
Other versions collated: MH(2); CR, 13 June 1863; printed program, *Order of Exercises at the Unitarian Festival, Faneuil Hall, Tuesday, May 26, 1863*; printed program, *Order of Exercises at the Unitarian Festival, at Music Hall, on Thursday, May 30, 1867*

58. The Tree of Liberty
Copy-text: MH
Other version collated: CR, 4 July 1863

644. Hymn: Our Country's Dead
Copy-text: MH
Other version collated: CR, 1 August 1863

298. The Intuitions Of The Soul
Copy-text: MH
Other version collated: MRM, 30 (August 1863): 90
MH is dated: 1863

436. Still a Day To Live
Copy-text: MH
Other version collated: CR, 19 September 1863
Precopy-text version: RPB

134. The Vagrant at the Church Door
Copy-text: NASS, 26 September 1863

364. Health of Body dependent on the Soul
Copy-text: MH
Other version collated: CR, 17 October 1863

847. The Crisis
Copy-text: MH
Other version collated: SG, 23 October 1863

794. The Forsaken Harvest Field
Copy-text: MH
Other versions collated: SG, 24 November 1863; CR, 13 November 1869
MH is dated: 1863.

757. The Freedmen of the Mississippi Valley
Copy-text: MH
Other version collated: CR, 26 December 1863

489. Dying Words of John Foster: "I Can Pray, And That's a Glorious Thing."
Copy-text: MH
Other version collated: CR, 17 July 1875
MH is dated: 1863.

848. Home and Heaven
Copy-text: MH

Other version collated: MRM, 31 (January 1864): 27
SG, 8 January 1864, prints the poem, attributing it to MRM.
MH is dated: 1864.

303. The Search For The Truth Not Vain
Copy-text: MH
Other version collated: CR, 20 February 1864
Precopy-text version: RPB

417. On The Three Hundredth Anniversary of Shakespeare's Birthday
Copy-text: MH
Other version collated: MRM, 31 (April 1864): 256
SG, 15 April 1864, prints the poem, attributing it to MRM.
MH is dated: April, 1864.

671. Hymn: The Way of the Righteous Easy
Copy-text: MH
Other version collated: CR, 7 May 1864
MH is dated: 1864.

658. Untimely Arguments
Copy-text: MH(1)
Other versions collated: MH(2); CR, 11 June 1864
MH(2) is a clear copy, probably based on MH(1), not in Very's hand.

300. Hymn: Ps. XLVI. 10: "Be still, and know that I am God."
Copy-text: MH
Other version collated: MRM, 31 (June 1864): 378
MH is dated: 1864.

843. The Voice of Nature In Youth And Age
Copy-text: MH(1)
Other version collated: SG, 15 July 1864
Precopy-text version: MH(2)

858. Hymn: Christ's Invitation in the Apocalypse
Copy-text: MH(1)
Other versions collated: MH(2); CR, 23 July 1864
It is uncertain whether MH(1) or MH(2) is the later version.

371. Hymn In Drought
Copy-text: MH
Other version collated: SG, 26 July 1864
MH is dated: July, 1864

549. The Rain
Copy-text: MH
Other version collated: CR, 20 August 1864
This is a much revised version of No. 550, of the same title.

478a. The Fair Morning
Copy-text: MH
Other version collated: CR, 3 September 1864
This is a revised version of an early poem, No. 478 of the same title, here treated as a
separate poem.

529. The Clouded Morning
Copy-text: MH
Other version collated: CR, 1 October 1864
The first four lines of this poem are similar to those of No. 530 of the same title.

349. Nature Repeats Her Lessons
Copy-text: MH
Other version collated: CR, 5 November 1864

774. What Is A Word?
Copy-text: MH
Other version collated: MRM, 32 (November 1864): 317
SG, 18 November 1864, 5 May 1865, and 23 June 1865, prints the poem, each time attributing it to MRM.
MH is dated: 1864.

810. To Charles W. Felt Esq. On His New Type-Setting Machine
Copy-text: RPB
In printing this previously unpublished poem, Bartlett erroneously transcribed the name as "Fell."
RPB is dated: Salem Dec^m 12th 1864.

566. The Young Drummer Boy of Libby Prison: An Incident Related by Capt. James Hussey.
Copy-text: MH
Other version collated: SG, 30 December 1864

840. Inward Direction
Copy-text: MH
Other version collated: CR, 7 January 1865
Precopy-text version: RPB

149. The Cherry Birds
Copy-text: MH
Other version collated: SG, 17 February 1865

563. The Soul's Questioning Of The Universe, And Its Beginning
Copy-text: MH(1)
Other versions collated: CR, 11 March 1865; SG, 4 June 1872
Precopy-text versions: RPB, MH(2)
Revisions in MH(1) are in a different hand from the remainder of the poem, possibly not Very's; yet, since SG generally follows MH(1) it seems clear that they were authorized by him.

374. Hymn: Sung at the Eulogy on Abraham Lincoln June 1st 1865.
Copy-text: MH
Other versions collated: printed program, *Order of Exercises at the Delivery of the Eulogy on Abraham Lincoln, Before the City Council of the City of Salem, June 1, 1865*; SG, 6 June 1865

193. Soul-Sickness
Copy-text: MH
Other version collated: CR, 3 June 1865

479. Song of The Early Spring
Copy-text: MH
Other versions collated: CR, 17 June 1865; SG, 17 April 1866

186. Sensibility to the Beauty and Fragrance of Flowers
Copy-text: MH
Other version collated: SG, 28 July 1865

776. What Is The Word?
Copy-text: CR, 12 August 1865

230. The Sight of the Ocean
Copy-text: MH
Other version collated: SG, 8 September 1865

401. Prayer For Rain
Copy-text: MH
Other version collated: SG, 15 September 1865

390. Hymn On The Logos: The Light Still Shining In The Darkness
Copy-text: MH(1)
Other version collated: CR, 23 September 1865
Precopy-text versions: RPB, MH(2)

764. Hath The Rain A Father? Or Who Hath Begotten The Drops of Dew? Job
38:28
Copy-text: MH(1)
Other version collated: CR, 16 June 1866
Precopy-text version: MH(2)
MH(1) is dated: October, 1865.

744. "It is vain to say, that this is the country of the 'white man.' It is the country of
man." Charles Sumner.
Copy-text: MRM, 34 (November 1865): 299

14. The East India Marine Museum
Copy-text: MH
Other version collated: SG, 15 December 1865
MH is dated: 1866.

811. Finishing The Work
Copy-text: MH
Other version collated: MRM, 34 (December 1865): 379

392. 'O Lord, How Long?'
Copy-text: HS
This hymn is taken, with slight alterations, from a longer poem, No. 723, "The
World."

447. Our Soldiers' Graves
Copy-text: MH
Probable date 1861–65 (based on content)

523. The Still Small Voice
Copy-text: MH

Probable date 1865 (based on content)

22. Indian Relics
Copy-text: MH
Other version collated: SG, 12 January 1866
Precopy-text version: RPB

817. The Veil upon the Heart
Copy-text: CR, 27 January 1866

420. True Knowledge Necessary for the Voyage of Life
Copy-text: CR, 26 May 1866

231. Sonnet: There is a natural body, and there is a spiritual body.—I. Cor. xv. 44.
Copy-text: MRM, 35 (June 1866): 389
Precopy-text version: MH

797. Nature's Help for the Soul
Copy-text: CR, 14 July 1866

290. Nature a Living Teacher
Copy-text: MH
Other version collated: SG, 10 August 1866

151. Primitive Worship
Copy-text: MH
Other versions collated: SG, 24 August 1866; CR, 4 September 1875
MH is dated: Aug. 24th, 1866.

233. The Holy Land
Copy-text: MH
Other version collated: CR, 1 September 1866
Precopy-text version: RPB

198. Standley's Grove
Copy-text: SG, 28 September 1866

30. October
Copy-text: MH
Other versions collated: CR, 3 November 1866; CR, 11 November 1871

567. The Soldier and the Statesman
Copy-text: MH
Other versions collated: SG, 27 November 1866; SG, 6 October 1868
Above title in MH and SG (1868) appears: Sonnets on Reconstruction / VI.
This series of six poems on Reconstruction, beginning with No. 425, "A Nation's
Life Of Slow Growth," was published in SG between 18 September and 6 October
1868. This is the only one to have been previously published.

66. The Triumphs of Science, And of Faith
Copy-text: MH
Other version collated: MRM, 36 (November 1866): 328
MH is dated: Nov., 1866

50. Christian Influence
Copy-text: MH

Other version collated: CR, 2 February 1867

378. The Reconciling Power
Copy-text: MH(1)
Other versions collated: MRM, 37 (February 1867): 99; CR, 21 September 1872
Precopy-text versions: RPB, MH(2)
MH(1) is dated: Feby, 1867.

335. The Heralds of the Spring
Copy-text: SG, 4 April 1867

173. The Bridge of Time
Copy-text: MH(1)
Other versions collated: CR, 6 April 1867; CR, 25 February 1871
Precopy-text version: MH(2)

356. Our Dear Mother
Copy-text: MH(1)
Precopy-text versions: MH(2), MH(3)
MH(3) (the earliest draft) is entitled "The Vacant Chair"; MH(2), "Our Mother."
MH(1) is dated: May, 1867.

363. Hymn: The Word Before All Things
Copy-text: MH
Other version collated: MRM, 37 (June 1867): 432
SG, 7 June 1867, prints the poem, attributing it to MRM.

451. The Whiteweed
Copy-text: MH
Other version collated: SG, 28 June 1867
MH is dated: June, 1867.

367. The Teachings of the Spirit
Copy-text: MH
Other version collated: CR, 3 July 1867

43. Hymn
Copy-text: MH
Other versions collated: CtY; MRM, 38 (October 1867): 310
Precopy-text version: RPB
It is uncertain whether MH or CtY is the later version.
RPB is dated: 1867. July.

181. The Help of the Spirit
Copy-text: MH
Other version collated: CR, 3 August 1867
Precopy-text version: RPB

466. The Birthright Church
Copy-text: MH
Other version collated: CR, 26 October 1867

745. Midas
Copy-text: MH
Other version collated: SG, 29 October 1867

26. Revelation
Copy-text: MH
Other version collated: CR, 7 December 1867
Precopy-text version: MH(2)

183. How come the Dead?
Copy-text: MH(1)
Other versions collated: MRM, 39 (January 1868): 28; SSLF
Precopy-text version: MH(2)

452. The Hacker School House
Copy-text: MH
Other version collated: SG, 27 March 1868
MH is dated: 1870.

768. The Houstonia
Copy-text: MH
Other version collated: SG, 12 May 1868

391. To The Salem Gazette, On The Completion Of Its First Century
Copy-text: MH
Other version collated: SG, 13 August 1869
MH is dated: 1870.
Headnote to SG version reads as follows:
   [The following sonnet, from a valued contributor, was furnished for publication a
   year ago; but accidentally mislaid and buried out of sight until the present time—
   an accident or carelessness which we greatly regret.]
The *Gazette*'s anniversary was 5 August 1868.

281. Ocean's Treasures
Copy-text: SG, 21 August 1868

425. A Nation's Life Of Slow Growth
Copy-text: MH
Other version collated: SG, 18 September 1868
For "Sonnets on Reconstruction," see Textual Note on No. 567 above, "The Sol-
dier and the Statesman," intended to be the sixth of the series, though it had been
previously published.

759. The Ends For Which A Nation Exists
Copy-text: MH
Other version collated: SG, 18 September 1868

28. Political Ambition
Copy-text: MH
Other version collated: SG, 25 September 1868

23. National Unity
Copy-text: MH
Other version collated: SG, 29 September 1868

788. Reflections on the History of Nations
Copy-text: MH
Other version collated: SG, 2 October 1868

446. Scepticism With Regard To The Gospels
Copy-text: MH(1)
Other version collated: CR, 31 October 1868
Precopy-text version: MH(2)

835. The Tide
Copy-text: MH(1)
Other versions collated: MH(2); MRM, 40 (October 1868): 289
Precopy-text version: RPB

713. The Spiritual Birth
Copy-text: MH
Other version collated: MRM, 40 (November 1868): 400
SG, 13 November 1868, prints the poem, attributing it to MRM.

827. The Youth and the Stream
Copy-text: MH(1)
Precopy-text version: MH(2)
Probable date: 1859–68, the period during which Very published poems in MRM.
MH(1) indicates that the poem was written for MRM, though it has not been
found there.

56. The Daily News
Copy-text: MH
Other version collated: CR, 9 January 1869

108. On A Hyacinth From Georgia
Copy-text: MH
Other version collated: SG, 29 January 1869
MH is dated: Jany 20th 1869.

836. Things Unseen
Copy-text: MH(1)
Other version collated: CR, 30 January 1869
Precopy-text version: MH(2)

611. The Oak And The Poplar
Copy-text: MH
Other version collated: CR, 6 March 1869

297. The Yellow Violets
Copy-text: MH
Other version collated: SG, 4 May 1869

202. The City of God
Copy-text: MH
Other version collated: CR, 5 June 1869

144. The Scholar Dreaming
Copy-text: MH
Other version collated: SG, 29 June 1869
Precopy-text version: RPB

534. Hymn: Sung at the Dedication of the Peabody Academy of Science, Salem,
Aug. 18, 1869.

Copy-text: MH(1)
Other versions collated: printed program at MSaE (title page missing); [untitled] in *Second and Third Annual Reports of the Trustees of the Peabody Academy of Science, for the Years 1869 and 1870* (Salem, 1871), p. 6
Precopy-text versions: MH(2), MH(3)

4. Spiritual Darkness
Copy-text: MH
Other version collated: CR, 9 October 1869
This poem is a revision of No. 5, "Spiritual Darkness," which is itself a revision of No. 3, "The Dark Day."

204. Friendship
Copy-text: MH(1)
Other version collated: CR, 1 January 1870
Precopy-text version: MH(2)

652. The Sparrows And The Crop of Weeds
Copy-text: MH
Other version collated: SG, 15 February 1870

81. Ye have hoarded up treasure in the last days.—James 5: 3.
Copy-text: CR, 26 February 1870
This is a significantly revised version of No. 80, "The First Shall Be Last," here treated as a separate poem.

87. Hymn: The Spiritual Body
Copy-text: MH
Other version collated: CR, 9 April 1870

400. Hymn: The Efficacy of a Mother's Prayer
Copy-text: MH(1)
Other versions collated: CR, 9 July 1870; SSLF
Precopy-text version: MH(2)

576. The Fireflies
Copy-text: MH
Other versions collated: SG, 19 July 1870; CR, 21 August 1875
Precopy-text version: RPB

62. Be Not Many Teachers
Copy-text: MH
Other version collated: CR, 6 August 1870

1. Military surprises and the capture of capitals, are the events of a by-gone age. D'Israeli.
Copy-text: SG, 9 September 1870
Other version collated: CR, 28 July 1877

600. The Bible Does Not Sanction Polygamy
Copy-text: MH
Other version collated: SG, 16 September 1870
MH is dated: Sept. 1871

627. Bitter-Sweet Rocks

Copy-text: MH(1)
Other version collated: *To-Day* (printed for the Institute and Oratorio Fair, Salem), no. 1 (31 October 1870): 2
Precopy-text version: MH(2)
Autumn Leaves, compiled by L. R. Swain (n.p., n.d.), prints the poem, attributing it to *To-Day*.

205. Humanity Mourning For Her Children Slain In War
Copy-text: PHC
Other versions collated: SG, 15 November 1870; SG, 13 December 1872
PHC is followed by this note to Charles W. Squires:
  Dear Sir I have copied the above poem of mine hoping that it may give you pleasure.
                                                                          Your friend
    Salem, Dec.ᵐ 9th, 1873.   Jones Very.
This poem is essentially the same as the last five stanzas of the eleven-stanza poem No. 141, "The Congress of Peace in Brussels."

320. The Poor Clergyman
Copy-text: MH
Other versions collated: SG, 13 December 1870; CR, 25 February 1871

822. The Teaching Of History Confirmed
Copy-text: MH
Other version collated: CR, 7 January 1871
MH is dated: 1871.

237. Childhood's Songs
Copy-text: MH
Other versions collated: CR, 18 March 1871; SSLF

38. Hymn, Sung at the Fiftieth Anniversary of the Essex Historical Society, Salem. April 21, 1871.
Copy-text: MH(1)
Other versions collated: MH(2); printed program, *Commemoration of the Semicentennial Anniversary of the Historical Department of the Essex Institute, Friday, April 21, 1871*

27. The Lessons of History Unlearned
Copy-text: SG, 16 June 1871

453. The Fulness of The Gentiles
Copy-text: MH
Other version collated: CR, 8 July 1871

813. To a Cloud
Copy-text: MH(1)
Other version collated: SG, 1 September 1871
Precopy-text version: MH(2)
Title in MH(2): To a Cloud In a Time of Drought

2. The Child's Dream of Reaching the Horizon
Copy-text: MH(1)
Other version collated: CR, 2 September 1871
Precopy-text version: MH(2)

296. Lead Me To The Rock That Is Higher Than I
Copy-text: MH
Other version collated: CR, 18 November 1871

18. Forevermore
Copy-text: SG, 24 November 1871

791. Man's First Experience of Winter
Copy-text: SG, 6 February 1872

302. Interpreting God's Ways
Copy-text: CR, 10 February 1872

251. I Prayed, Thy Kingdom Come
Copy-text: MH
Other version collated: CR, 20 April 1872

448. Justification By Faith
Copy-text: MH
Other version collated: CR, 4 May 1872

325. The First of May
Copy-text: SG, 7 May 1872

440. On the Great Divisions of the Christian Church, The Catholic, the Protestant, and the Greek
Copy-text: CR, 8 June 1872

726. The Nine O'Clock Bell
Copy-text: SG, 12 July 1872

426. "Are there Few that be Saved?" Luke 13:23.
Copy-text: CR, 24 August 1872

115. On Seeing the White Mountains from Cook's Hill, in West Peabody
Copy-text: SG, 30 August 1872

491. Signs in the Natural World
Copy-text: MH
Other version collated: CR, 5 October 1872

282. A Walk in Harmony Grove
Copy-text: SG, 25 October 1872
Other version collated: SG, 22 October 1872
Note at end of SG, 25 October 1872: [The above is reprinted, to correct an error, which spoiled the sense of a line.]

543. The Prayer of Jabez
Copy-text: CR, 9 November 1872

313. The Life of the Flower
Copy-text: MH
Other version collated: CR, 28 December 1872

25a. The Old Danvers Burying-Ground
Copy-text: SG, 18 February 1873

This poem differs substantially from No. 25, "Lines on the Old Danvers Burying Ground," in all but three of its eight stanzas and thus is treated as a separate poem.

162. Hymn: "He that loveth not, knoweth not God."
Copy-text: CR, 8 March 1873

35. Norman's Rocks
Copy-text: MH
Other version collated: SG, 20 June 1873
Precopy-text versions: RPB(1), RPB(2)

765. *On visiting the beautiful estate of* H. H. Hunnewell, Esq., *at Wellesley.*
Copy-text: SG, 1 July 1873

760. The Revelation of The Spirit Through The Material World
Copy-text: MH
Other versions collated: RPB; CR, 26 July 1873

666. And a little child shall lead them. Isaiah XI. 6.
Copy-text: MH
Other version collated: CR, 16 August 1873

189. The Blessing of Rain
Copy-text: MH
Other version collated: SG, 26 August 1873

164. On the Mountain Ash Tree In front of the house of the late Capt. Robert W. Gould
Copy-text: SG, 21 October 1873

177. October
Copy-text: SG, 7 November 1873

444. The Mound Builders. On Reading the work of the late J. W. Foster
Copy-text: MH
Other version collated: CR, 1 November 1873

187. Blessed are they that mourn: for they shall be comforted.
Copy-text: MH
Other version collated: SG, 12 December 1873

403. There shall be one Flock, one Shepherd
Copy-text: MH
Other version collated: CR, 17 January 1874

635. Old Houses of Salem Illustrated by George M. White
Copy-text: SG, 23 January 1874

64. Columbines and Anemones
Copy-text: MSaE
Other versions collated: MH; CR, 14 February 1874
MH is probably not in Very's hand.
Top of sheet on which MSaE is written has been cut off, apparently including the original title (and possibly a headnote); title provided in pencil, not in Very's hand, is "The Painted Columbine," indicating confusion with a different poem (No. 78) of that title.

751. The Hepatica in Winter
Copy-text: SG, 24 February 1874

762. Reverence
Copy-text: CR, 21 March 1874

331. Inward Phenomena
Copy-text: CR, 18 April 1874

15. To the Memory of Alpheus Crosby
Copy-text: Cl, p. 513

464. The Birds
Copy-text: MH
Other version collated: SG, 19 May 1874

194. Superfluities
Copy-text: CR, 23 May 1874

114. Arethusa Meadow
Copy-text: SG, 3 July 1874

442. The Night Blooming Cereus
Copy-text: SG, 24 July 1874

812. On The Wild Flowers of the Art Exhibition
Copy-text: SG, 24 July 1874

560. Interpreting Nature
Copy-text: CR, 25 July 1874

719. The Incarnation
Copy-text: CR, 8 August 1874

806. On a Lichen from North Cape Gathered by Mr. J. M. Richards, July 3d, 1874
Copy-text: SG, 18 August 1874

360. For we Walk by Faith, not by Sight
Copy-text: CR, 22 August 1874

851. On the Neglect of Public Worship
Copy-text: CR, 5 September 1874

265. The Solitary Gentian
Copy-text: SG, 13 October 1874

839. Indian Remains
Copy-text: SG, 1 December 1874

172. English Sparrows
Copy-text: SG, 25 December 1874

323. The Home
Copy-text: CR, 2 January 1875

634. Behold, I Make All Things New
Copy-text: MH
Other version collated: CR, 16 January 1875

113. Oliver C. Felton, Esq., of Brookfield
Copy-text: SG, 29 January 1875

758. On the Increase of Crime since the Late Civil War
Copy-text: CR, 20 February 1875
SG, 12 March 1875, prints the poem, attributing it to CR.

855. The Meteorologists
Copy-text: MH
Other version collated: CR, 6 March 1875

324. The Origin of Man
Copy-text: MH (ll. 1–14); CR, 20 March 1875 (ll. 15–28)
Other versions collated: CR, 20 March 1875 (ll. 1–14); SG, 9 May 1876
MH consists only of the first stanza (ll. 1–14) of the final version of the poem.

583. Sailing on Cakes of Ice in the North River
Copy-text: SG, 8 April 1875

369. Original Hymn
Copy-text: printed program, *Order of Services of the Twenty-Sixth Anniversary of the Children's Mission, at the Bulfinch Peace Chapel, Wednesday, May 16 [1875], at Three O'Clock* . . .
Other version collated: *Twenty-Sixth Annual Report of the Executive Committee of the Children's Mission to the Children of the Destitute in the City of Boston* . . . (Boston, 1875), 24.

71. The Faith of the First Christians
Copy-text: CR, 16 June 1875

717. On the Great Earthquake in New Grenada
Copy-text: SG, 29 June 1875

763. The Woodwax in Bloom
Copy-text: SG, 20 July 1875

68. On Visiting the Graves of Hawthorne and Thoreau
Copy-text: SG, 6 August 1875

45. On Viewing the Falls of Niagara, as Photographed by George Barker
Copy-text: SG, 3 September 1875

312. Knowledge and Truth
Copy-text: CR, 9 October 1875
Other version collated: MH(2)
Precopy-text version: MH(1)
MH(2) is not in Very's hand; MH(1) is a draft version from which someone constructed MH(2). Clearly there must have been a fair copy manuscript version, now lost, upon which CR is based.

190. Mt. Shasta. A Painting, by H. O. Young.
Copy-text: SG, 19 November 1875

245. Song: I Love the Light
Copy-text: MH
Other version collated: CR, 27 November 1875

Precopy-text version: RPB

740. Nature Teaches Us of Time and its Duration
Copy-text: CR, 18 December 1875

92. Take ye heed, watch and pray: for ye know not when the time is. Mark 13 : 33.
Copy-text: MH
Other version collated: SSLF
Alfred P. Putnam, compiler of SSLF, writes of this poem that it "had just been finished as the manuscript was placed in our hands" (p. 341).

643. The Ancient Burial Places in Peabody
Copy-text: MH
Other version collated: SG, 4 January 1876

200. Man's Need of a Spiritual Birth
Copy-text: CR, 5 February 1876

152. On some Eternals from a friend's garden
Copy-text: MH
Other version collated: SG, 11 February 1876

450. Hymn: The Rest of the Righteous
Copy-text: CR, 4 March 1876

130. "Tuesday night, the schooner Weaver, of Glen Creek, N.J., went to pieces near Sandy Hook, and her entire crew were lost."—*Transcript, March 22d.*
Copy-text: SG, 31 March 1876

321. The Purification of the Temple
Copy-text: CR, 22 April 1876

229. The May Flower
Copy-text: MH
Other version collated: SG, 2 May 1876
Precopy-text version: RPB

10. The International Exhibition at Philadelphia
Copy-text: CR, 6 May 1876

63. Evolution
Copy-text: SG, 12 May 1876
Other version collated: CR, 3 April 1875 (ll. 1–14)
CR consists only of the first stanza (ll. 1–14) of the final version of the poem.

769. Capt. Samuel Cook
Copy-text: SG, 30 May 1876

106. On the Beautiful Roses, In front of the Mansion of John Hodges, Esq.
Copy-text: SG, 23 June 1876

509. The Cows waiting at the Pasture Gate
Copy-text: MH
Other version collated: SG, 4 August 1876

485. Song: The Summer Day
Copy-text: CR, 5 August 1876

377. On some blue and golden Columbines from Pike's Peak, Colorado
Copy-text: MH
Other version collated: SG, 1 September 1876

299. The Stony Desert of Life
Copy-text: CR, 2 September 1876

459. Cadmus
Copy-text: CR, 16 September 1876
Other version collated: SG, 19 June 1877

357. The True Worshipers
Copy-text: CR, 7 October 1876

796. Song: We Have No Ship at Sea
Copy-text: SG, 10 October 1876

601. The Gospel the Reconciling Power
Copy-text: CR, 4 November 1876

6. Every Day a Day of Freedom
Copy-text: MH
Other version collated: CR, 25 November 1876

500. Hymn: Reflections at the Close of the Year
Copy-text: SG, 19 December 1876

821. On Hearing the Clock Strike, in Harmony Grove
Copy-text: SG, 29 December 1876

69. The Indians' Belief in a Future State
Copy-text: CR, 27 January 1877
Other version collated: SG, 26 February 1878

524. The Telephone
Copy-text: SG, 23 February 1877

191. Love Needing a Visible Object
Copy-text: CR, 10 March 1877

615. The Perfect Love that Casts out Fear
Copy-text: CR, 31 March 1877

171. The Glacial Marks on our Hills
Copy-text: MH
Other version collated: SG, 10 April 1877

415. The Future State of the Wicked and its Duration
Copy-text: CR, 14 April 1877

457. Faith in the Resurrection Confirmed
Copy-text: CR, 5 May 1877

525. Spring and Summer Flowers
Copy-text: SG, 11 May 1877

669. The Return of the Columbine
Copy-text: SG, 25 May 1877

201. Man's Accountability
Copy-text: CR, 2 June 1877

458. Hymn: The Cause of Peace
Copy-text: MH
Other version collated: CR, 16 June 1877

180. The Nodding Meadow Lily
Copy-text: SG, 20 July 1877

837. The Destruction of Public Property by Mobs
Copy-text: SG, 10 August 1877

461. The Barberry-Pickers
Copy-text: SG, 9 October 1877

41. Pompeii
Copy-text: SG, 16 October 1877

819. The Communion
Copy-text: SG, 23 November 1877

76. The Winter Night
Copy-text: SG, 25 December 1877

753. The Coasters
Copy-text: SG, 1 February 1878
Precopy-text version: MH

389. The Message
Copy-text: SG, 11 April 1878

326. Do Nations Ever Become Insane?
Copy-text: SG, 30 April 1878

815. Know Thyself: Suggested by hearing Dr. A. E. Miller's Lectures on the Human Body.
Copy-text: SG, 3 May 1878

823. The Blueberry Blossoms
Copy-text: SG, 28 May 1878

354. William Cullen Bryant
Copy-text: SG, 21 June 1878

514. "*Agriculture the Source of Individual and of National Prosperity.*"—Anne Pratt.
Copy-text: SG, 26 July 1878

834. Pleasure
Copy-text: SG, 16 August 1878

832. On The Late Tornado, At Wallingford, Conn.
Copy-text: SG, 30 August 1878

94-706. Hymn
Copy-text: MH(1)
Other versions collated: printed program, *Essex Institute, Salem. Order of Exercises at Mechanic Hall, Sept. 18, 1878, upon the Occasion of the Commemoration of the 250th*

Anniversary of the Landing of Governor Endicott at Salem (Salem, 1878); SG, 24 September 1878; *The Fifth Half Century of the Landing of John Endicott at Salem, Massachusetts: Commemorative Exercises by the Essex Institute September 18, 1878* (Salem, 1879), pp. 7–8.
Precopy-text versions: RPB(1), RPB(2), RPB(3), MH(2), MH(3)

174. On the Neglect of the Study of History
Copy-text: SG, 29 October 1878

395. Christ's Final Victory
Copy-text: SG, 26 November 1878

77. Thanksgiving Flowers
Copy-text: SG, 6 December 1878

767. Original Hymn
Copy-text: printed program, *Order of Exercises at the Installation of Rev. George Herbert Hosmer, over the East Church [Salem], Thursday, January 2, 1879*

578. Our Lighthouses
Copy-text: SG, 4 February 1879
Other version collated: MH
SG was chosen as copy-text because line 3 of MH is unfinished; SG must be based upon a later manuscript.

850. The African's First Sight of the Ocean
Copy-text: SG, 4 March 1879

443. The Zodiacal Light
Copy-text: SG, 28 March 1879

775. Education
Copy-text: SG, 11 April 1879

57. The Kingdom of Heaven In Its Growth and Coming a Mystery
Copy-text: SG, 6 June 1879

310. Azalea Swamp
Copy-text: SG, 27 June 1879

370. Guido's Aurora
Copy-text: SG, 25 July 1879

317. The Humming Bird
Copy-text: SG, 8 August 1879

86. Jupiter as the Evening Star
Copy-text: SG, 16 September 1879

507. The National Thanksgiving
Copy-text: SG, 27 November 1879

787. The Stock-Gilly Flowers
Copy-text: SG, 23 December 1879

638. Spiritual Intercourse
Copy-text: MH

Other version collated: SG, 3 February 1880

91. Invitation to the Robin
Copy-text: SG, 12 March 1880

435. The Influence of Channing
Copy-text: MH
Other version collated: SG, 8 April 1880

587. The Calling
Copy-text: MH
Precopy-text versions: RPB(1), RPB(2)
Above the title in RPB(1) and RPB(2) is written the title of the following series of sonnets: The Settlement of Naumkeck [Salem: RPB(2)] by the Puritans; a manuscript book at RPB containing many of the following poems is entitled "A Series of Sonnets On The Puritans."
This poem begins a series of thirty-eight sonnets on the Puritans that were not published during Very's life. They were probably conceived at around the time of the celebration of the 250th anniversary (September 1878) of the landing of Endicott's band in Salem (see No. 94-706, "Hymn") and intended for a similar celebration two years later (22 June 1880) of the arrival of John Winthrop at Salem (see *Essex Institute Historical Collections* 17 [July 1880]: 193–256). Very died two months before this event. Multiple versions of most of the sonnets exist in Very's papers; this, in addition to the fact that the poems were not published, suggests that Very was still working on them at the time of his death.

39. Endecott
Copy-text: RPB
The placement of this poem at this point in the series is conjectural. The fact that only one loose copy of this poem survives and that it is not included in either of the notebook versions of this series suggests that Very may have intended to omit it from the series. That possibility is strengthened by lines 9–10 of No. 587, "The Calling," which summarize the thought of "Endecott" and seem to make it superfluous:
    Why name, among those worthies brave and true,
    Brave-hearted Endicott, who led the van.

116. Farewell
Copy-text: MH
Precopy-text versions: RPB(1), RPB(2), RPB(3)
RPB(1) and RPB(3) are entitled: The Departure

476-581. The Departure
Copy-text: MH
Precopy-text versions: RPB(1), RPB(2)

96. The Petrels
Copy-text: MH
Precopy-text versions: RPB(1), RPB(2), RPB(3); in addition, the RPB(2) version of No. 476-581, "The Departure," contains seven lines that generally correspond to lines 2–8 of this poem and were probably its first version.
RPB(1) and RPB(2) are entitled "At Sea."

97. At Sea

Copy-text: MH
Precopy-text version: RPB

137. At Sea
Copy-text: RPB(1)
Other version collated: RPB(2)
Precopy-text versions: MH, RPB(3), RPB(4), RPB(5), RPB(6), RPB(7)
It is uncertain whether RPB(1) or RPB(2) is the later version.

79. The Sabbath
Copy-text: MH
Precopy-text version: RPB

646. Land
Copy-text: MH
Precopy-text versions: RPB(1), RPB(2), RPB(3)

647. Salem
Copy-text: MH
Other version collated: RPB(2)
It is unclear whether MH or RPB(2) is the later version.
Precopy-text version: RPB(1)

428-835a. The Landing
Copy-text: MH
Precopy-text version: RPB

359. The Old Planters
Copy-text: MH
Other version collated: RPB(1)
Precopy-text versions: RPB(2), RPB(3)
It is unclear whether MH or RPB(1) is the later version.

192. Paradise
Copy-text: MH
Precopy-text versions: RPB(1), RPB(2), RPB(3)
RPB(2) and RPB(3) are entitled "Autumn."

752. Naumkeck River
Copy-text: MH
Other version collated: RPB(1)
Precopy-text version: RPB(2)
It is unclear whether MH or RPB(1) is the later version.
RPB(2) is entitled "Exploration."

332. The Same
Copy-text: MH
Precopy-text version: RPB

539. Winter
Copy-text: RPB(1)
Precopy-text versions: MH, RPB(2)

845. Location
Copy-text: MH

Precopy-text version: RPB

412. The Home
Copy-text: MH
Precopy-text versions: RPB(1), RPB(2), RPB(3)

579. The Home
Copy-text: MH
Precopy-text versions: RPB(1); RPB(2); the RPB(3) version of No. 42 above, "The Home," has the earliest version of lines 9–14 of this poem.

842. Sickness
Copy-text: MH
Precopy-text version: RPB

196. Longing
Copy-text: MH
Other version collated: RPB
It is uncertain which is the later version.

83. Winthrop's Fleet
Copy-text: MH
Precopy-text versions: RPB(1), RPB(2), RPB(3)
RPB(1), RPB(2), and RPB(3) are entitled "Help."

53. Arabella Johnson
Copy-text: MH
Precopy-text versions: RPB(1), RPB(2)
RPB(2) is entitled "The Lady Arabella."

572. Spring
Copy-text: RPB(1)
Other versions collated: MH, RPB(2), RPB(3)
It is unclear which manuscript is the latest version.

637. Motive
Copy-text: MH
Precopy-text versions: RPB(1), RPB(2), RPB(3)

431. The Church
Copy-text: MH
Precopy-text versions: RPB(1), RPB(2), RPB(3), RPB(4)
RPB(2) and RPB(3) are entitled "Worship"; RPB(4) is entitled "The Church Organized."

84. Worship
Copy-text: RPB(1)
Precopy-text versions: MH, RPB(2)

648. Song
Copy-text: MH
Other version collated: RPB
It is unclear which is the later version.

170. [Untitled] (Here let the Church her holy mission prove)

Copy-text: RPB

641. The Puritan Church and State: I
Copy-text: MH(1)
Precopy-text versions: MH(2), RPB
Subtitle in MH(2) is "Forms."

352. The Puritan Church and State: II
Copy-text: MH(1)
Precopy-text versions: MH(2), RPB(1), RPB(2)
MH(2) is entitled "Progress."

361. The Puritan Church and State: III
Copy-text: MH(1)
Precopy-text versions: MH(2), RPB(1), RPB(2)
MH(2) is entitled "The State"; RPB(1), "State Growth"; RPB(2), "Form of Government."

857. Appeal
Copy-text: RPB(1)
Other versions collated: MH(1), MH(2), RPB(2)
Precopy-text version: RPB(3)
It is unclear which is the latest version.
The poem is entitled "The Puritan Church and State" in Clarke, though no extant manuscript gives that title. It is likely, however, that it was originally intended as No. IV (the only title given MH[2]) of the series of poems with this title (see above, Nos. 642, 352, and 361).

413. Influence of Puritanism
Copy-text: MH(1)
Other versions collated: MH(2), RPB(1)
Precopy-text version: RPB(2)
It is unclear which is the latest version.
This poem was originally intended as No. V of the series "The Puritan Church and State."

456. The Bible
Copy-text: MH
Precopy-text versions: RPB(1), RPB(2)

555. The Common School
Copy-text: MH
Precopy-text versions: RPB(1), RPB(2)

416. A Christian Commonwealth
Copy-text: MH
Precopy-text versions: RPB(1), RPB(2)

421. Discontent
Copy-text: RPB(1)
Precopy-text versions: MH, RPB(2), RPB(3)

99. Conclusion
Copy-text: MH

Other versions collated: RPB(2), RPB(4)
Precopy-text versions: RPB(1), RPB(3)
It is unclear which is the latest version.

82. The Old Organ Of The East Society Salem
Copy-text: MH

109. On Some Beautiful Crocuses In Front of the House of B. H. Silsbee, Esq.
Copy-text: Cl, pp. 436–37

318. The Return of the Savior
Copy-text: MH(1)
Precopy-text version: MH(2)

365. The Kingdom of the Truth
Copy-text: MH

379. Sunset after a Clouded Day in April
Copy-text: MH(1)
Precopy-text versions: MH(2), MH(3)

382. Hymn: Prayer for the Gift of the Holy Spirit
Copy-text: MH(1)
Incomplete fair copy (breaks off after line 14): MH(2)

394. Hymn
Copy-text: MH

414. Hymn: The Forms of Nature, and the Unity of their Origin
Copy-text: MH

449. Friendship: To J. M. S.
Copy-text: MH
Precopy-text version: RPB

462. Hymn: The Good Fight
Copy-text: MH

484. The Day calling us to a New Life
Copy-text: MH

499. To the Misses Williams, On seeing their beautiful Paintings of Wild Flowers
Copy-text: MH

538. Jacob wrestling with the Angel
Copy-text: MH

545. Rain Clouds
Copy-text: MH

569. The Soul in Dreams
Copy-text: MH
A notation on the manuscript indicates that the poem was intended for publication in CR, but no such publication has been located.

570. Our Native Sparrows
Copy-text: MH

590. Hymn: I Am The Way
Copy-text: MH(1)
Precopy-text version: MH(2)

636. Early Companions
Copy-text: MH

675. The Gift
Copy-text: MH

736. The Soul's Opportunities
Copy-text: MH

338. The Book of Life
Copy-text: MH

316. For the Sailors' Fair
Copy-text: MH

372. Parting Hymn
Copy-text: broadside (n.p., n.d.) at MWA

455. The Peace Congress the Promise of a Higher Civilization
Copy-text: Cl, pp. 463–64

589. Hymn to the Living
Copy-text: MH(1)
Other version collated: MH(2)
MH(2) is probably not in Very's hand.

562. Lines suggested by hearing the beach, at F. Peabody's Mills, South Salem.
December 21. 1833.

2 original reading: 'Far o'er the hills of snow;' 'Far' and 'the' cancelled; final version
of entire line interlined; all revisions in pencil

3 river silent] original reading 'silent river's'; 'river's' cancelled and 'river' interlined
with a caret before 'silent'; all revisions in pencil

5 too] 'too' interlined above cancelled 'now'; revisions in pencil

7 are hying] original reading: '[illegible word] heying'; '[illegible word] hey'
cancelled; 'are hying' interlined below; revisions in pencil

8 original reading: 'All now is hush'd'; 'now' cancelled and 'grows' interlined
above; final version of entire line interlined below in pencil

10 shining] original reading: 'clear and'; 'and' cancelled in ink and 'shining' inter-
lined in pencil

Cancelled fourth stanza (cancellation in pencil):

Or like the pine trees sighing,
At intervals
In the autumnal blast;
When <the> clouds before it flying
Are driven swift and fast.

Additional lines in pencil:

Within the mind returning,
The full orbed moon is shining[?]

418. A Song Composed by Mr J. Very, to be Sung at the Class-Supper of the Sopho-
more Class of 1834

2 min'] apostrophe written over erased 'd'

320a. Spring

2 snatched] written over illegible word
13 boughs] interlined above 'limbs'

528a. [Untitled] (The morn may lend its golden smile)

3 our] interlined above 'of'

Stanza 3: The following two lines are first written, then abandoned, and the stanza
rewritten as in text:

Yet still each glance that friendship gave
Shall beam with brighter ray

128. Eheu! fugaces, Posthume, Posthume, Labuntur anni.
    5 Beauty's] 'y' written over 'ie's'
    19 Beauty's] 'y' written over 'ie's'

399. A Withered Leaf—seen on a Poet's Table
MH:
Following the extra stanza in MH that succeeds stanza 2 (see Historical Collation), is the following stanza:
    Yes, that wither'd leaf can tell
    More than words strong power can say;
    On the Poet's ear there fell
    Other tones than sad decay.
The above stanza is then cancelled by enclosure in brackets and stanza 3 ("Not alone . . ."), written later in different ink, is substituted.
    16 list'ning] apostrophe written above cancelled 'e'

353. The Stars
    3 sons of air!] interlined above cancelled 'visions of air!'
Stanza 3 written in left margin to be inserted after stanza 2.
    17 lyre] 'y' over 'i'
    24 Too deep, too pure its source!] interlined below cancelled 'In God it finds its source.'

47. The Snow Bird
MH(2):
After stanza 7 the following stanza appears but is cancelled:
    And bid me feel that He, whose eye
        Thy wants doth pitying see;
    And through the wintry-time supply,
        Will surely succor me.
    31 thou'st] 'st' added below 'thou'
    31 left] interlined with a caret
    32 thou'st] 'st' interlined with a caret
MH(1):
    6 laugh] over illegible wiped out word

396. King Philip
MH:
Headnote: . . . Thatcher's Lives] 'v' written over 'f'

825. The Frozen Ship
    36 mortal] interlined with caret above cancelled 'silent'

343. My Mother's Voice
    2 brow,] top of semicolon erased to leave comma
    19 throng,] comma in pencil
    22 when, at eve,] commas in ink over pencil
    22 high;] pencilled alteration of comma to semicolon
    23 hear,] comma in ink over pencil
    26 Love] followed by a comma that was then erased

592. Hymn, Sung at the Dedication of The New Stone Church of The North Society In Salem June 22d, 1836.

Title: Salem] succeeding comma wiped out
Title: 22d,] comma in pencil
   7 To man Thou gavst] pencilled revision from original reading: Tis man's high gift
   18 On] written over wiped out illegible word
   18 height,] comma in pencil

695. The Winter Bird
   1 bough] 'gh' added in pencil
   2 now;] semicolon added in pencil
   3 voice, . . . rill,] commas added in pencil
   4 the] interlined in pencil above cancelled 'in'
   4 hill,] comma added in pencil
   5 ear,] comma added in pencil
   5 glided] interlined in pencil above uncancelled 'murmured'
   6 To join] originally 'And joined'; 'To' interlined above cancelled 'And'; 'ed' cancelled in 'joined'
   7 its sweetness] this original reading retained after substitution of 'thy' for 'its' and then substitution (in pencil) of 'thy music' for 'its sweetness'; these substitutions cancelled

24. The Boy's Dream: A Ballad
   9 for] inserted with a caret in pencil
   13 grow,] comma added in pencil
   17 original reading: 'Strange countries he saw, but none so dear,'; all of line except 'so dear,' cancelled; interlined above: 'But no land he found, that was'; 'land' cancelled and 'place' interlined above; all revisions in pencil
   23 on, and] comma added in pencil
   24 be.] period altered to exclamation point in pencil, then alteration cancelled in pencil
   25 those] inserted with a caret in pencil
   33 changed; he] comma cancelled, changed to semicolon in pencil; followed by 'and' cancelled in pencil

175. [Untitled] (Home of my youth! Where first my lot was cast)
   2 song] written over illegible word
   4 moved gaily] interlined above cancelled 'fled [illegible word]'
   10 tell] interlined above uncancelled 'bear'
   14 To] written over 'In'

160. [Untitled] (Haunts of my youth farewell! A while I leave)
   3 visit] interlined above cancelled 'dwell'

432. Death Decay and Change
   1 on] written over 'in'
   10 the knell] interlined above cancelled illegible word
   13 original reading: 'Where has fled that'; 'that' cancelled and 'from' interlined above; 'where' inserted with a caret after 'Where'; 'away' interlined above 'fled from'; 'me the face' added at end of line
   15 line begins with 'Why', which is cancelled
   15 clothed] interlined above cancelled 'hung around'
   16 wast] interlined (preceded by cancelled 'but') above cancelled 'didst camest'
   17 original reading: 'But a flower of brightest bloom'; interlined above 'But a' is

'Lo! See', with 'Lo!' cancelled; 'bud' is interlined above 'flower', and 'earliest' above 'brightest'; above 'earliest' is (in pencil) '[illegible word] rarest', cancelled in ink

20 original reading: 'Clouding oer my soul with night'; 'That' interlined above cancelled 'Clouding'; 'e' above cancelled 'y' in 'my'; 'had cast its' above cancelled 'soul with'

21 thee] 'too' [extraneous?] interlined above

22 all that] interlined above cancelled 'thou hast'

27 Each] interlined above cancelled '[illegible letter {E?}] All'

32 cannot] interlined above cancelled 'knows no'

309. The April Snow

2 Which] interlined above cancelled 'That'; revision in different ink

4 wear;] semicolon in different ink

5 from] originally 'how, from'; 'how,' cancelled in different ink

5 plain,] comma in different ink

6 sun;] semicolon in different ink

7 detain,] comma in different ink

8 which] interlined above cancelled 'that'; revision in different ink

8 run.] period in different ink

10 fill,] comma in different ink

11 And, with new life, from sun and kindly showers,] all commas in different ink

12 hill;] semicolon in different ink

14 bloom.] period in different ink

244. An Evening Walk

15 Which] interlined above cancelled 'That'

19 Till] interlined above cancelled 'Soon'

650. The Voice of God

RPB(2):

7 lightning] 'e' cancelled from original 'lightening'

11 'Twas,] comma added in pencil

12 nature,] comma added in pencil

17–20 This stanza originally written as follows:

'Tis only on the thankless heart
It breaks in thunder's pealing wrath:
To bid the wanderer's steps depart
And shun destruction's flaming path.

This version is cancelled and another is written on verso:

Tis only on the heedless ear
It breaks in thunder's pealing wrath
Quickening the wan[illegible letters] feet with fear
To shun destructions flaming path.

Final version appears in right margin, recto.

24 warbled] interlined above cancelled 'soaring'

MH:

15 called] written over erased illegible word

112. The Passage Bird

4 original reading: 'And call in soft murmurs and lure thee to stay.'; 'call ~ thee'

cancelled; 'wave with soft music their welcome' interlined above; 'voice' interlined above 'music'

    10 spread] interlined above cancelled 'lay'

    13 wander] interlined above cancelled 'murmur'

741. The Journey

    6 point] interlined above cancelled 'tell'

    7 travel] final second 'l' cancelled

    13 lies?] original comma altered to question mark

482. The Coming

    9 comes!] '!' in pencil

    12 Kingdom] interlined above cancelled 'riches'; revision in ink over pencil

    12 aye] interlined above cancelled 'e'er'

    13 Priests,] comma added in different ink

    14 of God] interlined below cancelled 'of Christ'; revision in ink over pencil

    14 joy] interlined above cancelled 'peace'; revision in ink over pencil

264. The Garden

    8 spirit's] apostrophe in pencil

789. The Song

    2 stretch] second 't' written over original 'a'

258. The Slave

    11 all–] comma originally followed 'all' and preceded dash; marked through in pencil

518. The Latter Rain

    1 rain,] comma added in pencil

598. The Word

    13 its praise] interlined above cancelled 'arise'

266. The Dead

    10 His] written over illegible word

269. The Presence

    4 Thou] mended from lower case

    8 Thou] mended from lower case

103. The Robe

    3 Lies] written over 'Lay'

256. The War

    8 fleecy] mended from 'fleacy'

306. Life

    6 rigid] 'riggid' written over illegible wiped out letters (possibly 'rug')

608. The Reaper

    7 bleed,] second 'e' written over illegible letter (possibly 'a')

616. Winter

    6 or] written over 'and'

    13 e'en] interlined above cancelled 'on'

781. John
  12 learn] 'ea' written over illegible wiped out letters
  13 Light] mended from lower case

218. The Flood
  10 rolled,] follows cancelled 'poured'

117. The Corrupt Tree
  11 wieldest] probably originally written 'wieldest', then 'ie' erased and replaced by 'ei'

125. The Pure in Heart
  2 Thou] upper case 'T' written over lower case
  11 Thou] upper case 'T' written over lower case

809. Whither shall I go from thy Spirit
Title: Whither] illegible letter(s) wiped out between 'W' and 't' and 'i' substituted (final reading: 'Wither')
  3 near,] question mark erased, replaced by comma
  8 nigh;] originally written 'night;'; 't' wiped out

672. Sacrifice
  2 lips,] comma added in different ink
  2 feel;] comma changed to semicolon in different ink
  3 hands, without the heart,] commas added in different ink
  4 lay] interlined above cancelled 'place' in different ink
  6 our] 'r' interlined above cancelled poorly formed 'r' in different ink
  7 But,] comma added in pencil
  7 keep, within,] commas added in ink over pencil
  10 Is {ms. reading}] 's' written over illegible wiped out letter
  11 which, who taste,] commas in different ink

618. The Ark
  2 Where'er] 'ere'e' written over illegible wiped out letters

700. The Father
  12 thine] 'ine' interlined above cancelled 'y'; revision in different ink

801. Rachel
  14 is] written over illegible wiped out word

526. The Hours
MH(1):
  7 they] 'the' written over illegible wiped out letters
MH(2):
  2 To bear] 'To' originally indented, then wiped out and rewritten at left margin; 'bear' written over wiped out 'To'
  2 His] 'H' written over wiped out 'h'
  14 dews,] 'ew' written over illegible wiped out letters

728. The Christ
  3 is] written over illegible wiped out word
  3 witness] interlined with a caret

574. Spring
3 breathed] 'bre' written over illegible wiped out false start

582. The Temple
MH(2):
8 chiselled] first 'l' inserted with caret in ink over pencil
9 repaired] 'i' inserted with caret in different ink

597. The White Horse
1 forth!] comma wiped out, exclamation point written over
14 joy] illegible letter wiped out, 'j' written over

698. The Tent
4 friendly] 'i' inserted with caret in different ink

472. Nature
MH:
3 know] 'k' added to original 'now'

522. Morning
14 a place to] 'a' and 'to' written over rubbed out 'their' and 'of', respectively

124. Change
5 overspread,] 'v' inserted with a caret
7 line surrounded by brackets, commonly Very's method of cancelling a line; in this case, nothing is substituted for the line

280. The Poor
14 and see] interlined above 'voice no'

681. They Who Hunger
2 Thou] mended from lower case
11 the] originally 'they'; 'y' wiped out

639. The Sign
MH:
2 'twould] 'tw' written over illegible wiped out letters
3 feel] followed by a period, which has been wiped out
6 Him,] comma added in different ink
13 ever] preceded by illegible wiped out letter

380. The Desert
MH:
9 earth] followed by comma that has been wiped out
RPB:
14 rich harvests still] interlined below cancelled 'the grateful crop'

386. Praise
4 his] 'h' written over wiped out illegible letter

136. Forgiveness
4 I] added in pencil
5 needy,] 'needy' written over illegible wiped out word

640. The Heavenly Rest

MH(1):
  4 dies.] period originally a semicolon; comma portion erased
  5 love!] exclamation point replaces erased comma
  8 which] interlined above cancelled 'that'
  10 which] interlined above cancelled 'that'

167. Compassion
  3 faltering] 'te' written over illegible wiped out letters

664. The Rock
  9 tear,] 'tea' written over illegible wiped out letters

739a. [Untitled] (To notice other days were pages given)
  2 stray,] comma originally a semicolon; top half wiped out
  5 these] followed by erased comma

490a. The Crocus
  16 May] word begun ('Ma') at left margin, then wiped out and indented

659a. The Plant
  3 furrowed] interlined with a caret
  12 draw life] interlined above cancelled 'proceed'

591. I am the Way
  8 an apparently incomplete attempt at revision: line is enclosed in pencilled paren-
thesis and revised line written in left margin in pencil: 'In wh. gained [?] thy feet
shall never wander more'; 'thy feet' cancelled and 'no soul' interlined above; 'stray or'
interlined above 'wander more'

498. To the pure all things are pure
  10 He] upper case written over erased lower case
  13 insect be] originally 'insect to shall be'; 'to shall' cancelled in pencil

235. Spring
  14 to] written over 'with'

802. The Warrior
  4 not; I breathe; ye fall before the blast.] all punctuation in pencil
  5 hills] 's' in pencil
  5 retire!] exclamation point in pencil
  6 now;] semicolon in pencil
  7 of battles—] 'of' and dash in pencil

556. The Acorn
Title: originally 'He that humbles himself shall be exalted'; 'The Acorn' written in
pencil in left margin
  1 started, who can stay it?] punctuation in pencil
  4 That rose beside it and] originally 'Beside it soon'; added in left margin in pencil
'That stood'; 'stood' cancelled and 'rose' added (in pencil); 'and' interlined above
cancelled 'soon'
  6 on! it cannot stop; its branches spread;] all punctuation in pencil
  8 find] interlined in pencil
  14 gave,] originally 'gave thee,'; 'thee' cancelled in pencil

279. The Husbandman
  4 guides] written over illegible wiped out word

820. The Last
  14 For he] 'he' written over illegible wiped out word
  14 ever] written over illegible word

93. The Call
  5 conflicts soon begin] 's' added to 'conflict' and 's' deleted from 'begins'
  7 gates] written over illegible wiped out word
  11 Him] upper case written over wiped out lower case
  14 He] upper case written over wiped out lower case

516. Joy
  12 however] written over 'howe'er'
  12 wide] written over illegible wiped out word

253. The Creation
  12 is] written over illegible word
  13 fly] written over 'come'

340. The Snare
  5 line begun as follows, then abandoned and new line (l. 5) written: 'The lightening shines e'en to the furthest w'
  13 brightness] written over illegible word

304. So is every one who is born of the spirit
  4 ye] originally 'yet'; 't' wiped out
  6 murmurs flow] originally 'music [illegible word]'; 'sic [illegible word]' cancelled; 'rmurs flow' interlined above
  11 approaching] 'appr' written over illegible wiped out letters

853. The Seed
  11 lustre] originally 'lustere'; first 'e' cancelled

240. The Guest
  3 owner] written over illegible wiped out word (first letter: 's')
  7 to] originally 'too', with final 'o' cancelled in pencil

490. The Eagles
  14 worshipped] second 'p' added in pencil

178. The Mourner
Title: written under the title in pencil: 'Hebs 12:'
  3 gone;] comma made semicolon in pencil
  5 Thy] preceded by bracket in pencil; pencilled line runs vertically through center of poem from this line to last line
  14 Prince] interlined above cancelled 'star'; revision in pencil
  14 Bethlehem.] followed by pencilled bracket

742. The Sower
  9 There] originally 'Their'; last three letters wiped out and 'ere' written over

783. Charity

4 line surrounded by pencilled parenthesis

5 thee] final 'e' added in pencil

631. The Created

8 thy Father too will be!] interlined beneath cancelled 'will be eternity!'; revision in pencil

159. The Unrevealed

Title: pencilled line drawn through title

4 joy;] written over erased 'hope'

8 spheres] final 's' erased, then restored

32. The Prisoner

2 line begins 'Find'; the word is cancelled and the line abandoned; line 2 restarted on next line

5 fixed] written over illegible wiped out word beginning with 'f'

6 move;] follows cancelled 'stir'

9 thus set] preceded by cancelled 'but'; 'set' inserted with a caret

10 short bounded] interlined above cancelled 'confined'

11 original reading: 'Within my orbit worlds untold will be'; this is cancelled, and final version written on next line

13 twinkling] interlined with a caret above cancelled 'move'; followed by cancelled 'glancing' (also interlined)

342. Eternal Life

5 find] followed by erased comma

13 name,] comma written over erased exclamation point

714. Hallowed be thy Name

Title: Hallowed] second 'l' inserted in pencil with a caret

261. The Children

6 They] interlined above cancelled 'Alike'

11 they] inserted with a caret

14 feasting] inserted with a caret

14 not Him] originally 'Him not'; 'not' cancelled and inserted with a caret before 'Him'

506. The New Man

2 eyes] followed by cancelled 'still'

5 see,] originally 'sees,'; final 's' cancelled

6 his] written over illegible erased word

6 shining] mended from original 'shiny'

7 bee,] originally 'bees,'; final 's' cancelled

8 Direct] originally 'Directs'; final 's' cancelled

732. The Veil of the Temple

5 he] written over illegible word

222. The Holy of Holies

12 My] lower case 'm' erased, replaced by upper case

704. The Fig Tree

8 wear'st] begun 'weare'; second 'e' cancelled, and ''st' added

9 The] originally 'Thee'; final 'e' erased
9 figs] 'fi' written over illegible letters
9 Father] followed by apparently stray mark resembling 's'

712. Not as the World giveth
6 grows,] originally 'grows;'; pencilled cancellation of top of semicolon
13 bring] originally followed by a comma, which is wiped out

782. The Good Gift
6 sure;] follows illegible erased word
10 gulf] 'lf' written over illegible letters

510. History
Title: original title, 'The Scriptures'; this cancelled and 'History' written above
8 original line begins 'But states beyond the', then is cancelled and abandoned
10 dust-soiled] 'i' inserted with a caret
13 man's] interlined above cancelled 'the'
13 still] preceded by cancelled 'still'
14 line originally reads: 'To me earth-born and him the heavens would claim.'; 'the heavens would claim.' cancelled and 'of higher name.' interlined above; then entire line cancelled and final version written on next line

393. The Spirit Land
9–12 written in pencil
9 line begun 'For tho' loud', then abandoned; then written on next line as 'Tho' now around me howls the raging blast,'; interlined above 'around' in ink is 'against'; interlined above 'howls' in ink is 'beats'; what is probably another version of line 9 appears at end of poem: 'Like thee I stand exposed to every blast'; 'exposed to' cancelled and 'the sport of' interlined above
11 shall] interlined above cancelled 'will'

689. Jacob's Well
2 clothe] written over illegible word
6 to] interlined above cancelled 'for'
9 gushing] interlined above cancelled 'flowing'

51. The Day of Denial
5 thou] interlined above cancelled 'ye'
8 hour by hour] original reading: 'day by day'; first 'day' cancelled and 'every' interlined above; 'every' cancelled and 'hour' interlined above; second 'day' cancelled and 'hour' interlined above
12 the] inserted with a caret
14 leave!] original illegible punctuation wiped out and exclamation point written over it

5. Spiritual Darkness
11 at the] 'the' inserted with a caret

532. The New World
3 The] interlined above cancelled 'And'
4 sea] preceded by cancelled 'tossing'
4 mighty] inserted with a caret
11 show] interlined above cancelled 'have'

14 laid] interlined above cancelled 'built'

588. The Word
5 speaking,] originally 'spoken'; 'en' cancelled and 'ing' interlined above
6 man] originally 'tongue'; this is cancelled and 'Word' interlined above; 'Word' cancelled and 'man' interlined
7 him] interlined above cancelled 'it'

604. The Apostles
3 where] interlined above cancelled 'to'
3 Death] upper case 'D' written over lower case
4 the earth] inserted with a caret
9 us,] comma added in pencil

216. The House
5 in] not in original line, but crowded in between semicolon and 'the'
8 Earth's] interlined above cancelled 'This'
12 on] interlined above cancelled 'in'
13 shine] followed by erased illegible punctuation
14 Light] lower case 'l' wiped out and written over in upper case

730. The Immortal
14 aside] originally 'asied'; interlined above are symbols apparently directing that the letters 'e' and 'd' be transposed

241. To-Day
RPB:
6 as] interlined above cancelled 'when'
MH:
Title: To The] lower case altered to upper case
9 brook] interlined above cancelled 'stream'
Following stanza 3: This stanza written at end in different ink to be inserted here:
The hill, which rises from the grassy plain,
Invites thy feet its breezy height to scale;
And view, with it, the blue encircling main,
And wite-winged ships, which o'er its bosom sail.

475. The Barberry Bush
1 which bears] interlined in ink over pencil above cancelled 'that has'
1 fruit,] comma added in different ink
4 find, e'en there,] commas in pencil; original reading of last two words was 'e'en there,' which was cancelled; 'on it' interlined above; then final reading interlined below; all these revisions in different ink
5 Salem, scattered wide,] commas in different ink
7 down] written over wiped out 'een'
10 name,] comma in pencil
11 know,] comma in different ink over pencil
12 *Me,*] comma in different ink
14 'Twill] written below cancelled 'Will'

210. Thy Better Self
13 visit] false start of letter following 's' wiped out; 'it' written over

470. The Glutton
   14 While] interlined above cancelled 'And', which is interlined above original cancelled 'For'
   14 foul] illegible letter wiped out at end of word
   14 upon thy dish has lit.] written below original 'has on thee lit.'

784. The Day not for Gain
   2 then?] question mark written over wiped out comma
   4 thee,] comma in different ink
   5 hours] followed by wiped out comma
   7 not] inserted with a caret, in different ink over pencil
   7 will] interlined above cancelled 'cannot', in different ink over pencil
   8 day, to thee, has past,] commas in different ink; 'has' originally 'hast', then 't' erased
   10 grow yellow in its ripening] surrounded by pencilled parenthesis; apparent tentative revision of line appears in pencil (not overwritten in ink) at end of poem: 'The grain may ripen in its golden rays'
   11 dusky] inserted with a caret above cancelled 'slow-paced'
   14 Day, a slave,] commas in different ink

613. The House Not made With Hands, Eternal In The Heavens
Title: above title is 'Hymn', cancelled in pencil
   14 final version is interlined above cancelled original: 'Which shows its adamantine walls;'

501. The Broken Bowl
MH:
   12 stream,] comma in pencil

271. Hymn: Home
   6 turned my feet;] 'bade me rove;' cancelled except for semicolon; 'go' written above 'rove', then cancelled; final version interlined above; all revisions in pencil
   8 Did my fond purpose still defeat.] first version reads: 'He whispered of a home above.'; this cancelled and 'He still another path would show.' interlined above; this remains uncancelled, but a third version interlined below reads: 'Did my fond purpose oft defeat', then 'still' interlined below cancelled 'oft'; all revisions in pencil

284. The Seasons
MH(1):
   17 Autumn's] followed by illegible erased word
   19 hangs] 's' added in pencil
MH(2):
Lines 1a–8a are in additional stanza included in MH(2); see Historical Collation.
   2a Our] written over illegible erased word
   8a fair,] interlined above cancelled 'sweet,'
   9 the] 'th' written over illegible wiped out letter(s)

614. The Silent
   16 Nature's] mended to upper case in different ink
   20 God!] period mended to exclamation point in different ink

683. [Untitled] (Thou know'st not what thy Lord will say)

2 entire line interlined above cancelled original 'Thou knowst not him but he knows thee'

3 unseen thou wert He] interlined above cancelled original 'from here he's'; 'He' written over 'thee'

4 entire line interlined above original 'Would seek thy motions every life[?]'

10 original reading: 'Quickly say the thing thou woust speak'; 'And' added in left margin; 'speak the flying word' interlined above cancelled 'say the thing thou woust speak'

586. The Good

3 original reading: 'From the deep truth the flower comes forth to view'; 'truth, the root,' interlined above 'deep truth'; 'puts' interlined above cancelled 'comes'; 'in' interlined above cancelled 'to'

8 whole] interlined above cancelled 'germ'

8 all that] originally 'all life that'; 'life' cancelled

15 Reveals] 's' written over original 'ed'

15 a] interlined above cancelled 'in'

15 Perfect Love will trace] interlined above original 'Time cannot de'; interlined below original is 'above times natal place'

16 entire line written below original 'Forever in the holy place of prayer.'; 'H' in 'House' written over original lower case

184. The Distant

Pencilled lines and fragments above and below the poem do not seem related to this poem.

561. A Word

MH(1):

26 deep,] comma added in pencil

263. The Dwellings of the Just

3 entire line interlined above original cancelled 'To give them light where'er they went'

5 none] interlined above cancelled 'nought'

7 who] followed by cancelled 'who'

7 taught] followed by illegible punctuation, wiped out

11 Who] written over 'And'; arrow directs reader to bottom of poem, where 'Who' is clearly written

15 these,] first 'e' written above cancelled 'o'; arrow directs reader to bottom of poem, where 'these' is clearly written

511. The Bee Hive

3 in a garden fenced around,] originally 'on a low and sunny mound'; 'in' interlined above cancelled 'on'; above cancelled 'low' illegible word interlined, then attempt made to change it to 'garden', which is finally rewritten above; 'fenced around,' interlined above cancelled 'sunny mound'

6 line is interlined below cancelled abandoned false start: 'Till she call'

8 Telling] 'ing' added with caret; 'Telling' rewritten in left margin

9 Are] interlined above cancelled 'Is'

9 dell] 'dell' cancelled, followed by 'field' cancelled; 'dell' then interlined above

10 their] interlined above cancelled 'its'

11 humming] originally 'huming'; 'ming' interlined with a caret above 'ing'

13 Do they bloom] 'Do' interlined above cancelled 'Have' and 'bloom' above cancelled 'grown'

14 the sheltered walks] interlined above cancelled 'where tread the feet'

15 line originally read 'There the generous flowers relieved', then cancelled and 'Not the smallest is concealed,' interlined below; 'smallest' cancelled and 'humblest' interlined above it

18 Thus] originally 'These'; 'ese' cancelled and 'us' interlined above

18 they] altered from 'their'

18 will,] interlined above cancelled 'tasks fulfil'; entire line rewritten at end of poem

20 go] interlined above cancelled 'serve'

661. The Absent
Title: The Absent] written above cancelled 'Not at Home'

5 Day] 'D' written over illegible wiped out letter

10 parlor] first 'r' inserted with a caret

11 Another] 'other' inserted with a caret above illegible cancelled letter

11 the] followed by cancelled 'narrow'

14 Look] originally 'Looks'; 's' cancelled

14 lighten] originally 'lightens'; 's' cancelled

748. The Pilgrim
RPB:

2 deep] interlined above cancelled 'thick'

5 a] interlined above cancelled 'the'

10 they had] interlined above cancelled 'that was'

MH:

2 path;] comma changed to semicolon in different ink

4 wrath.] comma scratched out; period added in different ink

8 restored.] comma scratched out; period added in different ink

9 him,] comma apparently first in ink, then overwritten in pencil

10 which] interlined in different ink above cancelled 'that'

351. The Baker's Island Light
7 its] 'it' written over wiped out 'th'

721. The Sepulchre Of The Books
8 cannot repent of their evil & sin] interlined in pencil above original abandoned line: 'They have done'

9 The good & the bad] interlined in pencil above original uncancelled 'This high stone pile it'

553. The Robin's Song
17 leaves,] comma added in pencil

18 tender,] comma added in pencil

19 begin,] 'be' written over illegible wiped out letter(s)

24 harm,] comma added in pencil

49. The Wounded Pigeon
Title: dimly pencilled above the title: 'The Dove That Perished In The Snow'

3 snow] pencilled above original 'rain'

6 lofty] pencilled above original cancelled 'leafy'

15 original reading: 'Nor rose the window by thee soft'; pencilled revision inter-

lined above: 'Thou heardst no welcome kind &'; 'kind' cancelled; 'voices' written below original line

16 original reading: 'With hands outstretched to save and bless.'; 'Thou sawst no' interlined above at beginning of line; 'to save' enclosed in parenthesis; all these revisions in pencil

29 our] pencilled in above cancelled 'the'

723. The World
MH:

2 in;] semicolon added in different ink
3 tell, when 'twas finished,] commas added in different ink
4 begin;] semicolon added in different ink
6 halls,] comma added in different ink
7 children,] comma added in different ink
9 meadow,] comma added in different ink
10 sky,] comma added in different ink
11 wood-land,] comma added in different ink
12 by;] semicolon added in different ink
13 many, too many,] commas added in different ink
14 eye, or for ear,] commas added in different ink
15 see,] comma added in different ink
17 weight, as of slumber,] commas added in different ink
18 mind;] semicolon added in different ink
19 train,] comma added in different ink
20 blind;] semicolon added in different ink
21 one,] comma added in different ink
22 show,] comma added in different ink
23 walk,] comma added in different ink
24 go.] period added in different ink
26 say,] comma added in different ink
28 song;] semicolon added in different ink
33–40 entire last stanza in different ink

668-697. The Cold Spring In North Salem
MH(OP):

2a entire line written over illegible erased line
MH-Ar:

19 Mix] written over illegible erased word
19 cooling] inserted with a caret
MH(2):

21 And] originally 'And', which is cancelled with 'Or' interlined above; then 'Or' is cancelled and 'And' written in the left margin in ink over pencil

617. God's Host
Title: underlined twice in pencil, probably by an editor of CE
4 the] cancelled in pencil, probably by an editor of CE

547. The White Dove And The Snow
Title: And] 'An' written over wiped out 'an'
11 ever] interlined above cancelled 'from'

182. Moses In Infancy
Title: written above title, but cancelled: 'Scriptural Sonnet'

750. Moses at the Bush
Title: written above title, but cancelled: 'Scriptural Sonnet'
    9 art] followed by erased comma

749. Moses As Leader Of Israel
Title: written above title, but cancelled: 'Scriptural Sonnet'
    11 land,] comma altered in pencil from original semicolon
    11 Thou, before,] commas added in different ink
    11 did'st] 'd's' written over illegible wiped out letters

708. The Autumn Flowers
    15 tints, how fair soever,] commas added in pencil
    16 take] interlined in pencil above 'steal', which is cancelled in pencil
    17 *They* will see *another*] underscoring in pencil
    21 Autumn,] comma added in pencil
    22 Bright, as now,] commas added in pencil
    26 Shall, unfading,] commas added in pencil
    26 bloom;] original comma altered to semicolon in pencil
    31 And, . . . continues,] commas added in pencil
    32 Still shall] interlined below 'There will', which has been cancelled in pencil

33. The Death of Man
    5 death, though,] commas in different ink apparently written over original ink
    5 wide] followed by erased comma
    7 Man's; . . . allied;] original commas altered to semicolons in different ink
    10 palace,] comma in different ink over original ink
    10 sky;] original comma altered to semicolon in different ink

593. The Indian's Retort
    7 fathers'] altered in pencil from 'father's'
9–12 stanza written at bottom of page to be inserted here
    17 length] altered in different ink from original 'last'
    21 "Thou steal'st!" "Thou . . . thief!"] single quotation marks altered to double in different ink
    23 proudly] interlined in different ink above 'calmly', which is cancelled in different ink
    23 answered;] original comma altered to semicolon in different ink
    28 I speak] originally 'He speaks'; attempted erasure and then cancellation of 'He'; 'I' interlined above; final 's' of 'speaks' erased

8. The Widow
    2 walls,] comma added in different ink
    5 there, alone,] commas added in different ink
    6 Book,] comma added in different ink
    6 all;] original comma altered to semicolon in different ink
    7 And, on her knees,] commas added in different ink
    8 light,] comma added in different ink
    8 strength,] comma written in different ink over pencil

12 She, through thy Son,] commas added in pencil
13 crowds,] comma added in pencil

477. Abdolonymus—The Sidonian
    1 arms,] comma added in pencil
    1 which] interlined above cancelled 'that'
    5 naught,] 'a' interlined above cancelled 'o' in ink over pencil; comma added in ink over pencil
    6 field;] 'fiel' written over illegible wiped out letters
    7 died;] comma altered to semicolon in different ink
    10 sway;] comma altered to semicolon in different ink
    11 arms,] comma added in ink over pencil
    12 and] interlined above cancelled 'or'
    14 lived,] comma added in ink over pencil

203. The Soul's Preparation For Adversity
    12 strength;] comma altered to semicolon in different ink
    12 hour,] comma added in different ink
    14 And they must] originally 'And must'; 'we' interlined, then erased; 'they' interlined in ink over pencil

156. Change In The Seasons
    6 opes] interlined above cancelled 'comes'
    8 blossoms] first 's' inserted with a caret
    14 freeze] followed by a final letter [s?] that has been wiped out and erased
    15 with] 'wi' written over illegible wiped out letters
    18 Astronomers] preceded by bracket in pencil
    21 great,] followed by bracket in pencil
    22 Has proved] 'Geology' interlined above in pencil
    22 the earth to have seen.] enclosed in pencilled brackets
    22 tropic] enclosed in pencilled parentheses; 'animals' interlined above in pencil
    23 Plants,] pencilled 'And' interlined above
    23 and animals] pencilled 'of tropic' interlined above
    26 pasturage] 'age' added in pencil

517. The Just Shall Live by Faith
    6 earth;] comma altered to semicolon in pencil
    7 And, with these words,] commas added in different ink
    8 birth.] original comma erased and replaced by period in different ink

469-573. Spring in the Soul
Title: originally 'Spring In'; 'In' wiped out; 'in the Soul' added in different ink
    1 which] interlined above cancelled 'that'; revision in different ink
    8 And, in the fruit you bear,] commas added in pencil
    8 proclaim.] period written over erased semicolon
    14 hearts,] comma added in different ink

166. Christ's Compassion
    4 road;] comma altered to semicolon in different ink
    5 burthens,] comma added in different ink
    8 arise!] period altered to exclamation point in different ink

9 Spirit] lower case altered to upper case in different ink
10 he, by works divine,] commas added in different ink

29. Hymn: Nevertheless, when the Son of Man cometh, shall he find faith on the earth? Luke XVIII:8.
Title: 'Hymn' written in different ink; 'Luke XVIII:8' originally written on separate line before quotation; pencilled instructions direct its placement after quotation
  1 Alas,] originally 'Alass,'; 'ss' wiped out and 's' written over
  8 more,] comma added in pencil
  10 spear,] written over wiped out and erased 'spear'
  15 or] written over wiped out 'and'
  22 Coming] lower case altered to upper case
  23 Coming] lower case altered to upper case

12. The Man of Science
  27 afraid,] originally 'affaid'; 'r' written over erased second 'f'

141. The Congress Of Peace At Brussels
  18 dwell, in peace,] commas added in different ink over pencil
  18 earth;] comma altered to semicolon in different ink over pencil
  28 time!] period altered to exclamation point in pencil
  32 wrongs,] comma added in different ink
  33 may] interlined above cancelled 'now' in pencil
  44 rest!] period altered to exclamation point in pencil

720. 'Tis A Great Thing to Live
  8 Which] interlined above cancelled 'Which'
  12 may, here,] commas added in different ink

515. The Indian's Petition
  8 display.] period written over illegible erased punctuation

13. The Struggle
  3 one,] comma erased, then replaced in pencil
  3 which] followed by erased comma
  6 prize,] comma added in pencil
  6 which] interlined above cancelled 'that'
  7 they,] comma added in different ink
  11 victors, with their dying breath,] commas added in different ink
  13 Which] interlined above cancelled 'that' in ink over pencil
  14 claims, as hers,] commas in different ink

292. The Things Before
  4 move.] original comma or semicolon erased, replaced by period.
  7 its] revised in pencil to 'their', then revision erased
  12 soul,] comma added in different ink over pencil
  12 here,] comma added in different ink
  13 Objects,] comma added in different ink over pencil
  13 which,] 'which' interlined above cancelled 'that'; revision in different ink over pencil
  13 itself,] comma added in different ink over pencil
  14 true, and lovely, just,] commas added in different ink over pencil

727. The Dying Leaf
    10 Which] interlined above cancelled 'That'; revision in different ink
    15 Which] interlined above cancelled 'That'; revision in different ink
    19 which] interlined above cancelled 'that'; revision in different ink

148. The New Body
    13 dead!] exclamation point replaces erased comma followed by dash
    16 Will] written over illegible wiped out word
    17 see'st] 'ee'' written over illegible wiped out letters

565. The Clock
    13 all] written over illegible erased word

176. On The Sudden Snow
    3 flung!] exclamation point in different ink over erased comma

268. The Funerals
    16 lost,] 'l' written over illegible erased letter(s)
Following line 16 this stanza appears, then is cancelled in pencil:
    What though no great, nor glorious deed
        Has left their names in History's page;
    Of which posterity may read,
        And hand it down from age to age?
    18 yon] interlined above cancelled 'the'; revision in different ink
    20 Unhonored] 'honored' interlined above cancelled 'welcomed' in different ink
    22 care;] originally 'cares;'; revision in different ink over pencil
    24 share.] originally 'shares.'; revision in different ink over pencil
    26 with] illegible word interlined above, then erased
    27 pride] interlined above cancelled 'joys'; revision in different ink
    30 honored] illegible word interlined above, then erased
    36 the sympathetic tear.] originally 'unseen the frequent tear.'; this phrase enclosed
in brackets; bracket following 'tear.' wiped out and erased; bracket added following
'frequent'; 'the sympathetic' interlined in different ink above
37–40 first version of this stanza (which was cancelled) follows:
    There, purified by grief, she views,
        The vail withdrawn, their blest abode;
    And <strengthened> quickened by the sight pursues
        With <quickened step> joyful hope her heaven-ward road.

657. The New Aqueduct
    12 sweet,] comma added in pencil
    19 deeds,] comma added in pencil
    20 hide;] comma altered to semicolon in pencil

504. The Soul's Freedom
Title: preceded on separate line by 'Hymn', cancelled in pencil
    19 mind;] original semicolon altered to comma by wiping out period; then period
restored in different ink

195. Looking Before And After
    2 purpose,] comma added in pencil, then in different ink
    2 done!] exclamation point written over illegible erased punctuation

5 behind;] semicolon written over illegible erased punctuation
8 complete;] comma altered to semicolon in pencil
12 Eternity's] lower case altered to upper case

212. The Succory
10 tone,] period of original semicolon wiped out
18 smile,] comma added in pencil

101. The Just
8 stain,] comma added in different ink

854. The Fugitive Slaves
1 who] interlined above cancelled 'that'
4 take.] period written over wiped out comma
8 stone.] period written over original erased semicolon

67. The Lost Sheep: Suggested by an Engraving
5 shepherd,] comma added in ink over pencil
10 valley,] comma added in ink over pencil
15 nor] altered from original 'or'
16 suffering,] comma added in pencil
After line 22 the following lines appear, then are cancelled:
With tender grass supplied, then homeward led,
And as his own the lost and wandering fed.
April 1851

188. Thoughts and Desires
Title: preceded on separate line by 'Hymn', which is then cancelled in pencil

52. Hymn, Sung at The Fourth anniversary Of The Evening Free School, In Salem,
May 15th, 1851.
Title Sung at] interlined above cancelled 'To'; revision in ink over pencil
8 hand!] 'd' written over illegible wiped out letter(s)
10 Man idly] originally 'He idle'; revision in pencil
Following line 16 this stanza appears but is cancelled:
The factory, ship, and <tapering> lofty spire,
   Alike proclaim his skill;
The steam-drawn car, the eletric fire,
   Are subject to his will.

407. The Soul's Rest
2 which] interlined above cancelled 'that'; revision in different ink
4 Christ, the King of your Salvation,] commas in different ink; 'K' and 'S' altered
from lower to upper case in different ink
7 cloud] 's' cancelled from original 'clouds' in different ink

564. The Sliding Rock
16 stand.] period written over erased semicolon
18 across] originally 'acrost'; 't' erased and 's' written over it
30 wide] followed by erased semicolon
38 watch] interlined above cancelled 'see'; revision in ink over pencil

347. The Potato Blight

7 best?] original comma wiped out and replaced by question mark

9 sight,] comma added in ink over pencil

25 'why, with a blighted vine,] commas added in pencil

30 whate'er he takes] originally 'whatever take'; apostrophe replaced by 'v' and 'he' inserted in different ink over pencil; 's' added to 'take' in different ink

849. Congregational Singing

35 love] followed by wiped out comma

295. Kossuth

1 who] 'w' written over illegible wiped out letter

14 consume] originally 'consumes'; 's' cancelled in pencil

139. John Woolman

1 mankind;] original exclamation point altered to semicolon in ink over pencil

2 He] interlined above cancelled 'Who'

2 feel;] comma altered to semicolon in different ink

3 his] interlined above cancelled 'thy'; revision in different ink

4 reveal.] semicolon altered to period in different ink

5 He] interlined above cancelled 'Who'

9 vain;] comma altered to semicolon in different ink

12 waves,] comma added in pencil

674. Hymn: Waiting For Christ

5 suffered, for his name,] commas added in ink over pencil

6 loss?] question mark written in different ink over illegible erased punctuation

7 nor] 'or' altered to 'nor' in pencil

13 He, too,] commas added in different ink

26 shalt] 't' written over erased second 'l'

27 fills] interlined in different ink above cancelled 'lights'

754. The Wild Rose of Plymouth

7 dwelling-place] followed by comma in pencil, which is cancelled in pencil

10 prime;] semicolon added in pencil

11 happy visions] interlined above cancelled 'thoughts and questions'; 'happy' enclosed in pencilled parentheses

11 Future] pencilled 'too' above, but 'Future' not cancelled

12 reach] interlined above cancelled 'stretch'

Wavy pencilled line drawn through lines 10–14.

At end the following pencilled fragments appear:

See within

<That> And wreath earths children in a flowery chain

358. Voting In The Old North Church

Title: The North] interlined, in different ink over pencil, above cancelled 'An' [unclear whether Very intended to cancel 'Old' as well, so that title would read 'Voting in The North Church']

9 purpose] inserted in different ink over pencil

After line 11 the following cancelled lines appear:

Assembling now to vote in such a place,

O may Religion consecrate our deed.

12 invade] interlined below cancelled illegible word

27 long years] interlined above cancelled 'a life'
29 set aside] interlined above cancelled 'overlooked'
45 which] interlined below cancelled 'that'

315. The Day Lily
After line 20 the following two stanzas appear, but are cancelled in pencil and in ink:
    Every seed thou sowest now
    Shall a future harvest bear,
    In the furrows <thou shalt <dost> plow> of thy plough
    Wave the wheat, or useless tare.
    Like a flower, the life man lives
    Quickly too must pass away;
    Heed the lesson which it gives,
    While as yet 'tis called to-day.

34. The Solitary Worshipper
Headnote: worship for some] 'for' interlined above
    10 meet,] period portion of original semicolon wiped out

542. Sonnet, To the Rev. James Flint, D.D., On reading his Collection of Poems.
Title: Sonnet,] period altered to comma in pencil
    1 often] 'en' added to 'oft'
    4 Which] interlined above cancelled 'That'
    4 us] written over and interlined above erased illegible word
    6 Which] interlined above cancelled 'That'
    9 propitious,] comma added in pencil
    10 flight,] comma added in different ink over pencil
    10 England's] 's' erased, then restored
    12 which] interlined above cancelled 'that'

276. The Mind The Greatest Mystery
Title: Greatest] interlined above cancelled 'Deepest'; revision in ink over pencil
    1 a cavern] 'a' interlined above cancelled 'the'; revision in ink over pencil

756. The Horsemen on the Sands
    4 delay.] period written over erased illegible punctuation or letter(s)

163. My Dear Brother Washington
    3 him,] comma added in pencil
    11 peaceful,] comma added in ink over pencil
    12 a] interlined above cancelled 'one'; revision in different ink over pencil
    12 doubt,] comma added in different ink over pencil
    15 as] written over illegible wiped out word
    19 be,] period altered to comma in pencil

705. On Seeing The Victoria Regia In Bloom, At The Garden of J. Fisk Allen Esq.
July 22d, 1853.
Title: Esq.] inserted in different ink over pencil
    9 ponds & streams] written in pencil at end to be substituted here for original
'northern streams'

846. On Finding the Truth
    12 crown!] exclamation point written over wiped out semicolon

14 lived] 'd' written over wiped out letter ('s'?)

735. A Sunset In Haverhill
14 above,] comma added in pencil
22 brighter,] comma added in pencil
27 western,] comma added in ink over pencil
27 clime,] comma erased, then restored

688. The Past
6 point'st] apostrophe substituted for cancelled 'e'
9 yesterday,] comma added in pencil
10 beckon'st] originally 'beconest'; apostrophe substituted for 'e'; revision in ink over pencil
14 impress,] comma added in pencil
14 rock;] comma altered to semicolon in pencil
15 clay;] interlined in pencil above cancelled 'earth,'
19 reeds,] comma added in pencil
27 countless] interlined above cancelled 'unknown'; revision in pencil
32 search,] comma added in pencil
33 And, of my soul,] commas added in ink over pencil
37 essence,] originally 'essense,'; third 's' wiped out and replaced by 'c'
43 Compel] originally 'And bid'; this cancelled in favor of 'Harness'; this cancelled in favor of 'Compel'; uncancelled 'yoke' interlined below; all revisions in pencil
After line 48 the following cancelled lines appear:
In God within myself, as in the world,
I would thy origin, O Past, explore.
51 to our weak] originally 'to our narrow'; revised to 'to man's weak'; 'man's' cancelled with the apparent intention of restoring 'our'; all revisions in pencil
54 our feeble, finite] interlined in pencil above original 'the weakness of our'
55 from beginning to] originally 'the beginning to'; 'from' interlined above cancelled 'the'; 'to' interlined above cancelled 'from'; all revisions in pencil
Cancelled phrase in pencil at end: 'weak imperfect'
Cancelled lines in pencil at end:
The origin of evil here doth lie
How wrong has left its mark and sin its stains
And hoary error dates its ancient birth
Here memory & conscience have their seats
Searching thy records for each secret thing
Condemning evil and approving good.

761. Hymn, Sung at the Thompson Jubilee, at Barre, Jany. 12, 1854.
Title: 12,] originally '12th,'; 'th' cancelled in pencil
After line 24 the following stanza appears, but is cancelled in ink over pencil:
Till, voiceless as the springing grain,
O'er all the earth the harvest wave;
And every hill and every plain,
Shall hail the Christ, who came to save.

422. On An Ear Of Wheat Brought, By My Brother, From The Field Of Waterloo
Title: From] 'F' written over erased 'f'
After line 12 the following stanza, cancelled in pencil, appears:

Welcome! as to Noah, once
   Was the olive-bearing dove;
As the beauteous bow, that spanned
   All the firmament above.

307. The Dead Elm
   1 amidst] 'st' inserted after original 'amid'
   2 graceful] originally 'dark, stiff'; 'naked' interlined above in pencil; 'graceful'
written over 'stiff' in ink
   3 which] interlined above cancelled 'that'
   7 Its roots have] interlined above cancelled 'The noble elm'
   8 limbs,] comma added in pencil

805. The Homeless Wind
   5 "I've] quotation marks added in ink over pencil
   6 wild] written over illegible wiped out word
   11 stay] interlined above cancelled 'stop'
   13 Now,] comma added in different ink
   17 there] inserted in ink over pencil
   20 mind."] quotation marks added in ink over pencil

40. The Age Changeful and Worldly
   7 over-anxious] hyphen added in pencil
   9 time] followed by wiped out comma
   14 And, in their places,] commas added in pencil

649. Hymn: So also will God, through Jesus, bring with him them who sleep.
   7 our sight] interlined above cancelled 'us now'; revision in pencil

179. "Blessed are they that mourn: for they shall be comforted." Math. 5:4.
Title: between the two lines of the title appears 'The Bow In', which is cancelled
   10 shower;] originally 'showers;' final 's' erased
   14 Promise] upper case written over lower case 'p'

314. The Woodwax
Following line 8 there are pencilled directions to insert a stanza; the only possibility
in the existing ms. is a pencilled stanza on the back of the sheet, here given as lines
9–12.

772. The First Telegraphic Message
   4 enquires.] word written in pencil

73. The Mission Of The Friends To The Emperor Nicholas
   14 by] interlined above cancelled 'with'; revision in ink over pencil

856. Be of Good Courage
   1 our] interlined above cancelled 'our', which shows evidence of attempt to mend
badly formed 'r'

828. To An Ancient Locust-Tree, Opposite Carltonville
Title: 'Opposite Carltonville' cancelled in pencil; 'in my garden' interlined above;
revision probably not in Very's hand
   2 gone?] question mark written over erased comma
   4 scenes] followed by erased comma

4 now] interlined above cancelled 'here'

7 Swift] originally 'The many'; 'many' cancelled and 'swift' interlined above; 'The' and 'swift' cancelled and 'Swift' interlined above

9 beautiful] followed by wiped out comma

7. A Walk In The Pastures
    11 insect's] apostrophe added in pencil

373. [Untitled] (O, cleave not to the things of earth)
    1 O,] originally 'Oh,'; 'h' cancelled in different ink
    8 store?] period altered to question mark in pencil

660. Nature Intelligible
    6 find;] 'find' written over original 'see'
    9 floor,] comma added in pencil
    10 height,] comma added in pencil
    14 finished,] comma added in pencil

585. The Great Facts Of Christ's History
    8 delay:] colon written over erased semicolon

734. Freedom National, Slavery Sectional
    4 quenchless] interlined above cancelled 'heavenly'
    8 oppressed.] period written over erased semicolon or comma
    12 birth,] comma added in pencil
    14 forth,] comma added in pencil
    14 That] lower case initial 't' altered to upper case in pencil

227. Christ Abiding Forever
    3 He] 'H' written over wiped out 'h'

330. The South River At Sunset
9–12 stanza written in left margin to be inserted here
    12 the earth] 'its banks' interlined below in pencil, but original not cancelled
    16 Paint with colors] interlined above cancelled 'Or to paint scene so'; interlined below original line is 'Touch with colors', which is cancelled; all revisions in pencil
17–20 these lines cancelled in pencil, but some of cancelling erased

654. Hymn Sung at the Dedication of Plummer Hall, Salem, Oct. 6, 1857
    5 Science,] comma added in pencil
    7 calm,] comma added in pencil

21. Philosophy and Religion
    2 lot,] comma added in pencil
    2 change] interlined above cancelled marred attempt at 'change'

217. Hindoo Converts: On the Domestic Trials of Hindoo Converts. Report of Unitarian Mission in India.
Title: Converts.] 'ts' written over illegible wiped out letters
    4 Truth] lower case 't' mended to upper case
    7 foresee,] 'e' inserted following 'r'

771. Nature Teaches only Love
    14 declares the Sacred Word.] originally 'is still their highest word.'; this cancelled and 'declares the sacred word.' interlined below, in ink over pencil; initial letter of

'sacred' and 'word' altered to upper case in yet a different ink
Following line 14 are two largely illegible pencilled lines.

841. The First Atlantic Telegraph
Title: First] inserted in different ink over pencil

25. Lines On The Old Danvers Burying Ground
Title: Lines On] inserted with a caret
    18 planet's] apostrophe added in pencil

145. On Seeing The Portrait of Helen Ruthven Waterston
    2 near!] exclamation point replaces cancelled semicolon; revision in pencil
    7 admiring] interlined above 'and ardent'; revision in pencil
    17 many mansions fair,] originally 'mansions bright and fair,'; 'many' inserted with a caret; 'bright and' cancelled; all revisions in pencil

785. Hymn: The Promise of The Spirit
Title: Hymn] this word cancelled, then rewritten above; all revisions in different ink
    10 I] interlined above cancelled 'He'
    11 But] interlined above cancelled 'He'll'

197. The Moss and Its Teachings
    13 made,] originally 'formed' followed by comma or semicolon that was erased; 'formed' cancelled and 'made,' interlined above; revision in different ink
    14 tree,] comma added in different ink
    14 mould;] comma altered to semicolon in different ink
    19 on] written over wiped out 'for'
    36 On] written over wiped out 'That'
    37 gloomy] 'glo' written over illegible wiped out letters

243. The Lament Of The Flowers
Title: Of] 'O' written over wiped out 'of'
    5 The] 'T' written over original 'A'
    6 Which] interlined above cancelled 'That'
    21 ghost,] 'gho' written over illegible letters
    22 dell,] period portion of original semicolon wiped out

20. The Voice In The Poplars
    6 Which] written over cancelled 'That' in different ink
    10 hour,] period portion of original semicolon wiped out
    13 That] 'Whi' written above but wiped out
    17 written] written over erased illegible word

366. The Set Times, And The Boundaries of Nations, Appointed By God
Title: By] upper case 'B' written over lower case
    1 States & Nations] upper case 'S' and 'N' written over lower case
    10 old,] period portion of original semicolon wiped out
    11 wise] followed by cancelled comma
    12 foretold;] period cancelled, followed by semicolon

770. The Cemetery of Harmony Grove
Title: written in pencil
After line 25 handwriting changes; see Textual Notes.
    31 Coming,] lower case altered to upper case

56 The] originally 'They'; 'y' wiped out

731. Hymn: The Dew
    13 gathered] interlined above cancelled 'lifted'; revision in pencil
    15 line in different ink
    15 humble trusting] interlined above cancelled 'trusting, humble'; revision in
pencil

165. The Triennial
    47 busy] 'bu' written over illegible wiped out letters

814. The Child's Answer
Title: original title: 'The Child's Answer'; written above this but cancelled in pencil:
'Hymn for Children'
    6 know] followed by wiped out comma
    12 being,] comma added in pencil

85. Freedom And Union
    2 things, not names,] commas added in pencil
    4 nobleness] enclosed in brackets, in pencil (probably indicates an abortive attempt
to revise)
    5 names,] comma added in pencil
    14 deeds,] comma added in pencil

404. The Cross
Title: original title: 'The Cross'; written above this but cancelled: 'Hymn.'; written
above this but cancelled in pencil: 'Hymn.'
    4 original line, which is cancelled in pencil: 'Making all things else but dross!'; writ-
ten below this and cancelled in pencil: 'Man's great gain, the world's sad loss!'; final
version written below this in pencil
    10 or] written over illegible wiped out letters
    11 uplifts] 'lifts' written over illegible wiped out letters
    13 faint,] comma added in pencil
    25–28 this stanza written at end to be inserted here

135. On reading the Memorial of John White Browne
    7 bow,] comma added in ink over pencil
    9 But, joined with these,] commas added in ink over pencil

368. Hymn: And God shall wipe away every tear from their eyes. Rev. xxi.4.
Title: Hymn] cancelled, then rewritten above
Title: xxi.] interlined above cancelled '21'; revision in pencil
    18 Father's] 'Fat' written over erased illegible letters
    23 joy,] comma added in pencil

54. One generation passeth away, and another generation cometh: but the earth
abideth for ever. Ecclesiastes 1:4.
    2 race;] semicolon in ink over pencil
    6 sea;] original comma altered to semicolon in ink over pencil
    10 fast;] original comma altered to semicolon in ink over pencil
    18 lie;] original comma altered to semicolon in ink over pencil
    19 stars,] comma added in pencil
    19 behold,] comma added in ink over pencil

21 believe,] comma added in ink over pencil
22 sight;] semicolon added in ink over pencil
24 cloudless] 'd' written over wiped out 'l'

481. The Hour Before The Dawn
8 mightier] interlined above cancelled 'greater'

830. State Rights
10 her] written over illegible wiped out word
13 seen,] comma added in pencil

838. The Rights of Man
7 theme,] comma written over illegible erased punctuation
14 boasts,] comma added in pencil

11. A Longing For The Spring
16 gladsome] interlined above cancelled 'merry'

142. The Abolition Of Serfdom In Russia
17 length] 't' written over illegible wiped out letter
22 strong] followed by wiped out comma

594. Fear not: for they that are with us are more than they that are with them.
2 Kings 6:16.
7 Word,] 'W' written over lower case letter

19. Hymn: Nature's Sympathy with Freedom
16 our] written over illegible wiped out word
18 save,] period portion of original semicolon wiped out

793. Christ's Capture In The Garden: A Paraphrase
Title: Paraphrase] 'Pa' written over wiped out 'Ph'
1 earth,] interlined above cancelled 'night,'

104. Song: Words Of Love To A Parent
Title: Song] added in ink over pencil
3 its] written over cancelled 'the'
7 sense,] 'se' written over illegible wiped out letter(s)

445. The Comet
7 aspires] 'ires' written over illegible wiped out letters

487. The Influence Of The Night on Faith And Imagination
10 quickened] 'k' written over illegible wiped out letter
35 there] 'ere' interlined in pencil above cancelled 'eir'
40 live.] 'v' written over illegible wiped out letter
47 dews,] comma added in pencil

653. Sunset in Derby's Woods
1 fitting] interlined above cancelled 'worthy'; revision in ink over pencil
After line 8 the following lines appear as stanza 3 but are cancelled, in pencil and
in ink:
Here the weary, troubled mind,
    Filled by day with vain unrest,
Doth at eve a shelter find,

With the bird that seeks its nest.
12 gentle,] comma added in pencil

437. Autumn Flowers
1 fade,] comma wiped out, then restored
2 rods] 's' added in ink over pencil
7 these,] comma in ink, overwritten in different ink
12 flowers,] comma added in different ink
18 heaven;] period portion of semicolon added in different ink
19 here, uncheered,] commas added in different ink
20 prized, in youth,] commas added in different ink
20 has] written over 'have' in pencil
22 found;] semicolon added in pencil
23 smile,] comma added in pencil
24 beguile.] period added in pencil

104. Hymn
12 He, pitying,] commas added in pencil
Following line 16 this stanza appears in MH, but is cancelled:
  Nor shalt thou walk alone,   1a
    For Christ shall walk with thee
  He shall to thee himself make known
    And thou his glory see.
2a walk with thee] originally 'with thee go'; 'walk' inserted with a caret and 'go' cancelled
4a glory see.] interlined above cancelled 'love shalt know'
Several incomplete cancelled lines written in margins.

826. The Poet's Plea
5 no,] comma written over erased exclamation point
5 rage!] exclamation point written over erased comma
12 harp] written over cancelled 'lyre'; revision in ink over pencil
14 lyres] written over cancelled 'harps'; revision in ink over pencil
22 crown,] comma added in pencil
23 sword,] comma written over erased exclamation point

454. On The Completion Of The Pacific Telegraph
11 strive] 've' written over illegible wiped out letters
12 Peace, and Liberty,] commas added in ink over pencil

584. The Traveller At The Depot
10 which] interlined above cancelled 'that'; revision in different ink

424. Salvation Is Of The Lord: The Book of Jonah ii.9.
11 deepening] 'en' written over illegible wiped out letter(s)

301. The Newspaper
4 yet, with careless glance,] commas added in pencil
8 speech,] 'ea' interlined above 'ee'
8 thought] 'h' written over illegible wiped out letter

9. E Pluribus Unum
4 lend.] period written over wiped out semicolon

5 which] interlined above cancelled 'that'
13 higher] written over illegible wiped out word

656. This Mortal Shall put on Immortality
3–4 lines are interlined above the following cancelled lines; revision in ink over pencil:
No more we see it with our eyes
    Upon the earth again.
11 whole] followed by wiped out comma

571. Hymn: The Spirit Itself Maketh Intercession For Us
Title: Hymn] cancelled, then restored in different ink
2 thought,] comma added in pencil
5 reach] interlined above cancelled 'pierce'; revision in ink over pencil
7 He] interlined above cancelled 'Who'; revision in ink over pencil
10 thought,] comma added in pencil
12 not, then,] commas added in pencil
14 comfort,] comma added in pencil
15 love,] comma added in pencil
16 brings] interlined above cancelled 'gives'; cancelled 'whispers to' written below 'gives'; all cancelling in pencil
18 then we] interlined above cancelled 'it doth'; cancelling in pencil
18 pray;] period portion of semicolon added in pencil

411. The Elm Seed
1 fly] 'ly' written over wiped out 'all'
4 care!] exclamation point replaces erased semicolon
6 which] interlined above cancelled 'that'
7 through] interlined above cancelled 'in'
13 and] interlined above cancelled '&'
The following aborted version of the poem appears on verso:
Scattered with every breeze I see you fly
This way and that upon the Summer air
To fall into the softened ground and die
Yet not without the great Creator's care
Your wingéd flight his Providence directs
That Providence which guides and governs all
The tiny seed though buried it protects
And in the Spring-time from its grave will call

468. The Cause
10 wrong,] comma written over erased question mark
14 greatness, like a shadow,] commas added in pencil

729. Outward Conquests Not Enough
10 light, and truth,] commas added in pencil
13 speak,] comma added in pencil

755. Philanthropy Before Nationality
1 Rights] 'R' written over wiped out 'r'
10 Power;] 'P' written over erased 'p'
12 appointed] interlined above cancelled 'fated'; revision in ink over pencil

14 *free*] followed by wiped out comma

111. The Falling Leaf
    18 the quiet] 'the' written over illegible erased word
    19 found, beneath its shade, a cool retreat,] commas added in pencil

252. Faith In Time Of War
Title: In . . . Of War] initial lower case letters altered to upper case
    6 alone?] question mark written over erased comma
    7 pain?] question mark written over erased comma
    9 heart!] interlined above cancelled 'soul!'
    13 sword may slay,] interlined above cancelled 'body dies,'
    13 save;] comma altered to semicolon in pencil
    14 line interlined below cancelled original line: 'And decks with flowers the lone, neglected grave.'

520. Hymn: The Light of Life
Title: Hymn] cancelled, then restored in different ink
    8 life, and light,] commas added in pencil
    10 wrought;] comma altered to semicolon in pencil
    13 God;] semicolon added in pencil
    15 sin,] comma added in pencil

17. Man's Heart Prophesieth Of Peace
    4 on] written over wiped out 'on'
    12 be!] exclamation point written in pencil over erased semicolon
    13 And] preceded by pencilled parentheses, as if to cancel in favor of alternate lines at end; but these alternate lines cancelled
    14 sword.] pencilled line under 'd', possibly to mark end of apparently abortive cancellation of last two lines. Following the poem these lines appear in pencil, and are cancelled in pencil:
    Have faith in God, and his prophetic Word,
    Men shall learn War no more, & sheathe the s.

777. Hymn: The New Life of Humanity
Title: Hymn] written in pencil
    18 poets'] 's' is preceded by erased apostrophe
    20 nobler] 'l' written over erased letter

438. The Statue of Flora, On the Grounds of R. Brookhouse Esq, Washington Street
    6 But] written over illegible erased word

37–42. Hymn: Sung At the Unitarian Festival, in Faneuil Hall, May 26th 1863
    13 relief,] period portion of semicolon erased

58. The Tree of Liberty
    1 which,] interlined above cancelled 'that,'
    13 which] interlined above cancelled 'that'
    14 destroy!] period altered to exclamation point in pencil

644. Hymn: Our Country's Dead
Title: Hymn] cancelled and then restored

298. The Intuitions Of The Soul

13 souls, unclouded and divine,] commas added in pencil

436. Still A Day To Live
    2 give;] 've' written over illegible wiped out letters
    19 timely] followed by wiped out comma

364. Health of Body dependent on the Soul
Title: 'Hymn' written on separate line above title, but cancelled in pencil
    6 sin?] question mark written over erased comma
    7 body, too,] commas added in pencil
    9 But,] comma added in pencil
    13–16 written at bottom of page to be inserted here

847. The Crisis
    2 party] 'y' written over illegible wiped out letter
    5 principles,] comma added in pencil
    9 day,] comma added in pencil
    9 prefer,] period portion of original semicolon wiped out
    12 Truth,] comma added in pencil

489. Dying Words of John Foster: "I Can Pray, And That's a Glorious Thing."
Title: Dying Words of John Foster] originally written on line below quotation, then cancelled; written above quotation in different ink
    7 To] interlined above cancelled 'Nor'
    7 them] interlined above erased 'of'
    8 name!] period altered to exclamation point in pencil
    9–12 written in pencil at end to be inserted here
    10 The dead] interlined above cancelled 'That all'
    16 man.] 'an' written over illegible erased letters
    17 now;] period portion of semicolon added in pencil
    28 Death,] comma added in pencil

848. Home and Heaven
    1 letter] followed by erased comma

417. On The Three Hundredth Anniversary of Shakespeare's Birthday
Title: Shakespeare's] first 'e' inserted in different ink
    1 Shakespeare] first 'e' inserted in different ink
    11 Jubilee,] lower case 'j' altered to upper case in different ink

671. Hymn: The Way of the Righteous Easy
Title: Hymn] cancelled, then restored in different ink
    15 spirit's] interlined in pencil above cancelled 'souls when'

658. Untimely Arguments
    3 That,] 'That' interlined above cancelled 'But'
    9 'Tis] preceded by pencilled bracket
    9 speech] second 'e' written over wiped out 'a'
    10 original reading: 'When hosts meet hosts upon the battlefield;'; 'hosts . . . battlefield;' cancelled; comma added after 'When'; 'like the waves, event event succeeds;' interlined above
    12 interlined above cancelled original version, which reads: 'And to the logic of Events must yield,'

13–14 interlined above cancelled original version, which reads:
Events that shall the Nation's fate decide—
The faithful from the faithless too divide.

300. Hymn: Ps. XLVI. 10: "Be still, and know that I am God."
Title: Hymn] cancelled, then restored in different ink
    4 And, in waiting trust,] commas added in different ink over pencil
    8 Naught] 'a' written over original 'o'
    8 naught] 'a' interlined above cancelled 'o'
    19 earth's] apostrophe added in pencil
    22 pride;] period portion of semicolon added in pencil
    24 Who, for all who live,] commas added in pencil
    28 And, in waiting trust,] commas added in ink over pencil

843. The Voice of Nature In Youth And Age
    38 relief] followed by erased comma
    40 Nature's] upper case 'N' written over lower case

858. Hymn: Christ's Invitation in the Apocalypse
Title: Hymn] added in pencil
    11 afar!] exclamation point replaces wiped out comma
    13 poor] 'oo' written over illegible wiped out letters

371. Hymn In Drought
    17 Nature's] upper case 'N' written over lower case
    24 daily] written over illegible erased word

549. The Rain
    5 Upon the river falls] interlined above cancelled 'The river swells beneath'
    6 drops,] 'op' written over illegible erased letter(s)
    7 The] 'T' written over illegible erased letter
    7 river] 'r' written over illegible erased letter

478a. The Fair Morning
    11 original reading: 'O'ertaking the long line of tinkling cows'; 'the long line of' cancelled and 'one by one the' interlined above; at end of poem a number of abortive pencilled versions of the line and the final one in ink, marked by asterisk; original attempt at final version: 'He hears far off the bells of tinkling cows,'; 'a' added before 'far' and 'off' cancelled in pencil

529. The Clouded Morning
    2 round,] period portion of original semicolon erased
    3 sail,] period portion of original semicolon erased
    9 and] written over erased illegible word

774. What Is A Word?
    2 the] interlined above cancelled 'a'
    5–8 stanza written at end in ink over pencil to be inserted here
    5 art] followed by comma in pencil only
Following line 12 these lines appear but are cancelled in pencil and ink:
    The symbol, thou, of Unseen Power,
      Which did all things create;

Which was before earth's morning hour,
    And knows nor age, nor date.

810. To Charles W. Felt Esq. On His New Type-Setting Machine
    4 day;] semicolon follows cancelled exclamation point

566. The Young Drummer Boy of Libby Prison: An Incident Related by Capt. James Hussey
    18 starving] interlined above cancelled 'sorrowing'

840. Inward Direction
    3 know)] parenthesis written over comma
    4 street!] exclamation point written over wiped out question mark
    9 whither] 'wh' written over original 'w'

149. The Cherry Birds
    4 teacheth] 'ea' written over illegible wiped out letters
    6 ash] written over illegible wiped out word

563. The Soul's Questioning Of The Universe, and Its Beginning
Title: written above title but cancelled, 'Hymn.'
    5–8 this stanza written in pencil at end (between pencilled stanzas 7 and 8) to be inserted here
    10 questions] final 's' added in pencil
    10 ask;] comma altered to semicolon in pencil
    14 we] interlined above cancelled 'they'; revision in pencil
    16 bewildered] 'en[quir?]ing' interlined below, then cancelled
    20 Word] upper case 'W' interlined above cancelled lower case in different ink
    20 is] interlined above cancelled 'we're' in different ink
    25–32 these two stanzas written in pencil at end to be inserted here
    32 interlined above but cancelled: 'And his greatness [illegible word] revere'
    36 sacred page.] upper case 's' and 'p' interlined in different ink above initial letters, then cancelled in pencil

374. Hymn: Sung at the Eulogy on Abraham Lincoln June 1st 1865
Title: written in different ink
All end-of-line punctuation in pencil except as noted.
    1 God!] exclamation point in different ink
    1 dost] 'st' interlined above cancelled 'th'; revision in different ink
    3 To thee we look,] interlined above cancelled 'We look to thee'; revision in pencil
    5 he,] comma in pencil
    6 Has] interlined above cancelled 'Is'; revision in pencil
    8 guide, to guard,] commas in pencil
    9 great,] comma in pencil
    12 And, by our Chief,] commas in pencil
    16 strife.] period in ink (unlike all other end-of-line punctuation)
    17 O,] comma in pencil
    21 Justice, Liberty,] commas in pencil
    23 land;] semicolon in pencil

193. Soul-Sickness
    2 conceal;] semicolon written over erased exclamation point

12 below!] comma altered to exclamation point in pencil

479. Song of The Early Spring
Title: Song of] interlined above cancelled 'Hymn On'; revision in ink over pencil
    6 in] interlined above cancelled 'with'; revision in pencil
    14 sun,] comma added in pencil
    17 dull,] comma added in pencil

186. Sensibility to the Beauty and Fragrance of Flowers
    4 none, who pass,] commas added in pencil
    13 haunts,] comma added in pencil

401. Prayer For Rain
Title: written above title but cancelled, 'Hymn.'

390. Hymn On The Logos: The Light Still Shining In The Darkness
    9 answered] 'n' inserted in different ink
    10 "Why] quotation marks in different ink
    14 face!] exclamation point written over wiped out semicolon
    21 love,] comma added in pencil
    24 bright,] comma added in pencil
    24 home."] quotation marks in different ink

764. Hath The Rain A Father? Or Who Hath Begotten The Drops of Dew? Job 38:28
    1 Slow of belief the Age;] original reading: 'An unbelieving Age!'; exclamation point cancelled and replaced by semicolon; interlined above: 'Oh' (cancelled); 'Slow of belief the Age;'; revisions in pencil
    2 Its very words] interlined above cancelled 'That by its words'; cancelled 'Whose' interlined below; all revisions in pencil
    10 Voice,] comma added in pencil

14. The East India Marine Museum
    4 wealth,] comma added in different ink
    14 far] interlined above cancelled 'e'en'

811. Finishing The Work
Headnote: just, . . . ourselves,] commas added in pencil
    1 with] written over illegible wiped out word
    10 precious] 'cious' written in different ink over erased illegible letters

447. Our Soldiers' Graves
Title: 'Hymn' written on line above title, but cancelled in pencil

523. The Still Small Voice
Title: written above cancelled 'The Lord on Sinai'
    3 trees,] comma added in pencil
    3 the strong blast,] interlined above cancelled 'its strong power'; then 'beneath the' (apparently an abortive revision) interlined in pencil above 'the strong blast'; comma added in pencil
    5 not;] semicolon added in pencil
    6 dire,] comma added in pencil
    7 base,] comma added in pencil
    9 But, after these,] commas added in pencil

10 heard;] semicolon added in pencil

11 face,] comma added in pencil

14 land;] comma altered to semicolon in pencil

15 fierce, consuming flame,] commas added in pencil

17 hear,] comma added in pencil

18 strife;] semicolon added in pencil

21 know that pardoning voice,] original reading: 'heed that still small voice,'; 'heed' cancelled and 'know' interlined above; 'still small' cancelled and 'gentle' interlined above then cancelled; then 'pardoning' interlined above

22 above!] exclamation point replaces cancelled semicolon

151. Primitive Worship

11 hemlock's shade] 'hemlocks shade' interlined in pencil above 'lofty grove'; 'lofty' cancelled (Very must have intended to cancel 'grove' as well.)

12 voices rose upon the air;] original reading: 'voices filled the summer air;'; 'voices' cancelled; 'singing' interlined above then cancelled in pencil; 'voices rose upon' interlined in pencil below (Very must have intended to cancel 'summer'; otherwise line has extra foot.)

233. The Holy Land

Between lines 8 and 9 a pencilled caret seems to indicate the insertion of a stanza written at end in pencil; but caret is cancelled in pencil.

15 holy] inserted with a caret

Following line 16 a pencilled caret seems to indicate the insertion of lines 17–20, written at end in pencil.

30. October

Following line 12, these lines appear but are cancelled:

Like Horeb's bush God's glory once illumed,

Each tree in splendor blazes, but unconsumed!

Lines 13–14 are written at bottom of sheet in pencil then rewritten above in ink.

567. The Soldier and the Statesman

2 When'er] wiped out apostrophe follows second 'e'

66. The Triumphs of Science, And of Faith

7 Faith,] upper case 'F' written over lower case

50. Christian Influence

8 nigh!] '!' written over erased 't'

12 as] written over wiped out 'as'

378. The Reconciling Power

7 hour,] comma added in pencil

20 voice!] exclamation point added, to replace period, in pencil

173. The Bridge of Time

16 pier.] period written over wiped out exclamation point

31 past] 'a' interlined above cancelled 'o'

356. Our Dear Mother

1 original reading: 'Our mother seems still in my sight,'; 'No more' interlined above 'Our mother' and 'meets our' above cancelled 'seems still in my'; revisions in pencil

4 final version interlined below cancelled original: 'But she has gone from earth away!'; revision in pencil

22 body,] comma added in pencil

363. Hymn: The Word Before All Things
Between lines 12 and 13 is written in pencil: 'Nor man ^', apparently a direction to insert a new stanza at this point; but see alteration at end of poem.

14 divine;] 'd' written over erased 'D'

15 heavens,] comma added in pencil

25 mind] followed by erased comma

26 dimmed] caret inserts pencilled interlineation above 'dimmed': '& [illegible word]'

30 shall] 'shal' written over illegible wiped out letters

31 time] followed by wiped out comma

At end of poem the following pencilled fragmentary stanza appears but is cancelled:
    Nor man himself with form erect
      <Was> When fashioned from the clod
    He

451. The Whiteweed
10 ever new] 'even' altered to 'ever' in different ink

15 Vain are] interlined above cancelled 'Living'

15 powers] followed by wiped out comma

367. The Teachings of the Spirit
Title: 'Hymn' appears on line above title but is cancelled in pencil
Each stanza is preceded by a pencilled number, in order from one to five.

15 Which] interlined above cancelled 'That'

16 they] interlined above cancelled 'those'

16 shall] interlined above cancelled 'them'; 'shalt' interlined in pencil below

17–20 written in pencil in left margin to replace the following cancelled original stanza:
    Grant us, O Lord, that birth divine,
      That we thy sons may be;
    That, though on earth, we may be thine,
      And here thy Kingdom see.

181. The Help of the Spirit
Title: 'Hymn' appears on line above title, but is cancelled in pencil
6 faint,] comma in pencil followed by comma in ink

466. The Birthright Church
5 In] written over wiped out 'The'

14 may] 'ay' wiped out, then restored

745. Midas
5 the] written over illegible wiped out word

26. Revelation
7 draw] followed by wiped out comma

183. How come the Dead?
Title: preceded on separate line by 'Hymn', cancelled in pencil

Title: come] 'c' written over erased 'C'
   11 Is it the mortal] interlined above cancelled 'For tis the mortal'
   11 mourn?] 'mourn' followed by comma, which has been partially erased, then by question mark
   17 whisper] 'h' inserted in pencil

768. The Houstonia
   10 blue,] comma added in different ink
   25 form,] comma added in different ink

391. To The Salem Gazette, On The Completion Of Its First Century
   3 many] followed by cancelled 'many'

759. The Ends For Which A Nation Exists
   2 be?] question mark written over wiped out comma

23. National Unity
   7 gives,] period portion of original semicolon wiped out
   14 length] 'th' written over illegible erased letters

788. Reflections on the History of Nations
Title: written on line above title, but marked through in blue pencil: 'Sonnets on Reconstruction'

446. Scepticism With Regard To The Gospels
   1 we know] interlined above cancelled 'is known'
   12 calls] 's' written over illegible wiped out letter(s)

713. The Spiritual Birth
Title: preceded on separate line by 'Hymn', which has been cancelled in pencil
   17 Spirit's] 'S' written over 's'

827. The Youth and the Stream
Written above title and cancelled in pencil: For the Monthly Magazine
Heading: *The Youth.*] underlined twice in pencil
Heading: *The Stream.*] underlined twice in pencil
   10 tide.] period replaces erased comma

836. Things Unseen
Title: preceded on separate line by 'Hymn', cancelled in pencil
   22 declare,] period portion of semicolon wiped out
   23 things!] 'things' followed by wiped out comma, then by exclamation point

611. The Oak And The Poplar
   2 tree;] comma altered to semicolon in pencil
   5 strong,] comma added in pencil
   8 Nor] 'No' written over erased 'Or'
   10 with] interlined above cancelled 'in'
   15 won;] period portion of semicolon added in pencil
   22 thick,] enclosed in pencilled parentheses, probably in order to cancel; no alternative reading given
   24 storm!] period altered to exclamation point in pencil
   25 stood] followed by erased comma
   33 there, around the parent tree,] commas added in pencil

34 stood;] comma altered to semicolon in pencil
37 And, on its boughs,] commas added in pencil
37 still] second 'l' written over illegible wiped out letter
43 "how] quotation marks in ink over pencil
44 once so] interlined in pencil above 'tall and'
45–48 written at end to be inserted here
45 made,] comma in ink over pencil
46 town,] comma in ink over pencil
47 shade,] comma in ink over pencil
49 For] written over erased illegible word
49 soon", they said, "its] quotation marks added in pencil
50 o'erthrew;"] quotation marks in ink over pencil
51 'tis] interlined above cancelled ''twas'; revision in ink over pencil

297. The Yellow Violets
    12 Bent] interlined above cancelled 'Turned'
    12 on] 'o' written over illegible erased letter
    15 search] written over illegible erased word

144. The Scholar Dreaming
    14 mind] interlined in pencil above original 'thoughts'

534. Hymn: Sung at the Dedication of the Peabody Academy of Science, Salem,
Aug. 18, 1869
Title: 'Hymn' written in original ink, but wiped out; remainder of title written in
different ink; 'Hymn' written below, but cancelled; 'Hymn' written above remainder
of title in different ink
    2 rare;] semicolon wiped out, then restored in different ink
    3 clime,] comma added in different ink
    11 study,] comma added in different ink

4. Spiritual Darkness
    7–14 original reading of these lines:
    Nor will it yield e'en to their strongest spell,
    Nor heed their gods though on their names they call.
    So, in eclipse, the sun withdraws its light,
    Or sheds a pale and ineffectual ray;   10
    The flowers close up, as at approach of night,
    And men, bewildered, wander from their way;
    The stars appear, and with faint lustre burn,
    Watching, from their far heights, the sun's return.
Lines 7–8 above cancelled, and the following substitute lines written at bottom
of page:
    In vain they seek by knowledge to dispel
    The gloom that shrouds the earth as with a spell.
Lines 9–14 above cancelled, and final version of lines 1–14 written on verso
    11 beam] originally 'beams'; 's' cancelled

204. Friendship
Title: preceded on separate line by 'Hymn', cancelled in pencil
    8 fond] original reading 'sweet'; this cancelled and 'sad' interlined above; this
cancelled and 'fond' interlined below

9–12 written at end to be inserted here

13–15 original version:

And, when again we wander there,　　　　　　　　　　　　　　　1a
　　They seem to us more fair;
And every flower and tree he loved,

1a And] interlined above cancelled 'Yet'; 'Oft as' written above 'And' and cancelled

1a again] inserted with a caret

1a there,] 'there' followed by cancelled 'again'

Final version of these lines written in pencil on back, with further alterations as indicated

13 the things] interlined above 'their forms'; 'their' cancelled

14 All] inserted at beginning of line before 'They', with apparent intention of substituting 'All' for 'They'

Another abortive, partially illegible stanza written in pencil at end

652. The Sparrows And The Crop of Weeds

14 long,] comma added in different ink

87. Hymn: The Spiritual Body

7 Like the] interlined above cancelled 'And with'

11 claiment] followed by wiped out comma

12 glorified!] period altered to exclamation point in pencil

15 Angels'] interlined above cancelled 'And the'

16 Powers that unto them] interlined above cancelled 'Which to angel powers'

19 doth] original reading: 'doth'; this cancelled and 'too' interlined above; this cancelled and 'doth' interlined above

19 reflection] followed by comma, marked through and erased

24 winter's] 'w' written over erased 'W'

24 gloom;] comma portion of semicolon added in pencil

25 which] interlined above cancelled 'that'

25 springeth] 'g' inserted in pencil

400. Hymn: The Efficacy of a Mother's Prayer

2 virtue's] interlined above cancelled 'wisdom's'

7 mid] interlined above cancelled 'in'; revision in ink over pencil

12 hatered,] interlined above cancelled 'error,'

20 recall!] period altered to exclamation point in pencil

23 Him,] comma added in pencil

576. The Fireflies

23 or] interlined above cancelled 'and'

62. Be Not Many Teachers

6 claim] interlined above cancelled 'seek'

600. The Bible Does Not Sanction Polygamy

8 Egypt's] originally 'AEgypt's'; 'A' cancelled

627. Bitter-Sweet Rocks

3 ferns,] 's' written over illegible wiped out letter

23 Has] 'H' written over illegible wiped out letter

27 please] interlined above cancelled 'charm'

822. The Teaching Of History Confirmed
6 give,] period portion of semicolon blotted out

237. Childhood's Songs
9 again] followed by erased comma
15 hours,] written over erased 'years'

38. Hymn, Sung at the Fiftieth Anniversary of the Essex Historical Society, Salem. April 21, 1871.
Title: Fiftieth] 'F' written over wiped out 'f'

453. The Fulness of The Gentiles
13 Come, Church Triumphant!] interlined above cancelled 'Church of the Future'

813. To a Cloud
8 Imploring] interlined above cancelled 'Look'

2. The Child's Dream of Reaching the Horizon
25 went] followed by wiped out comma
31 more] followed by erased comma

296. Lead Me To The Rock That Is Higher Than I
Title: preceded on separate line by 'Hymn', cancelled in pencil
2 nor] 'n' inserted in pencil
3 interlined above original reading, 'Guide me wandering Lord, and show me', which is cancelled in pencil; a third version interlined below in pencil, but erased
18 die!] exclamation point wiped out, then restored
19 me,] comma wiped out, then restored
23 ages,] comma cancelled, then restored

251. I Prayed, Thy Kingdom Come
8 Man] interlined above cancelled 'man'
11 strange!] exclamation point replaces wiped out comma

448. Justification By Faith
7 his] written over wiped out 'the'
11 From land to] written over erased 'Soon [illegible word] life'
11 quickly the] interlined above cancelled 'the joyful'
12 woke!] exclamation point follows cancelled semicolon

491. Signs in the Natural World
Following line 2 these lines appear, but are cancelled:
   The pastures withered, and the streams were dry;
   Fierce blazed the sun no rain from heaven was sent.
12 her] written over wiped out 'its'

313. The Life of the Flower
19 tell,] comma wiped out, then restored
25 For the] originally 'The'; 'For' inserted before 'The'; 'T' erased and replaced by 't'
27 Whole,] 'W' interlined above cancelled 'w'
28 love.] 'l' interlined above cancelled 'L'

35. Norman's Rocks
7 favorite] 'ite' interlined above cancelled 'ed'

8 In the warm] interlined above cancelled 'When come the'

33 original version: 'The rocks, to which the lichens cling,'; 'T' altered to 't'; 'to which the lichens cling,' cancelled; 'The lichens, cling to the rocks,' interlined above; 'cling' cancelled and 'clinging' interlined above; all revisions in pencil

41–44 written in pencil at end to be inserted here

45 And still] originally 'Still do'; 'do' cancelled; 'And' inserted in pencil before 'Still'

760. The Revelation of the Spirit Through The Material World

5 are] written over original 'is'

7 screen] 's' written over erased illegible letter

666. And a little child shall lead them. Isaiah XI. 6.

6 Dost] 'st' interlined above cancelled 'th'

13–18 written on next page to be inserted here

20 Forgotten] 'Fo' written over wiped out 'No'

20 rude] interlined above cancelled 'dread'

23 without painful] interlined in pencil above cancelled 'shall reward their'

24 Shall] interlined in pencil above cancelled 'And'

26 speech,] 'ee' interlined in pencil above cancelled 'ea'

27 No more] written originally at left margin, then erased and indented

34 guide,] exclamation point altered to comma

189. The Blessing of Rain

4 entire line interlined below cancelled original: 'And quick the hollow pool doth fill.'

18 grateful] 'at' written over illegible wiped out letters

19 In] written over illegible wiped out letters

444. The Mound Builders. On Reading the work of the late J. W. Foster

7 speech] second 'e' interlined in pencil above cancelled 'a'

11 Learning's] 'ing' written over erased 'g'

11 stores] written over illegible wiped out word

11 denied,] 'e' written over illegible wiped out letter

12 immortal] second 'm' inserted in pencil

13 graves,] 's,' interlined above cancelled 's,'

14 With thoughtful minds] interlined in pencil below 'Musing amid'

187. Blessed are they that mourn: for they shall be comforted.

2 this!] exclamation point follows cancelled semicolon

4 bliss.] comma portion of original semicolon cancelled

403. There shall be one Flock, one Shepherd

7 free] followed by wiped out comma

64. Columbines and Anemones

4 Anemone;] final 'e' written over 'y' in pencil

13 Flowers!] 'F' written over 'f' in different ink

464. The Birds

1 their] 'ir' added to original 'the', then wiped out; then interlined above between 'the' and 'songs'

9 suffering man,] interlined above cancelled 'human kind'

10 Whom] 'ich' interlined above 'om', then cancelled; all revisions in pencil

Between lines 12 and 13 two lines are added in pencil, then erased.

14 Would I your joy might] interlined above cancelled 'I would your joyance'

15 evil] followed by 's', which is cancelled in pencil

15 abounds,] 's' added in pencil

19 dimly now perceived,] original reading: 'now we see it not,'; 'dimly' interlined above 'now'; 'yet' interlined below 'yet', then cancelled; 'perceived,' interlined above cancelled 'we see it not,'; all revisions in pencil

21–24 stanza cancelled in pencil, then cancelling erased

Between lines 22 and 23 a pencilled revision has been added, but erased.

24 And] interlined in pencil above cancelled 'When'

Several cancelled and largely illegible pencilled lines follow the poem.

634. Behold, I Make All Things New

Title: Behold,] comma added in pencil

15 those happy years,] interlined above cancelled 'the glorious day,'; revision in pencil

18 seem,] comma added in pencil

29 nor pain, nor] 'nor' and 'nor' interlined above cancelled 'and' and 'and'

40 voice,] comma added in pencil

855. The Meteorologists

Title: Meteorologists] third 'o' written over 'i'; final 'i' inserted with a caret

6 make known;] interlined above cancelled 'explore;'

12 entire line inserted between lines 11 and 13

324. The Origin of Man

9 original reading (in pencil): 'With mind made dark by sin how should he know'; entire line cancelled in pencil; revision at end of poem in pencil to be substituted: 'With mind bewildered, dark how'; 'dark' cancelled and 'lost' interlined above; 'lost' cancelled and 'weak' interlined above

245. Song: I Love the Light

9 sunset hour,] interlined above cancelled 'parting day,'; revision in pencil

10 Which] interlined above cancelled 'That'; revision in pencil

11 Which] interlined above cancelled 'That'; revision in pencil

13 silvery] 'v' inserted with a caret

Written at the end in pencil, then cancelled in pencil:

I love the soft & silvery light
    Of moon, and stars, that keep

92. Take ye heed, watch and pray: for ye know not when the time is. Mark 13:33.

3 home,] period portion of original semicolon wiped out

8 glorious] interlined above cancelled 'coming'

21 faint] followed by comma, cancelled in different ink

21 not,] comma added in different ink

22 Nor] followed by erased comma

22 Coming] followed by erased comma

643. The Ancient Burial Places in Peabody

13–16 this stanza written in left margin to be inserted here

19 the] interlined above cancelled 'each'

20 are] interlined below cancelled 'is'

229. The May Flower

14 haunt the sweet May flower] interlined in pencil above 'natal spot the flower;'

17 an exile seems] interlined in pencil above cancelled 'remembered well'

18 'That longest for its country far away' interlined in pencil above cancelled 'The home, from which it was taken away;'; 'pined' interlined above cancelled 'longest'; 'his' interlined above cancelled 'its'; all revisions in pencil

25 So] interlined in pencil above cancelled 'And'

26 entire line interlined above cancelled 'And wanderers are on the earth,'

32 'That blossoms and blooms in his native spot.' interlined below cancelled 'That blossoms and blooms in his native spot.'; 'natal' interlined below cancelled 'native'

509. The Cows waiting at the Pasture Gate

6 entire line interlined above the following cancelled original line: 'Their drivers waiting too.'

7 entire line interlined above the following cancelled original line: 'How pleasant tis at close of day,'

8 entire line interlined above the following cancelled original line: 'The peaceful scene to view.'; 'herd' interlined in pencil below 'scene'

Written at end and enclosed in parentheses (as if to cancel): 'The pasture gate swings open wide'

377. On some blue and golden Columbines from Pike's Peak, Colorado

1 lovely] interlined above cancelled 'beauteous'

3 mountain] 'thy far' interlined above in pencil and cancelled in pencil

6 and vales more] interlined in pencil above cancelled 'how wondrous'

7 on hillside] interlined above cancelled 'in beauty'

8 Strange tho' the scene,] interlined above cancelled 'And makes its home,'

11 original reading: 'And, swift imaginations kindling power'; 'swift' cancelled and 'at the sight,' interlined above; 'kindling' cancelled

12 absent] interlined above wiped out and cancelled 'distant'

12 early] interlined above cancelled 'distant'

14 The] interlined in pencil below cancelled 'Thy'

6. Every Day a Day of Freedom

Title: Every Day] followed by 'is', circled in pencil, probably with intention of cancelling

Title: followed on next line by 'Ruskin', circled in pencil, probably with intention of cancelling

7 free,] 'ee' written over illegible wiped out letters

9 entire line interlined above cancelled 'A symbol of the dayspring to appear,'

10 The law] interlined above cancelled 'In it the'

171. The Glacial Marks on our Hills

13 boulders,] 'u' inserted with a caret

30 fade!] original semicolon wiped out, altered to exclamation point

At end of poem this stanza appears, cancelled in pencil:

The record of her rocky scroll
    Of countless ages passed away
Seems but a moment to the soul,
    That doth the boundless past survey.

458. Hymn: The Cause of Peace

Title: written in pencil

3 Cause] 'C' cancelled and lower case letter interlined above; this revision also cancelled; all revisions in pencil

4 original line: 'Who came of heavenly birth.'; line cancelled, except for 'birth.'; 'Announced' interlined below, then cancelled; 'Proclaimed e'en at his' interlined above; all revisions in pencil

5 time of] interlined above cancelled 'cause for'

7 'neath] apostrophe in pencil

9 passion] originally 'passions'; final 's' cancelled

16 still] interlined below cancelled 'none'; revision in pencil

94-706. Hymn

1 Though few, with] interlined above cancelled 'Conscious of'; comma added in pencil

13 The] originally 'They'; 'y' erased

24 fulfil.] originally 'fulfill.'; final 'l' cancelled in pencil

638. Spiritual Intercourse

1 us] followed by cancelled comma

19 they] followed by cancelled comma

21 memory's bright unbroken] originally 'memory with its'; ''s' added to 'memory'; 'with it' cancelled; 'bright unbroken' interlined above

22 heart,] period portion of original semicolon wiped out

28 high?] original exclamation point cancelled and replaced by question mark; revision in pencil

38 hurt,] comma added in pencil

39 time,] comma added in pencil

40 Their] interlined below cancelled 'Its'; revision in pencil

50 That higher] interlined below cancelled 'With them their'; revision in pencil

51 by them] interlined above cancelled 'on earth'; revision in pencil

52 Midst earthly] interlined above cancelled 'In suffering,'; revision in pencil

435. The Influence of Channing

1 Stern creeds and outward forms must] interlined above cancelled 'The outward form doth fade and'

2 Their] interlined above cancelled 'Its'

2 Life] upper case 'L' written over lower case

3 entire line interlined above cancelled original 'The immortal soul, that cannot know decay'

4 entire line interlined above cancelled original 'And doth o'er death and time the victory win!'

587. The Calling

Title: The Calling] written in ink over pencil

9 among] interlined in pencil above original 'amidst'

39. Endecott

8 hopes, like theirs,] interlined above cancelled 'trust, and hopes'

8 fixed] original reading: 'fixed'; this cancelled, and 'placed' interlined above; this cancelled, and 'fixed' interlined above

10 firm] interlined above cancelled 'fixed'

116. Farewell
    5 England's] upper case 'E' written over lower case
    7 loss &] interlined in pencil above original 'all their'

476-581. The Departure
    1 tall white] interlined in pencil above original 'chalky'
    8 As] preceded by unexplained superscript 'x' in pencil
    8 heart's] apostrophe added in pencil
    9 turn;] comma altered to semicolon in pencil

96. The Petrels
    4 nests.] original semicolon cancelled, followed by period; revision in pencil
    7 whate'er betide] 'whateer betide' interlined above cancelled 'on every side';
revision in pencil
    9 sustain;—] dash added in pencil
    14 alike,] comma added in pencil

97. At Sea
    4 original version: 'And civil and religious freedom gain.'; this cancelled in pencil;
interlined above in pencil: 'Christian Liberty in peace maintain.'; this also cancelled
in pencil; original version restored below in pencil
    5 timid] 'd' written over illegible wiped out letter(s)
    7 loud the] interlined above cancelled 'stormy'; revision in pencil
    12 ocean,] comma added in pencil
    13 desert] interlined above cancelled 'rocky'

137. At Sea
RPB(1):
    3 times,] comma added in pencil
    5 be!] exclamation point written over comma
    8 westward gaze with longing] interlined above cancelled 'anxious strain their
tearful'; 'tearful' written in pencil
    14 before,] comma added in pencil
RPB(2):
    4 As oft they view] interlined above cancelled 'While gazing on'

79. The Sabbath
    1 Bright is the morn] original version: ''Tis sabbath time'; this cancelled in ink;
four versions then interlined above in pencil: 'The Sabbath dawns'; 'Fresh dawns the
day'; 'Calm is the day'; 'Bright is the morn'; none are cancelled; the last of these I
have assumed to be the final version
    1 sound,—] dash added in pencil
    2 breast;—] dash added in pencil
    4 And, with the passengers,] commas in ink over pencil
    5 air,] comma added in pencil
    6 deep;] comma altered to semicolon in pencil
    8 As, on the ocean,] commas in ink over pencil
    8 keep:] colon written over wiped out semicolon
    12 text] interlined above cancelled 'truths'
    13 Trust] upper case 'T' written over erased lower case letter
    13 God; . . . land;] commas altered to semicolons in pencil

646. Land

3 rippling] enclosed by pencilled parentheses, as if with intention of cancelling, but no alternative reading provided

9 Lights on island, cape, or rock] interlined above cancelled 'friendly lights along the coast'

12 cheerful] interlined above cancelled 'friendly'; revision in pencil

Pencilled lines following the poem have been erased.

647. Salem

6 country] 'u' written over illegible wiped out letter

8 freedom,] comma added in pencil

12 blessings] 's' added in different ink

14 tyrants, for their race,] commas added in pencil

428-835a. The Landing

1–4 final version written in pencil above title; original version follows:

Soon from the anchored ship the shore they reach,
Their Country's banner floating in the breeze;
With grateful hearts they <gather on> shout along the beach,
<Then seek> Or sit beneath the <shade <amidst> beneath> shadow of the forest trees.

1 With flag unfurled] interlined above cancelled 'From stony point'

5 These] 'se' added in pencil

9 Their joy how full how deep] original reading: 'How deep how full their joy'; this cancelled in ink; 'great the Planter's joy,' interlined above, and cancelled in pencil; final version interlined below original line

11–14 written in pencil at end to replace these original lines:

And, with each day's new light, impatient grow,
While hopes and fears their minds alternate throng;
The trial's o'er! their <joy is now> happiness complete,
As they <their> old friends with hearty welcome greet!

359. The Old Planters

1 slightly] interlined in pencil above cancelled 'would I'

7 help,] comma added in pencil

10 gifts,] comma added in pencil

Erased pencilled lines follow the poem.

192. Paradise

2 groves,] 'ves' written over illegible wiped out letters; comma added in pencil

14 fishing,] comma added in pencil

752. Naumkeck River

Title: Naumkeck] 'ck' interlined in pencil above cancelled 'ag'

1 Up Naumkeck] 'Up Naumkeag' interlined above cancelled 'Now up the stream'; 'ck' interlined in pencil above cancelled 'ag'

1 explore,] comma added in pencil

9 strange birds unnumbered] interlined above cancelled 'they hear the sweet birds'

332. The Same

1 wide,] 'wide' written over illegible erased word

7 And,] comma added in pencil

7 slight] interlined above cancelled 'faint'

539. Winter
9 dwellings] interlined above cancelled 'shelter'

845. Location
2 leafy] interlined above cancelled 'hidden'
7 withstand;] period portion of semicolon added in pencil
13 Piety and Industry] upper case letters written above original lower case in pencil

412. The Home
5 cold,] 'cold' interlined above original 'storm,'
5 aged] enclosed in pencilled parentheses; illegible revision interlined in pencil above

579. The Home
1 books,] comma added in pencil
4 neighbor,] comma added in pencil
7 And now] enclosed in pencilled parentheses; illegible revision interlined in pencil above
8 simple,] comma added in pencil
9 that,] initial 't' originally upper case; this cancelled and lower case interlined above
13 wanderer,] comma added in pencil
14 sure,] comma added in pencil

842. Sickness
13 to sufferers] 'rers' written over illegible wiped out letters

196. Longing
4 again;] semicolon added in pencil

83. Winthrop's Fleet
9 comforts,] comma added in pencil
10 Which, in their strait,] commas added in pencil
13 want,] comma added in pencil

53. Arabella Johnson
6 band;] comma portion of semicolon wiped out, then restored
7 yonder shore] interlined above cancelled 'yon low mounds'; 's' in 'mounds' added in pencil
13 A ministering angel to] interlined above cancelled 'The weakest member of'
14 hardships] interlined above cancelled 'dangers'

637. Motive
4 track] 'k' written in pencil over original 't'
13 melt,] comma added in pencil
14 scanty] 'frugal' interlined below in very faint pencil, probably a tentative revision

431. The Church
6 pastor,] comma added in pencil
9 service,] comma added in pencil
10 waves,] comma added in pencil

11 comes;] semicolon added in pencil
12 love,] comma added in pencil

84. Worship
Title: written in ink over pencil
1 preserved] followed by comma, which is cancelled in pencil
1 care] followed by comma, which is cancelled in pencil

648. Song
5 God, in ancient times,] commas added in pencil
13 kept] written over illegible erased word
14 still, as theirs,] commas added in pencil

641. The Puritan Church and State: I.
3 aisle,] 'ais' written over illegible wiped out letters
8 youth.] top portion of original colon wiped out to make period
11 discipline] 'ine' written in pencil over original 'e'

857. Appeal
3 Learn, from the page of History,] commas added in pencil
8 bore,] comma added in pencil
11 God,] comma added in pencil
13 And,] comma added in pencil
13 name,] comma added in pencil

413. Influence of Puritanism
1 their] interlined in pencil above cancelled 'her'
2 state,] comma added in pencil
4 our] written over erased 'the'
9 African,] comma added in pencil

456. The Bible
2 Truth,] comma added in pencil
Written in pencil at end of poem: The Covenant

555. The Common School
1 build,] comma added in pencil
4 rough,] comma added in pencil
10 rich,] comma added in pencil
13 instruct,] comma added in pencil

416. A Christian Commonwealth
9 they unto] interlined above cancelled 'Elliot to'

421. Discontent
Title: written in pencil

318. The Return of the Savior
Title: preceded by 'Hymn On', which is cancelled in pencil
11 faith,] comma added in pencil
16 That we may] originally 'And we shall'; 'That' and 'may' interlined below in pencil

365. The Kingdom of the Truth
Title: preceded on separate line by 'Hymn', cancelled in pencil

Stanzas numbered in pencil, probably to make clear where lines 17–20 should be inserted.

3 whoever] originally 'whosoer'; 'ere' written over 'soer'; this cancelled and 'ever' interlined above

6 Love;] 'L' written over illegible wiped out letter

15 error] 'e' written over wiped out 'E'

15 pride] 'p' written over 'P'

17–20 stanza written in left margin in pencil to be inserted here

21 each a faithful witness bear] interlined above cancelled 'we that heavenly kingdom find'; revision in pencil

22 Truth's kingdom] interlined above cancelled 'Believe, and'; revision in pencil

23 And,] followed by 'e'en', which is cancelled, and 'all we', interlined above 'e'en', also cancelled

23 we] 'thy' interlined above, then cancelled

379. Sunset after a Clouded Day in April
20 fled!] originally 'fld!'; 'd' wiped out and 'ed' written over

382. Hymn: Prayer for the Gift of the Holy Spirit
15 line marked through in pencil, but no alternative reading provided

19 entire line interlined above original 'Then shall we find thy promise true,'; revision in pencil

394. Hymn
Stanzas numbered in pencil.

11 Autumn's] first 'u' inserted with a caret
Following line 12 these two stanzas appear; the first is numbered IV and is written in the margin; the second is numbered V; both are then cancelled:

The blessings of our homes so dear
   Our schools, and churches Lord are thine;
Thou watchest o'er them year by year
   And purgest still thy fruitful Vine.

Nor would we, when thou tak'st away,
   With discontented hearts repine;
But bow submissively, and say
   Thou gav'st, Thou tak'st; for all is Thine!

414. Hymn: The Forms of Nature, and the Unity of their Origin
1 not, in outward things,] commas added in pencil

12 original line: 'The work of One Creative Mind'; this cancelled, and 'Its order and its bounds defined.' interlined below; this cancelled, and final version interlined below in ink over pencil

21 powers,] period portion of original semicolon wiped out

27 us] inserted with a caret

30 every] interlined above cancelled 'all the'

30 form] followed by erased 's'
Pencilled fragments on back of sheet, largely illegible.

449. Friendship: To J. M. S.
12 with soul] written over illegible wiped out word

462. Hymn: The Good Fight

Title: written in pencil
    3 conflicts first begin] interlined in pencil above original 'victory we win,'
    4 entire line interlined in pencil above original 'The crown of Life we gain.'
    9–12 stanza preceded and followed by pencilled 'x', perhaps indicating an intention to cancel the stanza and substitute another for it; but this is not Very's usual method of cancellation
    17–20 stanza preceded and followed by pencilled 'x'; see note on lines 9–12 above
    18 thine,] period portion of original semicolon wiped out
    19 hour;] period portion of semicolon in pencil
    20 O,] comma in pencil
    20 seek] interlined in pencil below cancelled 'ask'
    21–24 stanza written in pencil in this point in left margin, its intended placement unclear; possibly it is intended to be substituted for either stanza 3 or 5; a single pencilled line through it may also indicate cancellation
    27 shall] interlined in pencil above cancelled 'will'
On back of sheet (following extraneous matter) appears the following stanza in pencil, which is then cancelled in pencil:
    Vain are his sword and shield
        And all his armor vain
    Vanquished by sin he quits the field
        Or in the fight is slain

484. The Day calling us to a New Life
    4 tells] 's' added in pencil

499. To the Misses Williams, On seeing their beautiful Paintings of Wild Flowers
    5 pleasant] first 'a' written over erased 's'

538. Jacob wrestling with the Angel
    13 thou] written over illegible wiped out word
    15 those] written over illegible wiped out word
    19 man] 'a' interlined above cancelled 'e'

545. Rain Clouds
    7 delays] 'lays' written over wiped out 'nies'
    12 his] 'h' written over illegible wiped out letter

570. Our Native Sparrows
    11–12 written in pencil
    13 of] written over wiped out 'from'
    20 feeble] written in pencil; 'when they' interlined below in pencil, apparently an incomplete revision

590. Hymn: I Am The Way
    24 And] interlined above cancelled 'Thou'

636. Early Companions
    1 dead,] comma added in pencil
    1 before!] exclamation point added in pencil
    2 remain;] semicolon added in pencil
    3 restore,] comma added in pencil
    6 Their] 'ir' written over 're' in pencil
    16 For each] interlined in pencil below cancelled 'That still'

16 love] 'd' added to end of word in pencil, then cancelled in pencil

19 bounds,] comma added in pencil

675. The Gift

Title: Gift] follows cancelled 'Offering'; revision in pencil

3 To restore] line originally began 'Restore'; 'To' added in left margin and 'r' written over 'R' in 'Restore'; revision in pencil

3 gifts] followed by exclamation point, cancelled in pencil

5 taught'st] ''st' added in pencil

7 do'st] apostrophe added in pencil

7 live;—] comma made into semicolon and dash added, both in pencil

9 gav'st] ''st' interlined above cancelled 'e'; revision in pencil

10 differing] interlined above cancelled 'various'; revision in pencil

11 selfishly presume] interlined above 'hide in night's dark gloom'; 'night's dark gloom' cancelled; revision in pencil (Very must have intended to cancel 'hide in' as well.)

12 made for] interlined below cancelled 'bid thy children' and second version (interlined below the first), '[illegible word] of all to', which is also cancelled; all revisions in pencil

16 entire line interlined below cancelled 'And not be found upon the gale?'; revision in pencil

17–20 entire stanza written in pencil

17 thy love] interlined above cancelled 'by Thee'

18 entire line interlined below cancelled 'Alike twas given to [illegible word] another'

Various pencilled incomplete stanzas and fragmentary lines in margins and at end.

736. The Soul's Opportunities

Title: written in ink over pencilled version: 'The Opportunities of the Soul'

13 state] written over wiped out 'Age'

14 in] 'i' written over illegible wiped out letter

338. The Book of Life

9 line followed by this cancelled line: 'Birds from out some thicket telling scaped to tell to the open'

12 Past!] upper case 'P' written over lower case

14 the] followed by a single diagonal mark (false start?) that is in turn marked through

316. For the Sailors' Fair

6 sails] interlined above cancelled 'steers'

8 for an armed foe he fears.] original reading: ''e'en the bravest foe he fears.'; this cancelled and 'fears though armed foe assails' interlined below; 'armed foe' interlined below in pencil, then cancelled; final version interlined above original line

10 frame,] period portion of original semicolon wiped out

19 or a home,] written over illegible wiped out words

21 Let] 'L' written over wiped out 'l[illegible letter]'

25 Love's] 'L' written over wiped out 'l'

589. Hymn to the Living

MH(1):

2 hand,] followed by cancelled 'and'

11 Radiant] originally 'Raydiant'; 'y' cancelled

13 lamp] interlined above cancelled 'light'

16 roll on] originally 'rolling'; 'on' interlined above cancelled 'ing'

19 Original reading:

For them. Spring and the Seasons too they give,
That thou mayst finish here thy work begun.

All following 'For them.' cancelled.

20 Forms] 'F' written over illegible erased letter

21 praise!] comma mended to exclamation point

30 amongst] originally 'among'; 'st' added

34 will not] originally 'cannot'; 'can' cancelled and 'will' interlined above

34 our] interlined above cancelled 'the'

35 Ye] originally 'Yet'; 't' cancelled

35 all;] semicolon written over illegible erased punctuation or letter(s)

36 weaves Spring's] interlined above uncancelled 'pushes forth'

39 Teachers!] 'T' mended from lower to upper case

40 letters] originally 'lessons'; 'ssons' cancelled and 'tters' interlined above

43 children] interlined above cancelled 'pupils'

46 pour] interlined above cancelled 'out'

46 burial] interlined above cancelled 'golden'

53 hear of] 'of' interlined in pencil

Following line 57 the following cancelled passage appears:

Our Elder Brothers! strengthen ye our hands,
With all the love the eldest-born must feel,
For one the youngest; feeble yet to bear
The weight of life, made lighter by your aid.

59 journeys] originally 'journies'; 'ey' written over 'ie'

Following line 64 the following passage (which runs one and one-half pages in the ms.) appears but is cancelled, in ink over pencil:

The roots men dig for, or what'er they stoop
To pick, or reach with their high hands;—berries
And fruits;—these nourish life, for Life it is
That gives them. Thou must live, else will thy gifts
Come toilless into men's hands; they will not
Dig to gain what thou hast never covered
In the earth, nor stoop amid the grass to find
The red, low berries on the bush or vine;
Thou canst not give them hands to reach on high
For Autumn's fruit all careless at them flung.
Canst thou send them, mariners, across the main;
When thou all idly livest in thine own home?
Thou givest them food that has no life from thee;
Their weak limbs hang palsied down, made feeble
By thy gifts. They come from out thy pasture
Lank and lean as Pharao's oxen, seen
In dream; for thou hast first been out to crop
The herbage, e'er thou turn'st them in. Not so
Great Teachers! ye who in your gifts make strong
The hands that take them from you; with swifter

Motion quicken the feet that seek your doors.
Heavy the baskets loaded with your grain;
Till stout our arms as yours the load to bear;
The sweat rolls down fast dropping from our brows,
While we your daily bounties homeward bring.
I have been out in your wide fields, fenced in
With jealous care, and home returned wearied
By the long walk, unable to see all.
You make us not your own, but strengthen us
To be ourselves with wrestling hard with you.
I have been welcomed where there was no meat,
And water tasted that I could not drink;
But ye have more than I can eat; water
And wine, that in me prove but springs gushing
The more I draw. With you there is no change;
The comings in and goings out of life
Are over. You always are. You always
Visit us, for we are not. Light of our dwellings
Air that girds us round, and earth beneath our
Feet; we tread amid your gifts, as common
Blessings of the One Great Hand upholding all.
Ye Unseen Messengers! Apostles sent
By Christ, moving and finding voice in words!
Forms! that visit human hearts as dwellings;
Be near us ever, ever be our guests!
65 Messengers!] exclamation point written over comma
Following line 72 these lines appear, but are cancelled:
The lamp burns feebly, and your Mighty Presence;
Seen e'en but dimly in its strongest rays,
Fades on my vision as too great for sight.
Have ye no eyes, but such as give us light
To see; no hands, but such as lose themselves
In offering us your gifts? Oh, lift us up
To take them from you! give the blind to see!
Lest we, as now, deem all your gifts chance-found.

311. "Ambitione inani pectus caret"
Title: *Italicized* SO
      3 know'st] knows't RPB, SO
      12 boy] ~. SO
      20 say] ~, SO
      21 its] it's SO
      22 sought'st] sought's RPB, SO
      23 fair.] ~, SO

778. [Untitled] (What more delightful than to wander forth)
      18 feel] ~, SO
      19 'twould] twould SO
      28 that which prompts] ~~ proms RPB; ~, ~~ SO
      29 stream,] ~; SO
      30 vault,] valt, RPB

418. A Song composed by Mr J. Very, to be sung at the Class-Supper of the Sopho-
more Class of 1834
Alternate lines indented in MH-Ar
Title: *omit* RPB
      3 remembered] remembere'd MH-Ar
      4 auld] *omit* MH-Ar
      5 o'] o'f MH-Ar
      5 glee,] ~^ MH-Ar
      6 kin';] kin'^ MH-Ar
      8 auld] *omit* MH-Ar
      9 meet,] ~^ MH-Ar
      10 clime;] ~, MH-Ar
      12 auld] *omit* MH-Ar
      16 auld] *omit* MH-Ar
      18 wine;] ~, MH-Ar
      20 auld] *omit* MH-Ar
      22 cheerfull] jolly MH-Ar
      24 t'] to MH-Ar
Chorus, ll. 25–28 *omit* RPB

746. Kind Words
 1 him,] ~^ BH
 6 his] no italics BH
 6 mind,] ~. SO
 7 turn'd] turned BH
 7 door,] ~^ BH
 9 find,] ~^ BH
 10 Nought] Naught BH
 10 scorn;] ~? BH
 12 born;] ~? BH
 13 heart;] ~, BH
 15 nought] naught BH
 16 canst] may'st BH
Stanzas 5–6 (ll. 17–24) *omit* BH
 25 So, drawn by thee,] And oft again BH
 26 thee;] ~, BH
 27 And, in thy breast, shall] ~^~~~^ will BH

419. Lines To ——— On the Death of His Friend
Title: *untitled* MH
Epigraph: *no italics* Harv
 1 Earth] earth Harv
 3 wind's] winds' Harv
 10 repose;] ~, Harv
 12 With joy, at day's still] When shades around it Harv
 13 there] no italics Harv
 17 Earth] earth Harv
 18 Her] no italics Harv
 19 drank] loved Harv
 20 fled, forever fled!] ~,—~~. Harv
 21 is] no italics Harv
 23 prayer,] ~,—Harv
 24 *tomb!] tomb.* Harv

128. Eheu! fugaces, Posthume, Posthume, Labuntur anni.
Alternate lines are indented in SO and E.
Title: Eheu! ~ anni.] "Eheu! ~ anni." SO
 2 away,] ~; SO; ~^ E
 3 sharing,] ~^ SO, E
 7 gone!] ~; E
 7 giver,] ~^ SO, E
 8 doomed] doom'd SO
 9 mayst] may'st E
 9 finger,] ~^ E
 11 linger,] ~^ E
 12 That] ~, SO
 12 canst not] *canst not* SO
 13 Love's] Loves MLi, SO
 13 awaken,] ~^ E
 15 live,] ~^ SO, E

16 may] can E
17 are] come E
19 Ah!] ah! E
20 your] thy SO
20 *soft blue eyes.*] soft blue eyes. SO; soft blue eyes! E

220. The Humming-Bird
Title: The Humming-Bird] To The Humming-Bird E
 1 that] thy SO, E
 2 prest,] ~; SO
 3 rear that] raise thy SO, E
 4 mate,] ~; SO
 5 his] thy SO, E
 7 him,] ~^ E
 7 hours,] ~^ E
 9 sip at morn] hover round SO, E
 9 flowers] ~, SO, E
 10 young,] ~; SO, E
 12 nest] ~, SO
 12 high-hung.] ~^~. SO, E
 13 care,] ~^ E
 15 dare] ~, SO
 16 spring] ~, SO, E
 17 sunny fields of] fields of sunny SO, E
 18 new-fledged] new-fledg'd SO; new fledged E
 19 wait] ~, SO
 20 fond, fond] ~^~ E
 22 eyes;] ~, SO
 23 Unseen] Unknown, SO, E
 23 fate!] ~, SO, E

399. A Withered Leaf—seen on a Poet's Table
Title: On a Withered Leaf MH; Lines To a Withered Leaf Seen on a Poet's Table E,
G, Waif
 2 wither'd] withered E, Waif
 3 Eye] eye MH, E, G, Waif
 4 *soul.*] soul. MH; soul, E, Waif; soul; G
 5 Though] True, MH
 5 trac'd] traced MH, E, G, Waif
 6 lore;] ~, E, G, Waif
 7 Love divine the page has grac'd,] Yet God's finger there was placed—MH;
  ~~~~~ graced,—E, G, Waif
 8 And can *man's* vain words teach more?] And the soul can learn far more^
  MH; What can words discover more? E, G, Waif
Following stanza 2 MH gives the following additional stanza:
 From yon dry and shrivel'd thing,
 Than from learning's proudest page;
 Though it deeds of heroes sing,
 Words repeat of hoary sage.
 9 Autumn's] Autum's MH; autumn's G

10 sear;] ~^ MH; ~,—E, G; sere,—Waif
11 Past] past G, Waif
12 poet's] Poets MH
13 Summer hours,] summer ~, E; summer-hours, G
14 murmur] murmur'd MH
14 by,] ~; E, G, Waif
15 Feather'd] Feathered E, Waif
15 song] songs E, G, Waif
15 bowers,] ~^ E, G, Waif
16 Draw] Drew MH
16 listening] list'ning MH, G
Stanza 5 *omit* E, G, Waif
17 above] beyond MH
17 soars,] soar'd, MH
18 Death] death MH
18 Decay;] decay; MH
19 above] before MH
19 adores,] ador'd, MH
20 Mid the spirit's native day.] Worship'd mid Eternal day. MH

353. The Stars
Title: followed on separate line by quotation in SO, "*The morning stars sang together.*"
1 wanderers!] ~, MH
2 bright;] ~, MH, SO
3 stooped,] stoop'd, MH, SO
3 air!] ~, SO
8 looked] lookd MH; look'd SO
8 it,] ~^ MH
8 smiled.] smil'd. MH, SO
9 come ye now,] have ye come, MH
10 listening] list'ning MH, SO
10 ear;] ~, MH, SO
14 earth's] earths MH
15 not, bright ones,] ~^~~^ MH, SO
15 rejoice] ~, MH, SO
18 slumbered] slumberd MH
20 numbered] number'd MH, SO
20 by] with MH
21 tearful eye] tear-lit Eye SO
23 divine] like thine MH; like Time SO
24 source!] ~. MH, SO
26 lyres] lines SO

47. The Snow Bird
2 White] blithe CR
2 wand'rer] wandr'er MH(2); wanderer Harv, CR
Following stanza 1 this stanza appears in MH(1):
The early sun, with gentle ray,
  Is pillowd on thy brest;
And tips thy wings with golden day,

And smiles upon thy crest.
     5 chirp,] ~^ MH(1), SO, Harv
     6 fear;] ~;— SO; ~, CR
    11 Winter] winter MH(1)
    11 learned] learnd MH(1)
    13 comes,] ~^ Harv
    14 shroud;] cloud; MH(1), SO
    16 hush'd] hushd MH(1); hushed Harv, CR
    17 driven, from each hidden nest,] ~^~~~^ MH(1), SO, Harv, CR
    18 comrades] comrads MH(1)
    18 air;] ~, CR
    19 banished] banish'd MH(1), SO
    19 wood's] woods MH(1), SO
    20 there,—] ~; MH(1); ~;—SO
    21 hoverest] hover'st MH(1), SO
    23 sweet,] ~; SO
    25 thee] ~, CR
    25 bird] ~—MH(1), SO, Harv; ~; CR
    25 He,] ~^ MH(1), SO, CR
    26 rude,] ~; SO
    27 Has] Hath MH(1)
    27 tenement] ~, MH(1), Harv
    28 gratitude;] ~. MH(1), SO, Harv, CR

After stanza 7 is the following stanza in CR (this stanza also appears with one minor
variation in MH(2) but was cancelled; see Alterations in the Manuscript):
    And bid me feel that He, whose eye
       Thy wants doth pitying see,
    And through the wintry-time supply,
       Will surely succor me.
    29 fled—] ~! CR
    29 gone, perhaps,] ~^~^ CR
    30 playmates] play-mates MH(1), SO
    31 thee—] ~; CR
    31 thou'st] thou SO, Harv, CR
    32 thou'st] thou MH(1), SO, Harv, CR

430. Memory
     1 waves,] ~^ E
     1 bounding,] ~^ E
     3 sounding,] ~^ E
     5 gladness,] ~^ E
Stanza 3 *omit* E
    13 'twill] t'will E
    17 *There*] no italics E
    17 vanish,] ~^ E
    20 *There*] no italics E

396. King Philip
Headnote in MH:
    "He fought and fell,—miserably, indeed, but gloriously,—the avenger of his own

household, the worshipper of his own gods, the guardian of his own honor, a martyr for the soil which was his birth-place, and for the proud liberty which was his birth-right."

Thatcher's Lives of the Indians

Headnote in Harv: follows CtY except for italicizing *Lives of the Indians*

1 white man's] whiteman's MH
2 Chilled] Chil'd MH
2 *thy*] *no italics* MH
2 breast?] ~—MH
3 unnerved] unnerv'd MH
3 *thy*] *no italics* MH
4 *thee*] *no italics* MH
5 *this*] *no italics* MH
6 Straight] Strait MH
7 thy] the MH
8 white man's] whiteman's MH
9 *this*] *no italics* MH
9 flew] ~, MH
10 Winged] Wing'd MH
10 lightning] light'ning MH
10 speed?] ~; MH
11 *this*] *no italics* MH
11 thy] my MH
12 Quivering] Quiv'ring MH
13 Yes—] ~, MH
13 hand,—] ~,^ MH
15 stand] ~, MH
17 brave,] ~,—MH
17 gathered] gather'd MH
18 fair!] ~; MH
19 their] your MH
20 They call me from] Ye stride along MH
21 son,—] ~^—MH
21 rise] ~, MH
22 In] Like MH
22 murmurs] murmers CtY
22 summer's] summers MH
23 darkened] darken'd MH
24 above,] ~^ MH
24 gleam.] gleem. CtY
25 wife?] ~,—MH
26 now.] ~; MH
29 wasted] wast'd MH
33 This] *This* MH
33 race!] ~, MH
34 will] can MH
35 urge] drive MH
35 chase,] chace, MH
36 Betrayed,] Betray'd, MH

36 abandoned,] abandon'd^ MH
38 drive] sweep MH
40 nerved] nerv'd MH
41 bow not:] fear not—MH
41 might,—] ~,^ Harv
43 gathered] gather'd MH
44 king.] *king.* MH
45 guard] gaurd CtY
46 grave;] ~;—MH
47 shalt] wilt MH
49 while] whilst MH
50 seat!] ~, MH
52 feet;] ~, MH
53 pine-clad] ~^~ MH
54 sweet;—] ~,—MH
55 own,] ~^ MH
55 father's grave,] fathers ~^ MH
56 'Twill rising] Twill gently MH

78. The Painted Columbine
Title: The Painted Columbine] To the Painted Columbine E, G, PF, PA, PG, LG, CAL, STC
      1 my] the E, G, PF, PA, PG, LG, CAL, STC
      1 years!] ~^ E, G, PF, PA, PG, LG, CAL, STC
      2 glowed] glow'd G, PF, LG
      4 swift-winged] ~-wing'd G, LG
      4 brow.] ~! E, G, PF, PA, PG, CAL, STC; ~^ LG
      5 painter's] painter s SO
      7 Nature's] nature's Harv
      9 thine,] ~; STC
      10 thee,] ~; G, PF, LG
      12 fond-remembered] fond-remember'd G, PF; fond^remember'd LG
      16 winds] wound Harv
      17 feathered] woodland E, G, PF, PA, PG, LG, CAL, STC
      18 tree,] ~; Harv
      19 And,] ~^ E, PA, PG, CAL
Stanza 6: *omit* Harv
      22 again;] ~, E, G, PF, PA, PG, LG, CAL, STC
      23 And,] ~^ PF
      24 glen.] ~, PF
      26 Touched] Touch'd G, LG
      26 withered] wither'd G, PF, LG
      27 hushed] hush'd G, LG
      31 And,] ~^ PF

825. The Frozen Ship
Title: Frozen] Ice MH(2)
Headnote: *omit* MH(2); CR includes longer headnote:
    "In 1775, Capt. Warrens, the master of a Greenland whale ship, fell in with an English ship surrounded by icebergs; which had been imprisoned for thirteen years. He was

struck with her strange and dismantled appearance. On going on board with his crew, they found the deck covered with snow to a considerable depth. In the fore part of the ship several sailors were discovered lying dead, and the body of a boy was crouched at the bottom of the gangway stairs. On entering the principal cabin, the first object that attracted their notice, was the dead body of a female, reclining on a bed in an attitude of deep interest and attention. Her countenance still retained the freshness of life, but a glance at the position of the limbs showed that her form was inanimate. Seated upon the floor was the corpse of an apparently young man, holding a steel in one hand and a flint in the other; as if in the act of striking fire upon some tinder, which lay beside him. In another apartment was the mate, reclining back on a chair. His pen was in his hand, and before him lay the log-book; the last sentence in whose unfinished page ran thus: 'Nov. 14, 1762. We have now been imprisoned in the ice seventeen days. The fire went out yesterday, and our master has been trying ever since to kindle it, but without success. His wife died this morning. There is no relief.' Capt. Warrens learned on his return to England that the ship had been missing thirteen years."

1 shout] ~, SO
3 out,] ~^ MH(2)
4 bright'ning sunbeams] ~ sun beams MH(2); brightning sun beams SO
5 life,] ~^ MH(2), CR
6 throng;] ~? MH(2)
7 joke,] ~^ MH(2), CR
7 joyance] joyaunce MH(2)
8 song?] ~. SO
9 Ah,] ~! SO
9 mailed] mail'd MH(2)
9 their bodies stand!] each body stands, MH(2); each body stands,—SO
10 Each fixed, and] The vacant, MH(2), SO; ~~^~ CR
11 Seems gazing on] Glares round upon MH(2), SO
11 wondering band,] ~ bands, MH(2); wond'ring bands, SO
12 gathered] gather'd MH(2), SO
15 lingered] linger'd MH(2)
16 wrestled] wrested CR
16 despair.] dispair. MH(2)
17 Speak,] ~^ MH(2), SO, CR
18 breast;] ~, MH(2)
19 *our* souls the tale] the tale *our* souls SO
21 your bosom rent,] ~ bosoms ~, MH(2); that ~~, SO; ~~~; CR
22 flickering fire,] flick'ring ~^ MH(2); flick'ring ~, SO; ~~^ CR
23 lent,] sent, MH(2), SO
25 your frame] that ~ SO
26 Claspt] Clasp MH(2)
26 cold, icy night;] ~^~~? MH(2); ~^~~; SO, CR
27 Gathered] gather'd MH(2)
27 flame,] ~^ MH(2), SO
28 Lighting] Light'ing MH(2)
29 When,] ~^ MH(2)
29 last loud cries of woe,] ~, ~~~~^ MH(2); ~~~~~^ CR
30 human] *human* SO

30 spoke;] ~, MH(2), CR
31 And, roaring deep,] ~^~~^ MH(2), CR; ~, waring-deep^ SO
34 Him,] *Him*^ SO; ~^ CR
34 sea;] ~, MH(2), SO
35 And triumph o'er your soul's despair] The realms of earth, the fields of air,
    MH(2), SO; And ~~~~, CR
36 And mortal] In silent MH(2), SO; And silent CR
37 can] shall MH(2), SO
38 breast;] ~, MH(2)
39–40 MH(2) and SO as follows:
Till the loud trump of God shall break
  The fetters of your rest!
41–44 *omit* MH(2), SO
    41 sphere,] ~^ CR
    43 fear,] ~^ CR

343. My Mother's Voice
Title: Voice] ~—TU
      1 mother's] Mother's TU
      1 now,] ~—TU
      3 when,] ~^ TU, CR
      3 heart-felt] heartfelt TU
      3 joy,] ~^ TU, CR
      4 praise,] ~^ TU
      6 boy.] Boy. TU
      7 mother's] Mother's TU
      7 voice!] ~—TU
      7 now,] ~^ TU; ~! CR
      8 brow,] ~^ TU
      9 hour;] ~, SO, CR, SG
     10 through] thro' TU
     11 fond] kind TU, CR
     11 pains,] ~^ TU; pain, SO
     12 power.] ~—TU
     13 mother's] Mother's TU
     13 voice!] ~—TU
     13 It] it SO
     14 men,] ~^ TU
     15 Patriarchs] Patriarch's SO
     15 old;] ~—TU; ~: SO; ~:—CR
     16 face,] ~^ TU
     17 trace] ~, CR
     18 told.] ~—TU
     19 comes,] ~—TU, Harv, SO, CR
     19 throng,] ~^ Harv, SG
     20 song,] ~—TU, Harv, SO, CR
     21 heart;] ~^ TU, CR; ~, SO, SG
     22 when, at eve,] ~^~~^ TU, Harv, SO, SG
     22 high;] ~^ TU; ~, SO, Harv

23 hear,] ~—TU; ~^ SO, CR, SG
23 she is nigh,] *italics* CR
24 depart.] ~—TU
25 all,] ~^ TU
25 beside,] ~^ TU, SO
26 Friendship,] friendship, CR
26 Love] ~, TU, SO, SG; love, CR
26 died;] ~^ TU; ~, Harv; ~,—CR
27 there;] ~^ TU; ~, CR
28 soft pillowed] ~ pillow'd TU; soft-pillowed Harv, SG
29 rest,] ~^ TU, SG
30 Or] ~, SO
30 prayer.] ~—TU

592. Hymn, Sung At The Dedication of The New Stone Church of The North
Society In Salem June 22d, 1836.
Title: Hymn, Sung] Hymn, / Hymn Sung MH(1)
Title: The North Society In Salem] the ~~, ~~, MSaE
Title: Dedication Hymn [entire title] MH(2), SO
 3 this, our temple,] ~^ *our* ~^ MH(2); ~^~~^ MSaE
 4 Till] 'Till SO
 4 days] years MH(2)
 4 tower shall] turrets MH(2)
 6 nature's] natures MH(2)
 7 To man Thou gavst] 'Tis man's high *gift* MH(2); 'Tis man's high gift
  MSaE, SO
 8 Thee] ~, MH(2), SO
 8 Father call:—] ~, ~. MH(2); ~~;—MSaE; ~, ~:—SO
 10 heart's] hearts MH(2)
 13 bad'st] badest MH(2)
 14 desire;] ~, SO
 16 sunbeam's] sun beam's MH(2)
 17 'Twill burn] Twill ~, MH(2); ~~, SO
 17 altar flame] altar-flame MH(2), SO; ~~, MSaE
 18 height,] ~^ MSaE, SO
 18 has] hath MH(2), SO
 19 earth's dark] dark earths MH(2); ~~, MSaE; dark earth's MH(2)
 23 O] Oh MSaE
 24 this,] ~^ MSaE, SO
 27 presence,] ~^ MH(2)

695. The Winter Bird
 1 bough] ~, SO
 2 Spring] spring SO
 3 rill,] ~^ SO
 4 breeze,] ~^ SO
 4 o'er meadow] oer medow RPB
 5 ear,] ~^ SO
 5 glided] murmured SO
 6 song] ~: SO

7 blast] ~, SO
9 Yet] *omit* SO
10 will] 'twill SO
11 brook] stream SO
11 voice] ~, SO
12 meadows] medows RPB; meadow SO
12 rejoice] ~; SO
13 Still] Yet SO
14 life's] lifes RPB

852. The Portrait
  2 beauty] Beauty Knick
  2 dwell;] ~, Knick
  3 glass,] ~—Knick
  4 smile] ~, Knick
  4 tell;] ~, Knick
  5 glance] ~, Knick
  7 no—] ~: Knick
  7 rest] ~, Knick
  9 Ocean's] ocean's Knick
  10 star] ~, Knick
  10 air] ~, Knick
  11 bosom] ~, Knick

221. The Canary Bird
Title: To the Canary Bird E; To the Canary-Bird SAP, G, LG
  1 others'] other's SO
  8 ravished] ravish'd SAP, G, LG
  14 bard like thee] ~, ~~, SAP, G; ~~~, LG

246. The Tree
  1 appear,] ~^ E, SG
  3 near] ~, E, SG
  6 robin's] robbin's SO
  7 skreen] screen SAP, SG; screen, G
  8 opprest;] oppress'd; G, SAP
  9 stript] stripp'd SAP
  10 smooth] ~, G
  11 nought] naught SAP, G

95. The Fossil Flower
Title: To the Fossil Flower] E
  2 their] thy E
  13 rolling] roling E
  14 mayest] may'st E
  17 on the] on E
  22 in] on E
  23 winds,] ~^ E
  24 oft as] as oft E
  24 wingéd] winged E
  26 man,] ~^ E

29 haunts] haunt E
33 Uncurb'd,] Uncurbed, E
36 demon] daemon E

309. The April Snow
Title: April Snow Knick; The Snow MH(2), CE
    1 stay!] ~—Knick; ~;—MH(2), CE
    1 white,] ~^ MH(2), CE
    2 Which] That Knick, MH(2), CE
    2 on] o'er Knick
    2 nature's] Nature's MH(2)
    3 moonbeams'] moonbeam's Knick, MH(2), CE
    4 such] pure Knick
    4 sainted] holy Knick, CE
    4 wear;] ~—Knick, MH(2); ~, CE
    5 Look,] ~^ MH(2), CE
    5 from the] how from Knick; how from th' MH(2), CE
    5 plain,] ~^ Knick, MH(2), CE
    6 sun;] ~! Knick; ~^ MH(2); ~, CE
    7 detain,] ~; Knick, MH(2), CE
    8 *entire line differs:* E'en there it will not stay—its task is done: Knick
    8 brooks, which] rills that MH(2), CE
    9 flowers] ~, Knick
    10 grass] ~, Knick
    11 And,] ~^ MH(2)
    11 life,] ~^ Knick, MH(2), CE
    11 showers,] ~^ MH(2)
    12 With beauty deck] Will deck again Knick; ~~ clothe MH(2), CE
    12 hill;] ~, Knick

348. Nature
    1 Nature,] Nature! SO, E
    5 my breast;] its breast—SO; its breast,—E
    6 Now] ~, E
    9 Then] ~, E
    9 city's] cities MH(OP), SO
    10 heights] height MH(OP)
    10 waters] water's SO
    12 swoln stream;] swollen ~, SO, E
    13 hold] ~, SO, E

244. An Evening Walk
    1 love] ~, SG
    3 *entire line differs:* From some high hill, to gaze around, SG
    5 see] ~, SG
    10 break;] breaks; SG
    13 *entire line differs:* Or catch, with listening ear intent, SG
    15 Which] That SG
Stanza 5 (ll. 17–20): *omit* SG
    24 care.] ~^ ViU

28 Enjoyed,] ~^ SG
28 alone.] ~^ ViU

232. Beauty
Title: Beauty] Love RPB
    1 face—] ~,—E, SSLF
    1 life,] ~^ E, SSLF
    3 every] weary SO 1837
    5 not,] ~^ SO 1837
    5 thee,] ~; SSLF
    6 trod,] ~; SSLF
    7 me,] ~: SSLF
    8 loved] love SSLF
    9 gaze—] ~,—E, SSLF
    14 Divine.] divine. SSLF

650. The Voice of God
    1 me—] ~, SO
    1 glad,] ~^ SO
    2 rejoice—] ~; MH; ~, SO
    3 me,] ~— MH
    5 that from] Him in MH
    6 monarch] Monarch SO
    6 o'er] of MH
    6 world,] ~; MH
    7 lightning] lightening MH
    7 by—] ~, MH
    8 *entire line differs:* And His the hand the red bolts hurled. MH
    9 I have learned] now I learn SO
    11 'Twas,] ~^ MH; 'Tis^ SO
    12 nature,] ~^ MH, SO
    12 caught,] ~. MH, SO
    14 sky,] heaven, SO
    17 heedless ear] thankless heart MH
    18 thunder's] thunders SO
    18 wrath] ~; MH; ~, SO
    19 Winging] Bidding MH
    19 steps with fear] steps depart MH; feet with fear SO
    20 To fly] And shun MH
    22 His voice in all that lives] In all that lives his voice SO
    24 warbled] soaring MH
    26 tear,] ~; MH
    27 rest,] ~^ MH, SO

684. The Wind-Flower
    1 meek,] ~^ MH(OP), SO 1837, SO 1838, E, CAL
    1 eye] ~, LG
    2 clouded] cloudy MH(OP)
    2 face,] ~; MH(OP)
    3 Unharmed,] ~^ MH(OP), SO 1837, SO 1838, E, CAL; Unharm'd, SAP;
        Unharm'd^ G, LG

3 by,] ~^ MH(OP), SO 1837, SO 1838, E, CAL

4 grace.] ~; MH(OP); ~^ E, LG

5 wisely!] ~—MH(OP)

5 in] In SAP

5 arrayed,] ~^ MH(OP), SO 1837, SO 1838, E, CAL; array'd, SAP, G, LG

6 King;] king; MH(OP), SAP, G, LG

7 faith was his,] was his faith MH(OP); ~~~^ SO 1837, SO 1838, E, SAP, CAL; ~~ His^ G, LG

7 whom] when SO 1837

7 betrayed;] ~, MH(OP); ~^ SO 1837, SO 1838, E; betray'd, SAP, G, CAL; betray'd^ LG

8 hear'st] hearst MH(OP); hearest SO 1837, SO 1838, G, LG

8 Spring,] ~^ MH(OP), SO 1837, SO 1838

9 While] When MH(OP)

9 call,] ~^ SO 1837, SO 1838, E, G, CAL, LG

10 brink,] ~^ MH(OP), SO 1837, SO 1838, E, SAP, G, CAL, LG

10 bare;] ~. E, SAP, G, CAL, LG

11 Thee] These CAL

12 childlike] child like MH(OP)

13 O'erjoyed,] ~^ SO 1837, SO 1838, E, SAP, CAL; Oe'rjoyed^ MH(OP); O'erjoy'd^ G, LG

14 Him,] ~^ G, LG; him^ MH(OP), SO 1837, SO 1838, E, SAP, CAL

580. The Sabbatia
    1 sweet briar] sweet-briar CR

710. A Sonnet
Title: A Sonnet] Thy Beauty Fades E, G, BS
        1 fades] ~, G, BS
        2 self-same] selfsame BS
        4 looked] look'd G
        6 dwell,] ~; G, BS
        7 strewed] strew SO, BS; strew'd G
        12 enthral,] enthrall, G, BS
        14 bloom] ~, G, BS

441. The Columbine
        1 long-fixed] long fixed E
        4 fan;] ~. E
        7 honey bells] honey-bells E
        13 Here,] ~^ E

686. The Robin
Title: Robin] Robbin FU, SO
        1 needst] need'st MH(OP), E, G, PA, PG, SG 1859, SG 1861, BS
        1 nest] ~, SO, E, G, PA, PG, SG 1859, SG 1861, BS
        2 hearst] hear'st E, G, SG 1859, SG 1861, BS
        2 by—;] ~; MH(OP), SO; ~, E, G, SG 1859, SG 1861, BS
        4 young's] youngs MH(OP); young E, G, PA, PG, SG 1859, 1861, BS
        4 unfinished] unfinish'd G
        7 pool's] pools FU, MH(OP)

7 now] ~, PA, PG, SG 1859, SG 1861, BS
8 straws] straw MH(OP)
9 out-pouring] out pouring MH(OP); outpouring SG 1859, SG 1861
9 joy,] ~^ MH(OP)
10 song;] ~, SO, E, G, PA, PG, SG 1859, SG 1861
12 else] ~, MH(OP)
12 along] ~, SG 1859, SG 1861, BS
13 light wings] light-wings MH(OP)
13 heart-ascending] heart ascending SG 1859
13 prayer] ~, MH(OP), SG 1859, SG 1861, BS
14 *no hanging indention* MH(OP), BS
14 learned] learn'd G
14 Heaven] heaven SO, SG 1859
14 joys] joyies MH(OP)

701. Hymn
1 keepst] keep'st MH(J)
2 meet;] ~, MH(J)
10 around,] ~; MH(J)
11 biddst] bidd'st MH(J)
15 needing] ~, MH(J)
20 'walk] 'Walk RPB(2)

228. The Stranger's Gift
2 guest,] ~; E
4 ozier] osier E
6 air,] ~; E
8 fair:] ~. E
10 Scattered along the path I love to go,] As sweetly scattered round my path they grow, E
14 bloom!] ~. E

722. The New Birth
1 'Tis] Tis MH(J)
1 life—] ~,—MH(J); ~;—E, Rosary, CAL, SSLF
1 did] ~, Rosary
2 steps] ~, Rosary
2 mind,] ~; MH(J), Rosary
3 on] ~, Rosary
4 wind;] ~^ E, CAL, SSLF; ~, Rosary
5 not,] ~^ SO, E, Rosary, CAL, SSLF
7 man's] man MH(OP); mans MH(J)
8 earth—] ~;—E, Rosary, CAL, SSLF
8 Their] their MH(J), SO, E, Rosary, CAL, SSLF
8 now—] ~. MH(J), Rosary, SSLF; ~.—E; ~,—CAL
9 crowding] pressing MH(J)
9 on] ~, E, Rosary, CAL, SSLF
9 claims] claiming MH(J); asks SO, E, Rosary, CAL, SSLF
9 strong,] ~; MH(J), E, Rosary, CAL, SSLF
10 shore] ~, E, Rosary, CAL, SSLF
12 through] from MH(J)

12 roar,] ~^ MH(J); ~; SO, E, Rosary, CAL, SSLF
13 I] ~, Rosary
13 God] ~, SSLF
13 free] ~, Rosary, SSLF
14 death's] deaths MH(OP), MH(J)
14 eternity.] Eternity. SO, E, Rosary, CAL, SSLF

120. "In Him we live, & move, & have our being"
Title: & move, &] and ~, and] SO; In Him We Live [entire title] E
1 live] ~, SO, E
2 thee] ~, E
3 give] ~, SO, E
4 wealth,] ~^ SO, E
6 bring,] ~; E
7 try] ~; SO; ~, E
9 bless] ~, SO, E
11 possess] ~, SO, E
13 prove] ~; SO; ~, E
14 &] and SO, E

242. Enoch
1 looked] look'd SAP, G
1 walked] walk'd SAP, G
1 God,] ~^ MH(OP)
2 the translated] to the Jewish MH(OP), SO
2 old;—] ~;^ MH(OP), SO, SAP
3 gladdened] gladened SO; gladden'd SAP, G
5 by] ~, SAP, G, Rosary
6 his] its MH(OP), SO, E, SAP, G, Rosary
7 high,] ~^ MH(OP)
8 none like David] ~, ~~, SAP
8 turned] turn'd SAP, G
9 walked alone unhonored] walk'd ~ unhonor'd SAP, G
10 stood,] ~; SAP, Rosary
11 soul] ~, SAP, G
11 birth] ~, SAP, G
12 and] & MH(OP)
13 unfinished] unfinish'd SAP, G
13 and] & MH(OP)

122. The Son
BH, HS, DHB, LSA, HTB, and SSLF print three four-line stanzas, omitting lines
13–14.
Title: The Son] 'I wait for the Lord; my soul doth wait.' BH, HS; "I wait for the
Lord; my Soul doth wait." LSA; "I wait for the Lord; my soul doth wait." HTB
1 Father!] ~^ SO, E, BH, HTB; ~, SAP, G
1 thy] Thy HS, LSA
1 word—the] word. The SO, E, SAP, G, BH, HS, DHB, LSA, HTB, SSLF
1 stand,] ~^ SO, E, SAP, G, BH, HS, DHB, LSA, HTB, SSLF
3 servant] ~, SO, E, SAP, G, BH, DHB, HTB, SSLF
3 thy command] thy ~, BH, DHB, SSLF; Thy ~, HS, LSA

4 rejoycing] rejoicing E, SAP, G, BH, HS, DHB, LSA, HTB, SSLF

4 way;] ~. BH, HS, DHB, LSA, HTB, SSLF

5 time] Time SAP

5 appointed] apointed MH(OP)

7 shower,] ~,—BH, DHB, SSLF

8 Then] ~, BH

8 thy call;] ~~. BH, DHB, HTB, SSLF; Thy ~. HS, LSA

9 bough] ~, SO, E, SAP, G, BH, HS, DHB, LSA, HTB, SSLF

10 unswollen] unswolen MH(OP)

10 song;] ~, SO, E, SAP; ~;—G, BH, HS, LSA, HTB, SSLF

11 thy] Thy HS, LSA

11 now] ~, BH, HS, DHB, LSA, HTB, SSLF

12 thy] Thy HS, LSA

12 along] ~, E, SAP, G; ~. BH, HS, DHB, LSA, HTB, SSLF

13 lengthened] lengthen'd SAP, G

14 *hanging indention* SO, E, SAP, G

14 Unuttered] Unutter'd SAP; unutter'd G

14 Word and Love] word and love G

213. Love

7 struggling] strugling SO

9 mountains'] mountains SO

11 led] ~, E

98. Day

1 Day] ~! E, CAL

3 rays] ~, E, CAL

4 confess;] ~. E, CAL

13–14 These lines differ entirely in E and CAL:
New rising still, though setting to mankind,
And ever in the eternal West my dayspring find.

275. Night

6 Thy] The E, CAL

6 labors] labours G

6 day] ~, E, G, CAL, PA, PG

9 thou see'st] thou seest G, PA, PG

9 burthened] burden'd G

9 love] ~, E, G, CAL, PA, PG

11 above] ~, E, G, CAL, PA, PG

13 darkened] darken'd G

482. The Coming

4 earth.] ~; SO

7 side,] ~^ SO

8 tears.] ~; SO

9 comes!] ~^ SO

9 give,] ~; SO

10 righteousness] purest white SO

12 Kingdom] riches SO

12 aye endure;] e'er ~, SO

13 Priests,] ~^ SO
14 God] Christ SO

725. The Morning Watch
No variants

264. The Garden
3 For] ~, Rosary
3 groves] ~, Rosary
10 Father's] father's E, Rosary
12 Him] him Rosary
14 pay.] ~^ Rosary

789. The Song
No variants

126. The Spirit Land
Title: The Spirit Land] ~ Spirit-Land G, BS, LWP
1 thy] Thy HBP
2 strayed;] stray'd; G
3 land] ~, G, HBP, BS, LWP
4 thine] Thine HBP
4 displayed;] display'd; G
5 thee] Thee HBP
7 we] ~, G, HBP, BS, LWP
7 sound,] ~; HBP
9 wander] wonder MH(1)
10 Mid] 'Mid BS
10 ruined] ruin'd G
11 dote,] doat, Rosary
13 bewildered] bewilder'd G
13 night] ~; BS

258. The Slave
14 view."] view^" MH(1)

319. The Bread from Heaven
Title: The Bread from Heaven] Bread [entire title] E
5 eat] ~, E
6 drink] ~, E
9 stranger's] strangers MH(1)
14 Father's] Fathers MH(1)
14 for evermore] forevermore E

518. The Latter Rain
1 rain,] ~,—PHi, E, G, CG, CAL, HBP, LWP
3 drops] droops MH(1)
3 waste] ~, PHi, E, G, CG, CAL
4 root's] roots MH(1), SO, SO offprint
4 repair;] ~! PHi
5 spring,] Spring, PHi, SO, SO offprint, E, CAL, HBP; Spring; CG;
~; LWP
6 thickening] tender PHi

7 mid] 'mid CG, CAL

7 sing] ~, G, CG, HBP, LWP

8 that . . . sheaves;] which . . . ~; PHi; ~ . . . ~: CG

9 still—] ~,—PHi, E, G, CG, CAL, HBP, LWP

9 fruit all ripened] ~, ~~, CG; ~~ripen'd G

10 chestnut burr] chestnut burr MH(1) SO, SO offprint; chestnut-burr G, CG, HBP, LWP

10 walnut shell,] walnut-shell, G, CG; walnut-shell; HBP, LWP

11 furrowed] furrow'd G

11 crops,] ~; HBP, LWP

12 tell,] ~; PHi, HBP, LWP

14 to man it was] that now it is PHi

598. The Word

1 Word!] word! SO, SO offprint

10 Father's] Fathers MH(1)

13 angels'] angels MH(1), SO, SO offprint

630. Worship

1 now—] ~,—E, Rosary

2 place;] ~! SO, SO offprint, E, Rosary

6 idol's] idols MH(1)

10 rush] leaps E, Rosary

10 shore;] ~: SO, SO offprint, E, Rosary

12 And hushed to peace] ~, ~~~, Rosary

13 keep] kept SO, SO offprint, E, Rosary

619. The Living God

1 each] Each SAP

2 still,] ~; SAP

3 see] ~, SAP

4 will;] ~. SAP

7 begun,] bugun, SAP

8 labor] labour SAP

9 pause] ~, SAP

12 shadows] shadow SO

14 forever] for ever SAP

622. Time

2 bower,] ~; SO, E

7 But waits] They wait SO, E

7 tongue,] ~^ SO, E

9 night] ~, SO, E

11 spirit songs] spirit-songs SO, E

11 swell,] ~^ SO, E

12 now;] ~, SO, E

13 angels'] angels MH(1), SO

699. The Violet

1 unspoken] upspoken SO

11 lest] least SO

612. The Heart
    4 daemon] demon G
    9 crystal] chrystal E

132. The Trees of Life
    1 Thee] THEE G
    2 Thee] THEE G
    3 Now] ~, G
    3 Thee] THEE G
    4 thy] THY G
    11 beam] ~, G
    12 brink,] ~^ E; ~; G
    13 grow] ~, G

168. The Soldier of the Cross
Title: The Soldier of the Cross] The Soldier [entire title] E, VTH
    4 breast-worn] breast worn VTH
    6 prayer;] ~;—VTH
    8 robes] ~, VTH
    10 forth] ~, VTH
    10 power;] ~: VTH
    12 dawn till] ~, to VTH

289. The Spirit
    4 again;] ~^ E
    5 hide themselves] hides itself E
    8 lest] least SO
    8 their] its E

266. The Dead
    1 them] ~,—E, VTH
    1 earth] ~—VTH
    2 Dry,] ~^ E, VTH
    2 no Autumn] ~ autumn SO; to autumn E, VTH
    7 have] has VTH
    7 know,] ~^ E, VTH
    8 th'] the VTH
    10 cheek;] ~. VTH
    11 words] ~, VTH
    12 speak;] ~: VTH
    13 live] ~, VTH

269. The Presence
    1 room] ~, E, SSLF
    2 loves] lov'st, E, SSLF
    4 Thyself] thyself SO, E
    4 keepst] keep'st E, SSLF
    7 thy] Thy SSLF
    8 Thou] thou SO, E
    9 watch,] ~^ SO, E, SSLF
    11 more] ~, SSLF

13 Thyself,] thyself, SO, E
13 Father's] father's SO, E, SSLF

651. The Lost
2 cries;] ~, SO
4 shepherd] shepard MH(1), SO
7 seen] near, SO
10 shepherd] shepard MH(1), SO
13 reigns] ~, SO

103. The Robe
2 rugged] ruggid MH(1), SO
3 Lies] Lie SO, E
6 not] nor SO
7 For 'neath] Beneath, E
11 plains] plaines MH(1)
12 Must e'er lay] Ever lie E
13 its] the E

169. The Will
6 bruise] bruse MH(1)
6 serpent's] serpents MH(1), SO
9 thy] Thy SO
10 When] Where SO
11 thy] Thy SO

256. The War
1 war] ~, SO, E
5 wills,] ~,—SO, E
6 within;] ~, E
7 leave unslain below,] left ~~,—E
8 skin;] ~;—E
9 peace;] ~,—E
10 ceased;] ~, SO; ~^ E
11 neighbour] neighbor SO, E
12 When John within our breasts has not decreased;] Ere haughty Self within
    us has deceased; E
13 kingdom] kindgdom SO
13 increase] ~, SO, E

306. Life
1 Thy] thy HA
2 But] ~, E, HA
2 still with deeper roots grow fixed] to grow fixed with deeper roots SO,
    E, HA
3 give] ~, E, HA
6 Where] Whose HA
6 moss-grown] moss grown SO
6 trunks] arms E, HA
6 rigid] riggid MH(1)
7 And full-faced] Where full faced SO

7 fruit] fruits E, HA
10 'tis] tis HA
11 Who while we eat] ~, ~~~, E, HA
12 That] Which E, HA

608. The Reaper
8 aggravate] aggravte MH(1)
11 descend,] decend, MH(1)
13 rest,] ~; SO

781. John
2 way";] ~;" SO
8 torn!] ~; SO
12 That] What SO

680. I Was Sick And In Prison
Title: I Was Sick And In Prison] Sympathy VTH
3 Thou] thou VTH
4 have] has E, VTH
6 note] notes VTH
7 Thou] thou VTH
10 dies;] ~, E, VTH
13 one new-born] ~, new born VTH
14 heaven] heav'n VTH

223. He Was Acquainted With Grief
3 reveal,] ~^ E
4 earth's] a E
6 sea;] ~, E
7 hymns] ~, E
8 thee;] ~. E
9 here,] ~^ E
11 hear,] ~^ E
12 spirit's] Spirit's E
12 above;] ~, E

677. The Rail Road
Title: Rail Road] Rail-road G
1 eye,] ~^ E, G
3 go'st,] goest, G
6 "prepare] "Prepare E, G
7 hurled,] hurl'd, G
9 valleys] vallies WM; ~, G
9 bed] ~, G
10 frowned] frown'd G
13 bidst] bid'st E; bidd'st G

334. Ye Gave Me No Meat
1 hungry,] ~,—E
1 food;] ~^ E
6 offerest,] ~^ E
10 should'st] shoulds't WM

703. The Disciple
    4 Thou] thou E
    4 sight;] ~. E
    5 Thee] thee E
    7 Thy] The E
    7 Thou sufferest too,] thou ~~^ E
    8 Thou] thou E
    9 Thou wilt] thou ~ E
    10 spirit] Spirit E
    12 fear;] ~, E

80. The First shall be Last
    8 knee;] ~: SO

234. Thy Brother's Blood
    1 Brother—] ~,—E
    3 And] ~, E
    3 brow] ~, E
    5 guilt;] ~;—E
    9 ear—] ~,—E
    10 Its] I'ts SO
    12 gore;] ~, E; son; SO
    13 gift—] ~;—E

339. The Graveyard
Title: Graveyard] Grave Yard E; Grave-Yard VTH
    2 speaks] spreads VTH
    6 not] ~, VTH
    7 this] ~, E, VTH
    7 too] ~, VTH
    10 cheek] ~, VTH
    14 body's] bodies SO

672. Sacrifice
    2 feel;] ~, SO
    4 altar] alter SO
    5 hands,] hand SO
    6 hear'st] hearest SO
    7 commands,] command, SO
    8 fill.] ~; SO
    10 Hangs clustering from] Is offered on MH
    10 sweet;] ~, SO
    11 which, who taste, unwillingly depart,] ~^~~^~~^ SO
    13 vine,] ~^ SO
    14 Him, who,] ~^~^ SO
    14 wants,] ~^ SO

568. The Son of Man
    1 son] Son SO
    4 land] ~, SO
    10 asks] ask MH

618. The Ark

    1 Thee,] ~; E, LSA; THEE; G
    2 go] ~, E, G, LSA
    2 same;] ~, LSA
    3 thy] Thy LSA
    4 thy most holy name;] Thy ~~ Name; LSA
    5 change;] ~, LSA
    6 shallows of] shadows on LSA
    6 storm-vexed] storm vexed SO; storm-vex'd G, LSA
    9 Thee] THEE G
    9 thy] Thy LSA
    11 And] ~, G, LSA
    11 dark] ~, SO, E, G, LSA
    12 hopes] hope LSA
    12 Christ] CHRIST G
    12 veil;] ~, SO
    14 rest to those who love] ~, ~~~~, SO

700. The Father
No variants

801. Rachel

    4 Me] me SO
    5 Me] me SO
    6 stocks] stacks SO
    8 Me] me SO
    14 sealed.] ~^ MH

59. Christmas

    4 imprisoned] emprisoned MH
    10 whom you] ~ ye SO

288. The Earth

    2 thy] Thy SO, E
    3 bread] ~, E
    5 and] or SO, E
    6 food;] ~, E
    7 Thou] thou SO, E
    10 built;] ~, E
    11 son] Son SO, E

526. The Hours
Alternate lines are indented in HC.

    2 love] ~, MH(2)
    4 Nor from] And never MH(2), CR, HC
    4 can they] *omit* MH(2), CR, HC
    4 alight;] ~. CR, HC
    5 me,] ~: HC
    6 Oh] O HC
    6 show;] ~, HC
    8 know;] ~. MH(2), CR; ~! HC
    10 thy] Thy SO

11 And] ~, MH(2)
11 comes] ~, MH(2)
11 blest] ~, MH(2), CR, HC
12 I a night to others] Thou wilt peaceful slumbers MH(2), CR, HC
12 give;] ~, HC
13 thy peace does to thy children] Thou dost to weary laborers MH(2), CR, HC
14 *entire line differs:* Whose sleep from Thee doth, with the dews, descend. MH(2); Whose sleep from Thee doth with the dews descend. CR, HC

728. The Christ
1 only] ~, SO
4 increase;] ~. SO
6 couldst not know;] could'st ~~, SO
9 bidst] bid'st SO

291. The Things Before
9 city's gate,] cities' gates, MH
11 wait,] waits, MH, SO
12 lived] live SO

467. The Cup
No variants

536. Old things are passed away
10 thy] Thy SO
13 Untill] Until SO
13 fade] fades MH, SO

645. The Harvest
10 o'er] oer MH
12 The] In SO

48. The City
No variants

554. The Rose
1 showst] show'st SO, E
5 shouldst] could'st SO, E
6 springs the bud] spring these buds E
6 its] the E
8 turnst] turnest SO, E
8 thine own self] thyself E
8 them;] ~, E
13 seed,] ~^ SO
14 O'er] Oer MH

620. Faith
5 sound,] ~^ SG
6 air;] ~, E, SG
8 prayer;] ~, SG
9 them Father] ~, ~, E, SG
9 word,] ~,—E

10 Thee] thee SO, E, SG
13 Thee] thee SO, E, SG

659. The Jew
    2 speech;] speach; MH
    4 reach;] ~, SO; ~. E
    9 guile,] ~^ E

574. Spring
    2 Encased] Enclosed SO
    13 Father's] father's SO

582. The Temple
Title: The Temple] The Temple of Humanity MH(2), CR
    2 earth] ~, MH(2), CR
    3 *entire line differs:* Nor blood of beasts with sprinkling make it clean; CR
    5 wrought,] ~^ MH(2), CR
    6 Him] ~, MH(2), CR
    8 chiseled] chiselled MH(2)
    8 away;] ~. MH(2), CR
    9–10 These lines differ entirely in MH(2) and CR:
The work of Sin [lower case in CR] in man shall be repaired,
Humanity to perfect manhood grow;
    11 son the work is to] nation shall the work MH(2), CR
    13 eternal shrine] Eternal Shrine MH(2), CR
    13 rise,] ~^ MH(2), CR

597. The White Horse
    1 Word] word SO
    8 and] & SO
    9 places] palaces SO
    13 judgement] judgment SO

698. The Tent
    12 they'll] they'l MH

285. My Sheep
    8 with out] without SO

474. The Corner Stone
    1 corner stone,] Corner Stone, MH(2)
    2 That I low down] Which deep MH(2); That deep CR
    2 have] must yet be MH(2), CR
    3 fall;] ~, MH(2)
    4 That in the building] Who, ~~~, MH(2)
    4 aid;] ~. MH(2), CR
    5 raise] ~, MH(2)
    5 sands] ~, MH(2), CR
    6 Houses that] ~, which MH(2)
    7 altars] ~, MH(2)
    7 Me] God MH(2), CR
    8 That] Which MH(2)
    12 laid] ~, MH(2)

599. The Good Ground
    1 Word] word SO
    4 feed?] ~; SO

663. The Beginning and The End
    8 son] Son SO
    11 sovereign's] Sovereign's SO
    13 descends] decends MH

472. Nature
    2 call;] ~, SO, E, CAL
    4 them] ~, G, HBP, LWP
    4 small;] ~. HBP, LWP
    5 flowers, which] flower that MH, E, G, CAL, HBP, LWP, RPST
    5 lovely] lonely HBP, LWP, RPST
    5 grow,] grows, SO; grows^ E, G, CAL, HBP, LWP, RPST
    6 Expect me there,] Expects ~~^ MH, E, G, CAL, HBP, LWP, RPST
    6 Spring] spring G, LWP
    6 their] its MH, E, G, CAL, HBP, LWP, RPST
    7 bush and tree] tree and bush MH, E, G, CAL, HBP, LWP, RPST
    7 know,] knows, MH, E, G, CAL, HBP, LWP, RPST
    8 heaven:] ~; MH, E, G, CAL, HBP, LWP, RPST
    9 he,] ~^ MH, E, G, CAL, HBP, LWP, RPST
    10 lord,] ~^ E, G, CAL, HBP, LWP, RPST
    10 Adam] ADAM G, LWP

522. Morning
    3 object,] ~,—E, G, Rosary
    3 skies,] ~,—E, Rosary
    4 th'] the G, Rosary, BS
    5 day—] ~,—E, G, Rosary; ~: BS
    5 filled] fill'd G
    7 all ready] already SO, E, G, Rosary
    7 stands] ~, Rosary
    9 gently too] ~, ~, Rosary
    9 breast—] ~,—E, G, Rosary, BS
    13 staff—] ~,—E, G, Rosary, BS
    14 a] their SO, E, G, Rosary, BS

693. The Temptation
    11 Life] life SO

702. Help
    2 Thou] thou SO
    4 'Thy will be done';] "~~~~," SO
    8 upholdst] upholdest SO
    10 Thee] thee SO
    11 sin] sins SO
    12 accord;] ~, SO

124. Change
Title: Change] God's Fatherly Care BH, HFS; *untitled, but headed with the following*

quotation: "God hath given to us eternal life, and this life is in His Son." CP; The Child of God HS, LSA

BH, HFS, DHB, CP, HS, LSA, HTB, HCC, and SSLF all print the poem in three four-line stanzas, omitting lines 13–14.

    1 Father!] ˜, BH, HFS, CP, HTB, SSLF

    1 Thee,] thee, BH, HFS, DHB, HTB, HCC, SSLF

    2 Christ] Thee HS, LSA; thee HTB

    2 day,] ˜; BH, HFS, DHB, CP, HS, LSA, HTB, HCC, SSLF

    3 hear,] ˜^ SO

    3 see] ˜, E, BH, HFS, DHB, CP, HS, LSA, HTB, HCC, SSLF

    4 My feet] My but SO; I but E, BH, HFS, DHB, CP, HS, LSA, HTB, HCC, SSLF

    4 rejoycing] rejoicing SO, E, BH, HFS, CP, HS, LSA, SSLF

    4 the way;] my ˜. BH, HFS, DHB, CP, HS, LSA, HTB, HCC, SSLF

    5 comes] ˜, BH, HFS, DHB, CP, HS, LSA, HTB, HCC, SSLF

    5 overspread,] ˜; SO, HFS

    6 I new-wakened] ˜, ˜, BH, HFS, DHB, CP, HS, HTB, HCC, SSLF; ˜, new-waken'd, LSA

    6 within;] ˜, CP

    8 hearst] hear'st E, BH, HFS, DHB, CP, HS, LSA, HTB, HCC, SSLF

    8 hymn;] ˜. BH, HFS, DHB, CP, HS, LSA, HTB, HCC, SSLF

    9 descend;] ˜, E, SSLF; ˜: CP

    10 me] ˜, E, BH, HFS, DHB, CP, HS, LSA, HTB, HCC, SSLF

    11 thy] Thy CP, HS, LSA

    11 their] thy SO, E; its BH, HFS, DHB, CP, HS, LSA, HTB, HCC, SSLF

    12 I a child] ˜, thy ˜, BH, HFS, DHB, HTB, HCC, SSLF; ˜, Thy ˜, CP, HS, LSA

    12 awhile on Thee;] in peace with thee. BH, HFS, DHB, HTB, HCC, SSLF; in peace with Thee. CP, HS, LSA

  13–14 *omit* BH, HFS, DHB, CP, HS, LSA, HTB, HCC, SSLF

280. The Poor

    3 in to] into SO, E

    4 hunger] ˜, E

    7 feed,] ˜^ E

    9 hear,] ˜^ E

    11 clear,] ˜^ E

    13 Father land,] Fatherland, E

    14 voice,] ˜^ SO, E

    14 beakoning] beckoning SO, E

681. They Who Hunger

    2 Thou] thou SO

    12 Rejoycing] Rejoicing SO

577. Who Hath Ears To Hear Let Him Hear!

Title: Hear!] ˜. E

    4 sight;] ˜. SG

    8 adores;] ˜. SG

    11 thee flesh-clothed the earth,] ˜, ˜, ˜˜^ SG

    12 declare:] ˜; E, SG

639. The Sign
    3–4 These lines differ entirely in MH:
While still no hunger of the soul they feel
For the True Bread, to all so freely given;
      6 him] Him, MH
      6 died,] ~; MH
      8 confide;] ~: MH
      9 Then] When MH
  10–12 These lines differ entirely in MH:
Shall they, with Christ, to a new life arise;
And learn their lower natures to deny,
And worldly power, and grandeur to despise;
      10 true] time SO
      13 still] ever MH
      14 heir] heirs MH
      14 His] his MH
      14 give.] ~? MH

277. The Tree
Title: The Tree] The Leafless Tree MH
      1 wait with thee] ~, ~~, MH
      1 spring,] Spring, MH
      2 bough,] ~; MH
      3 new grown] new-grown MH
      4 tore me now;] tear them now. MH
      5 stripped] striped SO
    5–7 These lines differ entirely in MH:
Though now against me beats the furious blast,
And o'er my head in scornful triumph rides;
I know the winter's bondage soon is past,
      8 the] his MH
      8 abides;] confides. MH
      9 And as his Father] ~, ~ the ~, MH
      9 returns,] ~^ MH
      10 dress,] ~; MH
      11 call] ~, MH
      12 Those who in patience] ~, ~, ~~, MH
      13 raiments] ~, MH

380. The Desert
      2 flower] ~, RPB
      3 thy] the RPB
      4 bough;] ~. RPB
      5 breathe] breath SO
      6 Though like the dead] ~, ~~~, RPB
      8 The] And RPB
      8 verdure] virdure MH
      9 Awake,] ~^ RPB
      9 earth] ~, SO
      11 come] came SO

14 to you the crop of peace] for you rich harvests still RPB

692. The Clay
    2 form'st] forms't MH, SO
    5 take,] ~^ E
    9 receive,] receives, E
    11 breathe,] breath, SO
    11 *entire line differs:* Above them Sleep their palm with poppy weaves, E
    12 The] Sweet E
    13 again,] ~^ E

385. The Altar
    1 Oh] O MH(2); ~, SO
    2 there] ~, MH(2)
    4 defile;] ~: MH(2)
    5 high,] nigh, MH(2), SO
    7 them] ~, MH(2)
    8 rod;] ~! MH(2)
    12 But at each word] For, ~~~, MH(2)
    13 Oh] O MH(2)
    14 name.] ~! MH(2)

386. Praise
    4 theirs] their's MH, SO
    9 triumph] triump MH
    12 wave;] ~! SO
    13 heaven uplifted] heaven-uplifted SO
    14 Kings] kings SO

625. Terror
    1 safety;] ~! SO
    6 fast!] ~; SO

119-123. The Prayer
    1 help] keep SO
    3 sight;] ~, SO
    9 more;] ~! SO

384. Humility
    14 servant yet a son,] ~, ~~~; SO

136. Forgiveness
    1 stand] ~, SO
    5 knowst] knowest SO
    5 blind] ~, SO
    7 Thee] thee SO
    10 gracious] gratious MH

640. The Heavenly Rest
Title: The Heavenly Rest] Heaven [entire title] MH(2), SO
    3 blest] blessed MH(2); bless'd SO
    4 nought] naught SO
    4 there, that ever dies.] ~^~~~; MH(2), SO; ~^~~~: CR

5 love!] ~—MH(2), SO, CR
5 hours,] ~! MH(2), SO, CR
6 tear, but that of joy,] ~^~~~~^ MH(2), SO, CR
6 the cheeks;] ~ cheek, MH(2), SO; their ~, CR
7 distill,] ~^ MH(2), SO
7 fragrance-breathing flowers,] fragrance breathing ~^ MH(2); fragrance-
   breathing~^ SO
8 which] that MH(2), SO, CR
8 speaks.] speak; MH(2); ~; SO
9 Oh, blessed the Parent, who] ~^~~~^ that MH(2), SO; ~^ bless'd ~~^
   that CR
10 joys, which] joy that MH(2), SO, CR
11 Oh, blessed] ~^~ MH(2), SO; ~^ bless'd CR
13 blessed the Lamb,] ~~ lamb^ MH(2); ~~~^ SO; bless'd ~~^ CR
14 with Him forevermore might reign.] in him forever might remain. MH(2),
   SO

167. Compassion
No variants

664. The Rock
   8 and] & SO
   11 thy] Thy SO
   13 and] & SO

498. To the pure all things are pure
   1 flowers I pass] ~, ~~, VTH
   1 me] ~, E, VTH
   2 spirit's] spirits RPB
   2 voice] ~, E, VTH
   3 see] ~, E, VTH
   4 rejoice] ~. E, VTH
   5 Come brothers] ~, ~, E, VTH
   5 hill] ~, E, VTH
   6 o'er] oer RPB
   6 fields] ~, E, VTH
   7 in] the E, VTH
   7 thy will] the ~; E, VTH
   8 And] Thence E, VTH
   8 yields] ~. E, VTH
   9 thine] ~, E, VTH
   10 Where He] When he E, VTH
   10 thee bid] ~, bids it E, VTH
   10 play] ~, E, VTH
   12 holyday] holiday, E, VTH
   13 plant and bird and insect] ~, ~~, ~~, E, VTH

556. The Acorn
   1 started,] ~,—E
   1 see] ~, E
   2 ground] ~; E

3 o'er] oer RPB
3 flowers its head,] ~, ~~; E
4 beside] Beside RPB
4 frowned] ~, E
5 Behold] ~! E
5 side] ~. E
7 pride] ~. E
8 bread] ~, E
9 heat] ~, E
10 kindreds tongues] ~, ~, E
11 contains] ~, E
13 away] ~; E
14 gave,] ~;—E

178. The Mourner
1 blessed] blest RPB
2 affliction's] afflictions' RPB
10 know'st] knowst RPB
12 death's] deaths' RPB
14 Prince] star RPB

689. Jacob's Well
1 Thou prayst] ~prays't RPB
1 thou prayst;] ~prays't, RPB
2 thyself] ~, RPB
3 sayst,] says't; RPB
8 controul;] control; RPB

816. The Call
1 awake] ~, E
5 awake] ~, E
9 sleepest] sleep'st E
10 vineyard,] ~;—E
10 toil;] ~, E

829. The Prayer
Title: The Prayer] Desires for God's Presence BH, HFS, DHB, HC, BW; God's Pres-
ence PL; Desire for God's Presence HCC; 'Visit Me With Thy Salvation' HS; Visit
Me With Thy Salvation LA; "Visit Me With Thy Salvation." LSA, HTB
1 Thou] thou SG, HFS, PL, DHB, CAL, HC, BW, HTB, HCC
2 thy] Thy HS, LA, LSA, SSLF
3 And every] Each BH, HFS, PL, DHB, HC, BW, HS, LA, LSA, HTB,
HCC, SSLF
3 see,] ~^ HC, HFS, DHB, HC, BW, HS, SSLF
4 thy] Thy HS, LA, LSA, SSLF
4 quickening] *omit* SO, SG, E ['quickening' inserted in Very's hand in a
number of copies of E seen by the editor], WM, CAL
4 drew.] grew. BH
5 Thou] thou SG, HFS, DHB, CAL, HC, BW, HTB, HCC
6 tone;] ~, HFS
8 Lend] Lends SG

8 voice,] ~,—HCC
8 Thee] thee SG, BH, HFS, PL, DHB, HC, BW, HTB, HCC
9 Come,] ~! BH, HFS, PL, DHB, HC, BW, HS, LA, LSA, HCC, SSLF;
  ~; HTB
9 thy] Thy HS, LA, LSA, SSLF
9 love;] ~, SG, E, WM, BH, PL, DHB, CAL, HC, HS, LA, LSA, HTB,
  HCC, SSLF; ~^ HFS; ~. BW
10 flower] ~, LA
10 rain,] ~; SG, E, WM, BH, HFS, PL, DHB, HC, BW, LA, LSA, HCC,
  SSLF; ~^ CAL
11 gently as] like BH, HFS, PL, HC, BW, HS, LA, LSA, HTB, HCC, SSLF;
  gentle ~ CAL
11 thy] Thy HS, LA, LSA, SSLF
11 dove;] ~, BH, HFS, PL, DHB, CAL, HC, BW, HS, LA, LSA, HTB,
  SSLF; Dove, HCC
11 thy] Thy HS, LA, LSA, SSLF
13–16 *omit* BH, HFS, PL, DHB, HC, BW, LA, LSA, HTB, HCC
14 thy . . . wrath;] Thy . . . ~; SSLF; ~ . . . ~, WM
16 thy] their SG; Thy SSLF
17 Yes,] ~! BH, PL, HFS; ~; DHB, HC, BW, HS, LA, LSA; ~: HTB
17 Thou] thou SG, HFS, PL, DHB, HC, BW, HTB, HCC
17 me:] ~; SG, E, WM, BH, HFS, PL, DHB, CAL, HC, BW, HS, HTB,
  HCC
18 thy parent eye delight so well;] thy eye delights ~~, SG, HC; thy eye ~~~, E,
  WM, CAL; thine eye delights ~~, BH, PL, DHB, HFS, BW, HTB, HCC;
  Thine eye delights ~~^ HS, LA, LSA; Thy eye delights ~~, SSLF
19 when from sin set free] ~, ~~~~, BH, HFS, PL, DHB, HC, BW, HS, LA,
  LSA, HTB, HCC, SSLF
20 My spirit loves] Man's spirit comes BH, HFS, PL, DHB, HC, BW, HS,
  LA, LSA, HTB, HCC, SSLF
20 thine] Thine HS, LA, LSA, SSLF

494. My Garden
6 thou'lt] thoul't MH, SO
8 thieves] theves MH
13 lily's] lilie's MH, SO
15 thou'lt] thoul't MH, SO
17 blade;] ~, SO
20 night's] nights MH

730. The Immortal
1 me,] ~^ SO
2 see,] ~; SO
19–24 *omit* SO

322. The Serving-Man
7 service] ~, SO
8 depart.] ~? SO
9 Servant] servant SO
14 past;] ~, SO

15 Thou] ~, SO
16 Wilt] Will SO
16 son] ~, SO

513. The Cottage
    1 left,] ~^ E
    2 Father e'er] parent still E
    2 down;] ~, E
    4 in] with E
    5 not,] ~^ E
    8 withstood;] ~. E
    9 years,] ~^ E
    9 rain,] ~^ E
    10 strength,] ~; E
    10 fell;] ~, E
    11 again,] ~,—E
    13 air,] ~^ E
    14 child;] ~, E
    16 was from all my grief] all my grief their love E
    17 field,] ~^ E
    19 kneeled,] ~^ E
    20 friend,] ~^ E
    20 Father,] friend and E

241. To-Day
Title: To-Day] The Present RPB; Nature's Invitation To The Passer-by MH, CR
    1 present,] Present, MH
    2 past] ~, RPB, MH, CR
    3 leafy] leavy SO
    4 away] ~, MH
    4 hear.] ~, RPB
    5 red] ~, MH
    6 thee] ~, MH
    8 there] here MH, CR
    9 stream] brook MH, CR
    9 thee, heed] ~^ heeds SO
    10 ear,] ~^ RPB
    11 shall] shalt MH

Following stanza 3 this stanza appears in MH (written at end of ms. in different ink
to be inserted here) and CR; the MH version is given first, and CR variations from it
follow:

    The hill, which rises from the grassy plain,   1a
    Invites thy feet its breezy height to scale;
    And view, with it, the blue encircling main,
    And wite-winged ships, which o'er its bosom sail.

1a hill,] ~^ CR
1a plain,] ~^ CR
2a scale;] ~, CR
3a view, with it,] ~^~~^ CR
4a wite-winged ships, which] white-winged ships^ that CR

13 hill, and grove, and flowers,] ~^&~^&~^ RPB
14 live with them,] grow as they RPB; ~~~^ MH, CR
15 awake] ~, MH, CR
16 life to-day] present life RPB
16 and] & RPB

308. The Withered Tree

Title: Withered] Unfruitful CR
    1 stands 'mid] stood midst CR
    2 are overgrown;] were ~, CR
    3 gash] blow CR
    3 has marked,] had ~; CR
    4 fruit] ~, CR
    5–8 *omit* CR
    9 rain] ~, CR
    10 Fell on it,] And dew fell on it; CR
    11 stirs] stirred CR
    12 could bring] brought it CR
    14 drink] draw CR
    17 axe,] ~^ CR
    17 chills,] chilled, CR
    18 blows, in haste it fell,] blows with echoing sound; CR
    19 the place it fills,] its place it filled, CR
    20 *entire line differs:* So long a cumberer of the ground. CR

552. The Old Road

    1 The] "~ SG
    1 left,] ~^ SG
    3 opened] ~, SG
    7 Where . . . grows?] "~ . . . ~^"—SG
    8 still,] ~^ SG
    10 travels, learn] ~; leave SG
    12 thee,] those ^ SG
    12 flow."] ~.^ SG
    13 "Man] ^~ SG
    14 blind] ~, SG
    15 days] ~, SG
    16 Me."] me.^ SG
    17 "Then] ^~ SG
    17 o'er,] ~^ SG
    19 more,] ~^ SG
    20 Me,] me, SG

267. The Plagues of Egypt

    1 land,] ~^ MH
    6 green;] ~^ MH
    13 born,] ~^ MH
    17 call,] ~^ MH
    20 Egypt's] Egypts SO, MH

502. The Frost

3 fingers] finger CE
4 their] its MH, CE
5 maple,] ~^ SO, CE
5 green,] ~^ CE
8 beauteous,] ~^ SO, CE
9 him,] Him, SO, CE

595. Autumn Days
2 late before them] ~, ~~, MH
2 walked] came MH
2 biting] bitting SO
4 twig and limb] the dead limbs MH
4 acrost;] ~. MH
7 And still the] The summer MH
8 grain] ~, MH
8 get;] ~. MH
11 And] But MH
11 smile] glance MH
12 *entire line differs:* Like smiling hope, when all beside is gone; MH
13 deepening] drifting MH

519. Autumn Leaves
4 see'st] seest RPB
5 many dyes] ~ dies SO; colors bright, RPB
6 That] Which RPB
6 eye;] ~, RPB
7 each leaf neglected lies,] such leaf ~~, SO; no longer please the sight, RPB
9–11 Lines differ entirely in RPB:
Yet mourn not for the leaves, of late so fair,
Which hung so gaily o'er the passer's head;
But learn the lesson, which is taught thee there,
13 see] ~, RPB

707. The Lost Sheep
Title: The Lost Sheep] The Shepherd in Distress MH
2 one] ~, MH
3 *entire line differs:* That from the flock has gone astray; MH
4 think'st] thin'kst SG
5 His] ~, MH
6 keep,] ~; MH
Following stanza 2 this additional stanza appears in MH:
Ah, hard the task the one to find,
Which once has left the sheltering fold;
O'er dreary hills and wilds it roves,
Exposed to darkness, storms, and cold.
11 seen] ~, MH
12 point him where his feet should] tell me where for him to MH

337. The Shepherd's Life
2 hills] ~, CR
3 Shepherd's] shepherd's CR

4 would'st] wouldst CR
11 quickly] softly CR
13 know,] ~^ CR
15 bid] bade CR
17 Shepherd's] shepherd's CR
19 sorrow,] ~^ CR
20 to the peace Christ gave him be] be to peace and innocence CR

475. The Barberry Bush
1 which bears] that has SO, Dial, Parnassus
1 briars,] ~^ SO, Dial; briers^ Parnassus
1 fruit,] ~: Parnassus
4 may'st] mays't SO; mayst Parnassus
4 find, e'en there,] ~^~~^ SO, Dial, Parnassus
4 bread.] ~; SO
5 Salem,] ~^ SO, Dial, Parnassus
6 Spring;] spring; Parnassus
7 And] ~, Parnassus
7 down] e'en SO, Dial, Parnassus
8 bunches] branches SO, Dial, Parnassus
10 What] That SO, Dial, Parnassus
11 know, that other fruit,] ~^~~~^ SO, Dial, Parnassus
11 sour,] ~^ Parnassus
12 *Me,* and *You;*] *Me*^~*You;* SO, Dial; *me*^~*you:* Parnassus
13 Yet,] ~^ SO, Parnassus
13 wait] ~, Parnassus
13 Autumn] autumn SO, Dial, Parnassus
13 see,] ~^ Parnassus
14 'Twill] Will SO, Dial, Parnassus

690. The Eye and Ear
9 hear;] hear) SG
13 full-born] full born RPB

210. Thy Better Self
Title: Thy Neighbor SO
1 self,] ~; SO
1 be,] ~^ SO
4 blade,] ~^ SO
4 plough.] ~; SO
5 built,] ~^ SO
8 ready to begin.] waiting ~~; SO
9 thyself,] ~; SO
12 would'st be,] wouldst ~^ SO
12 hast] have SO
14 alone,] ~^ SO

470. The Glutton
2 sums] sum RPB, SG
3 Father's] fathers' RPB; father's SG
5 feed;] ~, RPB, SG

7 drinkest,] ~^ RPB
8 'Tis] Tis RPB
11 fast,] ~^ SG
13 mightst] might'st RPB, SG
14 carrion-bird] carrion bird RPB, SG

784. The Day not for Gain
Title: The Slaveholder RPB, SG
2 then?] ~; RPB, SG
3 day,] ~^ RPB, SG
4 thee,] ~^ RPB, SG
4 been.] ~; RPB, SG
5 hours] ~, SG
6 thoughts,] ~^ RPB; ~; SG
7 not] *omit* RPB, SG
7 will] cannot RPB, SG
8 day, to thee, has] ~^~~^ hast RPB, SG
8 flown.] ~; RPB, SG
11 dusky] slow-paced RPB, SG
14 Day, a slave,] day^ ~~^ RPB, SG

613. The House Not Made With Hands, Eternal In The Heavens
Title: The Holy City SO
4 depart,] ~^ SO
5 gem,] ~^ SO
9 gold the] ~ its SO
10 affliction's] afflictions SO
12 *entire line differs:* For there alone to tread is sure. SO
14 *entire line differs:* That shows its adamantine walls; SO
14 its] the CR
16 Which] That SO
17 dwell,] ~^ CR
19 *entire line differs:* That house is called the House of Prayer, SO
20 There] Where SO

501. The Broken Bowl
2 stream;] ~, MH
4 dream?] ~. SG
5 broke;] ~, MH
7 old,] ~^ MH
8 I] We MH
8 truth like him] ~, ~~, MH
11–12 These lines differ entirely in MH:
For thou must from the fountain fill,
    And drink its heavenly stream, or die.
Stanza 4 *omit* MH
17 Ho] Come MH
17 come,] Come^ MH
19 Come,] Oh, MH
19 prophet's early] Savior's earnest MH
20 *entire line differs:* "Come every one that thirsts to me!" MH

271. Hymn: Home
Title: Hymn: Home] My Home MH(2), SG
    1 home;—] ~^—MH(2), SG
    4 *entire line differs:* And I was taught to call it good. MH(2), SG
    6 turned my feet;] bade me rove; MH(2), SG
    8 defeat.] ~^ MH(1); entire line differs in MH(2) and SG: He whispered of a home above.
    9 wandered;—] ~^—MH(2), SG
    10 me,] ~^ MH(2), SG
    16 broke,] ~^ MH(2), SG
    18 guide,] ~^ SG

284. The Seasons
    1 me] ~, MH(2), SO, CR
    2 seen,] ~; CR
    3 grass,] ~^ MH(2), SO, CR
    7 me,] ~—CR
Following stanza 1 this additional stanza appears in MH(2):
  For oft the chilly winds succeed
    Our pleasant, sunny, days;
  And winter's blustering trumpets drown
    The spring-birds early lays;
  And oft the snows, returning, fill
    Their half-built nests, and bowers;
  And hide from sight the smiling fields,
    And the fair, opening flowers.

5a

CR also includes the above stanza, with the following variations:
    2a sunny,] ~^ CR
    3a trumpets] trumpet's CR
    5a snows, returning,] ~^~^ CR
    6a nests,] ~^ CR
    7a fields,] ~^ CR
    8a fair,] sweet CR

    10 fall] ~. CR
    12 grass] ~, MH(2), CR
    13 stood,] ~^ SO
    15 But] As MH(2), CR
    16 will] must MH(2), SO, CR
    17 Autumn's] autumn's SO
    18 Is come, is] Has ~, has MH(2); Has ~^ has CR
    18 me,] ~; MH(2), SO, CR
    19 hangs] hang MH(2); CR; hang, SO
    21 that's owned of Spring,] ~~~ spring, SO; that decks the spring, MH(2), CR
    22 shall] may MH(2), CR
    23 shake] ~, MH(2), CR
    24 stalk] ~, MH(2)
    25 Then] Nor MH(2), SO, CR
    25 Winter's near,] ~ here, MH(2); winter's here, CR
    26 *entire line differs:* Though white with frost the ground; MH(2), CR

27 deep the] the deep MH(2), SO, CR
28 fields] ~, MH(2)
28 trees around;] hillocks round; MH(2), CR; hills around; SO
29 brook] ~, MH(2), SO
30 grove] ~, CR

614. The Silent
Title: Man's Sympathy with Nature MH, CR
    2 wave,] ~; MH
    3 understood] ~, MH
    4 tell in words] ~, ~~, MH
    5 it feels] we feel MH, CR
    5 tone,] ~^ CR
    7 *entire line differs:* Or listening through the night alone, MH, SG
    8 'Twould sound as does] As inland swells MH, CR
    9 wind swept] wind-swept MH, CR
    9 pine,] ~^ CR
    10 swell;] ~, CR
    11 sounds] ~, MH
    11 define,] ~; CR
    12 words] ~, MH, CR
    13 'Tis all unheard;] Thou hear'st in these MH; Thou hearest, man, CR
    13 Silent] Mighty MH, CR
    15 Bids bending reed] Bid sounding wood, MH; Bid sounding wood CR
    15 bird] wave MH, CR
    16 fills] fill MH, CR
    16 nature's] Nature's MH
    17 And] ~, MH
    17 speechless] speachless MH
    17 heart] ~, MH
    18 trod;] ~, MH, CR
    20 God.] ~! MH

737. The Way
    1 ask'st] askst RPB
    5 turn'st] turnst RPB
    8 seek'st] seekst, RPB
    9 *entire line differs:* Thou trackest one and all, yet findst it not; RPB

803. The Sun
    3 begin anew] anew begin RPB
    14 Shall] Shalt RPB

610. The Builders
    3 hope the brick,] ~, ~~^ SG
    3 long,] ~^ SG
    4 them,] ~^ SG
    6 firm] rough SG
    7 nest] ~, SG
    8 tempests] tempest, SG
  9–12 *omit* SG

15 passed, where] ~^ when SG
17 Time] years SG
23 fled,] ~^ SG
24 refuge,] ~^ SG

283. Give and it shall be given unto you.: Spiritual Debtors
Title: The Measure of Wheat MH(J), SG
    1 grieving,] ~^ MH(J)
    2 earth] Earth MH(J)
    3 voice,] ~^ MH(J), SG
    4 low:] ~. MH(J)
    13 They,] Thy MH(J)
    13 thee,] ~! MH(J), SG
    16 Grieve my child, then] ~, ~~. Then MH(J)

102. The Strangers
    2 sold;] ~, MH(E)
    3 men have] mankind MH(E)
    4 and spoke] &~ MH(E); ~ spake CR
    6 meet;] ~^ MH(E)
    7 though] tho' MH(E)
    7 way,] ~^ MH(E)
    8 'Tis] Tis MH(E)
    9 ear,] ~^ MH(E); ~; Parnassus, CR
    14 upon;] ~, MH(E)
    15 few,] ~^ MH(E), CR
    16 each act] ~~, MH(E)

259. The Light from Within
    2 my eye;] ~~^ BH, HS, HTB; ~~, HCC; mine ~^ SSLF
    3 forth] ~, BH, HS, HTB, HCC, SSLF
    3 my] the HS, HTB, SSLF
    5 shone still] still shone BH, HS, HTB, HCC, SSLF
    6 When] ~, HTB, SSLF
    6 farthest west] distant ~ BH, HS, HCC; distant ~, HTB, SSLF
    8 Forever] For ever BH, HTB, HCC
    9 walked] ~, BH, HS, HTB, HCC, SSLF
    9 night] ~, SO, BH, HS, HTB, HCC, SSLF
    10 day,] ~; SO, BH, HS, HTB, HCC, SSLF
    11 who by] to whom BH, HS, HTB, HCC, SSLF
    11 surer] shurer MB
    12 pointed] pointing BH, HS, HTB, HCC, SSLF
    13 noon-day's] noonday's BH, HS, HTB, HCC, SSLF
    13 beam,] ~; HTB
    14 within;] ~, SSLF
    15 lit] ~, BH, HS, HTB, HCC, SSLF
    15 heaven] ~, BH, HS, HTB, HCC, SSLF

561. A Word
Title: The History of a Word MH-Ar, MH(1)
    1 word,] Word, MH(1)

2 stream] tide RPB

2 along,] ~; MH(1)

3 sung] ~, MH-Ar, MH(1), RPB

3 heard,] ~; CR, SG

5 from] ~ out SG

5 soul's calm deep,] deep soul of man CR; deep soul of man, MH-Ar,
MH(1); ~~~^ RPB

6 the chastening] affliction's CR, MH-Ar; Affliction's MH(1), RPB

6 rod;] ~, CR, MH-Ar

7 *entire line differs:* And through the world its course began, CR; And angel
like its course began, MH-Ar, MH(1); As Eve flesh formed from Adam's
sleep SG

8 Touched by the hand] A messenger CR, MH-Ar, MH(1); *revised line
illegible* RPB

9 wandered] journied MH-Ar, MH(1)

9 o'er] through MH(1)

9 earth,] ~^ MH-Ar

10 war] ~, RPB

10 worn,] ~; RPB, SG

11 seen,] ~^ RPB, CR

11 birth;] ~, RPB, SG

12 Though] Through SG

14 hall;] ~, CR, MH-Ar

15 arms and strife] strife and arms CR, MH-Ar, MH(1); strife and woes RPB

15 forgot,] ~^ RPB, CR

17 peace] Peace MH-Ar

17 fail,] ~—SG

18 love] Love MH-Ar

19 mail,] ~; SG

21 took,] ~; SG

22 old] ~, CR, MH-Ar, MH(1), RPB, SG

23 to book;] ~~, CR, MH-Ar, MH(1), RPB, SG

24 as] like SG

24 gold.] ~; CR, MH(1)

25 furrow] ~, MH(1)

25 earth's] Time's CR, MH-Ar, RPB; Times MH(1)

25 field,] soil, CR, MH(1), RPB; soil^ MH-Ar; fields^ SG

26 deep,] ~^ MH-Ar, SG

26 sown] down SG

27 none] few MH(1), RPB

27 notice what it yields,] heed the Sower's toil, CR, MH(1), RPB; heed the
Sowers toil^ MH-Ar

28 its] the CR, MH-Ar, MH(1), RPB

28 harvest] Harvest MH-Ar, RPB

263. The Dwellings of the Just

3 night,] ~. WM

4 *omit* WM

5 upright] ~, WM

6 true] sure WM

465. The Birth-Day of the Soul

Title: Birth-Day] Birthday, MRM, MH(2); The Birth-Day [entire title] WM
      1 birth-day] birthday MH(2), MRM
      1 Soul] soul, MH(2), WM, MRM
      2 for all it] it ever WM
      4 sea] ~, MRM
      5 tribes] ~, MH(2), WM
      5 thick-swarming] thick swarming, MH(2), WM; thick swarming MRM
      6 born] come, WM
      6 grove,] ~; MH(2), WM, MRM
      7 song] ~, MH(2); hush, WM
      8 by gladsome] in song by WM
      8 rove.] ~; MH(2), WM, MRM
      9 all;—] ~;^ WM
      9 song] notes MH(2), MRM
     10 Bears witness also] Bear ~, ~, MH(2), MRM; Bear nobler witness WM
     11 please;] ~, MH(2), WM, MRM
     12 song] hymn WM
     12 sense,] ~^ WM
   13–14 Lines differ entirely in WM:
A strain too low for earth's loud tongue to raise,
The voice unheard of God's eternal praise.
     14 When from its wanderings] ~, ~~~, MH(2), MRM

511. The Bee Hive

Title: The Beehive WM
      2 sides;] ~, WM
      3 a] the WM
      4 she called Industry] ~, ~~, WM
      5 fly] ~, WM
      6 journeys] journies MH
      7 nigh] ~, WM
      9 crag or dell] ~, in ~, WM
     10 sweets,] ~; WM
     13 on] on the WM
     14 walks] plots WM
     15 humblest] smallest WM
     17 haste] ~, WM
     18 will,] ~; WM
     19 waste] ~, WM

480. Faith and Light

Title: Faith and Sight CR
      2 Light;] Sight^ CR
      8 old!] ~. CR
     11 storm-lashed waves,] storm-tost wave, CR
     12 lull;] ~, CR
     17 nought] naught CR
     17 hymn,] ~^ CR

661. The Absent

Alternate lines are indented in WM.
          3 hole] ~,WM
          8 stars'] stars MH

748. The Pilgrim
          1 winter] ~,WM, MH
          2 traveller's] traveler's WM
          3 saw] met WM, MH, CR
          3 on] ~,WM
          3 grey] ~,WM, MH, CR
          4 wrath;] ~. MH
          5 in] ~,WM, MH
          6 sit] set WM, MH, CR
          6 board,] ~; WM, MH
          7 Yet] But MH, CR
          7 begin] ~,WM, MH, CR
          8 restored;] ~. MH
          9 wondering] ~,WM, MH
          9 him,] ~^ CR
          9 not] ~,WM
          10 they had] which was MH, CR
          10 given;] ~, MH, CR
          11 forgot?] ~; MH, CR
          12 said;] ~,WM, MH, CR
          12 heaven;—] Heaven;^ WM
          14 offered] ~, MH

239. The Idler
Title: The Idler] Waiting The Divine Will Cl
          4 in] on Cl
          6 find,] ~; Cl
          7 his] His Cl
          8 designed.] ~; Cl
          9 wait] ~, Cl
          14 down] ~, Cl
          14 thy] Thy Cl

495. The Lost
          1 shone,] ~^ Cl
          4 be.] ~; Cl
          5 among] amidst Cl
          7 enjoys,] ~; Cl
          8 stem.] ~; Cl
          9 tree,] ~^ Cl

807. The Narrow Way
          1 know'st it] knowest Cl
          2 neighbor] ~, Cl
          4 Him] him Cl
          5 be,] ~^ Cl
          5 known;] ~, Cl

6 go'st,] ~^ Cl
7 the world thenceforth] thenceforth the world Cl
8 Broadening] And broader wear Cl
8 worn before?] wore? Cl
9 may'st] mayst Cl
9 me,] Me, Cl

531. The True Light
No variants

433. The Invitation
Title: Nature Pleads with the Traveller Cl
1 further] farther Cl
3 me] thee Cl
4 greet.] ~; Cl
5 on;—] ~? Cl
7 would'st] would Cl
9 here, as there,] ~^~~^ Cl
10 eve:] ~; Cl
12 weave;] ~, Cl
13 And many a pilgrim,] So weary pilgrims^ Cl
13 thou,] ~^ Cl
14 shade,] ~^ Cl

351. The Baker's Island Light
2 Light] Lights SG 1871
4 Rays] ~, SG 1871
4 light] pierce SG 1871
4 night.] nights. SG 1871
6 'Scaped] Scaped MH(1)
9 it shines,] they shine, SG 1871
11 the east with golden lines] the horizon's crimson line SG 1871
12 Marks] Tells SG 1871
13–16 Entire stanza differs in SG 1871:
Through the morning's dusky air
   Darts the sun's o'erpowering beams,
And the sailor's city fair
   In the golden radiance gleams!
14 near,] ~; SG 1840

553. The Robin's Song
4 by-gone] past-by SG
5 there;] ~, SG
5 mate;] ~, SG, CR
6 young';] ~', SG; ~;' CR
7 morn,] ~^ SG, CR
8 sung;—] ~. SG; ~;^ CR
10 year's] years MH
10 hold;] ~,' SG
13 twigs,] ~^ SG
13 grove,] ~; CR

17 soft, soft leaves,] ~^~~^ SG
17 line, within,] ~^~^ SG, CR
18 tender,] ~^ SG
19 love!] ~, SG, CR
19 begin,] ~^ SG
21 song,] ~^ SG
22 tree;] ~, SG
23 new-built, large] ~^ high SG
24 harm,] ~^ SG, CR

49. The Wounded Pigeon
Title: The Dove that Perished in the Snow Storm CR
1 yesternight] ~, CR
2 gale,] ~; CR
3 snow] rain SG; cold, CR
4 with] to SG
4 loud] ~, CR
4 wail!] ~; SG
6 lofty] leafy SG
6 low;] ~, SG
7 And,] ~^ SG
7 woof,] ~^ SG
8 To drive] Driving SG
9 Thee] ~, CR
12 Against our] 'Gainst our sharp SG
13 door man enters oft] ~, ~~~, SG
14 distress,] ~; CR
15 *entire line differs:* Nor rose the window by thee soft SG; Nor rose the window by thee soft, CR
16 *entire line differs:* With hands outstretched to save and bless; SG; With hands outstretched to save and bless. CR
16 to] and MH
17–20 *omit* CR
17 so,] ~^ SG
20 bark.] ~! SG
22 bill;] ~, CR
23 pangs,] ~^ SG; ~; CR
23 glowed,] ~^ SG
25–28 *omit* CR
26 place;] ~, SG
29 our] the SG
30 call,] ~; CR
31 we] they SG
31 keep] ~, CR
32 When, without aid, the weak must] When Innocence for aid must SG; When helpless Innocence may CR
33 heed] ~, CR
34 sufferer] mourner SG
34 door,] ~; CR

35 to] too SG
35 succour] succor CR

723. The World
Title: The World] How Long MH, CR
    1 show,] ~—HBP
    2 in,] ~; MH, HBP
    3 tell] ~, MH
    7 children] ~, MH
    8 picture-hung] picture hung CR
    10 sky,] ~—HBP
    11 wood-land,] woodland, CR, HBP
    13 too many] ~~, MH, CR
    14 eye] ~, MH, CR
    15 see,] ~^ CR
    17 weight as of slumber] ~, ~~~, MH
    18 mind,] ~; MH, HBP
    19 Life's train] ~~, MH; life's ~ CR, HBP
    20 its] it's CR
    21 one] ~, MH
    22 show,] ~—HBP
    23 walk] ~, Dial, MH, CR, HBP
    26 say] ~, MH
    26 'How long?'] "~~?" CR, HBP
    30 plain,] ~,—Dial, HBP
    32 shadow] shadows MH, CR
    32 remain!] ~? Dial, HBP
    33 long and] ~ ere Dial, HBP; ~, ere MH
    33 shine] ~, MH, HBP
    34 things] ~, MH
    35 Light] light CR; Light, MH, HBP
    35 prophet] prophets CR
    36 sings;] ~? HBP
    39 west] ~, MH
    40 Its] In its MH, CR
    40 run!] ~? CR

668–697. The Cold Spring In North Salem
Title: The Cold Spring [entire title] MH(OP); To The Cold Spring / In North Salem
MH-Ar; The Cold Spring* SG; The Cold Spring at the foot Of Liberty Hill, in
North Salem MH(2), CR
    1 small,] still MH(OP); still, SG; clear, MH(2), CR
    1 spring] ~, Pioneer, SG; Spring, MH(2), CR
    2 low hillocks round,] the rising ground, MH(2), CR
    3 oaks whose stretching branches] trees of varied leaf that MH(OP); trees of
       varied length that SG; triple oak, whose branches MH(2), CR
    4 on the ground;] all around; MH(2), SG
    5 upon] beside MH(OP), SG
    6 taste] drink MH(OP)

6 sweet,] ~; MH(OP), MH(2)

7 weary] ~, CR

9 thy] their MH(OP)

11 with them this fount] from thee each thing MH(OP), SG; ~~~ Fount CR

11 share] ~, SG, MH(2), CR

12 As the] The MH(OP), SG

14 still] ~, MH(OP), SG, MH(2), CR

14 flow;] ~, Pioneer

15 one] ~, CR

15 bliss] ~, CR

16 with] like MH(OP), SG

Stanzas 5 and 6 omitted in MH(OP), SG; the following stanza appears in MH(OP):

Farewell! the pilgrim sings to thee   1a
    Who stoops at thy waters clear,
That they who journey by may see
    And drink of a spring so dear.

Variants in SG from MH(OP) in above stanza:

1a to thee] of ~, SG

2a clear,] ~; SG

3a see] ~, SG

17 Sea,] sea^ MH-Ar, CR; sea, Pioneer, MH(2)

17 near] ~, MH(2)

18 tide,] ~^ MH-Ar; ~; MH(2)

19 clear] ~, MH-Ar, MH(2), CR

21 if perchance] ~, ~, MH(2), CR

22 swell,] ~; MH(2)

23 save] ~, MH-Ar, Pioneer, MH(2), CR

Footnote: *In Northfield. SG

617. God's Host

2 Holy Angels] holy angels MH(2), CE

4 dwells within a calm] ~, ~, ~ peace MH(2)

5 you] ~, MH(2)

5 street] ~, MH(2), CE

6 your shining dress,] thy ~~; MH(2)

7 robes] ~, MH(2)

7 greet] ~, MH(2), CE

8 like] as MH(2)

8 possess:] ~; MH(2), CE

9 thou] ~, MH(2), CE

9 like Jacob] as ~, MH(2)

9 heap] ~, MH(2)

10 journeyed] journied MH(1), MH(2), CE

10 Seir,] ~; MH(2)

12 God] ~, MH(2)

12 Fear;] ~, CE

13 Wouldst] Woulds MH(2)

13 aloud] ~, MH(2), CE

14 House] house MH(2), CE

14 God!] ~, MH(2)

547. The White Dove And The Snow
Title: White] *omit* CR
    1 quickly melting] quickly-melting CR
    2 street,] ~^ CR
    2 treads] ~, CR
    3 things,] ~^ CR
    6 Gazing,] ~^ CR
    9 His] his CR
    11 *entire line differs:* The wells that God has opened on our path, CR
    13 toil,] ~; CR
    14 loud, turbid] ~^ foaming CR

182. Moses In Infancy
Title: Scriptural Sonnet. / Moses. CR
    1 basket,] ~^ CR
    2 Moses,] ~^ CR
    2 side;] ~, CR
    3 her,] ~^ CR
    6 mother,] ~^ CR
    6 fear,] ~^ CR
    8 unbar,] ~^ CR
    9 *entire line differs:* To show the forms that sleep within the grave, CR
    10 far;—] ~: CR
    13 thine,] ~^ CR
    14 Memory,] ~^ CR

750. Moses at the Bush
Title: Scriptural Sonnet.—No. 2. / Moses. CR
    1 burning,] ~^ CR
    3 Jacob,] ~^ CR
    4 Spake, in the wild,] ~^~^~~^ CR
    9 palaces,] ~^ CR
    13 homes,] ~^ CR

749. Moses As Leader Of Israel
Title: Scriptural Sonnet.—No. 3. / Moses. CR
    1 man,] ~^ CR
    2 rest;] ~, CR
    3 wisdom,] ~^ CR
    7 not, by these, ~^~~^ CR
    9 'If . . . us,'] "~ . . . ~," CR
    10 'let] "~ CR
    11 Thou, before, did'st] ~^~^ didst CR
    13 Thou] thou CR
    14 Thee.'] ~." CR

609. The New Jerusalem
    1 are,] ~^ CR
    2 sky;] ~, CR

3 seen,] ~^ CR
5 there,] ~^ CR
7 here,] ~^ CR

33. The Death of Man
    1 wide] Wide CR 1846, CR 1850
    1 plain,] ~^ CR 1846, CR 1850
    2 eye;] ~, CR 1850
    4 grass, so green of late,] ~^~~~^ CR 1850
    5 though,] ~^ CR 1846, CR 1850
    7 Man's;] ~, CR 1850
    7 whom, in soul,] ~^~~^ CR 1846, CR 1850
    8 now, unnoticed,] ~^~^ CR 1846, CR 1850
    11 He] he CR 1846, CR 1850
    12 gorgeous] far-seen CR 1846
    12 wondering] wond'ring CR 1846
    12 eye;] ~, CR 1846, 1850

126a. God Not Afar Off
Alternate lines are indented in LSA and STC.
Title: God Not Afar Off] Heaven ~~~ HS, LSA, HTB; *entire title differs:* The Present
Heaven STC; *entire title differs:* The Spirit-Land SSLF
    1 Father! Thy] ~! thy PL, DHB, STC; ~, thy HTB
    2 strayed;] stray'd; LSA
    4 Thine] thine PL, DHB, HTB, STC, SSLF
    4 displayed.] display'd. LSA
  5–8 *omit* PL
    5 Thee] thee DHB, HTB, STC, SSLF
    5 found!] ~; HS, HTB, STC, SSLF
    6 Thee] thee DHB, HTB, STC, SSLF
    6 beside!] ~; HS, HTB, STC, SSLF
    9 see!] ~, STC, HTB
    10 ears] ~, STC
    10 Thy] thy PL, DHB, HTB, STC, SSLF
    10 hear!] ~; DHB; ~, STC, HTB
    12 Thy] thy PL, DHB, HTB, STC, SSLF
    12 us] ~, STC
    12 near;] ~. PL, HS, LSA, HTB, STC, SSLF
  13–16 *omit* PL, HS, LSA, HTB, STC, SSLF
    15 But] ~, DHB, SSLF
    16 Thy] thy DHB, SSLF

593. The Indian's Retort
Title: Retort] Lands CR
    1 soul,] ~^ SG
    1 gain,] ~! CR
    5 went,] ~^ CR, SG
    6 canoe;] ~^ CR; ~, SG
    8 White] white CR
  9–12 *omit* CR

10 a hot,] the ~^ SG
11 bring,] ~^ SG
12 back,] ~^ SG
14 Where] where SG
16 behind.] ~: SG
21 "Thou steal'st!" "Thou . . . thief!"] '~~!' '~ . . . ~!' CR; ^~~!^ ^~ . . . !^ SG
21 cried;—] ~: CR; ~;^ SG
23 *entire line differs:* And calm replied, while turning round CR
23 answered;] ~, SG
24 To meet] He met CR
25 "God] '~ CR
25 his sons,] ~~^ CR; His ~, SG
26 Indians,] ~^ CR
27 thief,] ~! CR
28 I speak] He speaks CR
28 truth,] ~^ SG
28 know."] ~.' CR, SG
29 White] white CR
32 steals, his] ~! His SG
32 name!"] ~!' CR; ~.^ SG

8. The Widow
1 Temple's] temple's CE
5 there, alone,] ~^~^ CE
6 Book, which] book that CE
6 all;] ~, CE
7 And, on her knees, . . . throne,] ~^~~~^ . . . ~^ CE
8 light, and strength, . . . need,] ~^~~^ . . . ~^ CE
10 vain;] ~;—CE
11 denied,] ~; CE
12 She, through thy Son,] ~^~~~^ CE
12 gain;] ~! CE
13 left by crowds,] crowds forsake, CE
13 near,] ~; CE

667. Impatience
1 wind, and snow, and sleet, and ice;] ~^~~^~~^~~, CR 1847
2 Spring,] ~^ CR 1847
3 see'st] seest CR 1869
5 hopes,] ~? CR 1869
6 ask?] ~. CR 1869
6 would] Would CR 1847
7 fail,] ~^ CR 1869
7 wind, and snow,] ~^~~^ CR 1847
9 powers,] ~^ CR 1869
10 else, with fatal haste,] ~^~~~^ CR 1847
10 grain,] ~^ CR 1869
12 O'ertook] O'ertaken CR 1869
12 frosts,] ~^ CR 1847, CR 1869
12 blasts,] ~^ CR 1847

15 ways,] ~; CR 1869
16 ordered, everywhere,] ~^~^ CR 1847, CR 1869
17 *thou*] *no italics* CR 1869
18–19 *omit* CR 1847

477. Abdolonymus—The Sidonian
 1 arms, which] ~^ that CR
 5 naught,] nought^ CR
 7 he, in old age, . . . died;] ~^~~~^ . . . ~, CR
 9 many,] ~^ CR
 10 princes, seeking kingly sway;] ~^~~~, CR
 11 Who, trained in arms,] ~^~~~^ CR
 11 War's proud school,] war's ~~^ CR
 12 and] or CR
 14 lived,] ~^ CR

203. The Soul's Preparation For Adversity
 1 tree] ~, CR
 5 So,] ~^ CR
 6 death;] ~, CR
 8 breath,] ~^ CR
 12 strength;] ~^ CR

156. Change In The Seasons
 2 That, in this northern clime,] ~^~~~~^ CR, SG
 4 mid December,] ~~^ CR; mid-December^ SG
 6 Full blown,] Full-blown^ CR, SG
 15 countries, . . . snow,] ~^ . . . ~^ CR, SG
 18 once thought] declare CR
 19 *entire line differs:* Approaches by degrees the ecliptic's; CR
 21 come.] [Remainder of line and lines 22 through 'Flowers.' of line 28 omit-
  ted.] CR
 21–22 Lines differ entirely in SG:
Would come. Geology has proved that earth
Hath witnessed changes as great. That tropic
 23 Plants,] ~^ SG
 23 here] *omit* SG
 26 pasturage] pasture SG
 29 vegetation] vegitation MH
 31 exchanged;] ~, CR
 37 year;] ~, CR
 39 earth, from month to month,] ~^~~~~^ CR, SG
 45 herself,] ~^ CR, SG
 48 hastens] hasten CR
 50 Spring] spring CR, SG

517. The Just Shall Live by Faith
 1 'The . . . faith'] "~ . . . ~" CR
 5 'The . . . faith,'] "~ . . . ~," CR
 6 earth;] ~, CR
 8 birth.] ~; CR

9 'The . . . faith'] "~ . . . ~" CR
13 it,] ~^ CR
14 long,] ~^ CR
14 ways!] ~. CR

72. Salem
2 Freedom's] freedom's CR
3 glory] ~, MH
8 warriors . . . done.] ~, . . . ~; MH
11 Justice's calls;] Justice' ~; NN; ~~, MH, CR
12 when in coming ages] ~, ~~~, MH
13 war and every blood-stained field,] ~, ~~~~; MH
Footnote: Boston being a closed port.] *omit* MH

469-573. Spring in the Soul
Title: Spring [entire title] CR
1 bough which] stem that CR
1 winter's] stormy CR
3 its cold and stormy months are] the winter's chilling breath is CR
4 The springing leaves] Its ~~, CR
4 show.] ~; CR
5 breath] wind CR
6 name;] ~, CR
8 And, . . . bear,] ~^ . . . ~^ CR
8 proclaim.] ~; CR
10 Who, with the seasons,] ~^~~~^ CR
12 fear;] ~! CR

166. Christ's Compassion
2 load;] ~, CR
5 burthens,] ~^ CR
8 arise!] ~: CR
9 Spirit] spirit CR
10 he, by works divine,] He^ ~~~^ CR

29. Hymn: Nevertheless, when the Son of Man cometh, shall he find faith on the
earth? Luke XVIII:8.
1 now,] ~^ CR
5 dead,] ~^ CR
6 seen;] ~, CR
8 more,] ~^ CR
11 fill,] ~; CR
21 appear,] ~^ CR
22 Coming see;] coming ~, CR
23 Coming] coming CR
24 And, in thy likeness,] ~^~~~^ CR

12. The Man of Science
1 man, . . . wise,] ~^ . . . ~^ CR
2 around;] ~, CR
7 naught,] nought, CR
8 sang!] ~. CR

9–12 *omit* CR
15 look without affright,] ~, ~ afright, CR
16 dread;—] ~. CR
17 musing,] ~^ CR
18 naught again;] nought ~, CR
19 *entire line differs:* And suns, and stars, and systems flee; CR
23 And] ~, CR
24 spoke.] ~; CR
25 thou,] ~^ CR
25 made?"] ~?' CR
26 "Where] '~ CR
26 be,] ~^ CR
27 afraid,] ~; CR
30 *entire line differs:* Unbidden through his troubled breast, CR
32 his] her CR
32 suppressed.] supprest. CR
35 he, in abstruse studies dreamed;] ~^~~~~, CR
37 sympathized] sympathised CR
38 decay;] ~, CR
39 Beheld far back] Looked back beyond CR
42 flower;] ~, CR
43 scarcely] scarely MH(1)
48 Science'] science' CR

141. The Congress Of Peace At Brussels
1 alarms,] ~^ CR
2 peace;] ~, CR
9 stream;] ~, CR
13 sword,] ~^ CR
15 fights,] ~^ CR
16 achieved,] acheived, CR
18 dwell, in peace,] ~^~~^ CR
18 earth;] ~, CR
19 others'] others MH
26 age,] ~^ CR
28 time!] ~. CR
32 wrongs,] ~^ CR
32 brother man] brother-man CR
44 rest!] ~. CR

720. 'Tis A Great Thing to Live
2 below;] ~, CR
4 light,] ~^ CR
8 Which] That CR
12 may, here,] ~^~^ CR
13 above,] ~^ CR

515. The Indian's Petition
Title: The Indian Calls CR
1 rest,] ~^ CR
2 wrong,] ~^ CR

8 display.] ~: CR
9 dream,] ~^ CR
10 heaven;] ~, CR
13 His love,] his ~^ CR

13. The Struggle
2 struggle,] ~^ CR
3 one,] ~^ CR
4 joys!] ~. CR
5 here,] ~^ CR
6 prize, which] ~^ that CR
7 they,] ~^ CR
8 life;—] ~;^ CR
13 Which] That CR
14 claims, as hers,] ~^~~^ CR

292. The Things Before
Poem is divided into two four-line and one six-line stanzas in CR.
2 path,] ~^ CR
5 sought,] ~; CR
10 mind;] ~! CR
12 soul, that slumbers here,] ~^~~~^ CR
13 Objects, which, . . . itself, endure;] ~^~^ . . . ~^~, CR
14 true, and lovely, just,] ~^~~, ~^ CR

727. The Dying Leaf
10 Which] That CR
11 And, to its being,] ~^~~~^ CR
12 bestowed.] ~: CR
13 thing!] ~; CR
15 Which] That CR
16 wave:] ~. CR
19 which] that CR

148. The New Body
5 feeble] lowly CR
6 Which] That CR
10 his realms above;] His ~~, CR
13 dead!] ~,—CR
15 But,] ~^ CR
17–20 *omit* CR
21 God's various power, which] His ~~^ that CR
22 seed;] ~, CR
26 Which now thou see'st] That ~~ seest CR
28 Which] That CR

565. The Clock
2 hours] ~, CR
6 rest;] ~, CR
11 past,] ~^ CR

176. On The Sudden Snow

2 white,] ~^ CR
3 flung!] ~; CR
4 bush, and tree,] ~^~~^ CR
20 And, . . . green,] ~^ . . . ~^ CR
21 surprise!] ~; CR
24 Good,] ~^ CR

129. On the late Disgraceful Scene in Congress
1 That] ~, CR
2 race;] ~, CR
9 few, and full of grace,] ~^~~~~; CR
10 loud, . . . tone;] ~^ . . . ~, CR
11 place,] ~; CR
13 tumult,] ~^ CR

268. The Funerals
2 Where,] ~^ CR, SG
2 grove,] ~^ CR
5 Winter's snows, and Summer's] winter's ~^~ summer's CR
9 there,] ~^ CR, SG
15 child,] ~; CR
15 wife;] ~, SG
16 early lost,] early-lost; CR
Following line 16 this stanza appears in CR:
  What though no great nor glorious deed
    Has left their names in History's page;
  Of which posterity may read,
    And hand it down from age to age?
21 deeds,] ~^ CR, SG
22 care;] cares; CR
24 share.] shares. CR
26 theirs, . . . swell;] ~^ . . . ~, CR
27 the] a SG
29 *Grove, whose name] ^grove^ ~~* CR
33 turn,] ~^ CR
35 wreath] wreathe CR
37 There,] ~^ CR
37 grief, she views,] ~^~~, CR; ~, ~~^ SG
38 (The vail withdrawn,)] ^~ veil ~,^ CR; (~ veil ~^) SG
39 And, quickened by the sight,] ~^ strengthened ~~~^ CR
40 joyful hope] quickened step CR

657. The New Aqueduct
3 years;] ~, SG
6 *no indention* SG
6 we throw them useless] so now we throw them SG
10 Abundantly,] ~^ SG
17 again,] ~^ SG
19 deeds,] ~^ SG
20 hide;] ~, SG
23 shine,] ~^ SG

25 kings] Kings SG
26 fame,] ~^ SG
27 these;] ~, SG
29 tell,] ~^ SG
32 homes,] ~^ SG

504. The Soul's Freedom
    1 wills,] will; CR; will, MRM 1867
    2 *entire line differs:* Beside the cottage door, CR
    3 *entire line differs:* And on the high head of the hill, CR
    3 and on the] on lofty MRM 1866, MRM 1867
    4 Which look the valleys] That looks the valley CR; That ~~~ MRM 1866,
       MRM 1867
    5 flows,] ~; CR
    6 directs,] ~^ CR, MRM 1867
    8 Forever] For ever MRM 1866
    9 wind, which] ~^ that CR, MRM 1866, MRM 1867
    10 bound;] ~: MRM 1866
    13 mark with narrow walls] ~, ~~~, CR, MRM 1866, MRM 1867
    14 scope;] ~: MRM 1866
    16 bounded is] is it barred CR
    17 Then fetter not with] Nor ~ thou ~ CR; ~~~ by MRM 1866, MRM 1867
    17 creed,] ~—MRM 1866
    18 hour,] ~—MRM 1866
    19 mind; which] ~^ that CR, MRM 1866, MRM 1867
    19 Word] word CR
    22 controul;] control; MRM 1866, MRM 1867
    23 bounds,] ~^ CR, MRM 1866

195. Looking Before And After
    2 purpose,] ~^ CR
    6 deed, when finished,] ~^~~^ CR
    8 complete;] ~^ CR
    9 work,] ~^ CR
    10 sight;] ~, CR
    12 But] And CR
    12 light!] ~; CR
    13 Say,] ~^ CR

212. The Succory
    1 name,] ~^ CR
    2 book*;] ~^; CR
    3 would'st] wouldst CR
    4 Flower!] ~, CR
After line 4 the following additional stanza appears in CR:
  Though thou by Learning's lofty seat
    Art scattered far and wide,
  I will not now the name repeat
    She gives thee in her pride.
    5 then of yon playful] that playful, little CR
    6 there;] ~, CR

7 thee,] ~^ CR
9 prattling tongue] infant words CR
10 tone,] ~^ CR
14 flower;] ~, CR
17 wake] ~, CR
18 smile,] ~^ CR
22 heart;] ~, CR
Footnote: *omit* CR

185. The Reapers Are The Angels
Title: The Reapers [entire title] CR
4 toil,] ~^ CR
5 Ah,] ~! CR
5 price] cost CR
6 seed field] seed-field CR
7 He,] ~^ CR
7 seed,] Word^ CR
10 Who, from the tares,] ~^~~~^ CR
10 wheat;] ~, CR
11 And,] ~^ CR
11 heavens,] heaven^ CR

427. The Sumach Leaves
17 boast,] ~^ CR
18 art;] ~, CR
22 Sumach's] sumach's CR

101. The Just
1 square,] ~; CR
4 Kingdom, more] ~^ mere CR
5 thee, with its earliest beam,] ~^ in ~~~^ CR
7 And,] ~^ CR
9 mayst] may'st CR
10 rise;] ~, CR
11 And,] ~^ CR

854. The Fugitive Slaves
1 who] that CR
2 laws,] ~^ SG, CR
3 your] you SG, CR
8 stone.] ~: SG; ~; CR
11 Where, in a freer land,] ~^~~~~^ SG, CR
13 Till] 'Till SG
14 wrath,] ~^ SG

67. The Lost Sheep: Suggested by an Engraving
3 thorns] ~, CR
5 shepherd,] ~^ CR
6 glade;] dale; CR
7 wander, parched and hungry,] ~^~~~^ CR
9 he, . . . searched,] ~^ . . . ~^ CR
15 nor] or CR

16 suffering,] ~^ CR
17 careth] cometh CR
17 lost] ~, CR
21 it, in his arms,] ~^~~~^ CR
25 Then,] ~^ CR
26 own] ~, CR

188. Thoughts and Desires
1 How,] ~^ CR
2 desires] ~, CR
3 controul,] control? CR
4 earth;] ~, CR
7 controul] control CR
10 Him,] ~^ CR
12 desires] ~, CR
16 purpose,] ~^ CR
19 Peace and Power] peace, and power CR
20 will] shall CR
21 give us strength] teach us how CR
24 unto] all to CR

407. The Soul's Rest
3 on] ~, CR
3 bourne,] ~; CR
4 Christ, the King of your Salvation,] ~^~ king ~~ salvation^ CR
10 star, or burning sun;] ~^~~~! CR
11 Rejoice!] ~, CR
12 God begun:] Good ~; CR
14 saints,] ~^ CR

564. The Sliding Rock
Headnote preceded by: Mr. Editor—SG
children,] ~^ SG
as smooth] *omit* ~ SG
from the hills] *omit* SG
5 Like glass, or steel,] like ~^~~^ SG
7 hobbly] hubbly SG
7 feel,] ~^ SG
13 now,] ~^ SG
14 merry,] ~^ SG
16 stand.] ~; SG
19 They, one by one,] ~^~~~^ SG
19 succeed,—] ~;—SG
25 weary] ~, SG
28 eye;] ~;—SG
31 herd, . . . wait,] ~^ . . . ~^ SG
33 number] ~, SG
35 lowings, long and loud,] ~^~~~^ SG
38 watch their play;] see ~~, SG
47 morn,] ~^ SG

347. The Potato Blight
  5 man,] ~^ CR
  6 'Thus] ʾThus CR
  6 be;'] ~;^ CR
  9 sight,] ~^ CR
  13 'ʾTis] "Tis CR
  13 laws,'] ~," CR
  14 Science,] ~^ CR
  15 'I] "~ CR
  16 skill.'] ~." CR
  17 'God] "~ CR
  18 hour;] ~, CR
  20 power.'] ~." CR
  21 heart,] ~^ CR
  23 wisdom,] ~^ CR
  25 'why,] "Why^ CR
  25 vine,] ~^ CR
  26 entwined?'] ~?" CR
  27 'How] "~ CR
  28 designed?'] ~?" CR
  30 whate'er he takes] whatever take CR
  35 to] 't CR

849. Congregational Singing
  3 heart,] ~^ CR
  12 met] ~, CR
  15 land,] ~; CR

295. Kossuth
  3 And, as thine own,] ~^~~~^ CR
  4 strong:] ~. CR
  5 winds] wind, CR
  6 nor the] ~ nor CR
  7 still] ~, CR
  9 Truth] truth CR
  13 Truth, or Right prevail,] ~^~~~^ CR
  14 sword,] ~^ CR

139. John Woolman
  1 mankind;] ~! CR
  2 He] Who CR
  4 reveal.] ~; CR
  5 He] Who CR
  8 word;—] ~. CR
  13 reapers, with their sickles stand,] ~^~~~~^ CR

674. Hymn: Waiting For Christ
  2 weary,] ~? CR
  3 strong,] ~; CR
  5–8 *omit* CR
  9 scoffers,] ~^ CR

10 'Where's . . . Lord?'] "~ . . . ~?" CR
11 'Who . . . day?'] "~ . . . ~?" CR
13 He, too,] ~^~^ CR
13 thee;] ~, CR
22 love;] ~, CR
24 faithless] failthless CR
27 fills] lights CR
28 has] hath CR

754. The Wild Rose of Plymouth
    1 blooms] ~, CR
    2 bay] ~, CR
    4 hour] ~, CR
    7 dwelling-place] ~, CR
    9 hour . . . springs] ~, . . . ~, CR
    10 prime;] ~, CR
    11 Future brings] future ~, CR
    12 time;] ~, CR
    14 Beauty] ~, CR

358. Voting In The Old North Church
Title: The Old North] An Old CR
    6 weal:] ~. CR
    7 foolish] reckless CR
    10 *Table] *table CR
After line 11 the following lines appear in CR:
  Assembling now to vote in such a place,
  O may Religion consecrate our deed.
    13 defiled,] ~^ CR
    14 bounds,] ~; CR
    15 Liberty;] ~, CR
    18 rights, which] ~^ that CR
    19 minds,] ~^ CR
    23 Knowledge, and in Virtue,] ~^~~~^ CR
    25 Ambition's] ambition's CR
    27 long years] a life CR
    28 history, and her laws;] ~^~~~, CR
    30 know, but to excell] ~^~~~excel CR
    32 Freedom, with her gifts,] ~^~~~^ CR
    33 people;] ~, CR
    35 such, in such a land,] ~^~~~~~^ CR
    38 votes!] ~. CR
    40 Country's] country's CR
    45 voice,] ~^ CR
    45 which says,] that ~; CR
    46 'Ye] ^~ CR
    52 wrong, . . . man.] ~^ . . . ~^ CR
    55 truths,] ~^ CR
    58 self-government] self government CR
    61 blessing, lasting and unmixed,] ~^~~~^ CR

62 race.'] ~." RPB; ~.^ CR

315. The Day Lily
Title: Day Lily] Day-Lily CR
        8 'Day . . . well.'] "~ . . . ~." CR
        17 ere] e're CR
Lines 21–24 differ entirely in CR:
  Like a flower, the life man lives
    Quickly too must pass away;
  Heed the lesson, which it gives,
    While as yet 'tis called to-day.

34. The Solitary Worshipper
Headnote: Friends, in Boston,] ~^~~^ CR, SG
      3 Where, once with him,] ~^~~~^ CR, SG
      8 tread.] ~^ SG
      9 loved,] ~^ CR
      10 meet,] ~; CR
      20 hearers spoke.] hearer ~; CR, SG
      21 those] these CR
      22 reverent] reverend CR
      26 Spirit] spirit CR
      26 implored;] ~, SG
      27 speech,] speach, MH
      32 Spirit] spirit CR
      33 Spirit] spirit CR
Lines 35–36 differ entirely in CR and SG:
  And on his lonely, darkened path
  It threw a heavenly light.
      39 God,] ~; CR
      40 Which saints] That ~, CR; That ~ SG
      43 young,] ~^ CR, SG
      43 innocence,] ~^ CR
      45 sorrow,] ~^ CR, SG
      49 peace] ~, CR
      52 controul.] control. CR, SG
      53 again, as when on earth,] ~^~~~~^ CR, SG
      55 And] ~, CR, SG
      55 made] ~, CR

276. The Mind The Greatest Mystery
      2 And listening] ~, ~, CR
      2 rebound;] ~. CR
      4 found;] ~. CR
      6 sank;] ~. CR
      8 below;] ~. CR
      12 afar;] ~. CR
      13 when, from these,] ~^~~^ CR
      13 mind,] Mind, CR

756. The Horsemen on the Sands

     5 night,] ~; CR
     8 And, with] ~^ at CR
     8 speed,] ~^ CR
     9 Time] ~, CR
    10 oft,] ~^ CR
    14 Shore] shore CR

833. Goliath
Title: Goliath] Goliah MH, CR
     1 bold,] ~^ CR
     2 forth,] ~^ CR
     3 strength,] ~^ CR
     9 oft, by feeblest arm,] ~^~~~^ CR
    12 prevails;] ~,—CR

735. A Sunset In Haverhill
     1 hill,] ~^ CR
     2 town;] ~, CR
     7 whole,] ~^ CR
    10 fair,] ~^ CR
    13 tell,] ~^ CR
  17–20 *omit* CR
    22 brighter,] ~^ CR
    23 hill-top] mountains CR

688. The Past
     1 whither] Whither CR
     1 lead] ~, CR
     2 away;] ~, CR
     3 Empires, and races,] ~^~~^ CR
     4 site,] ~; CR
     6 point'st] pointest CR
    10 beckon'st] becon'st MH; beckonest CR
    13 forms,] ~^ CR
    14 impress, left upon the rock;] ~^~~~~, CR
    15 clay;] earth; CR
    20 coal;] ~, CR
    22 nor] ~, CR
    27 countless] unknown CR
    28 sent!] ~. CR
    29 bewildered, . . . thought,] ~^ . . . ~^ CR
    31 origin;] ~, CR
    31 Past!] ~. CR
    32 search, I turn within;] ~^~~~, CR
    33 And, of my soul,] ~^~~~^ CR
    37 essence, who can tell,] ~^~~~? CR
    38 mark, by years,] ~^~~^ CR
    40 laws,] ~^ CR
    40 course,] ~; CR
    43 Compel] And bid CR
    46 ancient,] ~^ CR

49 rest,] ~; CR
50 Past,] ~^ CR
51 Though, to our weak view,] ~^~~ narrow ~^ CR
54 our feeble, finite] the weakness of our CR
55 from beginning to] the ~ from CR
60 determined,] ~^ CR

761. Hymn, Sung at the Thompson Jubilee, at Barre, Jany. 12, 1854
Title: Hymn for the Jubilee at Barre Broadside; Original Hymn. / By Jones Very /
Sung at the Thompson Jubilee CR; untitled in Thompson, *Discourse*
      1 Jubilee] jubilee Thompson
      2 Jubilee] jubilee Thompson
      6 enjoyed;] ~, Broadside, CR
      7 fill,] ~^ Broadside, CR, Thompson
     11 Fathers'] fathers' Broadside, Thompson
     13 Health, and Liberty, and Peace,] ~, ~~^~~, Broadside; health and liberty and
        peace Thompson
     15 O,] Oh^ Thompson
     16 forgot.] ~! Thompson
     18 Gospel] gospel Thompson
    20 above!] ~. Broadside, CR, Thompson
    24 still, as Thine,] ~^~~^ Broadside, CR; ~^~ thine^ Thompson
    24 Vineyard] vineyard CR, Thompson
After line 24 the following stanza appears in Broadside:
Till, noiseless as the springing grain,   1a
   O'er all the earth the harvest wave;
And every hill, and every plain
   Shall hail the Christ, who came to save.
CR prints the same stanza with the following variants:
     1a grain,] rain,
     3a plain] ~,
Thompson prints the same stanza with the following variants:
     3a hill,] ~^
     4a Christ,] ~^
     4a save.] ~!

     26 thy] the CR
     27 joys,] Joys, Broadside; ~^ CR, Thompson

422. On An Ear Of Wheat Brought, By My Brother, From The Field Of Waterloo
Title: Brought, By My Brother,] ~^~~~^ CR
     19 fail] cease, CR
     22 thy] Thy CR

307. The Dead Elm
     1 amidst] amid CR, SG
     2 graceful outline stretched] naked ~, stiff CR, SG
     3 suns,] ~^ CR, SG
     3 which] that CR, SG
     4 Blossoms,] ~^ CR, SG
     8 elm] ~, SG

9 sign] sin SG
10 world,] ~^ SG
12 When,] ~^ CR, SG
13 subtle] fatal CR, SG

155. Hymn Sung at the Celebration of the Fourth of July, in Salem, 1854.
Title: Original Hymn [entire title] Printed program; Love of Country PL
 7 Country's] country's Printed program, PL
 7 to] *omit* PL
 9 go] ~, PL
 11 Through] Thro' PL

118. The Camphene Lamp
 2 rich, and poor;] ~^~~, SG
 4 *entire line differs:* Lonely traveller on the moor. SG
 6 aid,] ~^ SG
 7 has] hast SG
 18 Sent] Gave SG
 22 king;—] ~. SG
 23 treat, with like neglect,] ~^~~~^ SG
 28 home] homes SG
After line 28 the following stanza appears in SG:
 Or; till science' morning ray
 With its noon-day lustre shine,
 And has come the perfect day,
 When her gifts all prove benign.
The footnote differs entirely in SG:
 *It has been stated that the aggregate destruction of human life annually in this country, from the use of Camphene, and other burning fluids, is greater than by all the accidents on steamers and railroads.

805. The Homeless Wind
Alternate lines are indented in CR.
 3 sad] ~, CR
Heading: Wind] ~. CR
 5 "I've] ^~ CR
 6 sea shore;] sea-shore; CR
After line 8 the following two stanzas appear in CR:
 I saw the sailor tossing
  Upon the stormy sea;
 He sighed, while ocean crossing,
  In sympathy with me.

 I've heard the roar of battle,
  And soldiers' dying wail!
 Men fell like herds of cattle,
  Beneath War's leaden hail.
 11 stay] stop CR
After line 12 the following stanza appears in CR:
 For still that wail pursued me,
  More sad, and deep, than mine;

No sounds upon the land or sea
  Its sadness can define.
      13 Now,] ~^ CR
      17 there] *omit* CR
      20 mind."] ~.^ CR

40. The Age Changeful and Worldly
      3 Present] present CR
      4 Past and Future] past, and future CR
      6 o'erthrown;] ~, CR
      10 day;] ~, CR
      13 Lord, from our hearts,] ~! ~~~^ CR
      14 *entire line differs:* That chokes the springing of Thy precious seed. CR

649. Hymn: So also will God, through Jesus, bring with him them who sleep.
Title: So . . . sleep.] "~ . . . ~." CR
       1 They, . . . sleep,] ~^ . . . ~^ CR
       4 he] He CR
       5 waking, we are one,] ~^~~~^ CR
       7 They,] ~^ CR
       7 our sight] us now CR
      10 soul] ~, CR
      13 then,] ~^ CR
      17 fair,] ~^ CR
      18 Who, in Christ,] ~^~~^ CR
      21 sting;] ~, CR
      23 God,] ~^ CR

179. "Blessed are they that mourn: for they shall be comforted." Math. 5:4.
Title: "Blessed] ~~ MH
Title: Math.] ~^ MH
Title: Blessed Are They That Mourn [entire title] MSaE
The Bow in the Cloud [entire title] CR
MSaE arranges the poem in four four-line stanzas.
       1 blessed] blest MSaE
       1 those,] ~^ MSaE
       2 Affliction's] Afflictions MSaE; affliction's CR
       4 Father, God!] Father-God! CR
       5 pain,] ~^ CR
       6 weep, for joy,] ~^~~^ MSaE, CR
       7 God, e'en on the sinful,] ~^~~~~^ MSaE, CR
       8 Son,] son, CR
       8 peace,] ~^ MSaE
       9 Thus,] ~^ MSaE, CR
       9 and, in the west,] ~^~~~^ MSaE, CR
      10 shower;] showers; MSaE; ~, CR
      11 far-off] far off CR
      12 bower;] bowers. MSaE; ~, CR
Instead of lines 13–14 the following stanza appears in MSaE:
  The bow of Promise in the opening sky
  Spans with its arch the green, rejoicing earth;

Fairer than when to Noah's wondering eye
It stood a sign of Nature's second birth.

44. To The Memory Of The Rev. James Chisholm
     1 Amidst] Amid'st CR
     6 state] State CR
     6 wide,] ~; CR
     7 free] ~, CR
     8 pride!] ~. CR
     9 manners] ~, CR
     9 heart] ~, CR
     11 Called, in mid-life,] ~^~~^ CR
     11 part;] ~, CR
     12 drop, in sympathy,] ~^~~^ CR

314. The Woodwax
     1 Laughing, midst] ~^ 'midst SG
     1 blooms,] ~^ SG
     2 consumes;] ~, SG
     3 year,] ~; SG
     5 side,] ~^ SG
     7 steep] ~, SG
  9–12 *omit* SG
     12 bring.] ~^ MH
     14 'Tis,] ~^ SG
     21 in] each SG
     23 blooms,] ~^ SG

772. The First Telegraphic Message
     1 What . . . wrought? What . . . wrought?] "~ . . . ~" "~ . . . ~" SG
     6 fulfil;] ~, SG
     8 skill.] ~? SG
     9 shore,] ~^ SG
     13 west] West, SG
     14 it stretching on,] ~, ~~^ SG
     15 rest,] ~; SG
     19 the] these SG
     21 North and South] north ~ south SG
     23 thought] thoughts SG
     24 Winter] winter SG
     25 each in his own tongue] ~, ~~~~, SG
     26 brought,] ~; SG
     27 say,] ~^ SG
     28 *Behold What*] "~ *what* SG
     28 *Wrought.*] ~?" SG

73. The Mission Of The Friends To The Emperor Nicholas
     2 splendor] ~, CR
     4 lower:] ~; CR
     7 king,] ~^ CR
     8 king, or people save.] ~^~~~; CR

9 pleaded, . . . man,] ~^ . . . ~^ CR
10 evils,] ~^ CR
12 By] With CR
12 agony] ~, CR
14 by] with CR

856. Be of Good Courage
This quotation appears in CR after the title: "They that are with us are more than they that are with them."
8 sound.] ~; CR
10 age,] ~^ CR
12 sublime;] ~: CR
14 near!] ~. CR

828. To An Ancient Locust-Tree, Opposite Carltonville
Title: Locust-Tree,] Locust Tree^ SG
1 mates,] ~^ SG
2 bank] banks SG
4 now alone!] here ~. SG
6 When] Since SG
6 tiny] slender SG
7 Swift cars] Streets, ~, SG
7 streets and work shops] noisy work-shops SG
8 groves] ~, SG
10 Man by his arts] ~, ~~~, SG

7. A Walk In The Pastures
7 grass] ~, SG
9 beast,] ~^ SG, CR
9 bird,] ~^ SG
16 song;] ~! SG

373. [Untitled] (O, cleave not to the things of earth)
Title: O, Cleave Not To The Things Of Earth CR
3 birth,] ~^ CR
7 disease] ~, CR
10 rich and rare,] ~, ~~; CR
11 naught] nought CR
12 not] scarce CR
13 build,] ~^ CR
14 alone;] ~, CR
15 filled,] ~; CR
21 Oh,] O, CR
23 birth,] ~^ CR

660. Nature Intelligible
2 sight;] ~, CR
4 Whilst thou] But fill CR
4 dost] with CR
7 mansion] mansions CR
8 One, Eternal Mind!] ~^~~. CR
9 floor,] ~^ CR

10 height, . . . stand;] ~^ . . . ~, CR

11 sky,] skies, CR

14 perfect] ~, CR

16 forms] ~, CR

18 proceeds,] ~^ CR

19 beast and bird,] ~, ~~^ CR

19 man their head,] ~, ~~; CR

22 year,] ~^ CR

23 Doth] Do CR

25 man!] ~, CR

27 word and letter trace,] ~, ~~~^ CR

29 humbly rise,] soring, ~^ CR

29 things,] ~^ CR

30 sublime;] ~, CR

585. The Great Facts of Christ's History

    1 traveller] traveler CR

    3 finds] ~, CR

    5 stand,] ~! CR

    8 delay:] ~; CR

    9 they] the CR

    10 ways,] ~; CR

    12 is] in CR

    14 heights,] ~^ CR

734. Freedom National, Slavery Sectional

    2 lakes, and mighty streams,] ~^~~~; CR

    4 stars in quenchless] ~, ~ heavenly CR

    5 *no italics* CR

    5 *to*] for CR

    8 oppressed.] opprest: CR

    9 laws,] ~^ CR

    11 jurists'] Jurists' CR

    12 Laws] And CR

    14 forth,] ~^ CR

    14 Free?] ~! CR

227. Christ Abiding Forever

    2 he] He CR

    6 sorrow] ~, CR

    11 foes] ~, CR

    12 He] he CR

    14 joy and peace] ~, ~~, CR

    14 his] God's CR

330. The South River At Sunset

Title: River] River In Salem CR

    3 distinct,] ~^ CR

    5 green,] ~^ CR

    8 sight.] ~! CR

  9–12 *omit* CR

11 Cropping] Croping MH
16 Paint with colors] Or to paint scene CR
17 calm,] ~^ CR

107. On Receiving A Flower From the Rev. C. H. A. Dall, in India.
      6 see,] ~; CR
      7 care;] ~, CR
      9 round,] ~^ CR
      11 mayest] mayst CR
      14 the whole] all the CR

654. Hymn Sung at the Dedication of Plummer Hall, Salem, Oct. 6, 1857.
Title: Hymn [entire title] Printed program, SG
      3 influence] usefulness Printed program, SG
      4 repay.] ~, Printed program, SG
      23 page,] ~^ Printed program, SG
      25 base] ~, Printed program, SG
      25 things] ~, Printed program
      27 high, with sun-bright wings,] ~^~~~^ Printed program, SG

21. Philosophy And Religion
      3 his] His CR
      4 derange;] ~: CR
      12 *entire line differs:* Tells them that parted friends shall meet again!
      13 who,] ~^ CR

483. The Day Begins To Dawn
      5 life,] ~^ SG
      6 faith, and hope] ~^~~, SG
      9 live,] ~^ SG
      10 Starlike] ~, SG
      14 flee] pass SG

844. On The Late Mild Winter
      13 course there is no change,] ~, ~~~~; CR
      14 occurs,] ~^ SG, CR
      14 "strange!"] "~." CR

294. The Evergreen
      3 way;] ~, CR
      4 thee,] ~^ CR
      5 thus.] ~; CR
      6 That,] ~^ CR
      7 hue;] ~, CR
      10 preserves, unchanged,] ~^~^ CR

217. Hindoo Converts: On the Domestic Trials of Hindoo Converts. Report of Unitarian Mission in India.
Title: of Unitarian Mission in] of the ~~ to CR
      3 beliefs,] ~^ CR
      4 Truth] truth CR
      9 *no italics* CR

13 danger, and the strife,] ~^~~~; CR
14 Crown of Life!] crown ~ life! CR

771. Nature Teaches only Love
    1 birds,] ~^ CR
    2 Love;] ~, CR
    3 feelings, . . . powers,] ~^ . . . ~^ CR
    5 fire,] ~^ CR
    9 man,] ~^ CR
    14 God is Love] "~~~" CR
    14 declares the Sacred Word.] is still their highest word. CR

841. The First Atlantic Telegraph
    2 end!] ~; CR
    4 tend.] ~; CR
    6 laid, from shore to shore,] ~^~~~~^ CR

25. Lines On The Old Danvers Burying Ground
Title: Lines On] *omit* SG
        Burying Ground] Burying-Ground SG
    8 dwellers] dweller SG
Lines 13–24 are omitted in SG; instead the following lines appear:
    There is no death in scene like this,
        Though mortal foes repose around;
    Our thoughts mount upward to the bliss
        The immortal soul with God has found.
    25 God!] Him! SG

785. Hymn: The Promise of The Spirit
Title: Hymn] *omit* MSaE, CR
        2 earth;] ~, CR
        9 I,] ~; MSaE, CR
        10 I] He MSaE, CR
        11 But] He'll MSaE
        12 you, in Me,] ~^~~^ MSaE, CR
    13–16 *omit* MSaE, CR
        17 mourn;] ~! MSaE, CR
        21 love,] ~^ MSaE
        23 Descending,] Decending, MH; Decending^ MSaE
        24 all,] ~^ MSaE, CR

197. The Moss and Its Teachings
        4 gaze,] ~^ SG
        5 Presence,] ~; SG
        9 man] men SG
        13 made,] formed, SG
        14 stalk, a tree,] ~^~~^ SG
        14 mould;] ~, SG
        16 forests,] ~^ SG
        17 black with dust,] thick ~~^ SG
        17 droops] ~, SG

22 oaks;] ~, SG
23 have, for centuries,] ~^~~^ SG
28 snow,] ~^ SG
31–34 *omit* SG
35 earth] ~, SG
35 the mosses grow,] through every clime, SG
Lines 36–37 differ entirely in SG:
  Oft where no other living thing is seen,
  On the lone mountain peak, the mosses grow;
39 care] ~, SG

243. The Lament Of The Flowers
1 flowers,] ~^ SG
4 haunts] spots SG
5 The alder and the] And the wild rose, and SG
6 Which] That SG
8 late.] ~! SG
10 destroys;] ~, SG
11 heard,] ~^ SG
15 strain,] ~^ SG
18 wind-flower] wind flower SG
21–24 *omit* SG
29 more, . . . side,] ~^ . . . ~^ SG
30 perfume;] ~, SG
33 "No] ^~ MH, SG
33 these, returning,] ~^~^ SG
34 charm;] ~, SG
35 bird, in early Spring,] ~^~~ spring, SG

20. The Voice In The Poplars
1 tree top breathes,] tree-top ~^ CR
2 ear;] ~, CR
3 amid'st its leaves,] amidst ~~^ CR
6 Which] That CR
7 call,] ~^ CR
11 things,] ~^ CR
11 to gross, dull minds unknown,] transcendent and unknown; CR
12 Power;] power, CR
13 speechless] speachless MH
After line 16 the following stanza appears in CR:
  For vain are human words to tell,
    Or language to define
  The sounds, which in the oak tree swell,
    Or whisper through the pine.
17 grows,] ~^ CR
18 birth;] ~, CR
20 new made] new-made CR
21 move,] blow, CR

110. How Faith Comes
1 Faith] "~ SG

1 Lord] ~, SG
1 find?] ~?" SG
3 made,] ~,, MH
6 *entire line differs:* The beauty of the wayside flower? CR, SG
8 His every deed,] his ~~^ SG
9 love,] ~^ CR
10 above.] ~; CR; ~? SG
12 night;] ~, CR
13 Which] That CR, SG
16 says Paul,] we read, SG
16 too,] ~; CR, SG
17 too] of SG
18 seen] ~, SG
21 Him,] ~^ CR
22 his] His CR

366. The Set Times, And The Boundaries of Nations, Appointed By God
Title: [only first and last words in upper case] SG
1 self-will] Self-will SG
1 & Nations born;] and ~~, SG
2 &] and SG
3 States] states SG
4 And, at his Word,] ~^~~~^ SG
8 Kingdoms] kingdoms SG
10 & the kings of old,] and ~~~~; SG
11 wise] ~, SG
12 foretold;] ~. SG
14 prophets'] prophet's SG

770. The Cemetery of Harmony Grove
Title: The Cemetery [entire title] MRM
1 cemetery called;] Cemetery ~, MRM, CR, SG
3 love;] ~, MRM
4 Him,] ~. MRM; him, CR
Instead of lines 5–12, these lines appear in MRM:
Without this hope, how sad the thought of death!
Of separation from the friends we love,
Their earthly forms commingling with the dust!
How does the spectacle of this our race,
With solemn march, forever moving on
In one procession to the silent tomb,
Oppress the mind, and lead it to despair!
5 wait,] ~^ CR
6–12 *omit* CR
9 seed,] seeds. SG
10 new] ~, SG
11 below,] ~; SG
Following line 12 these lines appear in SG:
Lost and bewildered by her countless forms,
But darkly could he of his own conceive.

13 For she,] Nature^ MRM, CR, SG

13 trust,] ~^ MRM, CR

13 grain,] ~^ CR

14 commit;] ~, CR

15 Yet tells him] But ~ us CR; But ~~ SG

15 not,] ~^ MRM, CR, SG

15 he] man CR

15 again;] ~, CR

17 *omit* CR

Instead of lines 18–25, these lines appear in MRM:

We need assurance from a higher source,

To look to Christ, and in his promise trust.

18 taught] ~, CR, SG

18 clearly see] learn indeed CR

19 countless] various SG

19 forms,] ~; CR

20 *omit* CR

22 be,] ~; CR

23 *omit* CR

23 succeed;] ~. SG

24 For] But CR

27 hundred fold,] hundred-fold, MRM

28 birds,] ~; MRM, SG

30 Resurrection,] ~^ MRM, CR

30 Life;] ~, CR

31 And,] ~^ MRM

31 Coming,] coming^ MRM

31 bring.] ~! CR

33 new clothed;] new-clothed; CR

Instead of lines 35–36, these lines appear in MRM:

Who here have sought and loved and served the Lord,

When He, with all his saints, shall be revealed

In glory brighter than the morning sun.

Instead of line 35, these lines appear in CR:

Who here have sought, and loved, and served their Lord;

E'en with celestial bodies, like his own,

36 He,] ~^ CR

36 our] their CR

36 Hope,] ~^ CR

37 are] is MRM; on SG

37 earth] ~, SG

38 bright,] ~^ CR

40 Coming] coming MRM, CR

42 voice,] ~^ MRM, CR

Instead of lines 43–58, these lines appear in MRM:

So shall the Saviour in his kingdom come,

And man, e'en here, transfigured be like him,

A pledge of that more glorious final change,

When God shall bring with Him the righteous dead.

Following line 43 this line appears in SG: In some lone spot, o'ergrown with weeds, or vines,

      44 all,] ~; SG
      45 resting place] resting-place CR
      51 scripture] Scripture CR, SG
      53 men] man CR

Following line 53, these lines appear in SG:
  Oft at the close of day I hither turn,
  To pass in pensive thought the twilight hour;
  Musing upon the future and the past.

      54 While thus] Here, as CR; And, while SG
      54 much frequented] much-frequented CR
      55 mourned;] ~, CR
      56 *entire line differs:* The dead and living seem to draw more near; CR, SG
      57 come] ~, SG
      58 death,] ~^ CR

731. Hymn: The Dew
      1 alone,] ~^ MRM
      2 parched] parchéd SSLF
      3 dews that nightly fall] ~, ~~~, MRM, SSLF
      5 unheard] ~, MRM, SSLF
      7 hills,] ~^ MRM, SSLF
      9 night] ~, SSLF
      11 grass . . . herb] ~, . . . ~, SSLF
      13 gathered] lifted MRM, SSLF
      13 blade] ~, MRM, SSLF
      14 dew-drops] dewdrops SSLF
      15 learn] ~, SSLF
      15 humble trusting faith] trusting humble ~ MRM; trusting humble ~, SSLF
      17 drop] ~, MRM, SSLF
      18 prayer;] ~, SSLF
      19 own that] ~, from MRM, SSLF
      19 by day] to ~, MRM, SSLF

165. The Triennial
      1 he reads] ~ read SG
      2 passed,] ~^ SG
      3 morn,] ~^ SG
      4 page,] ~^ SG
      5 beamed,] ~^ SG
      6 name;] ~, SG
      7 arose,] ~^ SG
      9 bays,] lays, MH
      10 heard;] ~, SG
      12 preferred;] ~, SG
      23 Now, on the starred page,] ~^~~~~^ SG
      25 there,] ~^ SG
      26 days;] ~, SG
      27 joys,] ~^ SG

29 dead, than the living,] ~^~~~^ SG
30 hall;] ~, SG
36 every where] everywhere SG
36 grave;] ~, SG
38 rock,] ~^ SG
38 life;] ~, SG
39 those,] ~^ SG
41 here,] ~^ SG
43 turns,] ~^ SG
45 days,] ~^ SG
46 Love;] ~, SG
48 above.] ~! SG

766. Welcome Written for the Essex Institute Fair, Held at Salem Sept. 4th, 1860.
Title: Welcome [entire title] Weal-Reaf
       13 oft,] ~^ Weal-Reaf
       19 still, from youth to age,] ~^~~~~^ Weal-Reaf
       21 Nature, to her children all,] ~^~~~~^ Weal-Reaf
       22 wide;] ~, Weal-Reaf
       23 Learning's] Learnings MH
       23 hall,] ~^ Weal-Reaf
       24 seek,] ~^ Weal-Reaf

814. The Child's Answer
    6 *entire line differs:* Who would by reasonings prove, CR
  7–10 *omit* CR
     11 the child] its thought CR
     12 being,] ~^ CR
     16 Name.] name. CR
     18 feet;] ~, CR
     19 men, everywhere,] ~^~^ CR
     20 Name] name CR
     21 a humble mind,] an ~~^ CR
     24 believe!] ~. CR

85. Freedom And Union
Title: Freedom and Union / A Sonnet for the Times SG
      2 things, not names,] ~^~~^ SG
      5 names,] ~^ SG
    10 good;] ~, SG
    11 And, by the fruit it bears,] ~^~~~~~^ SG
    11 tree,] ~; SG
    14 deeds,] ~^ SG

404. The Cross
      2 cross;] ~, MRM
      3 Savior's] Saviour's MRM
      4 *entire line differs:* Making all things else but dross! MRM
      6 seek;] ~, MRM
      9 others'] others MH
    10 wealth, . . . mine;] ~^ . . . ~, MRM

13 murmur faint,] ~, ~^ MRM

14 lot;] ~, MRM

18 wrong;] ~, MRM

21 Then,] ~^ MRM

21 vanish,] ~^ MRM

22 eye and from my thought;] ~, ~~~~, MRM

23 And, all glorified,] ~^ all-glorified^ MRM

23 my Savior] the Saviour MRM

25–28 *omit* MRM

368. Hymn: And God shall wipe away every tear from their eyes. Rev. xxi.4.
Title: Rev. xxi.4.] *omit* MRM

3 He] he MRM

4 Him] him MRM

9 Sin,] sin, MRM

10 forgive;] ~, MRM

13 know,] ~^ MRM

14 all-forgiven?] all forgiven? MRM

15 show,] ~^ MRM

17 the sinner's] our falling MRM

19 fears,] ~^ MRM

21 Memory's] memory's MRM

23 joy,] ~, MRM

54. One generation passeth away, and another generation cometh: but the earth abideth for ever. Ecclesiastes 1:4.
Title: One] "~ CR

for ever.] forever." CR

Ecclesiastes] Ecc. CR

15 God, through his Son,] ~^~~~^ CR

21 So, we believe,] ~^~~^ CR

21 still in heaven] ~, ~~, CR

22 forms, that] ~^ which CR

22 sight;] ~, CR

23 given] ~, CR

481. The Hour Before The Dawn
Alternate lines are indented in MRM.

1 earth,] ~^ MRM

2 dawn;] ~, MRM

6 hour;] ~, MRM

8 Kingdom] kingdom MRM

8 mightier] greater MRM

10 Kingdom] kingdom MRM

10 appear;] ~, MRM

11 foretold,] ~^ MRM

12 clear;] ~, MRM

830. State Rights

1 state] State SG

1 contends;] ~, SG

2 Country's] country's SG
4 obey.] ~, SG
11 separate] seperate MH(1)
13 seen,] ~^ SG
14 dream!] ~. SG

838. The Rights of Man
8 sing.] ~; SG
10 power;] ~, SG
12 Country,] ~^ SG
14 Whate'er] What e'er SG
14 great.] ~^ SG

11. A Longing For The Spring
5 freedom] ~, SG
15 tells, to many a leafy nook,] ~^~~~~~^ SG
16 gladsome] merry SG
18 swamp] ~, SG
19 welcome] welcomes SG
21 still,] ~^ SG
22 past;] ~, SG

142. The Abolition Of Serfdom In Russia
10 mind;] ~, CR
15 While, . . . favored,] ~^ . . . ~^ CR
23 noble, and the peasant,] ~^~~~^ CR

594. Fear not: for they that are with us are more than they that are with them. 2
Kings 6:16.
Title: Fear] "~ MRM
Title: them.] ~." MRM
Title: 6:16.] vi.16. MRM
2 meek] pure MRM
3 And, with fierce onset] ~^~~~, MRM
5 sword,] ~,—MRM
6 idols that cannot defend,] ~, ~~~^ MRM
10 hour;] ~: MRM
11 God, through his gracious love,] ~^~~~~~^ MRM
12 power;] ~, MRM
13 Who] Which MRM

19. Hymn: Nature's Sympathy with Freedom
7 swift-winged] swift winged SG
8 overcast!] ~. SG
9 rage,] ~^ SG
11 wage,] rage, SG
13 rise,] ~^ SG
14 domain;] ~, SG
17 still;—] ~, SG

793. Christ's Capture In The Garden: A Paraphrase
2 sight;] ~, MRM

3 Wisdom,] ~^ MRM
4 Light.] ~: MRM
5 forth] ~, MRM
10 When, in your sight and hearing,] ~^~~~~~^ MRM
16 And, leagued with Darkness,] ~^~~~^ MRM
19 light,] ~^ MRM

104. Song: Words Of Love To A Parent
Title: Song] *omit* CR
3 parent's] parents' CR
4 Descending] Decending MH
6 sight;] ~, CR
10 heart;] ~! CR
12 depart!] ~. CR

445. The Comet
3 night,] ~^ CR
4 thou, in terror clad,] ~^~~~^ CR
4 eye!] ~? CR
5 stars'] stars CR

773. Each Day a Prophecy
4 heavenly King;] Heavenly ~! MRM
6 That] Which MRM
7 thick] ~, MRM
14 Life and Joy] ~, ~~, MRM

487. The Influence Of The Night on Faith And Imagination
2 more, by its clear light,] ~^~~~~~^ MRM
4 fade] fades MH
12 years;] ~, MRM
17 space, which we call life,] ~^~~~~^ MRM
19 allied,] ~^ MRM
22 And, in the time to come,] ~^~~~~~~^ MRM
Lines 23–30 omitted in MRM; instead, the following lines are printed:
As fade from view the fading walls of time,
New stars and constellations will appear;
The central orb of systems I shall find,
Round which in tuneful choirs they all revolve.
Nor to the earth alone I think confined
34 life,] ~^ MRM
42 gifts;] ~, MRM
45 Thus as] As thus MRM
45 grow;] ~, MRM
47 And,] ~^ MRM

653. Sunset in Derby's Woods
1 fitting] worthy SG
2 art,] ~; SG
Following line 8 these lines appear in SG:
Here the weary, troubled mind,
Filled by day with vain unrest;

Doth at eve a shelter find,
    With the bird that seeks its nest.

131. My People are destroyed for lack of Knowledge.—Hosea 4:6.
Title: [all initial letters upper case] CR
        4 drought,] ~^ CR
        4 barrenness] barreness RPB
        9 Him,] ~^ CR
        10 his] His CR
        11 alone,] ~^ CR
        12 above;] ~;—CR
        13 mourn,] ~; CR
        14 fields,] ~^ CR

437. Autumn Flowers
        1 Summer-flowers] summer flowers CR 1861, CR 1866
        2 rods] rod CR 1861
        3 Exhaustless] exhaustless CR 1866
        7 year!] ~, CR 1861, CR 1866
        8 born] ~, CR 1861, CR 1866
        12 flowers,] ~^ CR 1861
        13 traveller!] ~, CR 1866
        18 his] His CR 1861
        19 here, uncheered,] ~^~^ CR 1861
        20 prized, in youth,] ~^~~^ CR 1861

826. The Poet's Plea
        1 sing,] ~^ MRM
        5 no,] ~! MRM
        5 rage!] ~, MRM
        7 foes,] ~^ MRM
        9 midst] 'midst MRM
        12 harp] lyre MRM
        12 strain;] ~,—MRM
        14 lyres] harps MRM
        21 reveals;] ~, MRM
        22 Life!] ~. MRM
        23 sword,] ~! MRM

454. On The Completion Of The Pacific Telegraph
Alternate lines are indented in SG.
        4 furthest west to furthest] farthest ~~ farthest SG
        12 Peace, and Liberty,] ~^~~^ SG
        13 light;] ~, SG

439. On the First Church Built by the Puritans in 1634.
Alternate lines are indented in SG.
        2 fane,] ~^ SG
        10 hymn,] ~^ SG
        13 Long] ~, SG
Footnote: Esq,] Esq., SG

535. The Barque Aurelia of Boston
Title: Aurelia] followed by cancelled semicolon RPB(2)
      4 *companion,] ~~, RPB(2)
      9 *entire line differs:* The ocean so lonely, so vast, and so grand RPB(2)
    22 Slaves,] ~^ RPB(2)
    30 fathers,] ~; RPB(2)
Footnote: Rev. William Hooper] *omit* RPB(2)

584. The Traveller At The Depot
      5 stay,] ~^ CR
      8 flower!] ~. CR
    10 which] that CR
    12 gone;] ~, CR

424. Salvation Is Of The Lord: The Book of Jonah ii.9.
Title: Jonah] ~, MRM
      1 arise] ~, MRM
      2 cried;] ~, MRM
    11 Name,] ~^ MRM

301. The Newspaper
      1 sheet,] ~^ CR, MRM
      2 deep] ~, MRM
      2 eye!] ~; CR; ~: MRM
      3 empire's] empires' MRM
      3 fate is found,] ~, ~~,—MRM
      4 yet, with careless glance,] ~^~~~^ CR, MRM
      5 Perchance,] ~^ CR, MRM
      5 find,] ~^ CR, MRM
      6 which through a long life] ~, ~~~~, MRM
      8 speech,] ~^ CR, MRM
      9 words,] ~^ MRM
      9 read,] ~^ CR, MRM
    10 Nature, or of man;] ~^~~ Man;—MRM
    11 Oft, in a single word,] ~^~~~~~^ CR, MRM
    13 But] ~, MRM
    14 Truth] truth MRM

9. E Pluribus Unum
Alternate lines are indented in CR.
      4 lend.] ~; CR
      5 which] that CR
      7 unity,] ~^ CR
    10 pride,] ~^ CR
    13 with] to CR

273. Song
      7 glen,] ~^ SG
    11 feet,] ~^ SG

656. This Mortal Shall put on Immortality
      7 day] ~, CR

11 whole] ~, CR
17 suffering, or disease,] ~^~~^ CR
19 we might our] he might his CR
20 our] his CR
22 man] we CR

571. Hymn: The Spirit Itself Maketh Intercession For Us
   2 thought,] ~^ MRM
   5 reach] pierce MRM
   7 He] Who MRM
   10 thought,] ~^ MRM
   11 light,] ~,—MRM
   12 not, then, alone.] ~^~^~! MRM
   14 comfort,] ~^ MRM
   15 love, and peace can tell,] ~^~~~~^ MRM
   16 brings] gives MRM
   16 soul!] ~. MRM
   18 prayer,] ~^ MRM
   18 then we pray;] it doth pray, MRM

411. The Elm Seed
   6 Providence, which] ~^ that SG
   6 &] and SG
   8 And, in the Spring-time,] ~^~~ spring time^ SG
   9 seed;] ~, SG
   12 elm;] ~, SG
   12 screen] ~, SG
   13 shade;] ~, SG
   14 that, in its boughs,] ~^~~~^ SG

468. The Cause
   10 wrong,] ~? CR
   12 prolong;] ~, CR

729. Outward Conquests Not Enough
   2 mind subdue;] ~, ~: MRM, CR
   3 foe, within,] ~^~^ MRM, CR
   3 harms,] ~^ MRM, CR
   4 armed] arméd MRM
   7 And, joined with them,] ~^~~~^ MRM, CR
   10 light, and truth, and love;] ~^~~^~~,—MRM, CR
   12 above:] ~,—MRM, CR
   13 speak,] ~^ MRM, CR

831. Ship Rock
   2 Burst] Bursts SG
   4 Hills, and fields,] ~^~~^ SG
   5 still, the ocean] ~^~ ocean's SG
   6 view;] ~, SG
   9 pond,] ~^ SG
   12 meadow] valley SG

14 far-off Arctic shore;] far off ~~, SG
15 various] curious SG
15 show,] ~^ SG
16 ago;—] ~; SG
18 race;] ~,* SG
25 word,] ~^ SG
26 father-land,] father-land^ SG
27 who, o'er the ocean wide,] ~^~~~~^ SG
Following line 28 the next two stanzas are reversed in SG (follows RPB).
29 Here,] ~^ SG
Lines 36–40 are omitted in SG; instead, these lines appear:
God was still their Rock, their Tower,
    They praised his goodness and his power;
And gained, while humbly toiling here,
    A fitness for a higher sphere.
This footnote is added in SG (follows RPB): *See Salem Gazette, Aug 23, 1859

792. The Light Of Freedom Necessary To National Progress
7 danger] dangers CR
14 Then like the traveller] ~, ~~~, CR

138. Ode to Freedom
10 conspire,] ~^ SG
16 Washington!] WASHINGTON! SG
18 post;] ~, SG
21 vain;] ~: SG

755. Philanthropy Before Nationality
1 first,] ~^ CR
8 name,] ~^ CR
9 strife] stife MH
10 Pride,] ~^ CR
12 appointed] fated CR

409-434. The King's Arm Chair
Title: Arm Chair] Arm-Chair SG 1862
3 stayed;] ~, SG 1862
6 *entire line differs:* From thy bold front its grace away; SG 1862
6 hoary] ancient, SG 1870
7 And] ~, SG 1862
7 feet] foot, SG 1862; foot SG 1870
7 borne,] ~^ SG 1862
10 bold] black, SG 1862
10 gainst] 'gainst SG 1862, SG 1870
12 lofty] towering SG 1862
13 arm chair,] arm-chair, SG 1862
17 Before me spread] Upon the right, SG 1862
17 green,] ~^ SG 1862
18 hills and meadows] rocky hills stretched SG 1862
19 Seaward] To where SG 1862
21 Beneath,] There oft SG 1862

21 tide,] ~^ SG 1862

22 hurrying] passing SG 1862, SG 1870

23 smooth-worn] smooth worn SG 1862

26 by,] ~; SG 1862

27 traveller] ~, SG 1862

29–32 *omit* SG 1862

37 Whose power restores] Who doth restore SG 1862

39 toil,] ~^ SG 1862

43 still,] ~^ SG 1870

44 gaze] gazed SG 1862

111. The Falling Leaf

15 When] ~, CR

15 spring,] Spring, CR

17 Summer,] summer, CR

18 We've] We CR

19 found, beneath its shade,] ~^~~~^ CR

19 retreat,] ~^ CR

21 bowers,] ~^ CR

22 lessons,] ~^ CR

26 controul,] control, CR

28 soul!] ~. CR

252. Faith In Time Of War

4 reply!] ~. CR

11 Living, . . . His,] ~^ . . . his, CR

13 save;] ~, CR

520. Hymn: The Light of Life

1 words,] ~^ MRM

2 him,] ~^ MRM

3 race,] ~^ MRM

6 Savior] Saviour MRM

8 life, and light,] ~^~~^ MRM

13 Him, who came from God;] ~^~~~~^ MRM

15 sin,] ~^ MRM

17 Him,] ~^ MRM

18 maze,] ~^ MRM

22 suffering, and of trial here;] ~^~~~, MRM

23 Life, on earth he saw,] ~^~~~~^ MRM

17. Man's Heart Prophesieth Of Peace

2 is,] ~; CR

2 dark hateful War,] ~, ~~, MRM; ~, ~~^ CR

5 History's] history's CR

10 need] ~, MRM

11 part,] ~,—MRM

12 be!] ~; MRM

Lines 13–14 differ entirely in CR:

Have faith in God, and his prophetic Word,

Men shall learn war no more, and shield the sword.

777. Hymn: The New Life of Humanity
     5 year,] ~^ CR
    12 rove?] ~! CR
    18 lyre;] ~, CR
    20 nobler] ~, CR
    22 perfect] ~, CR

438. The Statue of Flora, On the grounds of R. Brookhouse Esq, Washington Street.
    2 A] (~ SG
    2 throng!] ~!) SG
    5 though perchance] ~, ~, SG
    7 standst] stand'st SG
    9 day;] ~, SG
    10 o'er,] ~; SG
    13 And] When SG

37-42. Hymn Sung At the Unitarian Festival, in Faneuil Hall, May 26th 1863
Title: Faneuil] Fanuel MH(1)
Title: Hymn [entire title] MH(2); Original Hymn [entire title] Printed program
1863, CR, Printed program 1867
    1 Amidst] Amid CR
    2 sublime;] ~, Printed program 1863, CR, Printed program 1867
    3 glorious record] written over cancelled 'kindling glory' MH(2)
    4 time;] ~,—Printed program 1863, CR, Printed program 1867
    5 meet] ~, Printed program 1867
    7 Faith] faith Printed program 1867
    7 dear,] ~,—Printed program 1863, CR
    8 true!] ~!—Printed program 1863, CR; ~; Printed program 1867
    9 faith,] ~^ MH(2), Printed program 1863, CR, Printed program 1867
    9 that] which Printed program 1863, Printed program 1867
    12 sin:] ~. MH(2); ~; Printed program 1867
    13 Which, to the wounded,] ~^~~~^ MH(2), Printed program 1863, CR,
       Printed program 1867
    14 sufferer's] sufferers Printed program 1863
    14 pain;] ~, Printed program 1863, CR, Printed program 1867
    15 grief,] ~^ MH(2), Printed program 1863, CR, Printed program 1867
    16 hopes,] ~^ MH(2), Printed program 1863, CR, Printed program 1867
    16 sustain.] ~: Printed program 1863, CR; ~:—Printed program 1867
    17 that,] ~^ Printed program 1863, CR, Printed program 1867
    17 War,] ~^ Printed program 1863, CR; war^ Printed program 1867
    18 Peace;] peace; Printed program 1867
    20 Wrong and War] wrong ~ war Printed program 1867

58. The Tree of Liberty
    1 which,] that^ CR
    2 leaves,] ~^ CR
    6 Which] ~, CR
    8 clad,] ~^ CR
    14 fruits, at once destroy!] ~^~~~. CR

644. Hymn: Our Country's Dead

7 Cause,] ~^ CR
11 them] ~, CR
16 Is e'en on earth] ~, ~~~, CR
20 brave,] ~^ CR

298. The Intuitions Of The Soul
2 Beauty,] ~^ MRM
2 Power,] ~^ MRM
13 souls, unclouded and divine,] ~^~~~^ MRM

436. Still a Day To Live
3 what, in a day,] ~^~~^ CR
6 temptations,] ~^ CR
12 heart-spoken] heart spoken CR
19 deed,] ~^ CR

364. Health of Body dependent on the Soul
7 body, too,] ~^~^ CR
9 But,] ~^ CR
10 part;] ~, CR
14 clouded e'en our] dimmed the light of CR

847. The Crisis
5 principles,] ~^ SG
8 laid,] ~^ SG
9 day,] ~^ SG
14 honor,] ~^ SG

794. The Forsaken Harvest Field
1 farmer,] ~^ CR
1 fields,] ~^ SG, CR
5 flowers,] ~^ CR
7 Golden rods] Golden-rods SG
16 wind!] ~. SG, CR
17 ground,] field, CR
21 lessons,] ~^ CR
21 walks,] walk, CR
22 flowers!] ~, CR

757. The Freedmen of the Mississippi Valley
Alternate lines are indented in CR.
5 one,] ~^ CR

489. Dying Words of John Foster: "I Can Pray, And That's a Glorious Thing."
9 all at length] ~, ~~, CR
10 & live;] ~~!; MH; and ~; CR
16 fellow man.] fellow-man. CR
21 trod,] ~^ CR
23 soul,] ~^ CR
26 thing;"] ~"; CR
27 Grave,] grave, CR
28 Death,] death, CR

848. Home and Heaven
    1 letter] ~, MRM
    3 win,] ~^ MRM
    5 soul,] ~^ MRM
    7 whole,] ~^ MRM
    10 fro;] ~, MRM
    11 spot, . . . rest,] ~^ . . . ~^ MRM

303. The Search For The Truth Not Vain
    6 Truth,] truth, CR
    9 lead,] ~^ CR
    11 his] His CR
    12 inquire;] ~, CR
    13 he, who seeks the Truth,] ~^~~~~^ CR

417. On The Three Hundredth Anniversary of Shakespeare's Birthday
Title: Shakespeare's] Shakspeare's MRM
    1 Shakespeare,] Shakspeare, MRM
    2 mirth] ~, MRM
    3 roam;] ~,—MRM
    4 peer!] ~. MRM
    6 eye;] ~. MRM
    7 told,] ~; MRM
    9 tread;] ~,—MRM
    10 church,] ~^ MRM
    10 repose;] ~,—MRM
    11 throng,] ~^ MRM
    11 Jubilee,] jubilee, MRM
    12 fame, that,] ~^~^ MRM
    12 grows;] ~, MRM
    13 confined,] ~; MRM

671. Hymn: The Way of the Righteous Easy
    7 leadeth,] ~^ CR
    15 spirit's] souls, when CR
    18 plain;] ~, CR
    19 pleasure,] ~^ CR
    20 bondage,] ~^ CR
    23 summit,] ~^ CR

658. Untimely Arguments
    10 When,] ~^ MH(2)
    11 too] to MH(1)
    11 late,] ~^ CR

300. Hymn: Ps. XLVI. 10: "Be still, and know that I am God."
Title: XLVI.] xlvi. MRM
    1 armies,] ~^ MRM
    2 fill;] ~, MRM
    4 And, in waiting trust,] ~^~~~~^ MRM
    6 fall;] ~, MRM

8 Naught . . . naught] Nought . . . nought MRM
10 indeed;] ~, MRM
11 hearken,] ~^ MRM
15 Truth, and Justice,] ~^~~^ MRM
17 doeth!] ~!—MRM
20 love,] ~^ MRM
22 sins, and pride;] ~^~~, MRM
23 Savior's] Saviour's MRM
26 fulfil;] ~: MRM
27 Know my soul] ~, ~~, MRM
27 power,] ~^ MRM
28 And, in waiting trust,] ~^~~~^ MRM

843. The Voice of Nature In Youth And Age
2 earth, and sea, and air,] ~^~~^~~; SG
4 live",] ~^, SG
4 "with] ^~ SG
9 Come] ~, SG
15 And . . . freedom] ~, . . . ~, SG
15 goes;] ~:—SG
24 O'er] Oer MH(1)
26 range;] ~, SG
27 power,] ~^ SG
27 suffice;] ~! SG
40 Nature's] nature's SG

858. Hymn: Christ's Invitation in the Apocalypse
6 poor] ~, MH(2)
11 afar!] ~, MH(2), CR
12 me,] ~^ CR
12 live.] ~! MH(2), CR
15 While you] What though MH(2)
15 may find,] you find? MH(2)
18 gold] ~, MH(2)
18 fire,] ~; MH(2)
19 eyes] ~, MH(2)

371. Hymn In Drought
Title: In Drought] *omit* SG
7 brooks,] ~^ SG
9 hushed,] ~; SG
11 hand,] ~^ SG
13 Science] science SG
15 finds] ~, SG
16 fixed] ~, SG
17 Nature's laws,] nature's ~^ SG
17 Thee,] thee, SG
22 Thee] thee SG

549. The Rain
2 blade] ~, CR

4 waste.] ~! CR
9 think,] ~^ CR
10 rain drop] rain-drop CR

478a. The Fair Morning
4 rain;] ~. CR
11 afar the bells of tinkling cows,] far off the tinkling bells of cows CR
14 reecho] re-echo CR

529. The Clouded Morning
2 round,] ~; CR
3 sail,] ~; CR
6 dull] ~, CR
7 shrill,] ~^ CR
10 lost] ~, CR

349. Nature Repeats Her Lessons
3 light,] ~; CR
8 hear.] ~! CR

774. What Is A Word?
2 soul;] ~, MRM
4 controul.] control. MRM
25 Still] ~, MRM
25 tongue] ~, MRM
26 speech;] speach; MH
31 same,] ~^ MRM

566. The Young Drummer Boy of Libby Prison: An Incident Related by Capt. James Hussey.
Title: The] *omit* SG
6 answered;—] ~;^ SG
6 dream?] ~?" MH, SG
7 I] "~ SG
14 passed] past SG
17 few] ~, SG
18 starving] sorrowing SG
22 clime,] ~; SG
23 forever] for ever SG

840. Inward Direction
8 hopes,] hope^ CR
11 Unmindful] Forgetful CR
12 lent;] ~: CR

149. The Cherry Birds
3 cold,] ~^ SG
7 feed,] ~; SG
11 o'er,] ~^ SG
12 berries'] berries MH; berry's SG
18 lessons] lesson SG
19 again,] ~^ SG

563. The Soul's Questioning Of The Universe, And Its Beginning
Title: Universe,] ~^ CR
     5–8 *omit* CR
          6 forms 'mid] ~, midst SG
          7 are] came SG
          7 When began] when begin SG
          8 tell;] ~. SG
          10 ask;] ~, CR
          11 manhood and his age] ~, ~~~, SG
          14 we] they CR
          15 answer; that,] ~, ~^ CR; ~, ~, SG
          20 Word] word CR
          20 is] we're SG
     25–32 *omit* CR
          26 Godlike erect and free,] ~, ~, ~~; SG
          27 image it is said] ~, ~~~, SG
          30 here,] ~; SG
          33 And these] This world SG

374. Hymn Sung at the Eulogy on Abraham Lincoln June 1st 1865.
Title: Hymn [entire title] Printed program; [untitled] SG
          2 unknown;] unknon; MH; ~, SG
          3 thee] Thee Printed program, SG
          3 need,] ~; SG
          4 supplicant] suppliant Printed program
          6 fallen,] ~^ Printed program, SG
          7 thee] Thee Printed program, SG
          7 confide,] ~^ Printed program, SG
          8 guide, to guard,] guard, to guide, Printed program
          20 fail.] ~! Printed program, SG

193. Soul-Sickness
          2 conceal;] ~! CR
          7 decayed,] ~^ CR
          11 strength] strenth MH
          12 below!] ~, CR
          14 dream.] ~! CR

479. Song of The Early Spring
Title: Hymn On the Return of Spring [entire title] SG
          2 forms;] ~, CR, SG
     5–8 *omit* CR
          6 And in the balmy air] ~, ~~~~, SG
          10 Spring's] spring's SG
          10 see;] ~, SG
          11 sings,] ~; SG
          13 edge] ~, SG
          14 sun,] ~^ CR, SG
          15 fair May] ~~, SG
          17 dull,] ~^ CR, SG
          18 Spring;] spring; CR

19 above] ~, SG
20 offering] ~, SG
Following line 20 these lines appear in CR:
  Who without witness has not left
    Himself, in every clime;
  But doth to all earth's children give
    Glad Spring and Harvest Time.
21 birds,] ~^ CR, SG
21 thing,] ~^ CR
22 raise;] ~, CR

186. Sensibility to the Beauty and Fragrance of Flowers
  2 passer by!] passer-by! SG
  4 none, who pass,] ~^~~^ SG
  7 sense,] ~^ SG
  9 vale,] ~^ SG
  10 survey;] ~, SG
  13 haunts,] ~^ SG

230. The Sight of the Ocean
  5 mind;] ~, SG
  6 seemed, in the vast expanse,] ~^~~~~^ SG
  7 shore,] ~^ SG
  8 above,] ~^ SG
  23 height,] ~; SG

401. Prayer For Rain
  7 may'st] mayst SG
  9 earnest,] ~^ SG
  11 God] ~, SG
  19 O,] ~^ SG

390. Hymn On The Logos: The Light Still Shining In The Darkness
Title: Hymn On The Logos] *omit* CR
  4 man] men CR
  5 Essential, Uncreated,] the world it had created, CR
  13 But] "~ CR
  14 Savior's] Saviour's CR
  16 grace.] ~!" CR
  21 all] ~, CR
  24 home."] ~.^ CR

764. Hath The Rain A Father? Or Who Hath Begotten The Drops of Dew? Job
38:28
Title: Hath . . . Dew?] "~ . . . ~?" CR
  1 Slow of belief the Age;] An unbelieving Age! CR
  2 Its very words its] That by its words, its CR
  4 Spoken by men of faith] ~, ~~~~, CR
  5 extends;] ~, CR
  7 Science] science CR
  9 not] ~, CR
  10 Voice, which] voice that CR

10 man] Job CR
11 not in the clouds of heaven] ~, ~~~~~, CR
11 form,] ~; CR
12 Nor in his ceaseless works] ~, ~~~~, CR
12 behold;] ~, CR

14. The East India Marine Museum
4 wealth,] ~^ SG
14 far] e'en SG

811. Finishing The Work
Alternate lines are indented in MRM.
Headnote: just, . . . ourselves,] ~^ . . . ~^ MRM
Headnote: nations."] ~."—MRM
Headnote: Second Inaugural Address of] *italics* MRM
1 men] ~, MRM
7 dogmas] ~, MRM
12 life;] ~, MRM

22. Indian Relics
5 bones,] ~^ SG
6 chase;] ~, SG
7 arrow-heads,] ~^ SG
9 various] curious SG
11 bowl,] ~^ SG
21 they] ~, SG
32 cease!] ~. SG
34 deep,] ~; SG

290. Nature a Living Teacher
1 lore] ~, SG
3 *entire line differs:* But seek the hills and rocky shore, SG
4 Where] Whose SG
5 leaf,] ~^ SG
6 rose,] ~^ SG
7 leafy] forest SG
13 butterflies on rainbow wings] ~, ~~~, SG
14 watch] ~, SG
14 rove,] ~; SG
16 grove.] ~;—SG
17 forms with pain] ~, ~~, SG
18 bird's unruffled] bird, with joyless SG
20 rest!] ~. SG
23 fields,] ~^ SG

151. Primitive Worship
1 confined,] ~; CR
6 Peters] Peters* [but no accompanying note] CR
7 waves] ~, SG, CR
8 pines] ~, SG
9 Camp] camp CR

11 hemlock's] hemlocks MH
12 voices rose upon] singing filled SG
12 air;] ~, CR
13 mid] midst SG
14 temples,] Temples, SG
14 worshipped] worshiped CR

233. The Holy Land
　　2 those,] ~^ CR
Following line 4 CR prints the stanza appearing as lines 17–20 in MH.
　　6 in,] ~; CR
　　7 those,] ~^ CR
　　9 it,] ~^ CR
　　11 stars,] star, CR
　　16 Palestine] Palistine MH
　　17 Freedom, Truth prevail,] freedom, truth prevails, CR
　　18 Wherever] Where MH
　　19 Jehovah's land] ~~, CR
　　21 brighter] brigter MH
　　26 those,] ~^ CR

30. October
　　1 day,] ~^ CR 1866
　　1 bright,] ~^ CR 1866
　　6 hues, which] ~^ that CR 1866; ~^~ CR 1871
　　7 gazing] glorying CR 1866
　　8 canvass] canvas CR 1866, CR 1871
　　8 wondrous] fading CR 1866
　　9 seasons of the year return,] season ~~~ returns, CR 1866
　　11 burn,] burns CR 1866
　　12 shall] ~, CR 1866, CR 1871
　　12 last;] ~: CR 1866
Lines 13–14 differ entirely in CR 1866:
　Like Horeb's bush God's glory once illumed,
　Blazing with wondrous fire, but unconsumed!

567. The Soldier and the Statesman
　　5 safe;] ~, SG 1866, SG 1868

66. The Triumphs of Science, And of Faith
Title: Science,] ~^ MRM
　　4 Which] That MRM
　　5 Science] science MRM
　　6 have] hath MRM
　　7 Faith,] faith, MRM
　　13 forever] for ever MRM

50. Christian Influence
　　2 Kingdom] kingdom CR
　　2 peace;] ~? CR
　　4 cease.] ~, CR

5 the] its CR
8 Kingdom of the Lord] kingdom ~~ lord CR
12 spread;] ~, CR

378. The Reconciling Power
2 faith, and hope, and prayer;] ~^~~^~~, MRM
3 fulfil,] fulfill, CR
8 thou, in thine own keeping,] ~^~~~~^ MRM
10 youth;] ~, MRM
16 Millennial Rest.] millennial rest. MRM
20 voice!] ~. MRM

173. The Bridge of Time
1 which] that CR 1867
2 bridge, with musing steps,] ~^~~~^ CR 1867
6 builders,] ~^ CR 1867
6 away;] ~, CR 1867
13 For] ~, CR 1867
13 say,] ~^ CR 1871
14 hands,] ~^ CR 1871
15 gather, one by one,] ~^~~~^ CR 1867, CR 1871
15 moss-grown] mossy CR 1867
16 pier.] ~? CR 1867, CR 1871
17–28 *omit* CR 1867
24 bounds] bound CR 1871
25 mid] 'mid CR 1871
27 Their] Whose CR 1871
27 History] history CR 1871
28 midst] 'midst CR 1871
29 peaceful ends] some great end CR 1867
29 lived, and toiled,] labored, toiled^ CR 1867
29 died,] ~; CR 1871
30 For ends] An end CR 1867
32 Nor] Not CR 1867
33 high and safe] safe and sure CR 1867
33 deep, swelling] ~, broad CR 1867
34 mankind;] ~, CR 1867, CR 1871
Following line 36, these lines appear in CR 1867:
These ancient arches and deep-sunken piers
A tale of the old builders' lives can tell,—
What were their hopes, their aims, their faith,
And the dark mists, that hide the past, dispel.
37 not we,] we not CR 1867
37 Time's] Times MH(1)
38 builders'] builder's CR 1867; builders MH(1)
38 skill, and strength, and] strength and patient CR 1867; ~^~~^~ CR 1871

363. Hymn: The Word Before All Things
Title: Hymn] *omit* MRM
1 things,] ~^ MRM
1 behold;] ~, MRM

2 they,] ~^ MRM
7 bright,] ~^ MRM
10 insects' glittering throng,] insects ~ strong, MRM
11 birds,] ~^ MRM
12 song:] ~. MRM
15 Which] That MRM
15 heavens,] ~^ MRM
16 stars] sun MRM
17 it,] ~^ MRM
20 plan.] plain. MH
22 see;] ~, MRM
25 mind] ~, MRM
26 ray;] ~, MRM
28 day;] ~, MRM
30 reveal;] ~, MRM

451. The Whiteweed
3 waves,] ~^ SG
9 them,] ~^ SG
10 ever new] ever-new SG
15 Vain are fancy's] Living still man's SG

367. The Teachings of the Spirit
Title: preceded by 'Hymn' on separate line in CR
1 earth,] ~^ CR
6 dull,] ~^ CR
8 listening] lisening MH
12 name.] ~; CR
Lines 13–16 differ entirely in CR:
Grant us, O Lord, that birth divine,
    That we thy sons may be;
That, though on earth, we may be thine,
    And here thy kingdom see.

43. Hymn
1 green,] ~^ CtY
2 still;] ~^ CtY; ~, MRM
3 Lord,] God, CtY; ~! MRM
3 peace,] ~^ CtY
5 rock,] ~; CtY
9 disturbs,] ~^ CtY
11 peace, and rest,] ~^~~^ CtY; ~^~~, MRM
12 man's] Man's CtY
13 green,] ~^ CtY
14 rivers near;] ~; ~^ CtY; ~~, MRM
15 will,] ~^ CtY
16 love] Love CtY
16 hear.] ~, CtY, MRM
19 And, e'en] ~^ even CtY
19 waste,] ~^ CtY

181. The Help of the Spirit
Title is preceded by 'Hymn.' on separate line in CR.
    6 faint,] ~^ CR
    10 sight;] ~, CR
    11 fulfil] fulfill CR
    17 send,] ~^ CR
    18 mind, and heart;] ~^~~, CR
    20 depart!] ~. CR

466. The Birthright Church
    2 in;] ~, CR
    3 more,] ~^ CR
    4 doubt,] ~^ CR
    5 past] ~, CR
    6 moss,] ~^ CR
    12 mild, and peaceful light;] ~^~~~, CR
    13 Shining,] ~^ CR

745. Midas
    7 When] ~, SG
    10 soul;] ~, SG
    11 Which in its very richness] ~, ~~~~, SG
    13 they,] ~^ SG
    16 end;] ~, SG

26. Revelation
    2 True Religion] true religion CR
    4 controul.] control. CR
    8 things,] ~^ CR
    9 aspires;] ~, CR
    12 world,] ~^ CR
    13 See too] ~, ~, CR
    14 e'en Creation's] e'er creation's CR

183. How come the Dead?
Title is preceded by 'Hymn' on separate line in MRM.
    7 again] ~, MRM
    7 arms,] ~^ SSLF
    8 still,] ~^ SSLF
    9 question] questions MRM
    9 ask,] ~^ SSLF
Lines 10–11 differ entirely in MRM:
    Their answers to us give;
    'Tis but the mortal that we mourn,
    12 live.] ~! SSLF
    13 unperceived] unpercieved MH(1)
    18 heart;] ~, MRM, SSLF
    22 concealed;] ~, MRM, SSLF
    24 revealed!] ~. SSLF

452. The Hacker School House
    5 when] ~, SG

9 see,] see thee, SG
9 sight!] ~, SG
10 evergreen,] ~^ SG
11 sons'] sons MH
13 stand, flower-wreathed and fair] ~^ flower-wreathed, ~~, SG

768. The Houstonia
1 scent'st] scentest SG
10 blue, and look so mild,] ~^~~~~! SG
13 thee,] ~^ SG
25 form, and mild blue eye,] ~^~~~~^ SG
26 sympathy;] ~, SG
27 mild,] ~^ SG

391. To The Salem Gazette, On The Completion Of Its First Century
3 read,] ~^ SG
5 changes,] ~^ SG
5 flown;] ~, SG
6 wealth,] ~^ SG
10 round,] ~^ SG
10 sea;] ~, SG
14 deed,] ~^ SG

425. A Nation's Life Of Slow Growth
Heading: I.] *omit* SG
5 state;] ~, SG
7 debate;] ~, SG
10 soul;] ~, SG

759. The Ends For Which A Nation Exists
Heading: II.] *omit* SG
1 existence,] ~^ SG
3 scenes] ~, SG
12 cease.] ~, SG

28. Political Ambition
Heading: III.] *omit* SG
5 ends] ~, SG
13 no;—] ~;^ SG

23. National Unity
3 destiny;] ~, SG
7 gives,] ~; SG
11 shore,] ~; SG
13 thus] ~, SG
14 secure at length] ~, ~~, SG
14 man!] ~. SG

788. Reflections on the History of Nations
13 stray,] ~^ SG

446. Scepticism With Regard To The Gospels
2 Him] ~^ CR

2 Palestine;] Palistine; MH(1)
5 which] that CR
6 Him,] ~^ CR
7 death,] ~^ CR
9 Ah] ~, CR
9 which] that CR
10 noon-day] noonday CR
11 Which boasts its Science] That ~~ science CR
12 Gospel] gospel CR
14 blind!] ~. CR

835. The Tide
2 glide,] ~; MRM
3 Power,] ~^ MRM
5 thoughtless] ~, MH(2), MRM
7 Hand,] ~^ MRM
14 law;] ~, MH(2), MRM
21 law,] ~^ MRM
22 power;] ~, MRM

713. The Spiritual Birth
7 sense,] ~^ MRM
19 courts,] ~^ MRM

56. The Daily News
Alternate lines are indented in CR.
2 wave,] ~; CR
6 field,] ~^ CR
7 war,] ~; CR
10 see;—] ~. CR
13 Sacred Word,] sacred ~; CR
14 men,] ~—CR

108. On A Hyacinth From Georgia
5 not, how] ~^~, SG
8 ourselves] ~ a SG
19 out date,] outdate, SG

836. Things Unseen
5 real;—] ~, CR
10 Itself,] itself, CR
11 Oh] O CR
12 mine.] ~! CR
16 human power] things of time CR
17–20 *omit* CR
22 others too] ~, ~, CR

611. The Oak And The Poplar
7 shoots,] ~^ CR
16 [followed by extra line space] CR
17 passed.—] ~.^ CR
18 *its*] *no italics* CR

19 praise,] ~^ CR
20 passer by;] passer-by. CR
21 A] An CR
22 thick,] ~^ CR
23 lightning's] lightnings MH
26 side;] ~, CR
30 frame;] ~, CR
37 And, on its boughs,] ~^~~~^ CR
39 fill,] ~^ CR
42 there,] ~; CR
43 told, "how it increased,] ~^^~~~^ CR
49 soon", they said, "its] ~^, ~~, ^~ CR

297. The Yellow Violets
      6 tree;] ~, SG
     12 Bent] Turned SG
Following line 12 this stanza appears in SG:
  Their beauty charmed my youth
    To seek for them each year;
  Upon no other spot they grew,
    And to my home were near.
     15 search for] seek the SG
     17 childhood's] childhoods MH

202. The City of God
Alternate lines are indented in CR.
      3 night,] ~^ CR
     14 that to its scenes] ~, ~~~, CR

144. The Scholar Dreaming
      1 Gazing, listless,] ~^~^ SG
      6 cool, refreshing breeze;] ~^~~, SG
      7 Which] That SG
      9 hills so] hillside SG
     12 sport] fly SG
     14 mind] thoughts SG
     16 vanished] ~, SG
     21 Follow too] ~, ~, SG
   25–28 *omit* SG
     31 him far and wide] ~, ~~~, SG

534. Hymn Sung at the Dedication of the Peabody Academy of Science, Salem, Aug. 18, 1869.
Title: Hymn [entire title] Printed program; [untitled] Annual Reports
  Aug.] Aug MH(1)
     1 fathers] father's Printed program
     2 rare;] ~^ Printed program, Annual Reports
     3 clime,] ~^ Printed program, Annual Reports
     16 beneficence,] ~^ Printed program, Annual Reports

4. Spiritual Darkness
     2 mid day] midday CR

3 round,] ~^ CR
4 false] false, CR
10 hour,] ~^ CR
11 moment,] ~^ CR
13 eclipses] eclipes MH

204. Friendship
Title: Hymn [entire title] CR
2 more!] ~; CR
4 o'er.] ~! CR
8 fond] sweet CR
8 fill!] ~. CR
10 form we see;] ~, ~~, CR
13 *entire line differs:* Yet when we wander there again, CR
14 All] They CR
14 fair] ~, CR
15 *entire line differs:* And every flower and tree he loved; CR
18 complete;] ~, CR

652. The Sparrows And The Crop of Weeds
1 tall,] ~^ SG
2 found;] ~, SG
6 primal,] ~^ SG
10 plan;] ~, SG
14 cold;] ~, SG
15 light;] ~, SG
22 sow nor reap;] ~, ~~, SG

87. Hymn: The Spiritual Body
7 snow flakes] snow-flakes CR
10 aside;] ~. CR
11 claimant] claiment MH
12 glorified!] ~. CR
15 Angels'] And the CR
16 *entire line differs:* Which to angel powers belong. CR
22 sealéd] sealed CR
23 Summer's] summer's CR
24 gloom;] ~. CR
27 robe,] ~^ CR
28 shrub,] ~^ CR

400. Hymn: The Efficacy of a Mother's Prayer
7 mid] 'mid SSLF
10 council,] counsel, CR, SSLF
12 hatred,] hatered, MH(1)
12 lust,] ~^ CR
14 save] ~, SSLF
17 when] ~, SSLF
19 still] then CR
20 recall!] ~. CR, SSLF
23 Him, He] ~^~ CR; him, he SSLF

576. The Fireflies
     1 Summer's] summer's CR
Following line 4 these lines appear in SG:
  The birds their songs no longer sing,
    The bee has ceased to rove,
  The hum of insects on the wing
    No longer fills the grove.
      5 hay,] ~^ SG
      6 sight!] ~; SG
      11 fireflies] fire-flies CR
      11 show!] ~, CR
      12 pass;] ~. SG, CR
      13 kind;] ~, CR
      14 food;] ~, SG
      15 Or, by its light,] ~^~~~^ SG, CR
      17 Or,] ~^ CR
      22 power!] ~; SG
      23 hosts] ~, SG, CR
      25 whereere] where'er SG, CR

62. Be Not Many Teachers
Title: "Be not many teachers."—James 3:1. CR
      1 teachers;] ~, CR
      2 "in] ^~ MH
      4 teacher,] ~^ CR
      5 teachers".] ~." CR
      6 Wisdom,] wisdom^ CR
      10 fellow men;] fellow-men, CR
      11 grace,] ~^ CR
      12 speech;] speach; MH; ~, CR
      12 tongue,] ~^ CR
      13 they, as teachers,] ~^~~~^ CR

1. Military surprises and the capture of capitals, are the events of a by-gone age. D'Israeli.
Title: quotation enclosed in quotation marks in CR
      3 passions] ~, CR
      6 skill;] ~,—CR
      7 destruction's] destructions SG
      12 burnt,] burned, CR
      15 read,] ~; CR
      19 hosts; appeals to arms;] ~, ~~~, CR

600. The Bible Does Not Sanction Polygamy
      7 hardened like the King] ~, ~~ king SG
      13 quickens; gives the light,] ~, ~~~^ SG
      15 bliss,] ~^ SG
      16 unfold;] ~, SG
      19 Resurrection;—] ~;^ SG
      21 high;] ~, SG
      24 ties, which] ~^ that SG

627. Bitter-Sweet Rocks
    2 fingers,] ~-^ *To-Day*
    16 whose] above *To-Day*
    18 lie in confusion piled.] are ~~ heaped. *To-Day*
    27 please and charm;] charm the eye; *To-Day*
    29 Which rooted] ~, ~, *To-Day*
    32 hang;] ~, *To-Day*

205. Humanity Mourning For Her Children Slain In War
    2 sons] ~, SG 1872
    3 keep,] ~^ SG 1870
    7 ever flowing eyes] ever-flowing ~, SG 1872
    12 dismay.] ~^ PHC [ms. torn at edge]
    14 clime;] ~, PHC [ms. torn at edge]
    16 time.] ~^ PHC [ms. torn at edge]
    19 and] from SG 1870, SG 1872

320. The Poor Clergyman
    1 word] Word SG
    2 labored] labor CR
    4 come;—] ~:^ CR
    7 known;] ~, SG, CR
    8 heard,] ~^ CR
    10 days,] ~—SG; ~; CR
    10 knew;] ~—SG
    11 poverty,] ~^ SG
    12 day,] ~^ SG, CR

822. The Teaching Of History Confirmed
    3 When] While CR
    6 give,] ~; CR
    7 fall;] ~, CR
    10 Another] ~, CR
    10 to the very] in the CR
    11 Conqueror's] conqueror's CR
    12 trust!] ~; CR
    14 secure.] ~^ MH

237. Childhood's Songs
    5 far off] far-off CR, SSLF
    6 Mid] 'Mid SSLF
    6 childhood's] childhoods MH
    10 sweet;] ~, SSLF
    11 child again] little child SSLF
    12 feet!] ~. SSLF
    17 purify] ~, SSLF

38. Hymn, Sung at the Fiftieth Anniversary of the Essex Historical Society, Salem. April 21, 1871.
Title: Hymn [entire title] MH(2), Printed program
    1 swift] ~, Printed program
    2 voice] ~, Printed program

8 knowledge,] ~^ MH(2), Printed program
12 fame,] ~^ MH(2), Printed program
15 sons] ~, MH(2), Printed program
19 names,] ~^ Printed program

453. The Fulness of The Gentiles
Title: Fulness] Fullness CR
    4 grander Age] ~~, CR
    12 that] ~, CR
    12 Kingdom] kingdom CR
    13 Come, Church Triumphant!] Church of the future CR
    13 come;] ~, CR

813. To a Cloud
    1 Cloud!] ~? SG
    1 fraught,] ~,—SG
    2 brought;] ~,—SG
    3 way,] ~? SG
    10 gone!] ~, SG
    12 swift] ~, SG
    14 Controuling] Controlling SG
    16 laws;] ~, SG
    17 fillest] filleth SG
    17 dost] doth SG
    18 withholds alike] ~, ~, SG
    21 And,] ~^ SG

2. The Child's Dream of Reaching the Horizon
    1 o'er arching] o'er-arching CR
    10 what,] ~^ CR
    14 sped;] ~: CR
    19 where] ~, CR
    23 place,] ~^ CR
    26 sky,] ~; CR
    31 slow,] ~; CR

296. Lead Me To The Rock That Is Higher Than I
Title: Hymn: "Lead Me To The Rock That Is Higher Than I."—Psalms 61:2. CR
    2 tree,] ~^ CR
    4 *entire line differs:* Hear, O Lord, O hear my cry. CR
    15 me] ~, CR
    17 *entire line differs:* In a barren land I wander, CR

251. I Prayed, Thy Kingdom Come
Title: Prayer for the coming of God's Kingdom CR
    1 prayed,] ~^ CR
    3 wretchedness, and misery, war,] ~^~~, ~^ CR
    5 prayed, Thy] ~^ thy CR
    8 Man] man CR
    11 marvellous] marvelous CR
    12 wait] in CR

448. Justification By Faith
    1 thought,] ~^ CR
    4 Justified,] ~^ CR
    6 controul;] control; CR
    7 motives] motive CR
    9 By] "~ CR
    9 lives;] ~," CR
    13 forms,] ~^ CR

491. Signs in the Natural World
    1 sympathise!] sympathize! CR
    3 and from the cloudless skies] ~, ~~~~, CR
    4 fierce,] ~; CR
    4 sent:] ~; CR
    5 Now,] ~^ CR
    8 sound.] ~^ MH [ms. runs off page]
    10 signs;] ~, CR
    10 soul;] ~, CR
    12 controul;] control; CR

282. A Walk in Harmony Grove
    6 to human] to hum our SG, 25 October 1872

313. The Life of the Flower
    3 beauty?] ~, CR
    3 Power,] power^ CR
    6 past away;] passed ~, CR
    18 Science] science CR
    19 can'st thou by searching] canst ~, ~~, CR
    21 no:] ~; CR
    22 Mind;] ~^ CR

35. Norman's Rocks
    8 Summer] summer SG
    9 gives] ~, SG
    10 fields, and] ~^~ SG
    15 homes,] ~^ SG
    19 hues,] ~^ SG
    23 mid] 'mid SG
    23 woodwax] wood-wax SG
    27 bitter-sweet] bitter sweet, SG
    35 saxifrage,] ~^ SG
    36 seen;] ~, SG
    43 filled] ~, SG
    44 flower and plant] ~, ~~, SG
    48 sight;] ~, SG

760. The Revelation of The Spirit Through The Material World
Title: Sunset [entire title] CR
    2 gross,] ~^ RPB
    2 eyes;] ~, CR
    6 earth;] ~, RPB; ~? CR

10 mind;] ~? CR
12 refined;] ~, CR

666. And a little child shall lead them. Isaiah XI. 6.
Title: "And a Little Child Shall Lead Them." Isaiah 11:6. CR
    7 land,] ~^ CR
    11 power,] ~^ CR
    12 hurt,] ~^ CR
    13 The fields and pastures] Its ~, ~~, CR
    19 There] ~, CR
    23 Earth] ~, CR
    29 time;] Time; CR
    32 heavens] heaven CR
    32 we'll] well MH

189. The Blessing of Rain
    4 rain drops] raindrops SG
    5 leaves] ~, SG
    15 Which with unnumbered odors] ~, ~~~, SG
    20 good] ~, SG

444. The Mound Builders. On Reading the work of the late J. W. Foster
    1 past away,] passed ~! CR
    5 toiled] ~, CR
    8 history,] ~^ CR
    12 birth.] ~; CR
    13 tread] ~, CR
    14 minds] ~, CR

187. Blessed are they that mourn: for they shall be comforted.
Title: Blessed] "~ SG
Title: comforted.] ~." SG
    6 felt, and shared our] sympathized with SG
    12 them,] ~^ SG
    14 Savior] Saviour SG

403. There shall be one Flock, one Shepherd
Title: There] And There CR
    1 Unity, and Peace,] unity^ ~ peace, CR
    2 mind!] ~; CR
    5 Shepherd, and one Flock] ~^~~ flock CR
    6 watched,] ~^ CR
    8 by] by the CR
    11 home,] ~; CR
    13 Hasten ye Ages,] ~, ~ ages! CR
    13 fulfil] fulfill CR

64. Columbines and Anemones
Title: The Painted Columbine MSaE [see Textual Notes]
Headnote: *omit* MSaE [see Textual Notes]
Headnote: "Wild Flowers after water-color paintings by Miss Ellen Robbins." [entire headnote] MH

2 lea;] ~, MH
3 Columbines,] Columbine^ MH; columbines, CR
4 succeed] succeeds MH
4 Anemone;] anemone; MH, CR
6 rock;] ~, CR
9 fancy] ~, CR
11 shouts,] ~^ MH, CR
12 fields,] ~^ CR
12 hills] hill MH
13 dear;] ~, CR
14 Artist,] artist^ CR
14 bloom,] ~; MH, CR
15 storms,] ~^ CR
15 here,] ~^ MH
16 cold,] ~^ MH, CR

464. The Birds
9 man,] ~^ SG
23 *entire line differs:* When earth, and man, shall be restored, SG

634. Behold, I Make All Things New
1 new] ~, CR
2 heart,] ~^ CR
10 reason's] Reason's CR
12 passion's] Passion's CR
15 years,] ~^ CR
17 move,] ~; CR
24 Shall, even here,] ~^~~^ CR
25 adorned] ~, CR
26 man,] ~^ CR
27 Coworking] Co-working CR
27 our] one CR
28 healthful,] ~^ CR
31 enter,] ~^ CR
34 shadows] visions CR
35 himself] Himself CR
36 Light.] ~! CR
40 voice,] ~^ CR
42 above;] ~^ CR
43 quickly] ~, CR
43 fulfil] fulfill CR

855. The Meteorologists
8 phaenomena] phenomena CR
9 If,] ~^ CR

324. The Origin of Man
1 Origin;] origin; CR, SG
4 cave,] ~^ CR, SG
6 origin he came;] ~, ~~, CR, SG
7 here] ~, CR, SG

9 weak] ~, CR, SG
10 springs?] ~^ MH
12 record, and on outward things;] ~^~~~~, CR, SG
14 truths,] ~^ CR
20 weak;] ~, SG
25 Him he] ~ He SG
26 Oh] ~, SG
26 his] His SG
26 love!] ~; SG
28 find] ~, SG
28 dwell] ~, SG

369. Original Hymn
Title: [untitled] *Twenty-Sixth Annual Report* . . .

312. Knowledge and Truth
    2 *entire line differs:* For it is but in part and done away; MH(2)
    3 proud,] ~^ MH(2)
    3 born of] of the MH(2)
    6 prove possess] ~, ~, MH(2)
    8 young,] ~; MH(2)
    12 truth;] Truth, MH(2)
    14 truth] Truth MH(2)

245. Song: I Love the Light
    2 sky;] ~, CR
    5 noon-day sun,] noonday ~,—CR
    6 ray;] ~, CR
    7 That] Which CR
    9 hour,] ~^ CR

92. Take ye heed, watch and pray: for ye know not when the time is. Mark 13:33.
Title: The Coming of the Lord [on line above MH title] SSLF
Title: Take . . . is.] "~ . . . ~." SSLF
Title: 13:33.] xiii.33. SSLF
    5 deep,] ~; SSLF
    10 Thou] thou SSLF
    10 shall] shalt SSLF
    11 Thou] thou SSLF
    13 though, in slumber deep,] ~^~~~^ SSLF
    14 command;] ~, SSLF
    15 Coming] coming SSLF
    22 Coming] coming SSLF

643. The Ancient Burial Places in Peabody
    4 fill] ~. SG
    5 rest,] ~^ SG
    6 lives,] ~^ SG
    10 woods,] ~^ SG
    13 hands] ~, SG
  21–24 *omit* SG

152. On some Eternals from a friend's garden
        1 flowers,] ~^ SG
        2 Summer] summer SG
        3 Winter none would spare] winter ~~~, SG
        9 love,] ~^ SG
        11 gloom,] ~^ SG

229. The May Flower
        1 found] ~, SG
        1 hills] ~, SG
        6 wood wax] woodwax SG
        11 live-long] livelong SG
        12 bird's] birds' SG
        14 May flower;] May-flower; SG
        15 droops] droopes MH
        17 seemed] ~; SG
        20 sere;] ~, SG
        20 bloomed, once again,] ~^~~^ SG
        28 flowers] ~, SG
        30 lot;] ~, SG

63. Evolution
        3 lofty] ~, CR
        5 Or, from the egg,] ~^~~~^ CR
        5 bird,] ~^ CR
        10 see,] ~^ CR
        12 Nature] nature CR

509. The Cows waiting at the Pasture Gate
        3 Their] There MH
        14 dry;] ~: SG
        19 Till] ~, SG
        30 is] has SG

377. On some blue and golden Columbines from Pike's Peak, Colorado
        1 O] ~, SG
        3 Columbine,] columbine, SG
        4 beauty] ~, SG
        6 fair;] ~, SG
        7 Columbine] columbine SG
        8 tho'] though SG
        11 imagination's] imaginations MH

459. Cadmus
        2 teeth,] tooth, CR
        3 up; some] ~. Some SG

6. Every Day a Day of Freedom
CR gives the following title and quotation: "Every Day is a Day of Freedom." /
"Every day is a day of freedom."—Ruskin.
        2 sinful] ~, CR
        4 virtue] ~, CR

6 noon-day] noonday CR
10 The law of freedom, purity,] His perfect law of purity^ CR
11 Christ] ~, CR
11 taught] that MH, CR
14 love,] ~^ CR

69. The Indians' Belief in a Future State
5 cañons'] canyons' SG
15 weary,] ~^ SG

171. The Glacial Marks on our Hills
5 course] ~, SG
6 land,] ~; SG
7 steady,] silent SG
15 found,] ~; SG
16 hills,] ~^ SG
18 afar;] ~, SG
23 lies,] ~; SG
29 present,] ~^ SG

458. Hymn: The Cause of Peace
1 Ages pass;—] ages ~;^ CR
2 Cause of Peace] cause of peace CR
3 Cause] cause CR
3 Savior] Saviour CR
5 Angels sang] angels ~, CR
6 strains;] ~, CR
7 When] ~, CR
15 be,] ~; CR
18 Peace, and Truth, and Love;] peace, and truth, and love; CR
20 Angel-hosts] angel hosts CR

94-706. Hymn
Title: Original Hymn Printed program, *Fifth Half Century;* Hymns for the 250th Anniversary SG
3 frame,] ~^ Printed program, SG
4 country,] ~^ *Fifth Half Century*
7 courage,] ~^ Printed program, SG, *Fifth Half Century*
9 grown,] ~; Printed program, SG, *Fifth Half Century*
11 reap] ~, Printed program, *Fifth Half Century*
13 planted] ~, Printed program, SG, *Fifth Half Century*
14 fruit,] ~^ Printed program, SG, *Fifth Half Century*
16 Law] ~, Printed program
16 rights] right *Fifth Half Century*
18 hill-sides] hill-side Printed program, SG
19 wealth,] ~^ SG, *Fifth Half Century*
21 inspire,] ~; SG, *Fifth Half Century*
22 faith,] ~^ SG, *Fifth Half Century*
24 fulfil.] fulfill. *Fifth Half Century*

578. Our Lighthouses
Title: Our Light MH

1 Light,] ~^ MH
3 gathering gloom] darkling MH
11 *entire line differs:* For all who o'er the ocean sail MH
12 But] They MH
14 ray,] ~; MH
19 And] ~, MH

638. Spiritual Intercourse
　　7 come,] ~^ SG
　　21 memory's bright] Memory's ~, SG
　　27 leave,] ~^ SG
　　35 Disease, and pain,] ~^~~^ SG
　　37 And,] ~^ SG
　　52 earthly toil,] early ~^ SG
　　53 good,] ~^ SG

435. The Influence of Channing
　　6 hear, as once,] ~^~~^ SG
　　7 we] We SG
　　9 creed;] ~, SG
　　12 controul.] control. SG

137. At Sea
Title: [untitled] RPB(2)
　　4 While gazing on] As oft they view RPB(2)
　　5 be!] ~, RPB(2)
　　6 skies;] ~! RPB(2)
　　7 see,] ~? RPB(2)
　　8 ask?] ~, RPB(2)
　　8 westward gaze with longing] anxious strain their tearful RPB(2)
　　9 sight] ~, RPB(2)
　　11 But,] ~^ RPB(2)
　　14 Which] ~, RPB(2)

647. Salem
　　3 fair,] ~^ RPB(2)
　　5 hills, that] ~^ which RPB(2)
　　6 O'erlook] Oerlook RPB(2)
　　8 freedom,] ~^ RPB(2)
　　12 mankind;] ~, RPB(2)
　　14 tyrants, for their race,] ~^~~~^ RPB(2)

359. The Old Planters
　　1 slightly] <would I> lightly RPB(1)
　　5 Or] ~, RPB(1)
　　7 years.] ~? RPB(1)
　　12 descendant] decendant RPB(1)
　　14 poet's] poets MH

752. Naumkeck River
Title: Naumkeck] Naumkeag RPB(1)
　　1 Naumkeck] Naumkeag RPB(1)

1 explore,] ~^ RPB(1)
3 left,] ~^ RPB(1)
3 locusts] locust MH
4 Where on the sandy bank] ~, ~~~~, RPB(1)
5 grow,] ~; RPB(1)
6 high] ~, RPB(1)
10 squirrels leap] squirrel leaps RPB(1)

196. Longing
    1 oft, with homesick hearts,] ~^~~~^ RPB
    2 main;] ~, RPB
    7 e'en] ~, RPB
    10 o'er?] oer? MH
    12 fleet] ship RPB
    13 remain,] ~^ RPB

572. Spring
    1 returns,] ~; RPB(2)
    4 fell] ~, RPB(3)
    9 energy] ~, MH
    10 idle,] ~; RPB(3)
    12 heaviest] heavest RPB(1), MH, RPB(2), RPB(3)

648. Song
    4 were.] ~; RPB
    5 God, in ancient times,] ~^~~~^ RPB
    13 And] ~, RPB

857. Appeal
Title: IV. [entire title] MH(2)
    2 Industry] ~, RPB(2)
    2 sustained;] ~, MH(1)
    3 Learn, from the page of History,] ~^~~~~~^ MH(2), RPB(2)
    3 wise!] ~; MH(1), MH(2)
    8 want] ~, MH(1), MH(2), RPB(2)
    8 bore,] ~^ RPB(2)
    11 God,] ~^ MH(1)
    12 sure,] ~; RPB(2)
    13 And,] ~^ RPB(2)
    13 Massachusetts'] Massachusetts RPB(1), MH(1), MH(2); Massachusett's RPB(2)

413. Influence of Puritanism
Title: V. [entire title] MH(2)
    1 their] her MH(2), RPB(1)
    5 wandering] ~, MH(2)
    8 divine.] ~: RPB(1)
    13 the] the the MH(2)

99. Conclusion
Title: Conclusion] Concusion RPB(2); [untitled] RPB(4)
    1 Descendants] Decendants RPB(2), RPB(4)

7 which in after times] ~, ~~~, RPB(2), RPB(4)
8 bore;] ~, RPB(4)
10 'Gainst] Gainst RPB(4)

589. Hymn to the Living
2 foot,] ~^ MH(2)
6 wouldst] woulds't MH(2)
15 begun.] began. MH(2)
16 moving] ~, MH(2)
19 For them.] Included here in MH(2) are two lines cancelled in MH(1); see
   Alterations in the Manuscript.
21 nature's] natures' MH(2)
26 sight,] ~^ MH(2)
27 rise,] ~^ MH(2)
36 Spring's] Springs' MH(2)
38 they] those MH(2)
47 sun-beams] sunbeams MH(2)
56 Father's] Fathers' MH(2)
Following line 57 MH(2) includes four lines that are cancelled in MH(1); see Alterations in the Manuscript.
Following line 64 MH(2) includes forty-one lines that are cancelled in MH(1); see Alterations in the Manuscript.
65 Unseen] unseen MH(2)
Following line 72 MH(2) includes eight lines that are cancelled in MH(1); see Alterations in the Manuscript.
75 thy] Thy MH(2)
78 not;] ~, MH(2)

EDITORIAL EMENDATIONS

IN THE COPY-TEXT

492. [Untitled] (The earth is parched with heat, flowers droop and die)
  13 e'en] ee'n SO
  23 e'en] ee'n SO
  31 ought] aught SO
  32 joys] joyes SO

387. Lines, Written on Reading Stuart's Account of The Treatment of Slaves in Charleston
  2 o'er] oe'r SO
  7 e'er] o'er SO
  37 theirs] their's SO

423. Lines on Mount Auburn
  4 oft] of't SO
  10 ran] RPB; run SO
  18 musing,] ~. SO

562. Lines suggested by hearing the beach, at F. Peabody's Mills, South Salem. December 21. 1833.
Title: at F. Peabody's Mills, South Salem. December 21. 1833.] at Decem 21. 1833. F. Peabody's Mills, South Salem. RPB
  10 shining] clear shining RPB [Very probably intended to cancel 'shining' as well as 'and', which followed it; see Alterations in the Manuscript.]
  11 onward] on ward RPB

311. "Ambitione inani pectus caret"
  3 Know'st] Knows't RPB, SO
  22 sought'st] sought's RPB, SO

778. [Untitled] (What more delightful than to wander forth)
  28 prompts] SO; promps RPB
  30 vault,] SO; valt, RPB

418. A Song Composed by Mr J. Very, to be Sung at the Class-Supper of the Sophomore Class of 1834
Title: MH-Ar; *omit* RPB
Chorus, ll. 25–28 MH-Ar; *omit* RPB

161. Death of Lafayette
   17 fathers'] fathers SO

746. Kind Words
   6 mind,] BH ~. SO

150. Pleasure
   20 grotto's] grottos SO
   20 recess, deluded;] ~; ~, SO
   25 led] lead SO
   39 woos] wooes SO
   40 sink'st] sinks't SO

255. [Untitled] (I saw a child, whose eyes had never drank)
   25 zephyrs,] zephyr's, SO
   78 Unsparing] Unspairing SO

154. The Snow Drop
   7 boast'st] boast's SO
   10 ladies'] ladies SO

87a. [Untitled] (Cold cold thy lips my gentle boy)
   10 fittened] fittend RPB

320a. Spring
   8 Zephyrs] Zephers RPB
   12 catch] cathch RPB
   12 heaven's] heavens RPB
   14 Winter's] Winters RPB
   17 river's] rivers RPB
   18 Spring's] Springs RPB
   18 wardrobe] wardrob RPB

528a. [Untitled] (The morn may lend its golden smile)
   6 Life's] Lifes RPB
   9 Friendship's] Friendships RPB
   11 Life's] Lifes RPB

419. Lines To ——— On the Death of His Friend
Title: Lines to ——— On the Death of His Friend] Harv; [untitled] MH

199. North River
   14 swept] sweep SO

128. Eheu! fugaces, Posthume, Posthume, Labuntur anni.
   13 Love's] E; Loves MLi, SO

247. Nature
   1 hill's] hills SO
   4 O'er] MH-Ar; O'r SO

143. Religion
   8 aye] Cl; age SO
   22 Diamond's] Diamonds SO

47. The Snow Bird
  2 wand'rer] MH(1), SO; wandr'er MH(2); wanderer Harv, CR

429. Memory
  8 that's] thats MH
  24 destroy.] distroy. MH

396. King Philip
  22 murmurs] MH, Harv; murmers CtY
  24 gleam.] MH, Harv; gleem. CtY
  45 guard] MH, Harv; gaurd CtY

78. The Painted Columbine
  5 painter's] Harv, E, G, PF, PA, PG, LG, CAL, STC; painter s SO

592. Hymn, Sung At The Dedication of The New Stone Church of The North
Society In Salem June 22d, 1836.
Title: Hymn, Sung] MSaE; Hymn, / Hymn ~ MH(1); Dedication Hymn [entire
title] MH(2), SO

355. Song [For the Valedictory Exercises of the Senior Class of Harvard University, 1836]
  13–16 (Full Chorus repeated)] Chorus. Youth's cherished spot, &c. Printed program
  29–32 (Full Chorus repeated)] Chorus. We linger, &c. Printed program

673. The Autumn Leaf
  21 teachings] teaching SO

695. The Winter Bird
  4 o'er meadow] SO; oer medow RPB
  12 meadows] medows RPB; meadow SO
  14 life's] SO; lifes RPB

248. [Untitled] (I murmur not though hard the lot)
  12 passion's] passions MH

278. The Torn Flower
  18 robbed] robed MH

175. [Untitled] (Home of my youth! Where first my lot was cast)
  7 memory's] memorys RPB
  9 youth] yh RPB
  9 worthy] wor—— RPB
  11 o'er] oer RPB
  11 ocean's] ocn RPB
  12 India's] Indias RPB
  13 blessing] bless—— RPB
  13 thine] thi—— RPB
  15 Where'er] Whereer RPB
  15 whate'er] whatere RPB

160. [Untitled] (Haunts of my youth farewell! A while I leave)
  1 A while] Awile RPB

2 A while] Awile RPB
5 pour'st] pourst RPB
8 fast-receding] fast-receeding RPB
15 Beauty's] Beauties RPB
16 Goddess,] Godess, RPB
17 thee,] the, RPB
24 summer's] summers RPB
26 evening's] evenings RPB
26 approach] apprach RPB
29 Contemptuous] Contempteous RPB

432. Death Decay and Change
11 Reaper's] Reapers RPB
12 Autumn's] Autums RPB
13 If all uncancelled words in RPB are included, line reads as follows: Where where has fled away from me the face
20 o'er] oer RPB
23 Time's] Times RPB

221. The Canary Bird
1 others'] E, SAP, G, LG; other's SO

246. The Tree
6 robin's] E, SAP, G, SG; robbin's SO

348. Nature
9 city's] E; cities MH(OP), SO
10 heights] SO, E; height MH(OP)

244. An Evening Walk
24 care.] MH, SG; ~^ ViU
28 alone.] MH, SG; ~^ ViU

112. The Passage Bird
1 o'er] oer RPB
6 O'er] Oer RPB
10 o'er] oer RPB
12 Ocean's] Oceans RPB

710. A Sonnet
7 strewed] E; strew SO, BS; strew'd G

686. The Robin
Title: Robin] MH(OP), E, G, PA, PG, SG 1859, SG 1861; Robbin FU, SO
7 pool's] SO, E, G, PA, PG, SG 1859, SG 1861; pools FU, MH(OP)

722. The New Birth
7 man's] SO, E, Rosary, CAL, SSLF; man MH(OP); mans MH(J)
14 death's] SO, E, Rosary, CAL, SSLF; deaths MH(OP), MH(J)

741. The Journey
1 daily] dayly Myerson

122. The Son

5 appointed] SO, E, SAP, G, BH, HS, DHB, LSA, HTB, SSLF; apointed MH(OP)

10 unswollen] SO, E, SAP, G, BH, HS, DHB, LSA, HTB, SSLF; unswolen MH(OP)

213. Love
7 struggling] E; strugling SO
9 mountains'] E; mountains SO

126. The Spirit Land
9 wander] SO, SO offprint, E, G, Rosary, HBP, BS, LWP; wonder MH(1)

258. The Slave
14 view."] SO, SO offprint, E; view^" MH(1)

319. The Bread from Heaven
9 stranger's] SO, SO offprint, E; strangers MH(1)
14 Father's] SO, SO offprint, E; Fathers MH(1)

518. The Latter Rain
3 drops] PHi, SO, SO offprint, E, G, CG, CAL, HBP, LWP; droops MH(1)
4 root's] PHi, E, G, CG, CAL, HBP, LWP; roots MH(1), SO, SO offprint
10 chestnut burr] E, CAL; chesnut ~ MH(1), SO, SO offprint; chestnut-burr G, CG, HBP, LWP

598. The Word
10 Father's] SO, SO offprint; Fathers MH(1)
13 angels'] angels MH(1), SO, SO offprint

630. Worship
6 idol's] SO, SO offprint, E, Rosary; idols MH(1)

622. Time
13 angels'] E; angels MH(1), SO

699. The Violet
1 unspoken] E; upspoken SO
11 lest] E; least SO

289. The Spirit
8 lest] E; least SO

651. The Lost
4 shepherd] shepard MH(1), SO
10 shepherd] shepard MH(1), SO

103. The Robe
2 rugged] MH(2), E; ruggid MH(1), SO
11 plains,] SO, E; plaines, MH(1)

169. The Will
6 bruise] SO; bruse MH(1)
6 serpent's] serpents MH(1), SO

306. Life
6 rigid] SO, E, HA; riggid MH(1)

608. The Reaper
  8 aggravate] SO; aggravte MH(1)
  11 descend,] SO; decend, MH(1)

616. Winter
  4 summer's] summers MH
  8 surround] suround MH
  13 Christ's] Christs MH

677. The Rail Road
  9 valleys] E; vallies WM; ~, G

350. Nature
  5 woos] wooes WM

334. Ye Gave Me No Meat
  10 should'st] E; shoulds't WM

687. Labor and Rest
  3 dost] MH; does WM

250. The Watchman
  4 herald's] heralds WM
  9 yours] MH; your's WM
  11 sons,] sons MH; son's, WM

544. The Prison
  5 hast] MH; has WM

117. The Corrupt Tree
  11 wieldest] weildest MH(1)

809. Whither shall I go from thy Spirit
Title: Whither] Wither MH(1)

234. Thy Brother's Blood
  10 Its] E; I'ts SO
  12 gore;] E; son; SO

339. The Graveyard
  14 body's] E, VTH; bodies SO

672. Sacrifice
  10 Hangs clustering from] SO; Is offered on MH

568. The Son of Man
  10 asks] SO; ask MH

801. Rachel
  14 sealed.] SO; ~^ MH [Line runs off right edge of paper.]

59. Christmas
  4 imprisoned] SO; emprisoned MH

291. The Things Before
  9 city's gate,] SO; cities' gates, MH
  11 wait,] waits, MH, SO

536. Old Things are passed away
  13 fade] fades MH, SO

645. The Harvest
  10 o'er;] SO; oer; MH

554. The Rose
  14 O'er] SO, E; Oer MH

659. The Jew
  2 speech;] SO, E; speach; MH

698. The Tent
  12 they'll] SO; they'l MH

663. The Beginning and The End
  13 descends] SO; decends MH

639. The Sign
  10 true] MH; time SO

277. The Tree
  5 stripped] MH; striped SO

380. The Desert
  8 verdure] RPB, SO; virdure MH

692. The Clay
  2 form'st] E; forms't MH, SO

386. Praise
  4 theirs] their's MH, SO
  9 triumph] SO; triump MH

136. Forgiveness
  10 gracious] SO; gratious MH

591. I am the Way
  5 stretches] streches RPB
  11 Faithful] Fathful RPB

715. The Sabbath
  4 chastening] chasening RPB
  8 defer] differ RPB

606. The Preacher
  6 lead] led RPB
  11 wipe] whipe RPB

88. Come unto me
  2 Father's] Fathers RPB

528. Flee to the mountains
  2 burning] buring RPB

70. Blessed are they that mourn
  2 too] to RPB

157. Faith
    3 resist] oppose resist RPB
    5 but] by RPB

61. Redeeming the time
    7 leads] lead RPB
    10 withhold] withold RPB
    11 they'll] they'l RPB

724. 'Tis Finished
    4 broke] brook RPB

498. To the pure all things are pure
    2 spirit's] E, VTH; spirits RPB
    6 o'er] E, VTH; oer RPB

711. The Task
    2 E'en] Ee'n RPB
    11 temptation's] temptations RPB

235. Spring
    2 known] know RPB
    5 o'er] oer RPB
    6 heart] heat RPB
    7 Breathe] Breath RPB
    8 o'er] oer RPB

74. The Day
    14 day] *omit* RPB

623. The Strong Man
    5 reigns] regins RPB
    9 strengthens] strengthes RPB
    12 withstood] withstod RPB

556. The Acorn
    3 o'er] E; oer RPB
    4 beside] E; Beside RPB

279. The Husbandman
    13 thee] the RPB

820. The Last
    9 o'er] oer RPB
    9 thee] the RPB

75. Hope
    7 angel's] angels RPB

381. Relief
    10 heaviest] heavest RPB

253. The Creation
    8 calls] call RPB

340. The Snare

7 o'er] oer RPB
10 lightning] lightening RPB
11 branches] brances RPB
14 John's] Johns RPB

345. The Yoke
6 preferred] prefered RPB
8 unfold] unflold RPB

225. The Promise
3 O'er] Oer RPB

747. The Path of Peace
2 o'er] oer RPB
4 burning] buring RPB
12 fields] filds RPB
12 birds'] birds RPB
13 led] lead RPB

344. Obedience
3 earn] urn RPB

215. Grief
8 Thou'lt] Thoult RPB
10 sorrow's] sorrows RPB
11 learned] leared RPB

738. The Reward
5 I'll] Ill RPB

304. So is every one who is born of the spirit
10 through] though RPB

853. The Seed
10 givest] givests RPB
11 moment's] moments RPB

208. I am the Light of the World
2 lighteneth] ligtheneth RPB
6 hurrying] hurring RPB
7 word's] words RPB

209. I Am the Bread of Life
4 spirit's] spirits RPB

624. The Foe
3 givest] givests MH

508. Yet Once More
1 heavens] heaven MH
12 moment's] moments MH

240. The Guest
11 Father's] Fathers MH

490. The Eagles

11 talons] tallons MH

408. Repent for the kingdom of Heaven is at hand
5 descend,] decend, MH

503. The Giants
11 eagles'] eagle's MH

60. To the Fishermen
8 thou'lt] thoult MH

783. Charity
1 others'] others MH

159. The Unrevealed
5 surprize] MH(2); *omit* MH(1)

607. Sayings
4 Stretching] Streaching MH

405. Unto you is born a Saviour
14 this line cut off in MH; reading follows Cl

714. Hallowed be thy Name
1 hallowed,] halowed, MH

506. The New Man
6 high,] ~; MH
7 flies] fly MH
9 heaven,] ~; MH

133. The Brethren
4 wouldst] woulds MH

712. Not as the World giveth
11 other's] others MH
13 dwellst] dwelst MH

588. The Word
5 Speechless] Speachless MH
5 speaking,] spoking, MH

800. The Field and Wood
6 wily] whily MH

604. The Apostles
5 groping] grouping MH

216. The House
6 depths] deepths MH

829. The Prayer
4 quickening] BH, HC, HFS, DHB, PL, BW, HS, LA, LSA, HTB, HCC, SSLF; *omit* SO, SG, E ['quickening' inserted in Very's hand in a number of copies of E seen by the editor], WM, CAL

494. My Garden

6 thou'lt] thoul't MH, SO
8 thieves] SO; theves MH
13 lily's] lilie's MH, SO
15 thou'lt] thoul't MH, SO
20 night's] SO; nights MH

224. The Unripe Fruit
8 Yet] Ye SO
14 gav'st] gave'st SO
18 giv'st] gives't SO

260. The Still-Born
11 ceased] ceared SO

241. To-Day
3 leafy] RPB, MH, CR; leavy SO
9 thee, heed] RPB, MH, CR; ~^ heeds SO

211. The Hour
15 hers thou'lt] her's thoul't SO

267. The Plagues of Egypt
20 Egypt's] Egypts SO, MH

550. The Rain
12 duck's] ducks SO
14 theirs] their's SO

502. The Frost
4 their] SO; its MH, CE

595. Autumn Days
2 biting] MH; bitting SO

519. Autumn Leaves
5 dyes] dies SO
7 each] such SO

707. The Lost Sheep
4 think'st] MH; thin'kst SG

632. The Good Samaritan
Title: Samaritan] Samaratan SO

512. The Feast
20 refuse.] ~^ SG

541. The Ramble
4 ladies'] ladies SO
12 surprised] supprised SO

690. The Eye and Ear
9 hear;] RPB; hear) SG

733. Yourself
13 who's] whose SO

493. The World
  1 seest] sees't SG

501. The Broken Bowl
  4 dream?] MH; ~. SG

254. The Bunch of Flowers
  11 flowers'] flowers SO
  16 dropped] droped SO

271. Hymn: Home
  8 defeat.] ~^ MH(1)

257. The Worm
  8 biting] bitting SO

194a. The Miser
  11 thou dost] though dost NBEB

679. The Unfaithful Servants
  2 giv'st] MH; givs't SO
  3 others'] others SO
  7 parts,] MH; ~. SO

259. The Light from Within
  11 surer] SO, BH, HS, HTB, HCC, SSLF; shurer MB

683. [Untitled] (Thou know'st not what thy Lord will say)
  9 doest] doe'st RPB
  10 quickly] Quickly RPB

511. The Bee Hive
  6 journeys] WM; journies MH

661. The Absent
  8 stars'] WM; stars MH

553. The Robin's Song
  10 year's] SG, CR; years MH

49. The Wounded Pigeon
  16 to] and MH

329. The Swift
  3 kernels] kernals MWelC
  16 thee] the MWelC

270. Jonathan Huntington Bright
  23 rolls] roll's SG
  31 Whose] Whoose SG

617. God's Host
  10 journeyed] journied MH(1), MH(2), CE

559. The Arrival
  15 o'erjoyed,] 'oerjoyed, CR

156. Change In The Seasons
  29 vegetation] CR, SG; vegitation MH

72. Salem
  11 Justice's] MH, CR; Justice' NN

12. The Man of Science
  43 scarcely] CR, MH(2); scarely MH(1)

141. The Congress Of Peace At Brussels
  19 others'] CR; others MH

358. Voting In The Old North Church
  62 race.'] ~." RPB; ~.^ CR

34. The Solitary Worshipper
  27 speech,] CR, SG; speach, MH

833. Goliath
Title: Goliath] Goliah MH, CR

688. The Past
  10 beckon'st] becon'st MH; beckonest CR

179. "Blessed are they that mourn: for they shall be comforted." Math. 5:4.
Title: "Blessed] ^~ MH
Title: Math.] ~^ MH

314. The Woodwax
  12 bring.] ~^ MH

330. The South River At Sunset
  11 Cropping] RPB; Croping MH

89. The Soul's Invitation
  35 For] SG; Nor CR

147. Morning Hymn for a little Child
  3 grateful] gratful SG

785. Hymn: The Promise of The Spirit
  23 Descending,] CR; Decending, MH; Decending^ MSaE

243. The Lament Of The Flowers
  33 "No] ^~ MH, SG

20. The Voice In The Poplars
  13 speechless] CR; speachless MH

110. How Faith Comes
  3 made,] CR, SG; ~,, MH

165. The Triennial
  9 bays,] SG; lays, MH

766. Welcome Written for the Essex Institute Fair, Held at Salem Sept. 4th, 1860.
  23 Learning's] *Weal-Reaf*; Learnings MH

404. The Cross
  9 others'] MRM; others MH

830. State Rights
  11 separate] SG; seperate MH(1)

104. Song: Words Of Love To A Parent
  4 Descending] CR; Decending MH

487. The Influence Of The Night on Faith And Imagination
  4 fade] MRM; fades MH

131. My People are destroyed for lack of Knowledge.—Hosea 4:6.
  4 barrenness] CR; barreness RPB

755. Philanthropy Before Nationality
  9 strife] CR; stife MH

37-42. Hymn Sung At the Unitarian Festival, in Faneuil Hall, May 26th 1863
Title: Faneuil] Fanuel MH(1) (Word does not appear in title of other versions.)

489. Dying Words of John Foster: "I Can Pray, And That's a Glorious Thing."
  10 live;] CR; ~!; MH

658. Untimely Arguments
  11 too] MH(2), CR; to MH(1)

843. The Voice of Nature In Youth And Age
  24 O'er] SG; Oer MH

774. What Is A Word?
  26 speech;] MRM; speach; MH

566. The Young Drummer Boy of Libby Prison: An Incident Related by Capt. James Hussey
  6 dream?] ~?" MH, SG

149. The Cherry Birds
  12 berries'] berries MH; berry's SG

374. Hymn Sung at the Eulogy on Abraham Lincoln June 1st 1865.
  2 unknown;] Printed program; unknon; MH; ~, SG

193. Soul-Sickness
  11 strength] CR; strenth MH

151. Primitive Worship
  11 hemlock's] SG, CR; hemlocks MH

233. The Holy Land
  16 Palestine] CR; Palistine MH
  18 Wherever] CR; Where MH
  21 brighter] CR; brigter MH

198. Standley's Grove
  19 their] thy SG

173. The Bridge of Time

37 Time's] CR 1867, CR 1871; Times MH(1)
38 builders'] CR 1871; builder's CR 1867; builders MH(1)

363. Hymn: The Word Before All Things
20 plan.] MRM; plain. MH

367. The Teachings of the Spirit
8 listening] CR; lisening MH

183. How come the Dead?
13 unperceived] MRM, SSLF; unpercieved MH(1)

452. The Hacker School House
11 sons'] SG; sons MH

446. Scepticism With Regard To The Gospels
2 Palestine;] CR; Palistine; MH(1)

611. The Oak And The Poplar
23 lightning's] CR; lightnings MH

297. The Yellow Violets
17 childhood's] SG; childhoods MH

534. Hymn Sung at the Dedication of the Peabody Academy of Science, Salem,
Aug. 18, 1869.
Title: Aug.] Aug MH(1)

4. Spiritual Darkness
13 eclipses] CR; eclipes MH

87. Hymn: The Spiritual Body
11 claimant] CR; claiment MH

400. Hymn: The Efficacy of a Mother's Prayer
12 hatred,] CR; hatered, MH(1)

62. Be Not Many Teachers
2 "in] CR; ^~ MH
12 speech;] speach; MH; ~, CR

1. Military surprises and the capture of capitals, are the events of a by-gone age.
D'Israeli.
7 destruction's] CR; destructions SG

205. Humanity Mourning For Her Children Slain In War
12 dismay.] SG 1870, SG 1872; ~^ PHC [ms. torn at edge]
14 clime;] SG 1870, SG 1872; ~, PHC [ms. torn at edge]
16 time.] SG 1870, SG 1872; ~^ PHC [ms. torn at edge]

822. The Teaching Of History Confirmed
14 secure.] CR; ~^ MH

237. Childhood's Songs
6 childhood's] CR, SSLF; childhoods MH

491. Signs in the Natural World
8 sound.] CR; ~^ MH [ms. runs off page]

25a. The Old Danvers Burying-Ground
    23 image] inage SG
    32 light.] ~^ SG

666. And a little child shall lead them. Isaiah XI. 6.
    32 we'll] CR; well MH

177. October
    3 is] in SG

114. Arethusa Meadow
    9 azalea] azalia SG

806. On a Lichen from North Cape Gathered by Mr. J. M. Richards, July 3d, 1874
    23 bounds,] ~. SG

324. The Origin of Man
    10 springs?] CR, SG; ~^ MH

229. The May Flower
    15 droops] SG; droopes MH

509. The Cows waiting at the Pasture Gate
    3 Their] SG; There MH

377. On some blue and golden Columbines from Pike's Peak, Colorado
    11 imagination's] SG; imaginations MH

459. Cadmus
    2 teeth,] SG; tooth, CR

6. Every Day a Day of Freedom
    11 taught] that MH, CR

395. Christ's Final Victory
    8 all."] ~.^ SG

850. The African's First Sight of the Ocean
Subtitle: Livingstone] Livingston SG
    14 "I] ^~ SG

443. The Zodiacal Light
    11 meteor's] meteors SG

96. The Petrels
    2 waves'] waves MH
    7 whate'er] whateer MH
    12 find;] RPB(1), RPB(2); find, MH [page torn out and punctuation partially obscured]

97. At Sea
    6 sailors'] sailors MH

359. The Old Planters
    14 poet's] RPB(1); poets MH

192. Paradise
    7 pilgrims'] RPB(2); pilgrims MH

752. Naumkeck River
   3 locusts] RPB(1); locust MH

196. Longing
   10 o'er?] RPB; oer? MH

572. Spring
   12 heaviest] heavest RPB(1), MH, RPB(2), RPB(3)

352. The Puritan Church and State: II.
Title: II. [entire title] MH(1)

361. The Puritan Church and State: III.
Title: III. [entire title] MH(1)

857. Appeal
   13 Massachusetts'] Massachusetts RPB(1), MH(1), MH(2); Massachusett's
RPB(2)

456. The Bible
   3 princes'] RPB(2); princes MH
   4 prelates'] prelates MH

555. The Common School
   14 dungeons'] dungeons MH

538. Jacob wrestling with the Angel
   17 prevail;] ~, MH [semicolon probably intended; period portion may well have
gone off sheet]

570. Our Native Sparrows
   12 seed.] ~^ MH

ADDENDUM

The Word

There is no voice but that which speaks in Thee;
For This the world created and creates;
This was, before it bade the light to be;
It is; and is to come; it knows no dates;
By it, spring forth the time-born sons of earth,   5
That as the grass before the mower falls;
In it, are born the sons of heavenly birth,
And to itself their weary feet it calls;
There many mansions are for them prepared,
Within the Father's house where they shall dwell;   10
That Christ with all who love his word has shared,
That they with him the Father's love may tell
To millions that shall hear with loud acclaim,
And round the throne rejoicing praise His name.

Poem No. 629; late 1838–early 1839

Help

Thou wilt be near me, Father, when I fail,
For Thou hast called me now to be thy son;
And, when the foe within me doth assail,
Help me in Christ to say 'Thy will be done!'

This ever calms, this ever gives me rest,   5
And this consoles me in the house of grief;
Thou knowest for thy children what is best,
And send'st thy word to give them quick relief:
Swifter than light, or thought, thy message flies,
Where'er the suffering, or the weak may be;   10
And strength, and courage to their souls supplies,
Making their doubts, and foes before them flee;
And, when at last e'en flesh and heart shall fail,
With mightier power than Nature doth prevail.

Poem No. 702a; c. 27 May 1854

TEXTUAL NOTES

629. The Word
Copy-text: SO, 26 January 1839

702a. Help
Copy-text: MH
Other version collated: CR, 27 May 1854

ALTERATIONS IN THE MANUSCRIPT

702a. Help
    4 in Christ] originally followed 'say', then cancelled and interlined with a caret
following 'me'
    8 relief:] colon written over erased original semicolon

HISTORICAL COLLATION

702a. Help
    4 say 'Thy will be done!'] ~, "~~~~!" CR
    8 relief:] ~;—CR
    12 doubts,] ~^ CR

INDEX OF TITLES

Numbers in parentheses refer to poem numbers.

INDEX OF FIRST LINES

Numbers in parentheses refer to poem numbers.

By deeds not words we prove our inmost mind (85), 327

Calm o'er the hills the evening star (86), 529
Clothed upon with house from heaven (87), 429–30
Cold cold thy lips my gentle boy (87a), 22
Come all ye weary. I will give you rest (88), 132
Come, and enter Heaven, O soul! (89), 309–10
Come forth, come forth my people from the place (90), 82–83
Come, Robin, come, and sing to me (91), 532–33
Come suddenly, O Lord, or slowly come (92), 486–87
Come thou and labor with me I will give (93), 141

Dark fossil flower! I see thy leaves unrolled (95), 54–55
Day dawns again, with wondering gaze they see (96), 536
Day follows day, and week succeeds to week (97), 536
Day I lament that none can hymn thy praise (98), 67
Descendants of the Puritans! whose fame (99), 553
Disease that on thy body feeds (100), 223
Do all thy acts with strictest justice square (101), 264–65

Each care-worn face is but a book (102), 209–10
Each naked branch, the yellow leaf or brown (103), 79
Each word of love a child doth speak (104), 337

Fair damask roses! that, from year to year (106), 494–95
Fair flower! from one who toils in distant land (107), 305–6

Fair flower! that, from the southern skies (108), 420–21
Fair flowers! that open to the April sun (109), 554
Faith in the Lord how can I find? (110), 319
Fall, yellow leaf, for thy brief work is done! (111), 356–57
Far far o'er city & field thou art flying (112), 60–61
Far from his early charge, at four score years (113), 477
Far off, among the distant hills (114), 466–67
Far off I see, like a dim cloud, the hills (115), 448
"Farewell dear England, and thy Church farewell! (116), 535
Fast from thine evil growing will within (117), 99–100
Fatal Lamp! whose brilliant ray (118), 290–91
Father! help them who walk in their own light (119-123), 124
Father! I bless thy name that I do live (120), 65
Father, I thank Thee that the day begins (121), 102
Father! I wait thy word—the sun doth stand (122), 66
Father! there is no change to live with Thee (124), 118
Father, Thou wilt accept the pure in heart (125), 100
Father! thy wonders do not singly stand (126), 70
Father! Thy wonders do not singly stand (126a), 241
Fit emblem of th' immortal soul! though thou (127), 13–14
Fleeting years are ever bearing (128), 26
Fools! That when things of high import concern (129), 258
"For God's sake, help!" the drowning seaman cries (130), 490
For lack of Knowledge do my people die! (131), 341
For those who worship Thee there is no death (132), 75

509–10

How can we upward go (181), 408–9

How! canst thou see the basket, wherein lay (182), 236–37

How come the dead? we anxious ask (183), 410–11

How far hast thou travelled? Though many thy years (184), 212

How few the reapers in life's whitening fields! (185), 263

How freely do the flowers their wealth bestow (186), 385

How hard the truth of words like these to feel (187), 459

How, in the inmost soul (188), 267

How, like a blessing, falls the rain (189), 457

How, like a spiritual Presence, dost thou rise (190), 484–85

How love whom we see not, and cannot see (191), 503

How lovely in the warm September days (192), 540

How many of the body's health complain (193), 383–84

How many things there are in common life (194), 465–66

How much there is within this rich abode (194a), 205

How oft by passion, or by interest led (195), 262

How oft, with homesick hearts, their fancy flies (196), 544

How often pass we by the works of God (197), 315–16

How quick upon the eye and mind (198), 398–99

How quiet sleep the silent waves! (199), 25

How sayest thou we must be born again (200), 488

How shalt thou give account to God, O man (201), 508

How strange the thought, that in the very light (202), 424

How stript and bare is every bush and tree (203), 245

How sweet the memory of a friend (204), 427

Humanity laments, and still will weep (205), 435–36

Hurra, hurra, away they go (206), 20–21

I am the First and Last declare my Word (207), 149–50

I am the sun thine eye has seen the light (208), 149

I am thy life thou shalt upon me feed (209), 150–51

I am thy other self, what thou wilt be (210), 195

I ask not what the bud may be (211), 182–83

I ask not what the learned name (212), 262–63

I asked of Time to tell me where was Love (213), 66

I bear the prints of my ascended Lord (214), 161–62

I bid thee weep but mourn not at thy lot (215), 147

I build a house, but in this 'twill appear (216), 173

"I came to cast a fire into the earth" (217), 309

I cannot eat my bread; the people's sins (218), 99

I cannot find thy flowers, they have not blown (219), 90

I cannot heal that green gold breast (220), 26–27

I cannot hear thy voice with others' ears (221), 53

I cannot show thee that for which I live (222), 164–65

I cannot tell the sorrows that I feel (223), 85–86

I cannot wait, I cannot wait (224), 177–78

I come the rushing wind that shook the place (225), 145–46

I do not need thy food, but thou dost mine (226), 96

I followed Christ, and vainly hoped on earth (227), 304

I tore thee—thou who looked so sweet (278), 48–49

I waited long but now my joy is great (279), 140

I walk the streets and though not meanly drest (280), 118–19

I walked on the ocean beach (281), 413–14

I walked the grove where rest the mortal forms (282), 449

I was heavy-laden, grieving (283), 207

I will not call it Spring for me (284), 201

I will not look upon the lands you own (285), 114

I would adorn the day and give it voice (286), 93

I would be meek as He who bore his cross (287), 121

I would lie low, the ground on which men tread (288), 106–7

I would not breathe, when blows thy mighty wind (289), 76

I would not study Nature's lore (290), 396–97

I would not tarry, Look! the things before (291), 108

I would not tarry, Look! the things before (292), 254–55

I would weigh out my love with nicest care (293), 86

If here the imaginative Greek had lived (294), 308–9

Illustrious man! who doth to heaven appeal (295), 273

In a barren land I wander (296), 442

In a broad, grassy field (297), 423–24

In every soul is born some thought of God (298), 363

In far Australia's middle region lies (299), 497

In the shock of mighty armies (300), 372

In this one sheet, how much for thought profound (301), 347

Interpret not God's ways, unless his light (302), 444

Is that Philosophy, which doth declare (303), 369

It bloweth where it listeth hark the sound (304), 148

It does my heart with deepest sorrow fill (305), 100–101

It is not life upon Thy gifts to live (306), 80

It stands amidst the beauty of the Spring (307), 289

It stands 'mid other trees dry-barked (308), 182

It will not stay! the robe so pearly white (309), 56

Just o'er the stony wall (310), 527

Knowest thou what ambition gains (311), 9

Knowledge is not like truth, of heavenly birth (312), 484

Know'st thou the life of a single flower (313), 450–51

Laughing, midst its yellow blooms (314), 297–98

Learn O Man! the worth of time (315), 277–78

Like gallant barque, with canvas spread (316), 568–69

Like thoughts that flit across the mind (317), 528

Lo Christ returns! But where is love (318), 554–55

Long do we live upon the husks of corn (319), 71

Long had Christ's servant preached the word of truth (320), 436

Look! Winter now in trembling haste (320a), 23

Lord! cleanse thine inner temple, as of old (321), 490–91

Lord, thou hast many a serving-man (322), 179

Love builds for us a bower (323), 475

Man has forgot his Origin; in vain (324), 478–79

May has come, but flowers are rare (325), 445–46

May not whole nations, as the single man (326), 515–16

The Lord passed by! A mighty wind
(523), 391–92
The marvel of our age, the Telephone!
(524), 503
The mingling scent of flowers is in the
air (525), 506–7
The minutes have their trusts as they go
by (526), 107
The moon was shining on the deck
(527), 49–50
The morn is breaking see the rising sun
(528), 132–33
The morn may lend its golden smile
(528a), 23
The morning comes, and thickening
clouds prevail (529), 376–77
The morning comes; and thickening
fogs prevail (530), 184
The morning's brightness cannot make
thee glad (531), 221
The mortal body quickly dies (656),
348–49
The night that has no star lit up by God
(532), 171
The night was dark and I alone (533),
209
The noble hall our fathers planned
(534), 426
The old Barque's picture we took from
the wall (535), 345–46
The old creation Thou hast formed is
dead (536), 109
The organ smites the ear with solemn
notes (537), 229–31
The Patriarch wrestled with the angel
long (538), 562
The perils of the ocean safely o'er
(539), 541
The plant it springs it rears its drooping
head (540), 139–40
The plants that careless grow shall flower
and bud (541), 192
The Poet often strives, on eagle's wings
(542), 280
The prayer of Jabez, too, should be our
prayer (543), 450
The prison house is full, there is no cell
(544), 98
The promises they give, alas, to fail!
(545), 562–63
The Prophet speaks, the world attentive
stands! (546), 98–99
The quickly melting snow ran through
the street (547), 235–36
The rain comes down, it comes without
our call (548), 86–87
The rain descends; each drop some
drooping flower (549), 375–76
The rain descends; each drop some
drooping flowers (550), 186–87
The rightful name that thou art called by
(551), 155
The road is left, that once was trod
(552), 183
The robin has begun his early song
(553), 226
The rose thou showst me has lost all its
hue (554), 110–11
The School-house next they build, a
structure small (555), 551
The seed has started, who can stay it? see
(556), 138–39
The senseless drops can feel no pain, as
they (557), 87
The servant Thou hast called stands
ready shod (558), 84–85
The ship comes up the harbor. Every sail
(559), 244–45
The sights we see, the sounds we hear
(560), 468–69
The silent history of a word (561), 212–
13
The silent moon is rising (562), 7–8
The simple rustic's soul (563), 381–82
The Sliding Rock! that pleasant spot
(564), 269–70
The slowly-moving fingers minutes find
(565), 257
The slumberer wakes! "Are these the
walls (566), 379–80
The soldier to preserve his Country dies
(567), 400
The son of Man, where shall he find
repose? (568), 104
The soul heeds not, though darkest
night (569), 563–64
The sparrows still are lingering here
(570), 564

The Spirit doth our weakness aid (571), 349–50

The Spring returns, and, with fresh ardor filled (572), 545

The stem that long has borne the wintry blast (574), 112

The stones of time's old house with pelting storms (575), 216

The Summer's day has reached its close (576), 431–32

The sun doth not the hidden place reveal (577), 119–20

The sun has set; but lit the Light (578), 523–24

The supper o'er, with books, or converse sweet (579), 543

The sweet briar rose has not a form more fair (580), 60

The tall white cliffs of England fade away (476-581), 535

The temple shall be built, the Holy One (582), 112–13

The thick ice breaks, it floats away (583), 479–80

The traveller at the depot waiting stands (584), 346

The traveller sees afar the mountain rise (585), 303

The useful and the sweet the fair and true (586), 211

The Voice that spake to Abraham of old (587), 534

The voice that speaks when thou art in thy tomb (588), 171–72

The voiceless spirits, they who have given up (589), 570–72

The way! ah, who could tell, as well as thou (590), 565

The weight of years is on the pile (592), 42

The white man's soul, it thirsts for gain (593), 241–42

The wicked and the base do compass round (594), 335

The winds are out with loud increasing shout (595), 187–88

The wolf, why heeds he not the sportive lamb (596), 87–88

The Word goes forth! I see its con-quering way (597), 113

The Word! it cannot fail; it ever speaks (598), 72

The Word must fall; but where the well-tilled ground (599), 115

The Word of God doth sanction nothing ill (600), 433–34

The word the Gospel brought was love and peace (601), 499–500

The Word where is it? hath it voice (602), 218

The words I give thee they are not thine own (603), 141–42

The words that come unuttered by the breath (604), 172–73

The workman shall not always work; who builds (605), 208

The world has never known me bid them hear (606), 131

The world looks not the wider for thy travel (607), 159–60

There are no reapers in the whitening fields (608), 81

There are towers; where they are (609), 238

There are who wish to build their houses strong (610), 206–7

There grew upon a sandy hill (611), 422–23

There is a body, every joint and limb (611a), 205

There is a cup of sweet or bitter drink (612), 75

There is a house not built with hands (613), 197

There is a sighing in the wood (614), 202

There is a state that all may know (615), 504

There is a winter in the godless heart (616), 81–82

There is an order in our daily life (617), 234

There is no change of time and place with Thee (618), 104–5

There is no death with Thee! each plant and tree (619), 73

There is no faith; the mountain stands within (620), 111

be (670), 152

Thou dost make the pathway easy (671), 370–71

Thou dost prefer the song that rises pure (672), 103–4

Thou fair yet lifeless leaf! on whom decay (673), 45–46

Thou for Christ hast waited long (674), 274–75

Thou gav'st me many a fragrant flower (675), 566–67

Thou gladst my heart but not with oil and wine (676), 152–53

Thou great proclaimer to the outward eye (677), 88

Thou hast a moon for every cloudy night (678), 143–44

Thou hast no other hands than those that toil (679), 208

Thou hast not left the rough-barked tree to grow (680), 85

Thou hearst the hungry ravens when they cry (681), 119

Thou know'st not e'er the way to turn or go (682), 158–59

Thou know'st not what thy Lord will say (683), 211

Thou lookest up with meek, confiding eye (684), 59

Thou mak'st me poor that I enriched by Thee (685), 97

Thou needst not flutter from thy half-built nest (686), 62

Thou needst not rest, the shining spheres are thine (687), 93–94

Thou Past! What art thou? whither dost thou lead (688), 285–86

Thou prayst not, save when in thy soul thou prayst (689), 169–70

Thou readest, but each lettered word can give (690), 193

Thou ripenest the fruits with warmer air (691), 89

Thou shalt do what Thou wilt with thine own hand (692), 122

Thou shalt not live e'en by the bread alone (693), 117

Thou shalt the mountain move; be

strong in me (694), 94–95

Thou singest alone on the bare wintery bough (695), 46

Thou small, yet ever-bubbling spring (668-697), 231–32

Thou springest from the ground, and may not I (698), 113–14

Thou tellest truths unspoken yet by man (699), 74

Thou who first called me from the sleep of death (700), 105

Thou who keepst us each together (701), 62–63

Thou wilt be near me Father, when I fail (702), 117–18

Thou wilt be near me, Father, when I fail (702a), 865–66

Thou wilt my hands employ, though others find (703), 94

Thou wilt not give me aught though I am poor (704), 166

Thou wondrous Flower! in which, on grander scale (705), 282–83

Though few, with noble purpose came (94-706), 520–21

Though many, many sheep I have (707), 188–89

Though so fair, how soon they perish (708), 239

Though thou art dead and gone from mortal sight (709), 232–33

Thy beauty fades and with it too my love (710), 61

Thy cross is hard to bear it weighs me down (711), 136

Thy gifts are not the gifts that others give (712), 167

Thy knowledge cannot reach (713), 418

Thy name be hallowed, e'en thy Holy name (714), 162

Thy rest has come thy long expected rest (715), 130–31

Thy service Father! wants not aught beside (716), 95–96

Thy sudden terrors strike the world with dread (717), 481–82

Thy trespasses my heart has not forgiven (718), 96–97

Why cannot I make plain, to sinful men (817), 393–94

Why come you out to me with clubs and staves (818), 88–89

Why forms discuss, if that the soul is fled? (819), 512

Why hast thou tarried till the eleventh hour (820), 140–41

Why heard, amidst these shades, the tongue of time (821), 501–2

Why look we to the distant past to learn (822), 437

Why pluck their flowers? Each might have been (823), 516–17

Why readest thou? thou canst not gain the life (824), 89–90

Why rings not back the welcome shout (825), 36–38

Why sing, amidst the strife which reigns around? (826), 343

Why so swift thou hurrying tide (827), 419

Why stand'st thou here alone, when all thy mates (828), 300

Wilt Thou not visit me? (829), 175–76

Wisely each state for its own rights contends (830), 332

With a sudden, sweet surprise (831), 351–52

With aimless fury hurries on its path (832), 520

With bold, unblushing front the Giant Wrong (833), 283–84

With business haste, or with a worldly mind (834), 519

With daily ebb and flow (835), 417–18

With flag unfurled along the shore they sail (428-835a), 539

With higher thoughts, O God, uplift (836), 421

With madness seized men their own works destroy (837), 510

With narrow view each state its own would claim (838), 332–33

With ocean shell clasped to his breast (839), 473–74

With outward impulse, running to and fro (840), 380

With outward signs, as well as inward life (841), 311–12

With sickness and with famine they contend (842), 543

With sights of beauty rare (843), 373–74

With spring-like mildness passeth, day by day (844), 308

With sturdy blows the echoing woods resound (845), 542·

With sweet surprise, as when one finds a flower (846), 283

With the great thought, thy Country's cause, its life (847), 366

With the same letter heaven and home begin (848), 369

With the spirit Christians sung (849), 272–73

Without an end the world had seemed (850), 524–25

Worship declines; nor hidden is the cause (851), 471–72

Would I might stay those features as they pass (852), 53

Wouldst thou behold my features cleanse thy heart (853), 148–49

Ye sorrowing people! who from bondage fly (854), 265–66

Ye watch the appearance of the earth and sky (855), 478

Ye who against the evils of our lot (856), 300

Ye who behold the State in grandeur rise (857), 550

You, who confess that you are poor (858), 374